Ordnance Survey

STREET ATLAS
East
Sussex

Contents

III Key to map symbols
IV-V Key to map pages
VI Administrative and post code boundaries
1 Street maps
189 Extra-large-scale map of Brighton town centre
190 Town maps of Chichester and Crawley
191 Town maps of Horsham and Worthing
192 Index of hospitals, railway stations, schools, shopping centres, street names and universities
216 Town and village index

PHILIP'S

First edition published 1988
Fourth edition published 1994
First colour edition published 1997
Reprinted in 1998, 1999 by

Ordnance Survey® and George Philip Ltd, a division of
Romsey Road   Octopus Publishing Group Ltd
Maybush   2-4 Heron Quays
Southampton   London
SO16 4GU   E14 4JP

ISBN 0-540-07306-7 (hardback)
ISBN 0-540-07307-5 (spiral)

To the best of the Publishers' knowledge, the information in this atlas was
correct at the time of going to press. No responsibility can be accepted
for any errors or their consequences.

The representation in this atlas of a road, track or path is no evidence
of the existence of a right of way.

**The mapping between pages 1 and 191 (inclusive) in this atlas is
derived from Ordnance Survey® OSCAR® and Land-Line® data,
and Landranger® mapping.**

Ordnance Survey, OSCAR, Land-Line and Landranger are registered trade
marks of Ordnance Survey, the national mapping agency of Great Britain.

Printed and bound in Spain by Cayfosa

Digital Data

The exceptionally high-quality mapping
found in this book is available as digital
data in TIFF format, which is easily
convertible to other bit-mapped (raster)
image formats.

The index is also available in digital form
as a standard database table. It contains
all the details found in the printed index
together with the National Grid reference
for the map square in which each entry
is named and feature codes for places
of interest in eight categories such as
education and health.

For further information and to discuss
your requirements, please contact the
Ordnance Survey Solutions Centre on
01703 792929.

Motorway (with junction number)

Primary route (dual carriageway and single)

A road (dual carriageway and single)

B road (dual carriageway and single)

Minor road (dual carriageway and single)

Other minor road

Road under construction

Railway

Tramway, miniature railway

Rural track, private road or narrow road in urban area

Gate or obstruction to traffic (restrictions may not apply at all times or to all vehicles)

Path, bridleway, byway open to all traffic, road used as a public path

The representation in this atlas of a road, track or path is no evidence of the existence of a right of way

160
38
Adjoining page indicators

189
The map area within the pink band is shown at a larger scale on the page indicated by the red block and arrow

Acad	**Academy**	Mon	**Monument**
Cemy	**Cemetery**	Mus	**Museum**
C Ctr	**Civic Centre**	Obsy	**Observatory**
CH	**Club House**	Pal	**Royal Palace**
Coll	**College**	PH	**Public House**
Ent	**Enterprise**	Recn Gd	**Recreation Ground**
Ex H	**Exhibition Hall**	Resr	**Reservoir**
Ind Est	**Industrial Estate**	Ret Pk	**Retail Park**
Inst	**Institute**	Sch	**School**
Ct	**Law Court**	Sh Ctr	**Shopping Centre**
L Ctr	**Leisure Centre**	Sta	**Station**
LC	**Level Crossing**	TH	**Town Hall/House**
Liby	**Library**	Trad Est	**Trading Estate**
Mkt	**Market**	Univ	**University**
Meml	**Memorial**	YH	**Youth Hostel**

British Rail station

Private railway station

Bus, coach station

Ambulance station

Coastguard station

Fire station

Police station

Casualty entrance to hospital

Church, place of worship

H **Hospital**

i **Information centre**

P **Parking**

PO **Post Office**

Bexhill Coll **Important buildings, schools, colleges, universities and hospitals**

County boundaries

River Ouse **Water name**

Stream

River or canal (minor and major)

Water

Tidal water

Woods

Houses

Hastings Castle **Non-Roman antiquity**

ROMAN FORT **Roman antiquity**

■ The dark grey border on the inside edge of some pages indicates that the mapping does not continue onto the adjacent page

■ The small numbers around the edges of the maps identify the 1 kilometre National Grid lines

The scale of the maps is 5.52 cm to 1 km (3½ inches to 1 mile)

The scale of the map on page numbered in red is 11.04 cm to 1 km (7 inches to 1 mile)

0		¼		½		¾		1 mile

0								
	250 m	500 m	750 m	1 kilometre				

0		220 yards		440 yards		660 yards		½ mile

0								
	125 m	250 m	375 m	½ kilometre				

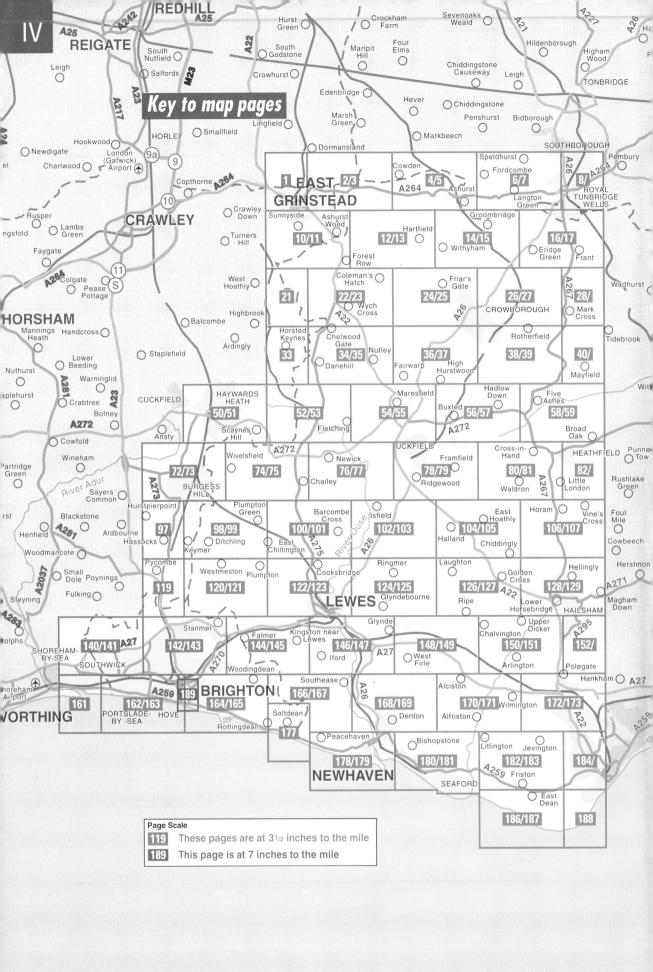

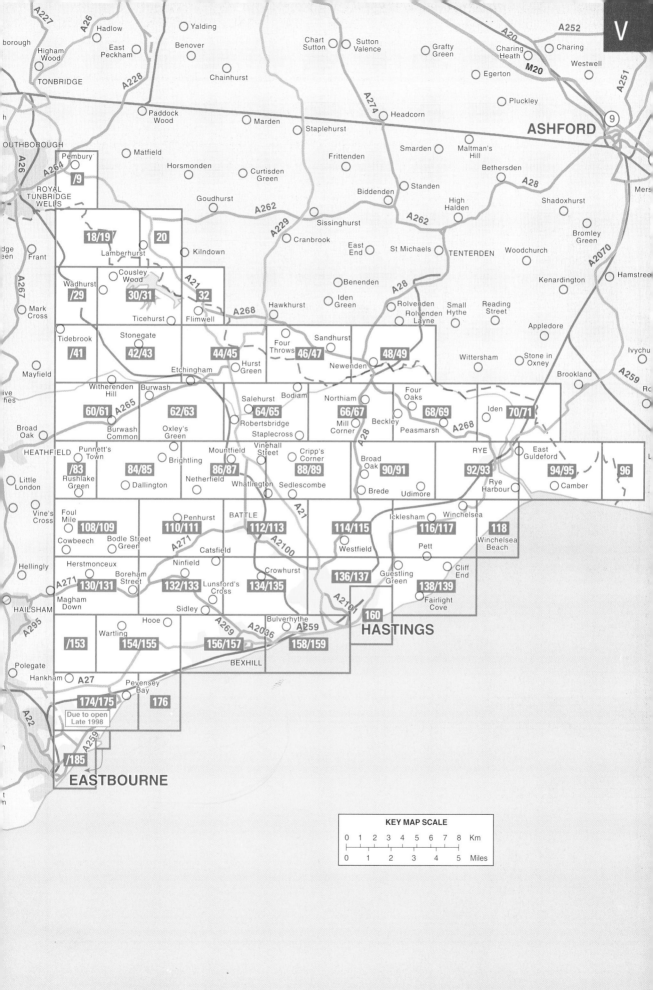

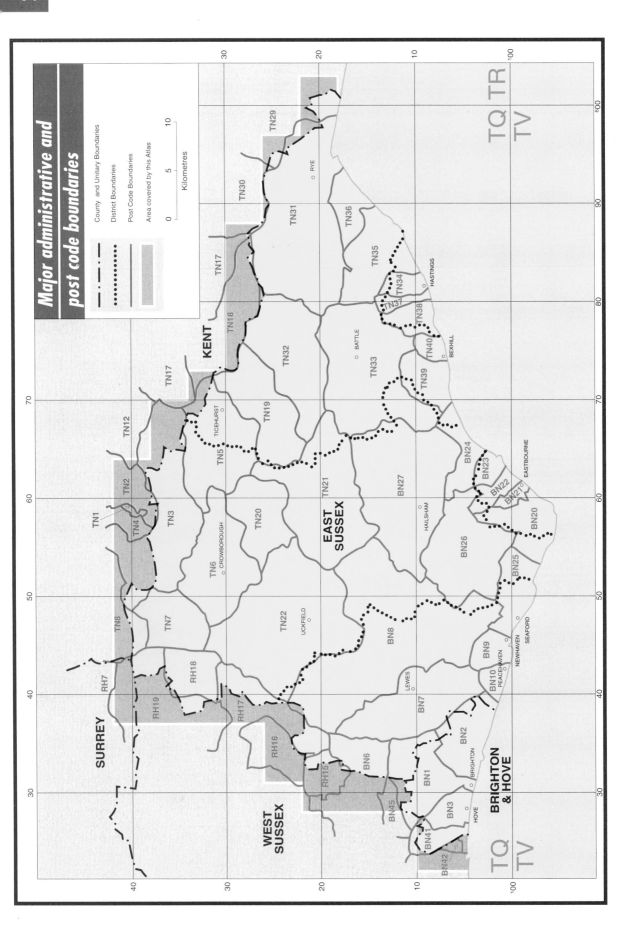

Major administrative and post code boundaries

County and Unitary Boundaries

District Boundaries

Post Code Boundaries

Area covered by this Atlas

Kilometres

0   5   10

SURREY

KENT

WEST SUSSEX

EAST SUSSEX

BRIGHTON & HOVE

TN1
TN2
TN3
TN4
TN5
TN6
TN7
TN8
TN12
TN17
TN18
TN19
TN20
TN21
TN22
TN29
TN30
TN31
TN32
TN33
TN34
TN35
TN36
TN37
TN38
TN39
TN40

RH7
RH16
RH17
RH18
RH19

BN1
BN2
BN3
BN6
BN7
BN8
BN9
BN10
BN20
BN21
BN22
BN23
BN24
BN25
BN26
BN27
BN41
BN42
BN45

TICEHURST
CROWBOROUGH
UCKFIELD
RYE
BATTLE
HASTINGS
BEXHILL
EASTBOURNE
HAILSHAM
LEWES
NEWHAVEN
SEAFORD
PEACEHAVEN
BRIGHTON
HOVE

TQ TR
TV

TQ
TV

30
20
10
100

40
30
20
100

600

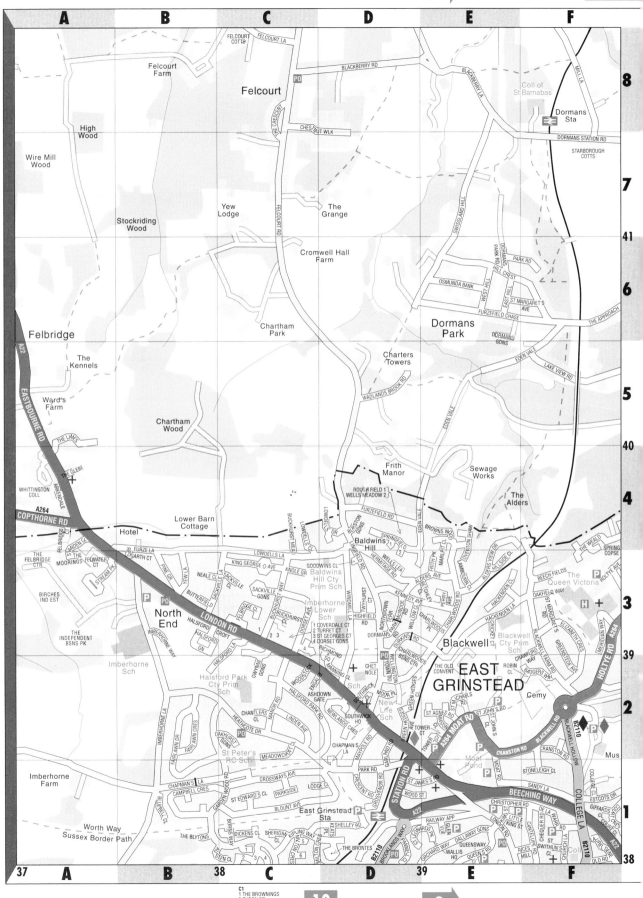

C1
1 THE BROWNINGS
2 BYRON GR
3 CHAUCER AVE
4 TENNYSON RISE
5 THE SAYERS
6 WORDSWORTH RISE

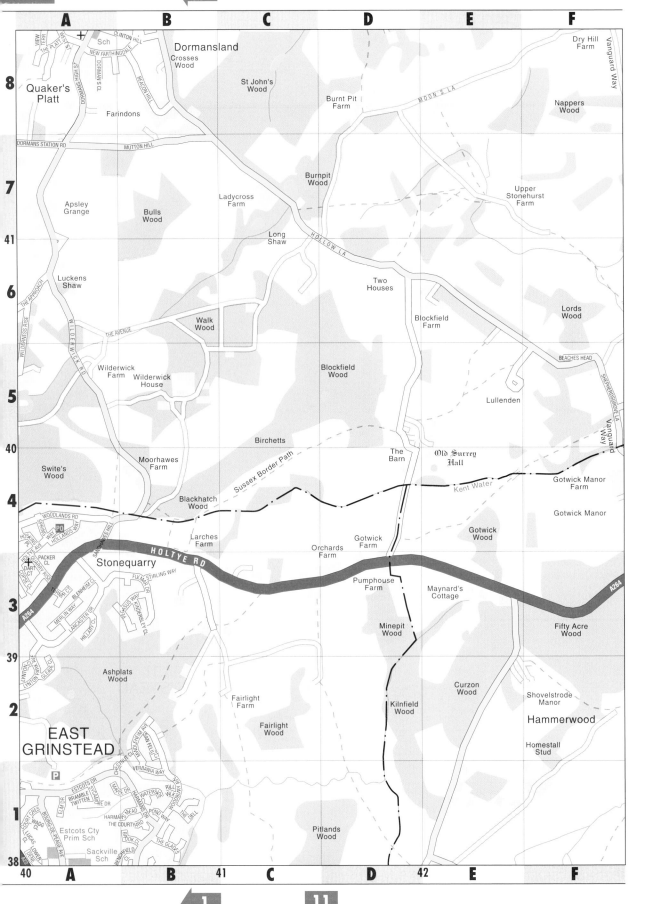

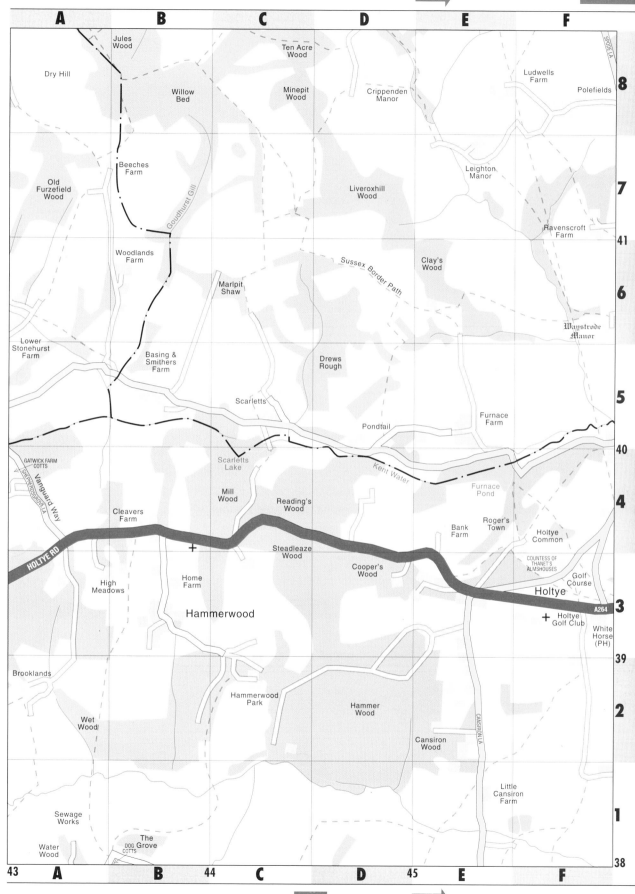

A B C D E F

Jules Wood

Dry Hill

Ten Acre Wood

Minepit Wood

Crippenden Manor

Ludwells Farm

Polefields

8

Willow Bed

Beeches Farm

Leighton Manor

Old Furzefield Wood

Liveroxhill Wood

7

Goudhurst Gill

Woodlands Farm

Ravenscroft Farm

41

Sussex Border Path

Clay's Wood

Marlpit Shaw

6

Maystrode Manor

Lower Stonehurst Farm

Basing & Smithers Farm

Drews Rough

Scarletts

5

Furnace Farm

Pondtail

GATWICK FARM COTTS

Scarletts Lake

40

Kent Water

Mill Wood

Reading's Wood

Furnace Pond

4

SHEPHERDSFORD LA

Vanguard Way

Cleavers Farm

Bank Farm

Roger's Town

Holtye Common

Steadleaze Wood

Cooper's Wood

COUNTESS OF THANET'S ALMSHOUSES

HOLTYE RD

High Meadows

Home Farm

Golf Course

Holtye

3

Hammerwood

A264

Holtye Golf Club

White Horse (PH)

Brooklands

39

Hammerwood Park

Hammer Wood

Wet Wood

CANSIRON LA

2

Cansiron Wood

Little Cansiron Farm

1

Sewage Works

Water Wood

The Grove
DOG COTTS

38

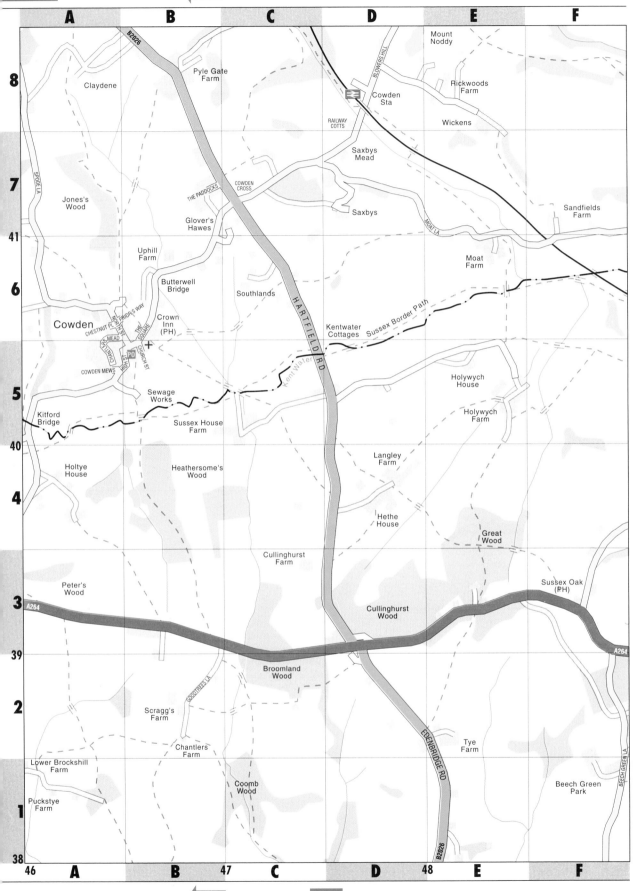

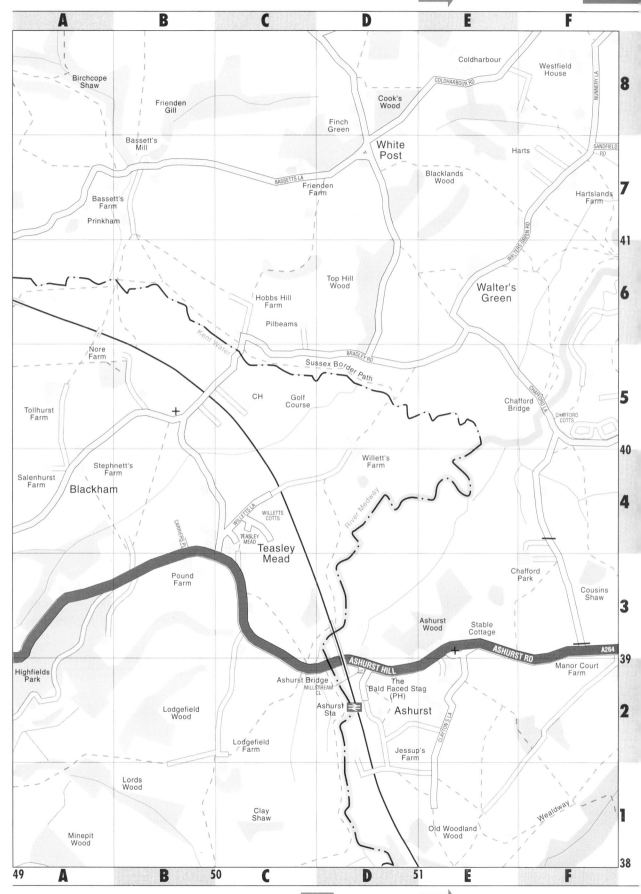

A B C D E F

8

Birchcope
Shaw

Coldharbour

Westfield
House

COLDHARBOUR RD

NUNNERY LA

Frienden
Gill

Cook's
Wood

Finch
Green

White
Post

Harts

SANDFIELD
RD

Bassett's
Mill

7

Blacklands
Wood

Hartslands
Farm

BASSETTS LA

Frienden
Farm

Bassett's
Farm

Prinkham

41

WALTERS GREEN RD

Top Hill
Wood

Walter's
Green

6

Hobbs Hill
Farm

Kent Water

Pilbeams

BRADLEY RD

Nore
Farm

Sussex Border Path

CHAFFORD LA

Chafford
Bridge

CHAFFORD
COTTS

5

CH

Golf
Course

+

Tollhurst
Farm

40

Salenhurst
Farm

Stephnett's
Farm

Willett's
Farm

4

Blackham

WILLETTS LA

CARRIERS PL

WILLETTS
COTTS

River Medway

TEASLEY
MEAD

Teasley
Mead

Chafford
Park

Cousins
Shaw

3

Pound
Farm

Ashurst
Wood

Stable
Cottage

+

ASHURST RD

A264

ASHURST HILL

39

Highfields
Park

Ashurst Bridge

MILLSTREAM
CL

The
Bald Faced Stag
(PH)

Manor Court
Farm

2

Lodgefield
Wood

Ashurst
Sta

Ashurst

CLAYTON S LA

Lodgefield
Farm

Jessup's
Farm

Lords
Wood

Clay
Shaw

Wealdway

1

Minepit
Wood

Old Woodland
Wood

38

49 A B 50 C D 51 E F

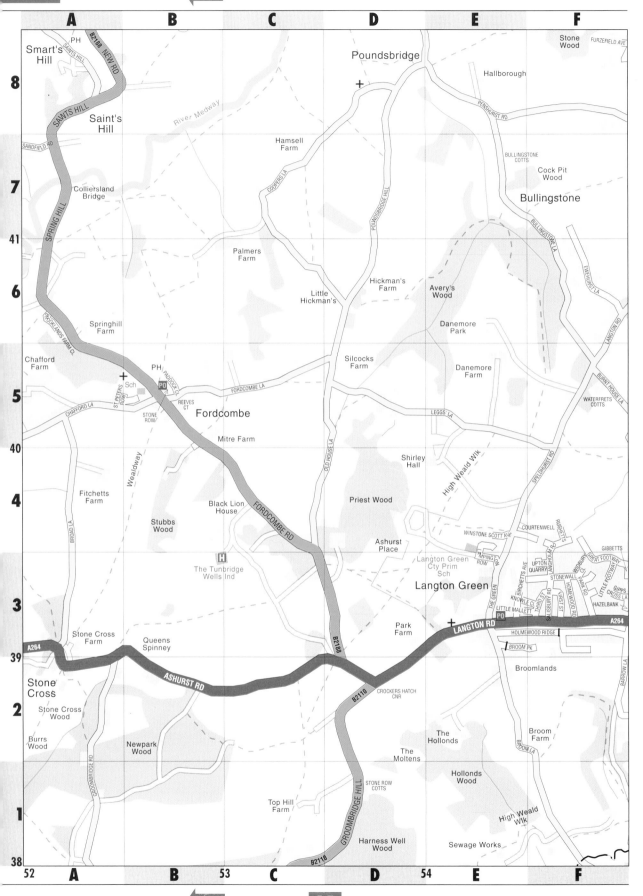

5

5

15

A   B   C   D   E   F

8

7

41

6

5

40

4

3

39

2

1

38

52   A   B   53   C   D   54   E   F

Smart's Hill

PH

B2188 NEW RD

SAINTS HILL

PH

SAINTS HILL

Saint's Hill

SANDFIELD RD

River Medway

Poundsbridge

Stone Wood

FURZEFIELD AVE

Hallborough

PENSHURST RD

BULLINGSTONE COTTS

Cock Pit Wood

SPRING HILL

Colliersland Bridge

Hamsell Farm

COOPERS LA

POUNDSBRIDGE HILL

Bullingstone

BULLINGSTONE LA

BROOKLANDS FARM CL

Springhill Farm

Palmers Farm

Little Hickman's

Hickman's Farm

Avery's Wood

Danemore Park

EWEHURST LA

LANGTON RD

Chafford Farm

CHAFFORD LA

BROAD LA

St PETERS ROW

Sch

PH

PADDOCK CT

PO

REEVES CT

STONE ROW

Fordcombe

FORDCOMBE LA

Mitre Farm

Silcocks Farm

Danemore Farm

LEGGS LA

BURNT HOUSE LA

WATERFRETS COTTS

Wealdway

Fitchetts Farm

Stubbs Wood

Black Lion House

FORDCOMBE RD

OLD HOUSE LA

Priest Wood

Shirley Hall

HIGH WEALD WLK

SPELDHURST RD

H

The Tunbridge Wells Ind

Langton Green Cty Prim Sch

WINSTONE SCOTT AVE

COURTENWELL

RUSHETTS

GIBBETTS

LITTLE FOOTWAY

GREAT FOOTWAY

UPTON CL

BIRCHETTS AVE

STONEWALL

WIDBURY RD

HOMEWOOD RD

PARK RD

FIRST ST

GIPPS CROSS LA

HAZELBANK

SALISBURY RD

KNOWLE CL

THIRD ST

LITTLE MALLETT

THE GREEN

Langton Green

Ashurst Place

TAMPING ROW

Park Farm

LANGTON RD

PO

A264

Stone Cross Farm

Queens Spinney

A264

ASHURST RD

B2188

HOLMEWOOD RIDGE

BROOM PK

Broomlands

BARROW LA

Stone Cross

Stone Cross Wood

Burrs Wood

GROOMBRIDGE RD

Newpark Wood

B2110

CROCKERS HATCH CNR

The Hollonds

The Moltens

Broom Farm

BROOM LA

Hollonds Wood

Top Hill Farm

GROOMBRIDGE HILL

STONE ROW COTTS

Harness Well Wood

B2110

Sewage Works

High Weald Wlk

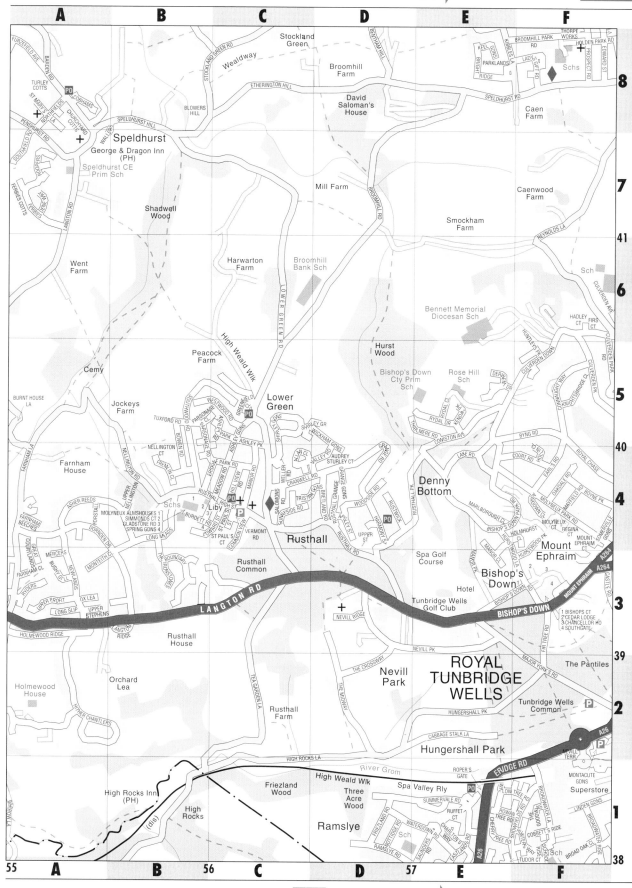

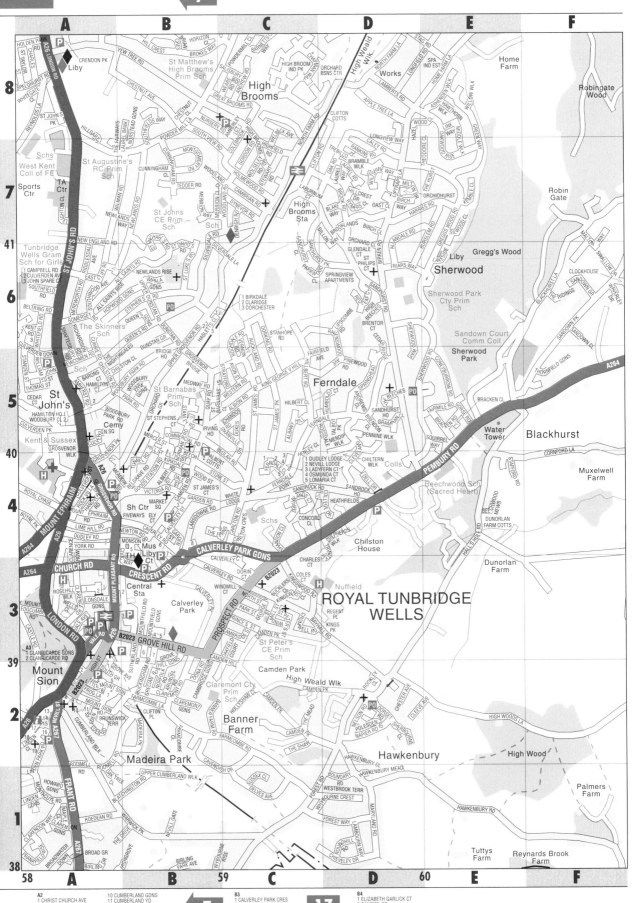

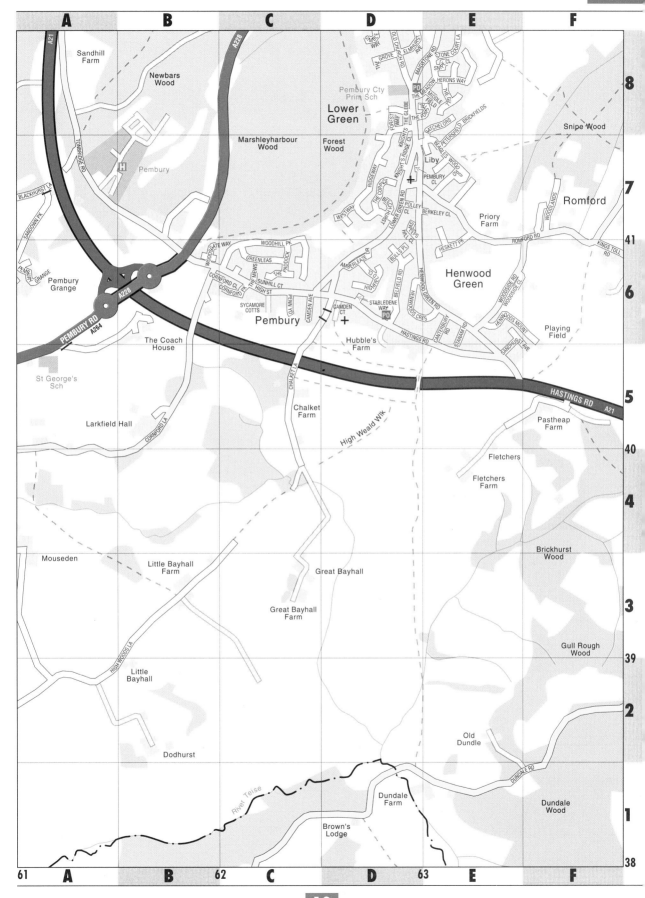

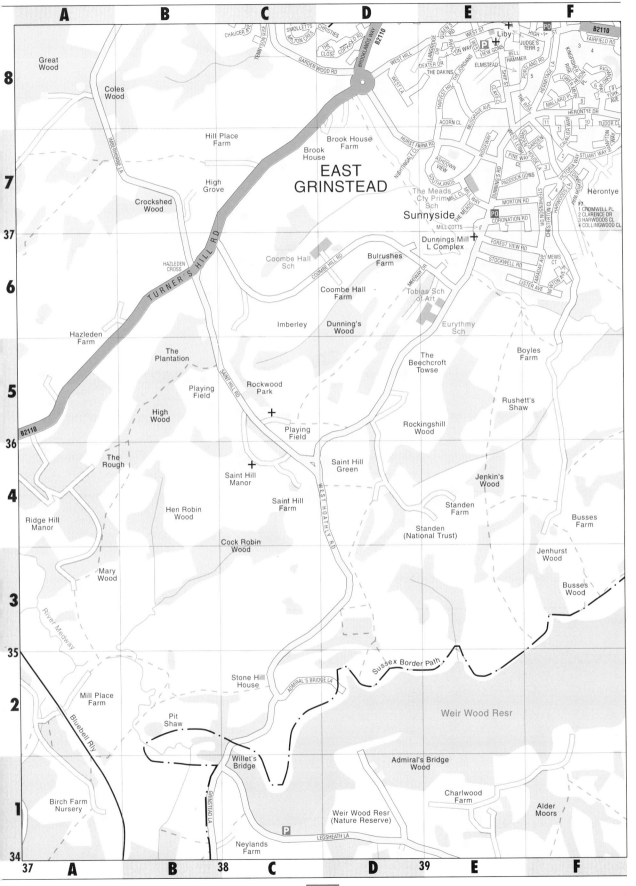

F8
1 MIDDLE ROW
2 FOREST LODGE
3 SACKVILLE CT
4 GREAT HOUSE CT
5 PORTLAND HO
6 CORNWALL GDNS
7 NORMANDY CL
8 WILLOW MEAD
9 KINGS COPSE
10 REGAL DR
11 BECKETT WAY

EAST
GRINSTEAD

Sunnyside

F7
1 CROMWELL PL
2 CLARENCE DR
3 HARWOODS CL
4 COLLINGWOOD CL

Herontye

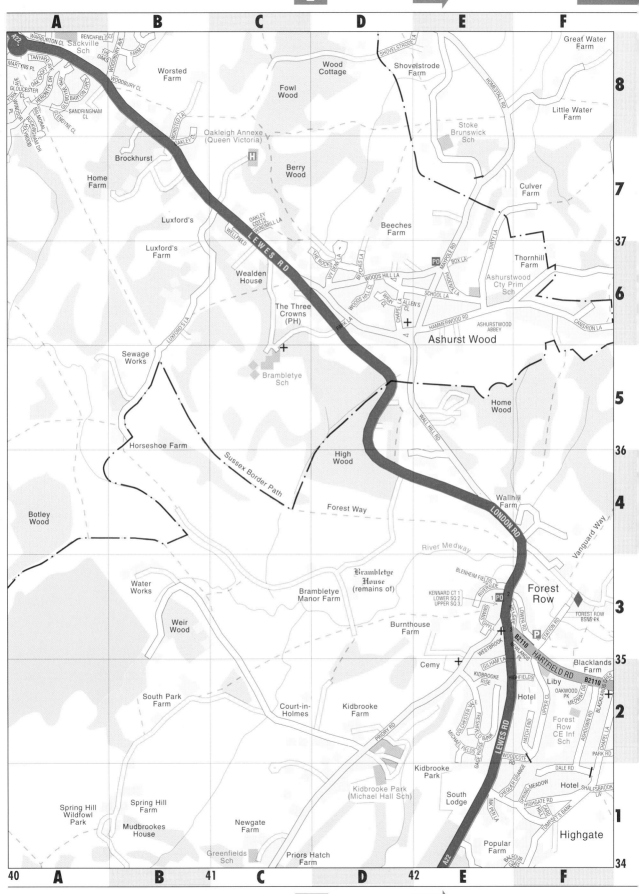

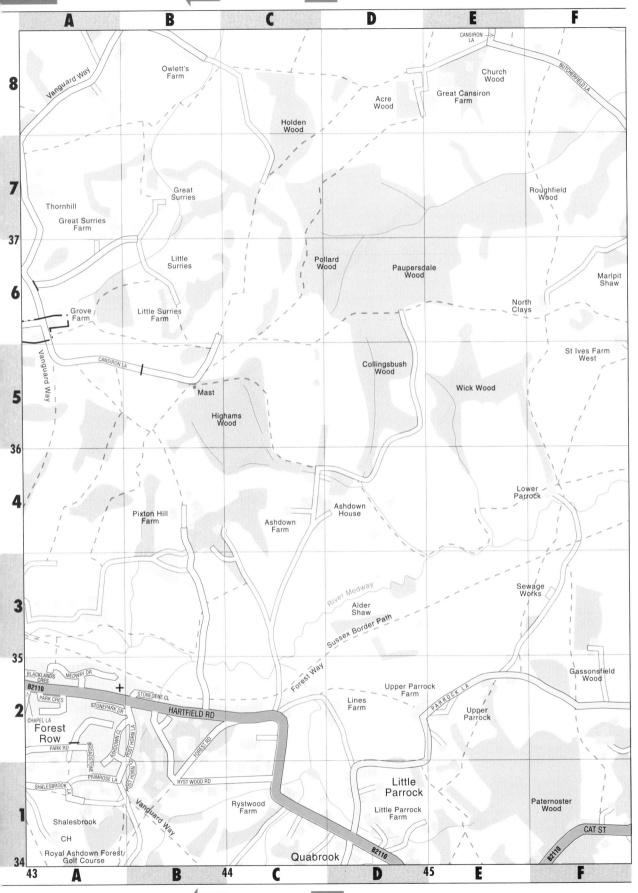

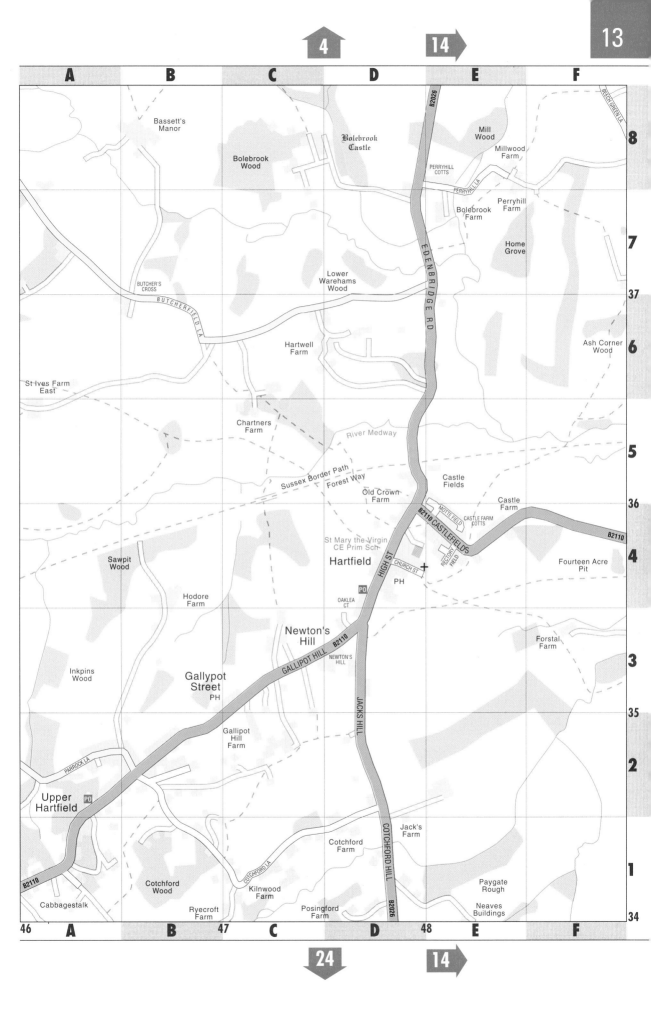

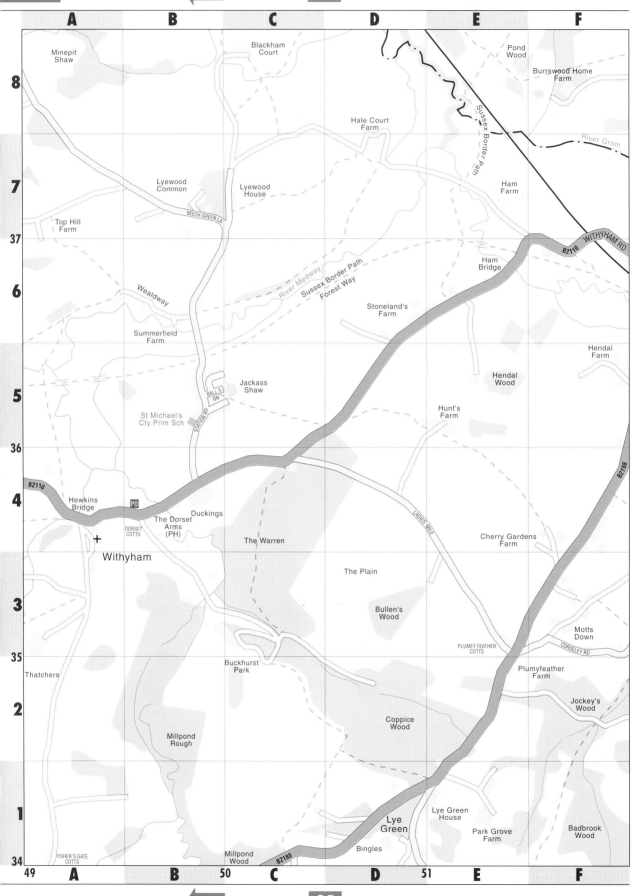

13
5

A B C D E F

8

Minepit
Shaw

Blackham
Court

Pond
Wood

Burrswood Home
Farm

Hale Court
Farm

Sussex Border Path

River Grom

7

Lyewood
Common

Lyewood
House

BEECH GREEN LA

Ham
Farm

37

Top Hill
Farm

WITHYHAM RD

B2110

6

Wealdway

River Medway

Sussex Border Path

Forest Way

Ham
Bridge

Stoneland's
Farm

Hendal
Farm

Summerfield
Farm

Hendal
Wood

5

BALL'S
GN

Jackass
Shaw

Hunt's
Farm

St Michael's
Cty Prim Sch

STATION RD

36

B2188

4

B2110

Hewkins
Bridge

PO

Duckings

Cherry Gardens
Farm

DORSET
COTTS

The Dorset
Arms
(PH)

The Warren

LADIES' MILE

+

Withyham

The Plain

Bullen's
Wood

3

Motts
Down

PLUMEY FEATHER
COTTS

CORSELEY RD

35

Buckhurst
Park

Plumyfeather
Farm

Thatchers

Jockey's
Wood

2

Millpond
Rough

Coppice
Wood

1

Lye Green
House

Lye
Green

Park Grove
Farm

Badbrook
Wood

34

FISHER'S GATE
COTTS

Millpond
Wood

B2188

Bingles

49 A B 50 C D 51 E F

13
25

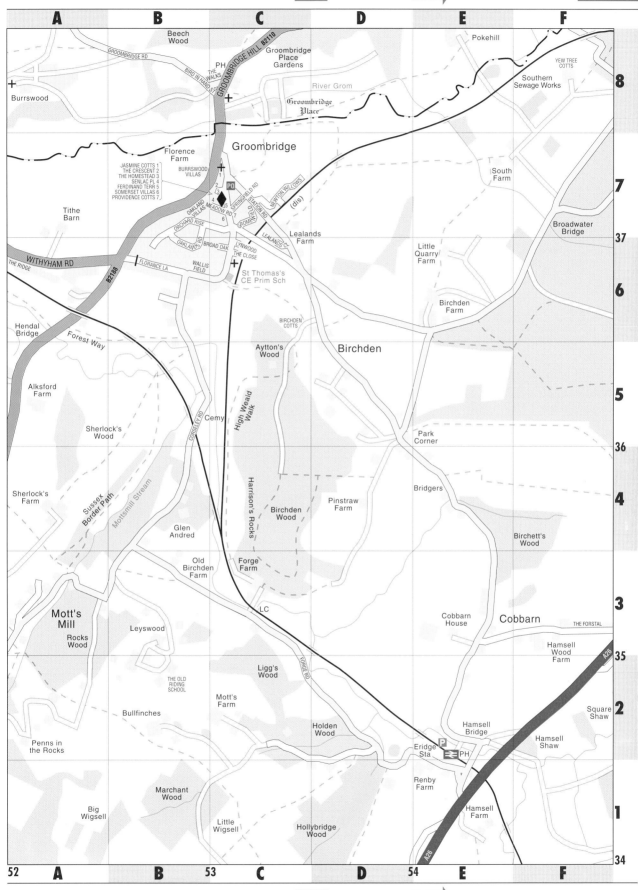

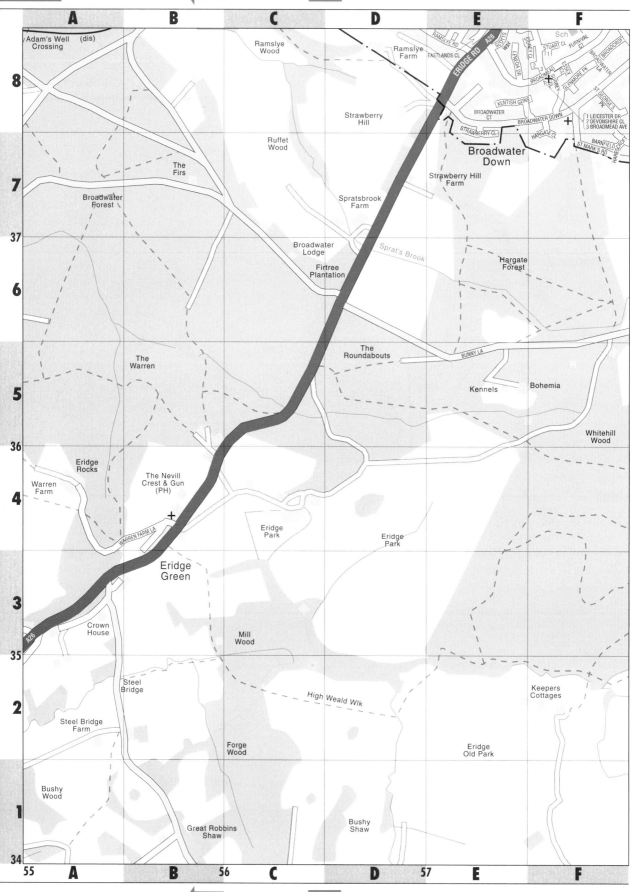

A **B** **C** **D** **E** **F**

Adam's Well (dis)
Crossing

Ramslye
Wood

Ramslye
Farm

Eastlands Cl

Sch

ERIDGE RD

A26

SCOTTS
WAY

SIDNEY
CL

STUART CL

FURNIVAL
CL

BROADCROFT

BROADCROFT

BROADWATER

8

Strawberry
Hill

BROADWATER
CT

KENTISH GDNS

BROADMEAD

SURREY

ESSEX CL

GLENMORE PK

ST GEORGE'S
PK

Ruffet
Wood

BROADWATER DOWN

1 LEICESTER DR
2 DEVONSHIRE CL
3 BROADMEAD AVE

The
Firs

Broadwater
Forest

7

Strawberry Cl

HARGATE CL

ST MARKS RD

BARNFIELD CROFT

HARESCROFT

Broadwater
Down

Strawberry Hill
Farm

37

Spratsbrook
Farm

Broadwater
Lodge

Sprat's Brook

Hargate
Forest

6

Firtree
Plantation

The
Warren

The Roundabouts

BUNNY LA

Bohemia

5

Kennels

Whitehill
Wood

36

Eridge
Rocks

Warren
Farm

The Nevill
Crest & Gun
(PH)

4

WARREN FARM LA

Eridge
Park

Eridge
Park

Eridge
Green

3

Crown
House

Mill
Wood

A26

35

Steel
Bridge

High Weald Wlk

Keepers
Cottages

2

Steel Bridge
Farm

Forge
Wood

Eridge
Old Park

Bushy
Wood

1

Great Robbins
Shaw

Bushy
Shaw

34

A **B** **C** **D** **E** **F**

55 56 57

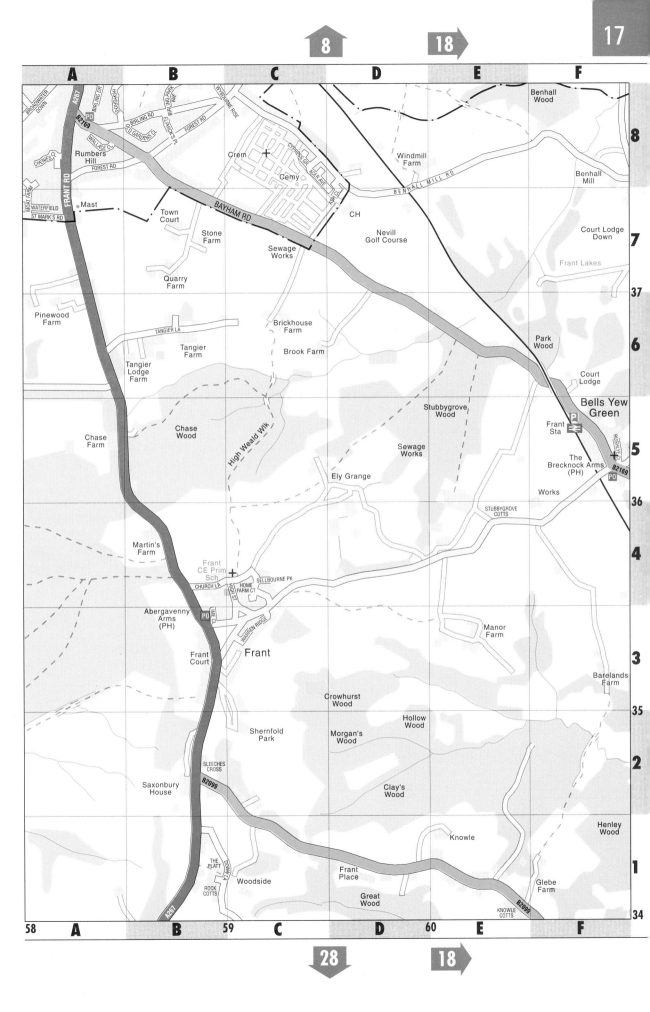

A B C D E F

8

Coker's Down

Sunninglye Farmhouse

Rushlye Down

Coneyburrow Wood

Furnace Wood

7

River Teise

Oxpasture Wood

Tollslye

The Bothy

37

6

Hollow Wood

Bayham Lake

Rushlye Farmhouse

Jews Wood

Great Coppice Wood

Abbots Down

Highfield

Diamonds

5

MIDDLE RD

Forest Lodge

B2169

Burnt Wood

Upper Sluice Wood

LITTLE BAYHAM COTTS

36

B2169

Bartley Mill Wood

Little Bayham

4

Higham Wood

Higham Farm

Verridge Wood

Bartley Mill

Churchfield Wood

Little Shoesmiths

Bartley House

Wickhurst Farmhouse

3

35

Sewers Bridge

Brookland Wood

Grigg's Wood

Shoesmith's Wood

Brick Kiln Wood

2

Camden Wood

Great Shoesmith Farm

Henley Wood

Sussex Border Path

Hewley Wood

1

WHITEGATES LA

34

Down Wood

DEWHURST LA

Sewage Works

61 A B 62 C D 63 E F

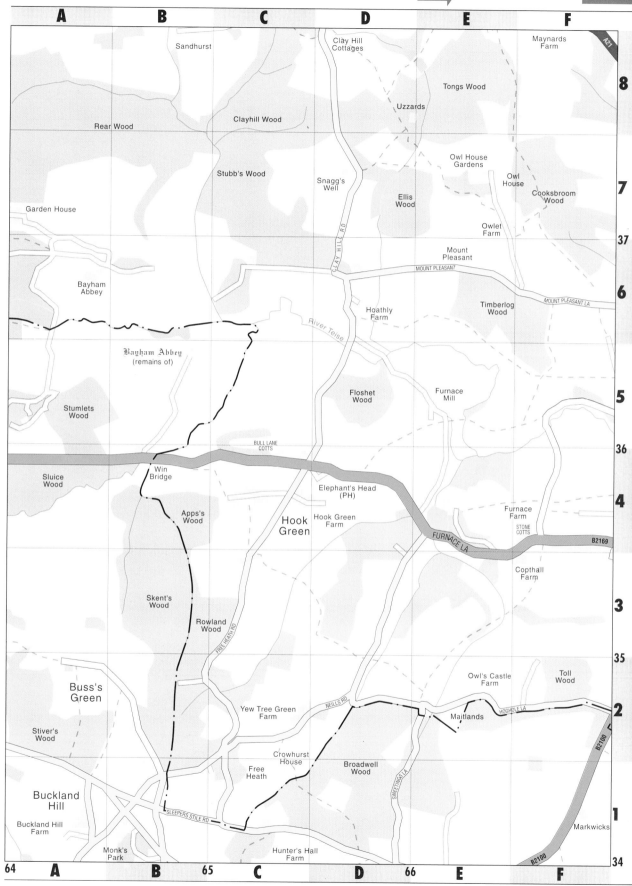

A   B   C   D   E   F

Sandhurst

Clay Hill Cottages

Maynards Farm

A21

Tongs Wood

8

Rear Wood

Clayhill Wood

Uzzards

Owl House Gardens

Owl House

Cooksbroom Wood

7

Stubb's Wood

Snagg's Well

Ellis Wood

Owlet Farm

37

Garden House

CLAY HILL RD

Mount Pleasant

MOUNT PLEASANT

Bayham Abbey

Mount Pleasant

Hoathly Farm

Timberlog Wood

MOUNT PLEASANT LA

6

River Teise

Bayham Abbey (remains of)

Floshet Wood

Furnace Mill

5

Stumlets Wood

BULL LANE COTTS

36

Sluice Wood

Win Bridge

Elephant's Head (PH)

Furnace Farm

4

Apps's Wood

Hook Green

Hook Green Farm

STONE COTTS

FURNACE LA

B2169

Copthall Farm

Skent's Wood

3

Rowland Wood

FREE HEATH RD

35

Buss's Green

Owl's Castle Farm

Toll Wood

Yew Tree Green Farm

NEILLS RD

Maitlands

HOGHOLE LA

2

Stiver's Wood

Crowhurst House

Broadwell Wood

SNEETLING LA

B2100

Free Heath

Buckland Hill

Buckland Hill Farm

SLEEPERS STILE RD

Markwicks

1

Monk's Park

Hunter's Hall Farm

B2100

34

64   A   B   65   C   D   66   E   F

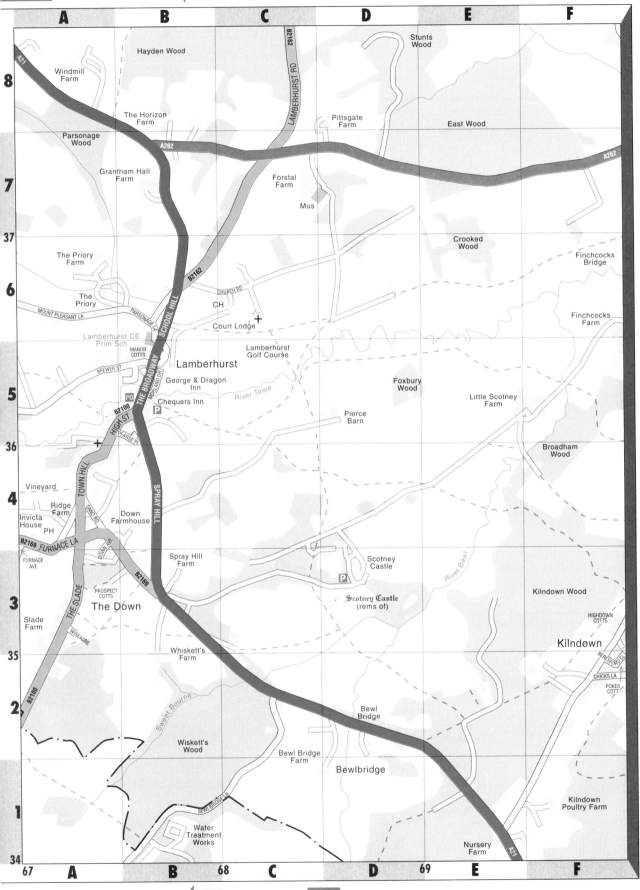

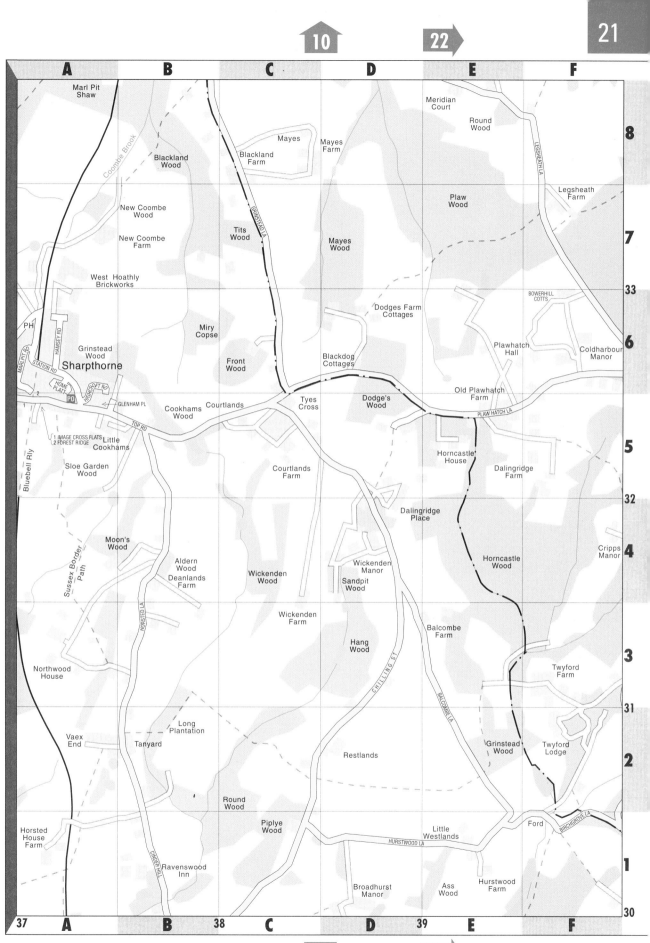

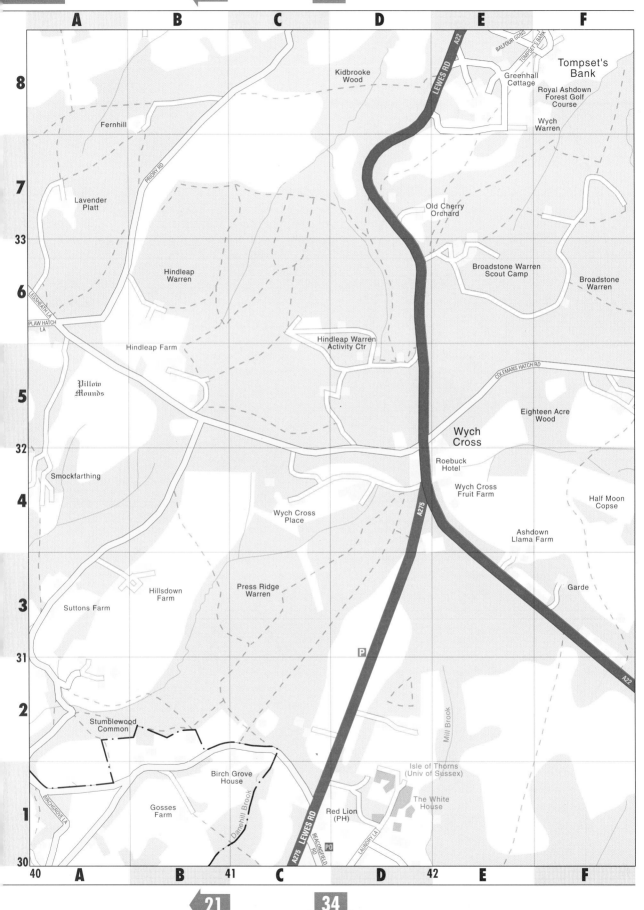

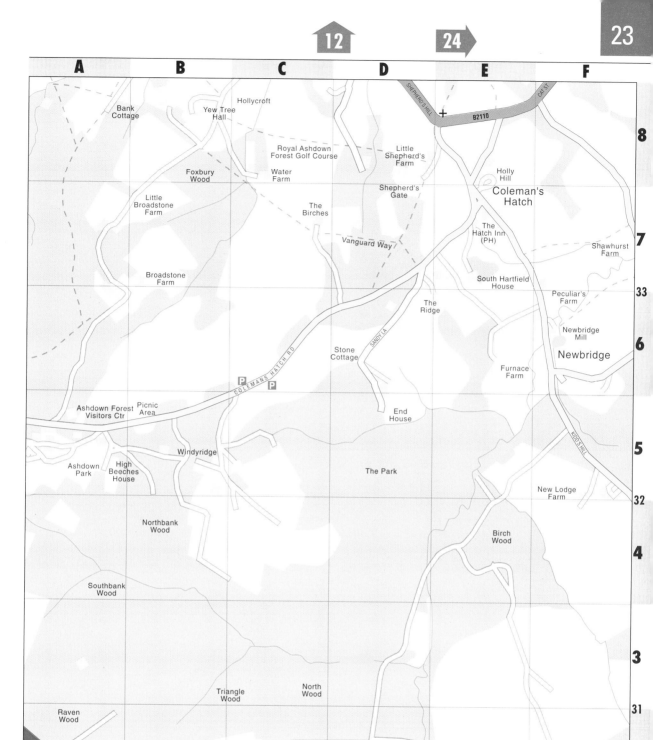

A   B   C   D   E   F

8

Bank
Cottage

Hollycroft

Yew Tree
Hall

Royal Ashdown
Forest Golf Course

Little
Shepherd's
Farm

SHEPHERD'S HILL

B2110

CAT ST

Foxbury
Wood

Water
Farm

Shepherd's
Gate

Holly
Hill

Coleman's
Hatch

7

Little
Broadstone
Farm

The
Birches

Vanguard Way

The
Hatch Inn
(PH)

Shawhurst
Farm

Broadstone
Farm

The
Ridge

South Hartfield
House

Peculiar's
Farm

33

COLEMANS HATCH RD

SANDY LA

Stone
Cottage

Newbridge
Mill

Newbridge

6

P
P

End
House

Furnace
Farm

Ashdown Forest
Visitors Ctr

Picnic
Area

5

Windyridge

The Park

KIDD'S HILL

Ashdown
Park

High
Beeches
House

New Lodge
Farm

32

Northbank
Wood

Birch
Wood

4

Southbank
Wood

3

Triangle
Wood

North
Wood

31

Raven
Wood

2

West
Wood

Pippingford
Park

P

Home
Farm

East
Wood

1

STABLE
CTYD

Old Lodge
Farm

Chelwood
Vachery

A22

30

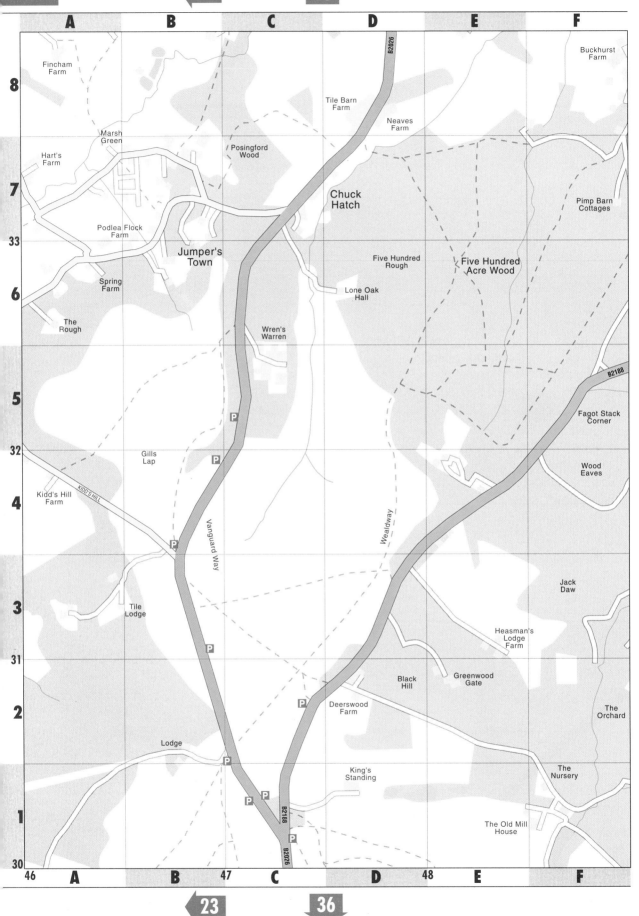

A   B   C   D   E   F

Buckhurst
Farm

Fincham
Farm

8

Tile Barn
Farm

Marsh
Green

Neaves
Farm

Hart's
Farm

Posingford
Wood

7

Chuck
Hatch

Pimp Barn
Cottages

Podlea Flock
Farm

33

Jumper's
Town

Five Hundred
Rough

Five Hundred
Acre Wood

Spring
Farm

6

Lone Oak
Hall

The
Rough

Wren's
Warren

B2188

5

Fagot Stack
Corner

Gills
Lap

32

Wood
Eaves

Kidd's Hill
Farm

KIDD'S HILL

4

Vanguard Way

Wealdway

Tile
Lodge

3

Jack
Daw

Heasman's
Lodge
Farm

31

Black
Hill

Greenwood
Gate

The
Orchard

2

Deerswood
Farm

Lodge

King's
Standing

The
Nursery

B2188

1

The Old Mill
House

B2026

30

46   A   B   47   C   D   48   E   F

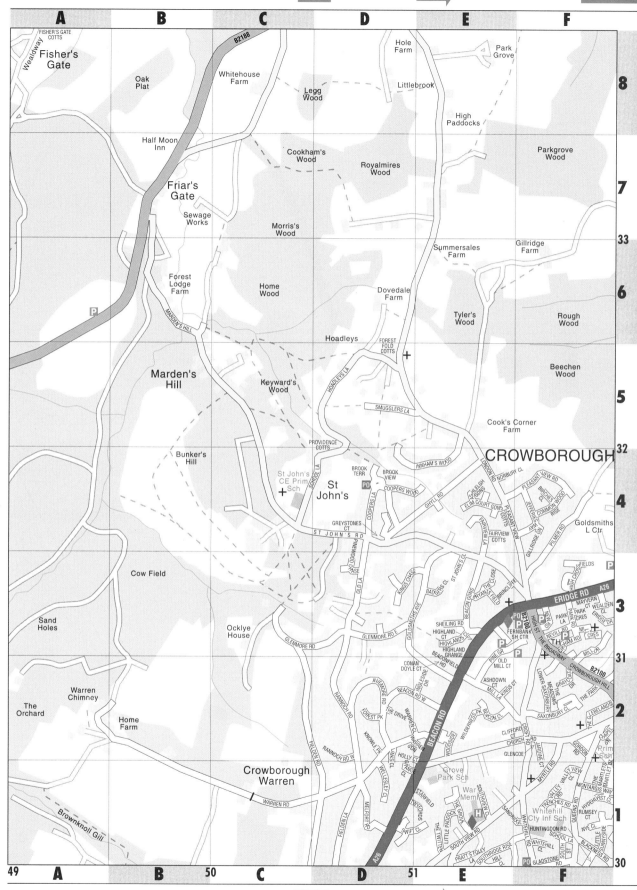

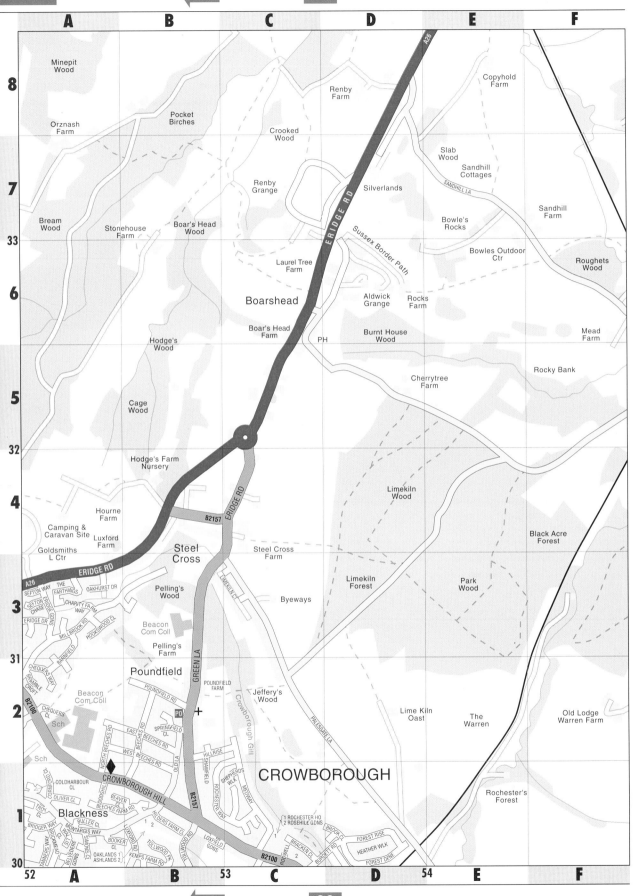

8

Minepit Wood

Orznash Farm

Pocket Birches

Crooked Wood

Renby Farm

Copyhold Farm

Slab Wood

Sandhill Cottages

Bream Wood

Stonehouse Farm

Boar's Head Wood

Renby Grange

Silverlands

Bowle's Rocks

Sandhill Farm

7

33

Laurel Tree Farm

Sussex Border Path

Bowles Outdoor Ctr

Roughets Wood

6

Boarshead

Aldwick Grange

Rocks Farm

Mead Farm

Boar's Head Farm

PH

Burnt House Wood

Rocky Bank

Hodge's Wood

Cherrytree Farm

5

Cage Wood

32

Hodge's Farm Nursery

ERIDGE RD

Limekiln Wood

Black Acre Forest

4

Hourne Farm

B2157

Camping & Caravan Site

Luxford Farm

Steel Cross Farm

Steel Cross

Limekiln Forest

Park Wood

Goldsmiths L Ctr

ERIDGE RD

A26

SEFTON WAY
THE FARTHWIGS
OAKHURST DR

Pelling's Wood

Byeways

3

SEFTON WAY
ERIDGE GDNS
ERIDGE CHASE

CHARITY FARM WAY

Beacon Com Coll

ERIDGE DR

MILLBROOK RD
HOOKSWOOD CL

GREEN LA

31

BARNFIELD

Pelling's Farm

Poundfield

CHEQUERS WAY
BRAMBLE CROFT

POUNDFIELD RD

Poundfield Farm

Jeffery's Wood

Crowborough Gill

PALESGATE LA

B2100

Beacon Com Coll

CHEQUERS CL

Sch

P O

SPRINGFIELD RD

2

+

NORTH BEECHES RD

EAST BEECHES RD
OLD LA

HILLRISE

SHAWFIELD

Lime Kiln Oast

The Warren

Old Lodge Warren Farm

Sch

WEST BEECHES RD

ROCHESTER WAY

SHEPHERDS WLK

MEDWAY

CROWBOROUGH

Rochester's Forest

COLDHARBOUR CL

CROWBOROUGH HILL

OLIVER CL

BEAVER CL
BEECHES FARM RD

HELDERS FARM CL

B2157

1 ROCHESTER HO
2 ROSEHILE GDNS

FOREST RISE

1

Blackness

BRIDGER WAY

BULLER CL

HILDERS FARM CL
TOLLWOOD PK

LOXFIELD GDNS

BROOK RD

BURDETT RD

HEATHER WLK

FOREST DENE

30

OAKLANDS
ASHLANDS

BOOKER CL

KEMPS FARM RD

B2100

ROOTWELL

BRACKEN CL

A B C D E F

8

7

33

6

5

32

4

31

3

2

1

30

Hamsell Manor

Rowland Wood

Stonewall Ghyll

Stitches Farm

Marchant's Wood

Redgate Mill Farm

Blackdon Hill Farm

Newhouse Farm

Sewage Works

The Cants

Hornshurst Wood

Highgate Farm

St Deny's Lodge

HIGHGATE FLATS

Biddenden Farm

Cemy

Little Millhole Wood

Big Millhole Wood

Sham Farm

Danegate

Stonewall

Sussex Border Path

Whitehouse Farm

BLACKDON HILL

Card's Wood

Hoth Wood

Town Row Green Farm

Chant Lane Farm

CHANT LA

HORNSHURST RD

B2100

STATION RD

NEW RD

Long Wood

Great Danegate

Hoth Farm

Entryhill Wood

Entry Hill

Heathfield Hall

Town Row

Highgate

DOUGLAS RD

STATION CL

THE OAKS

ASHLEY RD

PO

PH

BAINDEN CL

YENTRELLA

HOSMERS FIELD

Spring Wood

Lords Wood

Stone House Farm

The Gill

Greenhouse Farm

Orphanage Wood

Ashley Farm

Medway Farm

CATT'S HILL

CATT'S CORNER COTTS

BLETCHINGLYE LA

Rocks Wood

Saxonbury Wood

Saxonbury Hill

Ashets

Green Hedges Farm

BRICKYARD LA

Towers Lodge Farm

Forest Farm

Lodge Farm

Markhouse Farm

B2100

Bletchingley Wood

Bletchinglye Farm

55 A B 56 C D 57 E F

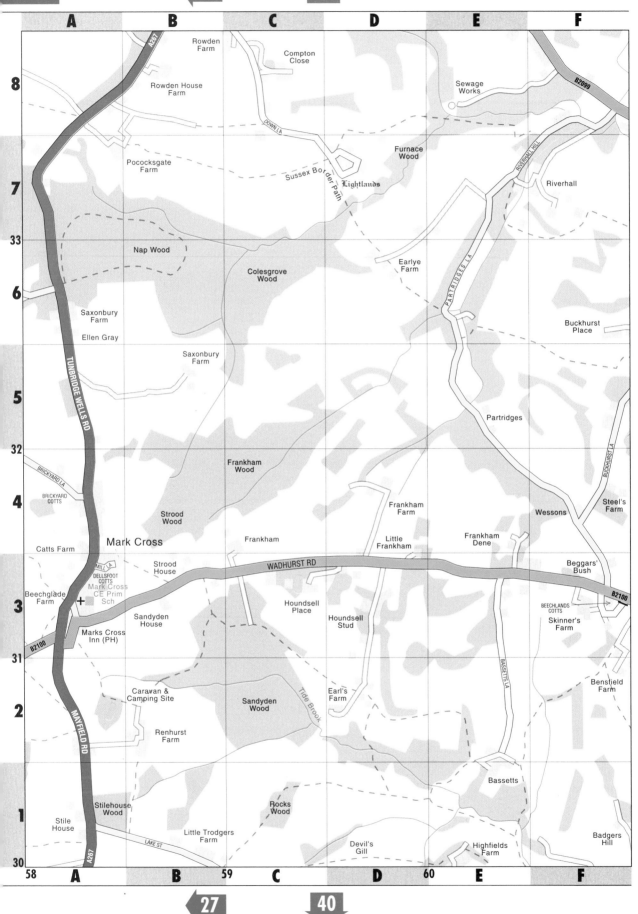

A 27

40

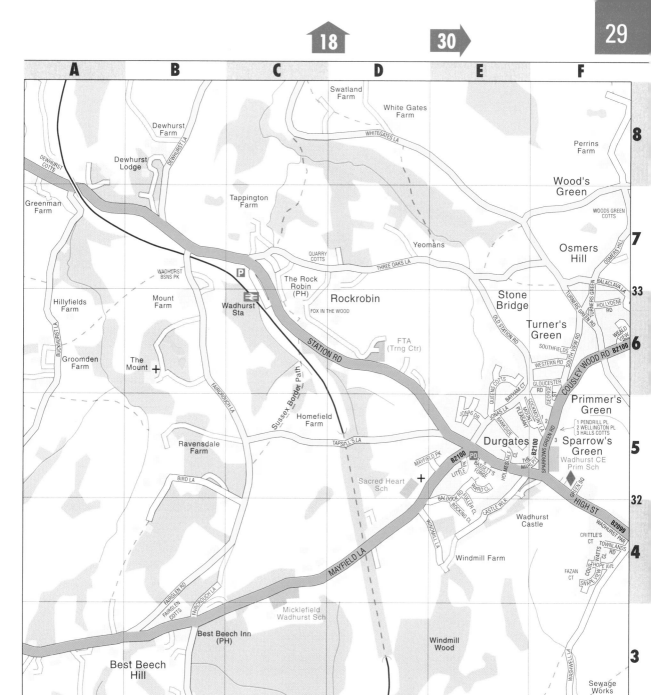

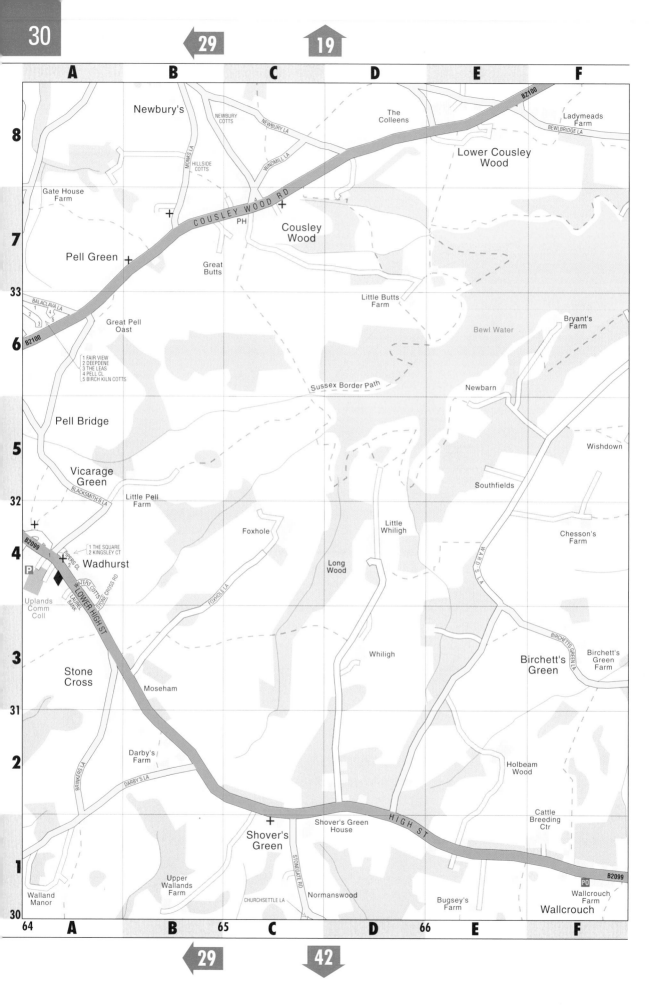

Cats Wood

Beal Barn Gardens

BEWLBRIDGE LA

Visitors Ctr

Slipway

River Bewl

Chingley Wood

8

Hook Farm

Activities Ctr

Chingley Manor

Hook House

A21

7

33

Stonecrouch

HOOK HILL LA

WARD'S LA

Beaumans Oast

Bewl Water

Sussex Border Path

ROSEMARY LA

6

Greenwoods

CLAPHATCH LA

Hazelhurst Farm

Rosemary Farmhouse

5

LOWER HAZELHURST

Nature Reserve

32

Tilehouse Bungalow

Overy's Farm

4

LOWER HAZELHURST

Rowley

Bakers & Strakes Farm

Norwoods Farm

Overy's Farmhouse

HUNTLEY MILL RD

LINTON HILL

Borders Farm

BOARDERS LA

Walter's Farm

3

Burnt Lodge

Three Leg Cross

TINKERS LA

31

BIRCHETTS GREEN LA

Tolhurst

CORONATION COTTS

BURNT LODGE LA

Broomden

Windmill Hill

CROSS LA

2

B2087

Landscapes Farm

Pickforde

Steellands Farm

PH

Dale Hill

VINEYARD LA

Ticehurst House

CROSS LANE GDNS

P

NEWINGTON CT

1-FRONT COTTS
2 CHAPEL PL
3 MARLPIT GDNS
4 REEVES TERR
5 LAVENDER GDNS

CH

Ridgeway Farm

HIGH ST

HILLBURY GDNS

Inn

PICKFORDE LA

FARTHING HILL

THE WARREN

Ticehurst

LOWER PLATTS

HORSEGROVE AVE

1

TAMDEN LA

Brick Kiln Farm

HAZELWOOD COTTS

PO

CHURCH ST

ST MARY'S LA

ST MARY'S CL

SPRINGFIELDS

ACRES RISE

B2087

MEADOWSIDE COTTS

UPPER PLATTS

B2099

30

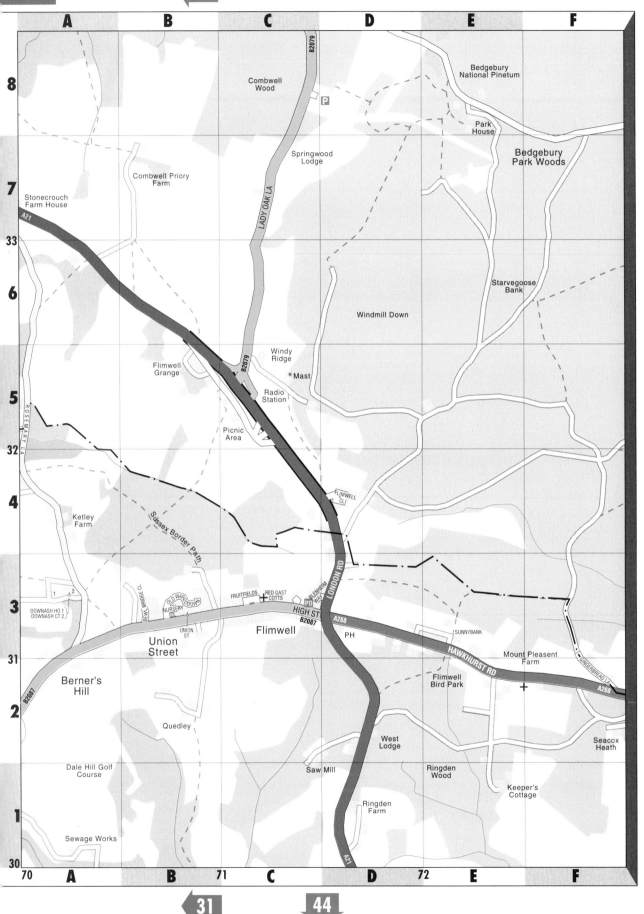

A   B   C   D   E   F

8

Bedgebury
National Pinetum

Combwell
Wood

B2079

P

Park
House

Springwood
Lodge

Bedgebury
Park Woods

7

Combwell Priory
Farm

LADY OAK LA

Stonecrouch
Farm House

A21

33

Starvegoose
Bank

6

Windmill Down

Windy
Ridge

Flimwell
Grange

B2079

Mast

5

Radio
Station

ROSEMARY LA

32

Picnic
Area

4

FLIMWELL
CL

Ketley
Farm

Sussex Border Path

1   2

3

DOWNASH HO 1
DOWNASH CT 2

BERM. BRIDGE CL

OLD WARDS DOWN
NURSERY CL

FRUITFIELDS
RED OAST
COTTS

BLENHEIM WAY

PO

LONDON RD

FLIMWELL CL

UNION
ST

HIGH ST
B2087

A268

PH

SUNNYBANK

Flimwell

HAWKHURST RD

Mount Pleasant
Farm

GINGERBREAD LA

31

Union
Street

A2087

B2087

Berner's
Hill

Flimwell
Bird Park

A268

2

Quedley

West
Lodge

Seacox
Heath

Dale Hill Golf
Course

Saw Mill

Ringden
Wood

Keeper's
Cottage

1

A21

Ringden
Farm

Sewage Works

30

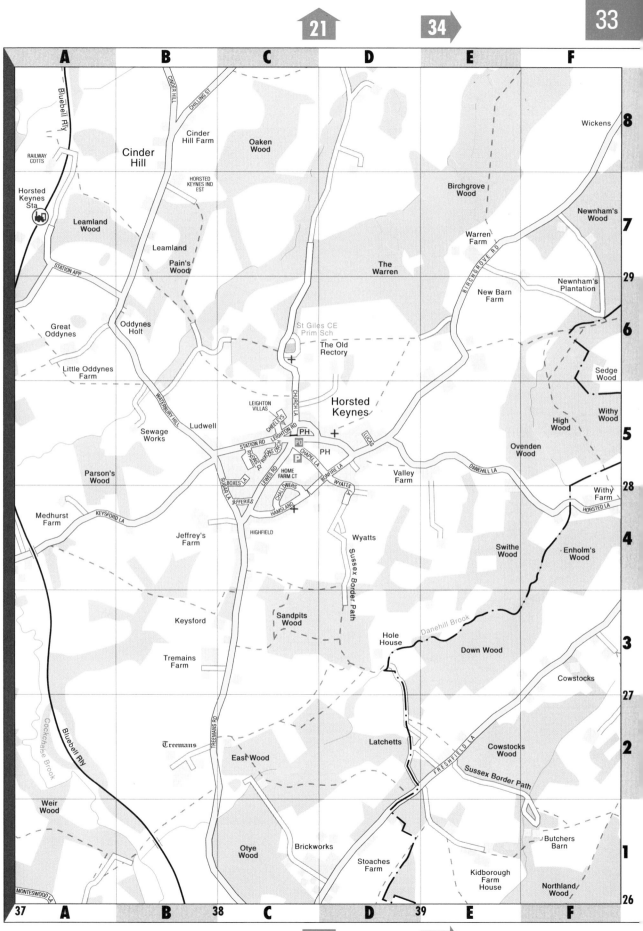

A B C D E F

8

7

29

6

5

28

4

3

27

2

1

26

37 A B 38 C D 39 E F

Bluebell Rly

RAILWAY COTTS

Horsted Keynes Sta

Leamland Wood

STATION APP

Great Oddynes

Little Oddynes Farm

CINDER HILL

CHILLING ST

Cinder Hill

Cinder Hill Farm

HORSTED KEYNES IND EST

Leamland

Pain's Wood

Oddynes Holt

Oaken Wood

St Giles CE Prim Sch

The Old Rectory

Horsted Keynes

Birchgrove Wood

Warren Farm

New Barn Farm

BIRCHGROVE RD

The Warren

Wickens

Newnham's Wood

Newnham's Plantation

Sedge Wood

High Wood

Withy Wood

Ovenden Wood

WATERBURY HILL

Ludwell

Sewage Works

Parson's Wood

Medhurst Farm

KEYSFORD LA

SUGAR LA

LEIGHTON VILLAS

CHEELYS

STATION RD

RIXONS CL

PARSONS ORCH

LEWES RD

BOXES LA

JEFFERIES

CHURCH LA

LEIGHTON RD

PH

PO

P

CHAPEL LA

HOME FARM CT

CHALLONERS

HAMSLAND

PH

BOWFIRE LA

WYATTS LA

LUCAS

Valley Farm

DANEHILL LA

Withy Farm

HORSTED LA

Jeffrey's Farm

HIGHFIELD

Wyatts

Sussex Border Path

Swithe Wood

Enholm's Wood

Keysford

Sandpits Wood

Danehill Brook

Hole House

Down Wood

Cowstocks

Tremains Farm

TREMANS RD

Tremans

East Wood

Latchetts

FRESHFIELD LA

Cowstocks Wood

Sussex Border Path

Cockhaise Brook

Bluebell Rly

Weir Wood

Otye Wood

Brickworks

Stoaches Farm

Kidborough Farm House

Butchers Barn

Northland Wood

MONTESWOOD LA

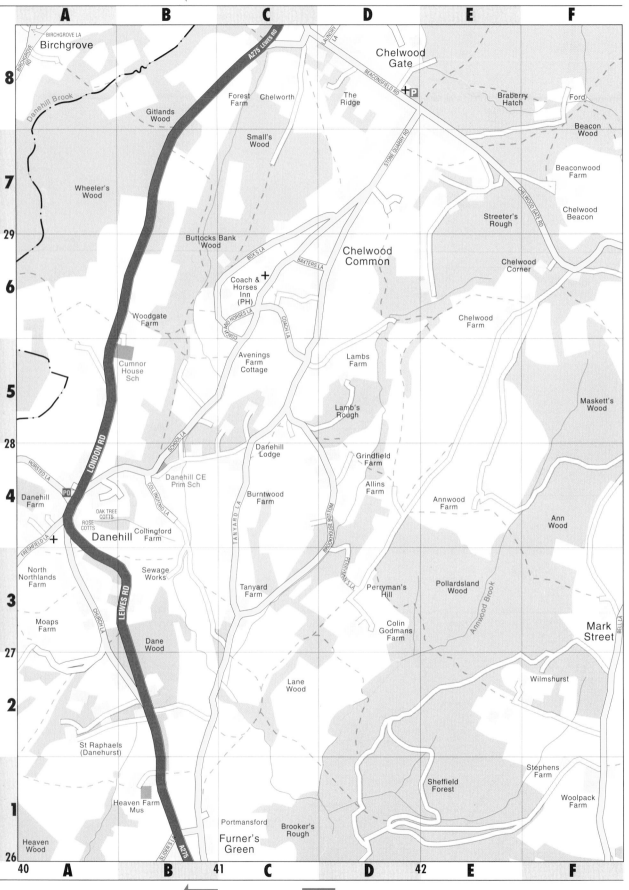

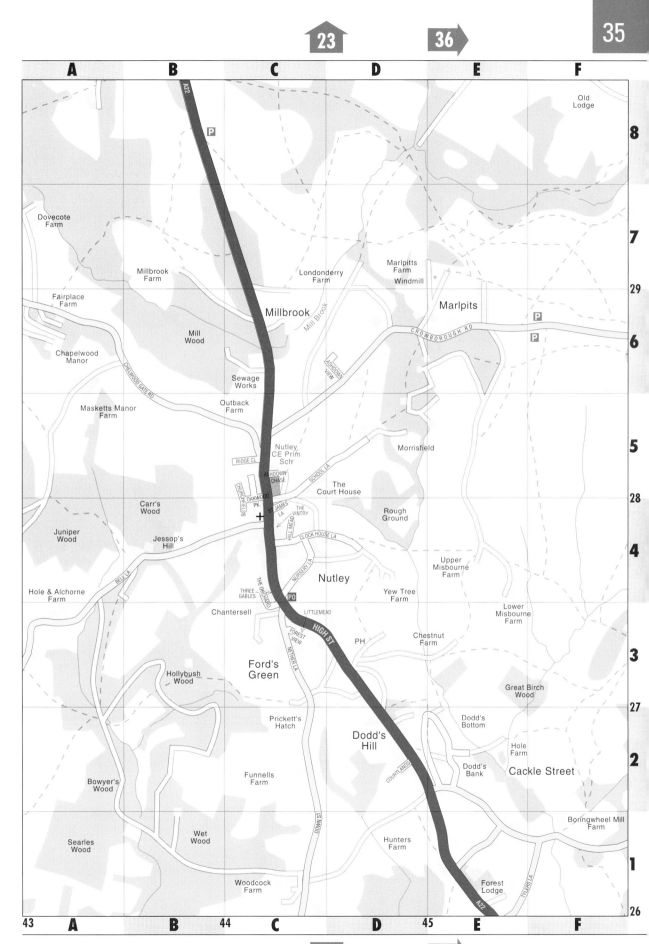

A B C D E F

8

7

29

6

5

28

4

27

2

1

26

Old Lodge

Dovecote Farm

Millbrook Farm

Londonderry Farm

Marlpitts Farm
Windmill

Marlpits

Fairplace Farm

Millbrook

Mill Brook

CROWBOROUGH RD

P
P

Chapelwood Manor

CHELWOOD GATE RD

Mill Wood

Sewage Works

ASHDOWN VIEW

Masketts Manor Farm

Outback Farm

Morrisfield

Nutley CE Prim Sch

SCHOOL LA

RIDGE CL

ASHDOWN CHASE

The Court House

Rough Ground

Carr's Wood

CHURCHFIELDS

OAKWOOD PK

ST JAMES LA

THE VINTRY

HILL MEAD

Juniper Wood

+

Jessop's Hill

CLOCK HOUSE LA

Upper Misbourne Farm

BELL LA

NURSERY LA

Nutley

Yew Tree Farm

Lower Misbourne Farm

Hole & Alchorne Farm

THREE GABLES

THE ORCHARD

PO

LITTLEMEAD

Chestnut Farm

Chantersell

HIGH ST

PH

Great Birch Wood

Hollybush Wood

Ford's Green

FOREST VIEW

NETHER LA

Dodd's Hill

Dodd's Bottom

Hole Farm

27

Prickett's Hatch

COURTLANDS

Dodd's Bank

Cackle Street

Bowyer's Wood

Funnells Farm

Searles Wood

Wet Wood

Hunters Farm

Boringwheel Mill Farm

Woodcock Farm

Forest Lodge

TYLERS LA

A22

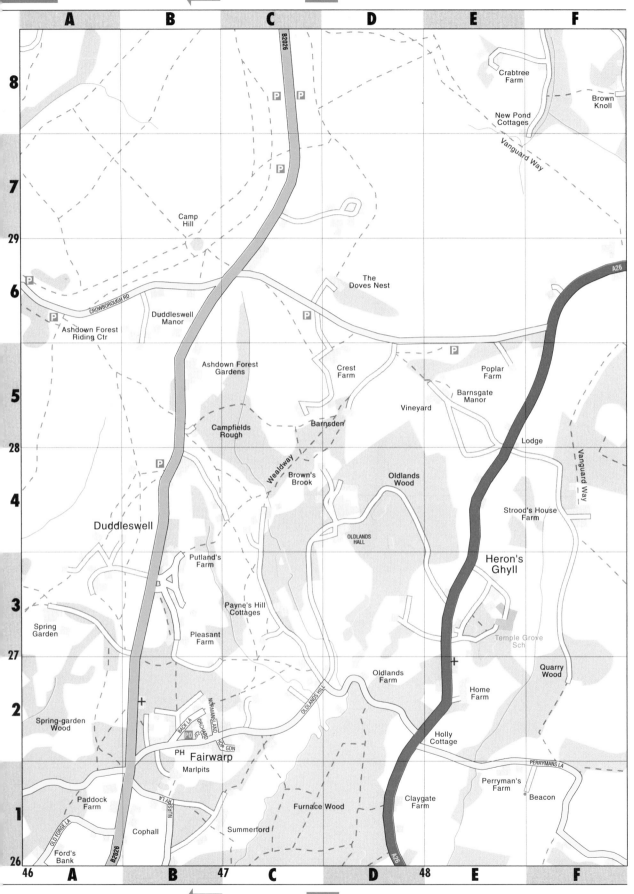

B2026

8

Crabtree
Farm

Brown
Knoll

New Pond
Cottages

Vanguard Way

7

Camp
Hill

29

The
Doves Nest

6

P

P

CROWBOROUGH RD

Duddleswell
Manor

A26

Ashdown Forest
Riding Ctr

P

Ashdown Forest
Gardens

Crest
Farm

Poplar
Farm

5

Barnsgate
Manor

Vineyard

Campfields
Rough

Barnsden

Lodge

28

Vanguard Way

P

Wealdway

Brown's
Brook

Oldlands
Wood

4

Strood's House
Farm

Duddleswell

OLDLANDS
HALL

Putland's
Farm

Heron's
Ghyll

Payne's Hill
Cottages

3

Spring
Garden

Pleasant
Farm

Temple Grove
Sch

27

Oldlands
Farm

Quarry
Wood

+

Spring-garden
Wood

NORMANSLAND

Home
Farm

2

BACK LA

ORCHARD CL

HDG GDN

PO

OLDLANDS HILL

PH

Fairwarp

Holly
Cottage

Marlpits

PERRYMANS LA

Paddock
Farm

NURSERY LA

FRY LA

Perryman's
Farm

Beacon

1

Furnace Wood

Claygate
Farm

Cophall

OLD FORGE LA

Summerford

26

Ford's
Bank

B2026

A26

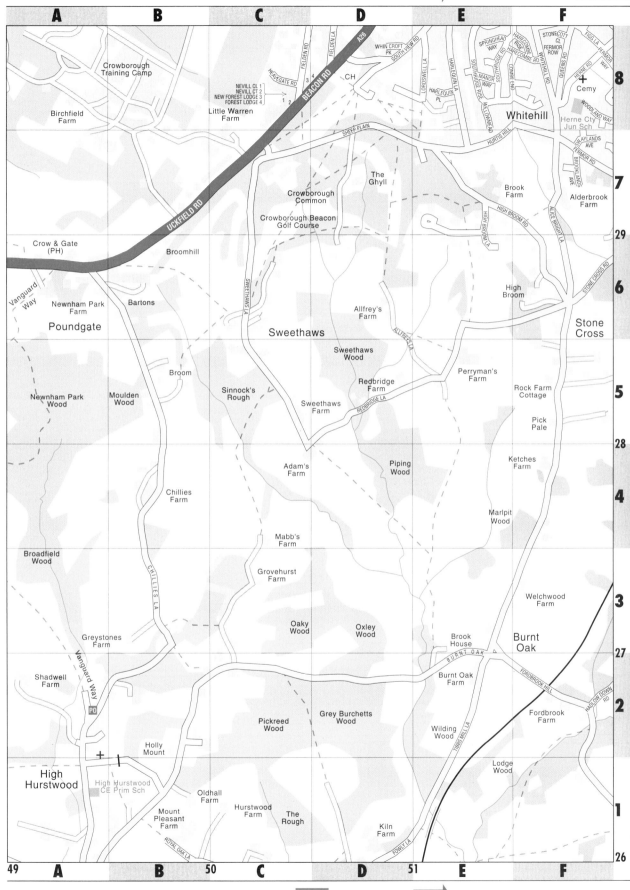

A B C D E F

BLACKNESS RD
ST MICHAELS CL
Jarvis Brook Ctry Pk
OSBORNE RD
OSBORNE HILL
WINDSOR RD
WINDSOR HILL
B2100
PO
LEXDEN LODGE IND EST
P

Jarvis Brook

1 Railway View
2 New Cotts

MILLBROOK IND EST

ROTHERFIELD RD
B2100

WYLE CL
HONEFORD
HERNE RD
DOWN
LUXFORD LA
1 2
3
Recn Gd

1 BLACKNESS VILLAS
2 COUNCIL COTTS
3 LUXFORD COTTS

LUXFORD DR
LUXFORD RD

BEACON BSNS PK
WEALDEN IND EST

SYBRON WAY
MILLBROOK BSNS PK

8

HERNE-HEIGHTS
DOWN
ROTHER CT
ST RICHARDS RD
FARNINGHAM RD

FERMOR RD
PO

Kemp's Farm

Plough & Horses (PH)

MOUNT PLEASANT

Crowborough Sta

PH

WESTERN RD
DALEHURST

KNOWLE CL
WESTERN GDNS
TUBWELL LA
MOTTINS HILL
CLACKHAMS LA

Alder Shaw

Rotherfield Hall

Golf Course

7

STONE CROSS RD
ALDERBROOK COTTS
ALDERBROOK CL

Alderbrook

Walsh Manor Farm

WALSHES RD

CROWBOROUGH

Tubwell Farm

VINE COTTS

Jarvis Brook Cty Prim Sch

29

ALDERBROOK WAY
ALDERBROOK PATH

Walsh Manor

Hayward's Farm

Lodgeland

Yewtree Wood

6

Sandhill Farm

Haywards Grange

Steep Hill Farm

Trebler's Farm

Castle Hill Farm

TREBLERS RD

5

Owlsbury Farm

HADLOW DOWN RD

28

Scaland Wood

Lodge Wood

Trebler's Wood

4

Rumsden Farm

Steep Park

Holly Grove Farm

Stumletts Pit Wood

STEEP RD

3

Sparrow Cottages

Marlpits Wood

Limney Farm

Great Dewlands

27

Inchreed Farm

Derridge Farm

Pinehurst

DEWLANDS HILL

Coe's Farm

2

Willinghurst

Stone Mill Farm

1

Stonehurst

STONEHURST LA

26

Hastingford Cottage

Huggett's Furnace

Fox Wood

52 A B 53 C D 54 E F

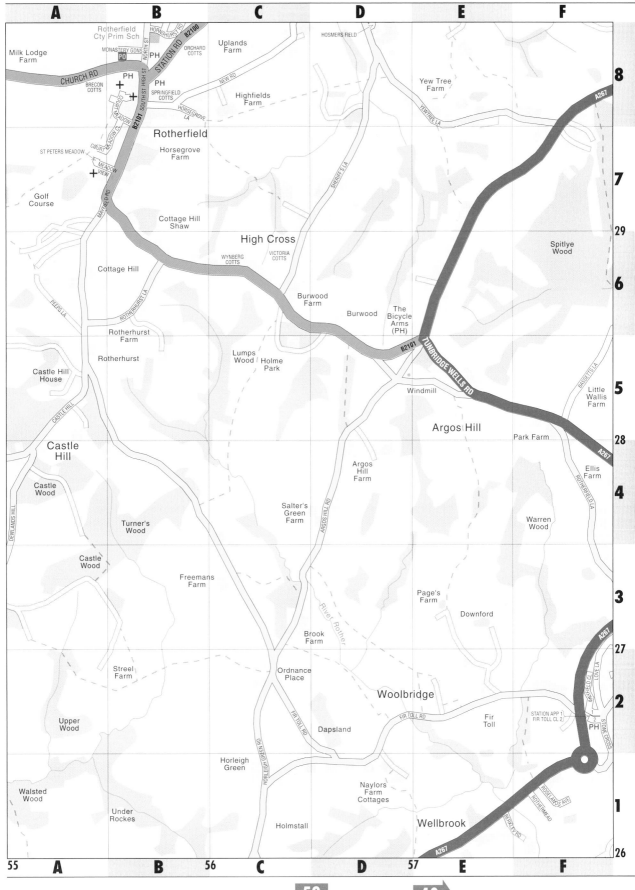

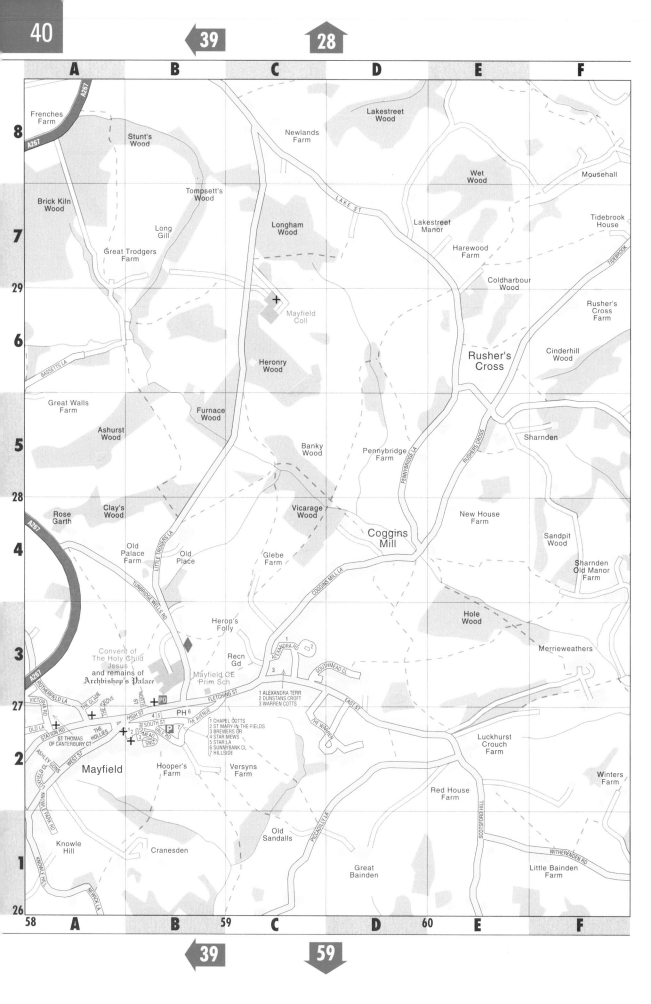

A **B** **C** **D** **E** **F**

8

Frenches
Farm

Stunt's
Wood

Lakestreet
Wood

Wet
Wood

Mousehall

7

Brick Kiln
Wood

Tompsett's
Wood

Long
Gill

Longham
Wood

Newlands
Farm

LAKE ST

Lakestreet
Manor

Tidebrook
House

TIDEBROOK

29

Great Trodgers
Farm

Harewood
Farm

Coldharbour
Wood

Rusher's
Cross
Farm

6

Mayfield
Coll

Rusher's
Cross

Cinderhill
Wood

BASSETTS LA

Heronry
Wood

5

Great Walls
Farm

Ashurst
Wood

Furnace
Wood

Banky
Wood

Pennybridge
Farm

PENNYBRIDGE LA

RUSHER'S CROSS

Sharnden

28

Rose
Garth

Clay's
Wood

Vicarage
Wood

New House
Farm

Sandpit
Wood

4

A267

Old
Palace
Farm

LITTLE TRODGERS LA

Old
Place

Glebe
Farm

Coggins
Mill

COGGINS MILL LA

Sharnden
Old Manor
Farm

TUNBRIDGE WELLS RD

Heron's
Folly

Hole
Wood

Merrieweathers

3

Convent of
The Holy Child
Jesus
and remains of
Archbishop's Palace

Recn
Gd

Mayfield CE
Prim Sch

ALEXANDRA RD

SOUTHMEAD CL

1 ALEXANDRA TERR
2 DUNSTANS CROFT
3 WARREN COTTS

EAST ST

ROTHERFIELD LA

FLETCHING ST

THE WARREN

27

VICTOR RD

THE GLADE

THE GROVE

NORTH ST

HIGH ST

PH 6

THE AVENUE

1 CHAPEL COTTS
2 ST MARY-IN-THE-FIELDS
3 BREWERS GR
4 STAR MEWS
5 STAR LA
6 SUNNYBANK CL
7 HILLSIDE

Luckhurst
Crouch
Farm

Old LA

STATION RD

ST THOMAS
OF CANTERBURY CT

THE HOLLIES

SOUTH ST

VALE RD

MEAD
SN

P

Winters
Farm

2

ASHLEY GDNS

COPPERFIELDS CL

WEST ST

Mayfield

Hooper's
Farm

Versyns
Farm

Red House
Farm

SCOTSFORD HILL

KNOWLE PARK RD

Knowle
Hill

Cranesden

Old
Sandalls

PICCADILLY LA

WITHERENDEN RD

Little Bainden
Farm

1

KNOWLE HILL

NEWICK LA

Great
Bainden

26

58 **A** **B** 59 **C** **D** 60 **E** **F**

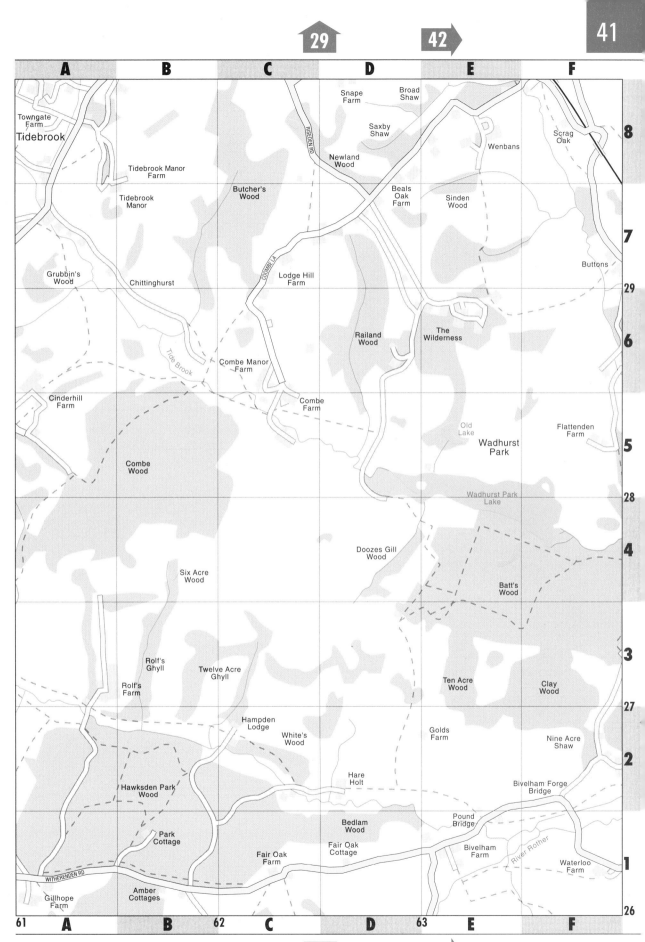

A	B	C	D	E	F

Towngate Farm
Tidebrook

Snape Farm
Broad Shaw

Saxby Shaw

Scrag Oak

8

Tidebrook Manor Farm

Butcher's Wood

Newland Wood

Wenbans

Tidebrook Manor

Beals Oak Farm

Sinden Wood

7

RISEDEN RD

Grubbin's Wood

Chittinghurst

COOMBE LA

Lodge Hill Farm

Buttons

29

Tide Brook

Combe Manor Farm

Railand Wood

The Wilderness

6

Cinderhill Farm

Combe Farm

Old Lake

Wadhurst Park

Flattenden Farm

5

Combe Wood

Wadhurst Park Lake

28

Doozes Gill Wood

4

Six Acre Wood

Batt's Wood

Rolf's Ghyll

Twelve Acre Ghyll

Ten Acre Wood

Clay Wood

3

Rolf's Farm

27

Hampden Lodge

White's Wood

Golds Farm

Nine Acre Shaw

2

Hawksden Park Wood

Hare Holt

Bivelham Forge Bridge

Park Cottage

Bedlam Wood

Pound Bridge

Bivelham Farm

River Rother

Fair Oak Farm

Fair Oak Cottage

Waterloo Farm

1

WITHERENDEN RD

Gillhope Farm

Amber Cottages

26

A B C D E F

8

Slidingfield Wood

Middle Wood

The Olives

CHURCHSETTLE LA

7

Bricklehurst Manor

Bricklehurst Farm

River Limden

Bardown

BARDOWN RD

Mabb's Hill Farm

29

Churchsettle Farm

Longfield Shaw

Bardown Farm

Stonegate

MABB'S HILL

Peartree Wood

Maplesden Farm

Cooper's Farm

Cock Farm

THE ACORNS

LYMDEN LA

6

Maplesden

LIMDEN CL

Coalpit Wood

FORGE FIELD

COTTENDEN RD

PO

STONEGATE CT

OWLS GDNS

Stonegate CE Prim Sch

5

Dens Wood

Hoadley Wood

Dens Farm

STATION RD

28

4

Dens Bridge

Tide Brook

Marchant's Wood

Peartree Hill

Church Wood Shaws

3

Batt's Wood Cottages

Hammerden

Stonegate Sta

Newbridge Wood

Witherenden Farm

27

Witherenden Mill

Cock's Wood

2

Bivelham Forge Farm

Witherenden Bridge

River Rother

Alder Wood

Orchard Shaw

High Wood

Witherenden Hill

Bines Farm

Round Wood

1

Bines Farm

Great Bines

Woodknowle Farm

Wreckery Bridge

26

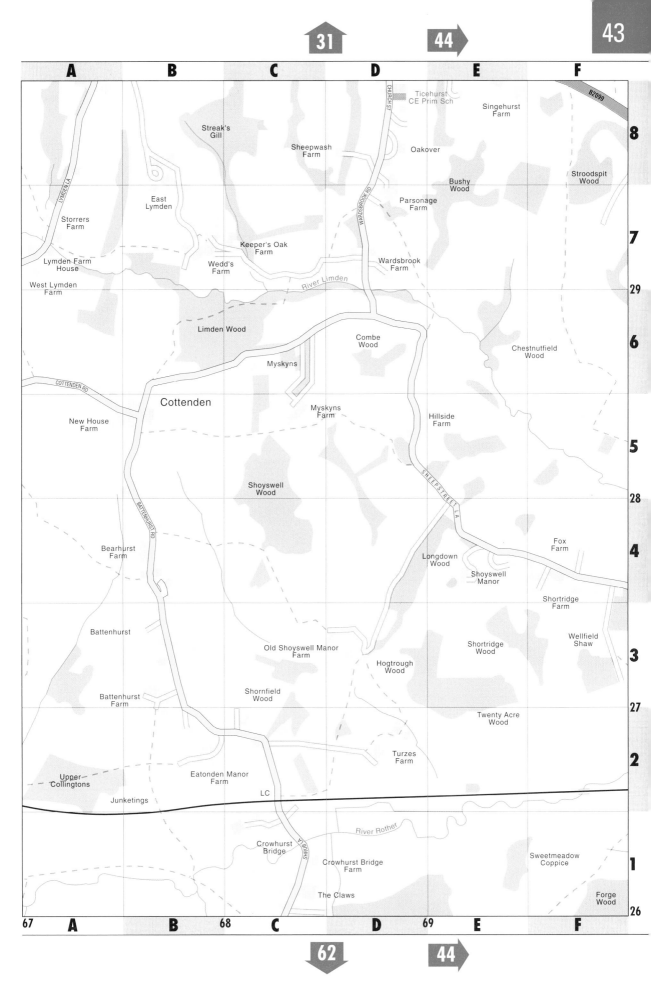

A B C D E F

8

Streak's
Gill

Sheepwash
Farm

Ticehurst
CE Prim Sch

Singehurst
Farm

B2099

Oakover

Stroodspit
Wood

East
Lymden

Storrers
Farm

Bushy
Wood

Parsonage
Farm

7

Keeper's Oak
Farm

Lymden Farm
House

Wedd's
Farm

Wardsbrook
Farm

29

West Lymden
Farm

River Limden

Limden Wood

6

Combe
Wood

Chestnutfield
Wood

Myskyns

COTTENDEN RD

Cottenden

Myskyns
Farm

New House
Farm

Hillside
Farm

5

Shoyswell
Wood

28

SHEEPSTREET LA

Fox
Farm

BATTENHURST RD

Bearhurst
Farm

Longdown
Wood

4

Shoyswell
Manor

Shortridge
Farm

Battenhurst

Shortridge
Wood

Wellfield
Shaw

Old Shoyswell Manor
Farm

3

Hogtrough
Wood

Battenhurst
Farm

Shornfield
Wood

Twenty Acre
Wood

27

Turzes
Farm

2

Upper
Collingtons

Eatonden Manor
Farm

LC

Junketings

SHMH LA

River Rother

Sweetmeadow
Coppice

Crowhurst
Bridge

1

Crowhurst Bridge
Farm

The Claws

Forge
Wood

26

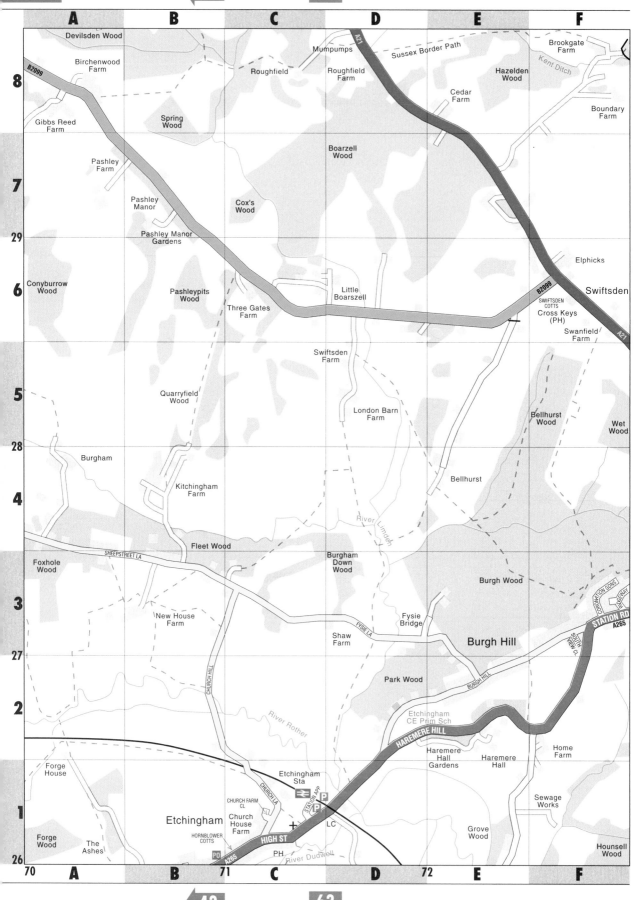

A   B   C   D   E   F

8

Devilsden Wood

Birchenwood Farm

B2099

Mumpumps

Roughfield

Roughfield Farm

Sussex Border Path

Brookgate Farm

Kent Ditch

Hazelden Wood

Gibbs Reed Farm

Spring Wood

Boundary Farm

7

Pashley Farm

Boarzell Wood

Cedar Farm

Pashley Manor

Cox's Wood

29

Pashley Manor Gardens

6

Conyburrow Wood

Pashleypits Wood

Three Gates Farm

Little Boarszell

B2099

SWIFTSDEN COTTS

Cross Keys (PH)

Swiftsden

Elphicks

Swanfield Farm

A21

5

Quarryfield Wood

Swiftsden Farm

London Barn Farm

Bellhurst Wood

Wet Wood

28

Burgham

Kitchingham Farm

Bellhurst

4

Foxhole Wood

Fleet Wood

River Limden

Burgham Down Wood

Burgh Wood

SHEEPSTREET LA

3

New House Farm

Fysie Bridge

FYSIE LA

Burgh Hill

STATION RD

A265

CORONATION GDNS

RIDGEWAY

27

Shaw Farm

Park Wood

BURGH HILL

SOUTH VIEW CL

2

CHURCH HILL

River Rother

Etchingham CE Prim Sch

HAREMERE HILL

Home Farm

Forge House

Etchingham Sta

P
P

STATION APP

Haremere Hall Gardens

Haremere Hall

Sewage Works

1

Etchingham

CHURCH FARM CL

CHURCH LA

Church House Farm

LC

Forge Wood

The Ashes

HORNBLOWER COTTS

PO

A265

HIGH ST

PH

River Dudwell

Grove Wood

Hounsell Wood

26

70   A   B   71   C   D   72   E   F

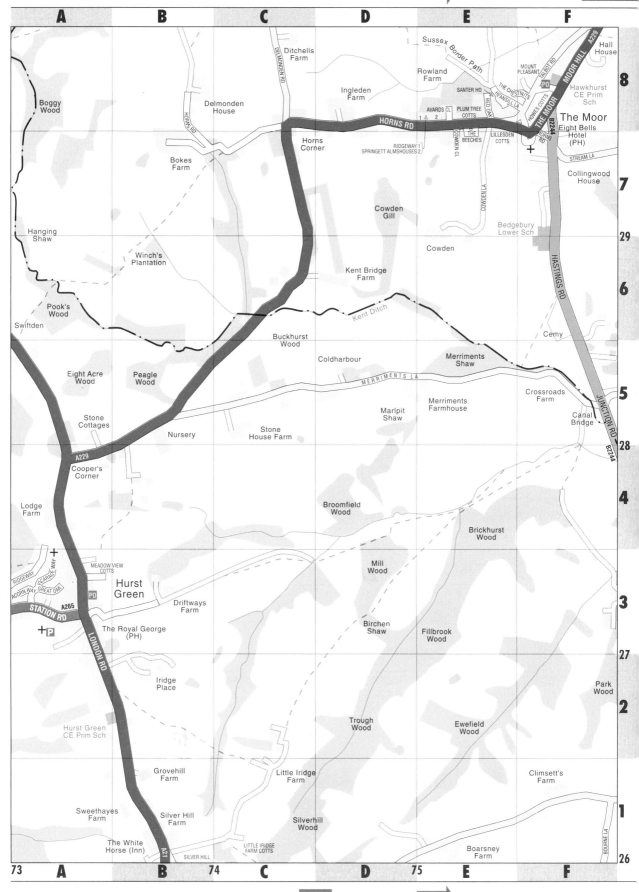

A B C D E F

8 7 29 6 5 28 4 27 2 1 26

Boggy Wood

Ditchells Farm

Delmonden House

Sussex Border Path

Rowland Farm

Ingleden Farm

Santer Ho

Mount Pleasant

The Chestnuts

Heansill La

Howes Cotts

Talbot Rd

Moor Hill

Hall House

Hawkhurst CE Prim Sch

The Moor

Eight Bells Hotel (PH)

Horns Rd

Delmonden Rd

Horns Rd

Horns Corner

Bokes Farm

Avards Cl
1 2

Plum Tree Cotts

Red Oak

Cowden Cl

The Beeches

Lillesden Cotts

Ridgeway 1
Springett Almshouses 2

Cowden La

Stream La

Collingwood House

Hanging Shaw

Winch's Plantation

Cowden Gill

Cowden

Bedgebury Lower Sch

Hastings Rd

Pook's Wood

Swiftden

Kent Bridge Farm

Kent Ditch

Buckhurst Wood

Coldharbour

Merriments Shaw

Cemy

Eight Acre Wood

Peagle Wood

Merriments La

Merriments Farmhouse

Crossroads Farm

Canal Bridge

Junction Rd

B2244

Stone Cottages

Nursery

Stone House Farm

Marlpit Shaw

A229

Cooper's Corner

Lodge Farm

Broomfield Wood

Brickhurst Wood

Meadow View Cotts

Ridgeway

Scarms Way

Acorn Way

Great Oak

Hurst Green

PO

A265

Station Rd

Driftways Farm

The Royal George (PH)

P

London Rd

Iridge Place

Mill Wood

Birchen Shaw

Fillbrook Wood

Park Wood

Hurst Green CE Prim Sch

Trough Wood

Ewefield Wood

Climsett's Farm

Grovehill Farm

Little Iridge Farm

Sweethayes Farm

Silver Hill Farm

Silverhill Wood

Boarsney Farm

Bourne La

The White Horse (Inn)

A21

Silver Hill

Little Iridge Farm Cotts

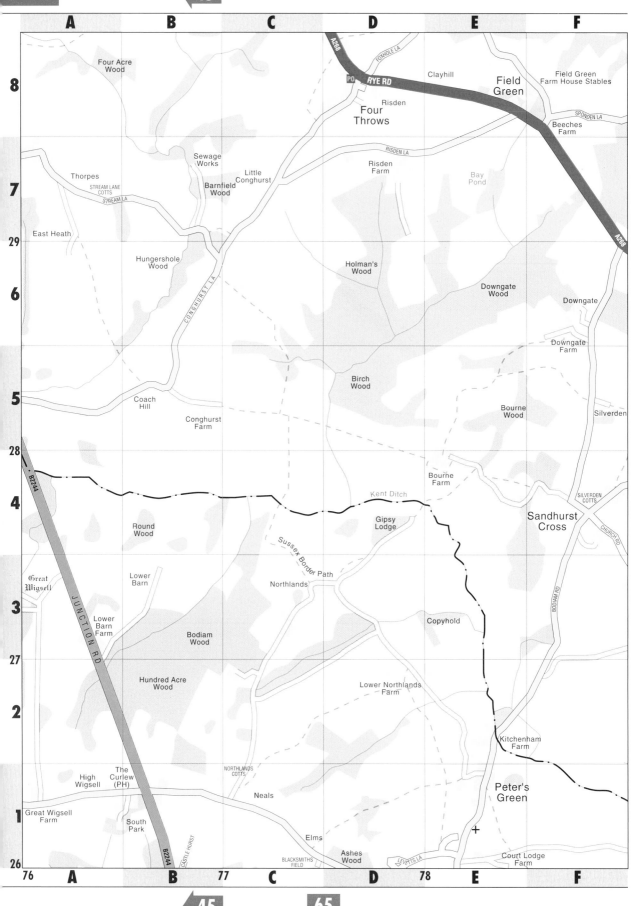

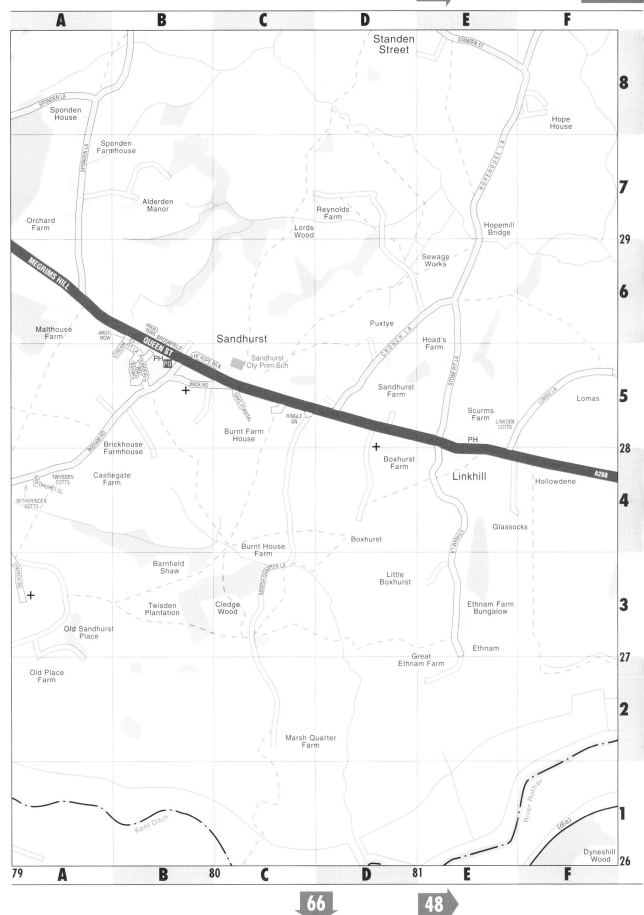

Standen Street

STANDEN ST

Hope House

SPONDEN LA
Sponden House

HOPEHOUSE LA

Sponden Farmhouse

Alderden Manor

Reynolds Farm

Hopemill Bridge

Orchard Farm

Lords Wood

Sewage Works

MEGRIMS HILL

Puxtye

Hoad's Farm

Malthouse Farm

ANGEL TERR.
ANGEL ROW
BROOKFIELD
Sandhurst

QUEEN ST

CROUCH LA

STONE PIT LA

Lomas

LOMAS LA

STREAM
PIT LA
PH
PO
PROVIDENCE RD
BACK RD
Sandhurst Cty. Prim. Sch.
LYE ROPE WLK

Sandhurst Farm

Scurms Farm

LINKDEN COTTS

Hollowdene

BODIAM RD
Brickhouse Farmhouse

OAK FORSTAL
Burnt Farm House

RINGLE GN

PH

A268

TWYSDEN COTTS
SANDHURST CL
Castlegate Farm

Linkhill

BETHERINDEN COTTS

Glassocks

CHURCH RD

Boxhurst

ETHNAM LA

Barnfield Shaw

Burnt House Farm

Little Boxhurst

MARSH QUARTER LA

Twisden Plantation

Cledge Wood

Ethnam Farm Bungalow

Old Sandhurst Place

Ethnam

Old Place Farm

Great Ethnam Farm

Marsh Quarter Farm

River Rother

Kent Ditch

(dis)

Dyneshill Wood

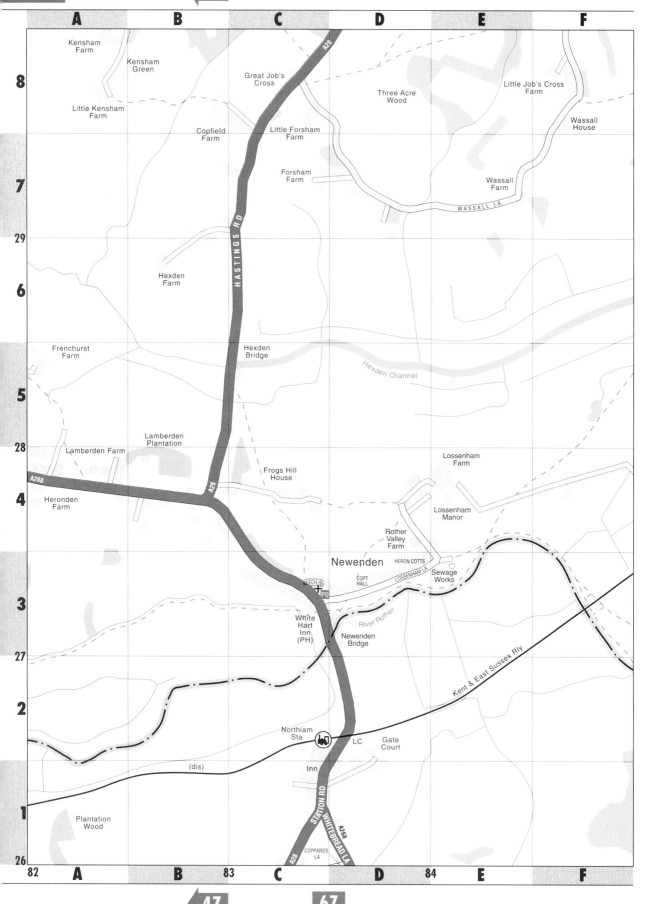

A   B   C   D   E   F

8

Kensham
Farm

Kensham
Green

Little Kensham
Farm

Great Job's
Cross

Three Acre
Wood

Little Job's Cross
Farm

Copfield
Farm

Little Forsham
Farm

Wassall
House

7

Forsham
Farm

Wassall
Farm

WASSALL LA

29

Hexden
Farm

HASTINGS RD

6

Frenchurst
Farm

Hexden
Bridge

Hexden Channel

5

Lamberden
Plantation

28

Lamberden Farm

Frogs Hill
House

Lossenham
Farm

A268

4

Heronden
Farm

A28

Lossenham
Manor

Rother
Valley
Farm

Newenden

HERON COTTS

Lossenham
Farm

3

BEECH
PO

COPT
HALL

LOSSENHAM LA

Sewage
Works

White
Hart
Inn
(PH)

Newenden
Bridge

River Rother

Kent & East Sussex Rly

27

2

Northiam
Sta

LC

Gate
Court

(dis)

Inn

1

Plantation
Wood

STATION RD

WHITEBREAD LA

A268

26

A28

COPPARDS
LA

82   A   B   83   C   D   84   E   F

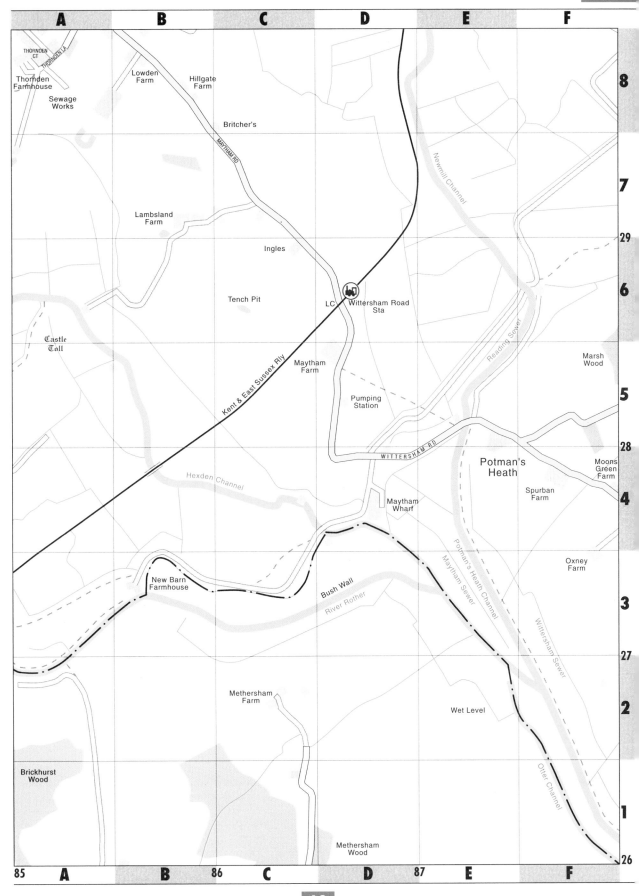

THORNDEN CT
THORNDEN LA

Thornden Farmhouse

Sewage Works

Lowden Farm

Hillgate Farm

Britcher's

MAYTHAM RD

Lambsland Farm

Ingles

Tench Pit

LC Wittersham Road Sta

Castle Toll

Kent & East Sussex Rly

Maytham Farm

Pumping Station

Newmill Channel

Reading Sewer

Marsh Wood

WITTERSHAM RD

Potman's Heath

Moons Green Farm

Spurban Farm

Hexden Channel

Maytham Wharf

Potman's Heath Channel

Maytham Sewer

Oxney Farm

Wittersham Sewer

New Barn Farmhouse

Bush Wall

River Rother

Methersham Farm

Wet Level

Brickhurst Wood

Otter Channel

Methersham Wood

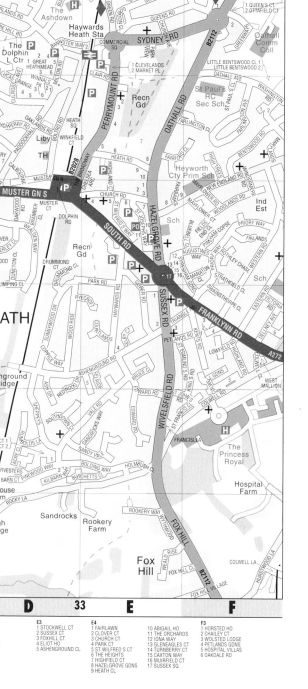

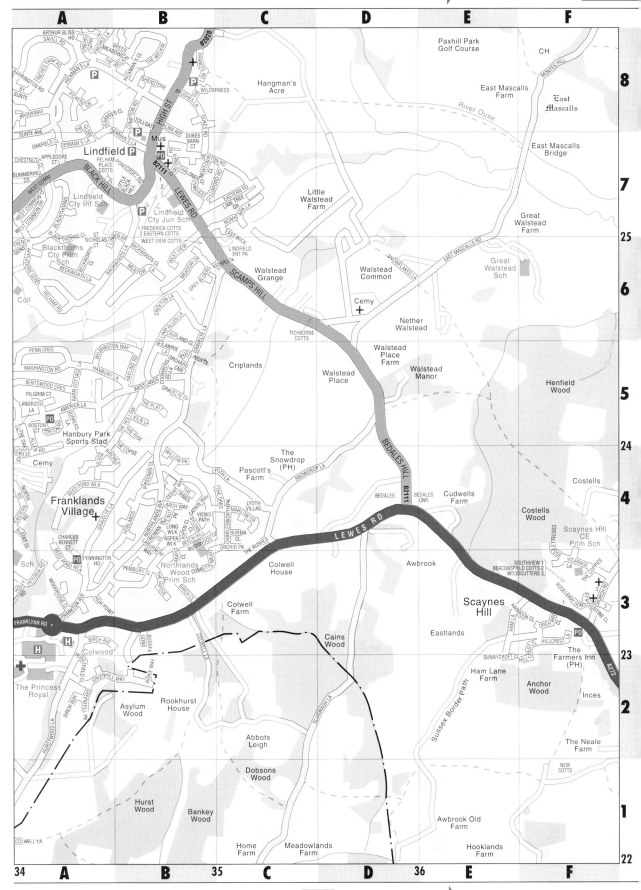

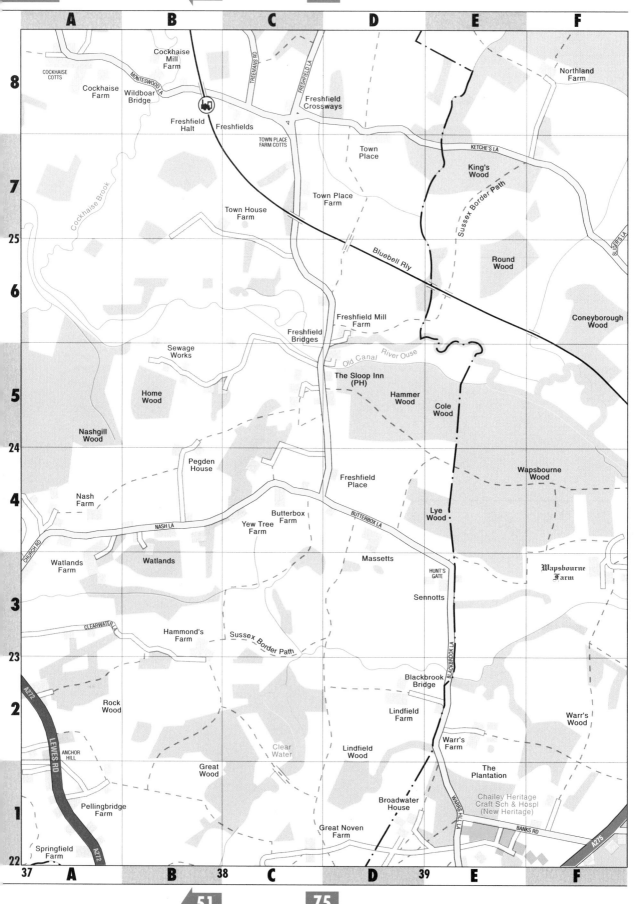

A B C D E F

8
COCKHAISE COTTS
Cockhaise Farm
Cockhaise Mill Farm
Wildboar Bridge
MONTESWOOD LA
TREEMANS RD
FRESHFIELD LA
Freshfield Halt
Freshfields
Freshfield Crossways
Northland Farm

7
TOWN PLACE FARM COTTS
Town Place
Town Place Farm
King's Wood
KETCHE'S LA
Sussex Border Path

25
Town House Farm
Bluebell Rly
Round Wood
SLUGERS LA

6
Freshfield Mill Farm
Coneyborough Wood

Sewage Works
Freshfield Bridges
Old Canal
River Ouse

5
Home Wood
The Sloop Inn (PH)
Hammer Wood
Cole Wood

24
Nashgill Wood
Pegden House
Wapsbourne Wood

4
Nash Farm
NASH LA
Butterbox Farm
Yew Tree Farm
Freshfield Place
BUTTERBOX LA
Lye Wood

Watlands Farm
Watlands
Massetts
HUNT'S GATE
Wapsbourne Farm

3
CLEARWATER LA
Hammond's Farm
Sussex Border Path
Sennotts
BLACKBROOK LA

23
Rock Wood
Blackbrook Bridge
Warr's Wood

2
A272
LEWES RD
ANCHOR HILL
Clear Water
Lindfield Farm
Lindfield Wood
Warr's Farm
The Plantation

1
Pellingbridge Farm
Great Wood
Broadwater House
Chailey Heritage Craft Sch & Hospl (New Heritage)
WARRS HILL LA
BANKS RD
A275

22
Springfield Farm
Great Noven Farm

Cockhaise Brook

CHURCH RD

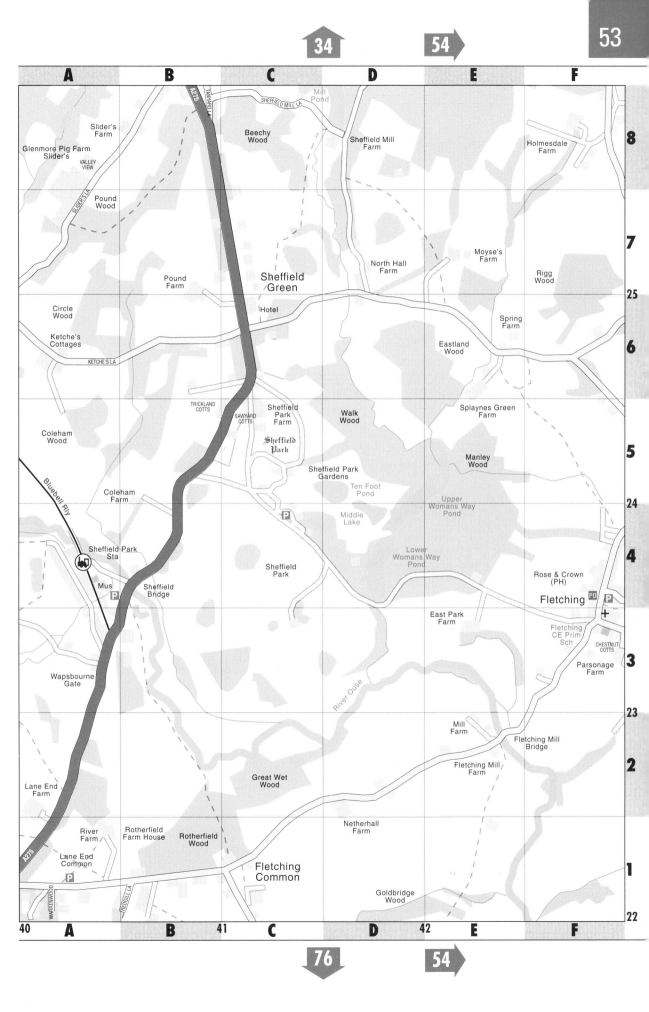

A   **B**   **C**   **D**   **E**   **F**

Searles

Searles
Lake

Courtland
Wood

Whitehouse
Farm

8

Black Ven
Farm

PICKETTS LA

Horney
Common

OLD FORGE LA

A22

Poultry
Houses

Marshall's
Farm

7

St Clears
Farm

Spring
Wood

Kennel
Wood

A22

25

Clapwater
Farm House

Marshall's
Manor

Lower Flitteridge
Wood

Ruttingham
Farm

High
Wood

Cave
Wood

6

Flitterbanks

Flitteridge
Farm

DOWN ST

Little Brown's
Wood

The
Wilderness

5   Splayne's
Green

Down
Street

Downstreet
Farmhouse

QUEENS DR

24

Knabb
Farm

Forge
Wood

A272

A22

Atherall's
Farm

Downstreet
Rough

4

Batt's
Farm

CHERRY
COTTS

Mallingdown
Farm

Batt's
Wood

Sewage
Works

Batt's Bridge Stream

Parsonage
Farm

White Barn
Farm

3

Grover's
Farm

23

Hungry
Hatch

Ruston
Wood

Oak Ferrars
Farm

Park Wood

2

CH

Pilt Down

Golf Course

Moses
Farm

Piltdown
Pond

Fairhazel
Wood

1

A272

Piltdown

Piltdown Man
(PH)

22

43   **A**   **B**   44   **C**   **D**   45   **E**   **F**

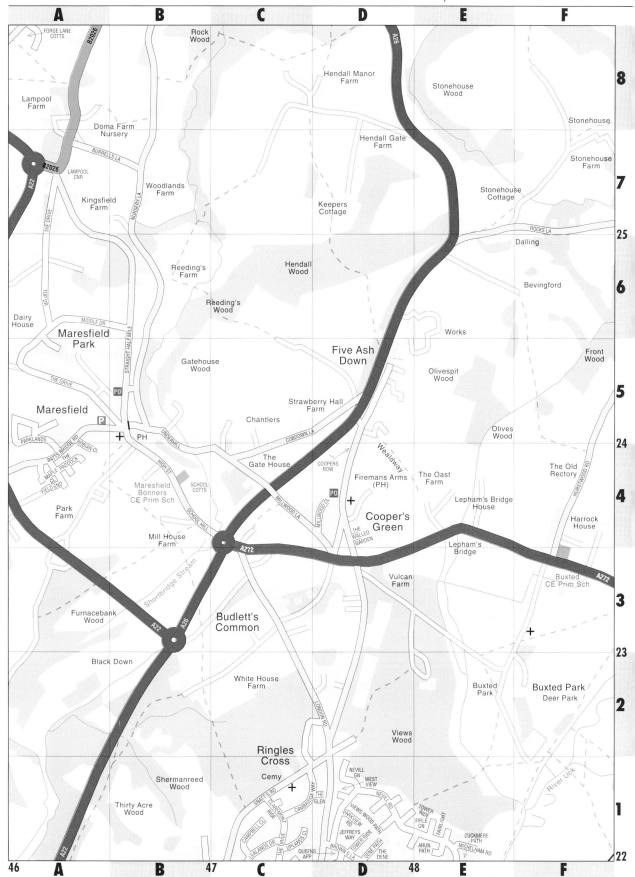

A **B** **C** **D** **E** **F**

8

FORGE LANE
COTTS

Rock
Wood

Hendall Manor
Farm

Stonehouse
Wood

Stonehouse

Lampool
Farm

Doma Farm
Nursery

BURRELLS LA

Hendall Gate
Farm

Stonehouse
Farm

7

B2026

LAMPOOL
CNR

NURSERY LA

Woodlands
Farm

Keepers
Cottage

Stonehouse
Cottage

ROCKS LA

Kingsfield
Farm

Dalling

25

A22

THE DRIVE

Reeding's
Farm

Hendall
Wood

Bevingford

6

TOP RD

Dairy
House

MIDDLE DR

Reeding's
Wood

Works

Front
Wood

Maresfield
Park

STRAIGHT HALF MILE

Gatehouse
Wood

Five Ash
Down

Olivespit
Wood

5

THE DRIVE

PO

Strawberry Hall
Farm

Olives
Wood

24

Maresfield

P

Chantlers

CORDOWN LA

Weald way

The Old
Rectory

PARKLANDS

PH

UNDERHILL

The
Gate House

COOPERS
ROW

Firemans Arms
(PH)

The Oast
Farm

Lepham's Bridge
House

Harrock
House

4

BATTS BRIDGE RD

ROBIAN CL

HIGH ST

Maresfield
Bonners
CE Prim Sch

SCHOOL
COTTS

PO

HURSTWOOD RD

MAPLE
PADDOCK
CL

THE

FIELD END

MILLWOOD LA

MILLWOOD CL

Cooper's
Green

Lepham's
Bridge

Park
Farm

SCHOOL HILL

Mill House
Farm

THE
WALLED
GARDEN

A272

Buxted
CE Prim Sch

3

A22

A26

Shortbridge Stream

A212

Vulcan
Farm

Furnacebank
Wood

Budlett's
Common

23

Black Down

White House
Farm

Buxted
Park

Buxted Park
Deer Park

2

LONDON RD

Views
Wood

River Uck

Ringles
Cross

NEVILL
GN

WEST
VIEW

Shermanreed
Wood

Cemy

NEVILL RD

TOWER
RIDE

1

SNATT'S RD

CAMBROOK WAY

THE
GLEN

VIEWS WOOD PATH

PARKVIEW
RD

FIRLE
GN

FAIRLIGHT

Thirty Acre
Wood

CLARETON
RIDE

THE DRIVE

UPLANDS CL

JEFFREYS
WAY

TOWER RIDE

CUCKMERE
PATH

MICHELHAM RD

CAMPBELL CL

LEALANDS DR

QUEENS
APP

BROWN'S LA

DENE PATH

THE
DENE

ARUN
PATH

22

46 **A** 47 **B** **C** 48 **D** **E** **F**

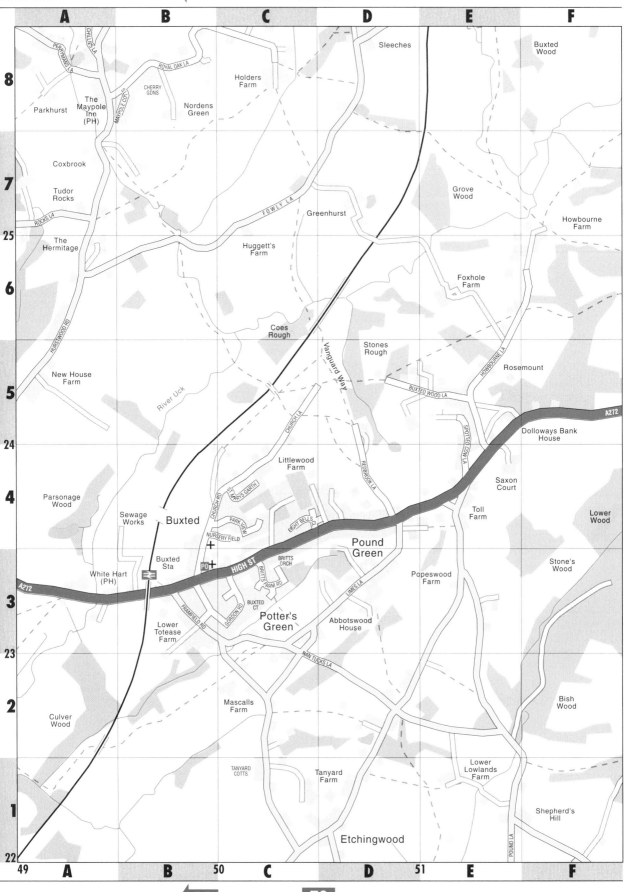

A **B** **C** **D** **E** **F**

8

Hastingford Farm

River Uck

Mill

Broadreed Wood

Grey's Wood

Stockland Wood

Broadreed View

STONEHURST LA

Broadreed Farm

7

Smallberry Hill

Gate House Farm

Stockland Farm

Pigsfoot Farm

Enclosure Wood

CRIERS LA

Brick Kiln Farm

Little Broadreed Farm

Stilereed Farm

25

6

Nashes Farm

Tully's Farm

SCHOOL LA

WASHORNS LA

Gillhope Bank Wood

WHEELERS LA

Old Croust Farm

DOG KENNEL LA

St Mark's CE Prim Sch

ST MARK'S FIELD

Hadlow Down

WHEELERS LANE COTTS

Hadlow House

5

A272

Five Chimneys

Upper Wood

Curtains Hill Farm

The New Inn (PH)

PO

South Beacon

24

Waste Farm

WILDERNESS LA

Wilderness Wood

Little England Farm

Hadlow Deep Wood

4

Waste Wood

Loudwell Farm

Hole Wood

WILDERNESS LA

Wilderness Farm

TINKER'S LA

Homegrove Wood

3

23

Hole Farm

Sleeves Wood

Spood's Farm

Wildings

Scocus Wood

2

Warren Farm

Crowpits

Harvest Hill Farm

Brookside Farm

Round Wood

1

Passalls Farm

Pounsley Wood

NURSERY LA

Malls Bank

22

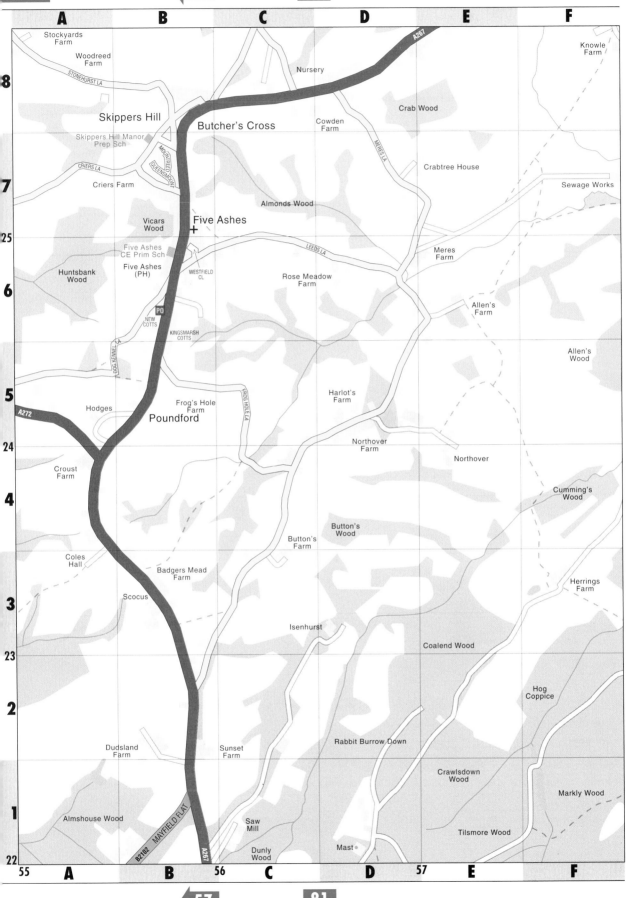

A B C D E F

Stockyards Farm
Woodreed Farm
STONEHURST LA
Skippers Hill
Skippers Hill Manor Prep Sch
CRIERS LA
Criers Farm
MOUNT REED
QUEENSMOUNT
Butcher's Cross
Nursery
A267
Cowden Farm
Crab Wood
MERES LA
Crabtree House
Sewage Works
Knowle Farm
Almonds Wood
Vicars Wood
Five Ashes
Five Ashes CE Prim Sch
Five Ashes (PH)
WESTFIELD CL
LEEDS LA
Rose Meadow Farm
Meres Farm
Huntsbank Wood
PO
NEW COTTS
KINGSMARSH COTTS
Allen's Farm
Allen's Wood
DOG KENNEL LA
Frog's Hole Farm
FROG HOLE LA
Poundford
Harlot's Farm
Northover Farm
Northover
Cumming's Wood
A272
Hodges
Croust Farm
Coles Hall
Scocus
Badgers Mead Farm
Button's Farm
Button's Wood
Herrings Farm
Isenhurst
Coalend Wood
Hog Coppice
Dudsland Farm
Sunset Farm
Rabbit Burrow Down
Crawlsdown Wood
Markly Wood
Almshouse Wood
MAYFIELD FLAT
B2102
A267
Saw Mill
Dunly Wood
Mast
Tilsmore Wood

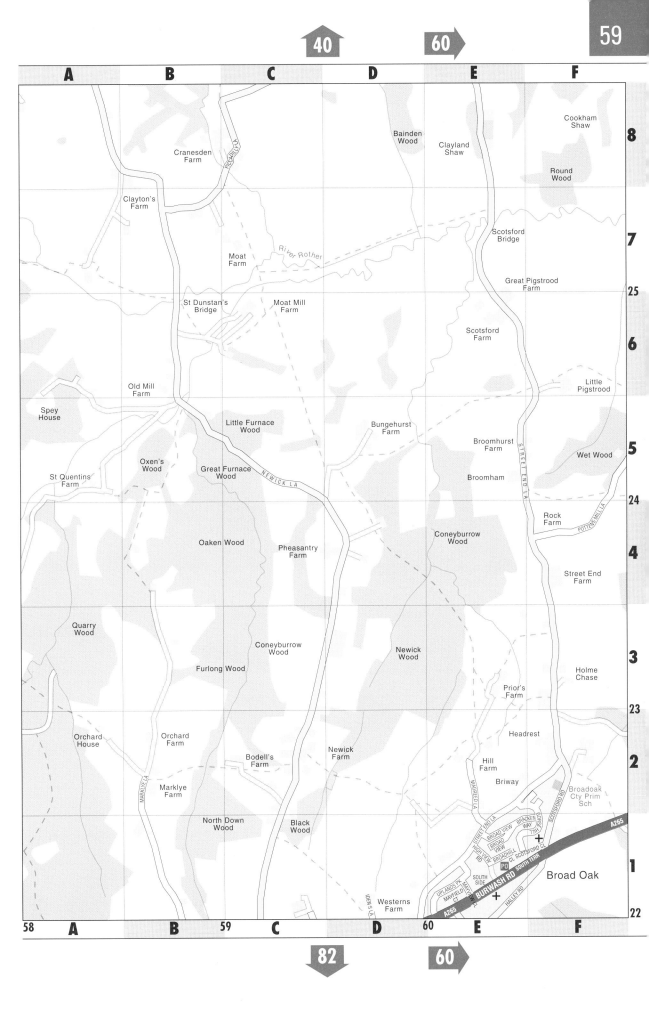

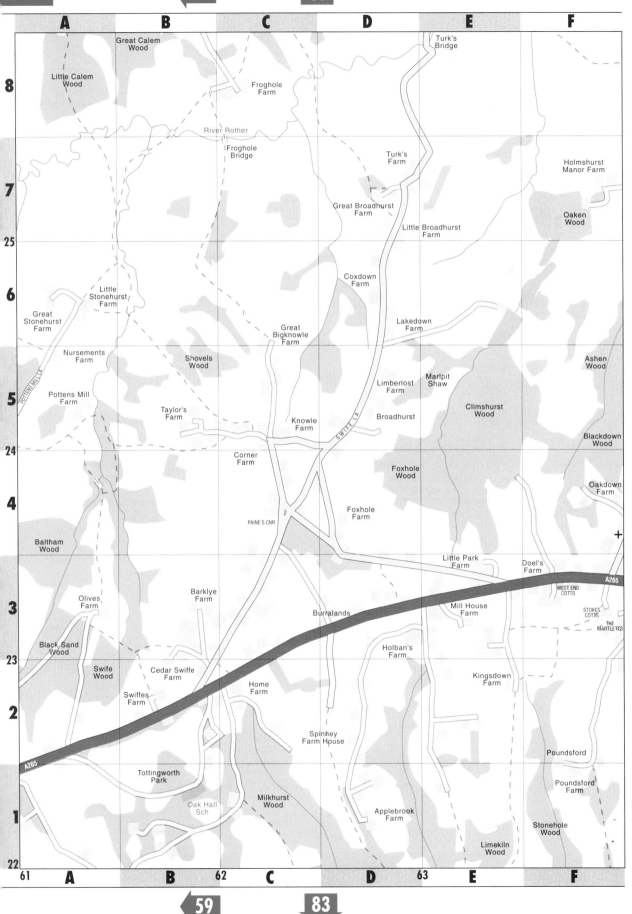

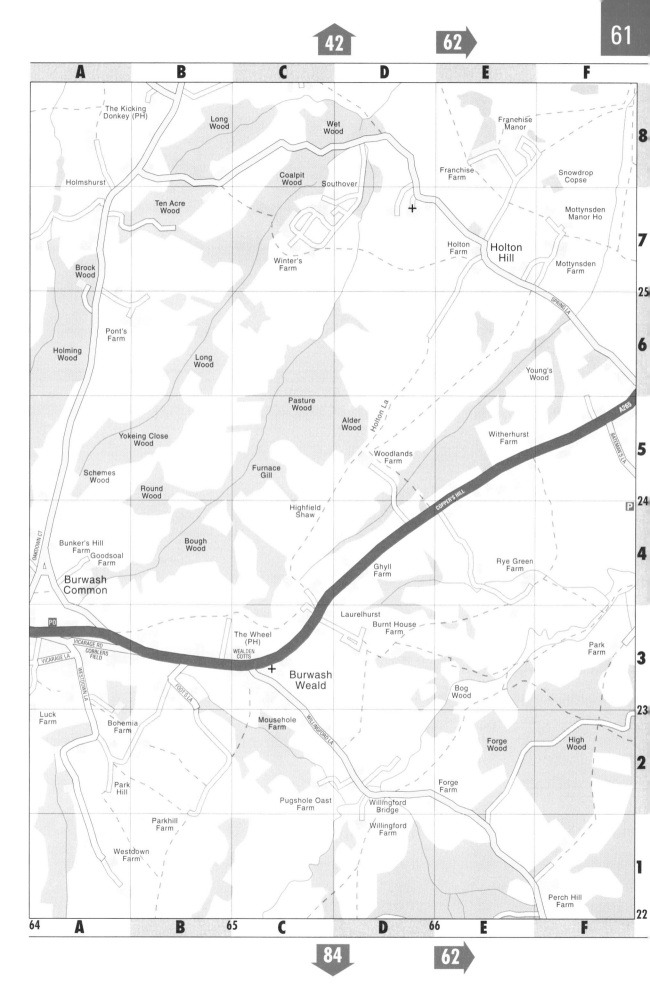

A B C D E F

8

Honeybrook
Wood

Brooksmarle

Shrub
Wood

Park
Wood

Court Lodge
Farm

A265

March
Farm

GREENFIELD RD

SHRUB LA

Little Park
Wood

Broomwood
Farm

7

HAM LA

STRAND MEADOW

BEECHWOOD CL

HOPFIELD

Dudwell
St Mary

Great Tott
Farm

BORDERS LA

Borders

25

VIEW

WEALDEN VIEW

Square
Farm

ROTHER CL

BROADS COTTS

Glebe
Ho

6

CORONATION
COTTS

PH

PO

HAM LA

EVERTON COTTS

ROTHER CL

HOPPERS
CROFT LA

RECTORY CL

P

PH

GARSTON PK

The Glebe
Farm

Tott
Wood

ST ANNES
GN

A265

HIGH ST

PH

VICTORIA
TERR

LIME TREE
TERR

P

SCHOOL HILL

GARSTON PK

Burwash CE
Prim Sch

Court Barn
Farm

Grandturzel

Little
Grandturzel

Church
Wood

Burwash

Ashlands

BELL ALLEY RD

River Dudwell

Fisher's
Farm

5

Dudwell
Farm

24

BATEMAN'S LA

Old
Dudwell
Mill

Dudwell
Bridge

Nepland
Pit

Old Brick
Farm

Glydwish
Wood

4

Bateman's

Oakhurst
Farm

Platt's
Farm

Glydwish
Hall

Northgate
Wood

Magpie's
Hall

KINGS HILL RD

FONTRIDGE LA

Drive
Cott

3

Park
Wood

Kemland
Wood

Fonthill
Farm

Socknersh
Manor

23

Kemland
Ho

Bowman's
Farm

Woodman's
Farm

Mill
Wood

2

Lower Leggett's
Wood

Brown's Oak
Farm

Oldhole
Wood

Kiln
Shaw

Leggett's
Wood

Perryman's
Farm

1

Stonepetty

Chilley's
Wood

Manor
Farm

22

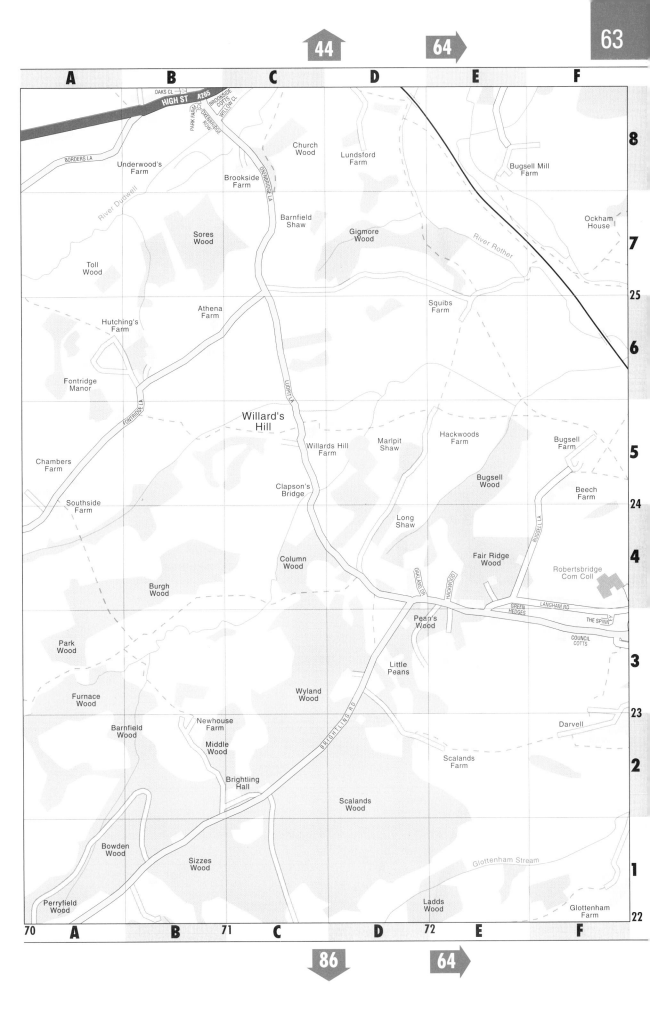

44
64
86
64

A   B   C   D   E   F

8
7
25
6
5
24
4
3
23
2
1
22

OAKS CL
HIGH ST   A265
PARK FARM CL
OXENBRIDGE ROW
BROOKSIDE COTTS
WILLOW CL

BORDERS LA

Underwood's Farm

Church Wood

Lundsford Farm

Bugsell Mill Farm

Brookside Farm

River Dudwell

Barnfield Shaw

Sores Wood

Ockham House

OXENBRIDGE LA

Toll Wood

Gigmore Wood

River Rother

Athena Farm

Squibs Farm

Hutching's Farm

Willard's Hill

LUDPIT LA

Fontridge Manor

FONTRIDGE LA

Willards Hill Farm

Marlpit Shaw

Hackwoods Farm

Bugsell Farm

Chambers Farm

Clapson's Bridge

Bugsell Wood

Beech Farm

BUGSELL LA

Southside Farm

Long Shaw

Column Wood

Fair Ridge Wood

Robertsbridge Com Coll

Burgh Wood

OAKLAND DR

HACKWOOD

GREEN HEDGES

LANGHAM RD

THE SPINN

Park Wood

Pean's Wood

COUNCIL COTTS

Little Peans

Furnace Wood

Wyland Wood

BRIGHTLING RD

Newhouse Farm

Darvell

Barnfield Wood

Middle Wood

Scalands Farm

Brightling Hall

Scalands Wood

Bowden Wood

Sizzes Wood

Glottenham Stream

Perryfield Wood

Ladds Wood

Glottenham Farm

70   A   B   71   C   D   72   E   F

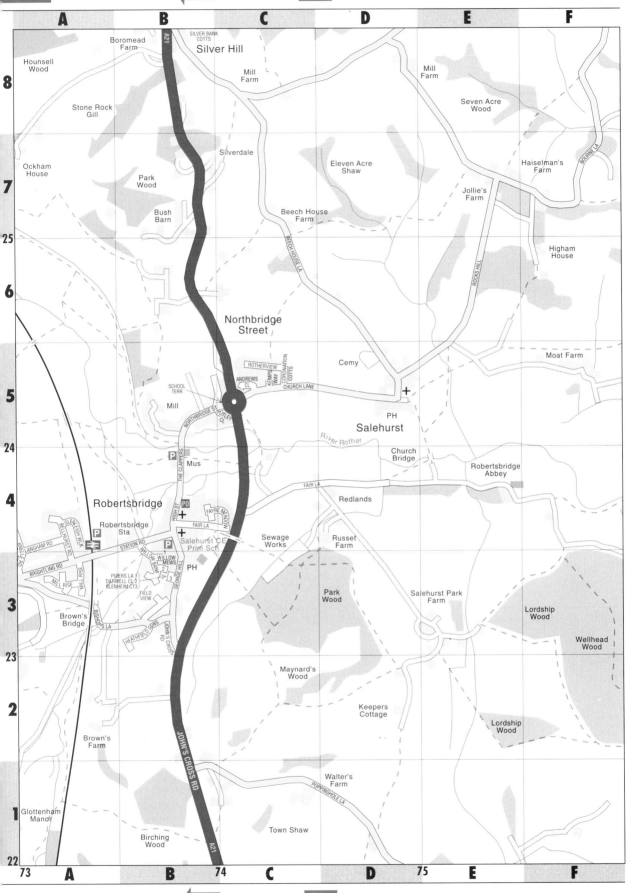

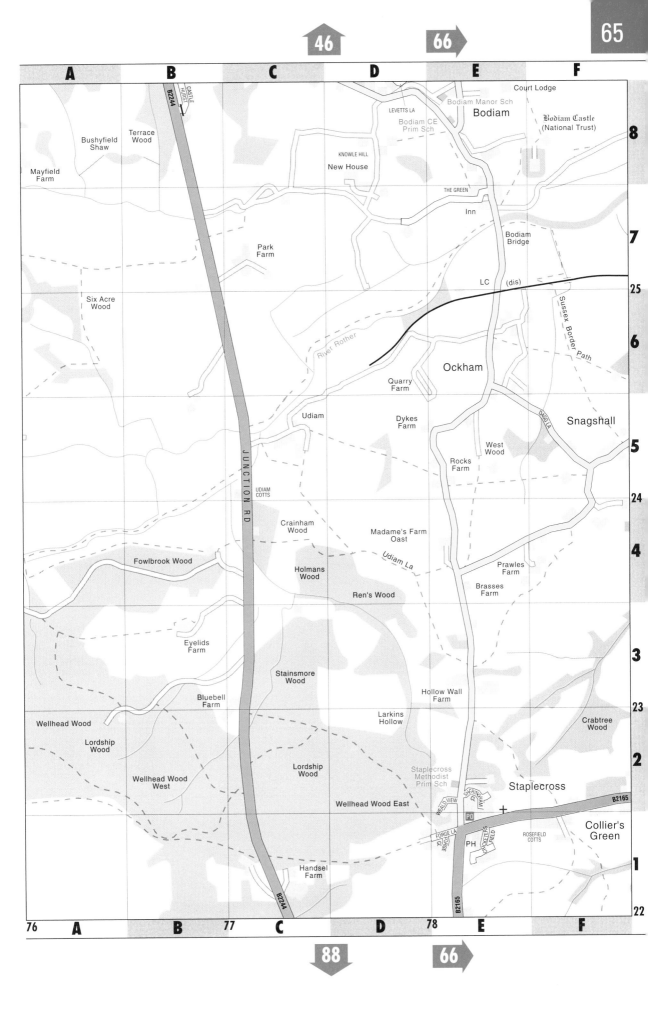

A B C D E F

8

Court Lodge
Bodiam Manor Sch
Bodiam
Bodiam Castle
(National Trust)

LEVETTS LA
Bodiam CE
Prim Sch

Bushyfield
Shaw
Terrace
Wood

Mayfield
Farm

KNOWLE HILL
New House

THE GREEN

Inn

7

Bodiam
Bridge

LC (dis)

25

Park
Farm

Six Acre
Wood

River Rother

6

Sussex Border Path

Ockham

Quarry
Farm

Snagshall

Udiam

Dykes
Farm

West
Wood

5

DAGG LA

UDIAM
COTTS

Rocks
Farm

24

Crainham
Wood

Madame's Farm
Oast

Fowlbrook Wood

Holmans
Wood

Udiam La

Prawles
Farm

4

Brasses
Farm

Ren's Wood

Eyelids
Farm

3

Hollow Wall
Farm

23

Stainsmore
Wood

Larkins
Hollow

Crabtree
Wood

Wellhead Wood

Bluebell
Farm

Lordship
Wood

2

Staplecross
Methodist
Prim Sch

Lordship
Wood

Staplecross

B2165

Wellhead Wood
West

WEALD VIEW

SHERINGHAM CL

Collier's
Green

Wellhead Wood East

PO

ROSEFIELD
COTTS

CROCKERS FIELD

FORGE LA
FORGE CL

PH

1

Handsel
Farm

B2165

76 A 77 B C 78 D E F 22

JUNCTION RD

B2244

CASTLE HURST

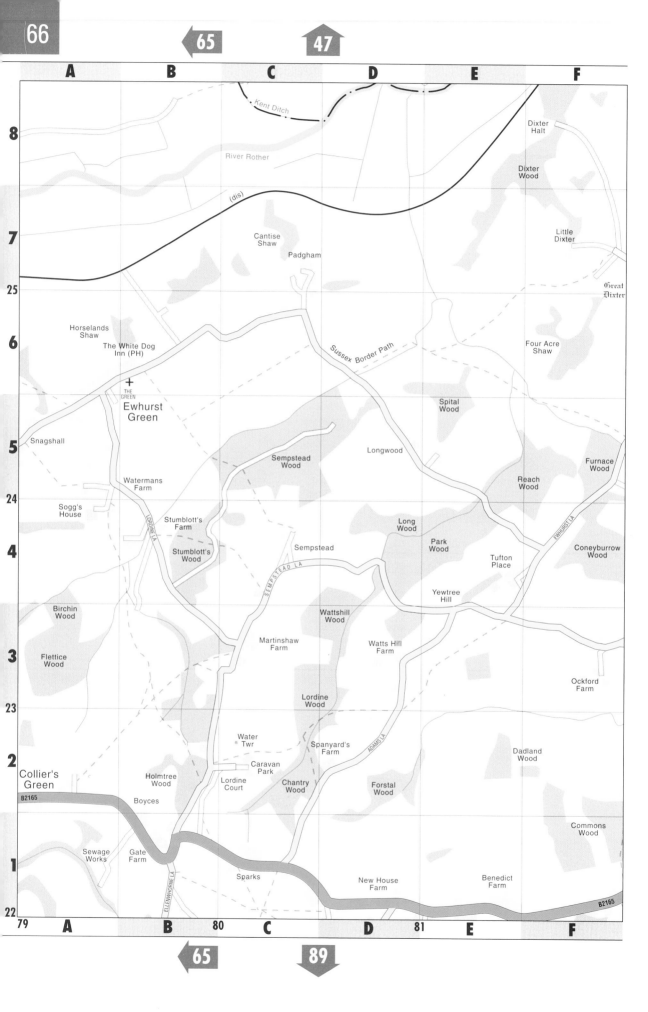

A B C D E F

8

Kent Ditch

Dixter
Halt

River Rother

Dixter
Wood

(dis)

7

Cantise
Shaw

Little
Dixter

Padgham

25

Great
Dixter

Horselands
Shaw

Sussex Border Path

Four Acre
Shaw

6

The White Dog
Inn (PH)

THE
GREEN

Spital
Wood

Ewhurst
Green

5

Snagshall

Sempstead
Wood

Longwood

Furnace
Wood

Watermans
Farm

Reach
Wood

24

Sogg's
House

Stumblott's
Farm

Long
Wood

Park
Wood

Coneyburrow
Wood

LORDINE LA

4

Stumblott's
Wood

Sempstead

Tufton
Place

EWHURST LA

Birchin
Wood

SEMPSTEAD LA

Wattshill
Wood

Yewtree
Hill

Watts Hill
Farm

3

Flettice
Wood

Martinshaw
Farm

Ockford
Farm

23

Lordine
Wood

Water
Twr

ADAMS LA

Dadland
Wood

2

Collier's
Green

Spanyard's
Farm

Caravan
Park

Holmtree
Wood

Lordine
Court

Chantry
Wood

Forstal
Wood

B2165

Boyces

Commons
Wood

Sewage
Works

Gate
Farm

1

ELLENWHORNE LA

Sparks

New House
Farm

Benedict
Farm

B2165

22

79 A B 80 C D 81 E F

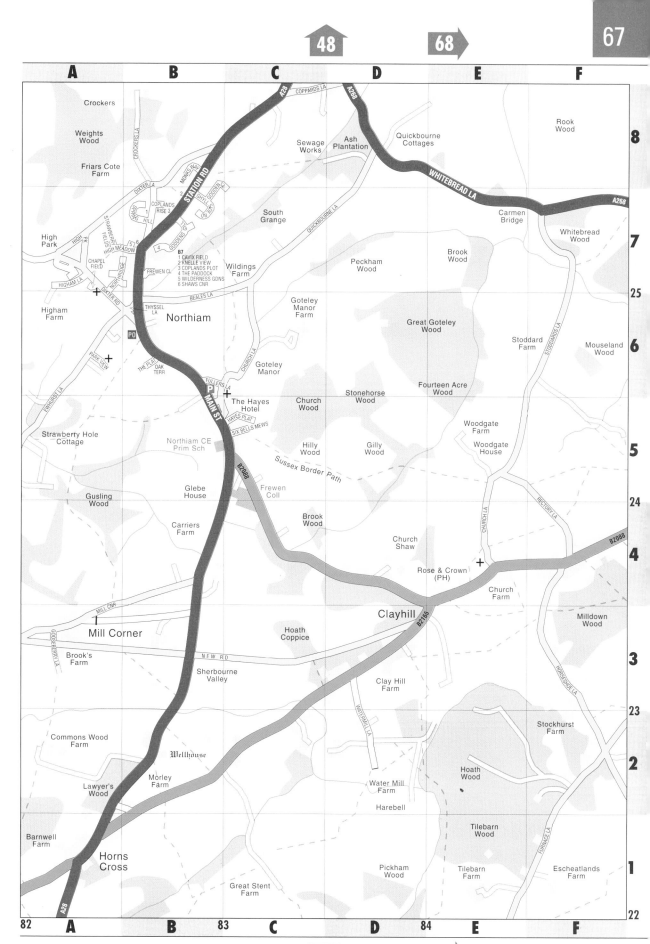

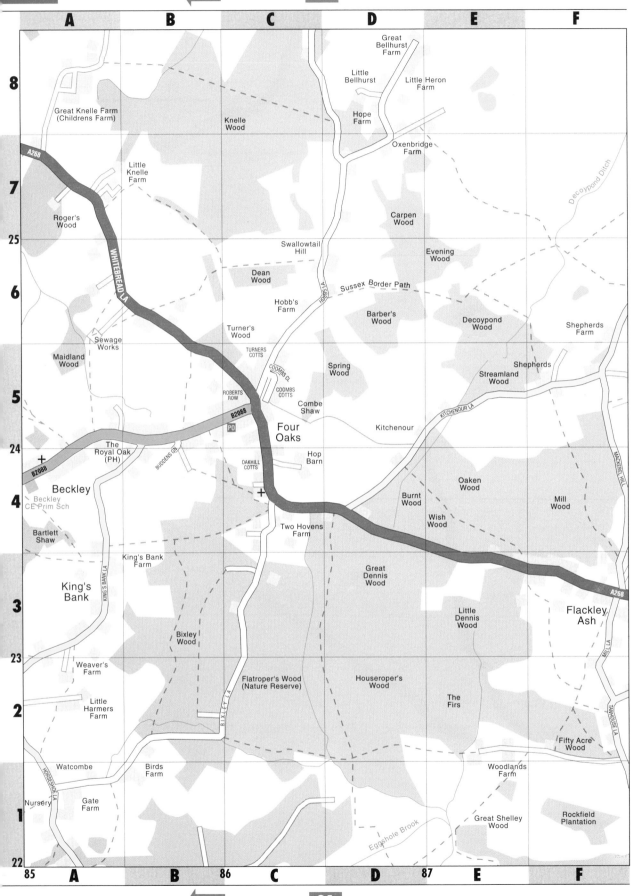

A B C D E F

8

7

25

6

5

24

4

3

23

2

1

22

85 A B 86 C D 87 E F

Great Bellhurst Farm
Little Bellhurst
Little Heron Farm
Hope Farm
Oxenbridge Farm
Great Knelle Farm (Childrens Farm)
Knelle Wood
A268
Little Knelle Farm
Roger's Wood
Carpen Wood
Decoypond Ditch
WHITEBREAD LA
Swallowtail Hill
Dean Wood
Evening Wood
Sussex Border Path
Hobb's Farm
A SB20
Barber's Wood
Decoypond Wood
Shepherds Farm
Sewage Works
Turner's Wood
Maidland Wood
TURNERS COTTS
COOMBS CL
Spring Wood
Streamland Wood
Shepherds
ROBERTS ROW
COOMBS COTTS
Combe Shaw
Kitchenour
KITCHENOUR LA
B2088
PO
Four Oaks
Kitchenour
The Royal Oak (PH)
BUDDENS GN
Hop Barn
Oaken Wood
Mill Wood
MACKEREL HILL
B2088
Beckley
Beckley CE Prim Sch
OAKHILL COTTS
Burnt Wood
Wish Wood
Bartlett Shaw
Two Hovens Farm
King's Bank Farm
KING'S BANK LA
Great Dennis Wood
King's Bank
Little Dennis Wood
Flackley Ash
Bixley Wood
MILL LA
Weaver's Farm
BIXLEY LA
Flatroper's Wood (Nature Reserve)
Houseroper's Wood
The Firs
Little Harmers Farm
TANHOUSE LA
Fifty Acre Wood
Watcombe
Birds Farm
Woodlands Farm
HORSESHOE LA
Nursery
Gate Farm
Eggshole Brook
Great Shelley Wood
Rockfield Plantation

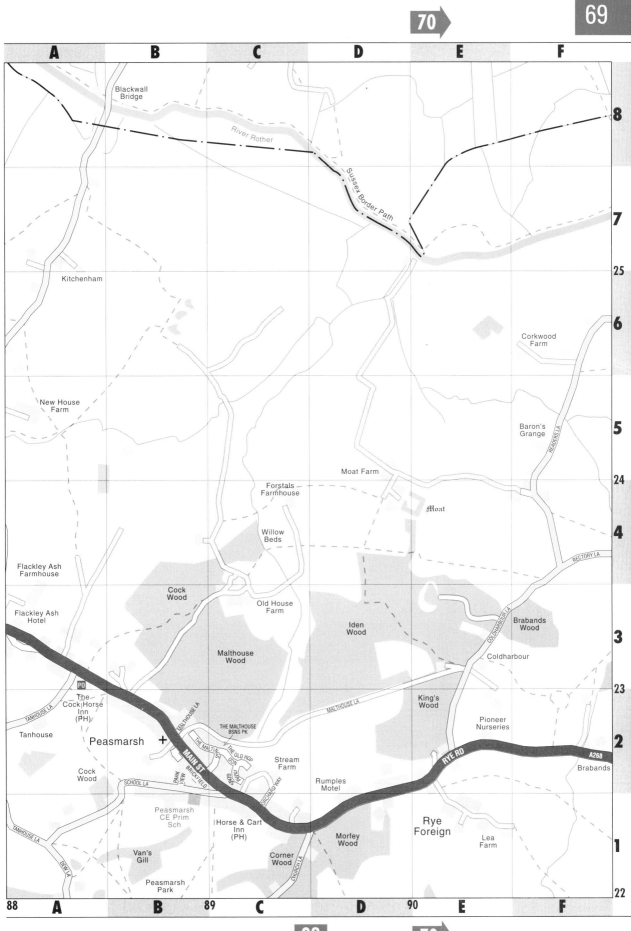

A B C D E F

8

7

25

6

24

5

4

23

3

2

1

22

Blackwall Bridge

River Rother

Sussex Border Path

Kitchenham

Corkwood Farm

New House Farm

Baron's Grange

READERS LA

Moat Farm

Forstals Farmhouse

Moat

Willow Beds

RECTORY LA

Flackley Ash Farmhouse

Cock Wood

Old House Farm

Iden Wood

Brabands Wood

COLDHARBOUR LA

Flackley Ash Hotel

Malthouse Wood

Coldharbour

TANHOUSE LA

PO

The Cock Horse Inn (PH)

MALTHOUSE LA

MALTHOUSE LA

King's Wood

Pioneer Nurseries

Tanhouse

Peasmarsh

THE MALTHOUSE BSNS PK

RYE RD

A268

Brabands

MAIN ST

THE MALTINGS GDN

THE OLD HOP

PARK

Stream Farm

Cock Wood

BRICKFIELD

SCHOOL LA

PARK VIEW

GDNS

ORCHARD WAY

Rumples Motel

Rye Foreign

Lea Farm

TANHOUSE LA

BEW LA

Peasmarsh CE Prim Sch

Van's Gill

Horse & Cart Inn (PH)

Morfey Wood

Corner Wood

CHURCH LA

Peasmarsh Park

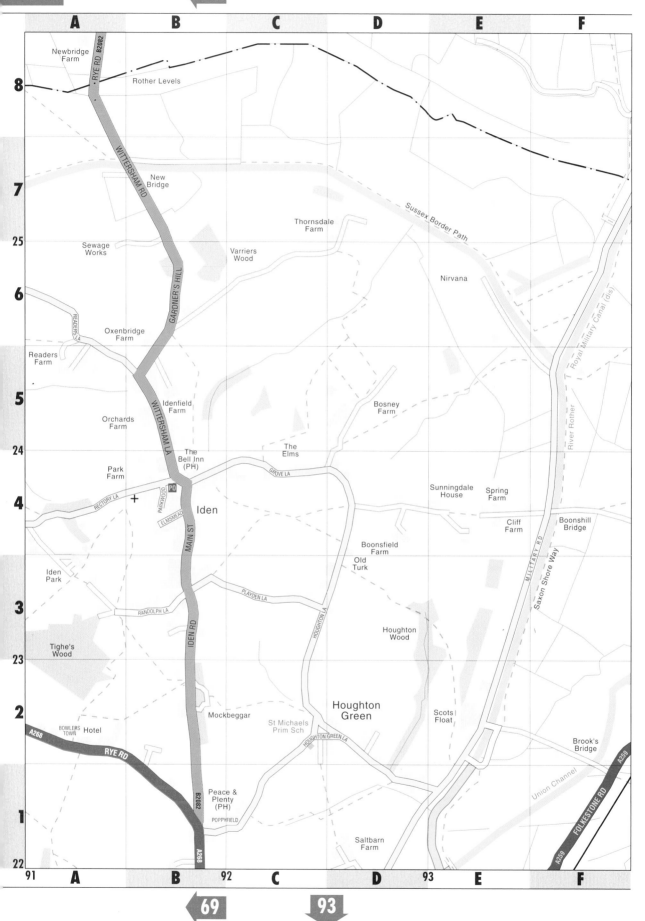

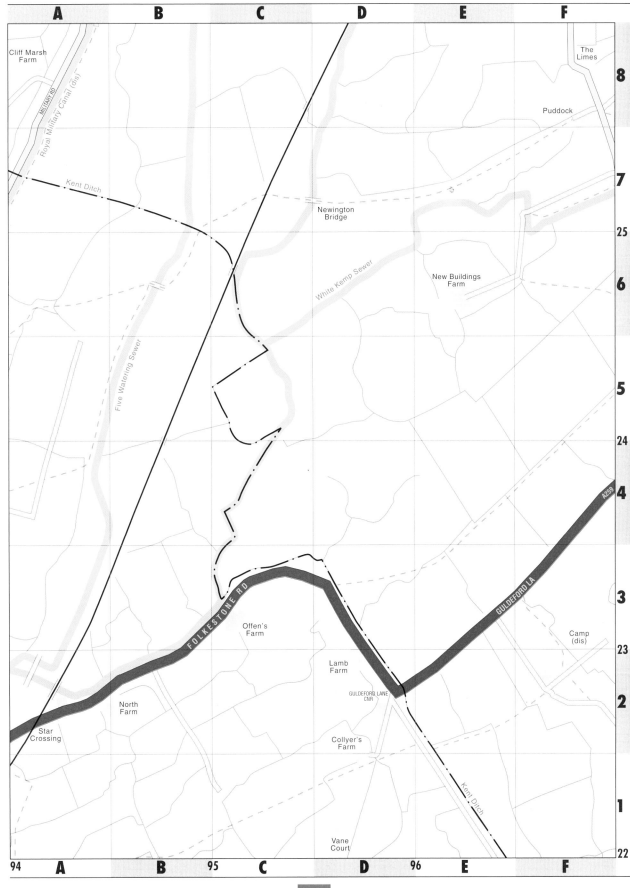

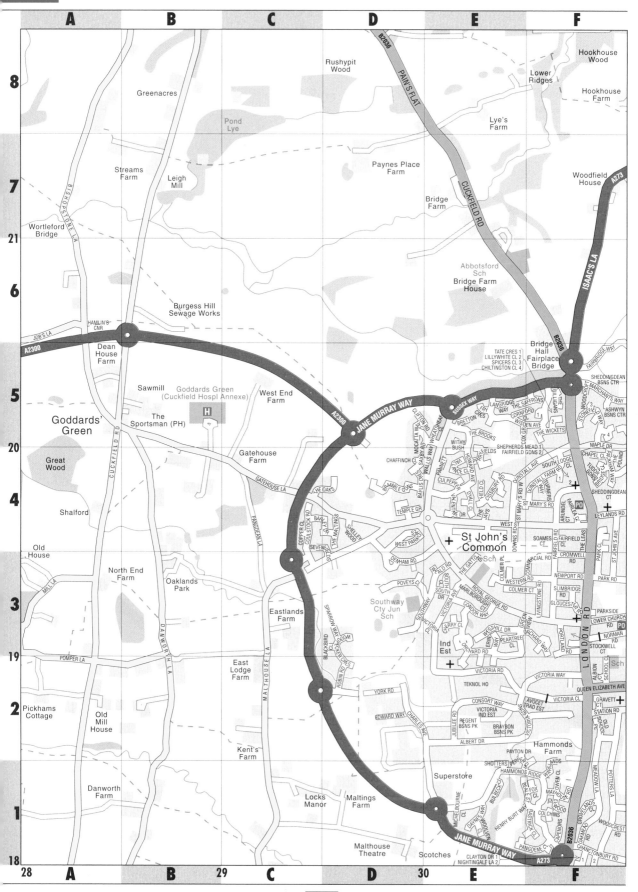

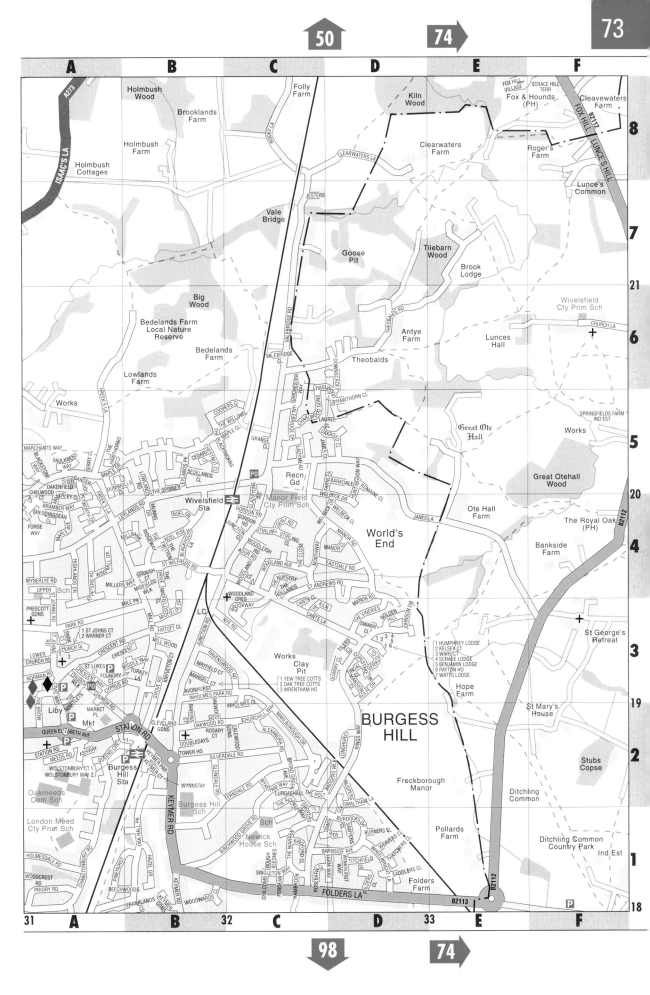

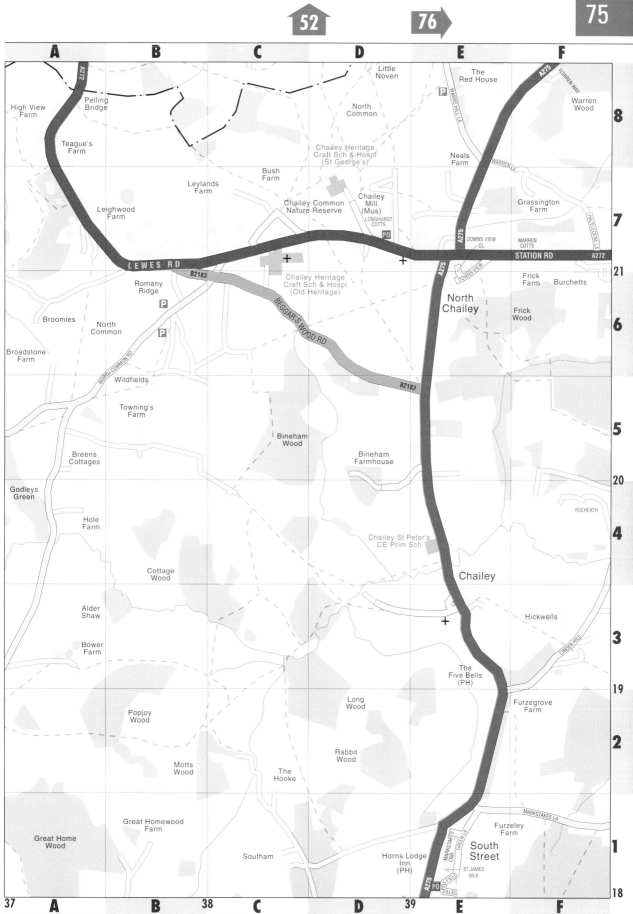

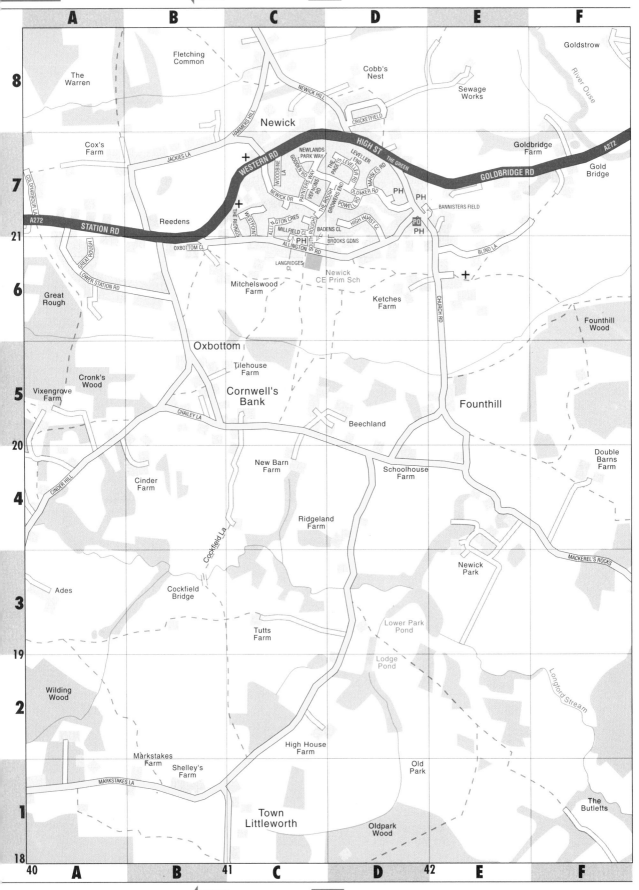

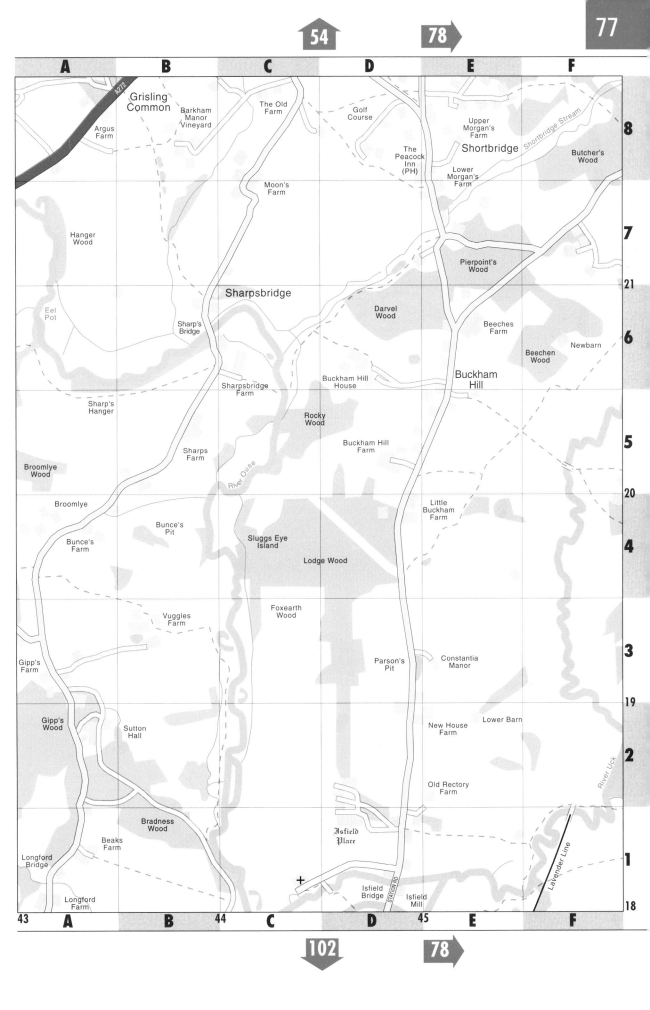

A   **B**   **C**   **D**   **E**   **F**

Grisling Common

Argus Farm

Barkham Manor Vineyard

The Old Farm

Golf Course

Upper Morgan's Farm

Shortbridge

Shortbridge Stream

Butcher's Wood

8

The Peacock Inn (PH)

Lower Morgan's Farm

Moon's Farm

Hanger Wood

7

Pierpoint's Wood

21

Sharpsbridge

Darvel Wood

Beeches Farm

6

Eel Pot

Sharp's Bridge

Beechen Wood

Newbarn

Sharpsbridge Farm

Buckham Hill House

Buckham Hill

Sharp's Hanger

Rocky Wood

Sharps Farm

Buckham Hill Farm

5

Broomlye Wood

River Ouse

20

Broomlye

Little Buckham Farm

Bunce's Pit

4

Bunce's Farm

Sluggs Eye Island

Lodge Wood

Vuggles Farm

Foxearth Wood

Parson's Pit

Constantia Manor

3

Gipp's Farm

19

Gipp's Wood

Sutton Hall

New House Farm

Lower Barn

2

Old Rectory Farm

River Uck

Bradness Wood

Beaks Farm

Isfield Place

Longford Bridge

+

Lavender Line

1

Longford Farm

Isfield Bridge

STATION RD

Isfield Mill

18

43   **A**   **B**   44   **C**   **D**   45   **E**   **F**

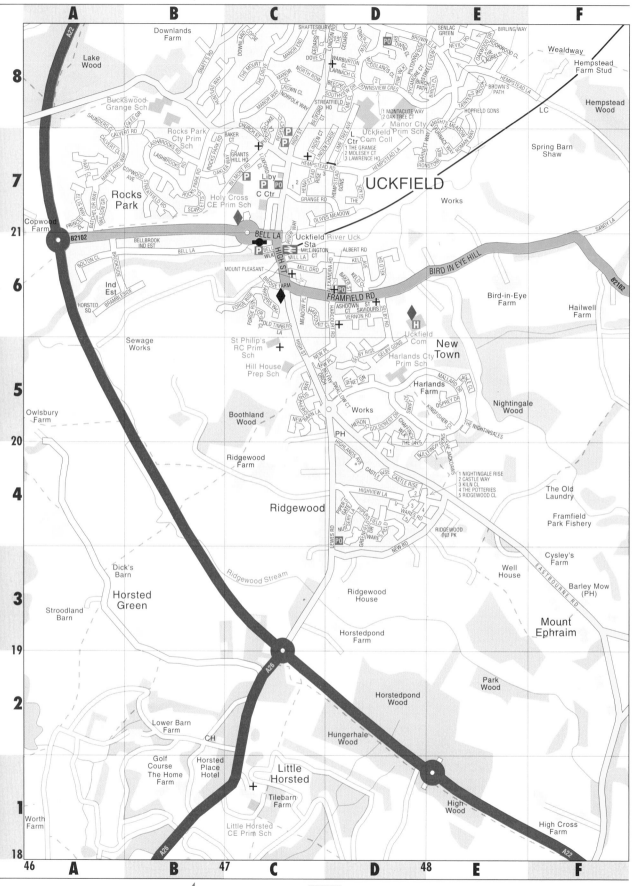

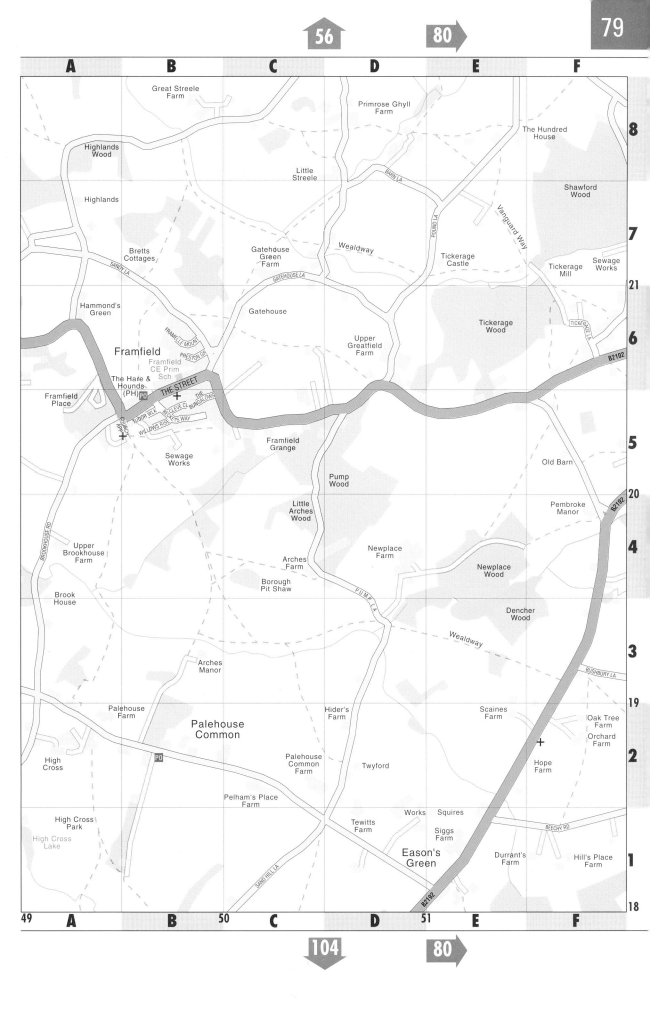

A   **B**   **C**   **D**   **E**   **F**

8

Pounsley

Springdene Farm

Waldron Down Farm

Baker's Common

Bosmere

NURSERY LA

Pounsley Manor

Waldron Down

Long Barn Motor Mus

B2102

MAYFIELD FLAT

POSSINGWORTH CL

7

YH
Shawford Farm

Tickerage Stream

CHAPEL LA

Burnthouse Farm

ST MARYS

Holy Cross Priory

21

Brookhurst Farm

GUN RD

Sharlands

Possingworth Park

6

B2102

JOHN DANN CL

MOUNT PLEASANT

STAR LA

PO

B2192

THE CLOSE

Browning's Manor

Possingworth Manor House

Oxpasture Wood

Roser's Cross

FOREST PL

WARREN LA

FIR GROVE RD

Sch

THE GREEN

LUDLOWS

MAPLES COTTS

Blackboys

5

Blackboys Inn (PH)

B2192

Kiln Wood

Possingworth Manor Farm

Dower House Farm

Brittenden

BRITTENDEN LA

Bryckden Place

NORTH ST

20

B2192

HOLLOW LA

4

Cider House Farm

Vanguard Way

Bushmere Stud

Butlett's Wood

Blackdown Wood

Catts Crouch Farm

Old Glebe

3

BUSHBURY LA

Bushbury

Hawkhurst Common Wood

Silveroaks Farm

Danesfield

Middle Wood

PO

Waldron

WHITEHOUSE LA

Waldron House

PH

St Georges Vineyard

Birchlands Farm

2

BEECHY RD

Wealdway

Little Goldsmith's Farm

Bonny's Farm

Holms Farm

MOAT LA

Moat Farm

Heronsdale Manor

The Grubs

Court Wood

Braysland Farm

1

Hawkhurst Common

Wenhams Farm

Foxhunt Green

Foxhunt Green Farm

18

52   **A**   **B**   **53**   **C**   **D**   **54**   **E**   **F**

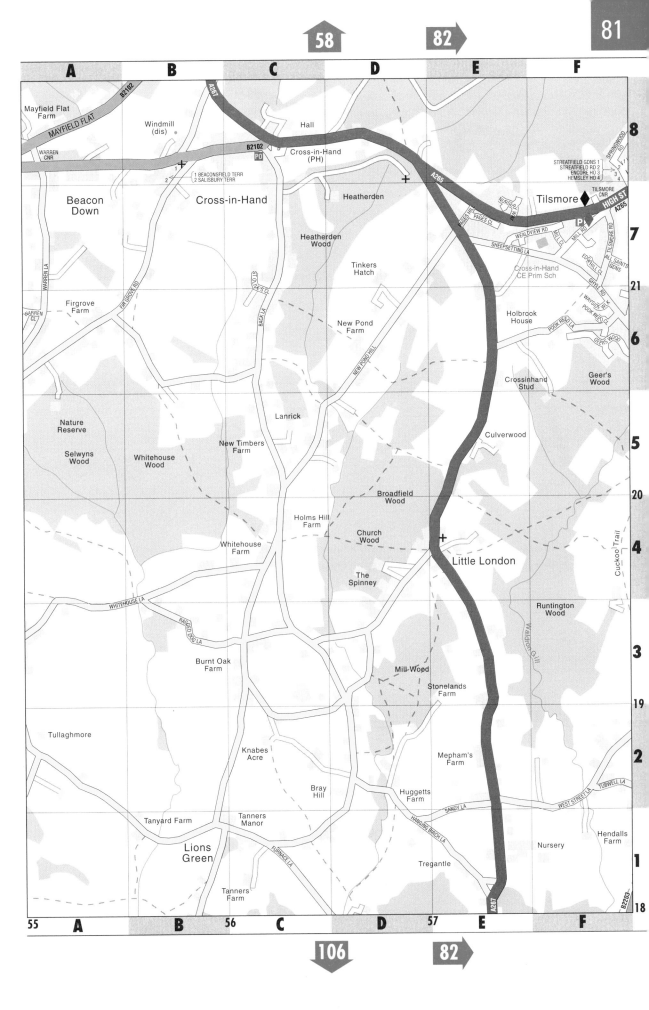

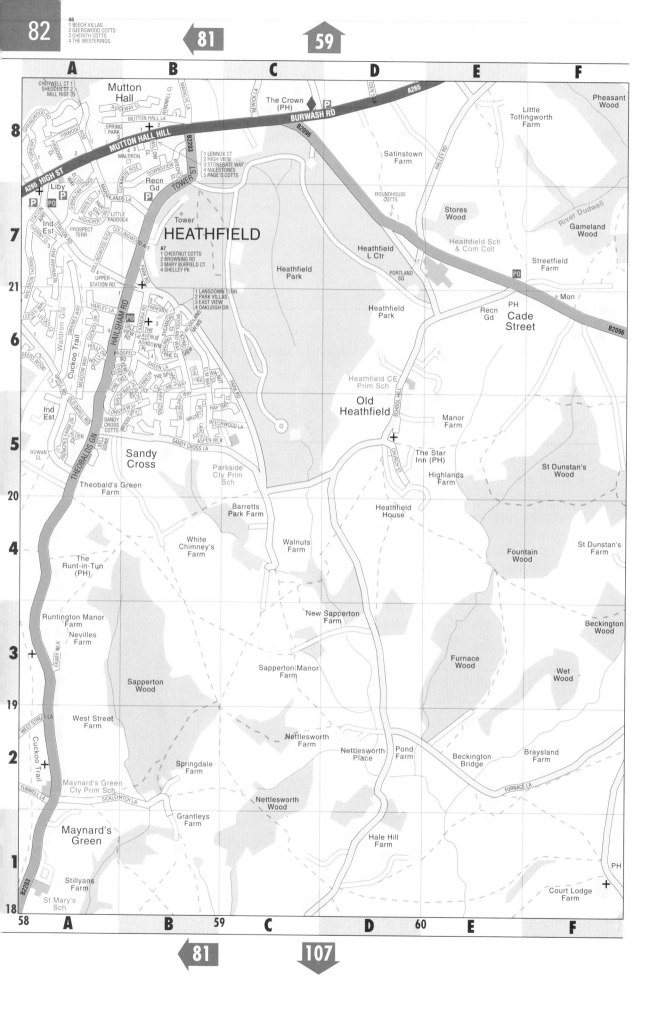

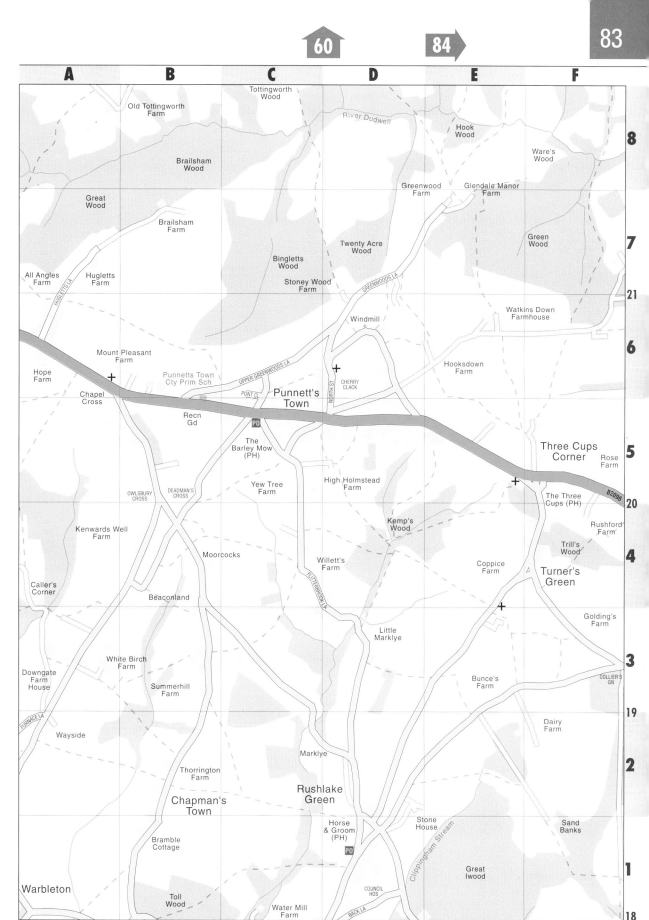

Tottingworth Wood
Old Tottingworth Farm
River Dudwell
Hook Wood
Ware's Wood
Brailsham Wood
Greenwood Farm
Glendale Manor Farm
Great Wood
Green Wood
Brailsham Farm
Twenty Acre Wood
Bingletts Wood
Stoney Wood Farm
GREENWOODS LA
21
Hugletts Farm
All Angles Farm
Watkins Down Farmhouse
HUGLETTS LA
Windmill
6
Mount Pleasant Farm
UPPER GREENWOODS LA
Hooksdown Farm
Hope Farm
Punnetts Town Cty Prim Sch
NORTH ST
CHERRY CLACK
Chapel Cross
PONT CL
Punnett's Town
Recn Gd
PO
Three Cups Corner
5
The Barley Mow (PH)
Rose Farm
OWLSBURY CROSS
DEADMAN'S CROSS
Yew Tree Farm
High Holmstead Farm
The Three Cups (PH)
B2096
20
Kenwards Well Farm
Kemp's Wood
Rushford Farm
Moorcocks
Willett's Farm
Trill's Wood
4
Caller's Corner
FLITTERBROOK LA
Coppice Farm
Turner's Green
Beaconland
Little Marklye
Golding's Farm
Downgate Farm House
White Birch Farm
Bunce's Farm
COLLIER'S GN
3
TURNACE LA
Summerhill Farm
19
Wayside
Dairy Farm
Thorrington Farm
Marklye
2
Chapman's Town
Rushlake Green
Stone House
Sand Banks
Bramble Cottage
Horse & Groom (PH)
Clippingham Stream
Warbleton
PO
Great Iwood
1
Toll Wood
Water Mill Farm
COUNCIL HOS
BACK LA

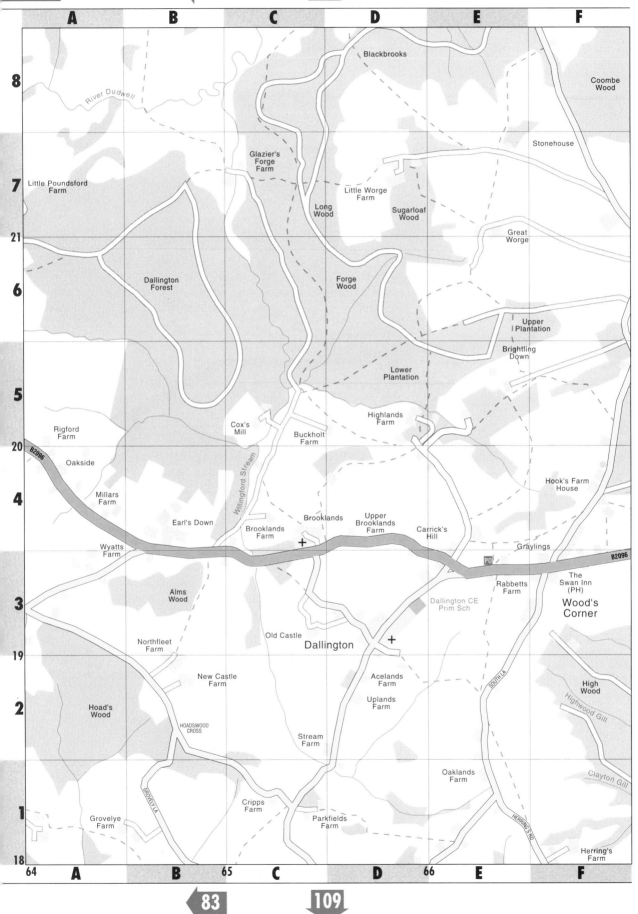

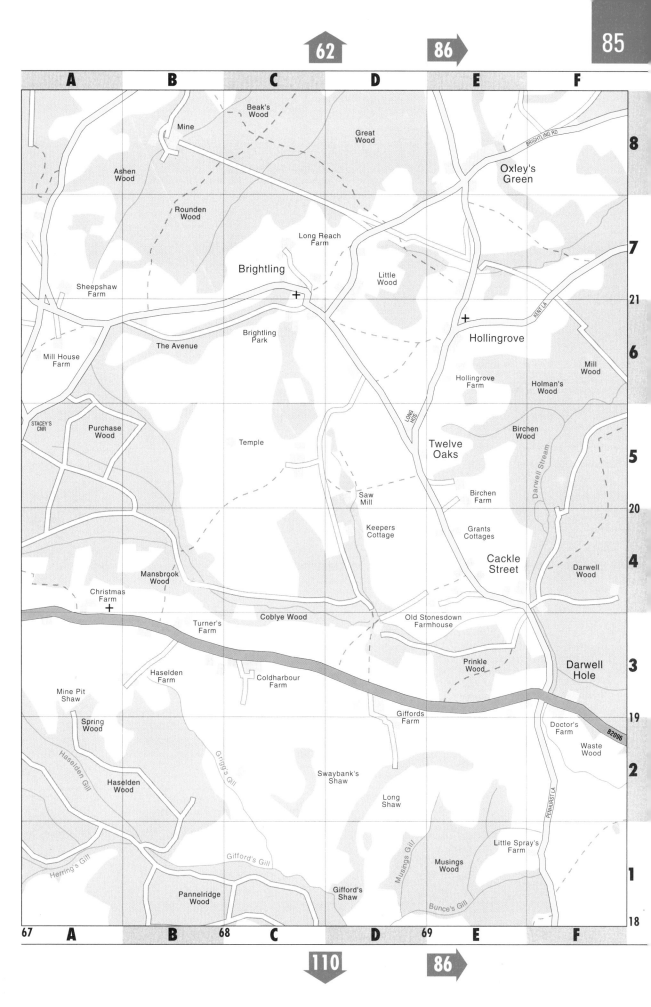

A B C D E F

8

Mine

Beak's
Wood

Great
Wood

BRIGHTLING RD

Oxley's
Green

Ashen
Wood

Rounden
Wood

7

Long Reach
Farm

Little
Wood

Brightling

KENT LA

21

Sheepshaw
Farm

The Avenue

Brightling
Park

Hollingrove

6

Mill House
Farm

Hollingrove
Farm

Holman's
Wood

Mill
Wood

STACEY'S
CNR

Purchase
Wood

Temple

LONG HOS

Twelve
Oaks

Birchen
Wood

Darwell Stream

5

Saw
Mill

Birchen
Farm

20

Keepers
Cottage

Grants
Cottages

Mansbrook
Wood

Cackle
Street

Darwell
Wood

4

Christmas
Farm

Coblye Wood

Old Stonesdown
Farmhouse

Turner's
Farm

Prinkle
Wood

Darwell
Hole

3

Haselden
Farm

Coldharbour
Farm

Giffords
Farm

Doctor's
Farm

B2096

19

Mine Pit
Shaw

Waste
Wood

Spring
Wood

PENHURST LA

Swaybank's
Shaw

2

Haselden Gill

Griggs' Gill

Haselden
Wood

Long
Shaw

Little Spray's
Farm

Musings Gill

Musings
Wood

1

Herring's Gill

Gifford's Gill

Pannelridge
Wood

Gifford's
Shaw

Bunce's Gill

18

A   **B**   **C**   **D**   **E**   **F**

BRIGHTLING RD

Swallowfield Farm

Mountfield Park Farm

Dray Shaw

8

Glottenham Stream

Park Pale

Coalbridge Shaw

Darwell Stream

Dens Wood

MOUNTFIELD LA

Coal Bridge

Bottonhold Wood

Hunters Farm

7

KENT LA

Darwell Resr

Tunstall Farm

Scaland Wood

21

Taylor's Cottage

Baldwin's Farm

6

Hightree Shaw

Furnace Shaw

The Banks

Castle Farm

Simmett's Wood

Banks Farm

5

Collier's Croft Wood

Castle Wood

Millham Wood

20

LC

Limekiln Wood

Factory

4

Darwell Wood

Shep's Wood

Mountfield Mine

3

River Line

Great Wood

Crowhurst Farm

19

Darwell Hill

DARVEL DOWN

Woodlands Farm

2

B2096

Netherfield CE Prim Sch

The Old Rectory

PO

Netherfield

Netherfield Court

NETHERFIELD WAY

EATENDEN LA

Homestead Farm

White Hart (PH)

NETHERFIELD RD

KANE HYTHE RD

Sandy Wood

Ivyland Farm

Netherfield Down

Kerry Farm

Eatenden Wood

1

Homestead Shaw

Ibrook Wood

B2096

Toll Wood

18

70   **A**   **B**   71   **C**   **D**   72   **E**   **F**

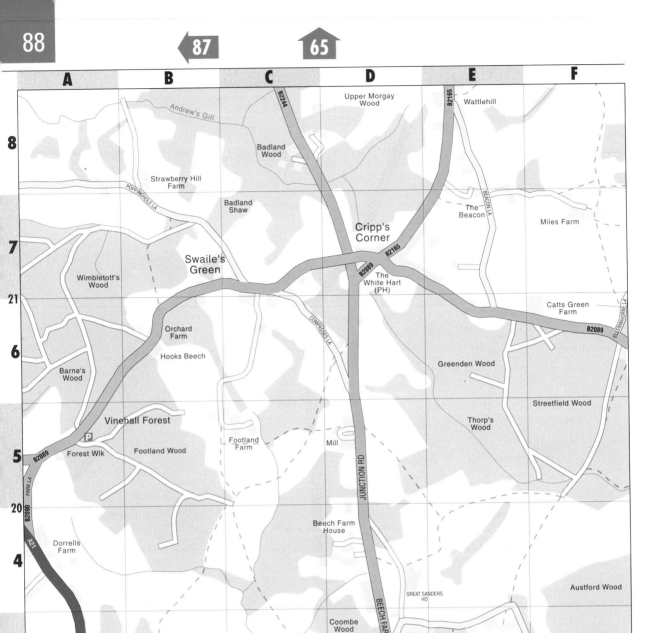

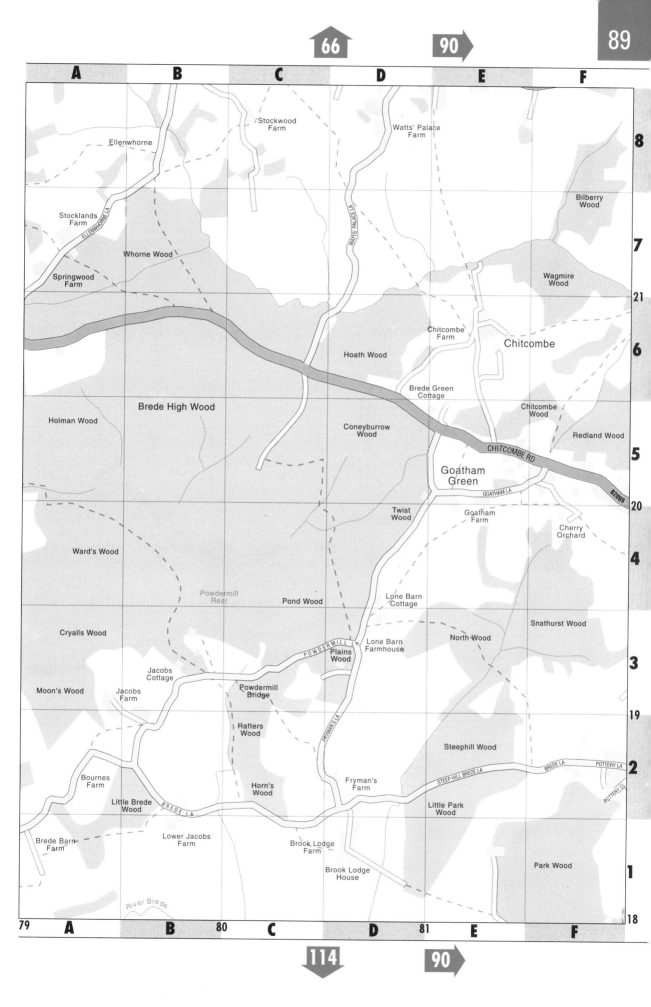

89
67

A B C D E F

8

Tanhouse
Farm

Doucegrove
Farm

Little
Doucegrove

Wharnham
Wood

Glass Eye
Farm

Garland
Wood

Moore's
Wood

MOORE'S LA

Osier
Gill

Greentiles
Farm

Sheepwash
Wood

Furnace
Wood

Beckley
Furnace

7

River Tillingham

Maplestone
Farm

NORTHIAM RD

Arnold Bridge

Conster
Manor

Wagmary
Wood

FURNACE LA

Furnace
Farm

21

Great Conster
Farm

Burnthouse
Wood

6

Austen's
Wood

West
Wood

Kicker
Wood

Birch
Wood

HOW'S CL

Twist
Wood

5

Hundredhouse
Bridge

Granary
Farm

BROAD OAK CL

THE TILLINGHAM VIEW
OAKHILL DR

THE HAWTHORNES

NORTHIAM RD

CHESTNUT
CL

REEDSWOOD RD
POND CL

FIELDWAY
THE ORCHARD
THE MARTLETS

Broad Oak

Spring
Wood

20

B2089

CHITCOMBE RD

PO

The
Rainbow Trout
(PH)

THE
CROSSWAYS

Brede
Cty Prim
Sch

Reysons
Farm

Gilly
Wood

Maidlands
Farm

HUNDREDHOUSE LA

4

Moorsholm
Farm

KING WOOD HILL

Reysons
Oasts

UDIMORE RD

Broadland Row

Broadlands
Wood

Sowdens
Farm

3

Cackle
Street

Well Wood

Broadlands
Wood

South Sowdens
Wood

B2089

19

ST MARY'S

POTTERY LA

CACKLE ST

Mill Wood

Springfield
Cotts

STUBB LA

Groaning
Bridge

Alder
Wood

2

POTTERY CL

Brede

Hillyfield

Hare
Cottages

Hare
Farm

Brede
Place

Stonelink
Farm

Pickdick
Farm

1

BREDE HILL

The
Red Lion Inn
(PH)

A28

18

82 A 83 B C 83 D 84 E F

91
69

A   **B**   **C**   **D**   **E**   **F**

Morebread Farm

Peasmarsh Place

CHURCH LA

Norland Wood

Leasam Wood

STARVECROW LA

DEW LA

8

Clayton Farm

Wr Twr

Cockney Hill Wood

Leasam House

TILLINGHAM LA

7

Secret Wood

21

Dew Farm

6

Tillingham Wood

River Tillingham

Ennets Wood

TILLINGHAM LA

Cottage Shaw

Tillingham Farm

5

Hooker's Wood

Calves Field Wood

20

Gillshaw Farm

CADBOROUGH CLIFF

B2089

Tillingham Bridge

OAST HOUSE DR

4

Wick Farm

Oaklands

Cadborough Farm

Turnpike Wood

Hotel

Wick Wood

Watlands

Cadborough Cliff

3

UDIMORE RD

Knellstone Wood

Farthing Wood

DUMB WOMAN'S LA

19

Cock Marling

1066 Country Wlk

B2089

2

The Plough (PH)

Nicholls Cottages

Newhouse Sewer

Padiam Sewer

Roadend Farm

WINCHELSEA LA

LC

Winchelsea Sta

STATION RD

1

Float Farm

STATION COTTS

18

88   **A**   **B**   89   **C**   **D**   90   **E**   **F**

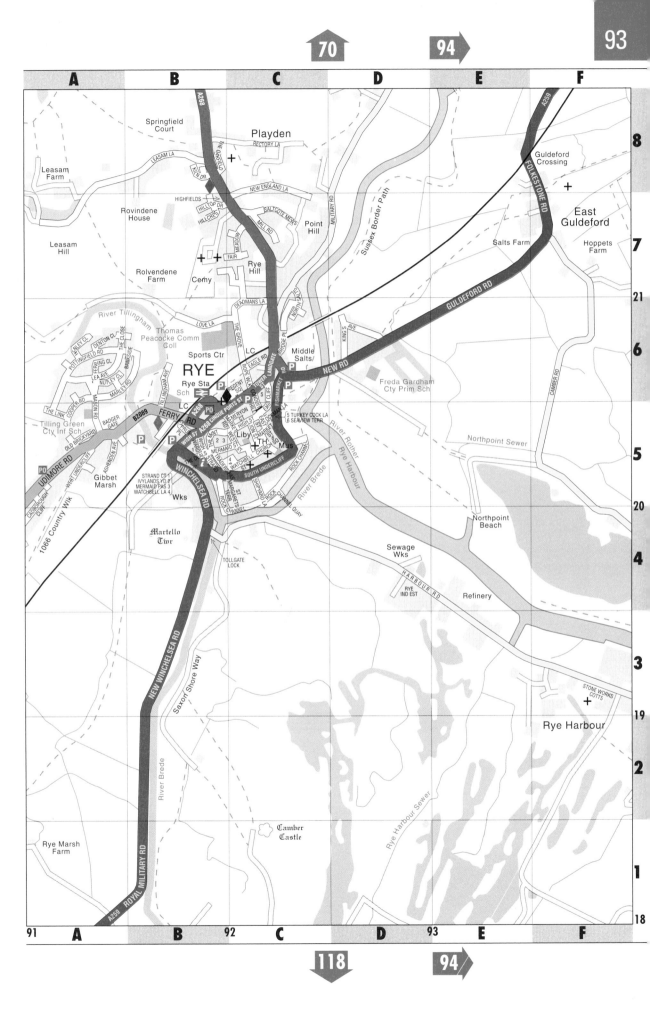

A   **B**   **C**   **D**   **E**   **F**

8

Kent Ditch

Barn Farm

7

Tressland

East Guldeford Level

Moneypenny

21

Black House Farm

6

Guldeford Sewer

5

20

Wainway Wall

4

Northpoint Beach

Guldeford Sewer

Point Farm

3

1 COASTGUARD SQ
2 PAINES COTTS
3 MARY STAMFORD GN

CAMBER RD

Pound Field Farm

CH

Holiday Centre

PH

FARM LA

19

IRB Sta

DRAFFIN LA

SCOTTS ACRE

HARBOUR RD

Rye Golf Links

COASTGUARD COTTS

OLD WORLD COTTS

LINKS WAY

NEW LYDD RD

Camber

TRAM RD

P

Martello Tower

River Rother

TONBRIDGE WAY

OLD LYDD RD

LYDD RD

SAM WAY

DENE

LYDD RD

MARCHANTS

DUNES AVE

DIXWELL WAY

FIRST AVE

SECOND AVE

PO

2

Caravan Park

Lime Kiln Cottage

Dunes

PETER JAMES CL

SEAFIELD WAY

Dunes

MARINE COTTS

P

1 COACH HOUSE COTTS
2 FLEETWAY CT

THE SUTTONS

1

Rye Harbour Nature Reserve

Rye Bay

East Pier

18

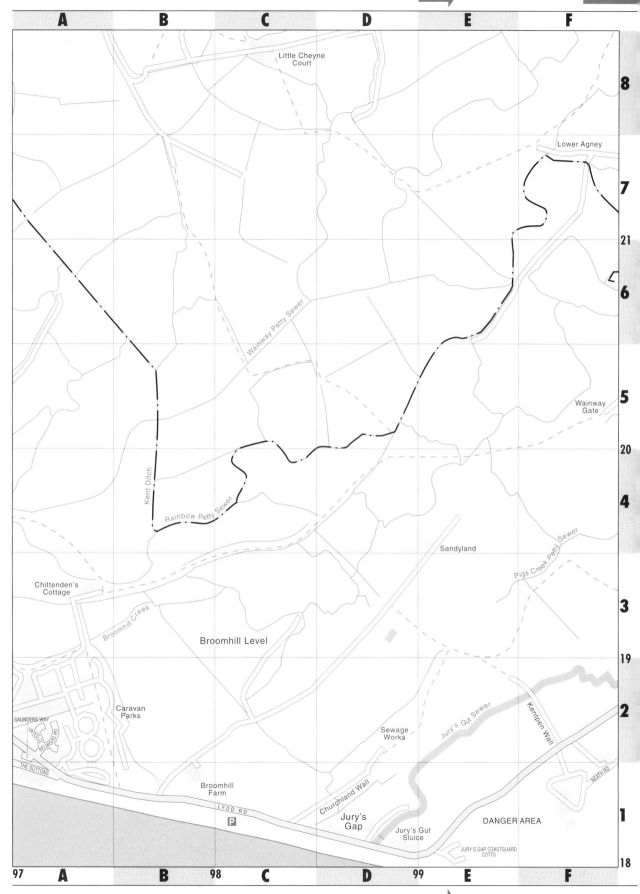

8

7

21

6

5

20

4

3

19

2

1

18

Little Cheyne Court

Lower Agney

Wainway Petty Sewer

Wainway Gate

Kent Ditch

Rainbow Petty Sewer

Sandyland

Pigs Creek Petty Sewer

Chittenden's Cottage

Broomhill Creek

Broomhill Level

Caravan Parks

SAUNDERS WAY

YATES CL

BELWOD RD

THE SUTTONS

Jury's Gut Sewer

Kenpen Wall

Sewage Works

Churchland Wall

Broomhill Farm

LYDD RD

P

Jury's Gap

Jury's Gut Sluice

JURY'S GAP COASTGUARD COTTS

HEATH RD

DANGER AREA

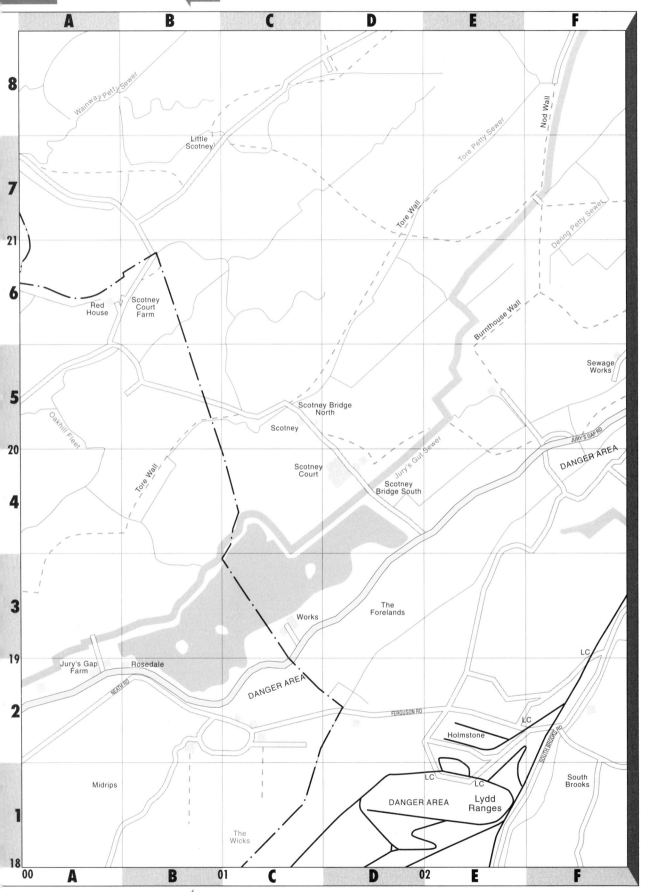

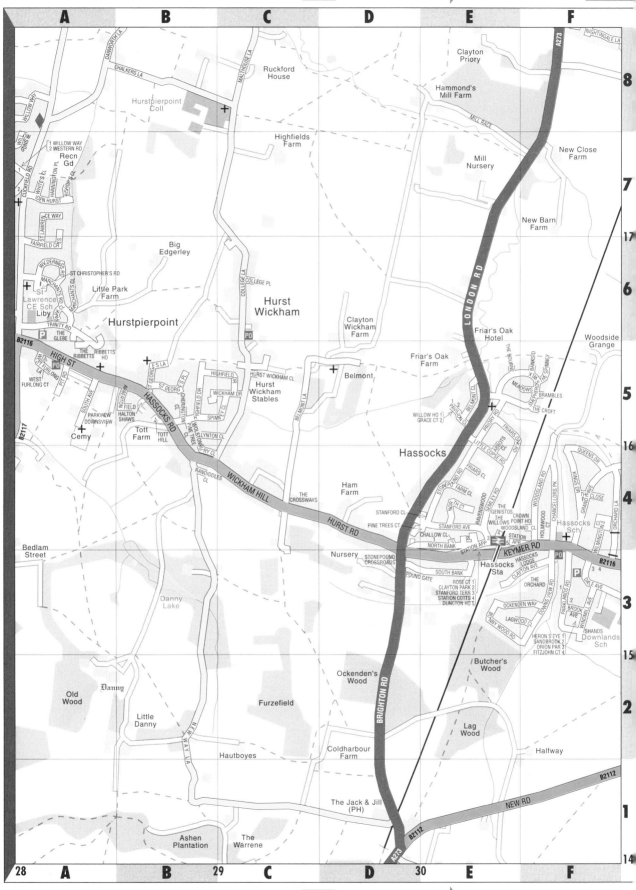

97
73

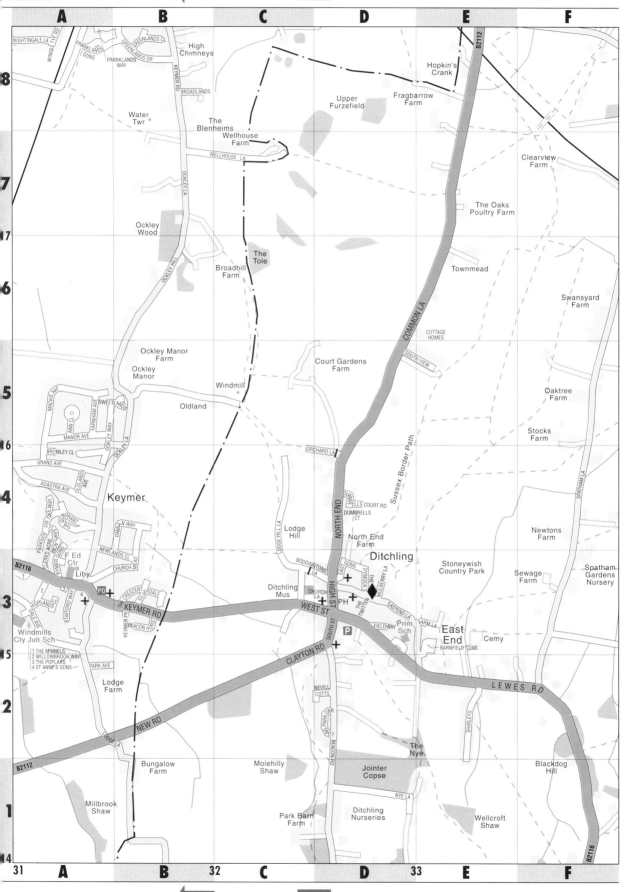

97
120

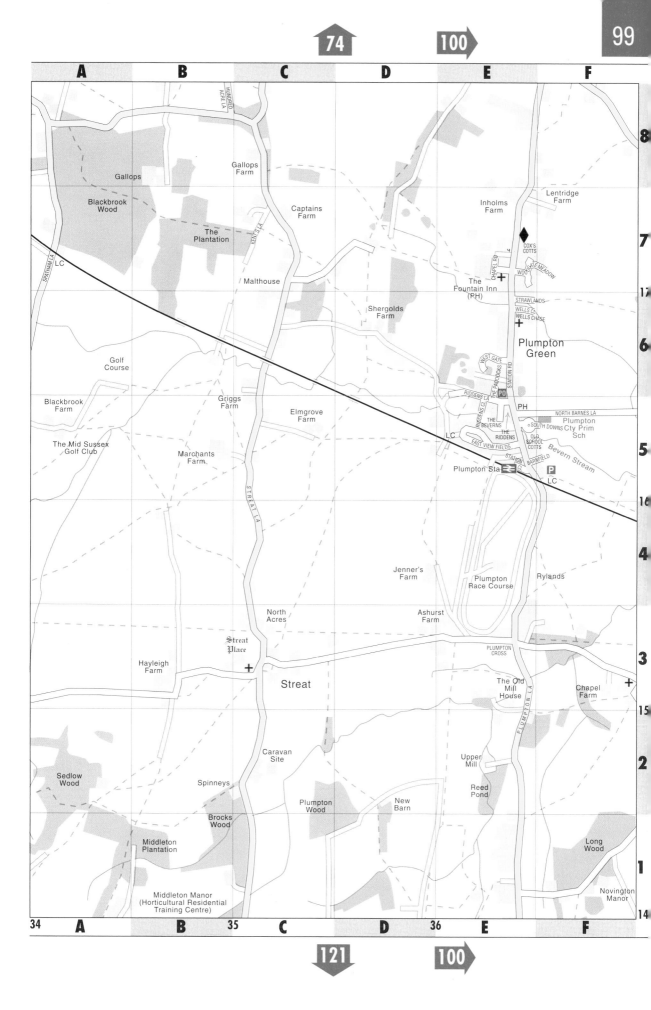

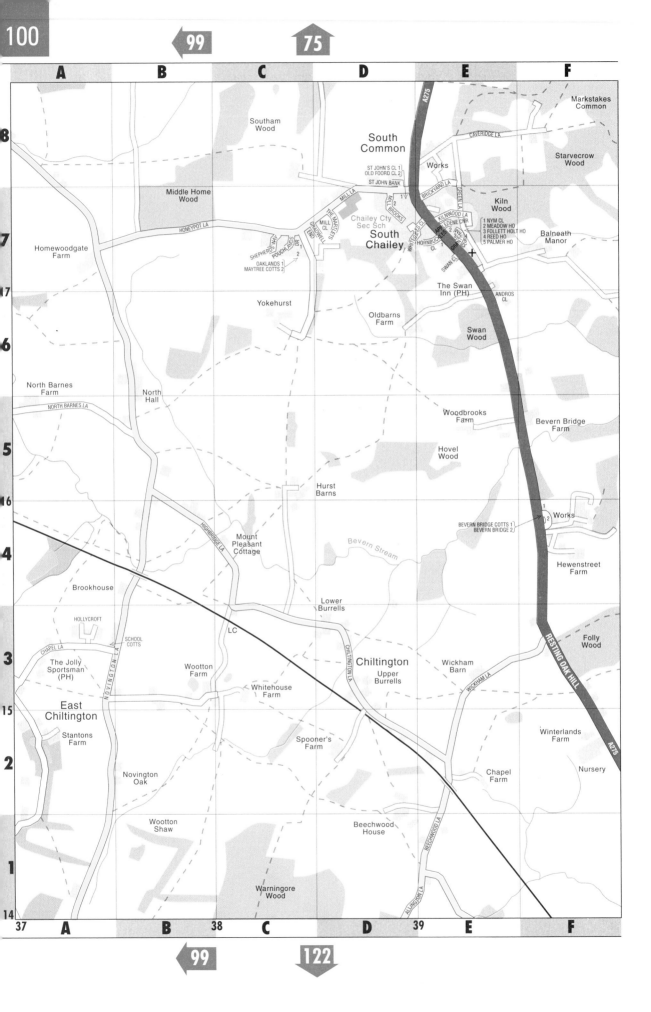

A B C D E F

8

Southam
Wood

South
Common

CAVERIDGE LA

Markstakes
Common

Starvecrow
Wood

Middle Home
Wood

Works

St JOHN'S CL 1
OLD FOORD CL 2

St JOHN BANK

BRICKYARD LA

Kiln
Wood

Balneath
Manor

HONEYPOT LA

7

Homewoodgate
Farm

Chailey Cty
Sec Sch
South
Chailey

HORNBUCKLES
CL

1 NYM CL
2 MEADOW HO
3 FOLLETT HOLT HO
4 REED HO
5 PALMER HO

SHEPHERDS WAY
POUCHLANDS DR

OAKLANDS 1
MAYTREE COTTS 2

Yokehurst

17

The Swan
Inn (PH)

ANDROS
CL

6

Oldbarns
Farm

Swan
Wood

North Barnes
Farm

NORTH BARNES LA

North
Hall

Woodbrooks
Farm

Bevern Bridge
Farm

5

Hovel
Wood

Hurst
Barns

16

HIGHBRIDGE LA

Mount
Pleasant
Cottage

Bevern Stream

BEVERN BRIDGE COTTS 1
BEVERN BRIDGE 2

Works

Hewenstreet
Farm

4

Brookhouse

Lower
Burrells

Folly
Wood

HOLLYCROFT

SCHOOL
COTTS

LC

CHILTINGTON LA

RESTING OAK HILL

3

CHAPEL LA

The Jolly
Sportsman
(PH)

NOVINGTON LA

Wootton
Farm

Whitehouse
Farm

Chiltington

Upper
Burrells

Wickham
Barn

WICKHAM LA

15

East
Chiltington

Stantons
Farm

Spooner's
Farm

Chapel
Farm

Winterlands
Farm

Nursery

2

Novington
Oak

BEECHWOOD LA

A275

1

Wootton
Shaw

Beechwood
House

Warningore
Wood

ALLINGTON LA

14

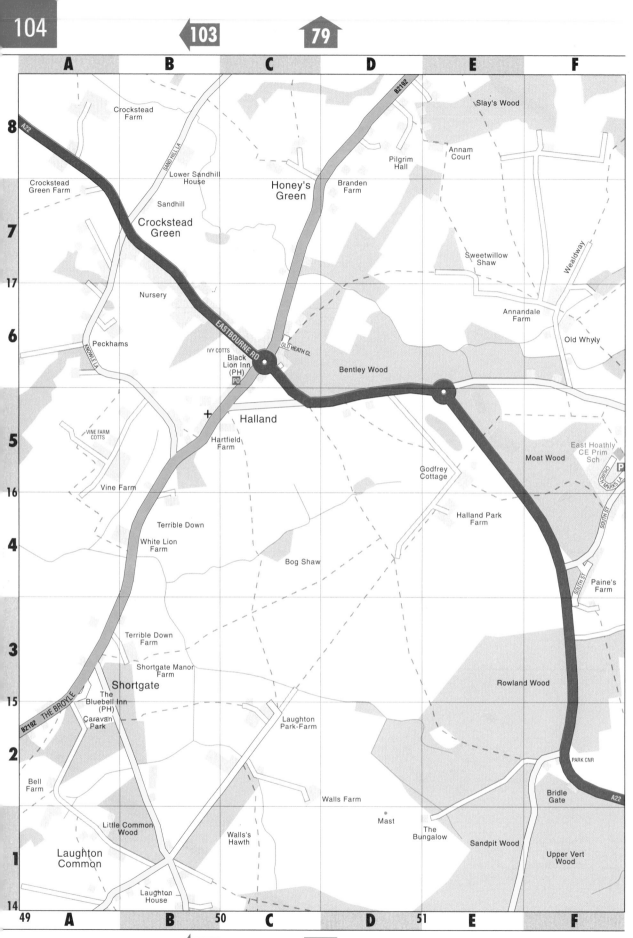
A B C D E F

8

Crockstead
Farm

B2192

Slay's Wood

Lower Sandhill
House

Annam
Court

Pilgrim
Hall

Crockstead
Green Farm

Honey's
Green

Branden
Farm

SAND HILL LA

Sandhill

Sweetwillow
Shaw

7

Crockstead
Green

Wealdway

17

Nursery

Annandale
Farm

EASTBOURNE RD

6

Peckhams

Old Whyly

KNOWLE LA

IVY COTTS

OLD HEATH CL

Black
Lion Inn
(PH)

Bentley Wood

PO

Halland

East Hoathly
CE Prim
Sch

5

VINE FARM
COTTS

Hartfield
Farm

Moat Wood

P

CHURCH MARKS LA

Godfrey
Cottage

16

Vine Farm

SOUTH ST

Terrible Down

Halland Park
Farm

4

White Lion
Farm

Bog Shaw

SOUTH ST

Paine's
Farm

3

Terrible Down
Farm

Shortgate Manor
Farm

Rowland Wood

Shortgate

15

The
Bluebell Inn
(PH)

THE BROYLE

Caravan
Park

Laughton
Park-Farm

2

B2192

PARK CNR

Bell
Farm

Walls Farm

Bridle
Gate

A22

Little Common
Wood

Mast

The
Bungalow

Sandpit Wood

Upper Vert
Wood

1

Laughton
Common

Walls's
Hawth

14

49 A B 50 C D 51 E F

Laughton
House

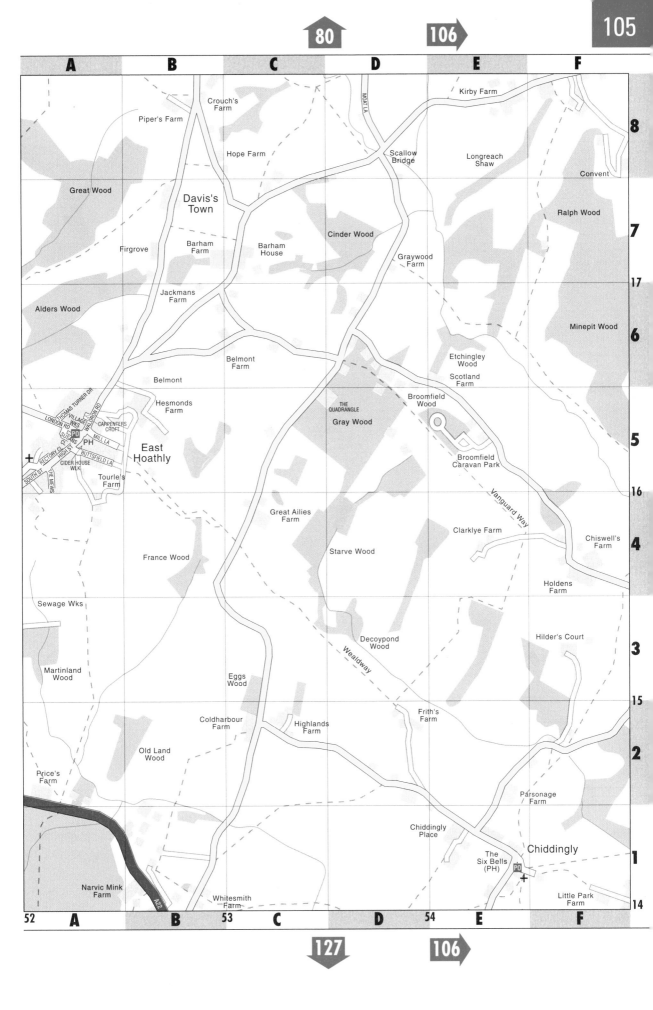

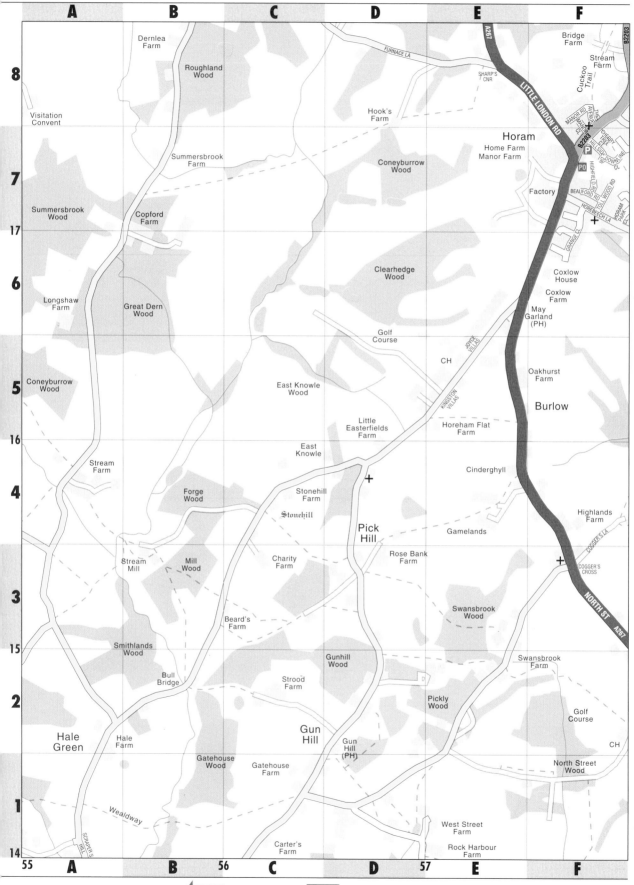

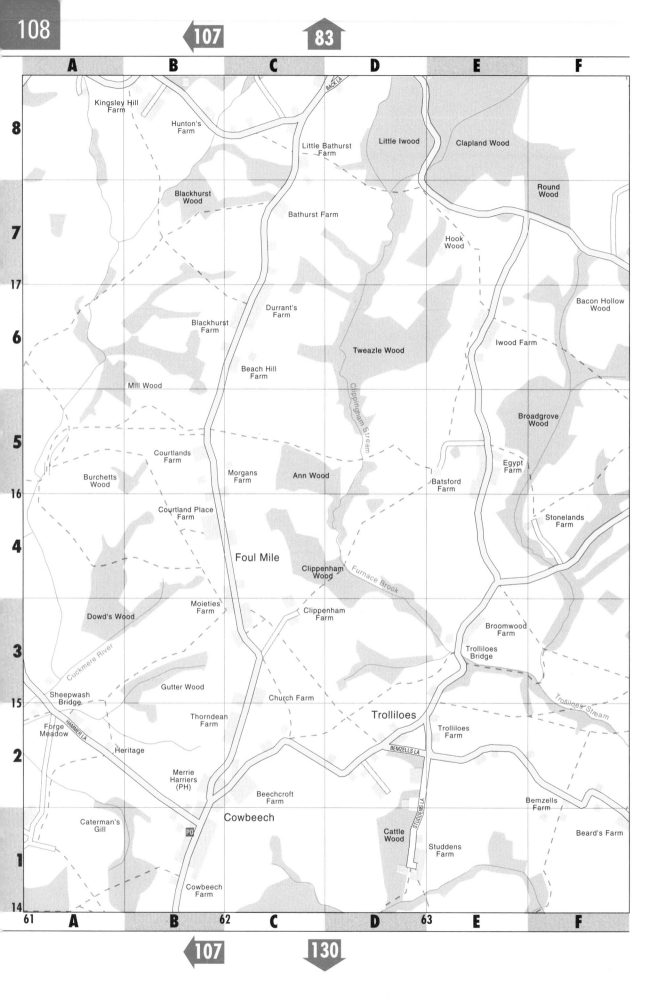

107
83

A   B   C   D   E   F

8

Kingsley Hill
Farm

Hunton's
Farm

Little Bathurst
Farm

Little Iwood

Clapland Wood

BACK LA

Round
Wood

Blackhurst
Wood

Bathurst Farm

7

Hook
Wood

17

Bacon Hollow
Wood

Durrant's
Farm

Blackhurst
Farm

6

Tweazle Wood

Iwood Farm

Mill Wood

Beach Hill
Farm

Clippingham Stream

Broadgrove
Wood

5

Courtlands
Farm

Morgans
Farm

Ann Wood

Egypt
Farm

Burchetts
Wood

Batsford
Farm

16

Stonelands
Farm

Courtland Place
Farm

4

Foul Mile

Clippenham
Wood

Furnace Brook

Moieties
Farm

Clippenham
Farm

Broomwood
Farm

Dowd's Wood

Trolliloes
Bridge

3

Trolliloes Stream

Cuckmere River

Gutter Wood

Church Farm

15

Sheepwash
Bridge

Trolliloes

HAMMER LA

Thorndean
Farm

Trolliloes
Farm

Forge
Meadow

BEMZELLS LA

2

Heritage

STUDDENS LA

Merrie
Harriers
(PH)

Beechcroft
Farm

Bemzells
Farm

Caterman's
Gill

PO

Cowbeech

Cattle
Wood

Beard's Farm

Studdens
Farm

1

Cowbeech
Farm

14

107
130

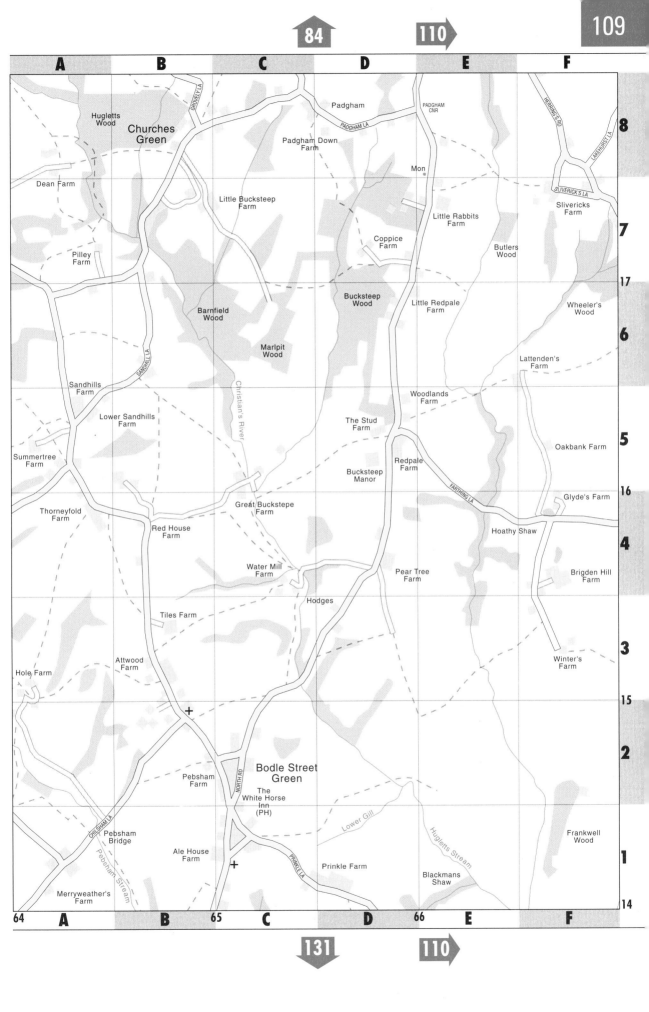

A   **B**   **C**   **D**   **E**   **F**

Pleasure House

LAKEHURST LA

Lakehurst

Pannelridge Wood

Bunce's Farm

Link Wood

Great Spray's Farm

8

Buckwell Wood

Buckwell Gill

Buckwell Farm

Spring Gill

Anderson's Wood

Rocks Farm

Foxearth Wood

7

Furnace Cottage

17

Thorndale Farm

Hogstye Wood

Allfrees Wood

Penhurst

Pollyspark Wood

6

Thornden Farm

Thornden Cottages

Church Farm

Manor House

PENHURST LA

Court Lodge

Malthouse Wood

1066 Country Walk

5

Izlebridge Wood

16

PO

Pontsgreen Wood

Forge Cottages

Ponts Green

Peens Wood

4

Reedlands Farm

Tent Hill

Reed Wood

Mon

Ash Bourne

3

The Bungalow

New Buildings Farm

15

Reservoir Pond

Ash Tree Inn (PH)

The Grove

2

Brownbread Street

Brownbread Stud

Pigknoll Farm

Ashburnham Place

Front Water

Walk Wood

1066 Country Walk

Linghams

The Pound

A271

1

Bray's Hill

Forty Acre Gill

Lingham's Farm

Broad Water

Burrage Wood

Baker's Wood

A271

14

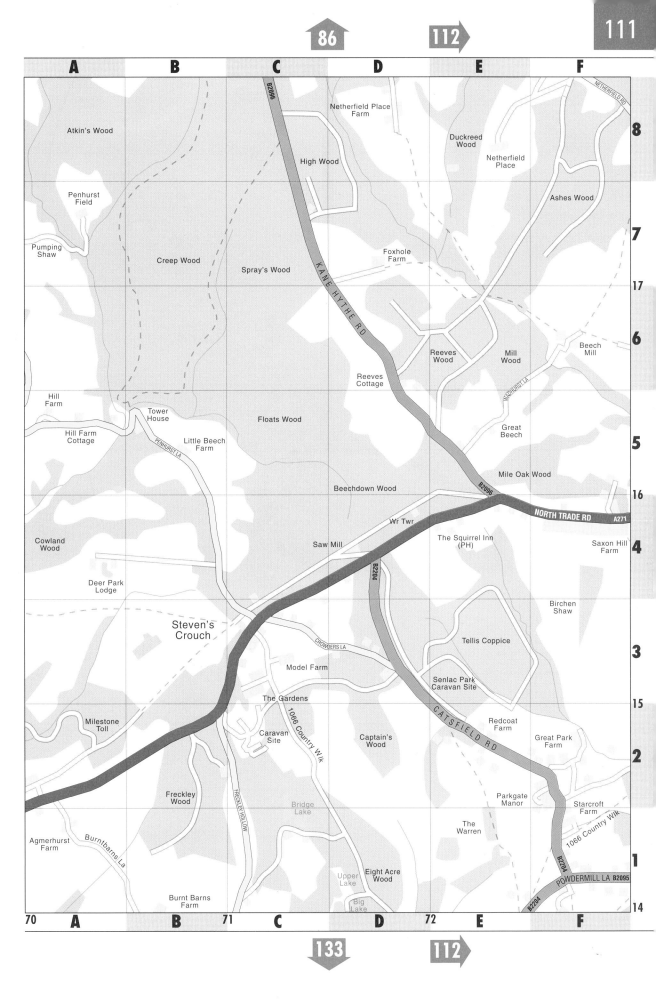

A **B** **C** **D** **E** **F**

8

Peacehaven Farm

Lower Gate Farm

Ringlett's Farm

Le Rette Farm

Canadia

CANADIA RD

Horseye Shaw

NETHERFIELD HILL COTTS

NETHERFIELD HILL

Gate Farm

WHATLINGTON RD

7

Beech Wood

NETHERFIELD RD

Black Firs Farm

Punch Bowl Farm

Somerby Farm

The Old Barrack Inn

Kingswell Farm

BEECH CL

OAKHURST RD

17

Beech Farm

WATTLE'S WISH

THE CLOISTERS

BOWBARNS

VIRGIN'S LA

VIRGIN'S CROFT

UCKHAM LA

Fuller's Farm

LONDON RD

A2100

6

Stream Farm

BOWMANS DR

DUKES HILL

Caldbec Hill

The Old Mill

1 WINDGROVE HO
2 WINDGROVE COTTS
1 2

Oast Cottage

Bailiffs Cottage

CALDBEC HILL

CALDBEC CT

SENLAC CT

Little Park Cotts

Coarsebarn Farm

5

Kelk Wood

CHAIN LA

NET LWGTON GDNS

VALE RD

BATTLE GATES

SAXONWOOD RD

MOUNT JOY

Liby

RUE DE BAYEUX

MARKET SQ

LEWINSCOURT

BATTLE

Little Park Farm

Sewage Works

CORONATION GDNS

Battle

H

North Lodge

A271

ALMONRY FIELDS

CLARVALE CL

HAMPDEN CL

ASTEN FIE

MKT RD

ABBEY WAY

WOODHAMS

ST MARTINS ABBEY CT

Mus

Cemy

NORMAN CL

LC

MARLEY LA

MARLEY RI

MARLEY GDNS

16

P

HIGH ST

PO

Mus

i

MEADOW BANK

WESTCL

FALCONER DR

WREN CT

SWALLOW DR

HARRIER LA

4

Claverham Com Coll

CLAVERHAM WAY

Almonry Farm

Battle & Langton CE Prim Sch

1066 Country Wlk

BULL RING

PARK

Battle Abbey (Sch)

UPPER LAKE

HARBOUR'S YD

Works

GRANARY COTTS

Battle Sta

ABB'ST CL

KINGSDALE CL

SHIRLEA VIEW

WALDEN TERR

PICARDY

SENLAC GDNS

LOWER LAKE

STATION APP

THE SPINNEY

THE GROVE

Battle Abbey (remains of)

Phipps's Gill

Saxon Wood

New Pond

Chapel Cotts

B2095

1
2
3
4
5
6
7
8
9
10

Starr's Green Farm

STARRS MEAD

STARR'S GREEN LA

STARR'S COTTS

3

Tower Hill

Horselodge Plantation

ST MARY'S FARMHOUSE 1
ST MARY'S GDNS 2
ST MARY'S VILLAS 3
CLIVE VILLAS 4
ST MARY'S TERR 5
GRAYS COTTS 6
HAROLD TERR 7
ST MARY'S COTTS 8
LAMBERTS COTTS 9
TANYARD COTTS 10

BATTLE HILL

HASTINGS RD A2100

GLENGORSE CT

GLENGORSE

Starr's Green

15

Farthings Farm

2

Farthing Pond

Warren Wood

Powdermill Lake

Powder Mills Hotel

Battle Abbey Farm

Hoathybank Wood

POWDERMILL LA

Malthouse Wood

1

Powdermill Wood

Water Works

Lower Telham

B2095

TELHAM LA

Stone Cottage

14

73 **A** **B** **74** **C** **D** **75** **E** **F**

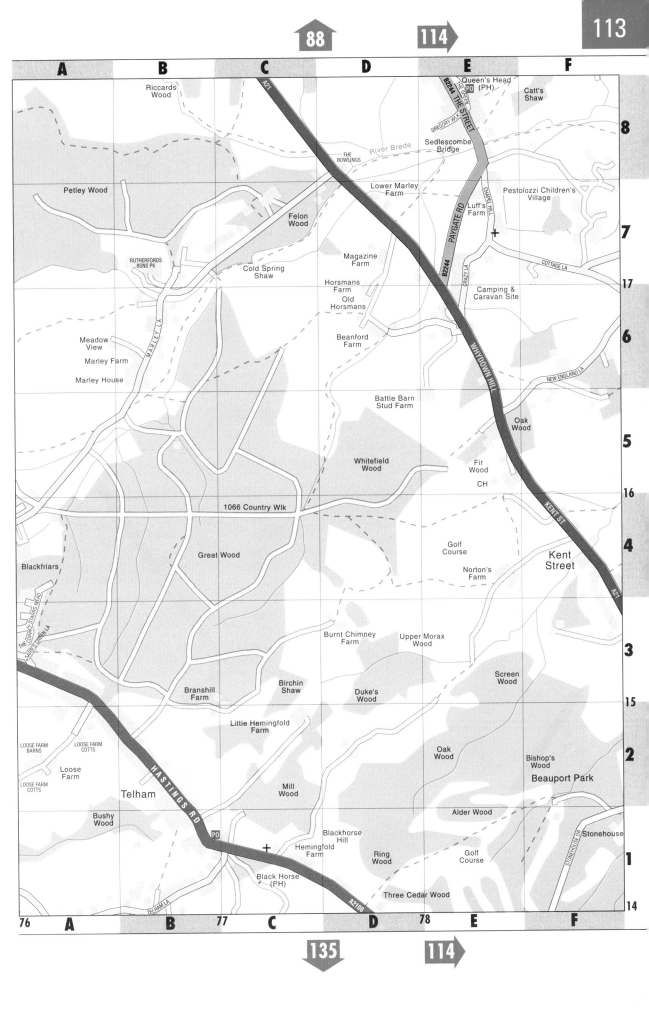

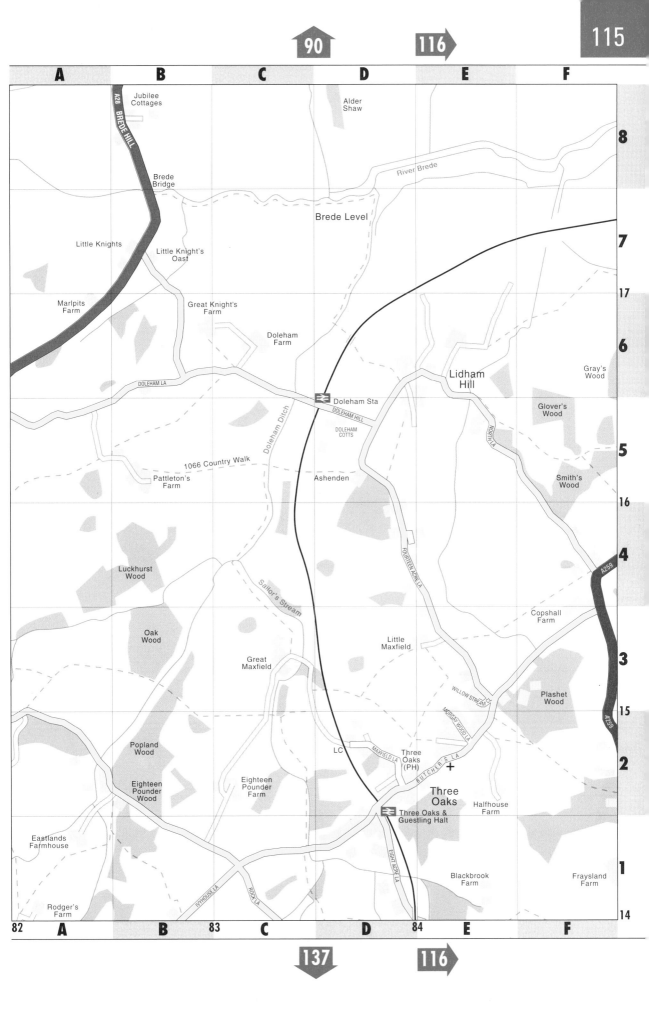

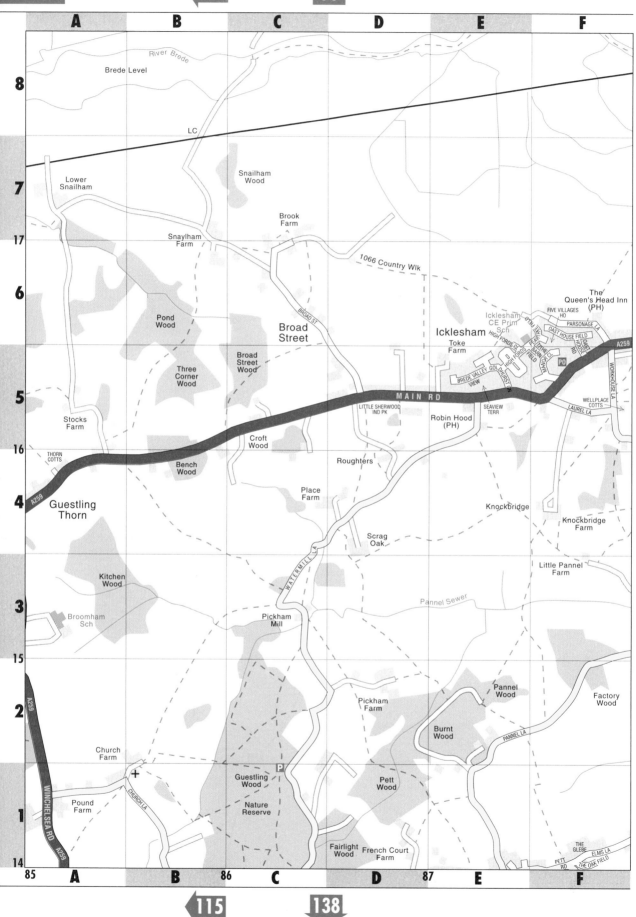

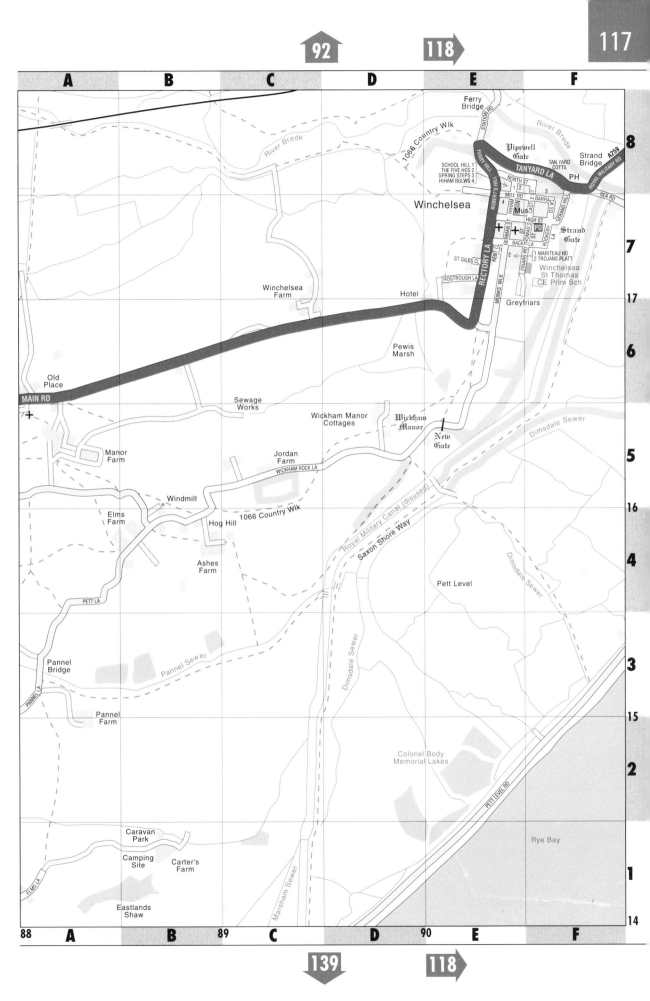

A   B   C   D   E   F

Ferry
Bridge

River Brede

1066 Country Wlk

River Brede

8

STATION RD

Pipewell
Gate

TAN YARD
COTTS

Strand
Bridge

A259

ROYAL MILITARY RD

TANYARD LA

PH

FERRY HILL

SCHOOL HILL 1
THE FIVE HOS 2
SPRING STEPS 3
HIHAM BGLWS 4

NORTH ST

ROBERT'S HILL

MILL RD

BARRA

SEA RD

3

Winchelsea

HIHAM
GERMAN ST

Mus

HIGH ST

STRAND HILL

PO

Strand
Gate

7

BACK
LA

CASTLE
ST THOMAS ST

RONKERY
LA

St GILES CL

KENT CL

1 MARITEAU HO
2 TROJANS PLATT

HOGTROUGH LA

RECTORY LA

2

FRIARS RD

Winchelsea
St Thomas
CE Prim Sch

Winchelsea
Farm

Hotel

Greyfriars

MONKS WLK

17

Pewis
Marsh

6

Old
Place

Sewage
Works

Wickham Manor
Cottages

Wickham
Manor

Dimsdale Sewer

MAIN RD

New
Gate

Manor
Farm

Jordan
Farm

5

WICKHAM ROCK LA

Windmill

Royal Military Canal (disused)

Dimsdale Sewer

16

Elms
Farm

Hog Hill

1066 Country Wlk

Saxon Shore Way

4

Ashes
Farm

Pett Level

PETT LA

Dimsdale Sewer

Pannel
Bridge

Pannel Sewer

3

PANNEL LA

Pannel
Farm

15

Colonel Body
Memorial Lakes

2

PETT LEVEL RD

Caravan
Park

Rye Bay

Camping
Site

Carter's
Farm

ELMS LA

Marsham Sewer

1

Eastlands
Shaw

14

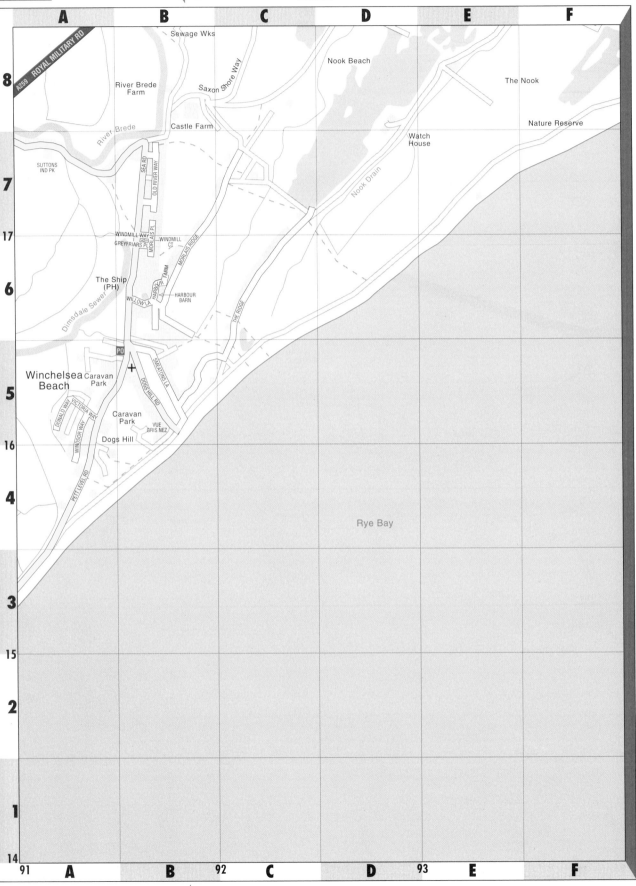

A   B   C   D   E   F

8   Sewage Wks

Nook Beach   The Nook

River Brede Farm

Saxon Shore Way

Nature Reserve

River Brede

Castle Farm

Watch House

7   SUTTONS IND PK

SEA RD   OLD RIVER WAY

Nook Drain

17   WINDMILL WAY   WINDMILL CT

GREYFRIARS PL   MORLANS PL   MORLANS RIDGE

6   The Ship (PH)

HARBOUR FARM

WILLOW LA   HARBOUR BARN

Dimsdale Sewer

THE RIDGE

PO

Winchelsea Beach   Caravan Park

SMEATONS LA

5   DONALD WAY   VICTORIA WAY

DOGS HILL RD

Caravan Park

VUE GRIS NEZ

16   WINDSOR WAY

Dogs Hill

4   PETT LEVEL RD

Rye Bay

3

15

2

1

14

91   A   B   92   C   D   93   E   F

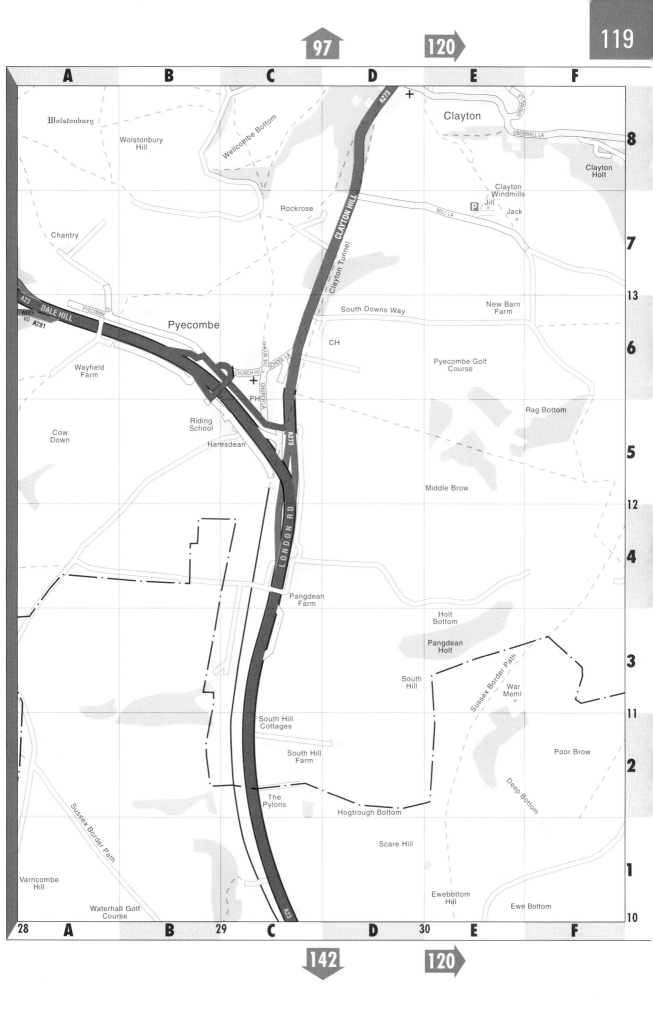

A B C D E F

Wolstonbury

Wolstonbury Hill

Wellcombe Bottom

Clayton

UNDERHILL LA

8

Clayton Holt

Rockrose

CLAYTON HILL

Clayton Windmills
Jill
Jack
MILL LA

P

7

13

Chantry

A23
WEST RD
DALE HILL
PYECOMBE
A281

Pyecombe

Clayton Tunnel

South Downs Way

CH

New Barn Farm

6

Wayfield Farm

THE WORTH
CHURCH HILL
SCHOOL LA
CHURCH LA
PH

Pyecombe Golf Course

Cow Down

Riding School

Haresdean

A273

Rag Bottom

5

Middle Brow

12

LONDON RD

4

Pangdean Farm

Holt Bottom

Pangdean Holt

South Hill

War Meml

Sussex Border Path

3

11

South Hill Cottages

Poor Brow

South Hill Farm

2

Deep Bottom

The Pylons

Hogtrough Bottom

Scare Hill

A23

1

Varncombe Hill

Sussex Border Path

Ewebottom Hill

Ewe Bottom

Waterhall Golf Course

10

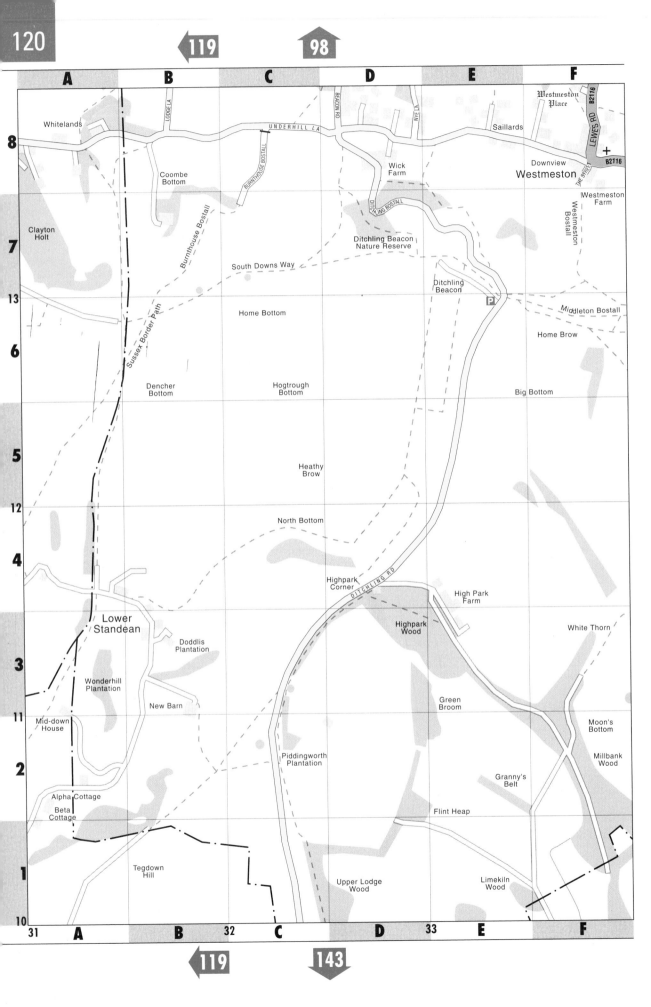

119
98

A **B** **C** **D** **E** **F**

Westmeston Place

B2116

LEWES RD

Whitelands

Saillards

UNDERHILL LA

Coombe Bottom

Wick Farm

Downview

Westmeston

THE STREET

B2116

Westmeston Farm

8

LODGE LA

BEACON RD

NYE LA

Westmeston Bostall

Clayton Holt

Burnthouse Bostall

BURNTHOUSE BOSTALL

Ditchling Beacon Nature Reserve

DITCHLING BOSTALL

7

Burnthouse Bostall

South Downs Way

Ditchling Beacon

Middleton Bostall

13

Sussex Border Path

Home Bottom

P

Home Brow

6

Dencher Bottom

Hogtrough Bottom

Big Bottom

5

Heathy Brow

12

North Bottom

4

Highpark Corner

DITCHLING RD

High Park Farm

Lower Standean

Highpark Wood

White Thorn

Doddlis Plantation

3

Wonderhill Plantation

Green Broom

Moon's Bottom

New Barn

11

Mid-down House

Millbank Wood

2

Piddingworth Plantation

Granny's Belt

Alpha Cottage

Flint Heap

Beta Cottage

1

Tegdown Hill

Upper Lodge Wood

Limekiln Wood

10

119
143

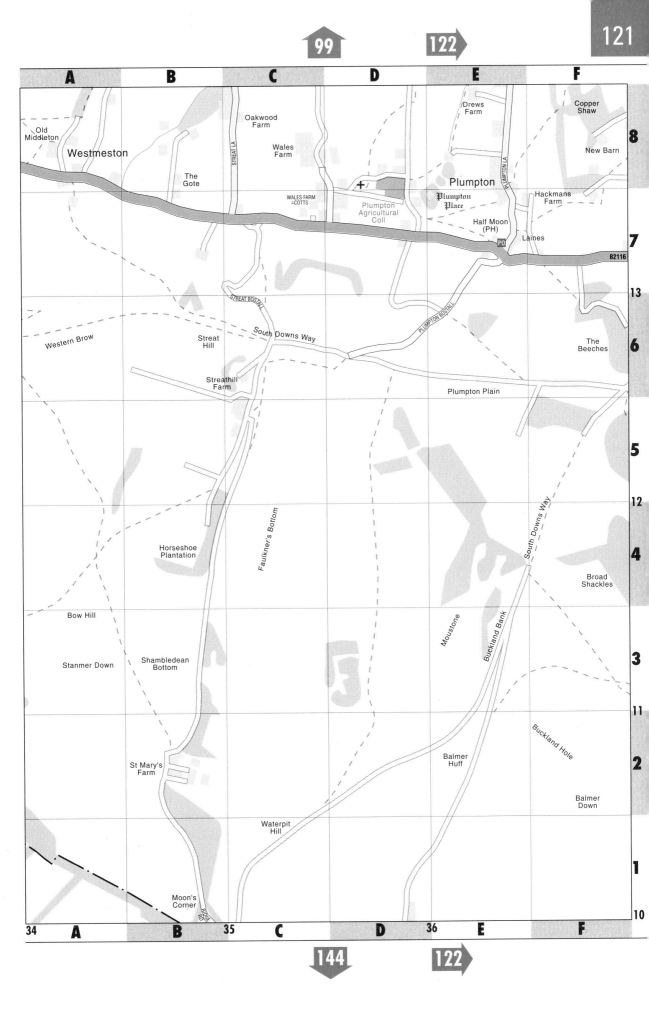

121
100

A **B** **C** **D** **E** **F**

8

Warningore
House

Lower Tulleyswells
Farm

BEECHWOOD LA

Warningore
Farm

NOVINGTON LA

Allington
Farm

ALLINGTON LA

Russet
Shaw

Tulleyswells
Farm

7

Newstead
Farmhouse

Watershoot
Shaw

B2116

A275

New
Barn

13

B2116

Warningore Bostall

Courthouse
Farm

Mount Harry
House

6

Offham
Farm

Offham
House

Blackcap

Mount
Harry

Coombe
Place

Offham

A275

5

Coombe
Plantation

Ashcombe
Bottom

Offham
Hill

12

4

Training Gallop

Landport
Bottom

3

HIGHDOWN RD

FIR.. CRES

Cuckoo
Bottom

11

Training Gallop

2

EAST
WAY

South Downs Way

Balmer
Down

1

10

37 **A** **B** 38 **C** **D** 39 **E** **F**

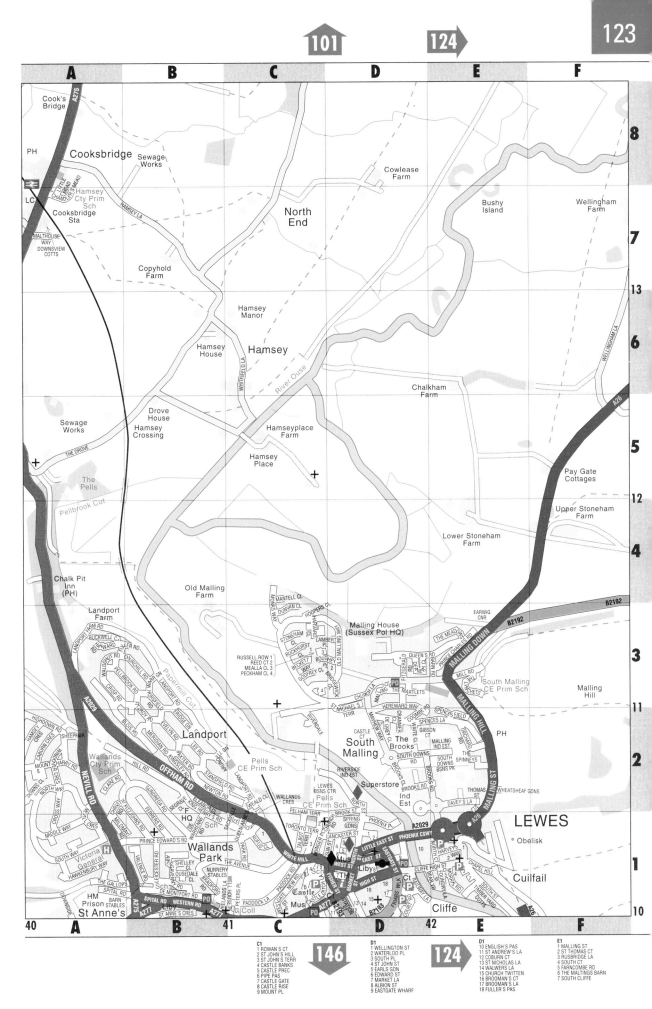

101
124

A B C D E F

8
7
13
6
5
12
4
3
11
2
1
10

Cook's Bridge
PH
Cooksbridge
LC
Little Mead
Chandlers Mead
Cooksbridge Sta
Malthouse Way
Downsview Cotts
Hamsey Cty Prim Sch
Hamsey La
Sewage Works
North End
Cowlease Farm
Bushy Island
Wellingham Farm
Copyhold Farm
13
Hamsey Manor
Hamsey
Whitfield La
River Ouse
Chalkham Farm
Wellingham La
A26
Sewage Works
The Drove
Drove House
Hamsey Crossing
Hamseyplace Farm
Hamsey Place
Pay Gate Cottages
The Pells
Pellbrook Cut
Upper Stoneham Farm
Lower Stoneham Farm
Chalk Pit Inn (PH)
Old Malling Farm
Mantell Cl
Monks Way
Dunvan Cl
Hoopers Cl
Harvard Cl
Malling House (Sussex Pol HQ)
EARWIG CNR
The Mead
B2192
B2192
B2192
Landport Farm
Landport Ham Rd
Buckwell Cl
Cluer Rd
Waldshut Rd
Churchill Rd
Ware Rd
Horsfield Rd
Bridge Gn
Papermill Cut
Stoneham Cl
Buckhurst
Lambert Pl
Boughey Pl
Old Malling Way
Queen's Rd
Fitzgerald Rd
Prince Charles Rd
Barn Rd
Mill Rd
Rachets
Malling Down
South Malling CE Prim Sch
Malling Hill
Peelbrook Rd
Crisp Rd
Blois Rd
Fitzroy Rd
Evelyn Rd
RUSSELL ROW 1
REED CT 2
MEALLA CL 3
PECKHAM CL 4
Beckett Way
Godfrey Cl
Brookdale
St Michael's Terr
Church La
The Martlets
Hereward Way
Cranmer Rd
De Grey Rd
Spences La
Gibson Rd
Spences Field
Mill Rd
Orchard Rd
PH
Malling Hill
Highdown Rd
Hillyfield
Cabburn Cres
Sheepfair
A2029
Nevil Rd
Landport
Meridian Rd
Kingsley Rd
Lee Rd
Offham Rd
Newton Rd
Landport Rd
Riverdale
Pells CE Prim Sch
South Malling
Mayhew Way
Castle Ct
The Brooks
South Downs
Malling Ind Est
Malling St
South Downs Bsns Pk
The Spinneys
Hamsey Cres
Downs Cl
North Way
Cross Way
Middle Way
Wallands Cty Prim Sch
Harry Rd
Clare Rd
Hill Rd
Stansfield Rd
Eleanor Cl
Ferrers Rd
Kenward Rd
Ousedale Cl
Wallands Cres
Pelham Terr
Toronto Terr
Spring Gdns
Phoenix Pl
Riverside Ind Est
Superstore
Ind Est
Brooks Rd
Thomas St
Wheatsheaf Gdns
Davey's La
LEWES
Obelisk
South Way
Victoria General H
Hawkenbury Way
De Montfort Rd
Shelley Cl
Prince Edward's Rd
Nunnery Stables
The Avenue
White Hill
St John's Terr
Park Rd
Leicester Rd
Valence Rd
Christie Rd
Mildmay Rd
Seagrave Cl
The Gallops
Spital Rd
Barn Stables
HM Prison
Western Rd
St Anne's
St Anne's Cres
Coll
Paddock La
Castle Mus
Talbot Terr
Friars Wlk
Lancaster St
Market La
West St
High St
Castle
Library
Fisher St
East St
Market St
Little East St
Eastgate St
Phoenix Cswy
Cliffe High St
A2029
Harveys
Cliffe
Court Rd
North St
Morris Rd
Chapel Hill
A26
Foundry La
Bear Rd
South Cliffe
Timber Yard
Cuilfail

40 A B 41 C D 42 E F

146
124

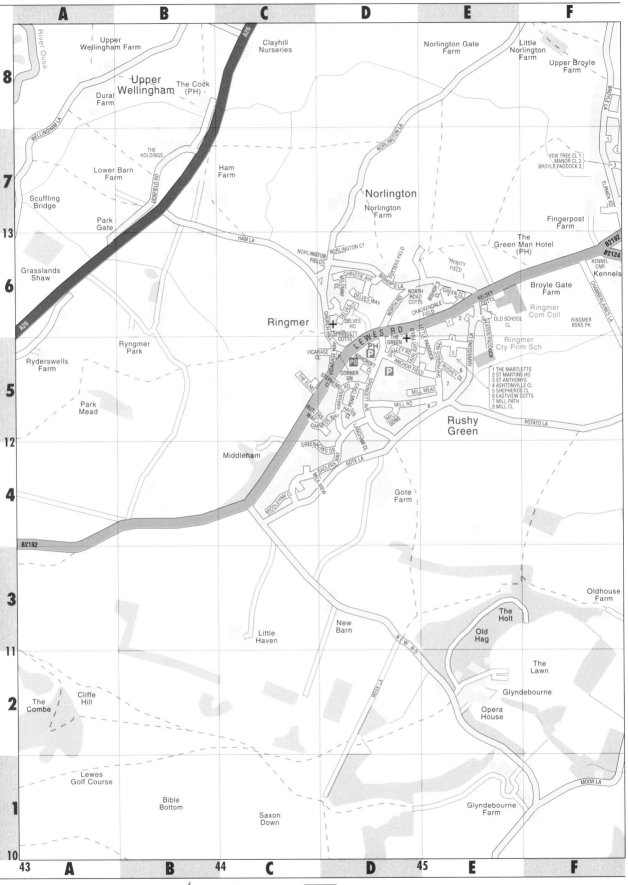

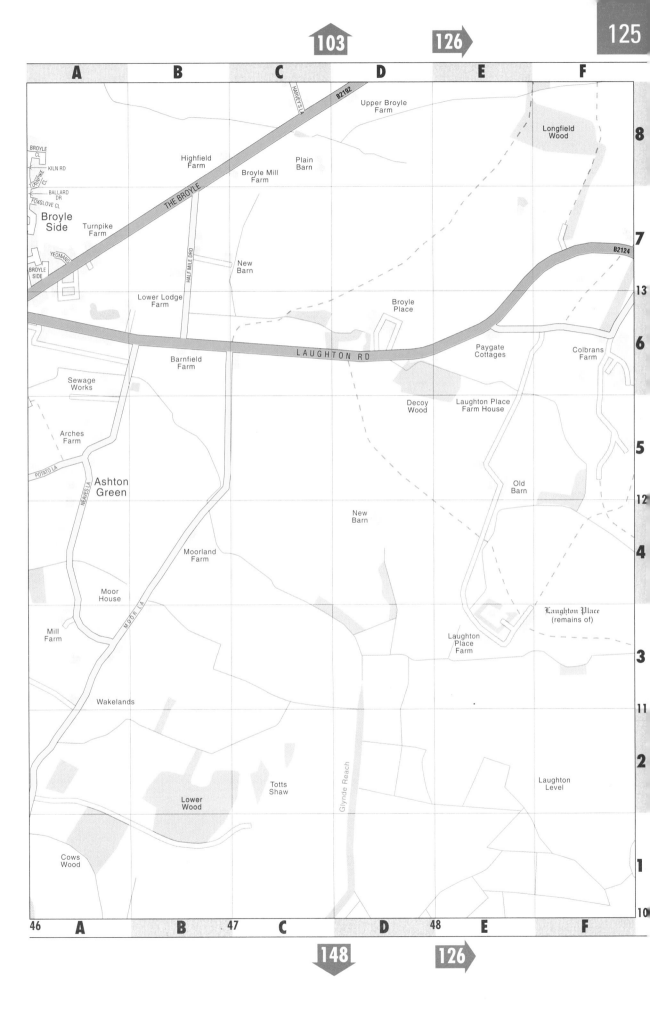

A B C D E F

8
7
13
6
5
12
4
3
11
2
1
10

BROYLE CL
KILN RD
TURNPIKE CL
BALLARD DR
FOXGLOVE CL
Broyle Side
YEOMANS
BROYLE SIDE
Turnpike Farm

HARVEY'S LA
B2192
Upper Broyle Farm
Longfield Wood

Highfield Farm
Plain Barn
Broyle Mill Farm
THE BROYLE

B2124

HALF MILE DRO
New Barn
Broyle Place
Paygate Cottages
Colbrans Farm

Lower Lodge Farm
LAUGHTON RD

Barnfield Farm

Sewage Works
Decoy Wood
Laughton Place Farm House

Arches Farm
Old Barn

POTATO LA
NEAVES LA
Ashton Green

New Barn

Moorland Farm

Moor House
Laughton Place (remains of)

MOOR LA
Laughton Place Farm

Mill Farm

Wakelands

Glynde Reach
Laughton Level

Totts Shaw
Lower Wood

Cows Wood

46 A B 47 C D 48 E F

A   B   C   D   E   F

8

Brickhurst
Wood

BRICKHURST LA

Laughton Common Wood

Lower Vert
Wood

Laughton
Lodge

Brickhurst
Farm

Saw
Mill

Averys Oak
Farm

Wood
Bungalows

The
Roebuck
(PH)

POUND LA

Helouan
Farm

7

Laughton
Manor

ELM
COTTS

PO

Queeake

B2124

LAUGHTON RD

ELM CL

13

Home
Farm

Bowen
Wood

Laughton

Laughton
Cty Prim
Sch

Coopers
Farm

Bowen
Farm

B2124

6

Black Shaw

Stone Cross
Farm

New House
Farm

Marchants
Farm

Milward's
Farm

5

Church
Farm

Harben's
Farm

12

Cleaver's
Farm

4

Muslins
Pit

Little Stream
Farm

Airfield

3

Cleggett's
Farm

Mill
Farm

11

RIPE LA

MARK CROSS

2

Curl's
Farm

Fowler's
Barn

1

Lamb
Inn
(PH)

PO

Ripe

CHANNERS LA

10

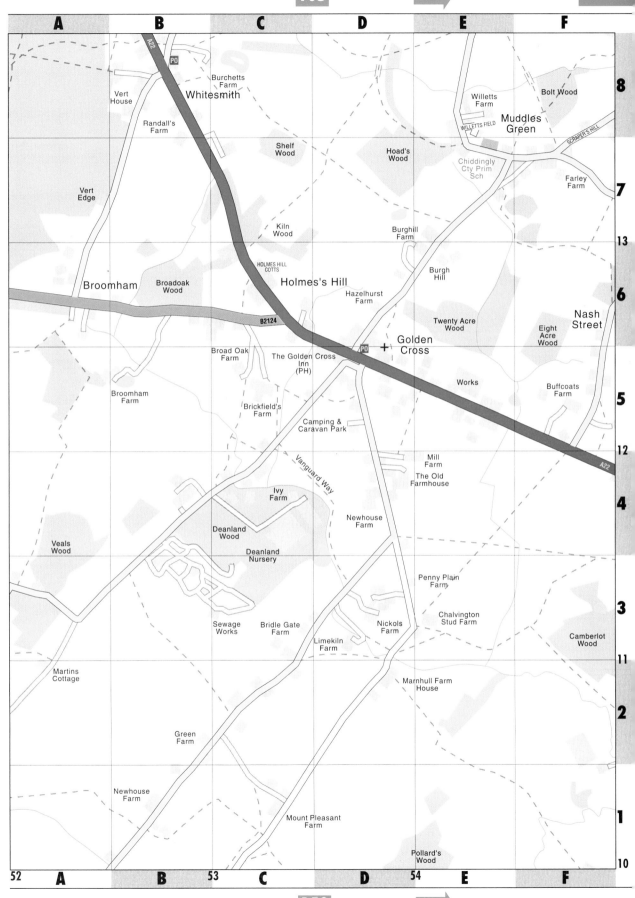

A B C D E F

8

Vert House

Burchetts Farm

Whitesmith

Randall's Farm

Willetts Farm

Bolt Wood

Muddles Green

WILLETTS FIELD

Chiddingly Cty Prim Sch

Shelf Wood

Hoad's Wood

Vert Edge

7

Farley Farm

SCRAPER'S HILL

13

Kiln Wood

Burghill Farm

Broomham

Broadoak Wood

HOLMES HILL COTTS

Holmes's Hill

Burgh Hill

6

Hazelhurst Farm

Nash Street

B2124

Twenty Acre Wood

Eight Acre Wood

Broad Oak Farm

The Golden Cross Inn (PH)

PO

Golden Cross

Works

Buffcoats Farm

5

Broomham Farm

Brickfield's Farm

Camping & Caravan Park

12

A22

Vanguard Way

Mill Farm

The Old Farmhouse

Ivy Farm

4

Deanland Wood

Newhouse Farm

Deanland Nursery

Veals Wood

Penny Plain Farm

Chalvington Stud Farm

3

Sewage Works

Bridle Gate Farm

Nickols Farm

Camberlot Wood

Limekiln Farm

11

Martins Cottage

Marnhull Farm House

2

Green Farm

Newhouse Farm

1

Mount Pleasant Farm

Pollard's Wood

10

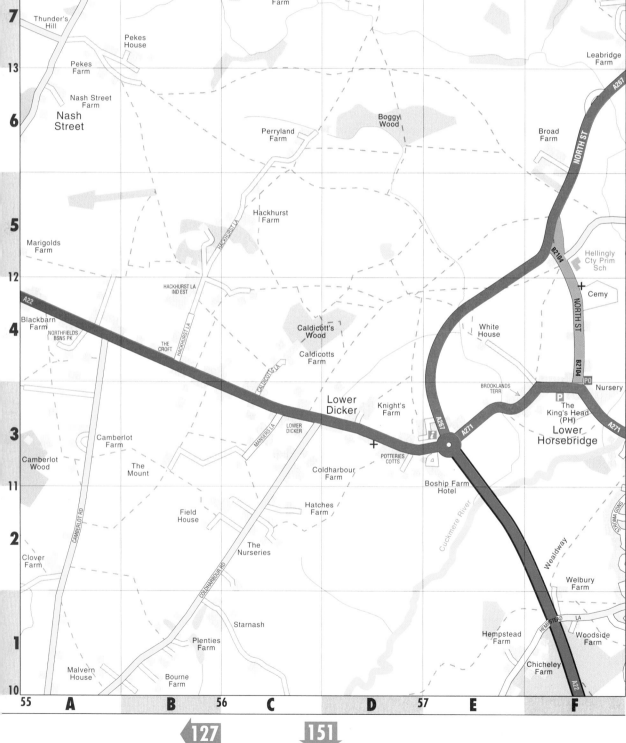

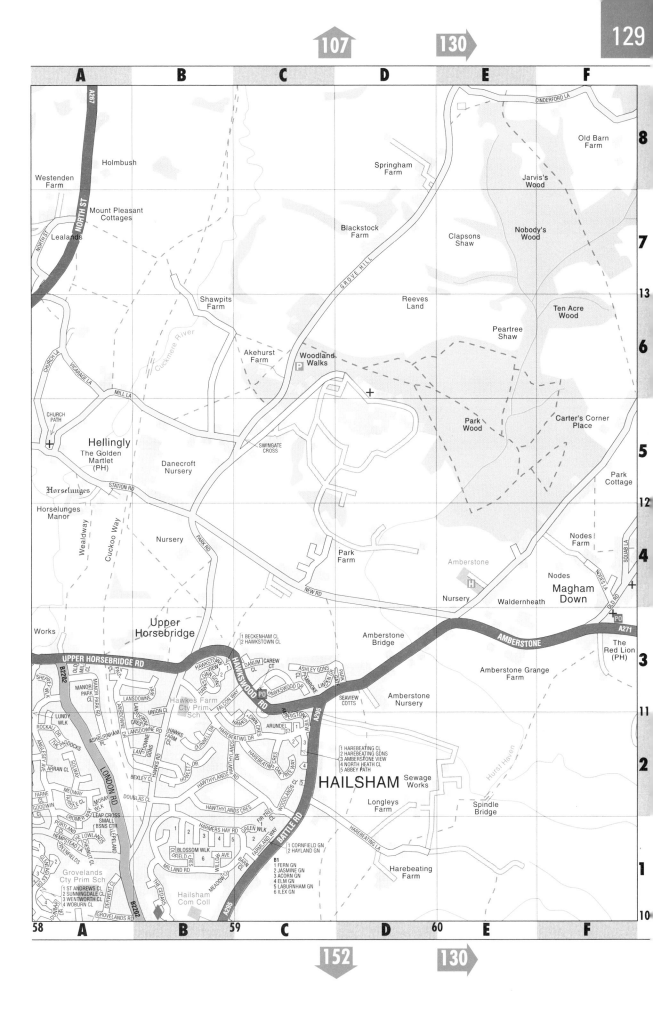

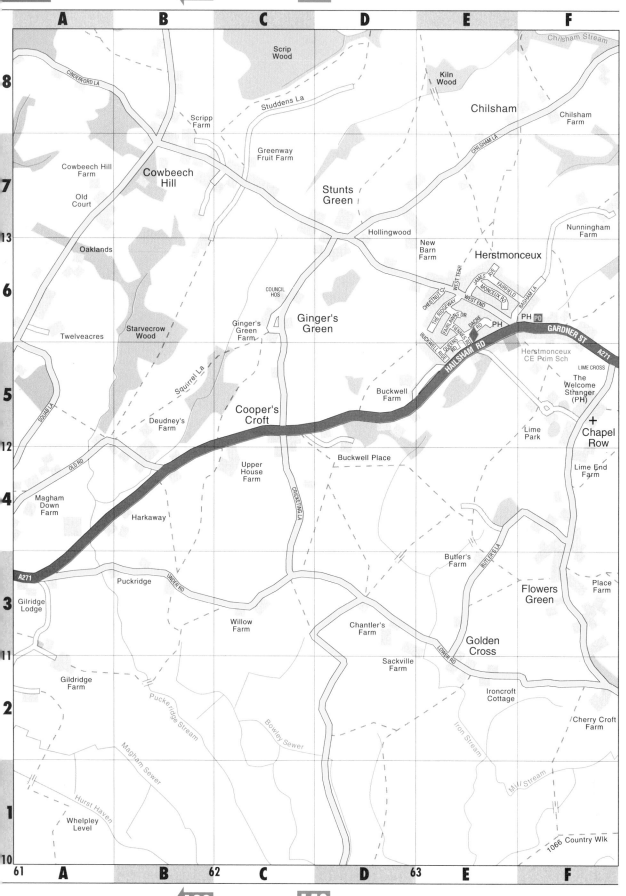
A B C D E F

8
Scrip Wood

CINDERFORD LA

Studdens La

Kiln Wood

Chilsham

Chilsham Stream

7
Cowbeech Hill Farm

Scripp Farm

Cowbeech Hill

Greenway Fruit Farm

Stunts Green

CHILSHAM LA

Chilsham Farm

Old Court

13
Oaklands

Hollingwood

New Barn Farm

Herstmonceux

Nunningham Farm

6
COUNCIL HOS

Ginger's Green

WEST TERR
JAMES AVE
FAIRFIELD
MONCEUX RD
BAGHAM LA
CHESTNUT CL
THE RIDGEWAY
WEST END
FAIRLAWNS DR
TWISSELL RD
FIENNES RD
DACRE RD
PH
PH PO
GARDNER ST
A271

Twelveacres

Starvecrow Wood

Ginger's Green Farm

BUCKWELL RISE
QUEENS RD
HAILSHAM RD

Herstmonceux CE Prim Sch

LIME CROSS

5
SQUAB LA

SQUIRREL LA

Cooper's Croft

Deudney's Farm

Buckwell Farm

Lime Park

The Welcome Stranger (PH)

Chapel Row

12
OLD RD

Buckwell Place

Lime End Farm

4
Magham Down Farm

Harkaway

Upper House Farm

CRICKETING LA

Butler's Farm

BUTLER'S LA

Flowers Green

Place Farm

3
A271

Gilridge Lodge

Puckridge

UNDER RD

Willow Farm

Chantler's Farm

LOWER RD

Golden Cross

11
Gildridge Farm

Sackville Farm

Ironcroft Cottage

Puckeridge Stream

2
Magham Sewer

Bowley Sewer

Iron Stream

Mill Stream

Cherry Croft Farm

1
Hurst Haven

Whelpley Level

1066 Country Wlk

10

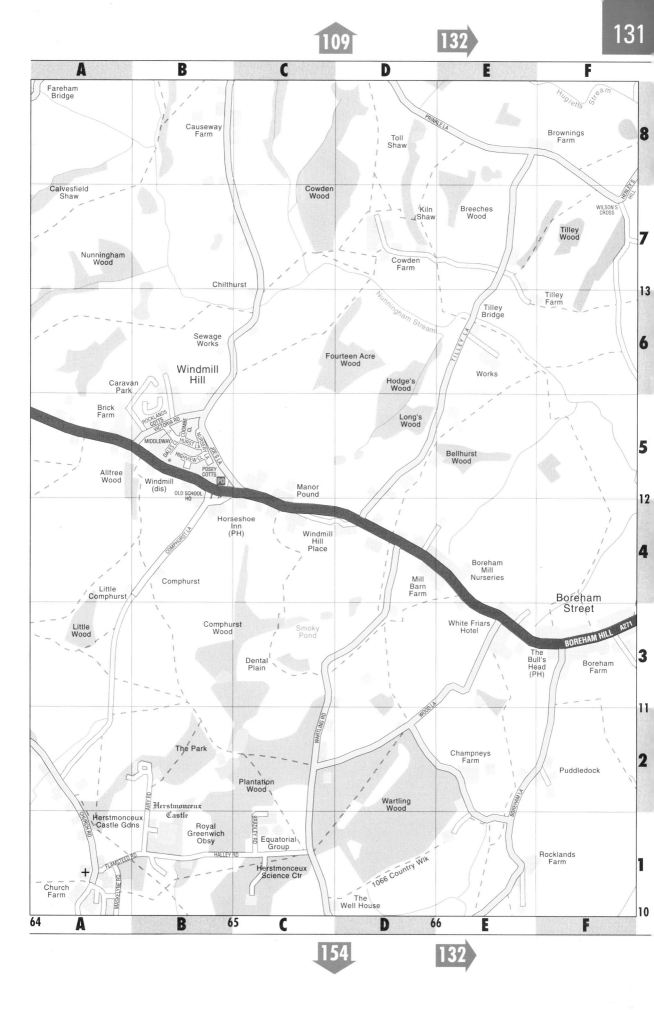

131
110

A **B** **C** **D** **E** **F**

1066 Country Wlk

Henley's Bridge

Northland Wood

Hammer Wood

The Old Kennels

A271

Compass Wood

Luxford's Wood

Combe Hill Farm

Combe Hill

Wilson's Farm

Ash Bourne

Spring Shaw

Kitchenham Farm

Wilding Wood

Combe Wood

Ninfield Stream

Lower Standard Hill Farm

STANDARD HILL CL 1
COOKSTOWN CL 2

COMBE LA

Wr Twr

HIGH ST A269

Gardners Farm

Standard Hill House

Standard Hill

MOORHALL DR

1066 Country Wlk

A269

Hazard's Green

Little Standard Hill Farm

Works

Moor Hall Farm

Moor Hall Hotel

Blackstock Bridge

Boreham Bridge

BOREHAM HILL

Wet Wood

Rough Wood

A271

Moorhall Stream

Hooe Level

White's Wood

B2095

New Barn

Waterlot Stream

Tanyard Farm

HOOE RD

Waller's Haven

Sandhall Farm

Red Lion (PH)

PO

ELIZABETHAN CL

Hooe Common

MILL LA

School Farm

Hogtrough Bridge

Bunts Barn

B2095

Sadlers Farm

Longdown Farm

67 **A** **B** **68** **C** **D** **69** **E** **F**

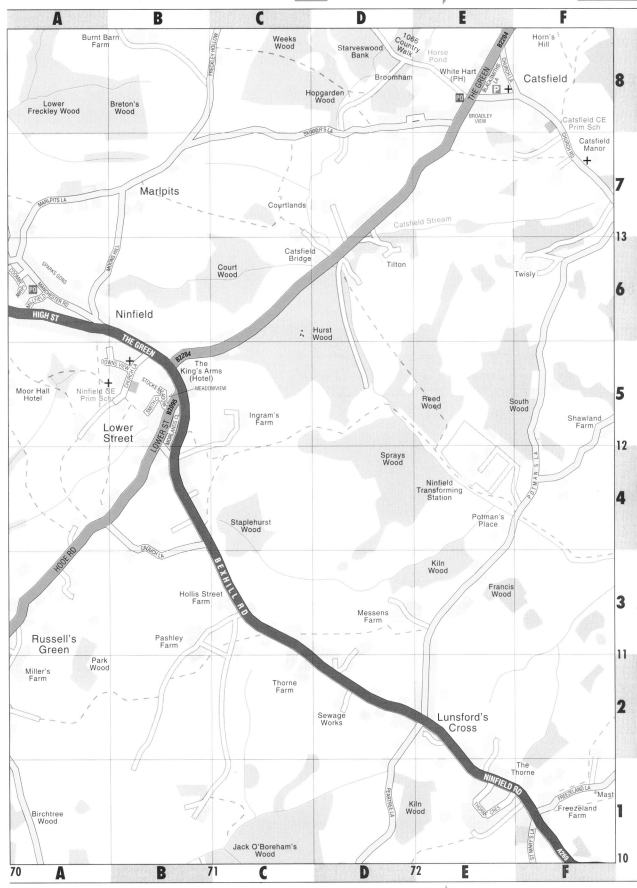

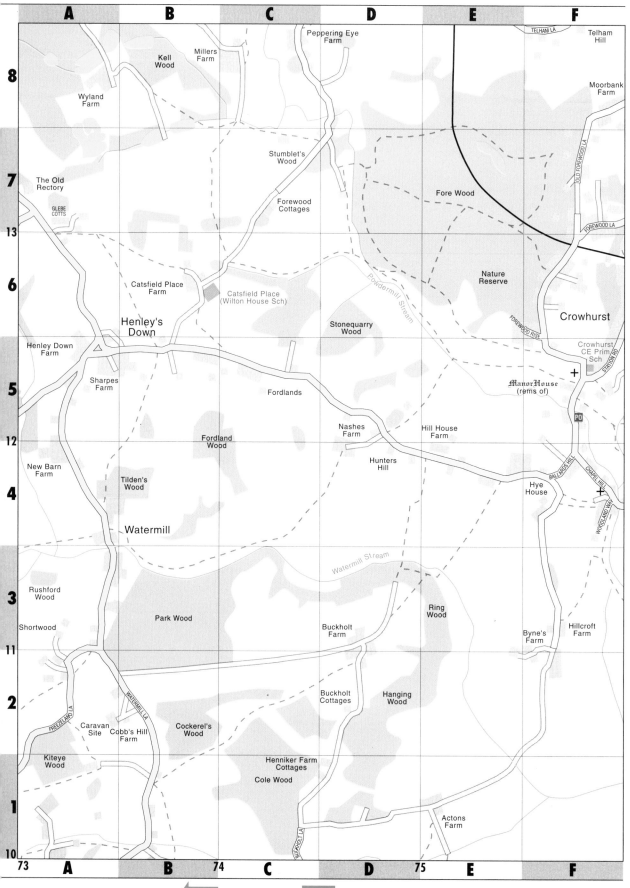

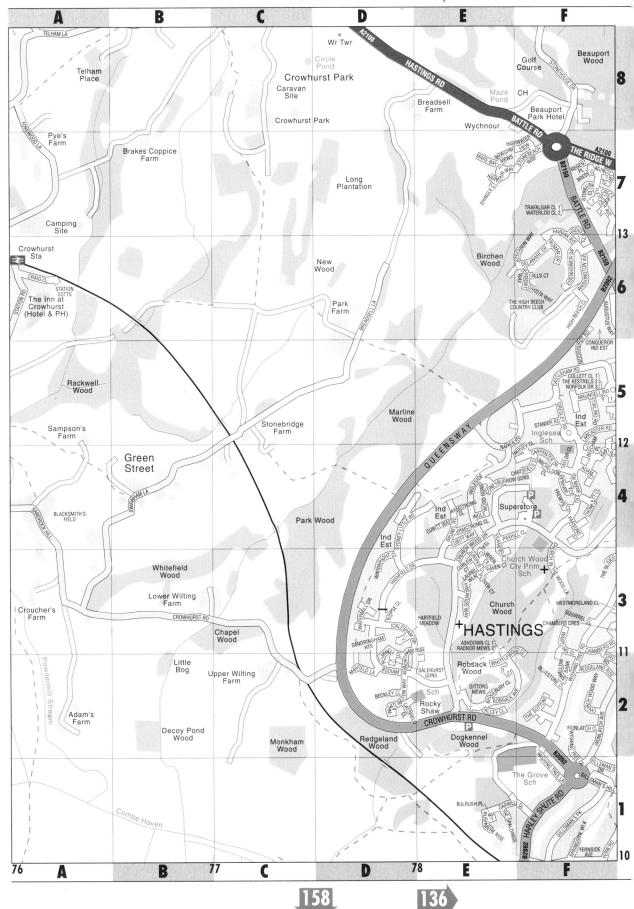

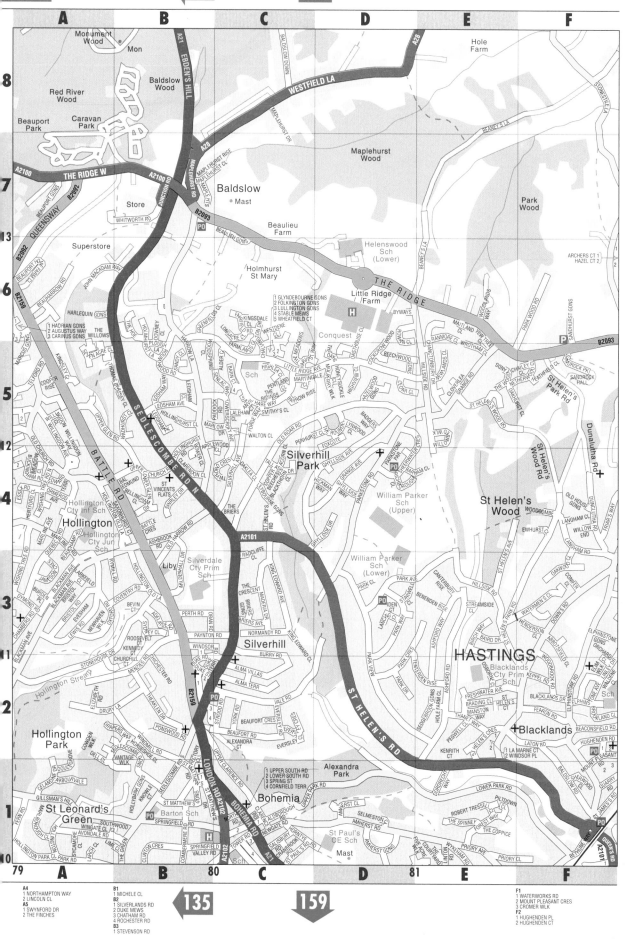

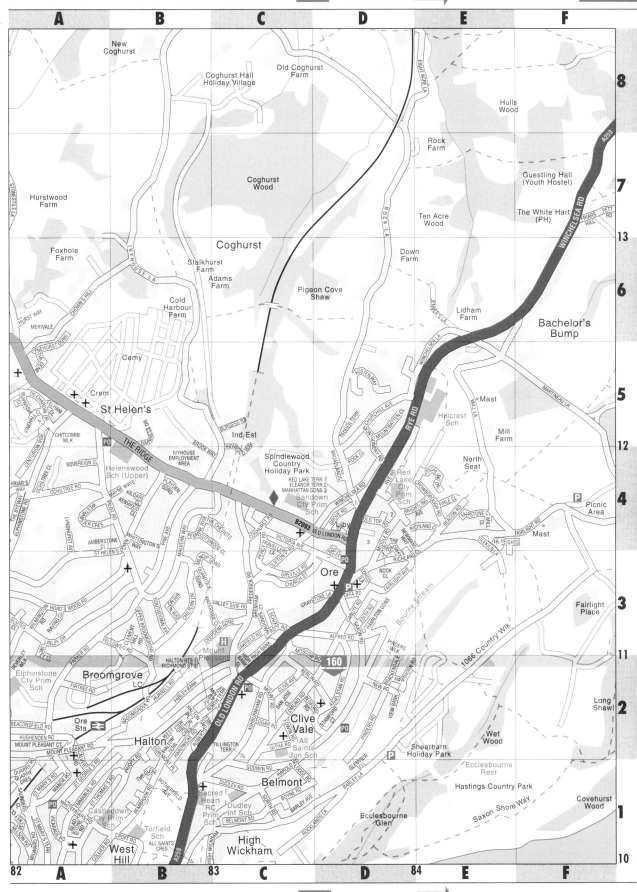

A B C D E F

8

Guestling-Bradshaw Prim Sch
The Hope (PH)
Guestling Green
Higham Farm
WINCHELSEA RD
THE THORNS
A259
Mount Pleasant Farm
CHAPEL LA
HIGHAM GDNS
Glebe Wood
CHURCH LA
Shellies Green
ALLARDS
PETT RD
WATERMILL LA
PO
Roughter's Wood
Church Farm
Pett
Gatehurst Farm

7

Friar's Hill
FRIAR'S CRES
FRIARS BANK
Lower Cherry Garden Farm
Winterstow Farm
Marsham Sewer
Lower New Barn Farm
New Barn Farm
ROSEMARY LA
Market Wood

13

FRIAR'S HILL TERR
1066 COUNTRY WK
Humphreys Farm
Birchen Knoll Plantation
Birchen Knoll Farm
PETER JAMES LA
Marsham Farm

6

The Hall
Cherry Garden Farm
Hoad's Wood
Stonelink Wood
Wakehams Farm
PETT LEVEL RD

5

Mallydams Wood (Nature Reserve)
The Mountain
BATTERY HILL
Stonelynk Farm
PO
FARLEY WAY
WAITES LA
Fairlight Cove
KNOWLE RD
BROAD WAY
CLINTON WAY
PRIMROSE HILL
CLIFF WAY
SEA RD

12

FAIRLIGHT RD
FAIRLIGHT LODGE HOTEL
Fairlight Lodge Hotel
MARTINEAU LA
P
Visitor Ctr
COASTGUARD LA
HILL RD
THE CLOSE
Fairlight
WARREN RD
NEW RD
Knowle Wood
WOODLAND WAY
MEADOW WAY
SHEPHERDS CT
SHEPHERDS WAY
FAIRLIGHT GDNS
LOWER WAITES LA
THE AVENUE
STOCK DALE
ROCK LA
ROAD RD
COMMANDERS WLK
CONSTABLE WAY
FYRSWAY
BLACKTHORN WAY
BRAMBLE WAY
HEATHER WAY
SMUGGLERS WAY
CHANNEL WAY

4

P
COASTGUARD LA

3

Place Farm
Hastings Country Park
FIREHILLS COTTS
Fire Hills
Saxon Shore Way

11

2

Covehurst Bay

1

10

85 A B 86 C D 87 E F

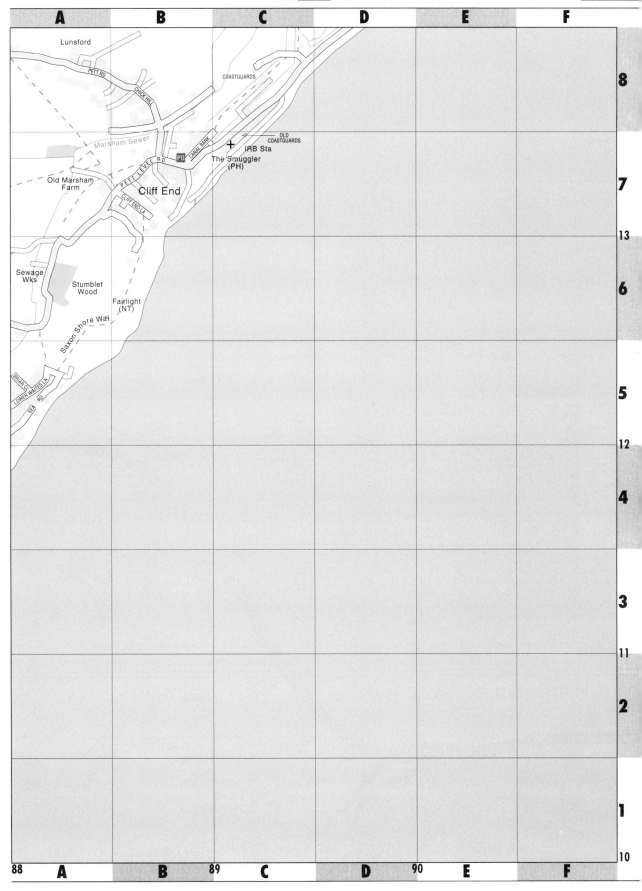

A   B   C   D   E   F

8

Lunsford

PETT RD

CHICK HILL

COASTGUARDS

Marsham Sewer

PO

CANAL BANK

OLD
COASTGUARDS

IRB Sta

+

The Smuggler
(PH)

PETT LEVEL RD

Old Marsham
Farm

Cliff End

7

CLIFF END LA

13

Sewage
Wks

Stumblet
Wood

6

Fairlight
(NT)

Saxon Shore Way

5

BRIAR CL

LOWER WAITES LA

SEA RD

12

4

3

11

2

1

10

88   A   B   89   C   D   90   E   F

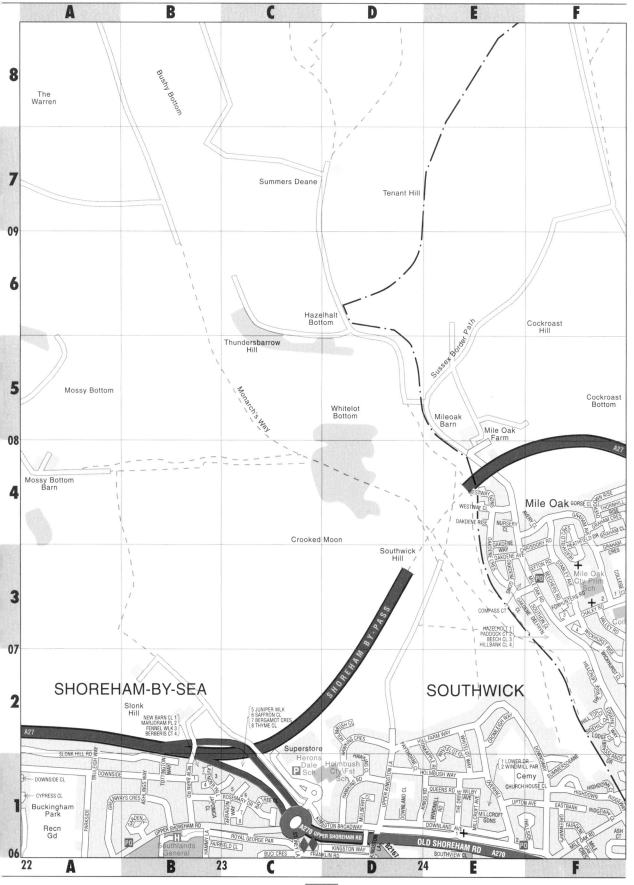

A **B** **C** **D** **E** **F**

8

7

09

6

5

08

4

07

3

2

07

1

06

The Warren

Bushy Bottom

Summers Deane

Tenant Hill

Hazelhalt Bottom

Thundersbarrow Hill

Mossy Bottom

Monarch's Way

Whitelot Bottom

Sussex Border Path

Cockroast Hill

Mileoak Barn

Mile Oak Farm

Cockroast Bottom

Mossy Bottom Barn

Crooked Moon

Southwick Hill

A27

WESTWAY GDNS
WESTWAY CL
OAKDENE RISE

Mile Oak

GORSE CL
DOWN RISE
THORNHILL RISE
GRAHAM AV
GRAHAM CRES
GRAHAM CL

NURSERY CL
AVERY CL
HEATHFIELD DR
CHRISDORY RD
GRAHAM CRES

OAKDENE WAY
OAKDENE GDNS
OAKDENE AVE

SEFTON RD
MILE OAK RD
STANLEY AVE
BEECHES RD
FOXHUNTERS RD

Mile Oak Cty Prim Sch

COLLEGE CL

OAKDENE CRES
OAKDENE DELVERN

SOUTHDOWN CL

COMPASS CT

HAZELHOLT 1
PADDOCK CT 2
BEECH CL 3
HILLBANK CL 4

CHALKY RD
VALLEY RD
WICKHURST RISE
WICKHURST RD

Col

SHOREHAM-BY-SEA

SOUTHWICK

Slonk Hill

NEW BARN CL 1
MARJORAM PL 2
FENNEL WLK 3
BERBERIS CT 4

5 JUNIPER WLK
6 SAFFRON CL
7 BERGAMOT CRES
8 THYME CL

SHOREHAM BY-PASS

A27

Superstore

Herons Dale Sch

Holmbush Cty Fst Sch

HILL FARM WAY
CROMLEIGH WAY
WHITELOT WAY

HILL TOP
SIDEHILL DR
LINE HILL WAY

CRES

HAWKINS CL
HAWKINS CRES
HAWKS RD

PANTHORNE RD
HOLMBUSH WAY
HOLMBUSH CL

HILLSIDE
LODGE

BRASS LANDS DR

SLONK HILL RD
TRULEIGH WAY
DOWNSIDE

GREENWAYS CRES
ASHLINGS WAY
TOTTINGTON WAY
NEW BARN RD

LAVENDER WL
JAPONICA CL

3

ROSEMARY DR
TARRAGON WAY

5

TREE CL

5 JUNIPER WLK

1 LOWER DR
2 WINDMILL PAR

Cemy

CHURCH HOUSE CL

SUMMERSDEANE

HIGHDOWN
RIDGEWAY

DOWNSIDE CL

CYPRESS CL

Buckingham Park

Recn Gd

PARKSIDE

GARDEN CT

PO

UPPER SHOREHAM RD

HAMMY LA

FAIRFIELD CL

Southlands General

H

PO

ROYAL GEORGE PAR

BUCI CRES

FRANKLIN RD

KINGSTON LA

SLONK HILL

SHOREHAM ST

KINGSTON BROADWAY

UPPER SHOREHAM RD

KINGSTON WAY

SOUTHVIEW CL

B2161

HANKINS RD

UPPER KINGSTON LA

MULBERRY CL

QUEENS RD

KINGS RD
WINDMILL RD

DOWNLAND CL

THE DRIVE

WILBY AVE
MILLCROFT AVE
OVERNE

DOWNLAND AVE

MILLCROFT GDNS

UPTON AVE

EASTBANK
GREENWAYS

FAIROAK

RIDGEWAY

OLD SHOREHAM RD

A270

PO

HILLSIDE

MILE OAK RD
FAIROAK
MILE CRES

ASH CT

A **B** **C** **D** **E** **F**

22 23 24

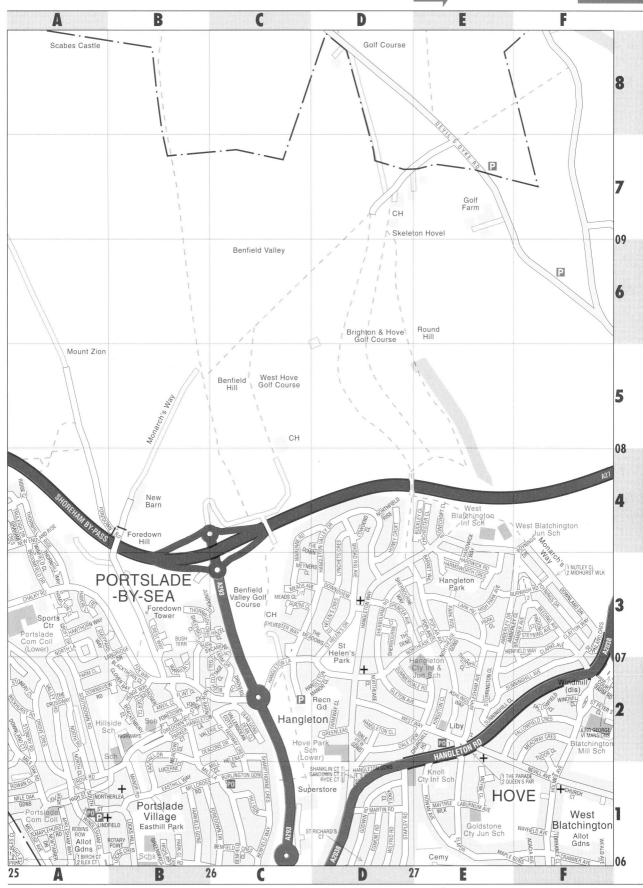

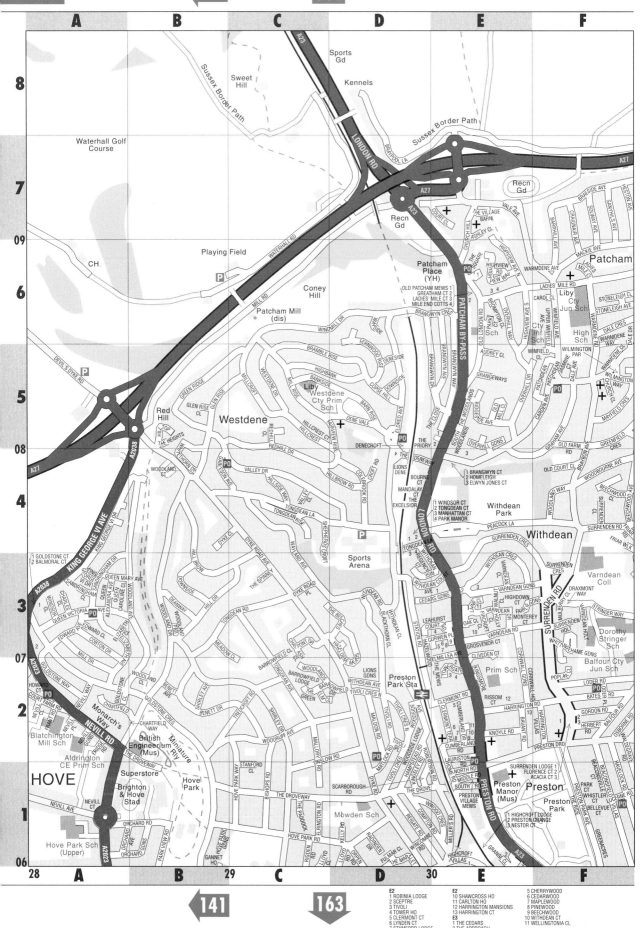

E2
1 ROBINIA LODGE
2 SCEPTRE
3 TIVOLI
4 TOWER HO
5 CLERMONT CT
6 LYNDEN CT
7 STAMFORD LODGE
8 CUMBERLAND LODGE
9 CENTENARY HO

E2
10 SHAWCROSS HO
11 CARLTON HO
12 HARRINGTON MANSIONS
13 HARRINGTON CT
E3
1 THE CEDARS
2 THE APPROACH
3 WITHDEAN HALL
4 LEAHURST CT

5 CHERRYWOOD
6 CEDARWOOD
7 MAPLEWOOD
8 PINEWOOD
9 BEECHWOOD
10 WITHDEAN CT
11 WELLINGTONIA CL

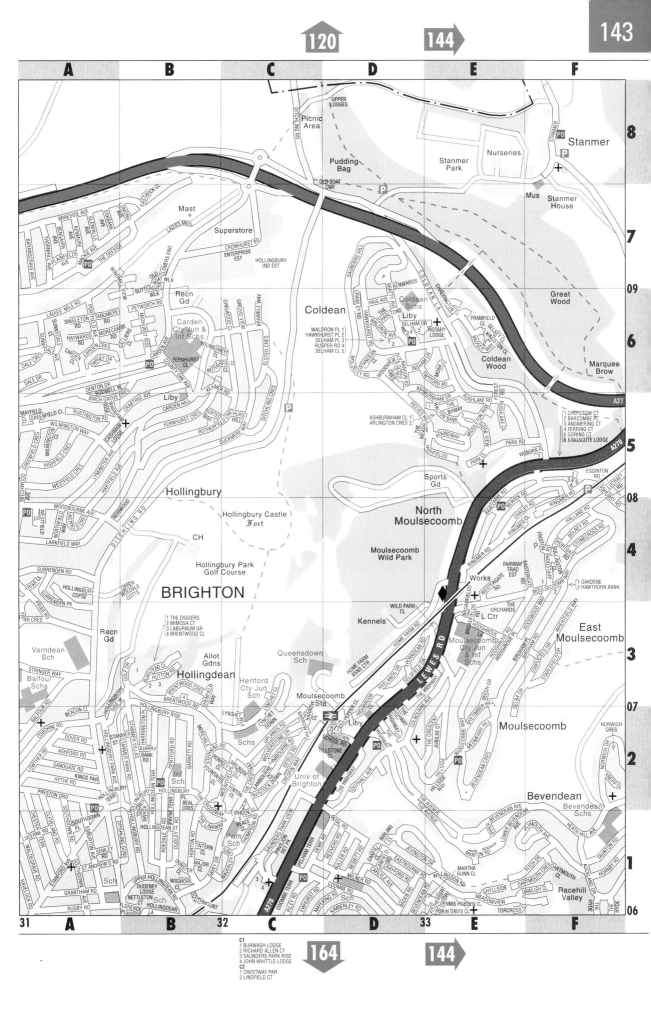

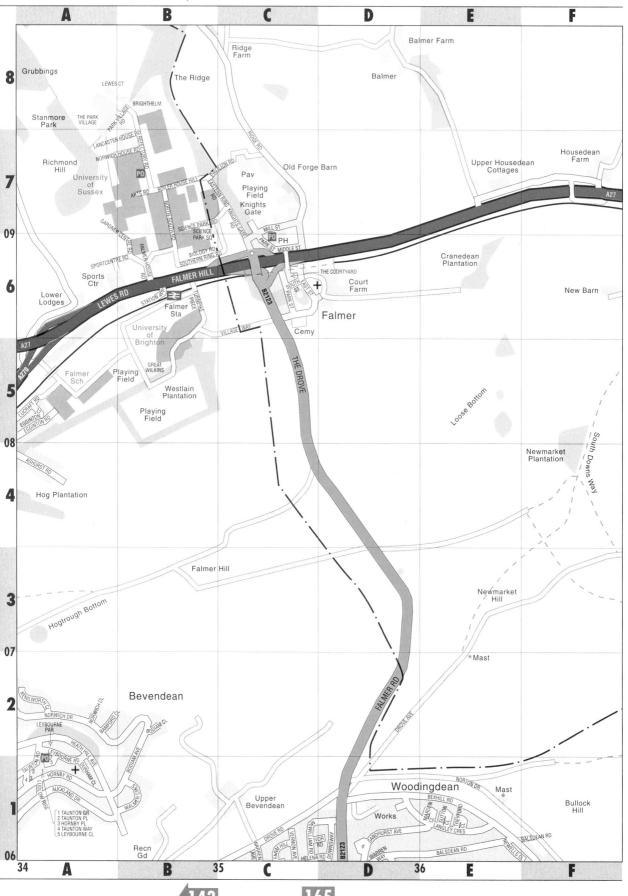

8 Grubbings

The Ridge

Ridge Farm

Balmer Farm

Balmer

7
Stanmore Park

THE PARK VILLAGE

Richmond Hill

University of Sussex

BRIGHTHELM

Old Forge Barn

Upper Housedean Cottages

Housedean Farm

A27

PO

ARTS RD

SCIENCE PARK SQ

Pav

Playing Field

Knights Gate

09

BIOLOGY RD

SOUTHERN RING RD

MILL ST

PO PH

MIDDLE ST

Cranedean Plantation

6
Lower Lodges

Sports Ctr

LEWES RD

FALMER HILL

STATION AV

Falmer Sta

B2123

THE COURTYARD

Court Farm

Falmer

New Barn

University of Brighton

VILLAGE WAY

SOUTH PARK ST

EAST ST

Cemy

Loose Bottom

Newmarket Plantation

South Downs Way

5
Falmer Sch

Playing Field

GREAT WILKINS

Westlain Plantation

Playing Field

A270

08

ASHURST RD

THE DROVE

4 Hog Plantation

Newmarket Hill

3
Hogtrough Bottom

Falmer Hill

07

FALMER RD

Mast

2
KENILWORTH CL

NORWICH DR

Bevendean

LEYBOURNE PAR

HEATH HILL AVE

BODIAM AVE

DROVE AVE

NORTON DR

Woodingdean

Mast

BEXHILL RD

Bullock Hill

PO

HORNBY RD

AUCKLAND DR

WALMER RD

Upper Bevendean

Works

LANGLEY CRES

BALSDEAN RD

1 TAUNTON GR
2 TAUNTON PL
3 HORNBY PL
4 TAUNTON WAY
5 LEYBOURNE CL

1

DROVE RD

FARM HILL

VERNON AVE

HELENA RD

WILLIAM RD

B2123

SANDHURST AVE

WARREN WAY

BALSDEAN RD

06
Recn Gd

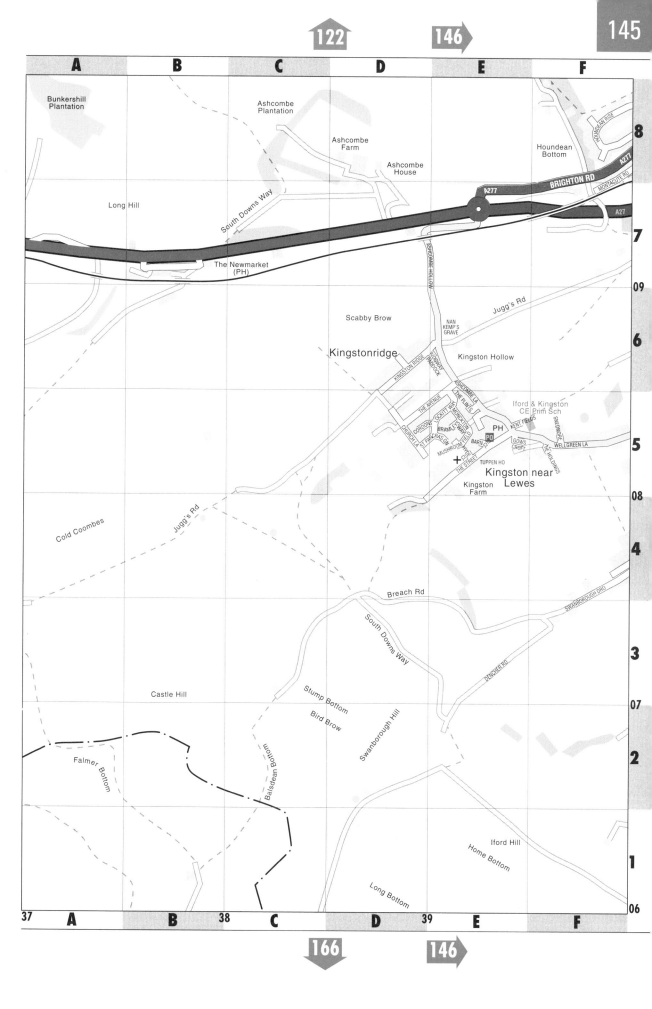

A B C D E F

Bunkershill
Plantation

Ashcombe
Plantation

Ashcombe
Farm

Ashcombe
House

Houndean
Bottom

HOUNDEAN RISE

A277

MONTAGUTE RD

BRIGHTON RD

A277

A27

8

Long Hill

South Downs Way

The Newmarket
(PH)

ASHCOMBE HOLLOW

Jugg's Rd

7

09

Scabby Brow

NAN
KEMP'S
GRAVE

Kingstonridge

Kingston Hollow

KINGSTON RIDGE

RIDGWAY PADDOCK

ASHCOMBE LA

THE FLINTS

THE AVENUE

COCKITT WAY

PADDOCK

Iford & Kingston
CE Prim Sch

SNEDMORE

KENT FIELDS

PH

PO

GOWS
CROFT

WELLGREEN LA

NEW HOLDINGS

CORDENS

CHURCH LA

ST PANCRAS DR

BRAML
CL

ELSWAY

MUSHROOM FIELD

BARN CL

TUPPEN HO

THE STREET

Kingston near
Lewes

6

5

Kingston
Farm

08

Cold Coombes

Jugg's Rd

SWANBOROUGH DRO

4

Breach Rd

South Downs Way

DENCHER RD

3

07

Castle Hill

Stump Bottom

Bird Brow

Swanborough Hill

Falmer
Bottom

Balsdean Bottom

2

Iford Hill

Home Bottom

1

Long Bottom

06

37 A B 38 C D 39 E F

145 123

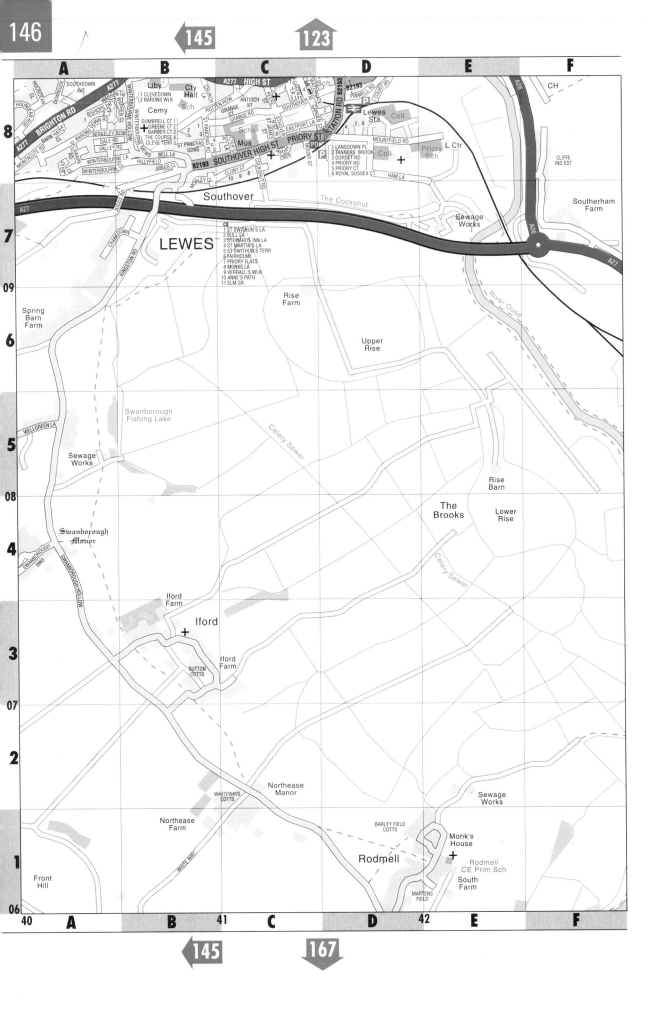

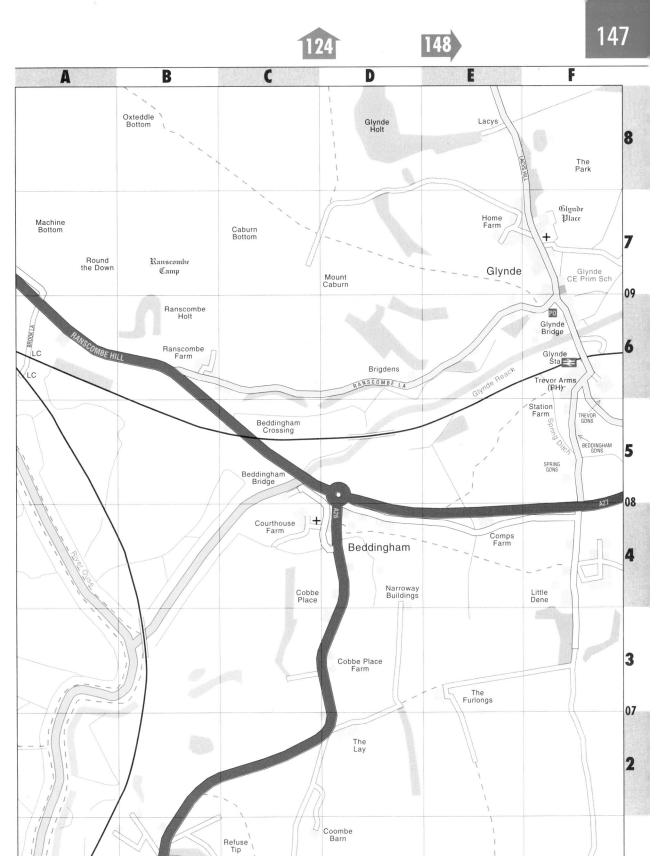

A   B   C   D   E   F

8   Decoy Wood   New Barn
Black Shaw

7   Willow Shaw   Glynde Reach   Barber's Wish

09   Burgh Shaw   Middle Barn

6   Loover Shaw   Burgh Bridge   LC   Bushy Lodge

Loover Barn   Bushy Lodge Farm

5   Garage   Newhouse Farm   BURGH LA   Stamford Buildings   Adder Wells

A27   Gibraltar   Wick Street   Middle Farm

08   Preston House   Dairy Farm   Decoy Pond

4   Firle CE Prim Sch   Firle Park   Petland Barn   A27

BOSTAL RD   P   Heighton Street   Compton Wood

Ram Inn (PH)   THE STREET   West Firle   Firle Tower

3   Newelm   PO   THE DOCK   Firle Place

Place Farm   +

07   Beanstalk

2   FIRLE BOSTAL   Round Hill

1   Firle Plantation   Roundhill Plantation

Beddingham Hill

06
46   A   B   47   C   D   48   E   F

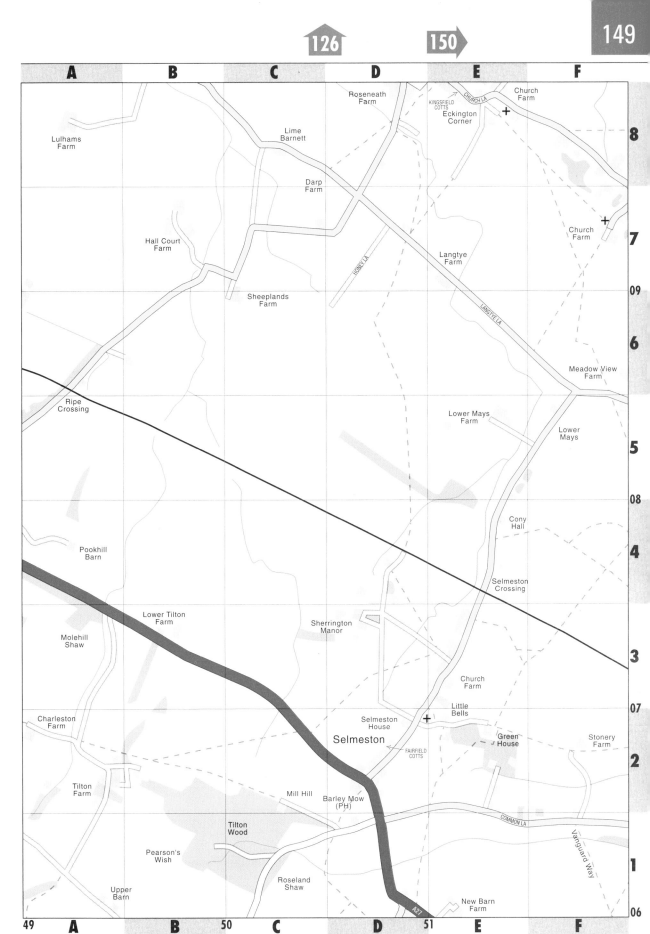

126
150

A B C D E F

8
7
09
6
5
08
4
3
07
2
1
06

Lulhams
Farm

Lime
Barnett

Roseneath
Farm

KINGSFIELD
COTTS
Eckington
Corner

CHURCH LA

Church
Farm

Darp
Farm

Hall Court
Farm

HONEY LA

Langtye
Farm

Church
Farm

Sheeplands
Farm

LANGTYE LA

Ripe
Crossing

Meadow View
Farm

Lower Mays
Farm

Lower
Mays

Pookhill
Barn

Cony
Hall

Lower Tilton
Farm

Selmeston
Crossing

Molehill
Shaw

Sherrington
Manor

Church
Farm

Charleston
Farm

Little
Bells

Selmeston
House

Green
House

Stonery
Farm

Selmeston

FAIRFIELD
COTTS

Tilton
Farm

Mill Hill

Barley Mow
(PH)

COMMON LA

Vanguard Way

Tilton
Wood

Pearson's
Wish

Roseland
Shaw

A27

New Barn
Farm

Upper
Barn

49 A B 50 C D 51 E F

170
150

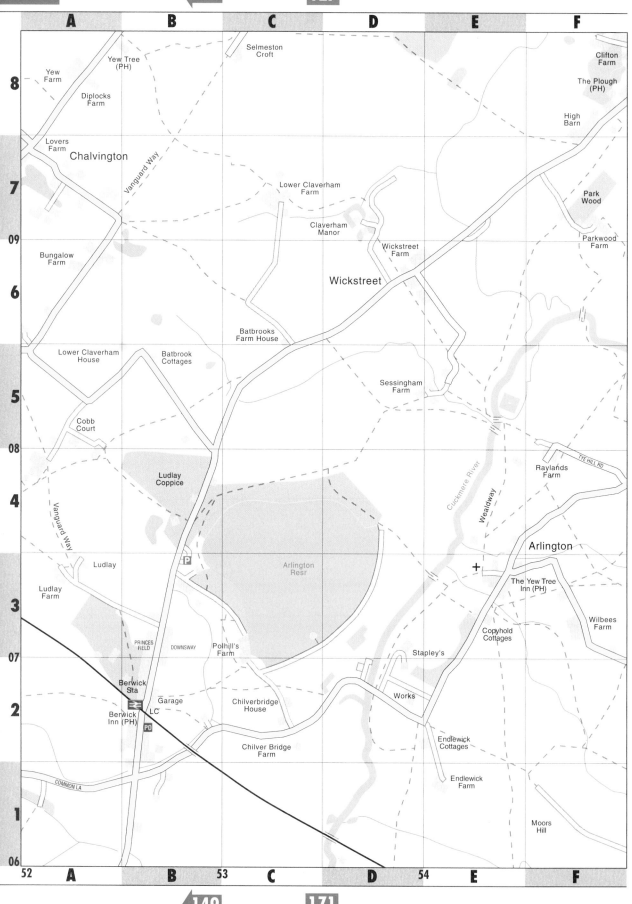

A   B   C   D   E   F

Yew Tree (PH)
Selmeston Croft
Clifton Farm
The Plough (PH)

8

Yew Farm
Diplocks Farm
High Barn

Lovers Farm
Chalvington
Vanguard Way
Park Wood

7

Lower Claverham Farm
Parkwood Farm

09

Bungalow Farm
Claverham Manor
Wickstreet Farm

Wickstreet

6

Batbrooks Farm House

Lower Claverham House
Batbrook Cottages
Sessingham Farm

5

Cobb Court

08

Ludlay Coppice
Cuckmere River
Raylands Farm
TYE HILL RD

Wealdway

4

Vanguard Way
Arlington

Ludlay
Arlington Resr
Arlington

Ludlay Farm
The Yew Tree Inn (PH)

3

Wilbees Farm

Copyhold Cottages

07

PRINCES FIELD
DOWNSWAY
Polhill's Farm
Stapley's

Berwick Sta
Garage
Works

2

Berwick Inn (PH)
LC
Chilverbridge House

PD
Endlewick Cottages

Chilver Bridge Farm

Endlewick Farm

1

COMMON LA
Moors Hill

06

52   A   B   53   C   D   54   E   F

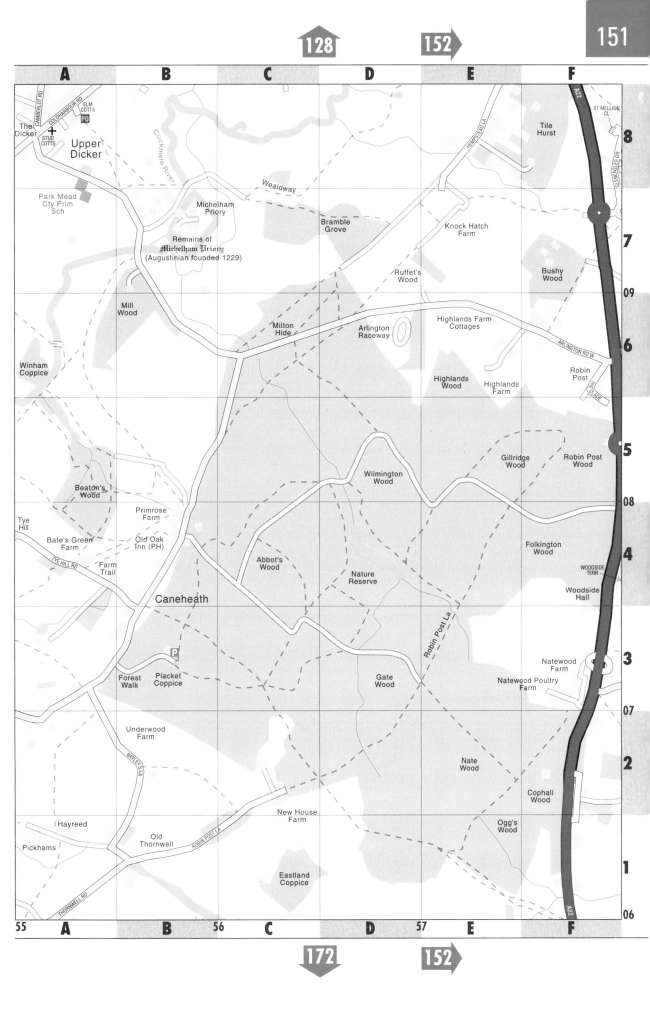

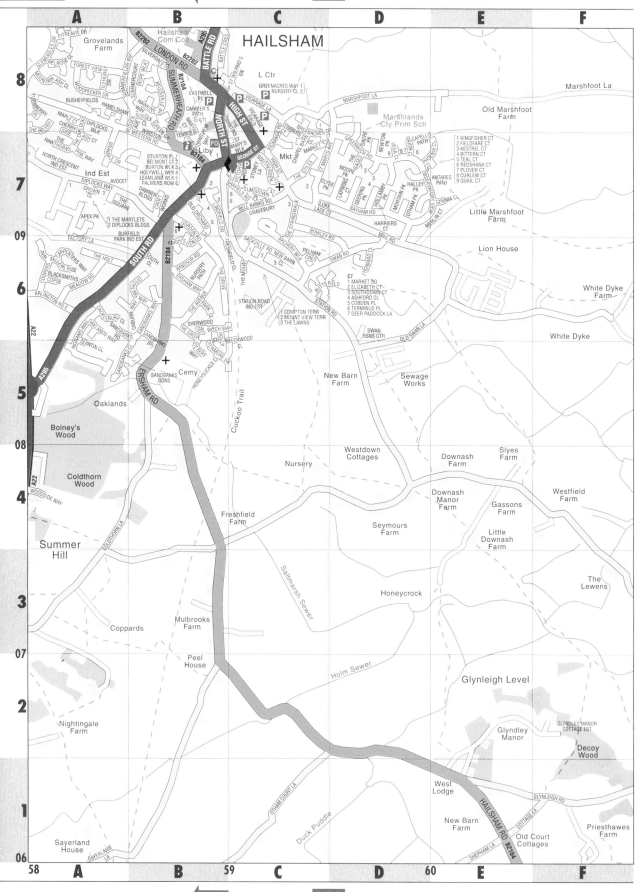

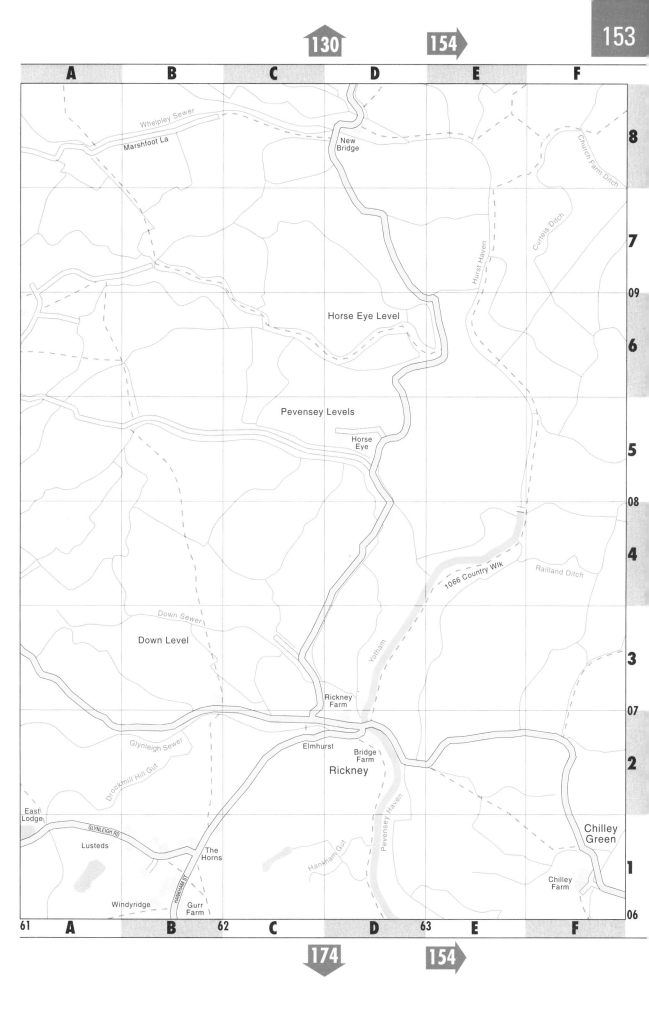

153
131

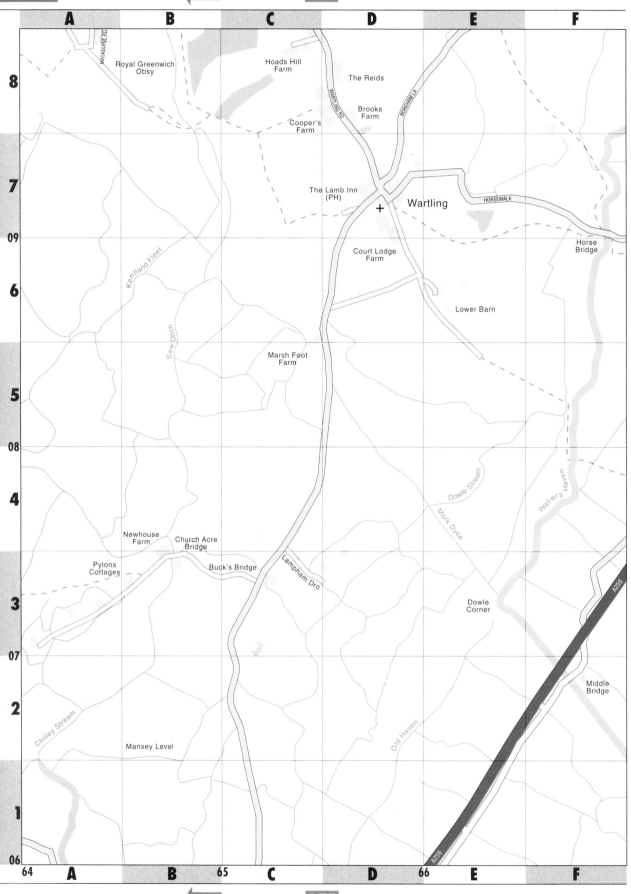

153
175

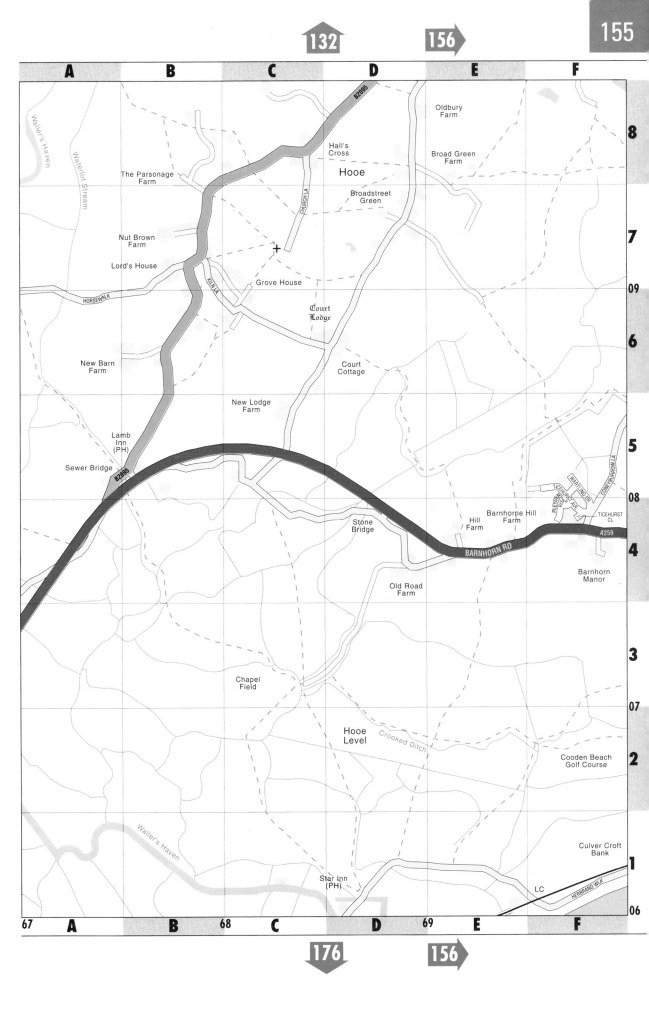

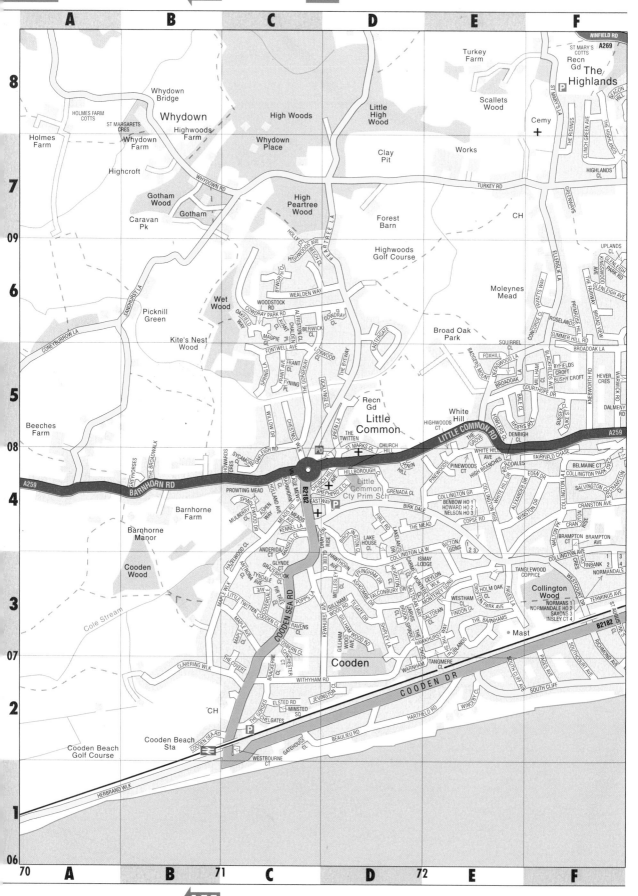

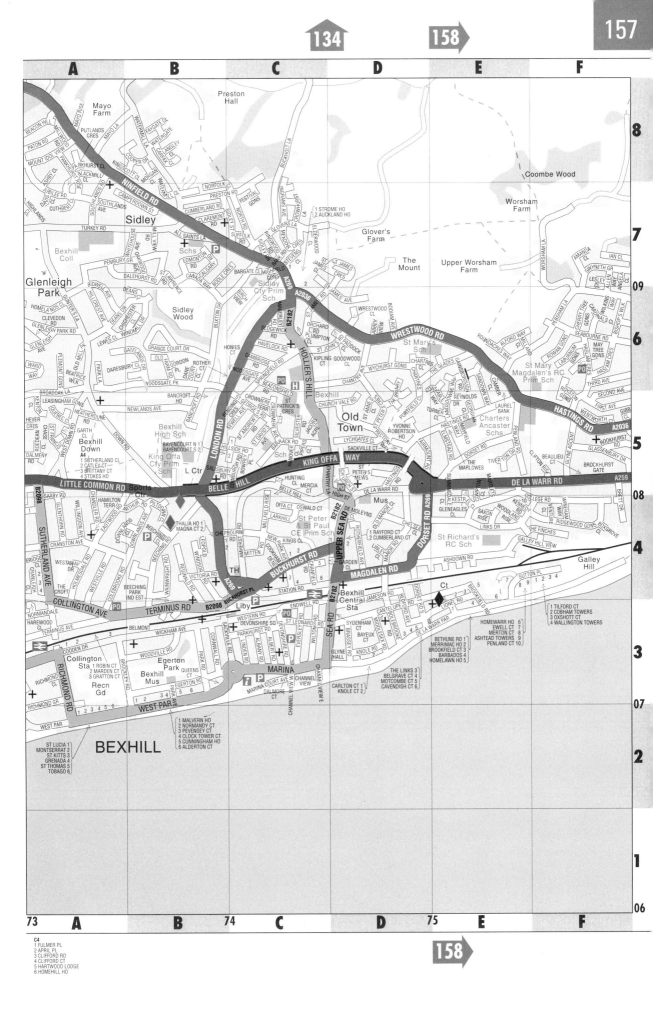

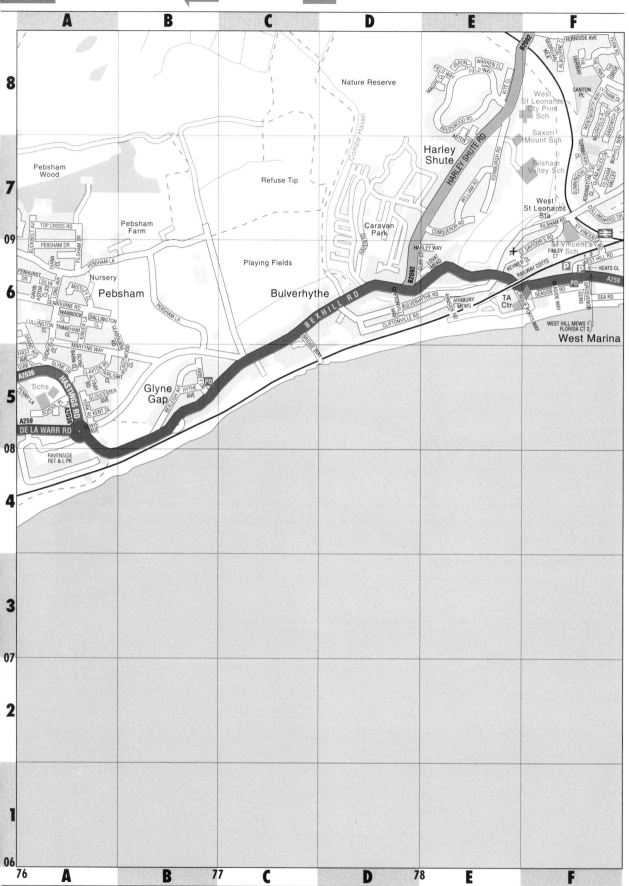

C7
1 STAINSBY ST
2 NORFOLK HO
3 ST RICHARDS HO
4 ROYAL TERR
5 EVERSFIELD MEWS N
6 ALAN CT

7 ASHLEY CT
8 ST MARY'S CT
9 CAVENDISH HO
10 DECIMUS BURTON WAY
11 UNION ST

F8
1 WATERWORKS COTTS
2 STONEFIELD PL
3 ELFORD ST
4 WALDEGRAVE ST
5 CORNWALLIS ST
6 ST ANDREW'S SQ

F8
7 ROBERT TRESSELL WKSHPS
8 SUSSEX CHAMBERS
9 MIDDLE ST
10 KINGS WLK
11 PORTLAND COTTS
12 STONE ST

13 PORTLAND PL
14 WELLINGTON TERR
15 PORTLAND TERR
16 PORTLAND VILLAS
17 WELLINGTON HO

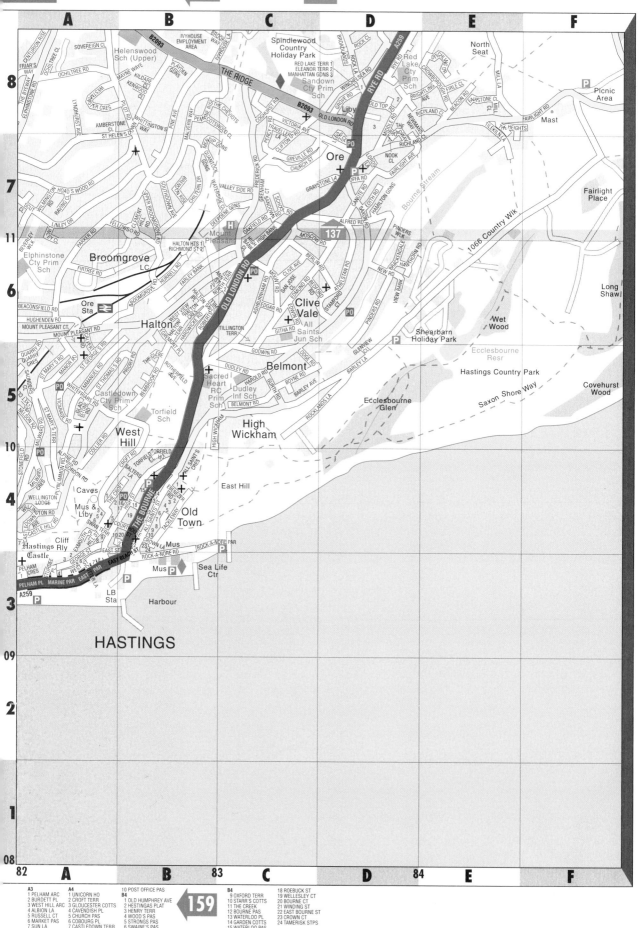

HASTINGS

◁159

A3
1 PELHAM ARC
2 BURDETT PL
3 WEST HILL ARC
4 ALBION LA
5 RUSSELL CT
6 MARKET PAS
7 SUN LA
8 SHELL LA

A4
1 UNICORN HO
2 CROFT TERR
3 GLOUCESTER COTTS
4 CAVENDISH PL
5 CHURCH PAS
6 COBOURG PL
7 CASTLEDOWN TERR
8 OAK PAS
9 SWAN AVE

10 POST OFFICE PAS

B4
1 OLD HUMPHREY AVE
2 HESTINGAS PLAT
3 HENRY TERR
4 WOOD S PAS
5 STRONGS PAS
6 SWAINE S PAS
7 EAST HILL PAS
8 TRAFALGAR COTTS

B4
9 OXFORD TERR
10 STARR S COTTS
11 THE CREEK
12 BOURNE PAS
13 WATERLOO PL
14 GARDEN COTTS
15 WATERLOO PAS
16 PHILIP COLE CL
17 SINNOOK SQ

18 ROEBUCK ST
19 WELLESLEY CT
20 BOURNE CT
21 WINDING ST
22 EAST BOURNE ST
23 CROWN CT
24 TAMERISK STPS

162
161
141

F7
1 MAINSTONE RD
2 EVEREST HO
3 ST PHILIPS MEWS
4 LION MEWS
5 RICHARDSON CT

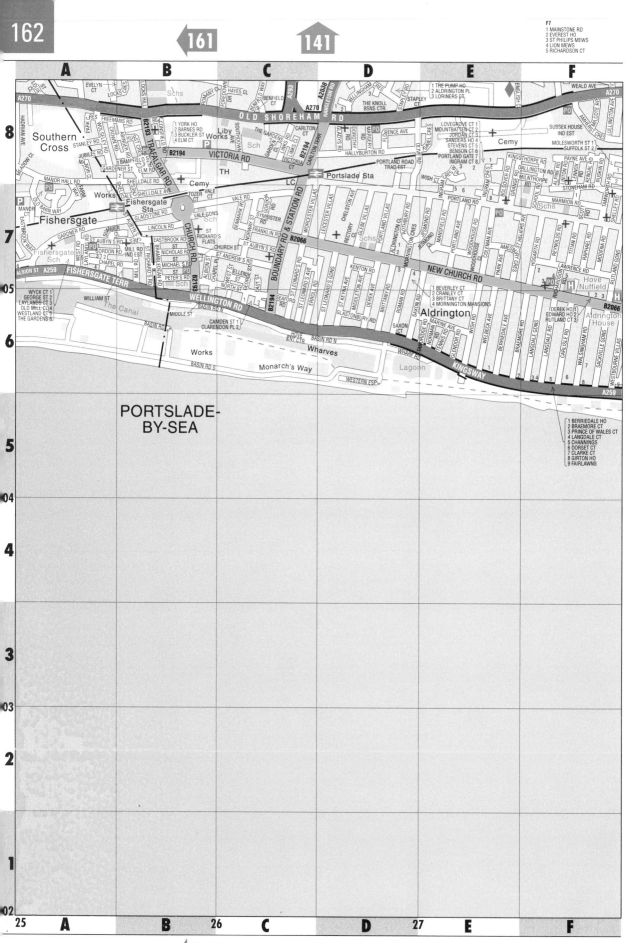

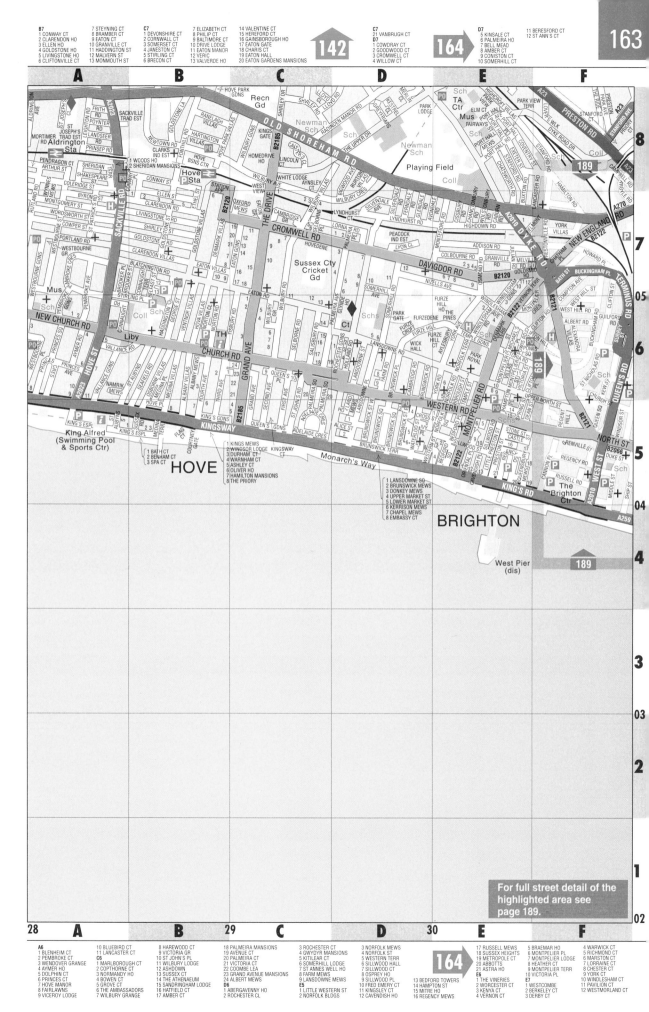

163

143

For full street detail of the highlighted area see page 189.

163

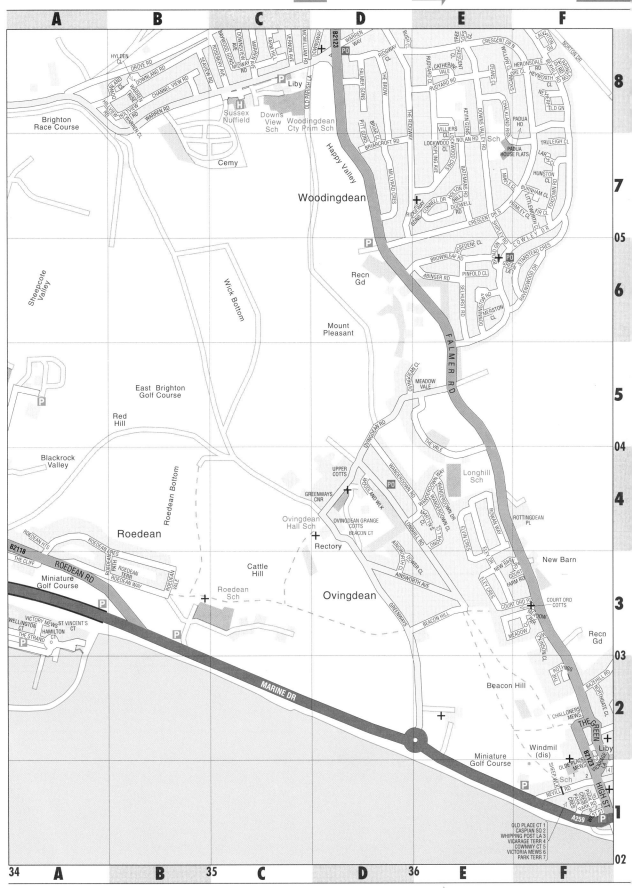

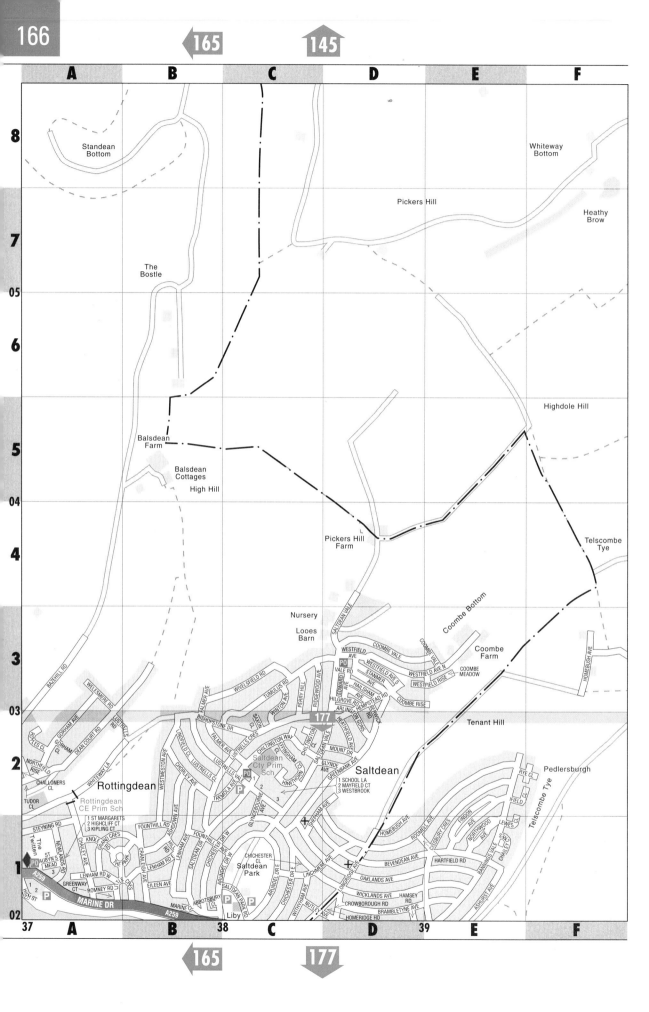

165
145

A B C D E F

8

7

05

6

Standean
Bottom

Whiteway
Bottom

Pickers Hill

Heathy
Brow

The
Bostle

5

04

4

3

03

2

1

02

Balsdean
Farm

Balsdean
Cottages

High Hill

Highdole Hill

Pickers Hill
Farm

Telscombe
Tye

Nursery

Looes
Barn

Coombe Bottom

Coombe
Farm

WESTFIELD
AVE

WESTFIELD RD

VALE RD

STANMER
AVE

HAILSHAM
AVE

EDWARD
AVE

HILGROVE RD

COOMBE VALE

COOMBE VALE

WESTFIELD AVE N

HEMPSTEAD RD

WESTFIELD RISE

COOMBE RISE

COOMBE
MEADOW

HOMEBUSH AVE

Tenant Hill

BAZEHILL RD

WELESMERE RD

LUSTRELLS

GORHAM
AVE

GORHAM
CL

RYLES CL

NORTHFIELD
RISE

DEAN COURT RD

CHALLONERS
CL

TUDOR
CL

Rottingdean

WHITEWAY LA

WESTMESTON AVE

CHORLEY AVE

ASHDOWN AVE

LINDFIELD CL

FALMER AVE

WIVELSFIELD RD

TUMULUS RD

BISHOPSTONE DR

FALMER
AVE

LUSTRELLS CRES

LUSTRELLS VALE

PERRY HILL

RIDGEWOOD AVE

SADDLESCOMBE

WINTON AVE

CHILTINGTON WAY

EFFINGHAM CL

CHILTINGTON CL

SALTDEAN VALE

MOUNT DR

ARLINGTON GDNS

BERWICK

HARTFIELD AVE

Saltdean
Cty Prim
Sch

GLYNDE AVE

GREENBANK AVE

HINTHORN

Saltdean

1 SCHOOL LA
2 MAYFIELD CT
3 WESTBROOK

177

Steyning Rd

Rottingdean
CE Prim Sch

1 ST MARGARETS
2 HIGHCLIFF CT
3 KIPLING CT

STEYNING RD

NEWLANS RD

CHAILEY AVE

GRAND CRES

KNOLE RD

THE PARK

LENHAM RD W

HERON

CRANLEIGH AVE

ROMNEY RD

LITTLE CRES

EILEEN AVE

ABBOTSBURY
CL

FOUNTHILL RD

LENHAM RD E

SALTDEAN DR

CHICHESTER DR W

CHICHESTER DR E

ARUNDEL DR W

CHICHESTER
CL

Saltdean
Park

ARUNDEL DR E

GLYNDEBOURNE AVE

SALTDEAN PARK RD

WITHAM AVE

NUTLEY AVE

SPEARHAM AVE

LINKMERE AVE

LONGRIDGE AVE

Bevendean Ave

Oaklands Ave

WICKLANDS AVE

CROWBOROUGH RD

HOMERIDGE HO

HAMSEY
RD

BRAMBLETYNE AVE

GOSSBURY CRES

FINDON
AVE

NORTHWOOD
AVE

ROOMEL AVE

HARTFIELD RD

ASHURST AVE

BANNINGS VALE

STACEY
CL

CHAILEY
CL

LEWES
CL

RYE CL

FIELD
CL

Telscombe Tye

Pedlersburgh

Coombe Vale

A259

The
Twitten

ST
AUBYN'S
MEAD

HIGH ST

GREENWAY
CT

MARINE DR

MARINE CL

A259

Liby

37 A B 38 C D 39 E F

165
177

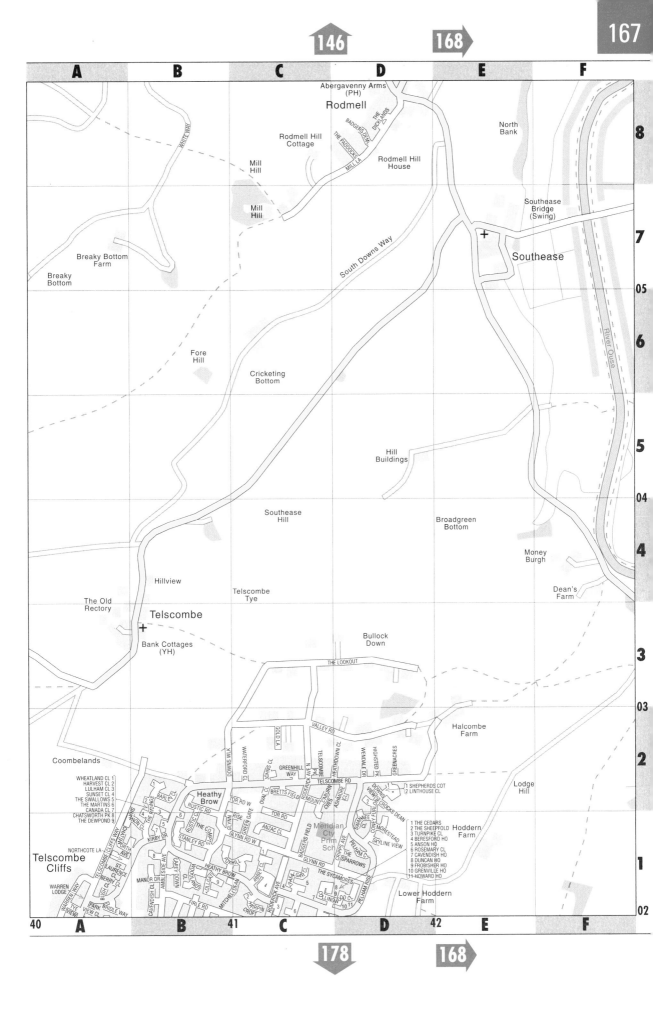

Abergavenny Arms (PH)

Rodmell

North Bank

Rodmell Hill Cottage

WHITE WAY

THE PADDOCKS

BADGERS TRK

THE DICKLANDS

MILL LA

Mill Hill

Rodmell Hill House

Southease Bridge (Swing)

Mill Hill

✛

Southease

South Downs Way

Breaky Bottom Farm

Breaky Bottom

05

Fore Hill

6

Cricketing Bottom

River Ouse

Hill Buildings

5

04

Southease Hill

Broadgreen Bottom

4

Money Burgh

Hillview

Dean's Farm

Telscombe Tye

The Old Rectory

Telscombe

✛

Bullock Down

Bank Cottages (YH)

3

THE LOOKOUT

03

Halcombe Farm

VALLEY RD

Coombelands

2

WHEATLAND CL 1
HARVEST CL 2
LULHAM CL 3
SUNSET CL 4
THE SWALLOWS 5
THE MARTINS 6
CANADA CL 7
CHATSWORTH PK 8
THE DEWPOND 9

Greenhill Way

Telscombe Rd

Lodge Hill

GOLD LA

DOWNS WAY

WATERFORD CL

SOPHUS CL

BRETTS FIELD

RODERICK AVE N

TELSCOMBE

HEATHDOWN CL

WENDALE DR

HIGHSTED PK

GREENACRES

1 SHEPHERDS COT
2 LINTHOUSE CL

Heathy Brow

BARLEY CL

RUSTIC RD

TOR RD W

OVAL CL

TELSCOMBE MOUNT

COBURN CRES

ASHMORE CL

DOWNS VIEW CL

CONEY FURLONG

CROCKS DEAN

1 THE CEDARS
2 THE SHEEPFOLD
3 TURNPIKE CL
4 BERESFORD HO
5 ANSON HO
6 ROSEMARY CL
7 CAVENDISH HO
8 DUNCAN HO
9 FROBISHER HO
10 GRENVILLE HO
11 HOWARD HO

THE RIVINGS

GREEN GATE

ANZAC CL

Meridian Cty Prim Sch

MORESTEAD

SKYLINE VIEW

Hoddern Farm

THE COPPICE

TOR RD

BADGERS FIELD

CRIPPS AVE

PELHAM CL

SWANBEE

NORTHCOTE LA

TELSCOMBE CLIFFS WAY

ST. LAURENCE CL

BUSH CL

SANNON CL

KIRBY DR

STANLEY RD

GLYNN RD W

RIBBE CL

THE SPARROWS

GLYNN RD

THE SYCAMORES

Telscombe Cliffs

WARREN LODGE

WARREN WAY

TYE VIEW

PARK VIEW CL

BRIDLE WAY

BERRY CL

MANOR DR

CAVENDISH CL

AMBLESIDE AVE

ABERGAVENNY

WOODLAND

SOLGATE

HEATHY BROW

MITCHELDEAN

FIRLE RD

RODERICK AVE

FOXHILL

PIRPIN CROFT

LARKHILL

COLLINGWOOD CL

PELHAM RISE

Lower Hoddern Farm

A   B   C   D   E   F

8

05

7

6

5

04

4

3

03

2

1

02

Mast
Radio Sta

White Lion Pond

Red Lion Pond

America Farm

LC
Southease Sta
Itford Farm
Itford Hill

South Downs Way

A26

Baydean

Baydean Bottom

Itford Bottom

Muggery Pope

Well Bottom

Cow Wish Bottom

Stock Cottages

Durham Farm

LC

Manor Farm

Court Farm

Tarring Neville

Page's New Barn

Caravan Park

Works

RODMELL HO

DOWNS VILLAS

South Heighton Farm

New Barn

River Ouse

Piddinghoe

COURT FARM CL

Royal Oak (PH)

BROOK...

The Wish

1 CEDARWELL CL
2 SHEPHERDS CL

PORTLAND TERR 1
FIRLE TERR 2
WEST VIEW TERR 3

HAMPDEN GDNS

E2
1 SOUTH VIEW
2 ORCHARD MEWS

South Heighton

WELLINGTON RD
THOMPSON RD
THE CLOSE

HARROD CL
LEONARDS
ST LEONARDS

CANTERCROW HILL

HEIGHTON RD
BRANDS CL

PO

THE GUINNESS TRUST HOLIDAY HOME

TARRING 2 CL
ST MARTINS

DENTON RISE

ROOKERY
VICARAGE CL

RY WAY
THE GROVE

PARK DRIVE

ACACIA

DENTON RD

Denton

Nore Down

Brookside Farm

LEWES RD

PIDDINGHOE MEAD

NEW RD

B2109

Mus

D1
1 MARTELLO CT
2 COTTAGE CL

Paradise Family L-Pk

AVIS RD

Denton Cty Prim Sch

GUINNESS CT

DENTON DR

KING'S AVE

MILL RISE
HILL RD

SEAVIEW RD
FAIRHOLME RD
CREST RD

Mount Pleasant

Cemy

NORTH QUAY RD

ESTATE RD
A26

AVIS WAY

Ind Est

AVIS RD
B2109
PO

STATION RD
ARUNDEL RD

SEAVIEW RD
BRESFORD RD

CLAREMONT RD

MOUNT RD

PALMERSTON RD
FALAISE RD
HOLMDALE RD
MOWBRAY

43   A   B   44   C   D   45   E   F

A   B   C   D   E   F

8

7

05

6

04

5

4

03

3

2

1

02

Males Burgh
Tumulus

FIRLE
BOSTAL
P

South Downs Way

Overhill
Lodge

Lord's Burghs
Tumuli

Well Bottom

Beacon Bottom

Tilton Bottom

Blackcap
Farm

Toy
Farm

Blackcap
Hill

Fore
Hill

Home Bottom

Heighton
Hill

Five Lord's Burgh
Tumulus

Blackstone Bottom

Snap
Hill

Stump
Bottom

Gardener's
Hill

Denton
Hill

Norton
Top

Poverty
Bottom

Well Bottom

Denton Hill
Farm

PALMERSTON RD

HOLMDALE RD

Norton
Bottom

Bishopstone
Nurseries

Devilsrest
Bottom

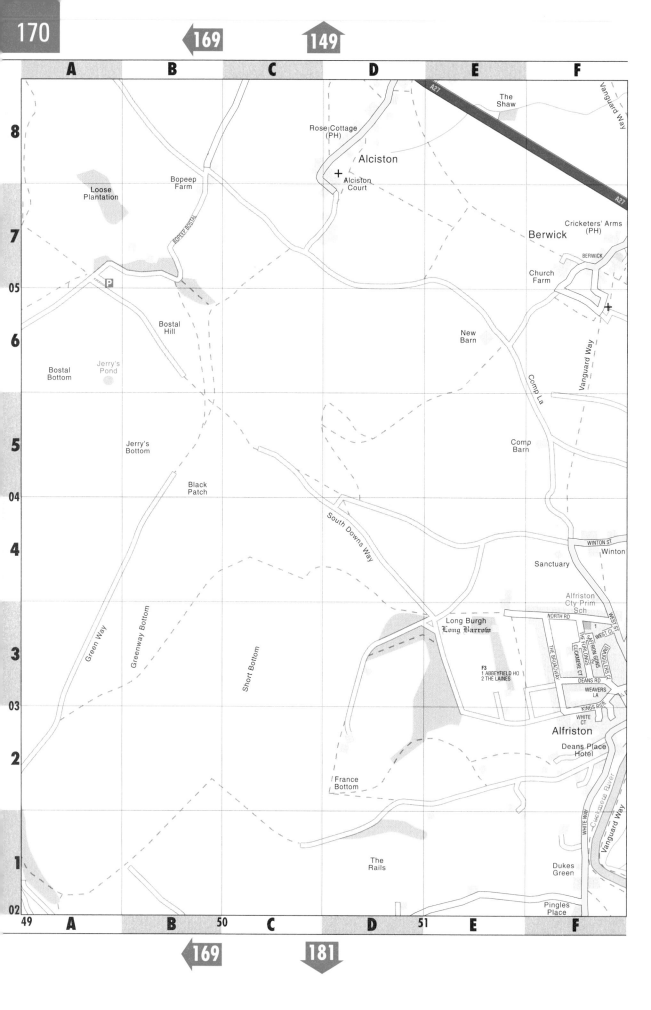

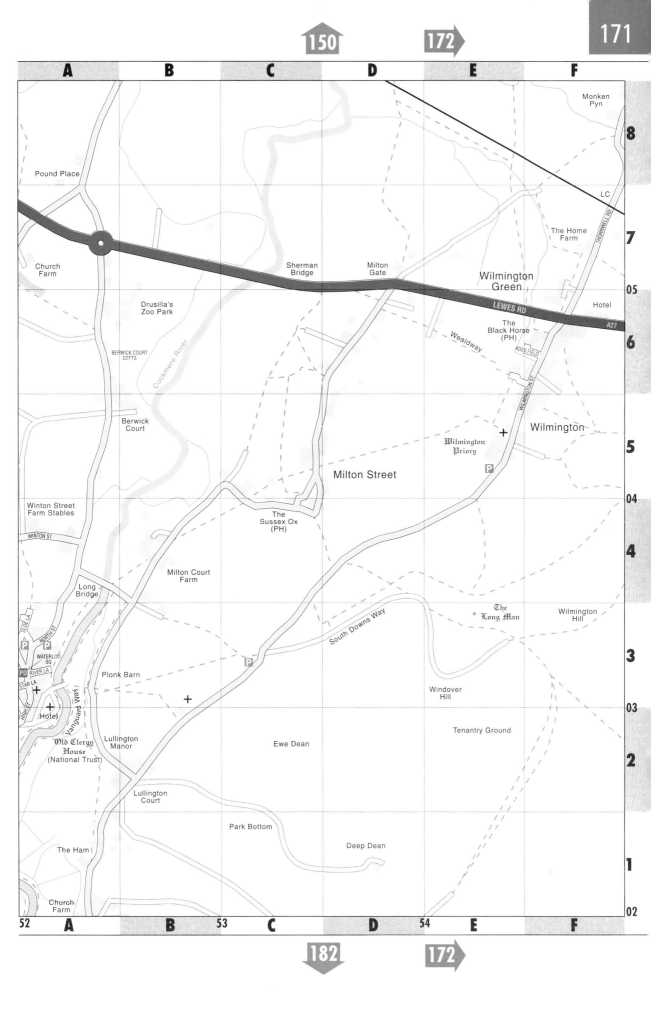

A B C D E F

8

THORNWELL RD
Warren Farm
Monkyn Pyn
Hide Farm
Cophall Farm
Cop Hall
BAY TREE LA
A22

7
Newbarn Farm
Wootton Manor
St Leonards Terr
POLEGATE BY-PASS
HAILSHAM RD
A27
HAVERLAND RD
GUARDSWELL
BROOKSIDE AVE
VICTORIA RD

05
DIPLOCK CL 1
GRAND PAR 2
SOUTHDOWN CT 3
THE BERNHARD BARON COTTAGE HOMES 4
BROOK ST
GOSFORD WAY
OLD DR

6
A27
LEWES RD
The Flint House
HYPERION AVE
SUNSTAR LA
GAINSBOROUGH LA
GOLDEN MILLER LA
BROWN JACK AVE
BAHRAM RD
REYNOLDSTOWN
A27
A22
PO
The Stud Farm

The Rough
HILERY CL
NORTHFIELD
BARONS WAY
WANNOCK DR
Recn Gd

5
Puddingham Wood
Folkington Manor Farm
The Links
Wannock Coppice
WANNOCK RD
SOUTHFIELD
GROSVENOR CL
FARMLANDS WAY

04
The Holt
Folkington Manor
FOLKINGTON RD
MAYFAIR CL
PADDOCK GDNS
LANCING WAY
MORTIMER GDNS
MILLSTREAM GDNS
THE MILLRACE
FARMLANDS AVE
PO

4
Folkington +
Wannock
MILL GDNS
MILL A
GLEN CL
Willingdon Sch
BROAD RD
+

Folkington Bottom
Middle Brow
Cranedown Bottom
Crane Down
MILL WAY
MILL CL
HOMEWALK CL
MILL GDNS
BROADWATER MEWS
FILCHING CL
GLEN COTTS
WANNOCK AVE
WANNOCK LA
THE PARAGON
THE GROVE

3

03
Folkington Hill
Ash Farm
JEVINGTON RD
WAYFARING DOWN
Dean Wood
Filching Manor Motor Mus
Hanging Hill
Willingdon Links

2
Hill Barn
Teddard's Bottom
WEALDWAY
Helling Down
1066 Country Wlk

South Downs Way

1
Hayward's Bottom
The Combe

Jevington Holt
Combe Hill
Wealdway

Holt Brow
02
Holt Bottom
GREEN LA

55 A B 56 C D 57 E F

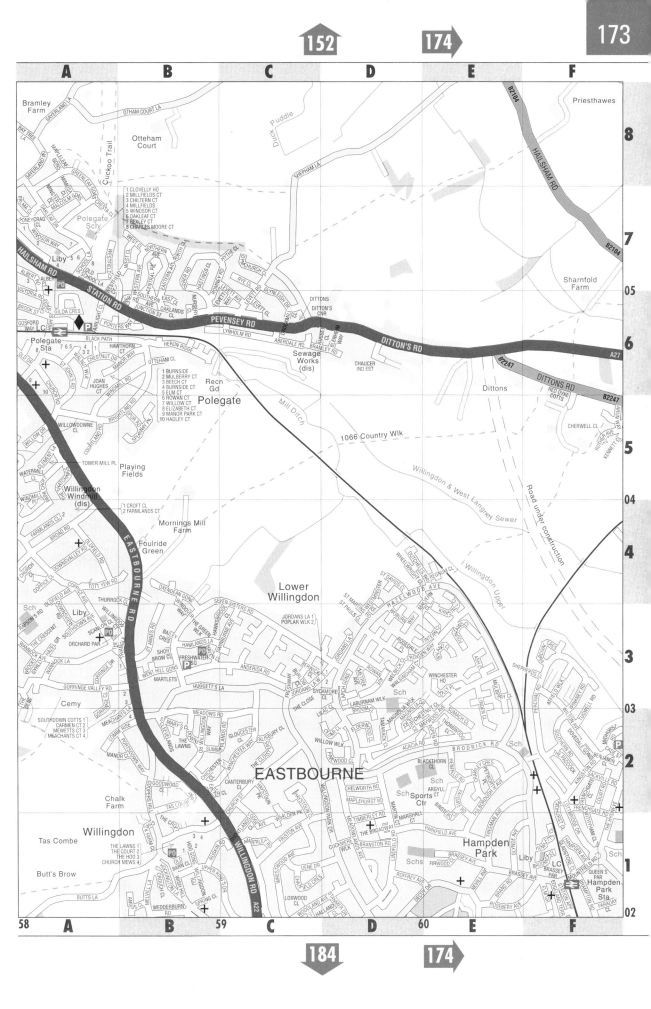

173 153

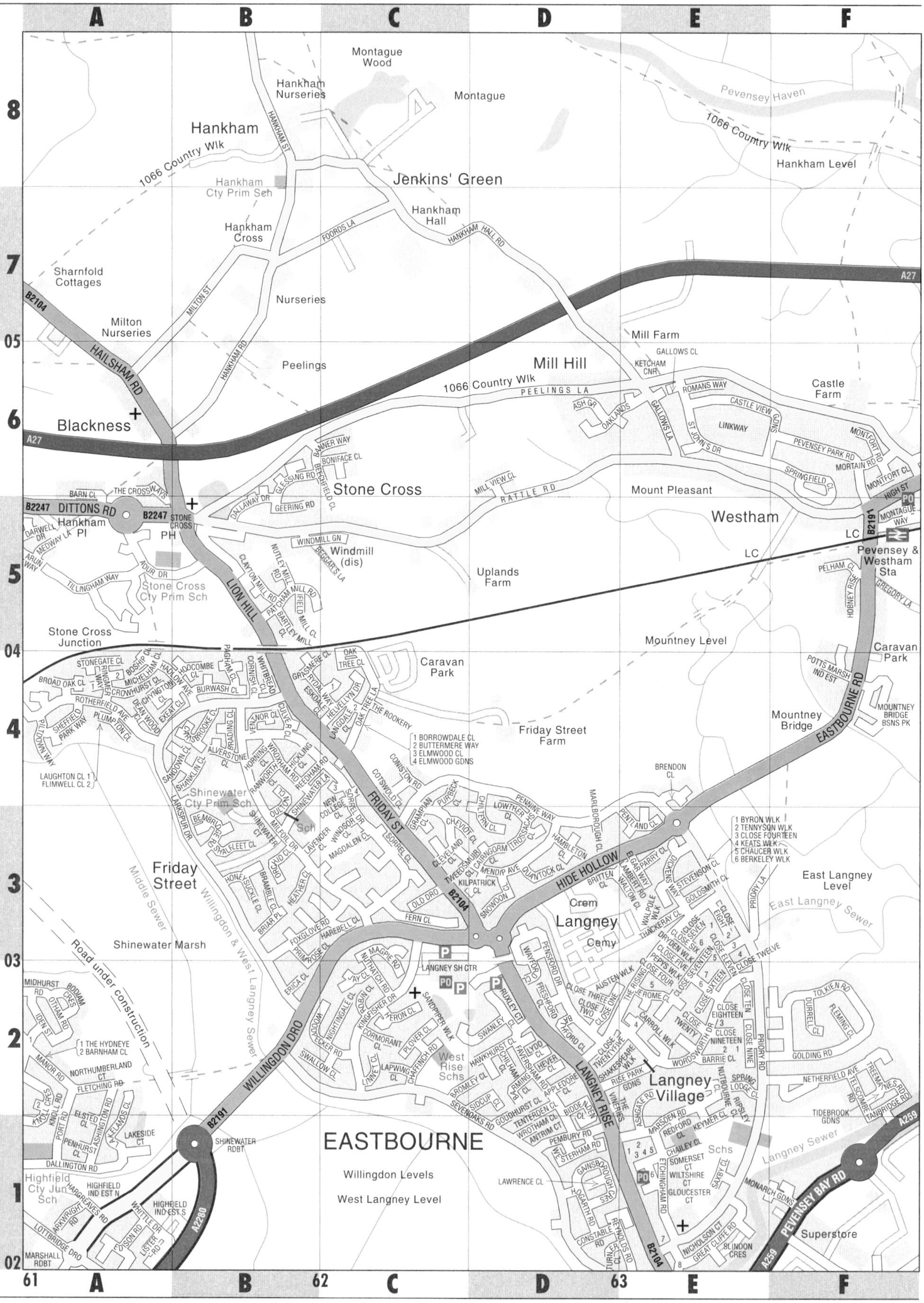

A B C D E F

8 7 05 6 05 04 04 03 02 (grid row markers)

Montague Wood
Hankham Nurseries
Montague
Pevensey Haven
Hankham
1066 Country Wlk
Hankham Level
1066 Country Wlk
Hankham Cty Prim Sch
Jenkins' Green
Hankham St
Hankham Cross
FOORDS LA
Hankham Hall
Hankham Hall Rd
A27
MILTON ST
HANKHAM RD
Sharnfold Cottages
Nurseries
Mill Farm
B2104
Milton Nurseries
Peelings
GALLOWS CL
KETCHAM CNR
Castle Farm
HAILSHAM RD
Mill Hill
1066 Country Wlk
PEELINGS LA
ROMANS WAY
GALLOWS LA
ASH GR
OAKLANDS
ST JOHN'S DR
LINKWAY
CASTLE VIEW GDNS
MONTFORT
Blackness
A27
BANNER WAY
BONIFACE CL
Mount Pleasant
PEVENSEY PARK RD
MORTAIN RD
SPRINGFIELD
MONTFORT CL
HIGH ST
B2247 DITTONS RD
BARN CL
THE CROSSWAYS
GLEESING RD
BECKFIELD LA
Stone Cross
MILL VIEW CL
RATTLE RD
Westham
B2191
PO
MONTAGUE WAY
Hankham PL
B2247
STONE CROSS
OAK LAWAY DR
GEERING RD
Pevensey & Westham Sta
DARWELL DR
MEDWAY LK
PH
WINDMILL GN
LC
LC
ARUN WAY
AVON DR
TILLINGHAM WAY
Stone Cross Cty Prim Sch
NUTLEY MILL RD
BEGGAR'S LA
Windmill (dis)
Uplands Farm
Mountney Level
PELHAM CL
HOONEY RISE
GREGORY LA
Caravan Park
LION HILL
CLAYTON MILL RD
CHAM MILL RD
FIELD MILL CL
PAT BARTLEY MILL
Caravan Park
Mountney Bridge
EASTBOURNE RD
POTTS MARSH IND EST
MOUNTNEY BRIDGE BSNS PK
Stone Cross Junction
STONEGATE CL
BROAD OAK CL
OAK TREE CL
GRASMERE RYDAL CL
OAK TREE LA
THE ROOKERY
Friday Street Farm
BRENDON CL
1 BYRON WLK
2 TENNYSON WLK
3 CLOSE FOURTEEN
4 KEATS WLK
5 CHAUCER WLK
6 BERKELEY WLK
SHEFFIELD PARK WAY
PLUMPTON CL
BISHOP CL
MICHELHAM CL
HAILSHAM CL
CROWHURST CL
CHYNGTON
WOOD
BURWASH CL
CORNISH CL
NOR CL
CLIVE
HELVELLYN DR
LANGDALE LA
1 BORROWDALE CL
2 BUTTERMERE WAY
3 ELMWOOD CL
4 ELMWOOD GDNS
PENNINE WAY
PENTLAND CL
1 BYRON WLK
ELGAR WAY
STEVENSON CL
East Langney Level
East Langney Sewer
ROTHERFIELD CT
PILTDOWN WAY
SANDOWN
ALVERSTONE
NORTH BROOKE CL
HORSTING CL
WHIDHAM CL
RANWORTH RD
NEW COLLEGE
GORSE CL
HINDOVER RD
CHEVIOT CL
GRAMPIAN
CAIRNGORM
TROSSACHS CL
HAMBLETON
MARLBOROUGH DR
PRIORY LA
GOLDSMITH CL
East Langney Level
LAUGHTON CL 1
FLIMWELL CL 2
Shinewater Cty Prim Sch
LAVENDER
WINDSOR CL
FRIDAY ST
COTSWOLD CL
PURBECK
CLEVELAND CL
LOWTHER
BRITTEN CL
Hide Hollow
WALTON CL
PARRY CL
AMBERLEY CL
ELGAR WAY
STEVENSON CL
1 BYRON WLK
Friday Street
Middle Sewer
BEAM CL
SHINEWATER CL
HONEYSUCKLE CL
BRAMBLE CL
BRIAR PL
MAGDALEN CL
SORREL CL
TRAMPAN
MENDIP AVE
KILPATRICK
SNOWDON
HIDE HOLLOW
Crem
Langney
Cemy
STEVENSON CL
CLOSE SEVENTEEN
CLOSE SIXTEEN
CLOSE ELEVEN
CLOSE TEN
CLOSE TWELVE
TOLKIEN RD
FLEMING CL
Shinewater Marsh
LARKSPUR DR
FOXGLOVE RD
HAREBELL CL
BRICK CL
PRIMROSE CL
OLD DRO
FERN CL
B2104
OLD DRO
MAGPIE CL
Langney SH Ctr
PO
LANGNEY RISE
AUSTEN WLK
ROME CL
CARROLL WLK
CLOSE FIVE
CLOSE FOUR
CLOSE SIX
CLOSE EIGHTEEN
CLOSE NINETEEN
CLOSE TWENTY
DURRELL RD
GOLDING RD
Road under construction
WILLINGDON DRO
Willingdon & West Langney Sewer
MIDHURST RD
BODIAM CRES
OTHAM CL
1 THE HYDNEYE
2 BARNHAM CL
NORTHUMBERLAND CT
FLETCHING RD
MANOR RD
AYLESBURY CL
NUTHATCH RD
KINGFISHER DR
KESTREL CL
SANDPIPER WLK
CORMORANT CL
SWALLOW CL
WOODPECKER RD
LAPWING CL
PLOVER CL
LINNET CL
BROMLEY CL
GODSHAWK RD
SEVENOAKS RD
West Rise Schs
SWANLEY CL
HAWKHURST RD
CHILTON CL
FAIRLYDO RD
HAMSEY
APPLEDORE
TENTERDEN CL
WROTHAM CL
ANTRIM RD
BIDDENDEN
PEMBURY RD
STERHAM RD
PRESCOTT RD
FRISTON CL
RISE PARK GDNS
THE
THAMESGATE
WORDSWORTH DR
BARRIE CL
MARSDEN RD
REDFORD CL
KEYMER CL
CHALEY CL
SOMERSET CT
WILTSHIRE CT
GLOUCESTER CT
SPRING CL
RIDGLEY
SHINEWATER RDBT
Highfield Cty Jun Sch
Highfield Ind Est N
Highfield Ind Est S
A2280
WHITTLE DR
LISTER RD
DALLINGTON RD
KYLE CL
PORT RD
ASHINGTON CL
PENHURST CL
KEJANS CL
LAKESIDE CT
LOTTBRIDGE DRO
MARSHALL RDBT
EASTBOURNE
Willingdon Levels
West Langney Level
LAWRENCE CL
GWINSBROUGH RD
HASGATH RD
CONSTABLE RD
REYNOLDS RD
B2104
NICHOLSON CL
GREAT CLIFFE RD
BLINDON CRES
LINDON CRES
Langney Village
Schs
PO
A259
Superstore
TIDEBROOK GDNS
NETHERFIELD AVE
PEVENSEY BAY RD
Langney Sewer
MONARCH GDNS
A259
PEVENSEY BAY RD

173 185

E1
1 HEREFORD CT
2 STAFFORD CT
3 RUTLAND CT
4 WARWICK CT
5 WORCESTER CT
6 HAMPSHIRE CT
7 WILLIAMS CT
8 PRIORY ORCH

E2
1 KIPLING WLK
2 BOSWELL WLK
3 SHELLY WLK
4 CLOSE TWENTYFOUR
5 BROWNING WLK
6 CLOSE FIFTEEN
7 COLERIDGE WLK

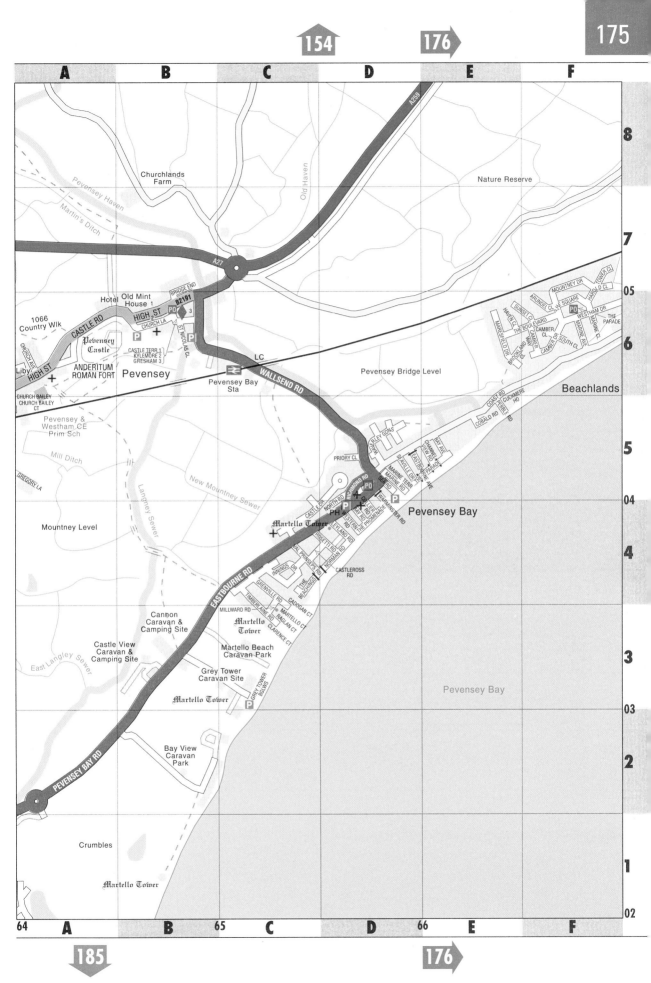

175
155

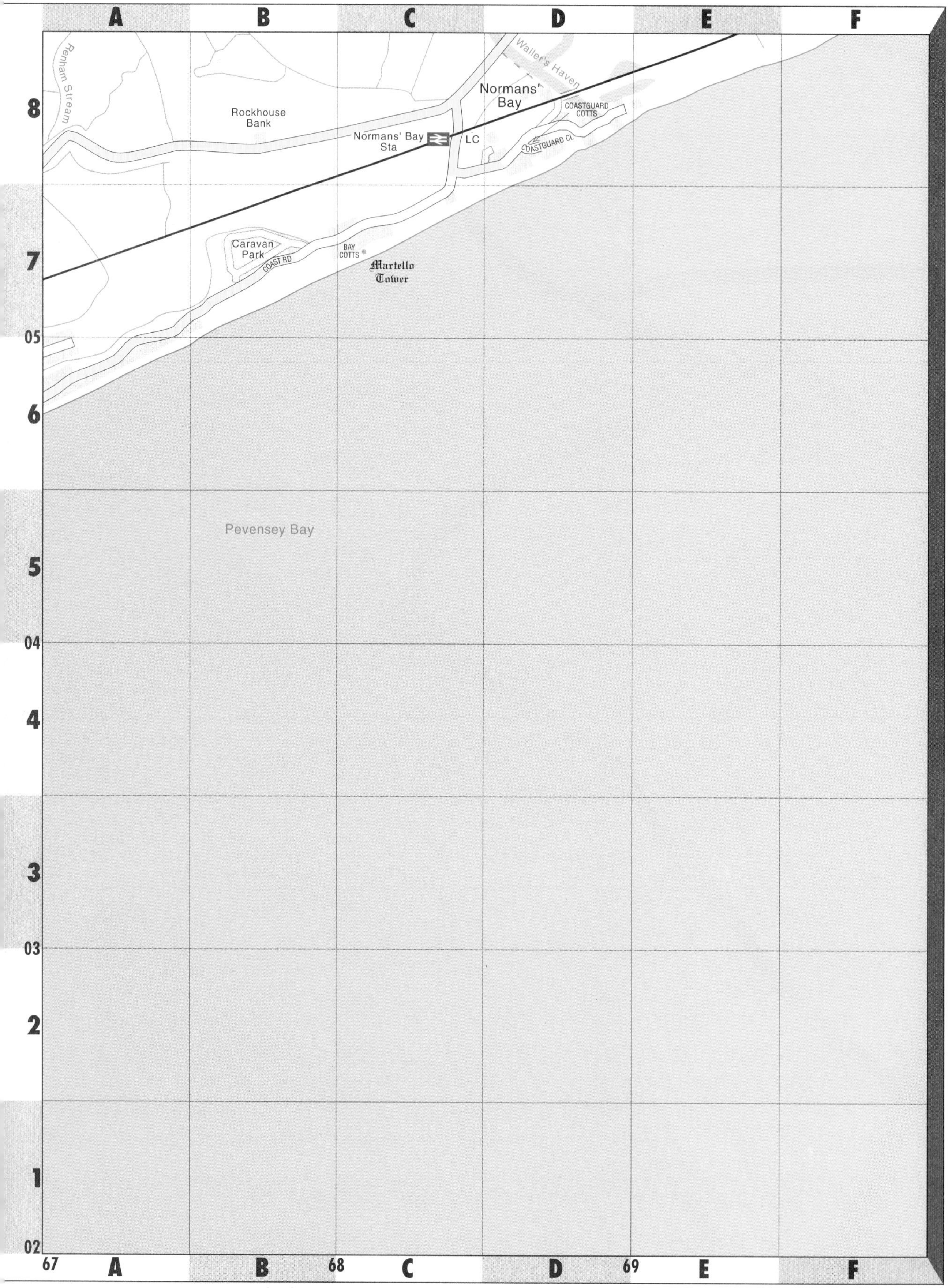
A
B
C
D
E
F
Renham Stream
Rockhouse Bank
Normans' Bay Sta
Waller's Haven
Normans' Bay
LC
COASTGUARD COTTS
COASTGUARD CL
Caravan Park
COAST RD
BAY COTTS
Martello Tower
Pevensey Bay
8
7
05
6
5
04
4
3
03
2
1
02
67
68
69

175

166 178

A B C D E F

8 Pickers Hill Farm Telscombe Tye

Nursery
Looes Barn
Coombe Bottom
Coombe Farm
7 WESTFIELD AVE
COOMBE VALE
WESTFIELD AVE S
WESTFIELD AVE N
STANMER AVE
COOMBE MEADOW
WESTFIELD RISE
COOMBE RISE
HOMEBUSH AVE

03
WIVELSFIELD RD
PERRY HILL
RIDGEWOOD AVE
166
VALE RD
HILGROVE RD
HEMPSTEAD RD
ARLINGTON GDNS
Tenant Hill

PALMEIRA AVE
TUMULUS RD
WINTON AVE
EDWARD AVE
HAILSHAM AVE
HAMSEY RD
COOMBE RISE

6 CHARLES CL
GORHAM AVE
DEAN COURT RD
LUSTRELLS RD
BISHOPSTONE DR
SAXON CL
CHILTINGTON WAY
EFFINGHAM CL
SALTDEAN VALE
MOUNT DR
Saltdean
Pedlersburgh
Saltdean City Prim Sch
GLYNDE AVE
GREENBANK AVE
RYE CL
IFIELD CL
FINDON

NORTHGATE RISE
CHALLONERS CL
Rottingdean
WHITEWAY LA
WESTMESTON AVE
CHORLEY AVE
LUSTRELLS CL
LUSTRELLS AVE
THEMOLA AVE
HAWTHORN
SHEPHAM AVE
1 SCHOOL LA
2 MAYFIELD CT
3 WESTBROOK
HOMEBUSH AVE
ROEDEAN CL
CISSBURY CRES
NORTHWOOD AVE
CHALEY AVE
LEWES
FINDON

TUDOR CL
Rottingdean CE Prim Sch
1 ST MARGARETS
2 HIGHCLIFF CT
3 KIPLING CT
FOUNTHILL RD
ASHDOWN AVE
FOUNTHILL AVE
SALTDEAN DR
CHICHESTER DR W
FOUNTHILL AVE
GLYNDEBOURNE AVE
BEVENDEAN AVE
HARTFIELD RD
Telscombe Tye

5 The Twitten
Steyning RD
NEWLANDS RD
CHAILEY AVE
KNOLE
GRAND CRES
The PARK
LENHAM AVE
CHICHESTER DR W
SALTDEAN PARK RD
ARUNDEL DR E
LINCHMERE AVE
OAKLANDS AVE
BARNING VALE
ASHURST AVE

A259
NEWLANDS RD
GREENWAY CT
LENHAM AVE RD W
CRANLEIGH AVE
EILEEN AVE
Saltdean Park
CHICHESTER DR E
WICKLANDS AVE
Telscombe Cliffs

HIGH ST
1 2
ROMNEY RD
THE CRES
Liby
ABBOTSBURY CL
SALTDEAN PARK RD
WITHYHAM AVE
BRAMBLETYNE AVE
SPRINGFIELD AVE
FAIRLIGHT CT

MARINE DR
MARINE CL
LYNWOOD RD
CROWBOROUGH RD
Homeridge Ho
HAMSEY RD
GORHAM WAY
HIGHVIEW RD
TYEDEAN RD
BROOMFIELD AVE
GRASSMERE AVE
CLIFF GDNS

02
CURZON HO 1
TEYNHAM HO 2
ROWANDEN CT 3
WALESBECK
NUTLEY AVE
CARDINGLY RD
COLVEN RD
TYE CL
GORHAM CT
AMHURST RD
OBLISKY
BUCKLEY
FAIRLIGHT AVE

4 THE GRANGE 1
MARTLET HO 2
REBA CT 3
SOUTH COAST RD
A259
TESCOMBE GRANGE
THE ESPLANADE
SUSSEX WAY
5/6 7

01
SEACLIFFE 1
FAIRHURST 2
TELSCOMBE CLIFFS WAY 3
AQUA CT 4
SUSSEX HO 5
MARINE CT 6
TUSCAN CT 7

2

1

00

178

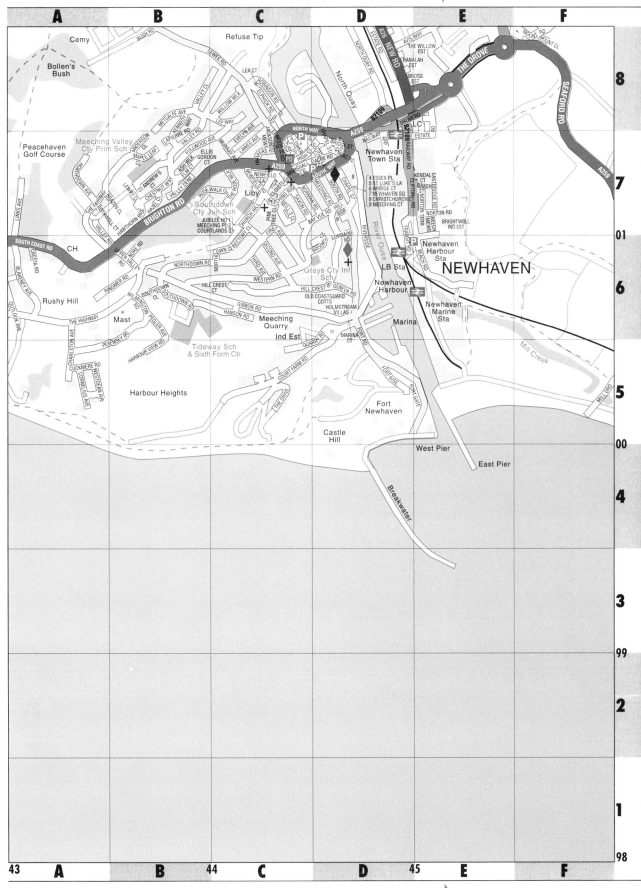

A B C D E F

8

Norton

Norton Farm

Blackstone Barn

Beacon Hill

Foxhole Farm

New Barn

Golf Course

Bullocks Barn

7

Stud Farm

Bishopstone Manor Farm

A259

SEAFORD RD

Rookery Hill

Bishopstone

GLENEAGLES CL
HOLMES CL
TROON CL
ELIZABETH CL
FREELAND CL
HURDIS RD
WINDSOR CL
HANOVER CL
ROSEMOUNT
ST JAMES RISE
MARGARET'S
VIKING CL
EDWARD
ROMAN CL
ANTONY CL
HARBOUR VIEW
ST ANDREWS DR
NORMAN CL
SEAGRAVE CL
MARINE DR
ROCKFORD WAY
ROOKERY WAY

CROWN HILL
THE LORDS
WHITEWAY CL
FLINT CL
DUCHESS DR
ROYAL DR
GORSE DR
CH
CHALVINGTON CL
LEXDEN DR
SEAGROVE WAY

Bowden House Sch
BOWDEN RISE
LUCORDA WAY
NORTH WAY
THE RIDINGS
OFFHAM CL

6

MILL DRO
LC

Pilgrims Sch
FIRLE RD
FIRLE GRANGE
THE HOLT
CHARTWELL CL
GRAND AVE

Newhaven RD

Tide Mills

5

HILL RISE

Motel

NEWHAVEN RD

BUCKLE BY-PASS

CLEMENTINE AVE
AUDREY CL
ISABEL CL
ELEANOR CL
KATHERINE WAY
ADELAIDE CL
ALEXANDRA CL
PRINCESS DR
CHURCHILL RD
CAROLINE CL
VICTOR CL
BEACON DR
BEACON CL

East Blatchington

FIRLE DR
THE BARN LA
ST PETER'S CL
ST ELIZABETH'S CL
NORTH CAMP LA
UPPER BELGRAVE RD
PINEWOOD CL
OLD BUCKLAND
NORTHFIELD CL
HOLTERS WAY
LOWER DR
BELGRAVE
LEXDEN RD

00

STATION RD
HAWTH HILL
HAWTH GR
HAWTH RISE
HAWTH PARK RD
HAWTH CRES
HAWTH CL
DUKES CL
CHARLES CL
KINGS RIDE
KINGS MEAD LA
KINGS MEAD
KINGSWAY
CARLTON RD
KINGSMEAD
KINGSMEAD WAY
BUCKINGHAM CL
HAMILTON HO
CARLTON CL
BELGRAVE RD
REGENT CL
FIRLE CL
ALCE'S DR
KIM CL
MORNINGSIDE CL
HOMEFIELD
MASON RD
ROSE WALK
ST BARNABAS CL
CHAPEL CL
WILKINSON WAY
FOSTER CL
BLATCHINGTON HILL
SHERWOOD CL
SHERWOOD RD
VALE RD
THE BYEWAYS
OLD BEN HOMES
NORTHCLIFFE

Buckle Caravan & Camping Park

Bishopstone Sta

Sunnyside Caravan Site

HAWTH PARK RD

Seaford Cty Prim Sch
CHICHESTER CL
SUTTON DRO
PONDSYDE CT
GLEBE CL
PO
SUTTON AVE
PARKSIDE RD
MILLFIELD
OLD ALBANY RD
GLEBE CL

4

MARINE PAR
KIMBERLEY RD
QUEENS PARK GDNS
BUCKLE
BUCKLE RISE
BUCKLE DR
SURREY RD
SURREY CL
BISHOPS
WESTDOWN RD
ASHLEIGH CL
GLEBE RD
WILTON
GROSVENOR RD
BEACON RD
SALISBURY RD
CHICHESTER RD
CHESTERTON RD
BLATCHINGTON RD
GROVE RD
GILREDGE RD
STAFFORD RD

SUTTON RD A259
HIGHLANDS RD
SUTTON PARK RD
CORNFIELD RD
MIDDLE RD
SOUTHDOWN RD

3

ALBANY RD
CONNAUGHT RD
EDINBURGH CT
PARK RD
CLAREMONT RD
BEAME CT
ST CRISPIANS
BEACH
STATION APP
i
BROOKLYN RD
VICARAGE CL
GUARDSWELL PL
CORNFIELD PL
BAINBRIDGE LA
HEATHFIELD RD

Libry
SUTTON PARK RD

1 HOMETYE HO
2 ST CRISPIANS CT

Recn Gd

Seaford Sta
RICHMOND RD
DANNFIELDS HO
DANE RD
GREEN LA
HIGH ST
CLINTON PLACE
PO
CHURCH
SOUTH ST
WEST ST
BRAMBER LA
DEAN RD

99

SEAFORD

Seaford Bay

DANE CL
WEST VIEW
CROUCH
GRAND
DANE HTS
PELHAM CT
CHATHAM PL
PELHAM YD
STEYNE RD
THE STEYNE
CORSICA RD
LIONS PL
MAURICE RD
GERALD RD
THE CLOSE

2

WEST VIEW
ESPLANADE
BRAKE
STEYNE
PINNER PL
MARINE CRES
THE COVERS
FRICKTFIELD RD
COLLEGE RD

Seaford Head Com Coll (Lower)

FITZGERALD PK
FITZGERALD AVE
CLIFF GDNS
CLIFF RD

Vanguard Way

Martello Tower Mus

CORSICA RD

E2
1 THE BOUNDARY
2 CUNNINGHAM CT
3 MALLETT CL
4 GRANVILLE CT
5 THE CAUSEWAY
6 RAYFORD CT
7 STRATHENDEN CT
8 WEST VIEW CT
9 STEYNE CT
10 DANE HTS
11 PELHAM CT
12 CHATHAM PL
13 THE HIGH SH HALL
14 PELHAM YD
15 TALLAND PAR

1

Groyne

98

46 A 47 B C 47 D 48 E F

C4
1 HAWTH VALLEY CT
2 SELMESTON CT
3 OFFHAM CT
4 LITLINGTON CT
5 RODMELL CT

E3
1 RICHMOND TERR
2 CLINTON LA
3 WELBECK CT
4 SUTTON CROFT LA
5 FITZGERALD HO
6 CROFT CT

F2
1 KINGSFOLD CT
2 CROUCHFIELD CL
3 BRAMBER CL
4 STEYNE CL

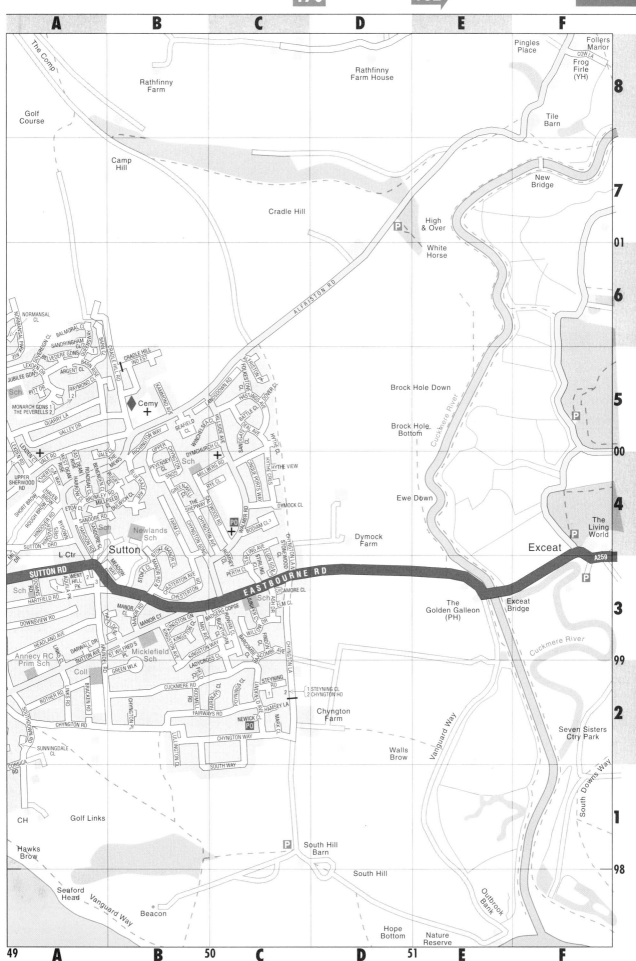

170   182

A   **B**   **C**   **D**   **E**   **F**

Winchester's Pond

Fore Down

Oldkiln Bottom

Lullington Heath
National Nature Reserve

8

Litlington

The Combe

PO

PH

CLAPHAM LA

Clapham
House

Clay Bottom

Oakmere River

Chamber's
Court

7

Clapham
Barn

01

Vanguard Way
South Downs Way

6

Charleston Manor

Long Brow

Charleston Manor
Gardens

Charleston Bottom

5

Snap
Hill

00

Beggar's Croft

Vanguard Way

4

Westdean

A259

Middle Brow

3

Friston Forest

Friston Hill

Exceat Hill

New Barn

Combe
Bottom

Sewage Works

99

South Downs Way

Newbarn Bottom

2

Friston
Place

Seven Sisters
Country Park

Scabs Island

Friston Bottom

Foxhole

Exceat
New Barn

1

Visitor
Centre

Foxhole Bottom

Newbarn Hill

A259

Hard Link

South Hill

98

52   **A**   **B**   53   **C**   **D**   54   **E**   **F**

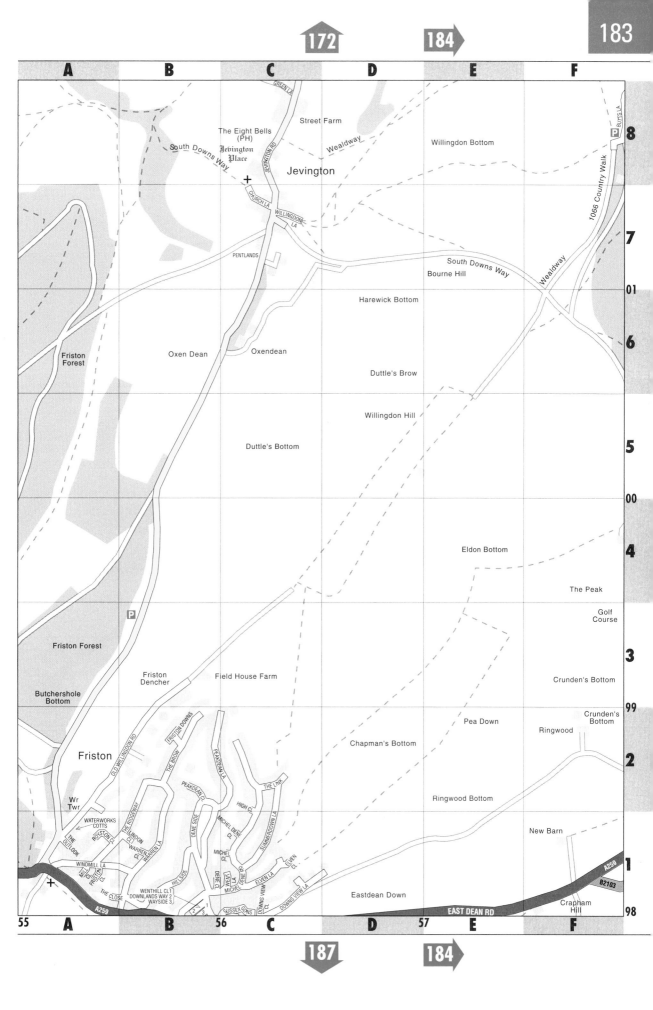

A B C D E F

GREEN LA

Street Farm

The Eight Bells
(PH)

Wealdway

Willingdon Bottom

South Downs Way

Jevington
Place

Jevington

BUTTS LA

P

1066 Country Walk

CHURCH LA

WILLINGDON
LA

PENTLANDS

South Downs Way

Bourne Hill

Wealdway

Harewick Bottom

Friston
Forest

Oxen Dean

Oxendean

Duttle's Brow

Willingdon Hill

Duttle's Bottom

Eldon Bottom

The Peak

Golf
Course

P

Friston Forest

Friston
Dencher

Field House Farm

Crunden's Bottom

Butchershole
Bottom

Crunden's
Bottom

Pea Down

Ringwood

Friston

FRISTON DOWNS

OLD WILLINGDON RD

THE BROW

PEAKDEAN LA

THE LINK

Chapman's Bottom

Ringwood Bottom

New Barn

A259

B2103

Wr
Twr

WATERWORKS
COTTS

THE LUNDON
CL

ROLSTON CL

THE RIDGEWAY

PEAKDEAN LA

DENE SIDE

HIGH CL

MICHEL DENE
CL

SUMMERDOWN LA

THE
OUTLOOK

WARREN
CL

WARREN LA

HILLSIDE

MICHEL
CL

DENER
CL

WEKT
LA

ELVEN LA

ELVEN
CL

DOWNS VIEW LA

WINDMILL LA

MILL CL

FRISTON CL

THE CLOSE

WENTHILL CL 1
DOWNLANDS WAY 2
WAYSIDE 3

SUSSEX GDNS

1
2
3

MICHEL
LA

TO PETER

DOWNS VIEW
CL

Eastdean Down

EAST DEAN RD

Crapham
Hill

183
173

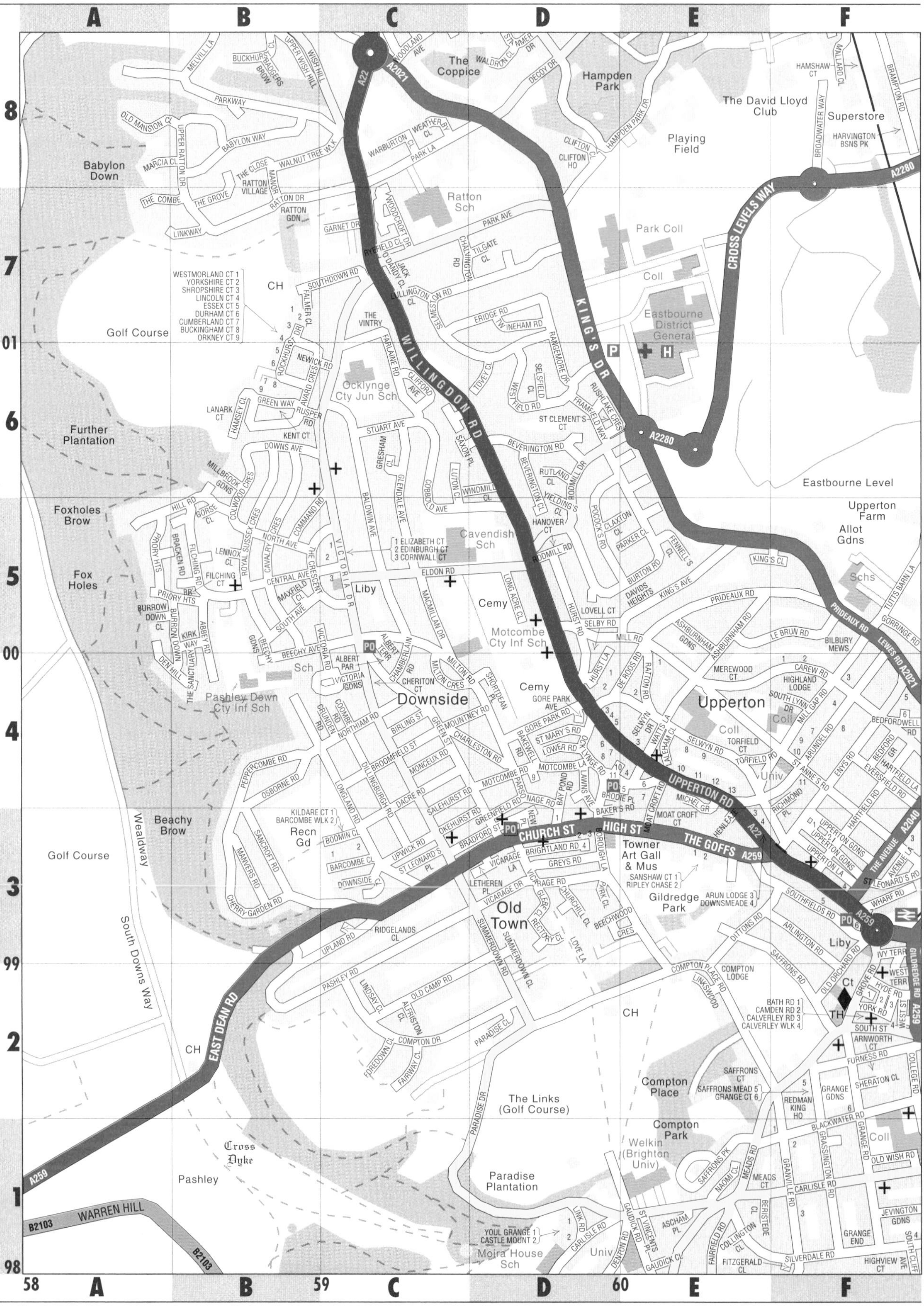
The Coppice
Hampden Park
The David Lloyd Club
Superstore
Playing Field
Babylon Down
Ratton Sch
Park Coll
Coll
Eastbourne District General
CROSS LEVELS WAY
KING'S DR
WILLINGDON RD
Golf Course
Ocklynge Cty Jun Sch
Further Plantation
Eastbourne Level
Foxholes Brow
Upperton Farm
Allot Gdns
Fox Holes
Cavendish Sch
Liby
Cemy
Motcombe Cty Inf Sch
Pashley Down Cty Inf Sch
Downside
Upperton
UPPERTON RD
Beachy Brow
Recn Gd
CHURCH ST
HIGH ST
THE GOFFS
Towner Art Gall & Mus
Gildredge Park
Old Town
South Downs Way
Wealdway
EAST DEAN RD
Compton Place
Compton Park
The Links (Golf Course)
Welkin (Brighton Univ)
Cross Dyke
Pashley
Paradise Plantation
WARREN HILL
Moira House Sch
Univ

183
188

D3
1 CHURCH LA
2 ST MARY'S CT
3 ST MARY'S CNR
4 ST MARY'S COTTS
D4
1 OCKLYNGE AVE
2 KINGSMERE CT
3 SHERBORNE CT
4 FARNOL HO
5 ARLINGTON HO
6 SELMESTON HO
7 JEVINGTON HO
8 CHALVINGTON HO
9 OLD MOTCOMBE MEWS
10 PROSPECT GDNS
11 CROWN ST
E4
1 ST HELENA'S CT
2 COLVILLE CT
3 LULLINGTON HO
4 RUSSELL COTTS
5 STAR RD
6 NEW UPPERTON RD
7 CROWNE HO
8 SELWYN PARK CT
9 SELWYN HO
10 SOUTH VIEW
11 THE CHANTRY
12 HAMILTON HO
13 THE LIMES
F1
1 PRIORY CT
2 GRANVILLE CT
3 CHELMSFORD CT
4 SOUTHDOWN HO
F3
1 BERNARD LA
2 BEATRICE LA
3 HOMEGATE HO
4 HADLEY HO
5 SOUTHFIELDS CT
6 STAFFORD HO
7 STATION PAR
F4
1 CAREW LODGE
2 CAREW VIEWS
3 HIGH TREES
4 ABBOT'S LODGE
5 LEWES HO
6 THE CONIFERS
7 FITZALAN HO
8 ARUNDEL KEEP
9 ELMWOOD
10 BELVEDERE CT
11 GLENTHORNE HO

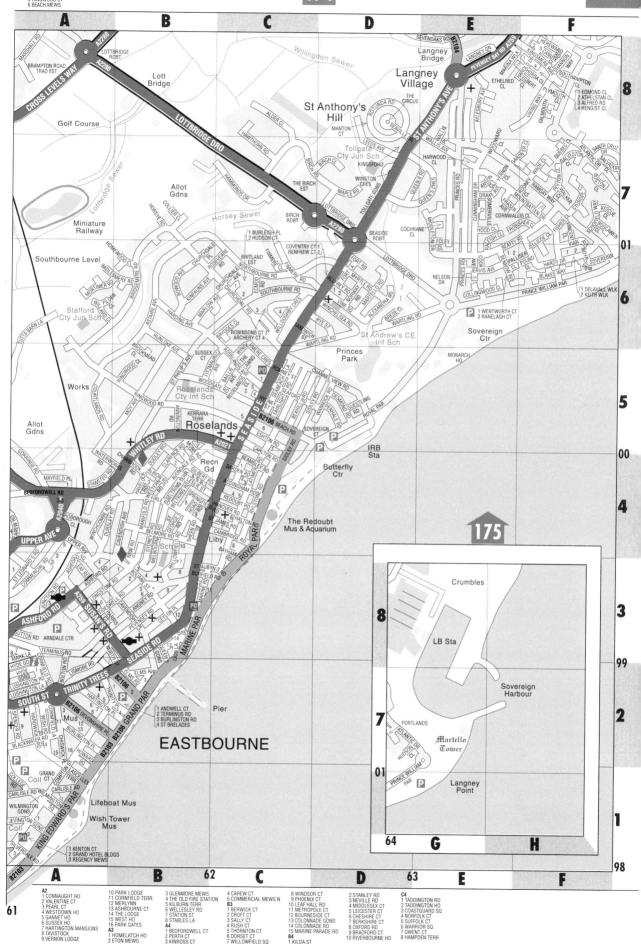

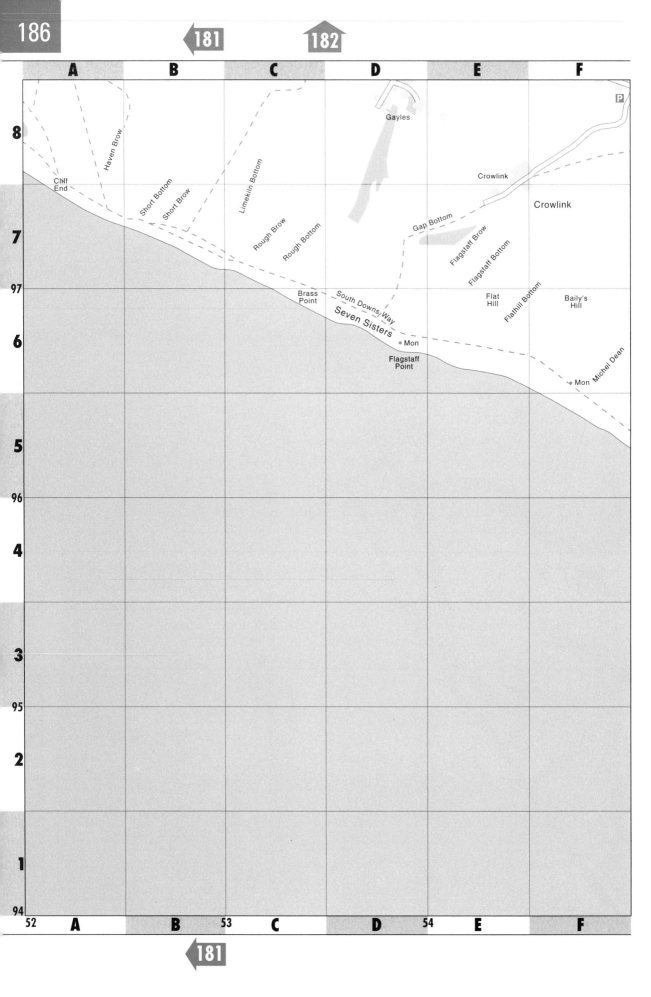

181
182
181

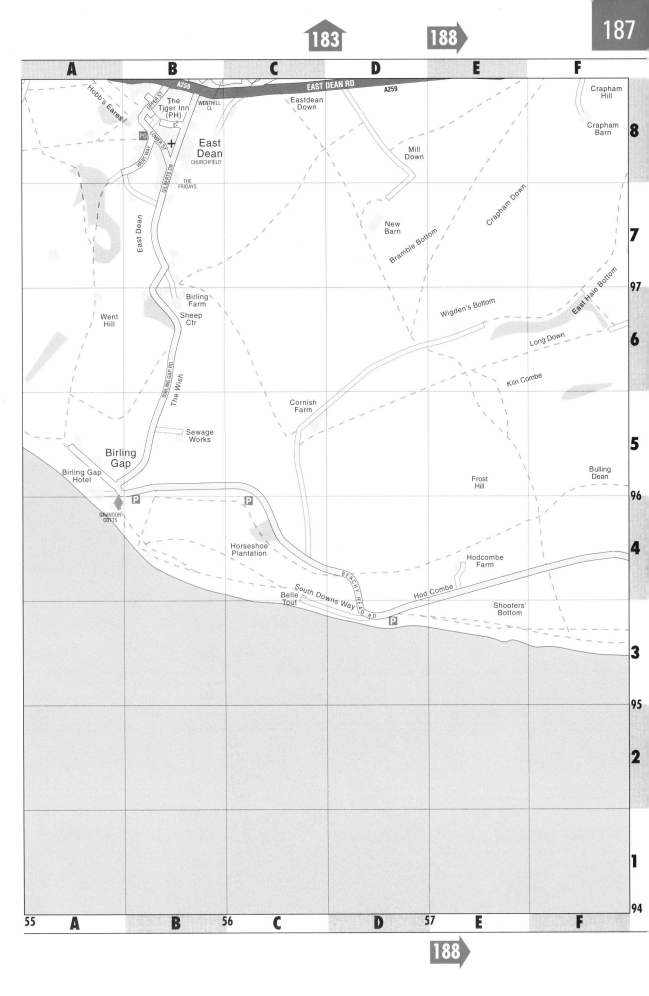

EAST DEAN RD

A259

A259

Hobb's Eares

Crapham Hill

UPPER ST

WENTHILL CL

Eastdean Down

Crapham Barn

8

The Tiger Inn (PH)

PO

LOWER ST

East Dean CHURCHFIELD

Mill Down

WENT WAY

GILBERT'S DR

THE FRIDAYS

New Barn

Crapham Down

7

East Dean

Bramble Bottom

97

Birling Farm

Wigden's Bottom

East Hale Bottom

Sheep Ctr

Long Down

6

Went Hill

BIRLING GAP RD

Kiln Combe

The Wish

Cornish Farm

5

Sewage Works

Frost Hill

Bulling Dean

Birling Gap

96

Birling Gap Hotel

P

P

GRANDON COTTS

Horseshoe Plantation

Hodcombe Farm

4

BEACHY HEAD RD

Hod Combe

Shooters' Bottom

South Downs Way

Belle Tout

P

3

95

2

1

94

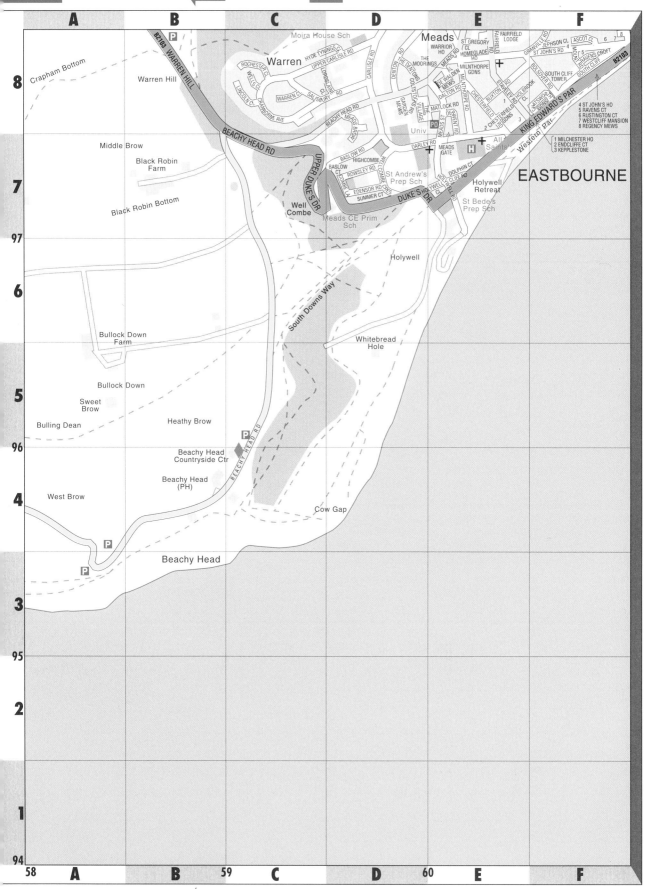

A B C D E F

8
7
97
6
5
96
4
3
95
2
1
94

Crapham Bottom

Warren Hill

Middle Brow

Black Robin Farm

Black Robin Bottom

Well Combe

Bullock Down Farm

Bullock Down

Sweet Brow

Bulling Dean

Heathy Brow

Beachy Head Countryside Ctr

Beachy Head (PH)

West Brow

Beachy Head

South Downs Way

Holywell

Whitebread Hole

Cow Gap

Warren

Moira House Sch

Meads

Univ

EASTBOURNE

St Andrew's Prep Sch

Meads CE Prim Sch

Meads Gate

Holywell Retreat

St Bede's Prep Sch

Holywell

King Edward's Par

Western Par

Fairfield Lodge

South Cliff Tower

St Gregory Homeglade

4 ST JOHN'S HO
5 RAVENS CT
6 RUSTINGTON CT
7 WESTCLIFF MANSION
8 REGENCY MEWS

1 MILCHESTER HO
2 ENDCLIFFE CT
3 KEPPLESTONE

BEACHY HEAD RD

WARREN HILL

UPPER DUKE'S DR

DUKE'S DR

B2103

B2103

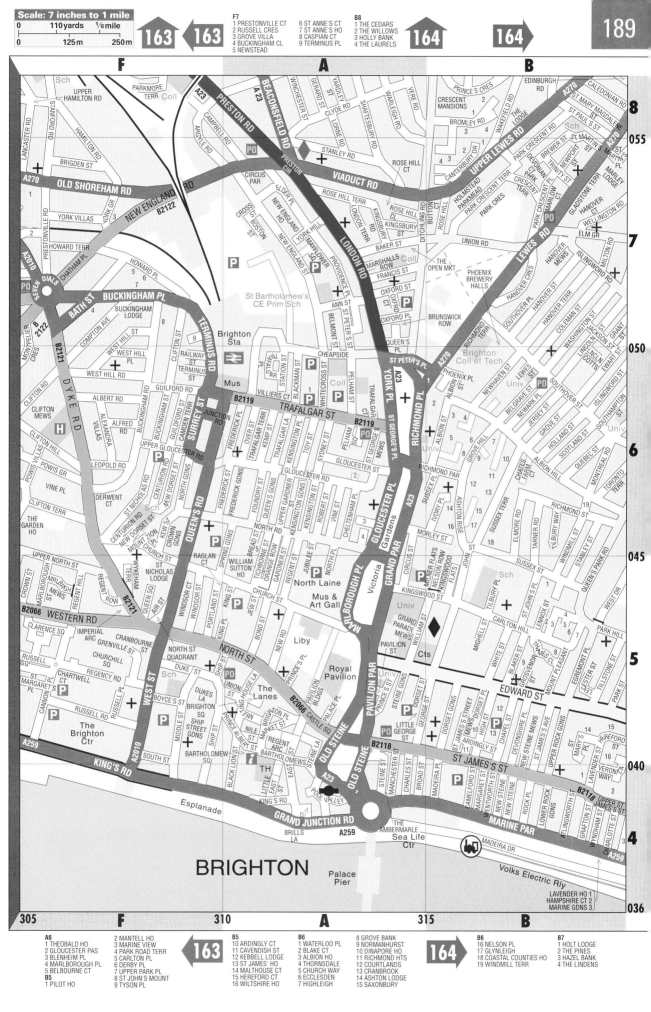

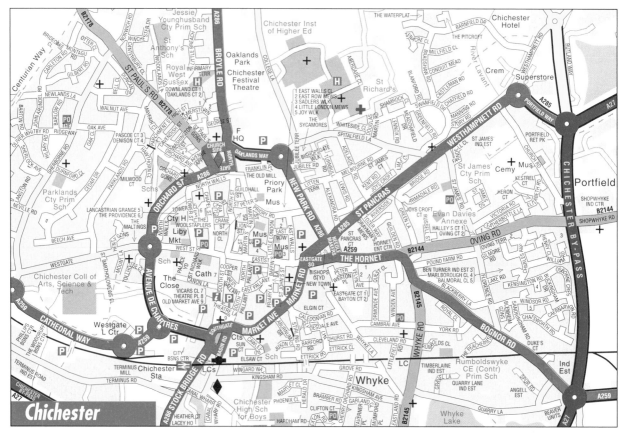

Chichester

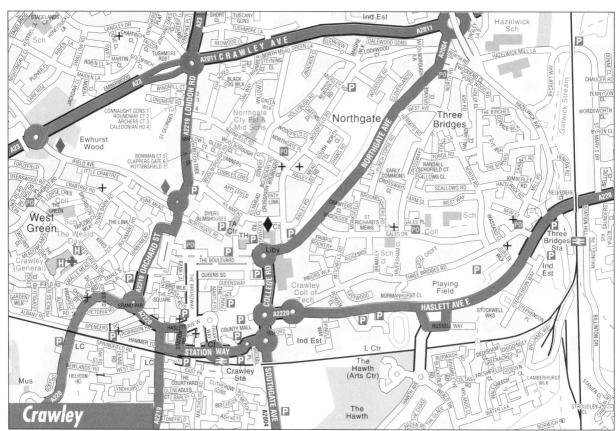

Crawley

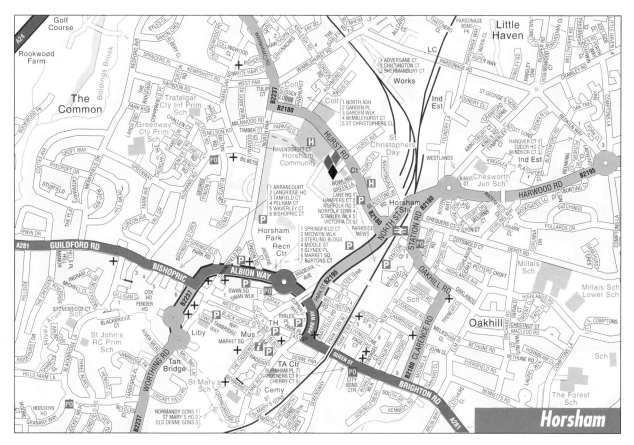

Horsham

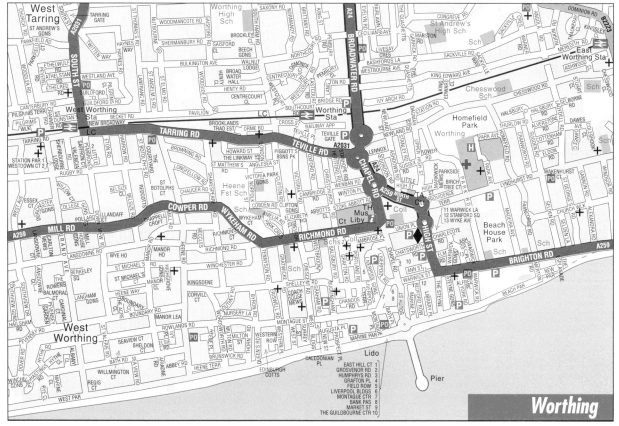

Worthing

Street names are listed alphabetically and show the locality, the Postcode District, the page number and a reference to the square in which the name falls on the map page

Neville Rd 3 Eastbourne BN22 . **185** B4

Full street name
This may have been abbreviated on the map

Location Number
If present, this indicates the street's position on a congested area of the map instead of the name

Town, village or locality in which the street falls.

Postcode District for the street name

Page number of the map on which the street name appears

Grid square in which the centre of the street falls

Schools, hospitals, sports centres, railway stations, shopping centres, industrial estates, public amenities and other places of interest are also listed. These are highlighted in magenta

Abbreviations used in the index

App **Approach**	Cl **Close**	Ent **Enterprise**	La **Lane**	Rdbt **Roundabout**
Arc **Arcade**	Comm **Common**	Espl **Esplanade**	N **North**	S **South**
Ave **Avenue**	Cnr **Corner**	Est **Estate**	Orch **Orchard**	Sq **Square**
Bvd **Boulevard**	Cotts **Cottages**	Gdns **Gardens**	Par **Parade**	Strs **Stairs**
Bldgs **Buildings**	Ct **Court**	Gn **Green**	Pk **Park**	Stps **Steps**
Bsns Pk **Business Park**	Ctyd **Courtyard**	Gr **Grove**	Pas **Passage**	St **Street, Saint**
Bsns Ctr **Business Centre**	Cres **Crescent**	Hts **Heights**	Pl **Place**	Terr **Terrace**
Bglws **Bungalows**	Dr **Drive**	Ho **House**	Prec **Precinct**	Trad Est **Trading Estate**
Cswy **Causeway**	Dro **Drove**	Ind Est **Industrial Estate**	Prom **Promenade**	Wlk **Walk**
Ctr **Centre**	E **East**	Intc **Interchange**	Ret Pk **Retail Park**	W **West**
Cir **Circus**	Emb **Embankment**	Junc **Junction**	Rd **Road**	Yd **Yard**

Abberton Field BN6 .... **97** B5
Abbey Cl BN10 .... **167** C1
Abbey Ct TN33 .... **112** D4
Abbey Dr TN38 .... **158** B5
Abbey Path BN27 .... **129** C2
Abbey Rd Brighton BN2 .... **164** D4
Eastbourne BN20 .... **184** B5
Abbey View TN40 .... **157** D6
Abbey Way TN33 .... **112** D5
Abbeyfield Ho **1** RH26 .... **170** F3
Abbot's Lodge **4** BN21 .... **184** E4
Abbots Cl Battle TN33 .... **112** F3
Hassocks BN6 .... **97** E4
Abbotsbury Cl BN2 .... **177** B5
Abbotsfield Ct TN34 .... **136** F3
Abbotsford Sch RH15 .... **72** E6
Abbotts **20** BN1 .... **163** E5
Aberdale Rd BN26 .... **173** C6
Aberdeen Rd BN2 .... **164** C8
Abergavenny Ho **1** BN3 .... **163** D6
Abergavenny Rd BN7 .... **123** B1
Abigail Ho **10** RH16 .... **50** E4
Abinger Pl BN7 .... **123** C1
Abinger Rd
Portslade-by-Sea BN41 .... **162** B8
Woodingdean BN2 .... **165** E6
Acacia Ave BN3 .... **141** F1
Acacia Ct BN1 .... **142** F2
Acacia Rd Eastbourne BN22 .... **173** D2
Newhaven BN9 .... **168** A4
Acer Ave TN2 .... **17** C8
Acorn Cl East Grinstead RH19 .... **10** E8
Hastings TN34 .... **136** C4
Acorn Gn **3** BN27 .... **129** B1
Acorn Way TN19 .... **45** A3
Acorns The TN5 .... **42** F6
Acre Cl RH16 .... **50** D2
Acres Rise TN5 .... **31** E1
Adam Ct TN38 .... **135** F4
Adams Cl BN1 .... **143** B2
Adams La TN31 .... **66** D2
Adastra Ave BN6 .... **98** A4
Addingham Rd BN22 .... **185** C4
Addington Cl TN38 .... **158** F7
Addison Rd BN1, BN3 .... **163** E7
Adelaide Cl BN25 .... **180** E5
Adelaide Cres BN3 .... **163** C5
Adelaide Rd TN37, TN38 .... **136** B3
Adelaide Sq BN43 .... **161** B7
Ades Field BN26 .... **171** F6
Admiral's Bridge La RH19 .... **10** C2
Adur Ct **10** BN43 .... **161** C8
Adur Dr
Shoreham-by-Sea BN43 .... **161** A7
Stone Cross BN24 .... **174** A5
Adur Rd RH15 .... **73** C4
Agincourt TN37, TN38 .... **135** F7
Agnes St BN2 .... **164** C7
Ainsworth Ave BN6 .... **165** D3
Ainsworth Cl BN2 .... **165** D3
Ainsworth Ho **1** BN2 .... **164** C7
Air St BN1 .... **189** F5
Airy Rd BN27 .... **131** B2

Alan Ct **6** TN37 .... **159** C7
Alan Way BN2 .... **164** F5
Albany Ct **3** TN34 .... **159** F7
Albany Hill TN2 .... **8** C5
Albany Mansions TN38 .... **159** B8
Albany Mews BN3 .... **163** B6
Albany Rd Bexhill TN40 .... **157** C3
Hastings TN38 .... **159** B7
Seaford BN25 .... **180** C3
Albany Villas Cuckfield RH17 .... **50** A6
Hove BN3 .... **163** B6
Albert Cl RH16 .... **51** A4
Albert Cotts TN1 .... **8** B4
Albert Dr RH15 .... **72** E2
Albert Mews **24** BN3 .... **163** C6
Albert Par BN21 .... **184** C4
Albert Pl BN26 .... **173** A7
Albert Rd Bexhill TN40 .... **157** C3
Brighton BN1 .... **189** F6
Hastings TN34 .... **159** F7
Polegate BN26 .... **173** A7
Uckfield TN22 .... **78** D6
Albert St TN1 .... **8** B4
Albert Terr BN21 .... **184** C5
Albion Ct RH15 .... **72** F2
Albion Hill BN2 .... **189** B6
Albion Ho **3** Brighton BN2 .... **189** B6
Southwick BN42 .... **161** F7
Albion La **4** TN34 .... **160** A3
Albion Rd Eastbourne BN22 .... **185** B4
Royal Tunbridge Wells TN1 .... **8** C5
Albion St Brighton BN2 .... **189** B6
8 Lewes BN7 .... **123** D1
Portslade-by-Sea BN41 .... **162** B7
Southwick BN42 .... **161** E7
Albourne Cl Brighton BN2 .... **164** F7
Hastings TN38 .... **158** F8
Alces Pl BN25 .... **180** E5
Aldborough Rd TN37 .... **136** C1
Alder Cl Eastbourne BN23 .... **185** C8
Hastings TN37 .... **136** C5
Heathfield TN21 .... **82** A5
Alderbrook Cl TN6 .... **38** A6
Alderbrook Cotts TN6 .... **38** A7
Alderbrook Path TN6 .... **38** A6
Alderbrook Way TN6 .... **38** A6
Alders Ave RH19 .... **1** E3
Alders View Dr RH19 .... **1** E3
Alderton Ct TN39 .... **157** B3
Aldervale Cotts TN6 .... **38** A7
Aldrich Cl BN2 .... **164** F6
Aldrington Ave BN3 .... **163** A8
Aldrington CE Fst Sch BN3 .... **162** F7
Aldrington CE Prim Sch BN3 .... **142** A2
Aldrington House (Hospl) BN3 .... **162** F6
Aldrington Pl BN3 .... **162** D8
Aldrington Sta BN3 .... **163** A8
Alexander Dr TN39 .... **156** E4
Alexandra Cl BN25 .... **180** E5

Alexandra Ct TN37 .... **136** C2
Alexandra Rd
Burgess Hill RH15 .... **73** C2
Eastbourne BN22 .... **185** D6
Hastings TN37 .... **159** C8
Heathfield TN21 .... **82** B6
Mayfield TN20 .... **40** C3
Uckfield TN22 .... **78** D6
Alexandra Terr TN20 .... **40** C3
Alexandra The TN37 .... **159** D7
Alexandra Villas BN1 .... **189** F6
Alford Way TN40 .... **157** E6
Alfray Rd TN40 .... **158** A5
Alfred Rd Brighton BN1 .... **189** F6
Eastbourne BN23 .... **185** F8
Hastings TN35 .... **137** D3
Alfred St TN37, TN38 .... **159** C7
Alfriston Cl Bexhill TN39 .... **156** C6
Brighton BN2 .... **164** F6
Eastbourne BN20 .... **184** C2
Alfriston Cty Prim Sch BN26 .... **170** F4
Alfriston Pk BN25 .... **181** C5
Alfriston Rd BN25, BN26 .... **181** D6
Alice Bright La TN6 .... **37** F7
Alice St BN3 .... **163** D5
All Saint's Cres TN34 .... **160** B4
All Saints CE Prim Sch TN39 . **157** B7
All Saints Gdns TN21 .... **81** F7
All Saints' Hospl BN20 .... **188** E7
All Saints Jun Sch TN35 .... **160** C6
All Saints La TN39 .... **157** B7
All Saints Rd TN4 .... **8** B6
All Saints Rise TN4 .... **8** A6
All Saints' St TN34 .... **160** B4
Allan Cl TN4 .... **7** C4
Allandale Rd TN2 .... **8** D7
Allards TN35 .... **138** C8
Allegria Ct TN38 .... **159** B7
Allen Rd RH16 .... **51** A4
Allen Way TN40 .... **157** F7
Allen's Cl RH19 .... **11** D6
Allfrey Rd BN22 .... **185** D6
Allfreys La TN6 .... **37** D6
Allington Cres BN8 .... **76** C7
Allington La BN7 .... **122** D7
Allington Rd BN8 .... **76** C6
Allwood Cres RH17 .... **74** C4
Alma Rd RH16 .... **51** B8
Alma Terr TN37 .... **136** C2
Alma Villas TN37 .... **136** C2
Almonry Fields TN33 .... **112** B4
Alpine Rd Hastings TN34 .... **160** A4
Hove BN3 .... **162** F8
Alverstone Cl BN23 .... **174** B4
Amanda Cl TN40 .... **157** F7
Ambassadors The **6** BN3 .... **163** C6
Amber Ct **17** Hove BN3 .... **163** C6
8 Hove BN3 .... **163** D7
Amberleaze Dr TN2 .... **9** D6
Amberley Cl Burgess Hill RH15 .... **73** A5
Haywards Heath RH16 .... **50** D4
Hove BN3 .... **141** E3
Amberley Ct TN4 .... **8** C8

Amberley Dr BN3 .... **141** E3
Amberley Lodge BN2 .... **189** A7
Amberley Rd BN22 .... **173** C1
Ambermarle The BN2 .... **189** A4
Amberstone BN27 .... **129** E3
Amberstone Cl TN34 .... **137** A4
Amberstone Hospl BN27 .... **129** E4
Amberstone View BN27 .... **129** C2
Ambleside Ave BN10 .... **178** A8
Ambleside Cl BN10 .... **178** A7
America La RH16 .... **51** A5
Amesbury Cres BN3 .... **162** E7
Amherst Cl TN37 .... **136** D1
Amherst Cres BN3 .... **162** F8
Amherst Gdns TN34 .... **136** D1
Amherst Rd Bexhill TN40 .... **157** C4
Hastings TN34, TN37 .... **136** D1
Royal Tunbridge Wells TN4 .... **8** A5
Amhurst Rd BN10 .... **177** F3
Anchor Field BN8 .... **124** D5
Anchor Hill RH17 .... **52** A2
Anchor La BN8 .... **102** B5
Anderida Ct TN39 .... **156** C4
Anderida Rd BN22 .... **173** C3
Anderson Cl BN9 .... **179** B7
Andrew Rd TN4 .... **8** C8
Andrews Cl
Northbridge Street TN32 .... **64** C5
Royal Tunbridge Wells TN2 .... **8** D5
Andros Cl BN8 .... **100** E6
Andwell St BN21 .... **185** B2
Angel Row TN18 .... **47** B5
Angel Terr TN18 .... **47** B6
Angela Cl TN40 .... **157** F7
Anglesea Terr TN37, TN38 .... **159** C8
Anglesey Ave BN27 .... **129** A2
Angmering Ct BN1 .... **143** F5
Angus Cl BN20 .... **173** B1
Ann Cl BN6 .... **98** A5
Ann St Brighton BN1 .... **189** A7
Hastings TN34 .... **160** C6
Anne's Path **10** BN7 .... **146** C8
Annecy RC Prim Sch BN25 .... **181** A2
Annington Rd BN22 .... **185** B5
Anscombe **5** RH16 .... **50** D6
Anson Cl BN23 .... **185** E7
Anson Ho BN10 .... **167** C1
Ansty Cl BN2 .... **164** E5
Antares Path BN27 .... **152** E7
Antioch St BN7 .... **146** C8
Antony Cl BN25 .... **180** B6
Antrim Ct BN23 .... **174** D1
Antrona Cl TN39 .... **156** C3
Anvil Cl BN41 .... **141** B2
Anvil Ct TN37 .... **136** C5
Anzac Cl BN10 .... **167** C1
Apex Pk BN27 .... **152** A7
Apple Tree La TN1, TN2 .... **8** D8
Appledene Cnr BN8 .... **100** E7
Appledore Cl BN23 .... **174** D2
Appledore Ct RH16 .... **51** A7
Appledore Gdns RH16 .... **51** A6
Appledore Rd BN2 .... **143** F4

Applesham Ave BN3 .... **141** E2
Applesham Way BN41 .... **141** A1
Applewood Cl TN37 .... **136** B5
Approach The
2 Brighton BN1 .... **142** E3
Dormans Park RH19 .... **1** F6
April Pl **2** TN40 .... **157** C4
Apsley St TN4 .... **7** D4
Aqua Ct BN10 .... **177** F3
Aquarius Cl BN10 .... **178** C6
Aquila Pk BN25 .... **181** A3
Arbor Ct **8** RH16 .... **50** E5
Arbourvale TN38 .... **136** A1
Archers Ct TN34 .... **136** F6
Archery Ct Eastbourne BN22 .... **185** C6
3 Hastings TN38 .... **159** B6
Archery Rd TN38 .... **159** B7
Archery Wlk BN27 .... **152** C6
Archie Ct **7** TN38 .... **159** B6
Ardingly Ct **10** BN2 .... **189** B5
Ardingly Rd BN2 .... **177** D4
Ardingly St BN2 .... **189** B5
Argent Cl BN25 .... **181** A5
Argos Hill Rd TN20, TN6 .... **39** D4
Argyle Rd BN1 .... **189** F8
Argyll Ct BN22 .... **173** E2
Arkendale RH19 .... **1** A4
Arkwright Rd BN22 .... **174** A1
Arlington Cres BN1 .... **143** E5
Arlington Gdns BN2 .... **177** D6
Arlington Ho **5** BN21 .... **184** D4
Arlington Rd BN21 .... **184** F3
Arlington Rd E BN27 .... **152** A6
Arlington Rd W BN27 .... **151** F6
Arlington Resr BN26 .... **150** C3
Armstrong Cl TN38 .... **135** E4
Arnbury Mews TN38 .... **158** E6
Arndale Ctr BN21 .... **185** A3
Arnold St BN2 .... **164** C7
Arnside Rd TN38 .... **158** E6
Arnworth Ct BN21 .... **184** F2
Arran Cl BN27 .... **129** A2
Arthur Bliss Ho RH16 .... **51** A8
Arthur Rd TN39 .... **157** B4
Arthur St BN3 .... **163** A8
Arts Rd BN1 .... **144** B7
Arun Ct **13** BN43 .... **161** C8
Arun Lodge BN1 .... **184** E3
Arun Path TN22 .... **55** E1
Arun Way BN24, BN26 .... **173** F5
Arundel Cl Beachlands BN24 .... **175** F6
Hailsham BN27 .... **129** C2
Shoreham-by-Sea BN43 .... **161** C8
Arundel Ct **6** Brighton BN2 .... **164** E4
Burgess Hill RH15 .... **72** F4
14 Shoreham-by-Sea BN43 .... **161** C8
Arundel Dr E BN2 .... **177** C5
Arundel Dr W BN2 .... **177** C5
Arundel Keep **8** BN21 .... **184** F4
Arundel Mews **10** BN2 .... **164** E4
Arundel Pl BN2 .... **164** E3
Arundel Rd Brighton BN2 .... **164** E4
Eastbourne BN21 .... **184** F4

Arundel Rd Newhaven BN9 ...... 168 F1
Peacehaven BN10 ...... 178 D7
Royal Tunbridge Wells TN1 ...... 8 B2
Seaford BN25 ...... 181 A3
Arundel Rd W BN10 ...... 178 B7
Arundel Road Central BN10 ... 178 B7
Arundel St BN2 ...... 164 E3
Arundel Terr BN2 ...... 164 E3
Arundell Gn BN7 ...... 123 B2
Ascham Pl BN20 ...... 184 E1
Ascot Cl BN20 ...... 188 F8
Ascot Mews TN38 ...... 159 A8
Ash Cl Eastbourne BN22 ...... 173 E3
Hove BN3 ...... 142 C3
Royal Tunbridge Wells TN2 ...... 17 D7
Ash Ct Hailsham BN27 ...... 152 A7
Southwick BN42 ...... 140 F1
Ash Dr BN25 ...... 181 C3
Ash Gr Haywards Heath RH16 ...... 50 D2
Westham BN24 ...... 174 D6
Ash Wlk BN9 ...... 179 B7
Ashbourne Ct 13 BN21 ...... 185 A2
Ashbrook Rd TN37 ...... 136 B4
Ashburnham Cl BN1 ...... 143 E5
Ashburnham Dr BN1 ...... 143 E5
Ashburnham Gdns BN21 ...... 184 E5
Ashburnham Pl BN27 ...... 129 A2
Ashburnham Rd
Eastbourne BN21 ...... 184 E5
Hastings TN34, TN35 ...... 160 C6
Ashby Cl TN39 ...... 157 A8
Ashcombe Dr TN39 ...... 156 D3
Ashcombe Hollow BN7 ...... 145 D7
Ashcombe La BN7 ...... 145 E5
Ashcroft 1 BN43 ...... 161 D7
Ashcroft Cl Ringmer BN8 ...... 124 D5
Shoreham-by-Sea BN43 ...... 161 D8
Ashdown 12 BN3 ...... 163 C6
Ashdown Ave BN2 ...... 177 B5
Ashdown Chase TN22 ...... 35 C5
Ashdown Cl Forest Row RH18 ... 12 A2
Hastings TN38 ...... 135 E2
Haywards Heath RH16 ...... 51 B4
Royal Tunbridge Wells TN4 ...... 7 F4
Ashdown Ct Crowborough TN6 ... 25 E2
Uckfield TN22 ...... 78 D6
Ashdown Forest Riding Ctr
TN22 ...... 36 B6
Ashdown Forest Visitors Ctr
RH18 ...... 23 A5
Ashdown Gate RH19 ...... 1 D2
Ashdown Hospl The RH16 ...... 50 D6
Ashdown Llama Farm RH18 ...... 22 E4
Ashdown Pl TN21 ...... 82 B6
Ashdown Rd Bexhill TN40 ...... 157 E4
7 Brighton BN2 ...... 164 B8
Forest Row RH18 ...... 11 F2
Ashdown View
East Grinstead RH19 ...... 10 E7
Nutley TN22 ...... 35 D6
Ashenden Ave TN31 ...... 93 A5
Ashenden Wlk TN2 ...... 8 E8
Ashenground Cl 5 RH16 ...... 50 E3
Ashenground Rd RH16 ...... 50 E3
Asher Reeds TN3 ...... 7 A4
Ashford Cl 4 BN27 ...... 152 C7
Ashford Rd Brighton BN1 ...... 143 A2
Eastbourne BN21 ...... 185 A4
Hastings TN34 ...... 136 E2
Ashford Sq BN21 ...... 185 A3
Ashford Way TN34 ...... 136 E3
Ashgate Rd BN23 ...... 174 E2
Ashington Ct BN2 ...... 164 F6
Ashington Gdns BN10 ...... 178 F6
Ashington Rd BN22 ...... 174 A1
Ashlands TN6 ...... 26 B1
Ashleigh Glegg Ho BN25 ...... 180 D4
Ashleigh Gdns TN6 ...... 25 E4
Ashley Cl BN1 ...... 142 E7
Ashley Ct 7 Hastings TN37 ...... 159 C7
Hove BN3 ...... 163 C5
Ashley Gdns Hailsham BN27 ...... 129 C3
Mayfield TN20 ...... 40 A2
Rusthall TN4 ...... 7 C5
Ashley Park TN4 ...... 7 C5
Ashley Pk TN4 ...... 7 C5
Ashley Rd TN6 ...... 27 D1
Ashlings Way Hove BN3 ...... 141 E2
Shoreham-by-Sea BN43 ...... 140 B1
Ashmore Cl BN10 ...... 167 D2
Ashstead Towers TN40 ...... 157 E4
Ashton Lodge 14 BN2 ...... 189 B6
Ashton Rise BN2 ...... 189 B6
Ashtonville Cl BN8 ...... 124 E5
Ashurst Ave BN2 ...... 177 E5
Ashurst Hill TN3 ...... 5 D2
Ashurst Rd Brighton BN1, BN2 ... 143 F5
Seaford BN25 ...... 180 F2
Stone Cross TN3 ...... 6 B2
Ashurst Sta TN3 ...... 5 D2
Ashurstwood Abbey RH19 ...... 11 E6
Ashurstwood Cty Prim Sch
RH19 ...... 11 E6
Ashway RH15 ...... 73 A2
Ashwyn Bsns Ctr RH15 ...... 72 F5
Aspen Cl RH16 ...... 51 B4
Aspen Rd BN22 ...... 173 E2
Aspen Way TN39 ...... 156 C4
Aspen Wlk
Haywards Heath RH16 ...... 51 B4
Heathfield TN21 ...... 82 B5
Astaire Ave BN22 ...... 185 B6
Asten Cl TN38 ...... 158 E7
Asten Fields TN33 ...... 112 C4
Astra Ho 21 BN1 ...... 163 E5
Atfield Wlk BN22 ...... 173 F3
Athelstan Cl BN23 ...... 185 F8
Athelstan Rd TN35 ...... 160 D6

Athenaeum The 14 BN3 ...... 163 C6
Atlantic Dr BN20 ...... 185 F7
Atlingworth St BN2 ...... 189 B4
Attree Ct 6 BN2 ...... 164 C6
Attree Dr BN2 ...... 164 C6
Auckland Dr BN2 ...... 143 F1
Auckland Ho TN40 ...... 157 C7
Auckland Rd TN1 ...... 8 C5
Audrey Cl Brighton BN1 ...... 142 E5
Seaford BN25 ...... 180 D5
Audrey Sturley Ct TN4 ...... 7 D4
Augustines Way RH16 ...... 50 F4
Augustus Way TN38, TN37 ...... 135 F6
Austen Cl RH19 ...... 1 B1
Austen Way TN35 ...... 137 D5
Austen Wlk BN23 ...... 174 D2
Avard Cres BN20 ...... 184 B6
Avards Cl TN18 ...... 45 E8
Avenue Ct 19 BN3 ...... 163 C6
Avenue La BN1 ...... 184 F3
Avenue The Brighton BN2 ...... 143 E1
Dormansland RH19 ...... 2 B6
Eastbourne BN21 ...... 184 F3
Fairlight Cove TN35 ...... 138 F4
Hailsham BN27 ...... 152 B6
Heathfield TN21 ...... 82 B6
Horam TN21 ...... 106 F8
Kingston near Lewes BN7 ...... 145 D5
Lewes BN7 ...... 123 C1
Mayfield TN20 ...... 40 B2
Avery Cl BN41 ...... 140 F4
Aviemore Rd TN6 ...... 25 D2
Avis Cl BN9 ...... 168 E1
Avis Rd BN9 ...... 168 E1
Avis Way BN9 ...... 168 E1
Avocet BN27 ...... 152 A7
Avocet Trad Est RH15 ...... 72 F2
Avon St TN1 ...... 8 C5
Avondale Rd
Eastbourne BN22 ...... 185 B4
Hastings TN38 ...... 136 A1
Hove BN3 ...... 163 D7
Seaford BN25 ...... 180 F3
Avonhurst RH15 ...... 73 B3
Awbrook Cl RH17 ...... 51 F3
Aylesbury Bsns 163 E6
Aylesbury Ave BN23 ...... 185 E8
Aymer Ho 4 BN3 ...... 163 A6
Aymer Rd BN3 ...... 163 A6
Aynsley Cl BN3 ...... 163 C8
Ayscue Cl BN23 ...... 185 F7

Babylon Way BN20 ...... 184 B8
Back La Cross-in-Hand TN21 ...... 81 C6
Fairwarp TN22 ...... 36 B2
Rushlake Green TN21 ...... 83 D1
Winchelsea TN36 ...... 117 E7
Back Rd TN18 ...... 47 B5
Backwoods Cl RH16 ...... 51 B6
Backwoods La RH16 ...... 51 B6
Baden Rd BN2 ...... 143 D1
Badens Cl BN8 ...... 76 C6
Badger Cl BN41 ...... 141 B2
Badger Dr RH16 ...... 50 C5
Badger Gate TN31 ...... 93 A5
Badger Way BN1 ...... 143 E6
Badgers Brow BN20 ...... 184 B8
Badgers Cl TN6 ...... 25 E3
Badgers Copse BN25 ...... 181 C3
Badgers Dene BN7 ...... 167 D8
Badgers Field BN10 ...... 178 F6
Badgers Mount TN39 ...... 156 E5
Badgers Way
East Grinstead RH19 ...... 1 F2
Hastings TN34 ...... 136 D5
Badgers Wlk RH15 ...... 73 D2
Badlesmere Rd BN22 ...... 185 B6
Bagham La BN27 ...... 130 F6
Bahram Rd BN26 ...... 172 F6
Bailey Cres BN22 ...... 173 B3
Baillie Ave BN22 ...... 185 C5
Bainbridge Cl BN25 ...... 180 F3
Bainden Cl TN6 ...... 27 D1
Baird Dr TN34 ...... 136 E3
Baird Ho TN37 ...... 159 C8
Baker Ct TN22 ...... 78 C7
Baker St Brighton BN1, BN2 ...... 189 A7
Newhaven BN9 ...... 179 E7
Uckfield TN22 ...... 78 D6
Baker's Rd BN21 ...... 184 D3
Bakewell Rd BN21 ...... 184 D4
Bal Edmund TN37 ...... 158 A8
Balaclava La TN5 ...... 30 A6
Balcombe Cl BN10 ...... 178 C8
Balcombe Gn TN33 ...... 88 E1
Balcombe La RH17, RH19 ...... 21 E2
Balcombe Rd
Haywards Heath RH16, RH17 ...... 50 D7
Peacehaven BN10 ...... 178 B8
Baldings Cotts RH17 ...... 74 B5
Baldock Rd TN5 ...... 29 E4
Baldslow Down TN37 ...... 136 C8
Baldslow Rd TN34 ...... 136 F1
Baldwin Ave BN20, BN21 ...... 184 C5
Baldwins Hill Cty Prim Sch
RH19 ...... 1 D1
Bale Cl TN39 ...... 156 E5
Balfour Cty Inf Sch BN1 ...... 143 A3
Balfour Cty Jun Sch BN1 ...... 143 A3
Balfour Gdns RH18 ...... 11 E1
Balfour Rd BN1 ...... 143 A2
Ball's Gn TN7 ...... 14 B5
Ballard Dr BN8 ...... 125 A7
Ballards Hill TN33 ...... 134 F4
Ballsocks La TN21 ...... 107 C8
Balmoral Rd RH19 ...... 11 A8
Balmoral Cl BN25 ...... 181 A6
Balmoral Ct BN3 ...... 142 A3

Balsdean Rd BN2 ...... 144 E1
Baltimore Ct 9 BN3 ...... 163 C7
Bamford Cl BN2 ...... 144 A2
Bampfield St BN41 ...... 162 B8
Bancroft Ho TN39 ...... 157 B5
Bancroft Rd TN39 ...... 157 B5
Bank Rd TN39 ...... 157 C7
Banks Rd BN8 ...... 52 F1
Bankside Brighton BN1 ...... 142 C5
Hassocks BN6 ...... 97 F5
Rye TN31 ...... 93 B6
Sparrow's Green TN5 ...... 29 E5
Banner Cl BN24 ...... 174 C6
Banner Farm Rd TN2 ...... 8 B2
Banner Way BN24 ...... 174 C6
Bannings Vale BN2 ...... 177 E5
Bannister Way BN24 ...... 174 C6
Bannisters Field BN8 ...... 76 D7
Baranscraig Ave BN1 ...... 143 A7
Barbados BN40 ...... 157 E3
Barber Ct BN7 ...... 146 B8
Barclay Ho 2 BN2 ...... 164 C7
Barcombe Ave BN25 ...... 181 C3
Barcombe CE Prim Sch
BN8 ...... 101 D5
Barcombe Cl
Eastbourne BN20 ...... 184 C3
Seaford BN25 ...... 181 C3
Barcombe Mills Rd BN8 ...... 101 E4
Barcombe Pl BN1 ...... 143 F5
Barcombe Rd BN1 ...... 143 E4
Barcombe Wlk BN20 ...... 184 C3
Barden Rd Eastbourne BN22 ...... 185 C4
Speldhurst TN3 ...... 7 A8
Bardown Rd TN5 ...... 42 E7
Bargate TN40 ...... 157 C7
Barham Cl TN34 ...... 136 D4
Barkdale RH15 ...... 73 D5
Barkham Manor Vineyard
TN22 ...... 77 B8
Barley Ave TN35 ...... 160 C5
Barley Cl BN10 ...... 167 B2
Barley Dr BN6 ...... 72 C4
Barley Field Cotts BN7 ...... 146 D1
Barley La TN35 ...... 160 D5
Barming Cl BN23 ...... 174 D2
Barn Cl Hailsham BN27 ...... 129 C1
Kingston near Lewes BN7 ...... 145 E5
Seaford BN25 ...... 181 A6
Stone Cross BN24 ...... 174 A6
Barn Cottage La RH16 ...... 51 A5
Barn Cotts 2 BN25 ...... 181 A3
Barn Ct TN37 ...... 136 C5
Barn Field Gdns 8 BN2 ...... 164 C6
Barn Hatch Cl BN7 ...... 146 A8
Barn Ho The BN25 ...... 180 E5
Barn La TN2 ...... 79 D8
Barn Rd BN7 ...... 123 E3
Barn Rise Brighton BN1 ...... 142 D5
Seaford BN25 ...... 181 A5
Barn Stables BN7 ...... 123 B1
Barnard Gate RH16 ...... 50 E7
Barnes Rd BN41 ...... 162 B8
Barnet Way BN3 ...... 141 E3
Barnett Rd BN1 ...... 143 B2
Barnetts Way TN4 ...... 8 C8
Barnfield Crowborough TN6 ...... 26 A3
Plumpton Green BN7 ...... 99 E5
Royal Tunbridge Wells TN2 ...... 16 F7
Barnfield Cl TN34 ...... 159 D8
Barnfield Gdns BN6 ...... 98 E3
Barnham Cl BN22 ...... 174 A2
Barnhams The TN39 ...... 156 E3
Barnhorn Cl TN39 ...... 156 C4
Barnhorn Rd TN39, TN33 ...... 156 B4
Barnmead RH16 ...... 50 D7
Barnsgate Manor Vineyard
TN22 ...... 36 E5
Barnside Ave RH15 ...... 73 D1
Barons Cl BN25 ...... 180 C5
Barons Ct Burgess Hill RH15 ...... 73 B2
Royal Tunbridge Wells TN4 ...... 8 A5
Barons Down Rd BN7 ...... 146 A8
Barons Way BN26 ...... 172 F5
Barrack Rd TN40 ...... 157 C5
Barrack Sq TN36 ...... 117 F7
Barracks Cotts TN32 ...... 87 C7
Barrhill Ave BN1 ...... 142 F7
Barrie Cl BN23 ...... 174 E2
Barrington Cl RH16 ...... 50 F8
Barrington Rd RH16 ...... 51 A8
Barrington Wood RH16 ...... 50 F8
Barrow Cl BN1 ...... 143 C2
Barrow Hill BN1 ...... 143 C2
Barrow La TN3 ...... 6 F1
Barrow Rise TN37 ...... 136 C5
Barrowfield Cl BN3 ...... 142 C3
Barrowfield Dr BN3 ...... 142 D2
Barrowfield Lodge BN3 ...... 142 C2
Barry Wlk BN2 ...... 164 C6
Bartholomew Sq BN1 ...... 189 A5
Bartholomews BN1 ...... 189 A5
Bartley Mill TN3 ...... 18 E4
Bartley Mill Rd BN24 ...... 174 B5
Barton Cres RH19 ...... 11 A8
Barton St TN38 ...... 136 B1
Basin Rd N BN41 ...... 162 B6
Basin Rd S BN3, BN41 ...... 162 B6
Baslow Cl BN20 ...... 188 D7
Baslow Rd BN20 ...... 188 D7
Bassett's Forge TN5 ...... 29 E5
Bassetts La Argos Hill TN20 ...... 39 F5
Mark Cross TN6 ...... 28 E2
White Post TN11, TN8 ...... 5 C7
Batchelor Way TN2 ...... 78 A7
Batchelors TN2 ...... 9 E8
Bateman's TN19 ...... 62 A4

Bateman's La TN19 ...... 62 A4
Batemans Rd BN2 ...... 165 E2
Bates Rd BN1 ...... 142 F2
Bath Cl BN23 ...... 163 A5
Bath Rd BN21 ...... 184 F2
Bath St BN1 ...... 189 F7
Bathford Cl BN23 ...... 174 D2
Battenhurst Rd TN5 ...... 43 B4
Battery Hill TN35 ...... 138 D5
Battle Abbey TN33 ...... 112 D4
Battle Abbey (Sch) TN33 ...... 112 D4
Battle Cl BN23 ...... 181 C5
Battle Cres Hailsham BN27 ...... 152 B8
Hastings TN33 ...... 136 B4
Battle Gates TN33 ...... 112 B5
Battle Hill TN33 ...... 112 E3
Battle Hospl TN33 ...... 112 A4
Battle & Langton
CE Prim Sch TN33 ...... 112 C4
Battle Rd Hailsham BN27 ...... 129 C1
Hastings TN33, TN37, TN38 ...... 136 A4
Battle Sta TN33 ...... 112 E4
Batts Bridge Rd TN22 ...... 55 A4
Bavant Rd BN1 ...... 142 E2
Baxter Rd BN7 ...... 123 B2
Baxter St BN2 ...... 164 C7
Baxters La RH17 ...... 34 C6
Bay Ave TN35 ...... 175 E5
Bay Cotts BN24 ...... 176 C7
Bay Pond Rd BN21 ...... 184 D4
Bay Rd BN24 ...... 175 D4
Bay Tree Cl Heathfield TN21 ...... 82 C5
Shoreham-by-Sea BN43 ...... 140 C1
Bay Tree La BN26 ...... 172 F8
Bay Vue Rd BN9 ...... 179 D7
Bayencourt N TN40 ...... 157 C5
Bayencourt S TN40 ...... 157 C5
Bayeux Ct Bexhill TN40 ...... 157 D3
Hastings TN37 ...... 159 D8
Bayhall Rd TN2 ...... 8 C3
Bayham Abbey TN3 ...... 19 B5
Bayham Cl TN5 ...... 29 E6
Bayham Rd Eastbourne BN22 ... 185 C4
Hailsham BN27 ...... 152 D7
Royal Tunbridge Wells TN2, TN3 ... 17 C7
Bayley's La TN26 ...... 151 B2
Baylis Cres RH15 ...... 72 F4
Bayview Rd BN10 ...... 178 E5
Baywood Gdns BN2 ...... 165 C8
Bazehill Rd BN2 ...... 165 F2
Beach Cl BN25 ...... 180 D3
Beach Ct 10 BN43 ...... 161 A6
Beach Mews BN2 ...... 165 C5
Beach Rd Eastbourne BN22 ...... 185 C5
Newhaven BN9 ...... 179 E6
Beachings The BN24 ...... 175 C4
Beachy Head Countryside Ctr
BN20 ...... 188 B4
Beachy Head Rd
Beachy Head BN20 ...... 188 C4
Eastbourne BN20 ...... 188 D8
Beacon Bsns Pk TN6 ...... 38 C8
Beacon Cl Brighton BN1 ...... 143 A2
Crowborough TN6 ...... 25 E2
Seaford BN25 ...... 180 D5
Beacon Com Coll
Crowborough TN6 ...... 26 A2
Crowborough TN6 ...... 26 B3
Beacon Ct BN2 ...... 165 D4
Beacon Dr BN25 ...... 180 E5
Beacon Gdns TN6 ...... 25 E3
Beacon Hill Bexhill TN39 ...... 157 A8
Dormansland RH7 ...... 2 B8
Ovingdean BN2 ...... 165 E3
Beacon Hurst BN6 ...... 98 B3
Beacon La TN32 ...... 88 E7
Beacon Rd Crowborough TN6 ...... 25 E2
Ditchling BN6 ...... 98 D2
Hastings TN35 ...... 137 E4
Seaford BN25 ...... 180 D4
Beacon Rd W TN6 ...... 25 D2
Beaconfield Ho TN6 ...... 25 E2
Beaconsfield Cotts RH17 ...... 51 F3
Beaconsfield Rd Bexhill TN40 ... 157 C6
Brighton BN1 ...... 164 A8
Chelwood Gate RH17 ...... 34 D8
Hastings TN34 ...... 136 F2
Portslade-by-Sea BN41 ...... 162 B8
Beaconsfield Terr TN21 ...... 81 B8
Beaconsfield Villas BN1 ...... 142 F1
Beaconsville Ct BN1 ...... 142 F1
Beagles Wood Rd TN2 ...... 9 E7
Beal Cres BN1 ...... 143 B2
Beale St RH15 ...... 72 F1
Beales La TN31 ...... 67 B6
Beame Ct BN25 ...... 180 D3
Beamsley Rd BN22 ...... 185 C4
Beaney's La TN34 ...... 136 E6
Bear Rd BN2 ...... 164 D8
Bear Yd BN7 ...... 123 D1
Beatrice La 2 BN21 ...... 184 F3
Beatrice Wlk TN39 ...... 157 A6
Beatty Ave BN1 ...... 143 D6
Beatty Rd BN23 ...... 185 E7
Beauchamp Rd TN38 ...... 136 A4
Beauford Rd TN21 ...... 106 F7
Beaufort Cres TN37 ...... 136 C2
Beaufort Rd TN37 ...... 136 C2
Beaufort Terr BN2 ...... 164 C6
Beauharrow Rd TN37 ...... 136 A6
Beaulieu Ct TN40 ...... 157 F5
Beaulieu Gdns TN36 ...... 136 C6
Beaulieu Rd TN36 ...... 156 D2
Beauport Gdns TN37 ...... 136 A4
Beauport Home Farm Cl
TN37 ...... 136 A6
Beaver Cl TN6 ...... 26 A1
Beckenham Cl BN27 ...... 129 B3

Becket Cl TN34 ...... 160 A5
Beckets Way TN22 ...... 79 B5
Beckett Way
11 East Grinstead RH19 ...... 10 F8
Lewes BN7 ...... 123 C3
Beckley CE Prim Sch TN31 ...... 68 A4
Beckley Cl Brighton BN2 ...... 164 E5
Hastings TN38 ...... 135 D2
Beckworth Cl RH16 ...... 51 A6
Beckworth La RH16 ...... 51 A6
Bedales RH16 ...... 51 D4
Bedales Cnr RH16 ...... 51 D4
Bedales Hill RH16 ...... 51 D4
Beddingham Gdns BN8 ...... 147 F5
Bedelands RH15 ...... 73 C6
Bedelands Farm
Local Nature Reserve RH15 ... 73 B6
Bedford Ave TN40 ...... 157 D3
Bedford Ct TN22 ...... 78 C8
Bedford Gr BN21 ...... 184 E4
Bedford Pl BN1 ...... 163 E5
Bedford Rd TN35 ...... 160 C6
Bedford Sq BN1 ...... 163 E5
Bedford St BN2 ...... 164 C4
Bedford Terr 9 TN1 ...... 8 A2
Bedford Towers 15 BN1 ...... 163 E5
Bedfordwell Ct 1 BN22 ...... 185 A4
Bedfordwell Rd BN21, BN22 ... 185 A4
Bedgebury Cl TN38 ...... 135 E2
Bedgebury Lower Sch TN18 ... 45 F7
Bedgebury National Pinetum
TN17 ...... 32 E8
Bee Rd BN20 ...... 178 C8
Beech Cl Battle TN33 ...... 112 C7
Bexhill TN39 ...... 156 C6
Portslade-by-Sea BN41 ...... 140 F4
Beech Ct BN26 ...... 173 A6
Beech Farm Rd TN33 ...... 88 D3
Beech Fields RH19 ...... 1 F3
Beech Gr BN2 ...... 143 E3
Beech Green La TN7 ...... 14 B7
Beech Hill RH16 ...... 51 B4
Beech House La TN32 ...... 64 C6
Beech Hurst TN2 ...... 9 D7
Beech Hurst Cl RH16 ...... 50 D4
Beech Mews BN9 ...... 179 E7
Beech Rd RH18 ...... 48 C3
Beech St TN1 ...... 8 B4
Beech Villas 1 TN21 ...... 82 A6
Beecham Pl TN38 ...... 135 F4
Beechers Rd BN41 ...... 140 F3
Beeches Cl Heathfield TN21 ...... 82 B8
Uckfield TN22 ...... 78 D8
Beeches Farm Rd TN6 ...... 26 A1
Beeches Head RH19 ...... 2 F5
Beeches La RH19 ...... 11 D6
Beeches Rd TN6 ...... 26 B2
Beeches The
Brighton BN1, BN3 ...... 142 D3
Royal Tunbridge Wells TN2 ...... 8 D5
The Moor TN18 ...... 45 E7
Beechfield Cl BN24 ...... 174 B6
Beeching Cl TN39 ...... 157 B4
Beeching Park Ind Est TN39 ... 157 B4
Beeching Rd TN39 ...... 157 B4
Beeching Way RH19 ...... 1 E1
Beechlands Cotts TN6 ...... 28 F3
Beechwood 9 BN1 ...... 142 E3
Beechwood Ave BN2 ...... 142 F4
Beechwood Cl Brighton BN1 ...... 142 F4
Burwash TN19 ...... 62 B7
Hailsham BN27 ...... 152 C5
Beechwood Cres BN20 ...... 184 D3
Beechwood Gdns TN37 ...... 136 D5
Beechwood La
Cooksbridge BN7, BN8 ...... 122 F8
Heathfield TN21 ...... 82 B5
Beechwood Mews TN2 ...... 8 E4
Beechwood Sch
(Sacred Heart) TN2 ...... 8 E4
Beechwoods RH15 ...... 73 A1
Beechy Ave BN20 ...... 184 B5
Beechy Gdns BN20 ...... 184 B5
Beechy Rd TN2 ...... 80 A2
Beeding Ave BN3 ...... 141 F3
Beeding Ct 4 BN43 ...... 161 B8
Beggar's La BN24 ...... 174 B5
Beggar's Wood Rd BN8 ...... 75 C6
Belbourne Ct 5 BN1 ...... 189 A6
Belfast St BN3 ...... 163 B7
Belfield Rd TN2 ...... 9 D6
Belfry Orch TN22 ...... 78 D5
Belfry The BN27 ...... 152 A8
Belgrave Cres BN25 ...... 180 F5
Belgrave Ct TN40 ...... 157 D3
Belgrave Pl 11 BN2 ...... 164 D4
Belgrave Rd
Royal Tunbridge Wells TN1 ...... 8 B4
Seaford BN25 ...... 180 E4
Belgrave St BN2 ...... 189 B6
Belgrove 5 TN1 ...... 8 A2
Bell Alley Rd TN19 ...... 62 B5
Bell Banks Rd BN27 ...... 152 C7
Bell Hammer RH19 ...... 10 E8
Bell La Lewes BN7 ...... 146 B8
Nutley TN22 ...... 35 A4
Uckfield TN22 ...... 78 B6
Uckfield TN22 ...... 78 C6
Bell Mead 7 BN3 ...... 163 D7
Bell Tower Ind Est 7 BN2 ...... 164 E4
Bell Wlk TN22 ...... 78 C6
Bell Wood Ind Est TN22 ...... 78 B6
Belle Hill Bexhill TN40 ...... 157 B5
Bexhill TN40 ...... 157 C5
Belle Vue Ct BN2 ...... 164 D5

Belle Vue Rd **4** BN22 .... 185 C5
Bellevue Cotts BN2 .... 164 F8
Bellevue Ct Brighton BN1 ...... 142 F1
2 Eastbourne BN22 .... 185 C5
Bellevue Gdns BN2 .... 164 D4
Bellhurst Rd TN32 .... 64 A4
Bellingham Cl TN37 .... 136 B4
Bellingham Cres BN3 .... 162 D8
Belmaine Ct TN39 .... 156 F4
Belmont Bexhill TN39 .... 157 B3
Brighton BN1, BN3 .... 163 E7
Belmont Cl BN6 .... 97 C5
Belmont Ct BN27 .... 152 B7
Belmont La BN6 .... 97 C5
Belmont Rd Hastings TN35 ..... 160 C5
Uckfield TN22 .... 78 C7
Belmont St BN1 .... 189 A6
Belmore Rd BN22 .... 185 B4
Belton Rd BN2 .... 164 B8
Beltring Rd Eastbourne BN2 .. 185 B4
Royal Tunbridge Wells TN4 .... 8 A6
Beltring Terr BN22 .... 185 B4
Belvedere Ct **10** BN21 .... 184 F4
Belvedere Gdns
Crowborough TN6 .... 26 A1
Seaford BN25 .... 181 A5
Belvedere Pk TN38 .... 159 A8
Bembridge Rd BN23 .... 174 B3
Bembridge St BN2 .... 164 C8
Bembrook Rd TN34 .... 160 B5
Bemzells La BN27 .... 108 D2
Benbow Ave BN23 .... 185 E6
Benbow Ho TN39 .... 156 E4
Benchfield Cl RH19 .... 2 B1
Bending Cres TN39, TN40 .... 157 C5
Benenden Cl BN25 .... 181 A4
Benenden Rise TN34 .... 136 E3
Benett Ave BN3 .... 142 B2
Benett Dr BN3 .... 142 B2
Benfield Cl BN41 .... 141 C1
Benfield Cres BN41 .... 141 C1
Benfield Rd BN41 .... 162 C8
Benfield Cty Jun Sch BN41 ... 162 C8
Benfield Valley Golf Course
BN3 .... 141 C3
Benfield Way BN41 .... 141 C1
Bengairn Ave BN1 .... 143 A7
Benhall Mill Rd TN2, TN3 .... 17 D8
Benham Ct BN3 .... 163 B5
Benjamin Cl BN22 .... 173 F2
Benjamin Lodge RH15 .... 73 D3
Bennett Memorial
Diocesan Sch TN4 .... 7 E6
Bennett Rd BN2 .... 164 E4
Benson Ct BN3 .... 162 E7
Bentham Hill TN3 .... 7 D8
Bentham Rd BN2 .... 164 C7
Bentley Motor Mus BN8 .... 103 F5
Bentley Wildfowl Reserve
BN8 .... 103 F4
Bentswood Rd RH16 .... 51 A5
Bentswood Rd RH16 .... 50 F5
Berberis Ct BN17 .... 140 B1
Beresford Cl TN17 .... 20 F2
Beresford Ct **11** BN3 .... 163 D7
Beresford Ho BN10 .... 167 C1
Beresford Rd Brighton BN2 ... 164 D5
Newhaven BN9 .... 168 E1
Bergamot Cres BN43 .... 140 C1
Beristede Ct BN20 .... 184 E1
Berkeley Cl TN2 .... 9 E7
Berkeley Ct **2** BN3 .... 163 E7
Berkeley Rd **7** TN1 .... 8 A2
Berkeley Row BN7 .... 146 A8
Berkeley Wlk BN23 .... 174 E3
Berkley Rd TN20 .... 39 E1
Berkshire Ct **7** BN22 .... 185 B4
Berlin Rd TN35 .... 160 C6
Bernard La **1** BN21 .... 184 F3
Bernard Pl BN2 .... 164 C7
Bernard Rd BN2 .... 164 C7
Bernhard Baron
Cottage Homes The BN26 ... 172 F6
Bernhard Gdns BN26 .... 172 F5
Berriedale Ave BN3 .... 162 E6
Berriedale Ho BN3 .... 162 E6
Berry Cl Burgess Hill RH15 ..... 73 A6
Telscombe Cliffs BN10 .... 167 A1
Berwick BN26 .... 170 F7
Berwick Cl Bexhill TN39 .... 156 C6
Lower Willingdon BN22 .... 173 C3
Seaford BN25 .... 180 D4
Berwick Court Cotts BN26 ... 171 A6
Berwick Ct **1** BN22 .... 185 B3
Berwick Rd BN2 .... 166 D3
Berwick Sta BN26 .... 150 B2
Betchley Cl RH19 .... 1 E3
Betherinden Cotts TN18 .... 47 A4
Bethune Rd TN40 .... 157 E3
Bethune Way TN34 .... 136 F1
Beulah Rd TN1 .... 8 C4
Beuzeville Ave BN27 .... 152 B8
Bevendean Ave BN2 .... 177 D5
Bevendean Cres BN2 .... 143 E2
Bevendean Prim Sch BN2 ..... 143 F1
Bevendean Rd BN2 .... 143 D1
Beverington Cl BN21 .... 184 D6
Beverington Rd BN21 .... 184 D6
Beverley Ct BN3 .... 162 D7
Beverley Wlk TN34 .... 160 A6
Bevern Bridge BN8 .... 100 F4
Bevern Bridge Cotts BN8 ..... 100 F4
Beverns The BN7 .... 99 E5
Bevin Ct TN38 .... 136 B3
Bewl Bridge Cl TN5 .... 32 B3

Bewl Water TN5 .... 31 C6
Bewl Water Visitors Ctr TN5 .. 31 B7
Bewlbridge La
Bewlbridge TN3, TN5 .... 20 B1
Lower Cousley Wood TN5 .... 30 F8
Bexhill Central Sta TN40 ...... 157 C4
Bexhill Coll TN39 .... 157 A7
Bexhill High Sch TN39 .... 157 B5
Bexhill Hospl TN40 .... 157 C5
Bexhill Mus TN39 .... 157 B3
Bexhill Rd Eastbourne BN22 .. 185 C5
Hastings TN38, TN40 .... 158 D6
Lower Street TN33, TN39 .... 133 C3
Woodingdean BN2 .... 144 E1
Bexleigh Ave TN38 .... 158 B5
Bexley Cl BN27 .... 129 B2
Bexley Ct BN26 .... 173 A7
Bicton Gdns TN39 .... 156 E4
Biddenden Cl BN23 .... 174 D2
Bidwell Ave BN27 .... 157 A7
Bigwood Ave BN3 .... 163 D8
Bilbury Mews BN21 .... 184 F5
Billingham La TN31 .... 91 C3
Binstead Cl BN22 .... 173 E1
Biology Rd BN1 .... 144 B6
Birch Ave RH16 .... 51 A3
Birch Cl Eastbourne BN23 ..... 185 D7
Haywards Heath RH16 .... 51 B3
Royal Tunbridge Wells TN1 .... 8 D7
Uckfield TN22 .... 78 E8
Birch Ct BN42 .... 141 A1
Birch Est The BN23 .... 185 C7
Birch Grove Cres BN1 .... 143 A5
Birch Kiln Cotts TN5 .... 30 A6
Birch Path TN22 .... 78 D8
Birch Rd BN22, BN23 .... 185 C7
Birch Rdbt BN22, BN23 .... 185 C7
Birch View TN39 .... 157 C6
Birch Way Hailsham BN27 ..... 152 B6
Hastings TN34 .... 136 E3
Haywards Heath RH16 .... 51 A2
Heathfield TN21 .... 82 A5
Royal Tunbridge Wells TN1, TN2 .. 8 D7
Birchden Cotts TN3 .... 15 C6
Birchen La RH16 .... 50 F8
Birches Ct TN6 .... 25 F4
Birchetts Ave TN3 .... 6 E3
Birchetts Green La TN5 .... 31 A2
Birchgrove La RH17 .... 22 A1
Birchgrove Rd RH17 .... 33 E7
Birchington Cl TN39 .... 156 D4
Birchwood Grove
Cty Prim Sch RH15 .... 73 C1
Birchwood Grove Rd RH15 ... 73 C1
Bird in Eye Hill TN22 .... 78 E6
Bird in Hand St TN3 .... 15 B8
Bird La TN5 .... 29 B5
Birdham Pl BN2 .... 143 F3
Birdham Rd BN2 .... 143 F3
Birk Dale TN39 .... 156 C4
Birkdale TN4 .... 8 B6
Birken Rd TN1, TN2 .... 8 D6
Birling Cl Brighton BN2 .... 143 D1
Seaford BN25 .... 180 D4
Birling Dr TN2 .... 8 A1
Birling Gap Rd BN20 .... 187 B6
Birling Park Ave TN2 .... 17 B8
Birling Rd TN2 .... 17 B8
Birling St BN20, BN21 .... 184 C1
Birling Way TN22 .... 78 E8
Bishop Bell CE Sch BN23 ...... 174 E1
Bishop's Cl Hurstpierpoint BN6 .. 97 A7
Ringmer BN8 .... 124 E6
Bishop's Down TN4 .... 7 F3
Bishop's Down Cty Prim Sch
TN4 .... 7 E5
Bishop's Down Park Rd TN4 .... 7 F4
Bishop's Down Rd TN4 .... 7 F4
Bishop's La Ringmer BN8 .... 124 D6
Robertsbridge TN32 .... 64 A3
Bishop's Wlk TN40 .... 157 F6
Bishops Cl BN25 .... 180 C4
Bishops Ct TN4 .... 7 F3
Bishops Dr BN7 .... 146 A8
Bishops Rd BN3 .... 142 C1
Bishopstone Dr BN2 .... 177 B6
Bishopstone La BN6, RH17 .... 72 A7
Bishopstone Rd BN25 .... 180 C6
Bishopstone Sta BN25 .... 180 B4
Bittern Ct BN27 .... 152 D7
Bixley La TN31 .... 68 B2
Black Hill RH16 .... 51 A7
Black Lion St BN1 .... 189 A4
Black Path BN26 .... 173 A6
Blackberry La RH7 .... 1 E8
Blackberry La RH19, RH7 .... 1 D8
Blackbird Cl BN6 .... 72 D3
Blackboys CE Prim Sch TN22 .. 80 A6
Blackbrook La BN8 .... 52 E2
Blackdon Hill TN3, TN6 .... 27 B6
Blackfields Ave TN39 .... 156 F5
Blackhouse La RH15 .... 73 B4
Blackhurst La TN2 .... 8 F6
Blacklands TN33 .... 88 F1
Blacklands Cres RH16 .... 11 F2
Blacklands Cty Prim Sch
TN34 .... 136 E2
Blacklands Dr TN34 .... 136 F2
Blackman Ave TN34, TN38 ... 136 A3
Blackman St BN1 .... 189 A6
Blackmill Cl TN39 .... 157 A8
Blackness Rd TN6 .... 38 A8
Blacksmith's Field TN33 ...... 135 A4
Blacksmith's La TN5 .... 30 A5
Blacksmiths Copse BN27 ..... 152 A6
Blacksmiths Field TN32 .... 46 C1
Blacksmiths La TN33 .... 133 E8

Blackstone Way RH15 .... 73 A5
Blackthorn Cl Brighton BN1 .. 142 D3
Eastbourne BN22 .... 173 E2
Hastings TN37 .... 136 C4
Portslade-by-Sea BN41 .... 141 B2
Blackthorn Way TN35 .... 138 F4
Blackthorns BN16 .... 51 A7
Blackthorns Cl RH16 .... 51 A6
Blackthorns Cty Prim Sch
RH16 .... 51 A6
Blackthorns The TN35 .... 73 B5
Blackwater Rd BN20, BN21 .. 184 F1
Blackwater Cty Prim Sch RH19 . 1 E3
Blackwell Farm Rd RH19 .... 1 F3
Blackwell Hollow RH19 .... 1 F2
Blackwell Rd RH19 .... 1 F2
Blake Ct **2** BN2 .... 189 B6
Blake Way TN1 .... 8 D7
Blakeney Ave BN10, BN9 ...... 179 A6
Blaker St BN2 .... 189 B5
Blakes Way BN23 .... 185 F6
Blatchington Cl BN25 .... 180 F4
Blatchington Hill BN25 .... 180 E4
Blatchington Rd Hove BN3 ... 163 B7
Royal Tunbridge Wells TN1 ...... 8 B1
Seaford BN25 .... 180 E3
Blenheim Cl RH19 .... 2 A3
Blenheim Ct **1** Hove BN3 ... 163 A6
Robertsbridge TN32 .... 64 B3
Blenheim Fields RH18 .... 11 E3
Blenheim Pl **3** BN1 .... 189 A6
Blenheim Way Flimwell TN5 .... 32 C3
Polegate BN26 .... 173 D6
Bletchinglye La TN6 .... 27 E1
Bletchley Ct BN1 .... 164 A8
Blind La BN8 .... 76 E6
Blois Rd BN7 .... 123 B2
Blomfield Rd TN37 .... 159 D8
Bloomsbury Pl **17** BN2 ...... 164 C4
Bloomsbury St **16** BN2 .... 164 C4
Blossom Wlk BN27 .... 129 B1
Blount Ave TN1 .... 1 C1
Blowers Hill Cowden TN8 .... 4 D8
Speldhurst TN3 .... 7 B8
Blue Haze Ave BN23 .... 181 B4
Bluebell Cl East Grinstead RH19 ... 1 B1
Haywards Heath RH16 .... 50 F4
Bluebell Rly RH17, RH19, TN22 .. 21 A5
Bluebell Rly Mus TN22 .... 53 A4
Bluebird Ct **10** BN3 .... 163 A6
Bluemans La TN33 .... 114 A4
Bluestone Cl TN38 .... 135 F2
Blunts Wood Cres RH17 .... 50 B6
Blunts Wood Rd RH17 .... 50 C6
Blytons The RH19 .... 1 B1
Boarders La TN5 .... 31 C3
Boast La BN8 .... 101 F5
Boath Mus of Natural History
BN1 .... 163 E6
Bocking Cl TN5 .... 29 E4
Boddingtons La BN6 .... 98 D3
Bodiam Ave Bevendean BN2 . 144 B1
Bexhill TN40 .... 157 D6
Bodiam Castle (NT) TN32 ...... 65 E8
Bodiam CE Prim Sch TN32 .... 65 E8
Bodiam Cl Bevendean BN2 ... 144 B2
Seaford BN25 .... 181 C4
Bodiam Cres BN22 .... 174 A2
Bodiam Ct **2** RH16 .... 50 E5
Bodiam Dr TN38 .... 135 D2
Bodiam Manor Sch TN32 .... 65 E8
Bodiam Rd TN18, TN32 .... 46 F3
Bodle Cres TN39 .... 157 B7
Bodmin Cl BN20 .... 184 C3
Bohemia Rd TN34, TN37, TN38 . 159 D8
Boiler House Hill TN34 .... 144 B7
Bolding Way RH16 .... 50 E2
Bolebrooke Rd TN40 .... 157 D3
Bolney Ave BN10 .... 178 C6
Bolney Rd BN2 .... 143 F4
Bolnore RH16 .... 50 B4
Bolnore Rd RH16 .... 50 C6
Bolsover Rd Eastbourne BN20 . 188 F8
Hove BN3 .... 162 E8
Bolton Cl TN22 .... 78 A6
Bolton Rd BN21 .... 185 A2
Boltro Rd RH16 .... 50 D5
Bonchurch Rd BN2 .... 164 C7
Bond St BN1 .... 189 A5
Bonfire La RH17 .... 33 D5
Boniface Cl BN2 .... 174 C6
Bonny Wood Rd BN6 .... 97 E3
Booker Cl TN6 .... 26 A1
Bopeep Bostal BN26, BN8 .... 170 B7
Borders La TN19 .... 62 F7
Boreham Hill BN27 .... 132 A4
Boreham La BN27 .... 131 E2
Borodales TN39 .... 156 E4
Borough La BN20, BN21 .... 184 D3
Borough St BN1 .... 163 E6
Borrow King Cl BN2 .... 164 D8
Borrowdale Ct BN23 .... 174 C4
Boscawen Ct BN23 .... 185 F7
Boscobel Ct TN38 .... 159 A6
Boscobel Lodge TN38 .... 159 B7
Boscobel Rd TN38 .... 159 A7
Boscobel Rd N TN38 .... 159 A7
Boship Cl BN23 .... 174 A4
Bostal Rd BN8 .... 148 B4
Boston Cl BN23 .... 185 F7
Boston Ct RH16 .... 51 A5
Boston Rd BN16 .... 51 A5
Boston St BN1 .... 189 A7
Boswell Wlk **2** BN23 .... 174 E2
Bough Beeches RH15 .... 73 C1
Boughey Pl BN7 .... 123 C3
Boulevard The BN24 .... 175 F6

Boundary Pas **6** BN3 .... 163 E6
Boundary Rd Brighton BN2 ... 164 F4
Portslade-by-Sea BN3, BN41 . 162 C7
Royal Tunbridge Wells TN2 ...... 8 D1
Boundary The
Langton Green TN3, TN4 .... 7 B3
1 Seaford BN25 .... 180 E2
Bourg-de-Peage Ave RH19 ...... 2 A1
Bourne Ct Brighton BN1 .... 142 D4
20 Hastings TN34 .... 160 B4
Bourne Cty Prim Sch BN22 .. 185 B3
Bourne La TN32 .... 64 F7
Bourne Pas **12** TN34 .... 160 B4
Bourne St BN21, BN22 .... 185 B3
Bourne The Hassocks BN6 ...... 97 E5
Hastings TN34 .... 160 B4
Bourneside Ct **12** BN22 ..... 185 B3
Bowden House Sch BN25 ..... 180 F6
Bowden Rise BN25 .... 180 E6
Bowen Ct **4** BN3 .... 163 C6
Bowen Rd TN4 .... 7 B4
Bower Cl TN37 .... 136 B4
Bower The RH16 .... 50 D5
Bowerhill Cotts RH19 .... 21 F6
Bowlers Town TN31 .... 70 A2
Bowley Rd BN27 .... 152 C7
Bowlings The TN33 .... 113 D8
Bowmans Dr TN33 .... 112 D6
Bowood Ave BN22 .... 185 B6
Bowrey Pl TN40 .... 157 C5
Bowring Way BN2 .... 164 D4
Bowsprit Mews TN38 .... 135 E7
Box La RH16 .... 11 E6
Box's La RH17 .... 34 C5
Boxes La RH17 .... 33 C5
Boxgrove Cl TN40 .... 157 F4
Boyce's St BN1 .... 189 F5
Boyne Pk TN4 .... 7 F4
Boyne Rd TN35 .... 160 C5
Bracken Cl Crowborough TN6 . 26 C1
Royal Tunbridge Wells TN2 ...... 8 E5
Bracken Rd Eastbourne BN20 .. 184 B5
Royal Tunbridge Wells TN2 ...... 8 E5
Seaford BN25 .... 181 A2
Bracken Way TN31 .... 59 E1
Brackenbury Cl BN41 .... 141 B2
Brackendale TN35 .... 160 D6
Brackerne Cl TN39 .... 156 C2
Bradford Ct **9** BN22 .... 185 B4
Bradford Rd BN7 .... 123 B1
Bradford St BN20, BN21 .... 184 D3
Brading Cl Eastbourne BN23 . 174 B4
Hastings TN34 .... 136 E2
Brading Rd BN2 .... 164 C7
Bradley Rd Wartling BN27 ..... 131 C1
White Post TN3 .... 5 D5
Braemar Ho **6** BN1 .... 163 E6
Braemore Ct BN3 .... 162 E6
Braemore Rd BN3 .... 162 E6
Braeside Ave BN1 .... 143 A7
Bramber Ave Hove BN3 .... 141 F3
Peacehaven BN10 .... 178 C7
Bramber Ave N BN10 .... 178 C8
Bramber Cl
Haywards Heath RH16 .... 50 D4
Peacehaven BN10 .... 178 C8
3 Seaford BN25 .... 180 F2
Bramber Ct **6** Hove BN3 ... 163 B7
2 Shoreham-by-Sea BN43 . 161 B8
Bramber La BN25 .... 180 F2
Bramber Rd BN25 .... 180 F2
Bramber Way RH15 .... 73 A4
Bramble Cl BN23 .... 174 B3
Bramble Croft TN6 .... 26 A2
Bramble Dr BN27 .... 152 A7
Bramble Gdns RH15 .... 72 C4
Bramble Rise BN1 .... 142 C5
Bramble Twitten RH19 .... 2 A1
Bramble Way Brighton BN1 ... 143 C6
Fairlight Cove TN35 .... 138 F4
Bramble Wlk TN1 .... 8 D7
Brambledean Rd BN41 .... 162 B7
Brambles BN6 .... 97 F5
Brambles The TN17 .... 50 A6
Brambleside TN22 .... 78 A6
Brambletye Sch RH19 .... 11 C5
Brambletye Ave BN2 .... 177 D5
Bramley Rd BN26 .... 173 D6
Bramleys BN7 .... 145 E5
Brampton Ave TN39 .... 156 F4
Brampton Ct TN39 .... 156 F4
Brampton Rd BN22 .... 184 F8
Brampton Road Trad Est
BN22 .... 185 A8
Brand Rd BN22 .... 173 E1
Brands Cl BN9 .... 168 E2
Brangwyn Ave BN1 .... 142 E5
Brangwyn Cres BN1 .... 142 E6
Brangwyn Ct BN1 .... 142 E5
Brangwyn Dr BN1 .... 142 E5
Brangwyn Way BN1 .... 142 E5
Branksome Rd TN38 .... 159 A8
Branston Rd BN22 .... 173 D1
Brassey Ave BN22 .... 173 E1
Brassey Par BN22 .... 173 F1
Brassey Rd TN40 .... 157 D3
Brasslands Dr BN41 .... 140 F1
Braybon Ave BN1 .... 142 F4
Braybon Bsns Pk RH15 .... 72 E2
Braybrooke Cl TN38 .... 159 E8
Braybrooke Rd TN38 .... 159 F8
Braybrooke Terr TN34 .... 159 E8
Braypool La BN1 .... 142 D7
Brazen Cl BN9 .... 179 B7
Bread St BN1 .... 189 A6
Breadsell La TN33, TN38 ...... 135 D6
Brecon Cotts TN6 .... 39 A8
Brecon Ct **6** BN3 .... 163 C7

Brecon Ct **6** BN3 .... 163 C7
Brede Cl Brighton BN2 .... 164 F5
Eastbourne BN22 .... 185 D6
Brede Hill TN31 .... 115 B8
Brede Cty Prim Sch TN31 ...... 90 B4
Brede La Cackle Street TN31 .. 89 F2
Sedlescombe TN31, TN33 .... 89 B2
Brede Valley View TN36 .... 116 E5
Breeds Pl TN34 .... 159 F7
Brendon Cl Eastbourne BN23 . 174 E4
Royal Tunbridge Wells TN2 ...... 8 D5
Brendon Rise TN34 .... 137 B3
Brentor Ct TN2 .... 8 D6
Brentwood Cl BN1 .... 143 B3
Brentwood Cres BN1 .... 143 B3
Brentwood Rd BN1 .... 143 B3
Bretland Rd TN4 .... 7 D4
Brett Dr TN40 .... 157 F4
Bretton RH15 .... 72 E5
Bretts Field BN10 .... 167 C2
Brewer St Brighton BN2 .... 189 B7
Lamberhurst TN3 .... 20 A5
Brewers Gr TN20 .... 40 B2
Brian Cres TN4 .... 8 B8
Briar Cl Fairlight Cove TN35 .. 139 A5
Woodingdean BN2 .... 165 D7
Briar Pl BN23 .... 174 B3
Briarcroft Rd BN2 .... 165 D7
Briary The TN40 .... 157 D5
Brickfield TN31 .... 69 B2
Brickfields TN2 .... 9 E8
Brickhurst La BN8 .... 126 C8
Brickmead TN6 .... 26 A1
Bricky The BN10 .... 178 D8
Brickyard Cotts TN6 .... 28 A4
Brickyard La Mark Cross TN6 .. 27 E5
South Chailey BN8 .... 100 E7
Bridge Cl Burgess Hill RH15 ... 72 F4
Horam TN21 .... 107 A7
Bridge Ct BN9 .... 179 D7
Bridge End BN24 .... 175 B7
Bridge Farm Rd TN22 .... 78 C6
Bridge Ho TN4 .... 8 B5
Bridge Pl TN31 .... 93 C6
Bridge Rd RH16 .... 50 F6
Bridge Road Bsns Pk RH16 .... 50 F7
Bridge St BN9 .... 179 D7
Bridge Way TN38 .... 158 C6
Bridgelands BN8 .... 101 D4
Bridgemere Rd BN22 .... 185 B6
Bridger Way TN6 .... 26 A1
Bridgersmill RH16 .... 50 D6
Bridgewick Cl BN7 .... 123 D3
Bridle Way BN10 .... 167 A1
Briers Ave TN37 .... 136 C3
Briers Gdns TN37 .... 136 C3
Briers The TN37 .... 136 C4
Brigden St BN1 .... 189 F7
Bright Ridge TN4 .... 7 E8
Brighthelm BN1 .... 144 B8
Brightland Rd BN20 .... 184 D3
Brightling Ave TN35 .... 137 E4
Brightling Rd Polegate BN26 . 173 B5
Robertsbridge TN32 .... 63 D2
Brighton Coll BN2 .... 164 C5
Brighton Coll of Tech
Brighton BN1 .... 189 A6
Brighton BN1 .... 189 B7
Brighton BN1 .... 189 B8
Brighton Ctr The BN1 .... 189 F5
Brighton General Hospl BN2 . 164 D7
Brighton & Hove
Golf Course BN41 .... 141 D6
Brighton & Hove
High Sch for Girls BN3 .... 163 E6
Brighton & Hove Stad BN3 ... 142 B1
Brighton, Hove & Sussex
Sixth Form Coll BN3 .... 163 B8
Brighton Marina BN2 .... 164 F2
Brighton Marina Village BN2 . 164 F3
Brighton Mus & Art Gall BN1 . 189 A5
Brighton Pl BN1 .... 189 A5
Brighton Race Course BN2 ... 165 A3
Brighton Rd Hassocks BN6 ..... 97 D2
Lewes BN7 .... 146 A8
Newhaven BN9 .... 179 B7
Shoreham-by-Sea BN43 .... 161 B7
Brighton Sea Life Ctr BN1 .... 189 A4
Brighton Sq BN1 .... 189 A5
Brighton Sta BN1 .... 189 A6
Brightwell Ind Est BN9 .... 179 E7
Brills La BN1, BN2 .... 189 A4
Brincliffe TN6 .... 25 C3
Brinkers La TN5 .... 30 A2
Bristol Gate BN2 .... 164 D4
Bristol Gdns BN2 .... 164 E4
Bristol Mews **3** BN2 .... 164 E4
Bristol Pl BN2 .... 164 E4
Bristol Rd Brighton BN2 .... 164 C4
Hastings TN38 .... 136 A3
Bristol St BN2 .... 164 E4
Bristol Way TN38 .... 136 A3
British Engineerium (Mus)
BN3 .... 142 B2
Britland Est BN22 .... 185 C6
Brittany Ct **3** Bexhill TN39 . 157 A4
Hove BN3 .... 162 D7
Brittany Mews TN38 .... 159 B7
Brittany Rd Hastings TN38 ... 159 B8
Hove BN3, BN41 .... 162 D6
Britten Cl BN23 .... 174 C3
Brittenden La TN11 .... 80 E5
Britts Farm Rd TN22 .... 56 C3
Britts Orch TN22 .... 56 C3
Broad Gn BN2 .... 165 C6
Broad Gr TN2 .... 8 A1
Broad Green Ave RH15 .... 73 C2

Broad La TN3 ... 6 A4
Broad Oak TN3 ... 15 C6
Broad Oak Cl Broad Oak TN31 ... 90 B5
  Eastbourne BN22 ... 174 A4
  Royal Tunbridge Wells TN2 ... 7 F1
Broad Rd BN20, BN22 ... 173 A4
Broad Rig Ave BN3 ... 141 D3
Broad St Brighton BN2 ... 189 A4
  Cuckfield RH17 ... 50 A6
  Icklesham TN36 ... 116 C6
  Seaford BN25 ... 180 E3
Broad View Bexhill TN39 ... 156 F6
  Broad Oak TN21 ... 59 E1
Broad Way TN35 ... 138 F5
Broadcroft TN2 ... 16 F8
Broadfields BN2 ... 143 E3
Broadfields Rd BN2 ... 143 E3
Broadhill Cl TN21 ... 59 E5
Broadlands Burgess Hill RH15 ... 98 B8
  Hastings TN35 ... 137 D4
Broadley View TN33 ... 133 E8
Broadmead TN2 ... 16 F8
Broadmead Ave TN2 ... 16 F8
Broadoak Cty Prim Sch TN21 ... 59 F2
Broadoak La Bexhill TN39 ... 156 E5
  Bexhill TN39 ... 156 F5
Broads Cotts TN19 ... 62 B6
Broadstone RH18 ... 12 A2
Broadview Cl BN20 ... 172 F4
Broadwalk The TN39 ... 156 B4
Broadwater Ct TN2 ... 16 E8
Broadwater Down TN2 ... 16 F8
Broadwater Down Cty Prim Sch TN2 ... 16 F8
Broadwater La
  Royal Tunbridge Wells TN2, TN4 ... 7 F1
  Royal Tunbridge Wells TN2 ... 16 F8
Broadwater Mews BN26 ... 172 E3
Broadwater Rise TN2 ... 7 F1
Broadwater Way BN22 ... 184 F8
Broadway [11] BN43 ... 161 C8
Broadway The Alfriston BN26 ... 170 F3
  Crowborough TN6 ... 25 F3
  Eastbourne BN22 ... 173 D1
  Hastings TN35 ... 137 D4
  Haywards Heath RH16 ... 50 D4
  Lamberhurst TN3 ... 20 B5
Brockhurst TN2 ... 164 F7
Brockhurst Gate TN40 ... 157 F5
Brockley Rd TN39 ... 157 A3
Brocks Gyhll BN20 ... 173 A3
Brodie Pl BN1 ... 141 E4
Brodrick Cl BN22 ... 173 F1
Brodrick Rd BN22 ... 173 E2
Brokes Way TN4 ... 8 B8
Bromley Cl Eastbourne BN23 ... 174 C2
  Keymer BN6 ... 98 A4
Bromley Rd Brighton BN2 ... 189 B8
  Seaford BN25 ... 181 A4
Brompton Cl BN1 ... 142 E6
Brontes The RH19 ... 1 D1
Brook Ave BN6 ... 97 F3
Brook Cl Crowborough TN6 ... 26 D1
  East Grinstead RH19 ... 2 B1
Brook La Beddingham BN8 ... 147 A6
  Haywards Heath RH16 ... 50 F8
Brook Rd TN1 ... 8 D7
Brook St Hastings TN34 ... 159 F8
  Lewes BN7 ... 123 D1
  Polegate BN26 ... 172 F6
Brook Terr TN6 ... 25 D4
Brook View TN6 ... 25 D4
Brook Way TN34 ... 137 B4
Brooker Pl BN3 ... 163 A7
Brooker St BN3 ... 163 A7
Brookfield TN18 ... 47 B5
Brookfield Ct TN40 ... 157 E4
Brookfield Rd TN40 ... 157 E4
Brookhouse Bottom RH17 ... 34 D4
Brookhouse Rd TN22 ... 79 A4
Brookland Cl Beachlands BN24 ... 175 E6
  Hastings TN34 ... 136 F2
Brooklands TN1 ... 8 D7
Brooklands Ave TN6 ... 37 F7
Brooklands Farm Cl TN3 ... 6 A6
Brooklands Terr BN27 ... 128 E3
Brooklands Way RH19 ... 10 D8
Brooklyn Rd BN26 ... 180 E3
Brookmead Cl BN22 ... 185 B5
Brooks Cl Lewes BN7 ... 123 D2
  Newhaven BN9 ... 179 D6
Brooks Gdns BN8 ... 76 D6
Brooks Rd BN7 ... 123 D2
Brooks The RH15 ... 72 E5
Brookside Piddinghoe BN9 ... 168 B2
  Uckfield TN22 ... 78 A6
Brookside Ave BN26 ... 172 F7
Brookside Cotts TN19 ... 63 B8
Brookway Burgess Hill RH15 ... 73 C3
  Haywards Heath RH16 ... 51 A8
Broom Cl BN22 ... 173 D2
Broom La TN3 ... 6 E2
Broom Pk TN3 ... 6 E3
Brooman's Ct [16] TN7 ... 123 D1
Broomans La BN7 ... 123 D1
Broomfield Ave BN10 ... 177 F4
Broomfield Dr BN41 ... 141 A3
Broomfield St BN20, BN21 ... 184 C4
Broomgrove Rd TN34 ... 160 B6
Broomham Sch TN35 ... 116 A3
Broomhill Bank Sch TN3 ... 7 C6
Broomhill Park Rd TN4 ... 7 F8
Broomhill Rd TN3 ... 7 D7
Bross Est BN9 ... 179 D8
Brow The Burgess Hill RH15 ... 73 A2
  Friston BN20 ... 183 A1
  Woodingdean BN2 ... 165 D8
Brown Jack Ave BN26 ... 172 F6

Brown's La TN22 ... 78 D8
Browning Rd [2] TN21 ... 82 A7
Browning Wlk [5] BN23 ... 174 E2
Brownings The [1] RH19 ... 1 C1
Brownleaf Rd BN2 ... 165 E6
Browns Cl TN22 ... 78 D8
Browns Wood RH19 ... 1 E4
Broyle Cl BN8 ... 125 A8
Broyle La BN8 ... 124 F8
Broyle Paddock BN8 ... 124 F7
Broyle Side BN8 ... 125 A7
Broyle The BN8 ... 125 B7
Bruce Cl RH16 ... 50 E3
Brunel Rd TN38 ... 135 E4
Brunswick Mews BN3 ... 163 D5
Brunswick Pl BN3 ... 163 D6
Brunswick Rd BN3 ... 163 D6
Brunswick Row BN1 ... 189 A7
Brunswick Sq BN3 ... 163 D5
Brunswick St E BN3 ... 163 D5
Brunswick St W BN3 ... 163 D5
Brunswick Terr
  Hove BN1, BN3 ... 163 D5
  Royal Tunbridge Wells TN1 ... 8 A2
Brushes La RH16 ... 51 B8
Bryants Field TN6 ... 25 E3
Brydges Cl BN22 ... 185 C6
Buchanan Hospl TN38 ... 136 B1
Buci Cres BN43 ... 140 C1
Buckholt Ave TN40 ... 158 A7
Buckholt La TN39 ... 157 C8
Buckhurst Cl
  East Grinstead RH19 ... 1 C3
  Eastbourne BN20 ... 184 B8
  Lewes BN7 ... 123 C3
Buckhurst La TN5 ... 29 A6
Buckhurst Mead RH19 ... 1 C1
Buckhurst Pl TN39, TN40 ... 157 C4
Buckhurst Rd Bexhill TN40 ... 157 C4
  Telscombe Cliffs BN10 ... 177 F3
Buckhurst Way RH19 ... 1 C3
Buckingham Cl
  [4] Brighton BN1 ... 189 F7
  Seaford BN25 ... 180 E4
  Shoreham-by-Sea BN43 ... 161 A8
Buckingham Dr RH19 ... 11 A8
Buckingham Lodge BN1 ... 189 F7
Buckingham Pl BN1 ... 189 F7
Buckingham Rd Brighton BN1 ... 189 F6
  Hastings TN38 ... 136 A4
  Royal Tunbridge Wells TN1 ... 8 B2
Buckingham St BN1 ... 189 F6
Buckland Rd BN25 ... 180 F5
Buckle By-Pass BN25 ... 180 C4
Buckle Cl BN25 ... 180 C4
Buckle Dr BN25 ... 180 C4
Buckle Rise BN25 ... 180 C4
Buckler St BN41 ... 162 B8
Bucklers Cl TN2 ... 8 C3
Buckley Cl BN3 ... 141 E4
Buckswood Grange Sch TN22 ... 78 B8
Buckthorn Cl BN25 ... 181 C3
Buckwell St BN7 ... 123 A3
Buckwell Rise BN27 ... 130 E5
Buddens Gn TN31 ... 68 B5
Bugsell La TN32 ... 63 F4
Bulbeck Cl RH15 ... 72 E1
Bull La [2] BN7 ... 146 C8
Bull Lane Cotts TN3 ... 19 C4
Bull Ring TN33 ... 112 D4
Buller Cl TN6 ... 26 A1
Buller Rd BN2 ... 143 D1
Bullfinch Gdns TN22 ... 78 E4
Bullingstone Cotts TN3 ... 6 F7
Bullingstone La TN3 ... 6 F7
Bulls Pl TN2 ... 9 D6
Bulrush Pl TN38 ... 135 E1
Bulverhythe Rd TN38 ... 158 B6
Bungalows The TN22 ... 79 B5
Bunny La TN3 ... 16 E5
Burchetts Cl RH16 ... 50 E2
Burden Pl TN38 ... 136 A3
Burdett Pl [2] TN34 ... 160 A3
Burdett Rd Crowborough TN6 ... 26 C1
  Rusthall TN4 ... 7 B4
Burdocks Dr RH15 ... 73 D1
Burfield Park Ind Est BN27 ... 152 B6
Burfield Rd BN20 ... 185 B3
Burgess Hill Sch RH15 ... 73 B2
Burgess Hill Sta RH15 ... 73 B2
Burgess Rd TN34 ... 137 C5
Burgh Hill TN19 ... 44 E2
Burgh La BN8 ... 148 E5
Burhill Way TN38 ... 158 F7
Burleigh Pl BN22 ... 185 C6
Burlington Gdns BN41 ... 141 C1
Burlington Pl BN21 ... 185 A2
Burlington Rd BN21 ... 185 B2
Burlington St BN2 ... 164 C4
Burlow Cl Brighton BN2 ... 164 E5
  Lower Willingdon BN22 ... 173 C3
Burma Cl RH16 ... 51 C4
Burners Cl RH15 ... 73 D1
Burnham Cl BN2 ... 165 F7
Burns Way RH19 ... 1 C1
Burnside BN26 ... 173 A6
Burnside Cl BN26 ... 173 A6
Burnt House La TN3 ... 7 A5
Burnt Lodge La TN5 ... 31 B2
Burnt Oak Rd TN22, TN6 ... 37 E2
Burnthouse Bostall TN22 ... 120 C8
Burrell Rd BN22 ... 50 D6
Burrells La TN22 ... 55 A7
Burrells The BN43 ... 161 B6
Burrow Down BN20 ... 184 B5
Burrow Down Cl BN20 ... 184 A5
Burrswood Villas TN3 ... 15 B7

Burry Rd TN37 ... 136 C3
Burslem Rd TN2 ... 8 E7
Burstead Cl BN1 ... 143 B3
Burston Gdns RH19 ... 1 D4
Burton Rd BN21 ... 184 E5
Burton Villas BN3 ... 163 D8
Burton Way TN38 ... 159 B6
Burton Wlk BN27 ... 152 B7
Burwash CE Prim Sch TN19 ... 62 B6
Burwash Cl Eastbourne BN23 ... 174 B4
  Hastings TN37 ... 137 A5
Burwash Lodge [1] BN1 ... 143 C1
Burwash Rd Broad Oak TN21 ... 82 C8
  Hove BN3 ... 141 F3
Bush Cl Telscombe Cliffs BN10 ... 167 A1
  Woodingdean BN2 ... 165 D8
Bush Farm Dr BN41 ... 141 C3
Bush Rd BN9 ... 179 B8
Bushbury La TN22 ... 80 A3
Busheyfields BN27 ... 152 A8
Bushy Croft TN39 ... 156 F5
Bushy Gill TN7 ... 7 A3
Butcher's Cross TN7 ... 13 B7
Butcher's La TN35 ... 115 E2
Butcherfield La TN7 ... 13 B6
Bute St BN2 ... 164 D5
Butler's Green Ho RH16 ... 50 B4
Butler's Green Rd RH16 ... 50 C4
Butler's La BN27 ... 130 E3
Butlers Way BN8 ... 124 C5
Butterbox La BN8, RH17 ... 52 D4
Buttercup Wlk BN1 ... 143 B7
Butterfield RH19 ... 1 B3
Butterfly Ctr BN22 ... 185 D4
Buttermere Way BN23 ... 174 C4
Button Cl BN2 ... 189 B7
Butts Field BN27 ... 152 C6
Butts Rd BN42 ... 161 E7
Buttsfield La BN2 ... 105 A5
Buxted CE Prim Sch TN22 ... 55 F3
Buxted Cl BN2 ... 56 C3
Buxted Rise BN1 ... 143 B5
Buxted Sta TN22 ... 56 B3
Buxted Wood La TN22 ... 56 E5
Buxton Dr TN6 ... 157 B6
Buxton Rd Brighton BN1 ... 163 E7
  Eastbourne BN20 ... 188 E8
By Sunte RH16 ... 50 F8
Bye-law Cotts BN8 ... 101 E6
Byeway The Bexhill TN39 ... 156 D5
  Hastings TN34 ... 137 A4
Byeways The BN25 ... 180 F4
Byfields Croft TN39 ... 156 F5
Byland Cl BN22 ... 173 E3
Bylands BN2 ... 164 F5
Byng Rd TN4 ... 7 F5
Byron Ct [1] RH16 ... 50 D5
Byron Gr [2] RH19 ... 1 C1
Byron St BN3 ... 163 A7
Byron Wlk BN23 ... 174 E3
Byway The BN1 ... 143 E5
Byways TN34 ... 136 D6
Byworth Cl Bexhill TN39 ... 156 C6
  Brighton BN2 ... 164 F6

Cabbage Stalk La TN4 ... 7 E2
Caburn Cres BN7 ... 123 A2
Caburn Rd BN3 ... 163 E7
Caburn Way BN27 ... 152 B6
Cackle St TN31 ... 90 A2
Cacklebury Cl BN27 ... 152 A6
Cadborough Cliff TN31 ... 93 A4
Cade St TN21 ... 173 F2
Cadogan Cl BN8 ... 101 E6
Cadogan Gdns [6] TN1 ... 8 B4
Cairngorm Cl BN23 ... 174 D3
Cairo Ave BN10 ... 178 A8
Cairo Ave S BN10 ... 178 A7
Caister's Cl BN3 ... 163 C8
Caius Ct [16] BN43 ... 161 C8
Calbourne RH16 ... 50 D5
Caldbec Ct TN33 ... 112 D5
Caldbec Hill TN33 ... 112 D5
Caldicotts La BN27 ... 128 C4
Caledonian Rd BN2 ... 189 B8
Caley Rd TN1 ... 8 D7
Calgary Rd TN39 ... 157 B7
Calverley Ct TN2 ... 8 B3
Calverley Park Cres [1] TN1, TN2 ... 8 B3
Calverley Park Gdns TN1, TN2 ... 8 B3
Calverley Pk TN1, TN2 ... 8 B3
Calverley Rd Eastbourne BN21 ... 184 F2
  Royal Tunbridge Wells TN1, TN2 ... 8 B3
Calverley St TN1 ... 8 B4
Calverley Wlk BN21 ... 184 F2
Calvert Cl TN22 ... 78 A7
Calvert Rd Hastings TN34 ... 160 A6
  Uckfield TN22 ... 78 A7
Camber Cl Beachlands BN24 ... 175 F6
  Bexhill TN40 ... 157 E6
  Brighton BN2 ... 164 F5
Camber Dr BN24 ... 175 F6
Camber Rd TN31 ... 94 B3
Camberlot Rd BN27 ... 128 A2
Cambrian Rd TN4 ... 8 C7
Cambridge Gdns
  Hastings TN34 ... 159 E7
  Royal Tunbridge Wells TN2 ... 8 B2
Cambridge Gr BN3 ... 163 C7
Cambridge Rd
  Bexhill TN39, TN40 ... 157 C6
  Eastbourne BN22 ... 185 C4
  Hastings TN34 ... 159 E7
  Hove BN3 ... 163 D6
Cambridge St TN2 ... 8 C3

Cambridge Way TN22 ... 55 C1
Camden Ave TN2 ... 9 C6
Camden Ct Pembury TN2 ... 9 D6
  [2] Royal Tunbridge Wells TN1 ... 8 B4
Camden Hill TN1, TN2 ... 8 B4
Camden Pk TN2 ... 9 C6
Camden Rd Eastbourne BN21 ... 184 F2
  Royal Tunbridge Wells TN1 ... 8 A6
Camden St BN41 ... 162 C6
Camden Terr BN1 ... 189 F6
Camelford St BN2 ... 189 B4
Campbell Cl TN22 ... 55 C1
Campbell Cres RH19 ... 1 B1
Campbell Ct TN38 ... 159 A8
Campbell Rd Brighton BN1 ... 189 F8
  Royal Tunbridge Wells TN4 ... 8 A6
Camperdown St TN39 ... 157 B7
Canada Cl BN10 ... 167 B1
Canada Way TN39 ... 157 B7
Canadia Rd TN33 ... 112 D8
Canal Bank BN3 ... 139 B7
Canfield Cl BN2 ... 143 D1
Canfield Rd BN2 ... 143 D1
Canning St BN2 ... 164 D5
Cannon Pl BN1 ... 189 F5
Cansiron La
  Ashurst Wood RH19 ... 11 F6
  Holtye TN7, TN8 ... 3 E2
Cantelupe Rd Bexhill TN40 ... 157 D3
  East Grinstead RH19 ... 1 F1
Canterbury Cl BN22 ... 173 C2
Canterbury Dr [5] BN2 ... 189 B7
Canterbury Rd TN2 ... 9 E6
Canterbury Rise TN34 ... 136 E3
Cantercrow Hill BN9 ... 168 F2
Canton [3] RH16 ... 50 D6
Canton Pl TN38 ... 158 F8
Cants Cl RH15 ... 73 C3
Cants La RH15 ... 73 C3
Canute Cl BN23 ... 185 F8
Canute Rd TN35 ... 137 D3
Capel Ave BN10 ... 178 D7
Capello Path BN27 ... 152 D7
Capenors RH15 ... 72 F1
Caple Ct TN38 ... 159 B8
Caple Gdns TN38 ... 159 B7
Card Hill RH18 ... 11 F1
Carden Ave BN1 ... 143 B6
Carden Cl BN1 ... 143 A6
Carden Cres BN1 ... 143 A6
Carden Cty Inf Sch BN1 ... 143 B6
Carden Cty Jun Sch BN1 ... 143 B6
Carden Hill BN1 ... 143 B5
Cardiff Rd TN38 ... 159 C7
Cardinal Newman Sch BN3 ... 163 D8
Cardinals Cl TN40 ... 157 F6
Carew Cl BN21 ... 185 A4
Carew Lodge [1] BN21 ... 184 F4
Carew Rd BN21 ... 184 F4
Carew Views [2] BN21 ... 184 F4
Carey Down BN10 ... 167 B1
Carfax Cl TN39 ... 157 B8
Carinus Gdns TN38 ... 136 A4
Carisbrooke Cl BN23 ... 174 B4
Carisbrooke Rd Brighton BN2 ... 164 D7
  Hastings TN38 ... 159 C7
Carlisle Par TN34 ... 159 F7
Carlisle Rd
  Eastbourne BN20, BN21 ... 184 F1
  Hove BN3 ... 162 F6
Carlton Cl BN25 ... 180 E4
Carlton Cres TN2 ... 8 C4
Carlton Ct Bexhill TN40 ... 157 D3
  Portslade-by-Sea BN3 ... 162 C8
Carlton Hill BN2 ... 189 B5
Carlton Hill Cty Prim Sch BN2 ... 189 B5
Carlton Pl [5] BN2 ... 189 B5
Carlton Rd Eastbourne BN22 ... 185 C4
  Royal Tunbridge Wells TN2 ... 8 C4
  Seaford BN25 ... 180 D4
Carlton Terr BN3 ... 162 C8
Carlyle Ave BN2 ... 143 D1
Carlyle St BN2 ... 164 C7
Carmel TN39 ... 156 D3
Carmen Ct BN20 ... 173 B3
Carol Cl BN1 ... 142 F6
Caroline Cl BN25 ... 180 C5
Carpenter Dr TN38 ... 135 F4
Carpenters Croft BN8 ... 105 A5
Carpenters Way BN27 ... 152 A6
Carrier's Path BN27 ... 152 B8
Carriers Pl TN3 ... 5 B3
Carroll Wlk BN23 ... 174 E2
Cashman Lodge BN1 ... 143 A5
Caspian Cl [8] BN1 ... 189 F7
Caspian Sq BN2 ... 165 F1
Castle Banks [4] BN7 ... 123 C1
Castle Cl BN7 ... 123 D2
Castle Ditch La BN7 ... 123 C1
Castle Farm Cotts TN7 ... 13 E4
Castle Gate [7] BN7 ... 123 C1
Castle Gdns [10] TN34 ... 159 F7
Castle Hill TN20 ... 39 A5
Castle Hill Pas TN34 ... 159 F8
Castle Hill Rd TN34 ... 159 F7
Castle Hurst TN32 ... 65 A1
Castle Mount BN20 ... 184 C4
Castle Prec [5] BN7 ... 123 C1
Castle Rd TN4 ... 8 A3
Castle Rise [8] Lewes BN7 ... 123 D2
  Uckfield TN22 ... 78 D4
Castle Sq BN1 ... 189 A5
Castle St Brighton BN1 ... 163 E5
  [9] Hastings TN34 ... 159 F7
  [2] Royal Tunbridge Wells TN1 ... 8 A2

Castle St
  Winchelsea TN36 ... 117 F7
Castle Terr BN24 ... 175 B6
Castle View Gdns BN24 ... 174 E6
Castle Way TN22 ... 78 D4
Castle Wlk TN5 ... 29 C4
Castledean Sch BN2 ... 143 C2
Castledown Ave TN34 ... 160 A4
Castledown Cty Prim Sch TN34 ... 160 A5
Castledown Terr [7] TN34 ... 160 A4
Castlefields TN7 ... 13 E4
Castleham Rd TN38 ... 135 F4
Castleross Rd BN24 ... 175 C4
Cat St TN7 ... 12 F1
Catherine Pl [7] TN1 ... 8 B4
Catherine Vale BN2 ... 165 E8
Catkin Way RH16 ... 51 B4
Catley Ct [2] TN39 ... 157 A4
Catsfield CE Prim Sch TN33 ... 133 F8
Catsfield Cl TN38 ... 135 D2
Catsfield Place
  (Wilton House Sch) TN33 ... 134 B6
Catsfield Rd TN33 ... 111 E2
Catt's Corner Cotts TN6 ... 27 D1
Catt's Hill TN6 ... 27 E1
Causeway The Brighton BN2 ... 164 D6
  [5] Seaford BN25 ... 180 E2
Cavalier Way RH19 ... 10 F7
Cavalry Cres BN20 ... 184 B5
Cavell Ave BN10 ... 178 B7
Cavell Ave N BN10 ... 178 C8
Cavendish Ave Eastbourne BN22 ... 185 B4
  Hastings TN38 ... 159 A7
Cavendish Cl TN40 ... 167 B1
Cavendish Ct TN40 ... 157 D3
Cavendish Dr TN2 ... 8 B1
Cavendish Ho
  [12] Brighton BN1 ... 163 E5
  [9] Hastings TN37 ... 159 C7
  Peacehaven BN10 ... 167 C1
Cavendish Pl Brighton BN1 ... 163 E5
  Eastbourne BN21 ... 185 B3
  [4] Hastings TN34 ... 160 A4
Cavendish Sch BN21 ... 184 C5
Cavendish St [11] BN2 ... 189 B5
Caveridge La BN8 ... 100 E8
Caverley Rd TN1 ... 8 B4
Caves Rd TN38 ... 159 A6
Cavix Field [1] TN31 ... 67 B7
Caxton Way [15] TN31 ... 50 E4
Cedar Cl Burgess Hill RH15 ... 73 B5
  Eastbourne BN22 ... 173 D2
  Hastings TN37 ... 136 D5
Cedar Ct TN4 ... 8 A5
Cedar Lodge TN4 ... 7 F3
Cedar Ridge TN2 ... 8 D5
Cedar Way RH16 ... 51 B4
Cedars Cl TN22 ... 78 C8
Cedars Gdns BN1 ... 142 E3
Cedars The [1] Brighton BN2 ... 189 B8
  [1] Brighton, Withdean BN1 ... 142 E3
  Hailsham BN27 ... 129 B1
  Haywards Heath RH16 ... 50 D7
  Peacehaven BN10 ... 167 C1
  Uckfield TN22 ... 78 D8
Cedarwell Cl BN9 ... 168 B2
Cedarwood [6] BN1 ... 142 E3
Celandine Dr TN38 ... 136 A1
Centenary Ho [9] BN1 ... 142 E2
Centenary Ind Est [6] BN2 ... 164 B8
Central Ave Eastbourne BN20 ... 184 B5
  Polegate BN26 ... 173 B7
  Telscombe Cliffs BN10 ... 178 A8
Central Sta BN1 ... 8 A3
Centurion Rd BN1 ... 189 F6
Centurion Rise TN34 ... 137 A4
Ceylon Pl BN21, BN22 ... 185 B3
Ceylon Wlk TN39 ... 156 E3
Chadborn Cl BN2 ... 164 D5
Chaffinch Cl RH15 ... 72 D4
Chaffinch Rd BN23 ... 174 C2
Chaffinch Wlk TN22 ... 78 D5
Chafford Cotts TN3 ... 5 F5
Chafford La TN3 ... 5 F5
Chailey Ave TN2 ... 177 A5
Chailey Cl Eastbourne BN23 ... 174 E1
  Hastings TN34 ... 136 F5
Chailey Common
  Nature Reserve BN8 ... 75 D7
Chailey Cres BN2 ... 177 E5
Chailey Ct [2] RH16 ... 50 F3
Chailey Cty Sec Sch BN8 ... 100 D7
Chailey Heritage Craft Sch &
  Hospl (New Heritage) BN8 ... 52 E1
Chailey Heritage Craft Sch &
  Hospl (Old Heritage) BN8 ... 75 C7
Chailey Heritage Craft Sch &
  Hospl (St George's) BN8 ... 75 D7
Chailey La BN8 ... 76 B5
Chailey Rd BN1 ... 143 E4
Chailey St Peter's
  CE Prim Sch BN8 ... 75 E4
Chailey Windmill
  Rural Life Mus BN8 ... 75 D7
Chain La TN33 ... 112 C5
Chalden TN39 ... 156 C6
Chalfont Dr BN3 ... 142 C3
Chalk Farm Cl BN20 ... 173 B1
Chalkers La BN6 ... 97 B8
Chalket La TN2 ... 9 C5
Chalkland Rise BN2 ... 165 E8
Chalky Rd BN41 ... 141 A3
Challoners RH17 ... 33 C4

Challoners Cl BN2 .... 177 A6
Challoners Mews BN2 .... 165 F2
Challow Cl BN6 .... 97 E4
Chaloner Cl RH16 .... 51 B7
Chaloner Rd RH16 .... 51 B7
Chalvington Cl Brighton BN1 ... 143 E6
  Seaford BN25 .... 180 F6
Chalvington Dr TN37 .... 136 C6
Chalvington Ho 6 BN21 .... 184 D4
Chalvington Rd BN21 .... 184 C7
Chamberlain Rd BN21 .... 184 C4
Chamberlaines La BN8 .... 124 F6
Chambers Cres TN38 .... 135 F3
Chambers Rd TN38 .... 135 F3
Chancellor Ho TN4 .... 7 F3
Chancellors Pk BN6 .... 97 F4
Chanctonbury Dr TN34 .... 136 E5
Chanctonbury Rd
  Burgess Hill RH15 .... 73 A1
  Hove BN3 .... 163 E7
Chandler Rd TN39 .... 157 A4
Chandler's Mead BN8 .... 123 A7
Chandos Rd TN1 .... 8 C5
Channel View Bexhill TN40 .... 157 C3
  13 Southwick BN42 .... 161 E7
Channel View E TN40 .... 157 C3
Channel View Rd
  Eastbourne BN22 .... 185 D5
  Pevensey Bay BN24 .... 175 E5
  Woodingdean BN2 .... 165 B8
Channel View W TN40 .... 157 C3
Channel Way TN35 .... 138 E3
Channers La BN8 .... 126 D1
Chant La TN6 .... 27 B1
Chantlers Cl RH19 .... 1 C2
Chantlers Mead TN8 .... 4 A5
Chantry Ave TN40 .... 157 D6
Chantry Cty Inf Sch TN40 .... 157 C5
Chantry La TN40 .... 157 C5
Chantry The 11 BN21 .... 184 E4
Chapel Barn Cl BN27 .... 152 C7
Chapel Cl Burgess Hill RH15 .... 72 F4
  Seaford BN25 .... 180 E4
Chapel Cotts Battle TN33 .... 112 B3
  Mayfield TN20 .... 40 B2
Chapel Field TN31 .... 67 A7
Chapel Gn TN6 .... 25 F2
Chapel Hill Crowhurst TN33 ..... 134 F4
  Lewes BN7 .... 123 E1
  Sedlescombe TN33 .... 113 E7
Chapel La Ashurst Wood RH19 .... 11 D6
  Blackboys TN22 .... 80 B7
  East Chiltington BN7 .... 100 A3
  Forest Row RH18 .... 11 F2
  Guestling Green TN35 .... 138 A8
  Horsted Keynes RH17 .... 33 C5
Chapel Mews BN3 .... 163 D5
Chapel Park Rd TN37 .... 159 C8
Chapel Pl
  Portslade-by-Sea BN41 .... 162 B7
  8 Royal Tunbridge Wells TN1 ... 8 A2
  Ticehurst TN5 .... 31 E1
Chapel Rd Plumpton Green BN7 .. 99 E7
  Southwick BN41 .... 162 A7
Chapel St Brighton BN2 .... 189 B5
  Newhaven BN9 .... 179 D7
Chapel Terr 2 BN2 .... 164 D4
Chapman Way TN4 .... 8 C8
Chapman's La
  East Grinstead RH19 .... 1 B1
  East Grinstead RH19 .... 1 D1
Charis Ct 15 BN3 .... 163 C7
Charity Farm Way TN6 .... 26 A3
Charles Ave RH15 .... 72 D2
Charles Bennett Ct RH16 .... 51 A4
Charles Cl Hove BN3 .... 142 A3
  Seaford BN25 .... 180 E4
Charles Ct TN2 .... 8 C3
Charles Moore Ct BN26 .... 173 A7
Charles Rd TN38 .... 159 C8
Charles Rd W TN38 .... 159 B8
Charles St Brighton BN2 .... 189 A4
  Royal Tunbridge Wells TN4 .... 8 A8
Charleston Farm BN8 .... 149 A2
Charleston Manor Gdns
  BN25 .... 182 A6
Charleston Rd BN21 .... 184 D4
Charlesworth Pk RH16 .... 51 C4
Charlotte St BN2 .... 189 B4
Charlston Ave BN9 .... 179 A5
Charlton's Way TN4 .... 7 E1
Charltons The BN1 .... 143 D6
Charlwood Gdns RH15 .... 73 C5
Charlwood Rd RH15 .... 73 D6
Charlwoods Bsns Ctr RH19 .... 1 D2
Charlwoods Pl RH19 .... 1 E3
Charlwoods Rd RH19 .... 1 E3
Charters Ancaster Sch TN40 .. 157 F5
Charters Ancaster Sch
  (Jun Dept) TN40 .... 157 F5
Chartfield BN3 .... 142 A2
Chartfield Way BN3 .... 142 B2
Chartres TN40 .... 157 D6
Chartres Cl TN40 .... 157 D6
Chartwell Cl BN25 .... 180 E6
Chartwell Ct BN1 .... 189 F5
Chates Farm Ct BN2 .... 189 B6
Chatfield Cres BN22 .... 173 C1
Chatfield Rd RH17 .... 50 A6
Chatham Pl Brighton BN1 .... 189 F7
  12 Seaford BN25 .... 180 E2
Chatham Rd 3 TN37 .... 136 B2
Chatsfield Cl TN38 .... 135 F4
Chatsworth Ave BN10 .... 167 A1
Chatsworth Cl BN10 .... 178 A8

Chatsworth Gdns BN20 .... 188 F8
Chatsworth Pk BN10 .... 167 B1
Chatsworth Rd BN1 .... 163 E8
Chaucer Ave 3 RH19 .... 1 C1
Chaucer Ct 2 RH16 .... 50 D5
Chaucer Ind Est BN26 .... 173 D6
Chaucer Wlk BN23 .... 174 E3
Chawbrook Rd BN41 .... 185 B4
Cheal Cl BN43 .... 161 A6
Cheapside BN1 .... 189 A6
Cheeleys RH17 .... 33 C5
Chelgates TN39 .... 156 C2
Chelmsford Ct 3 BN20 .... 184 F1
Chelsea Arc RH16 .... 50 E4
Chelsea Cl TN40 .... 157 D4
Chelston Ave BN3 .... 162 D7
Cheltenham Pl BN1 .... 189 A6
Chelwood Cl BN1 .... 143 C6
Chelwood Ct RH15 .... 73 A4
Chelwood Gate Rd TN22 .... 35 B6
Chene Rd BN10 .... 178 F6
Chenies Cl TN2 .... 17 A8
Chepbourne Rd TN40 .... 157 C4
Chepstow Ct BN1 .... 143 F5
Chequer Grange RH18 .... 11 E1
Chequer Rd RH19 .... 1 F1
Chequers Cl TN6 .... 26 A2
Chequers Way TN6 .... 26 A2
Cherith Cotts 3 TN21 .... 82 A6
Cherrie Ct BN20 .... 184 C4
Cherry Cl RH15 .... 72 E3
Cherry Clack TN21 .... 83 D6
Cherry Cotts TN22 .... 54 A4
Cherry Garden Rd BN20 .... 184 B3
Cherry Gdns Heathfield TN21 ..... 82 B5
  High Hurstwood TN22 .... 56 B8
Cherry Side BN27 .... 152 A7
Cherry Tree Cl TN37 .... 159 D8
Cherry Tree Ct TN21 .... 106 F7
Cherry Tree Gdns TN40 .... 157 F4
Cherry Tree Rd TN2 .... 7 E1
Cherrywood 5 BN1 .... 142 E3
Cherwell Cl BN26 .... 173 F5
Cherwell Ct TN21 .... 82 A8
Cherwell Rd TN21 .... 82 A8
Chesham Pl BN2 .... 164 D4
Chesham Rd BN2 .... 164 D4
Chesham St BN2 .... 164 D4
Cheshire Ct 6 BN22 .... 185 B4
Chesnut Cl BN27 .... 129 A1
Chester Ave TN2 .... 8 D2
Chester Ct 8 BN3 .... 163 E7
Chester Terr BN1 .... 143 A1
Chesterfield Gdns BN20 .... 188 E8
Chesterfield Rd BN20 .... 188 E8
Chesterton Ave BN25 .... 181 B3
Chesterton Cl RH19 .... 10 F7
Chesterton Dr BN25 .... 181 B3
Chestnut Ave TN4 .... 8 B8
Chestnut Cl Broad Oak TN31 ...... 90 B5
  Burgess Hill RH15 .... 73 B5
  East Grinstead RH19 .... 2 A1
  Eastbourne BN22 .... 173 E2
  Herstmonceux BN27 .... 130 E6
  Royal Tunbridge Wells TN4 .... 8 B7
Chestnut Cotts Fletching TN22 .. 53 F3
  11 Heathfield TN21 .... 82 A7
Chestnut Dr BN26 .... 173 A6
Chestnut Pl TN8 .... 4 A5
Chestnut Wlk Bexhill TN40 .... 157 C5
  Felcourt RH19 .... 2 B8
Chestnuts Cl RH16 .... 51 A7
Chestnuts The
  Haywards Heath RH16 .... 50 F7
  The Moor TN18 .... 45 F8
Chet Nole RH19 .... 1 D2
Cheviot Cl BN23 .... 174 C3
Cheviots The TN34 .... 137 C4
Cheyne Ct BN43 .... 161 C7
Chichester Cl Bexhill TN39 .... 157 B6
  15 Brighton BN2 .... 164 D4
  Eastbourne BN22 .... 173 B2
  Hove BN3 .... 141 E4
  Peacehaven BN10 .... 178 F7
  Saltdean BN2 .... 177 C5
  Seaford BN25 .... 180 E3
Chichester Ct TN39 .... 156 C3
Chichester Dr E BN2 .... 177 C5
Chichester Dr W BN2 .... 177 B5
Chichester Rd Hastings TN38 ... 136 B2
  Seaford BN25 .... 180 E3
Chichester Terr 16 BN2 .... 164 D4
Chichester Way RH15 .... 73 C5
Chick Hill TN35 .... 139 B8
Chicks La TN17 .... 20 F2
Chiddingley Cl BN2 .... 164 F5
Chiddingly Cty Prim Sch BN8 ... 127 E7
Chieveley Dr TN2 .... 8 D1
Chilcomb RH15 .... 73 C1
Chilham Ct RH15 .... 174 D2
Chillies La TN22, TN6 .... 37 B3
Chilling St RH19 .... 21 D3
Chillis Wood Rd RH16 .... 50 C5
Chilsham La BN27 .... 130 E7
Chilston Cl TN4 .... 8 A5
Chilston Rd TN4 .... 8 A5
Chiltern Cl Eastbourne BN23 .... 174 C3
  Shoreham-by-Sea BN43 .... 161 C8
Chiltern Dr BN26 .... 173 A7
Chiltern Rd TN37 .... 137 B3
Chiltern Wlk TN2 .... 8 D4
Chiltington Cl Burgess Hill RH15 .. 72 F5
  Saltdean BN2 .... 177 C6
Chiltington La BN7 .... 100 D3

Chiltington Way BN2 .... 177 C6
Chiswick Pl BN2 .... 185 A2
Chitcombe Rd TN31 .... 89 E5
Chitcombe Wlk TN34 .... 137 A5
Chorley Ave BN2 .... 177 B6
Chown's Hill TN34 .... 137 A6
Chownes Mead La RH16, RH17 .. 50 B4
Chrisdory Rd BN41 .... 140 F3
Christ Church Ave 1 TN1 .... 8 A2
Christ Church CE Prim Sch
  TN37 .... 136 C1
Christie Ave BN8 .... 124 D6
Christie Rd BN7 .... 123 A2
Christies RH19 .... 10 D8
Christopher Rd RH19 .... 1 E1
Church App TN22 .... 79 B5
Church Ave
  Haywards Heath RH16 .... 50 E6
  Westham BN24 .... 175 A6
Church Bailey BN24 .... 175 A5
Church Bailey Ct BN24 .... 175 A5
Church Cl Brighton BN1 .... 142 F5
  Burgess Hill RH15 .... 73 A3
  Lower Willingdon BN20 .... 173 A4
Church Ct
  3 Haywards Heath RH16 .... 50 E4
  Hove BN3 .... 141 F1
Church Farm Ct TN19 .... 44 C1
Church Gn BN43 .... 161 C7
Church Hill Bexhill TN39 .... 156 D4
  Brighton BN1 .... 142 E7
  Etchingham TN19 .... 44 B2
  Newhaven BN9 .... 179 C7
  Pyecombe BN45 .... 119 C6
  Ringmer BN8 .... 124 D6
Church Hill Ave TN39 .... 156 D4
Church House Cl BN42 .... 140 F1
Church in the Wood La TN38 .. 135 F3
Church La
  Burgess Hill RH16, RH17 .... 73 A6
  Buxted TN22 .... 56 C5
  Catsfield TN33 .... 133 E8
  Clayhill TN31 .... 67 E4
  Danehill RH17 .... 34 A3
  Ditchling BN6 .... 98 D3
  East Grinstead RH19 .... 1 F1
  11 Eastbourne BN21 .... 184 D3
  Etchingham TN19 .... 44 C1
  Frant TN3 .... 17 B4
  Guestling Green TN35 .... 116 B1
  Hellingly BN27 .... 129 A6
  Hooe TN33 .... 155 C7
  Horsted Keynes RH17 .... 33 C5
  Jevington BN26 .... 183 C7
  Kingston near Lewes BN7 .... 145 D5
  Lewes, South Malling BN7 .... 123 D3
  Lewes, St Anne's BN7 .... 146 B8
  Ninfield TN33 .... 133 B5
  Northbridge Street TN32 .... 64 C5
  Northiam TN31 .... 67 C6
  Peasmarsh TN31 .... 92 B8
  Pevensey BN24 .... 175 B6
  Pyecombe BN45 .... 119 C6
  Ripe BN27, BN8 .... 149 E8
  Seaford BN25 .... 180 E2
  Southwick BN42, BN43 .... 161 D7
  Westfield TN35 .... 114 E3
Church Marks La BN8 .... 104 F5
Church Mead BN6 .... 98 B3
Church Mews BN20 .... 173 B1
Church Pas 5 TN34 .... 160 A4
Church Path BN27 .... 129 A5
Church Pl BN2 .... 164 E4
Church Rd Barcombe BN8 .... 101 E2
  Burgess Hill RH15 .... 73 A3
  Buxted TN22 .... 56 B4
  Catsfield TN33 .... 133 F7
  Crowborough TN6 .... 25 F2
  Flowers Green BN27 .... 131 A1
  Hastings TN37 .... 159 D7
  Haywards Heath RH16 .... 50 E4
  Hove BN3 .... 163 B6
  Lamberhurst TN3 .... 20 C6
  Lewes BN7 .... 123 C1
  Mountfield TN32 .... 87 B5
  Newick BN8 .... 76 E6
  Polegate BN26 .... 173 A6
  Portslade-by-Sea BN41 .... 162 B7
  Rotherfield TN6 .... 39 A8
  Royal Tunbridge Wells TN1, TN4 .. 8 A3
  Sandhurst Cross TN18 .... 46 F4
  Scaynes Hill RH17 .... 51 F3
Church Sq TN31 .... 93 C5
Church St Bexhill TN40 .... 157 D5
  Brighton BN1 .... 189 A5
  Cowden TN8 .... 4 B5
  Eastbourne BN20, BN21 .... 184 D3
  Hartfield TN7 .... 13 D4
  Hastings TN35 .... 137 C3
  Old Heathfield TN21 .... 82 D5
  Portslade-by-Sea BN41 .... 162 B7
  Seaford BN25 .... 180 E2
  Ticehurst TN5 .... 31 D1
  Uckfield TN22 .... 78 C7
  Willingdon BN20, BN22 .... 173 C2
Church Twitten 15 BN7 .... 123 D1
Church Vale Rd TN40 .... 157 D5
Church Way 5 BN2 .... 189 B6
Church Wlk RH15 .... 73 A3
Church Wood Cty Prim Sch
  TN38 .... 135 F3
Church Wood Dr TN38 .... 135 E4
Church Wood Way TN38 .... 135 F2
Churchdale Ave BN22 .... 185 C6
Churchdale Pl BN22 .... 185 B6
Churchdale Rd BN22 .... 185 C6
Churchfield East Dean BN20 .... 187 B8
  Westfield TN35 .... 114 D3

Churchfields TN22 .... 35 C4
Churchill Ave TN35 .... 137 D5
Churchill Cl BN20 .... 184 D3
Churchill Ct TN38 .... 136 B2
Churchill Ho BN3 .... 141 E2
Churchill Rd Heathfield TN21 ..... 82 B6
  Lewes BN7 .... 123 B3
  Seaford BN25 .... 180 D5
Churchill Sq BN1 .... 189 F5
Churchland La TN33 .... 88 E3
Churchsettle La TN5 .... 42 B7
Churchyard Cotts TN3 .... 7 A8
Chyngton Ave BN25 .... 181 B4
Chyngton Cl BN23 .... 174 A4
Chyngton Cty Prim Sch BN25 .. 181 B4
Chyngton Gdns BN25 .... 181 B4
Chyngton Ho BN25 .... 181 C2
Chyngton La BN25 .... 181 C3
Chyngton La N BN25 .... 181 C3
Chyngton Pl BN25 .... 181 B2
Chyngton Rd BN25 .... 181 A2
Chyngton Way BN25 .... 181 C2
Cider House Wlk BN8 .... 105 A5
Cinder Hill Chailey BN8 .... 75 F3
  Cinder Hill RH19 .... 21 B1
Cinderford La BN27 .... 129 F8
Cinque Ports St TN31 .... 93 B5
Cinque Ports Way
  Hastings TN38 .... 158 E6
  Seaford BN25 .... 181 C4
Cinquefoil BN10 .... 178 C8
Circus Par BN1 .... 189 A7
Circus St BN2 .... 189 A5
Circus The BN23 .... 185 D8
Cissbury Ave BN10 .... 178 E7
Cissbury Cres BN2 .... 177 E5
Cissbury Rd Burgess Hill RH15 ... 72 E4
  Hove BN3 .... 163 E7
Civic Way Burgess Hill RH15 .... 73 A3
  Royal Tunbridge Wells TN1 .... 8 A3
Clackhams La TN6 .... 38 D7
Clair Ct 1 RH16 .... 50 E5
Clair Rd RH16 .... 50 E5
Clanricarde Gdns 1 TN1 .... 8 A3
Clanricarde Rd 2 TN1 .... 8 A3
Clapham La BN26 .... 182 A8
Claphatch La TN5 .... 31 A5
Clappers The TN32 .... 64 B4
Clare Rd BN7 .... 123 A2
Clare Wlk BN2 .... 164 D5
Claremont 9 TN34 .... 159 E7
Claremont Cty Prim Sch TN2 ..... 8 B2
Claremont Gdns TN1, TN2 .... 8 B2
Claremont Rd Bexhill TN39 ...... 157 B7
  Newhaven BN9 .... 168 F1
  Royal Tunbridge Wells TN1 .... 8 B2
  Seaford BN25 .... 180 D3
Claremont Rise TN22 .... 55 C1
Claremont Sch TN33 .... 114 B1
Clarence Ct BN24 .... 175 C3
Clarence Dr 2 RH19 .... 10 F7
Clarence Rd Eastbourne BN22 .. 185 B4
  Hastings TN37 .... 136 C1
  Royal Tunbridge Wells TN1, TN4 .. 8 A3
Clarence Row TN1 .... 8 A3
Clarence Sq BN1 .... 189 F5
Clarendon Cl TN37 .... 136 B4
Clarendon Gdns TN2 .... 8 A1
Clarendon Ho 2 BN3 .... 163 B7
Clarendon Pl 15 Brighton BN2 .. 164 C4
  Portslade-by-Sea BN41 .... 162 C6
Clarendon Rd Hove BN3 .... 163 B7
  Shoreham-by-Sea BN42, BN43 .. 161 D8
Clarendon Terr 16 BN2 .... 164 D4
Clarendon Villas BN3 .... 163 B7
Clarendon Way TN2 .... 8 A1
Claridge TN4 .... 8 B6
Clarke Ave BN3 .... 141 F3
Clarke Ct BN41 .... 162 F6
Clarks Ind Est BN3 .... 163 B8
Claverham Cl TN33 .... 112 B4
Claverham Com Coll TN33 ...... 112 A4
Claverham Way TN33 .... 112 B4
Clavering Wlk TN39 .... 156 B2
Claxton Cl BN21 .... 184 D5
Claxton Rd TN40 .... 158 A5
Clay Corner BN8 .... 101 F6
Clay Hill Rd TN3 .... 19 D6
Clayfields BN10 .... 178 B7
Clays Cl RH19 .... 10 E8
Clayton Ave BN6 .... 97 F3
Clayton Dr RH15 .... 72 F1
Clayton Hill BN45, BN6 .... 119 D7
Clayton Mill Rd BN24 .... 174 B5
Clayton Pk BN6 .... 97 E4
Clayton Rd Brighton BN2 .... 164 D7
  Ditchling BN6 .... 98 C3
Clayton Way BN3 .... 141 F3
Clayton's La TN3 .... 5 E2
Clearwater Rd RH17 .... 52 A3
Clearwaters La RH15 .... 73 D8
Cleeve Ave TN2 .... 8 D2
Cleevelands BN22 .... 173 B2
Clement Hill Rd TN34 .... 137 B3
Clement La BN26 .... 173 A6
Clementine Ave TN35 .... 180 D5
Clerks Acre Keymer BN6 .... 98 A3
  Keymer BN6 .... 98 A4
Clermont Ct 5 BN1 .... 142 E2
Clermont Rd BN1 .... 142 E2
Clermont Terr BN1 .... 142 E2
Cleve Cl TN22 .... 79 B5
Cleve Terr BN7 .... 123 B2
Clevedon Rd TN39 .... 157 A6
Clevedown BN7 .... 146 A8
Cleveland TN2 .... 8 D4
Cleveland Cl BN23 .... 174 C3

Cleveland Gdns RH15 .... 73 B2
Cleveland Rd BN1 .... 143 A1
Clevelands RH16 .... 50 E6
Cliff App BN2 .... 164 F4
Cliff Ave BN10 .... 178 E5
Cliff Cl BN25 .... 180 F1
Cliff Ct TN38 .... 158 D6
Cliff End La TN35 .... 139 B7
Cliff Gdns Seaford BN25 .... 180 F1
  Telscombe Cliffs BN10 .... 177 F4
Cliff Park Cl BN10 .... 178 F7
Cliff Rd Brighton BN2 .... 164 F4
  Eastbourne BN20 .... 188 E7
  Seaford BN25 .... 180 F1
Cliff The BN2 .... 164 F4
Cliff Way TN35 .... 138 F5
Cliffe High St BN7 .... 123 D1
Cliffe Ind Est BN7 .... 146 F1
Clifford Ave BN21 .... 184 C6
Clifford Ct 4 Bexhill TN40 ...... 157 C4
  Crowborough TN6 .... 25 F2
Clifford Rd 3 TN40 .... 157 C4
Clifton Cl BN22 .... 184 D8
Clifton Cotts TN1 .... 8 D8
Clifton Ct TN34 .... 159 E8
Clifton Hill BN1 .... 189 F6
Clifton Ho BN22 .... 184 D8
Clifton Mews BN1 .... 189 F6
Clifton Pl Brighton BN1 .... 163 E6
  Royal Tunbridge Wells TN1 .... 8 B2
Clifton Rd Brighton BN1 .... 189 F6
  Burgess Hill RH15 .... 72 D5
  Hastings TN35 .... 137 C3
  Newhaven BN9 .... 179 D7
  Royal Tunbridge Wells TN1 .... 8 C7
Clifton Rise TN40 .... 157 F5
Clifton St BN1 .... 189 F7
Clifton Terr BN1 .... 189 F6
Clifton Way BN10 .... 178 A8
Cliftonville Ct 6 BN3 .... 163 B7
Cliftonville Rd TN38 .... 158 D6
Cliftonville Way TN38 .... 158 D6
Climping RH16 .... 50 D3
Clinch Green Ave TN39 .... 156 F7
Clinton Cres TN38 .... 136 B1
Clinton Hill RH7 .... 2 A8
Clinton La BN25 .... 180 E3
Clinton Pl BN25 .... 180 E3
Clinton Way TN35 .... 138 F5
Clive Ave TN35 .... 160 C6
Clive Villas TN35 .... 112 E3
Cliveden Ct BN1 .... 142 E3
Clock House La TN22 .... 35 C4
Clock Tower Ct TN39 .... 157 B3
Clockhouse TN2 .... 8 F6
Cloisters BN9 .... 179 C7
Cloisters The Battle TN33 .... 112 D6
  Eastbourne BN22 .... 173 C2
  Hastings TN37 .... 159 D7
Close Eight BN23 .... 174 E3
Close Eighteen BN23 .... 174 E3
Close Eleven BN23 .... 174 E3
Close Fifteen 6 BN23 .... 174 E3
Close Five BN23 .... 174 E2
Close Four BN23 .... 174 E2
Close Fourteen BN23 .... 174 E2
Close Nine BN23 .... 174 E3
Close Nineteen BN23 .... 174 E2
Close One BN23 .... 174 D2
Close Seven BN23 .... 174 E2
Close Seventeen BN23 .... 174 E2
Close Six BN23 .... 174 E3
Close Sixteen BN23 .... 174 E3
Close Ten BN23 .... 174 E2
Close The Blackboys TN22 .... 80 B6
  Brighton BN1 .... 142 E5
  Burgess Hill RH15 .... 73 C4
  Crowborough TN6 .... 25 E3
  East Grinstead RH19 .... 10 D8
  Eastbourne BN20 .... 184 B8
  Fairlight TN35 .... 138 C4
  Friston BN20 .... 183 A1
  Groombridge TN3 .... 15 C6
  Hassocks BN6 .... 97 F4
  Lower Willingdon BN22 .... 173 C3
  Newhaven BN9 .... 168 F2
  Rye TN31 .... 93 A6
  Seaford BN25 .... 180 F2
Close Three BN23 .... 174 D2
Close Twelve BN23 .... 174 E2
Close Twenty BN23 .... 174 E2
Close Twentyfive BN23 .... 174 D2
Close Twentyfour 4 BN23 .... 174 E2
Close Two BN23 .... 174 D2
Cloudesley Rd TN37 .... 159 C8
Clovelly Ho BN26 .... 173 A7
Clover Ct 2 RH16 .... 50 E4
Clover Way BN41 .... 141 B2
Cloverlea TN34 .... 136 E5
Clovers End BN1 .... 143 B7
Cluny St BN7 .... 146 C8
Clyde Pk BN27 .... 152 C7
Clyde Rd Brighton BN1 .... 189 A8
  Hastings TN37, TN38 .... 159 C4
Coach and Horses La RH17 .... 34 C6
Coach & Horses Pas 16 TN2 ...... 8 A2
Coach La RH17 .... 34 C6
Coast Rd BN24 .... 176 B7
Coastal Counties Ho 18 BN2 .. 189 B6
Coastguard Cotts
  Camber TN31 .... 94 D2
  Normans' Bay BN24 .... 176 D8
Coastguard La TN35 .... 138 C4
Coastguard Sq
  3 Eastbourne BN22 .... 185 C4
  Rye Harbour TN31 .... 94 A3
Coastguards TN35 .... 139 C8

Coates Ct 11 BN42 .... 161 E7
Cobald Rd BN24 .... 175 E5
Cobbett's Ride TN2 .... 7 F1
Cobbetts Mead RH16 .... 51 B3
Cobblers Field TN19 .... 61 A3
Cobbold Ave BN21 .... 184 C5
Cobden Pl 5 BN27 .... 152 C7
Cobden Rd BN2 .... 164 C7
Cobdown La TN22 .... 55 C5
Cobham Towers TN40 .... 157 F4
Cobhams TN3 .... 7 A8
Cobourg Pl 6 TN34 .... 160 A4
Cobton Dr BN3 .... 142 A3
Coburn Ct 12 BN27 .... 123 D1
Cochrane Cl BN23 .... 185 E7
Cockcrow Wood TN37 .... 136 D5
Cockfield La BN8 .... 76 B3
Cockhaise Cotts RH16 .... 52 A8
Cockmount La TN5 .... 29 F5
Cockshut Rd BN7 .... 146 C8
Cogger's Cross TN21 .... 106 F3
Cogger's La TN21 .... 106 F4
Coggins Mill La TN20 .... 40 D4
Coghurst Rd TN35 .... 137 C4
Colbourne Ave BN2 .... 143 D2
Colbourne Rd BN3 .... 163 E7
Colchester Vale RH18 .... 11 E2
Colchins RH15 .... 72 F1
Coldean Cty Inf Sch BN1 .... 143 D6
Coldean Cty Jun Sch BN1 .... 143 D6
Coldean La BN1 .... 143 E6
Coldharbour La TN31 .... 26 A1
Coldharbour La Newick BN8 .... 76 A7
Rye Foreign TN31 .... 69 E3
Coldharbour Rd
Lower Dicker BN27 .... 128 B2
White Post TN11 .... 5 E8
Coldthorn La BN26, BN27 .... 152 A4
Coldwaltham La RH15 .... 73 D2
Colebrook Rd Brighton BN1 .... 142 D4
Royal Tunbridge Wells TN4 .... 8 C8
Southwick BN42 .... 161 F7
Colebrooke Rd TN39 .... 157 A4
Coleman Ave BN3 .... 162 E7
Coleman St BN2 .... 189 B7
Colemans Hatch Rd RH18, TN7 .... 23 C6
Coleridge St BN3 .... 163 A8
Coleridge Wlk 7 BN23 .... 174 E2
Coles Ct TN2 .... 8 C3
Colgate Cl BN2 .... 164 F6
Coll of St Barnabas RH7 .... 1 F8
Coll of the Holy Child Jesus
TN37 .... 159 D7
College Cl East Grinstead RH19 .... 1 F1
Portslade-by-Sea BN41 .... 140 F3
College Dr TN2 .... 8 D4
College Gdns BN2 .... 164 C4
College La East Grinstead RH19 .... 1 F1
Hurst Wickham BN6 .... 97 C6
College Pl Brighton BN2 .... 164 C4
Hurst Wickham BN6 .... 97 C6
College Rd Bexhill TN40 .... 157 F5
Brighton BN2 .... 164 C4
Eastbourne BN21 .... 184 F2
Haywards Heath RH16 .... 50 E7
Seaford BN25 .... 180 F2
College St 1 BN2 .... 164 C4
College Terr BN2 .... 164 D5
Collett Cl TN38 .... 135 F5
Collier Cl BN22 .... 185 B7
Collier Rd Hastings TN34 .... 160 A5
Pevensey Bay BN24 .... 175 D4
Collier's Gn TN21 .... 83 F3
Collingford La RH17 .... 34 B4
Collington Ave TN39 .... 156 F3
Collington Cl BN20 .... 184 E1
Collington Gr TN39 .... 156 E4
Collington La E TN39 .... 156 E4
Collington La W TN39 .... 156 D3
Collington Park Cres TN39 .... 156 F4
Collington Rise TN39 .... 156 E4
Collington Sta TN39 .... 157 A3
Collingwood Ave TN21 .... 82 B7
Collingwood Cl
4 East Grinstead RH19 .... 10 F7
Eastbourne BN23 .... 185 E6
Peacehaven BN10 .... 167 D1
Collingwood Rise TN21 .... 82 A7
Collinstone Rd TN38 .... 159 A7
Collinswood Dr TN38 .... 159 A7
Colmer Ct RH15 .... 72 E3
Colmer Pl RH15 .... 72 E3
Colonnade Gdns BN22 .... 185 B3
Colonnade Rd BN22 .... 185 B3
Coltstocks Rd BN20 .... 188 D8
Colville Ct 2 BN21 .... 184 E4
Colwell Cl RH16 .... 50 F3
Colwell Gdns RH16 .... 50 F3
Colwell La
Haywards Heath RH16, RH17 .... 51 B3
Haywards Heath, Fox Hill
RH16, RH17 .... 50 F1
Colwell Rd RH16 .... 50 F2
Colwood Cres BN20 .... 184 B6
Colwood Hospl RH16 .... 51 A3
Combe End TN6 .... 37 E8
Combe La Eastbourne BN20 .... 188 D7
Ninfield TN33 .... 132 F6
Combe Rise BN20 .... 173 A2
Combe The BN20 .... 184 A7
Combermere Rd TN38 .... 136 B1
Command Rd BN20 .... 184 B5
Commanders Wlk TN35 .... 138 E4
Commercial Mews N 5 BN21 .... 185 A4
Commercial Rd
Burgess Hill RH15 .... 72 F3
Eastbourne BN21 .... 185 A3
Royal Tunbridge Wells TN1 .... 8 B5

Commercial Sq RH16 .... 50 E6
Common La Ditchling BN6 .... 98 D6
Selmeston BN26 .... 149 E1
Common View TN4 .... 7 C4
Compass La BN41 .... 140 E3
Comphurst La TN27 .... 131 B4
Compton Ave BN1 .... 189 F7
Compton Cl TN40 .... 157 E5
Compton Dr BN20 .... 184 C2
Compton Lodge BN21 .... 184 E2
Compton Place Rd
BN20, BN21 .... 184 E2
Compton Rd Brighton BN1 .... 142 D1
Haywards Heath RH16 .... 51 B8
Compton St BN20, BN21 .... 185 A1
Compton Terr BN27 .... 152 C6
Compts The BN10 .... 167 B1
Conan Doyle Ct TN6 .... 25 E2
Concord Cl TN2 .... 8 C4
Concorde Ct TN39 .... 156 F6
Condor Way RH15 .... 72 E3
Conduit Hill TN31 .... 93 C6
Coney Furlong BN10 .... 167 D1
Coneyburrow Gdns TN38 .... 135 E4
Coneyburrow La TN39 .... 155 F5
Coneyburrow Rd TN2 .... 8 E5
Conifer Cl TN34 .... 136 F3
Conifers The 6 BN21 .... 184 F4
Coniston Ave TN5 .... 7 E5
Coniston Ct 9 BN3 .... 163 D7
Coniston Rd BN23 .... 174 C4
Connaught Ctr Brighton Coll of
Tech & F Ed BN3 .... 163 A6
Connaught Rd
1 Eastbourne BN21 .... 185 A2
Hove BN3 .... 163 A6
Seaford BN25 .... 180 C3
Connaught Terr BN3 .... 163 B7
Connaught Way TN4 .... 7 F5
Connell Dr BN2 .... 165 E7
Conqueror Ind Est TN38 .... 135 F6
Conqueror Rd TN38 .... 158 E7
Conqueror Terr TN33 .... 88 F1
Consort Hospl TN37 .... 136 D6
Consort Way RH15 .... 72 E2
Constable Rd BN23 .... 174 D1
Constable Way TN40 .... 157 E5
Convent of The Holy
Child Jesus TN20 .... 40 A3
Conway Ct 9 Hastings TN38 .... 159 B6
1 Hove BN3 .... 163 B7
Conway Pl BN3 .... 163 A8
Conway St BN3 .... 163 B8
Cooden Beach Golf Course
TN39 .... 156 A2
Cooden Beach Sta TN39 .... 156 D2
Cooden Cl TN39 .... 156 C3
Cooden Dr TN39 .... 156 C3
Cooden Sea Rd Bexhill TN39 .... 156 B2
Bexhill TN39 .... 156 C3
Cook Ave BN23 .... 185 E6
Cookham Dene TN40 .... 157 C4
Cooksbridge Rd BN2 .... 164 E6
Cooksbridge Sta BN8 .... 123 A7
Cookstown Ct TN33 .... 132 F6
Coolham Dr BN2 .... 164 E7
Coombe Cl BN27 .... 131 B5
Coombe Hall Sch RH19 .... 10 D6
Coombe Hill Rd RH19 .... 10 D6
Coombe Lea BN3 .... 41 C7
Coombe Lea 22 BN3 .... 163 C6
Coombe Meadow BN2 .... 166 E3
Coombe Rd Brighton BN2 .... 143 D1
Eastbourne BN20 .... 184 C4
Lewes BN7 .... 123 D2
Coombe Rise BN2 .... 166 D3
Coombe Road Cty Prim Sch
BN2 .... 143 D1
Coombe Shaw TN33 .... 133 A6
Coombe Terr BN2 .... 143 C1
Coombe Vale BN2 .... 166 D3
Coombers La RH16 .... 51 B5
Coombs Cl TN31 .... 68 C5
Coombs Cotts TN31 .... 68 C5
Cooper Dr TN39 .... 157 B8
Cooper Rd TN31 .... 93 A5
Cooper Rise TN38 .... 136 A5
Coopers Cl RH15 .... 73 C5
Coopers Hill BN20 .... 173 A4
Coopers La Crowborough TN6 .... 25 D4
Poundsbridge TN11, TN3 .... 6 C7
Coopers Row BN2 .... 55 D4
Coopers Way BN27 .... 152 A6
Coopers Wood TN6 .... 25 D4
Copestake Dr RH15 .... 73 D3
Coplands Plot 3 TN31 .... 67 B7
Coplands Rise TN31 .... 67 B7
Coppards Cl RH17 .... 74 C4
Coppards La TN31 .... 67 C8
Copper Beeches TN37 .... 136 C4
Copper Cl BN6 .... 72 C4
Copper's Hill TN19 .... 61 E4
Coppice Ave BN20 .... 173 A4
Coppice Cl BN20 .... 173 A4
Coppice The Battle TN33 .... 113 A3
Hastings TN34 .... 136 E1
Pembury TN2 .... 9 D7
Scaynes Hill RH17 .... 51 F3
Coppice View TN21 .... 82 B6
Coppice Way RH16 .... 50 D3
Copse Cl East Grinstead RH19 .... 2 A3
Hastings TN35 .... 135 D3
Copse Hill BN1 .... 142 D5
Copse Rd TN39 .... 156 F2
Copse The RH16 .... 51 B5
Copt Hall TN18 .... 48 D3

Copthorne Ct 2 BN3 .... 163 C6
Copthorne Rd RH19 .... 1 A4
Copwood Ave TN22 .... 78 B7
Copyhold La RH17 .... 50 A4
Copyhold Rd RH19 .... 10 D8
Corbyn Cres BN43 .... 161 A7
Cordons BN7 .... 145 D5
Cormorant Cl BN23 .... 174 C2
Corn Ct 7 BN2 .... 164 C6
Cornelius Ave BN9 .... 179 A5
Corner Gn BN8 .... 124 D5
Cornfield Cl BN25 .... 180 F3
Cornfield Gn BN27 .... 129 C1
Cornfield La BN21 .... 185 A2
Cornfield Rd Eastbourne BN21 .... 185 A2
Seaford BN25 .... 180 F3
Cornfield Terr
11 Eastbourne BN21 .... 185 A2
Hastings TN37 .... 136 C1
Cornford Cl Burgess Hill RH15 .... 72 E5
Crowborough TN6 .... 26 A1
Pembury TN2 .... 9 B6
Cornford La TN2 .... 9 B5
Cornford Pk TN2 .... 9 C6
Cornish Cl BN23, BN24 .... 174 B4
Cornmill Gdns BN26 .... 172 E4
Cornwall Ave BN10 .... 178 E6
Cornwall Ct Eastbourne BN20 .... 184 C5
2 BN3 .... 163 C7
Cornwall Gdns Brighton BN1 .... 142 E2
6 East Grinstead RH19 .... 10 F8
Cornwall Ho BN1 .... 142 E2
Cornwall Rd TN39 .... 157 B3
Cornwallis Cl BN23 .... 185 F7
Cornwallis Gdns TN34 .... 159 E8
Cornwallis St 5 TN34 .... 159 F8
Cornwallis Terr TN34 .... 159 E8
Coronation Cotts
Berner's Hill TN5 .... 31 F2
Burwash TN19 .... 62 A6
Northbridge Street TN32 .... 64 C5
Coronation Gdns Battle TN33 .. 112 F5
Hurst Green TN19 .... 44 F3
Coronation Rd RH19 .... 10 E7
Coronation St 7 BN2 .... 164 C7
Corseley Rd TN3 .... 15 B5
Corsica Cl BN25 .... 180 F2
Corsica Rd BN25 .... 180 F1
Costells Edge RH17 .... 51 F3
Costume Mus TN20 .... 157 D4
Cotchford Hill TN7 .... 13 D1
Cotchford La TN7 .... 13 C1
Cotswold Cl Eastbourne BN23 .... 174 C4
Hastings TN34 .... 137 B4
Cotswold Pl 7 BN2 .... 164 F5
Cotswolds The BN42 .... 161 E7
Cottage Bush Cl BN41 .... 141 C2
Cottage Ct 2 BN9 .... 168 D1
Cottage Homes BN6 .... 98 E6
Cottage La Hankham BN24 .... 152 E1
Westfield TN33, TN35 .... 114 D7
Cottenden Rd TN5 .... 43 A6
Cottesmore St Mary's
RC Prim Sch BN3 .... 163 D8
Coulstock Rd BN6 .... 72 C4
Council Cotts TN32 .... 63 F3
Council Hos
Ginger's Green BN27 .... 130 C6
Rushlake Green TN21 .... 83 D1
Countess of Thanet's
Almshouses TN8 .... 3 F3
County Oak Ave BN1 .... 143 B6
Courcels BN2 .... 164 E3
Course The BN7 .... 146 B8
Court Cl Brighton BN1 .... 142 E7
East Grinstead RH19 .... 1 F1
Court Cres RH19 .... 1 F1
Court Farm Cl BN9 .... 168 A2
Court Farm Rd Hove BN3 .... 142 A2
Newhaven BN9 .... 179 C5
Rottingdean BN2 .... 165 F3
Court Meadow TN6 .... 39 B8
Court Meadow Cl TN6 .... 39 B7
Court Meadow Sch RH17 .... 50 A8
Court Ord Cotts BN2 .... 165 F3
Court Ord Rd BN2 .... 165 F3
Court Rd Eastbourne BN22 .... 173 F2
Lewes BN7 .... 123 D1
Royal Tunbridge Wells TN4 .... 7 F4
Court The BN20 .... 173 B1
Courtenwell TN3 .... 6 E4
Courthope Ave TN5 .... 29 F4
Courthope Dr TN39 .... 156 F5
Courthouse St TN34 .... 160 B4
Courtland Rd BN26 .... 173 A5
Courtlands 12 Brighton BN2 .... 189 B6
Dodd's Hill TN22 .... 35 D2
5 Hastings TN38 .... 159 B6
Haywards Heath RH16 .... 50 E3
Newhaven BN9 .... 179 C2
Courtlands Rd BN22 .... 185 A5
Courtney Gate BN3 .... 163 B5
Courtney King Ct 8 BN2 .... 164 C5
Courtney King Ho 1 BN2 .... 164 D4
Courtyard The
East Grinstead RH19 .... 2 B1
Falmer BN1 .... 144 D6
Hastings TN34 .... 136 E1
Cousley Wood Rd TN5 .... 30 C7
Coventry Ct BN22 .... 185 D6
Coventry Rd TN37, TN38 .... 136 B3
Coventry St BN1 .... 163 E8
Coverdale Ave TN39 .... 156 C3
Coverdale Ct RH19 .... 1 C3
Covers The BN25 .... 180 F2
Covert The TN39 .... 156 C2
Cow BN26 .... 181 F8

Cowden Cl TN18 .... 45 E8
Cowden Cross TN8 .... 4 C7
Cowden La TN18 .... 45 E7
Cowden Mews TN8 .... 4 A5
Cowden Rd BN2 .... 177 D4
Cowden Sta TN8 .... 4 D8
Cowden Wlk TN38 .... 136 A2
Cowdens Cl BN3 .... 141 D4
Cowdray Cl TN39 .... 156 D6
Cowdray Ct 1 BN3 .... 163 D7
Cowdray Park Rd TN39 .... 156 C6
Cowfold Rd BN2 .... 164 E5
Cowley Dr BN2 .... 165 F7
Cownwy Ct BN2 .... 165 F1
Cowper St BN3 .... 163 A7
Cox Gr RH15 .... 72 E5
Cox's Cotts BN7 .... 99 E7
Crabtree Ave BN1 .... 143 B5
Crabtree Ho 1 TN38 .... 159 B6
Crackendale Field BN8 .... 124 E6
Cradle Hill Cty Prim Sch
BN25 .... 181 A5
Cradle Hill Ind Est BN25 .... 181 B5
Cradle Hill Rd BN25 .... 181 B5
Craig Cl TN33 .... 135 A6
Craignair Ave BN1 .... 142 F7
Cranborne Ave BN20 .... 188 C8
Cranbourne St BN1 .... 189 F5
Cranbrook 13 BN2 .... 189 B6
Cranbrook Rd TN37 .... 136 C1
Cranedown BN7 .... 146 B7
Cranfield Rd TN40 .... 157 C4
Cranleigh Ave BN2 .... 177 B5
Cranleigh Cl TN39 .... 157 A4
Cranley Ct BN3 .... 162 D7
Cranmer Ave BN3 .... 141 F1
Cranmer Cl BN7 .... 123 D2
Cranston Ave TN39 .... 157 A4
Cranston Cl TN39 .... 156 F4
Cranston Rd RH19 .... 1 F2
Cranston Rise TN39 .... 156 F4
Cranwell Rd TN4 .... 7 C4
Craven Rd BN2 .... 164 D6
Crawfurd Way RH19 .... 1 F3
Crawley Cres TN39 .... 173 E2
Crawley Rd BN1 .... 143 D6
Crayford Rd BN2 .... 143 D1
Crazy La TN33 .... 113 E7
Crecy Cl TN37, TN38 .... 135 F7
Creek The 11 TN34 .... 160 B4
Crendon Pk TN4 .... 8 A8
Crescent Cl Burgess Hill RH15 .... 73 B3
Woodingdean BN2 .... 165 E8
Crescent Dr N BN2 .... 165 E8
Crescent Dr S BN2 .... 165 E7
Crescent Mansions BN2 .... 189 B8
Crescent Pl BN2 .... 164 C4
Crescent Rd Brighton BN2 .... 164 B8
Burgess Hill RH15 .... 73 A3
East Grinstead RH19 .... 1 D1
Royal Tunbridge Wells TN1, TN2 .... 8 B3
Crescent The Brighton BN2 .... 143 E2
Eastbourne BN20, BN21 .... 184 B5
Felcourt RH19 .... 1 C8
Groombridge TN3 .... 15 C7
Hastings TN37 .... 136 C3
Keymer BN6 .... 98 B3
Lower Willingdon BN20 .... 173 A3
Southwick BN42 .... 161 B8
Crescent Way BN1 .... 143 A1
Crespin Way BN1 .... 143 C2
Crest Rd BN9 .... 168 F1
Crest Way BN41 .... 141 B3
Cresta Cl BN26 .... 173 A7
Cresta Rd BN9 .... 179 A6
Crestway Par 1 BN1 .... 143 C2
Crestway The BN1 .... 143 C2
Cricket Rd RH19 .... 1 E3
Cricketers Field TN32 .... 65 E1
Cricketfield BN8 .... 76 D8
Cricketfield Rd BN25 .... 180 F2
Cricketing La BN27 .... 130 C4
Criers La TN20, TN22 .... 57 E6
Crink Hill BN8 .... 101 F3
Cripland Cl RH16 .... 51 B6
Cripps Ave BN10 .... 167 D1
Crisp Rd BN7 .... 123 A3
Crittle's Ct TN5 .... 29 F4
Crockers Hatch Cnr TN3 .... 6 D2
Crockers La TN31 .... 67 B8
Crocks Dean BN10 .... 167 D2
Croft Ave BN42 .... 161 F7
Croft Cl BN26 .... 173 A4
Croft Ct 2 Eastbourne BN22 .... 185 B3
6 Seaford BN25 .... 180 E3
Croft Dr BN41 .... 141 A3
Croft La BN25 .... 180 E3
Croft Rd Brighton BN1 .... 142 D4
Crowborough TN6 .... 25 F2
Hastings TN34 .... 160 A4
Croft Terr 2 TN34 .... 160 A4
Croft The Bexhill TN39 .... 157 A4
Hassocks BN6 .... 97 F5
Hastings TN34 .... 160 A4
Lower Dicker BN27 .... 128 B4
Southwick BN42 .... 161 E8
Willingdon BN20 .... 173 B1
Croft Works BN27 .... 152 B7
Crofton Park Ave TN39 .... 156 E3
Croham Rd TN6 .... 25 F3
Cromer Way BN27 .... 129 A1
Cromer Wlk 3 TN34 .... 136 F1
Cromleigh Way BN42 .... 140 E2
Cromwell Ct 3 BN3 .... 163 D7
Cromwell Pl 1 RH19 .... 10 F7
Cromwell Rd Burgess Hill RH15 ..... 72 F3
Hove BN3 .... 163 D7
Royal Tunbridge Wells TN2 .... 8 C3

Cromwell St BN2 .... 164 C7
Crooked La BN25 .... 180 F2
Cross La TN5 .... 31 D2
Cross Lane Gdns TN5 .... 31 D1
Cross Levels Way BN21, BN22 .. 184 C4
Cross Rd BN42 .... 161 D8
Cross St Brighton BN1 .... 189 A7
Hastings TN37 .... 159 C7
Hove BN1, BN3 .... 163 D5
Polegate BN26 .... 173 A6
Cross Way BN7 .... 123 A3
Cross-in-Hand CE Prim Sch
TN21 .... 81 F7
Crossbush Rd BN2 .... 164 E6
Crossroad Cl BN42 .... 161 D8
Crossway The Brighton BN1 .... 143 B2
Portslade-Sea BN41 .... 141 A2
Royal Tunbridge Wells TN4 .... 7 D2
Crossways Ave RH19 .... 1 C1
Crossways The
Broad Oak TN31 .... 90 B4
Hassocks BN6 .... 97 C4
Stone Cross BN24 .... 174 A4
Crouch Cl BN20 .... 173 B1
Crouch La Linkhill TN18 .... 47 D6
Lower Street TN33 .... 133 B3
Seaford BN25 .... 180 E2
Crouchfield Cl 2 BN25 .... 180 F2
Crowborough Beacon
Golf Course TN6 .... 37 C7
Crowborough Hill TN6 .... 26 B1
Crowborough Rd
Hastings TN35 .... 137 E4
Marlpits TN22 .... 35 E6
Saltdean BN2 .... 177 D4
Crowders La TN33 .... 111 D3
Crowhurst CE Prim Sch TN33 .. 134 F5
Crowhurst Cl BN23 .... 174 A4
Crowhurst La TN39 .... 157 C7
Crowhurst Rd Brighton BN1 .... 143 C7
Green Street TN33, TN38 .... 135 B3
Hastings TN38 .... 135 C2
Crowhurst Sta TN33 .... 135 A6
Crowmere Ave TN40 .... 157 C5
Crowmere Terr TN40 .... 157 C5
Crown Cl Hailsham BN27 .... 152 A7
Uckfield BN20 .... 78 C8
Crown Ct 23 TN34 .... 160 B4
Crown Gdns BN1 .... 189 F5
Crown Hill 4 Brighton BN2 .... 164 C6
Seaford BN25 .... 180 E2
Crown La TN34 .... 160 B4
Crown Point Ho BN6 .... 97 F4
Crown Rd
Portslade-by-Sea BN41 .... 162 A8
Shoreham-by-Sea BN43 .... 161 B8
Crown St Brighton BN1 .... 189 F5
11 Eastbourne BN21 .... 184 D4
Crowne Ho 7 BN21 .... 184 E4
Croxden Way BN22 .... 173 D3
Croxton La RH16 .... 51 B6
Crump's Cnr TN22 .... 103 D6
Crunden Rd BN20 .... 184 C4
Cubitt Way TN38 .... 135 E4
Cuckfield Cl TN40 .... 158 A5
Cuckfield Rd
Burgess Hill RH15, RH17 .... 72 E7
Goddard's Green BN6, RH17 .... 72 A4
Cuckmere Cl BN26 .... 170 F3
Cuckmere Ho BN24 .... 175 E5
Cuckmere House Sch BN25 ..... 181 C3
Cuckmere House Sch
(Tower House Annexe)
BN25 .... 181 A3
Cuckmere Path TN22 .... 55 E1
Cuckmere Rd Newhaven BN9 ... 179 A5
Seaford BN25 .... 181 B2
Cuckmere Rise TN21 .... 82 B8
Cuckmere Way BN1 .... 143 C5
Cuckmere Wlk BN22 .... 173 D1
Cuckoo Dr TN21 .... 82 A6
Culpepper RH15 .... 72 E4
Culpepper Cl BN2 .... 143 D2
Culross Ave RH16 .... 50 D5
Culver Cl BN23 .... 174 B4
Culverden Ave TN4 .... 8 A6
Culverden Down TN4 .... 7 F5
Culverden Park Rd TN4 .... 7 F5
Culverden Pk TN4 .... 7 F5
Culverden Sq TN1, TN4 .... 8 A5
Culverden St TN1 .... 8 A4
Cumberland Ct Bexhill TN40 .. 157 F4
Eastbourne BN20 .... 184 B6
Cumberland Dr BN1 .... 142 E7
Cumberland Gdns
Hastings TN38 .... 159 B8
10 Royal Tunbridge Wells TN1 .. 8 A2
Cumberland Lodge 8 BN1 ..... 142 E2
Cumberland Mews 12 TN1 ..... 8 A2
Cumberland Rd Bexhill TN39 .. 157 B7
Brighton BN1 .... 142 E2
Cumberland Wlk TN1 .... 8 A2
Cumberland Yd 11 TN1 .... 8 A2
Cumnor House Sch RH17 .... 34 B5
Cunningham Cl 1 BN25 .... 180 E2
Cunningham Dr BN23 .... 185 E7
Cunningham Ho TN39 .... 157 B3
Cunningham Rd TN4 .... 8 B7
Curlew Ct Hailsham BN27 .... 152 D7
Hastings TN38 .... 135 E3
Curlews The BN43 .... 161 A8
Currie Rd TN4 .... 8 A5
Curwen Pl BN1 .... 142 E3
Curzon Ho BN2 .... 177 C4

Cuthbert Cl TN39 .... 157 A7
Cuthbert Rd BN2 .... 164 C5
Cutter La TN34 .... 160 A3
Cypress Cl Hastings TN38 ...... 159 A7
  Shoreham-by-Sea BN43 .... 140 A1
Cypress Gr TN2 .... 17 C8
Cyprus Pl TN31 .... 93 B5
Cyprus Rd RH15 .... 73 A3

D'aubigny Rd BN2 .... 164 B8
Dacre Pk BN27 .... 152 D7
Dacre Rd
  Eastbourne BN20, BN21 ...... 184 C4
  Herstmonceux BN27 .... 130 E6
  Newhaven BN9 .... 179 D7
Dagg La TN32 .... 65 F5
Dakins The RH19 .... 10 E8
Dakota Way TN38 .... 135 F6
Dale Ave Brighton BN1 .... 142 F5
  Keymer BN6 .... 98 A3
Dale Cres BN1 .... 142 F6
Dale Dr BN1 .... 143 A6
Dale Hill BN45 .... 119 A6
Dale Rd Forest Row RH18 ...... 11 F1
  Lewes BN7 .... 146 A8
Dale St TN1 .... 8 B4
Dale View BN3 .... 141 D2
Dale View Gdns BN3 .... 141 D2
Dalehurst TN6 .... 38 C7
Dalehurst Rd TN39 .... 157 B7
Dales Cl BN27 .... 131 B5
Dalewood Gdns RH15 .... 73 C2
Dallas La BN8 .... 101 F6
Dallaway Dr BN24 .... 174 B5
Dallaway Gdns RH19 .... 1 E1
Dallington CE Prim Sch TN21 .. 84 D3
Dallington Cl TN40 .... 158 A6
Dallington Rd
  Eastbourne BN22 .... 174 A1
  Hove BN3 .... 162 F8
Dalmeny Rd TN39 .... 157 A5
Dalmore Ct TN40 .... 157 C3
Dalton Rd BN20 .... 188 E8
Damian Way BN6 .... 98 B4
Damon Cl BN10 .... 178 C7
Dana Lodge BN10 .... 178 A7
Dane Cl BN25 .... 180 D2
Dane Court Cl TN39 .... 157 B6
Dane Hts **10** BN25 .... 180 E2
Dane Rd Hastings TN38 .... 159 B8
  Seaford BN25 .... 180 E3
Danehill CE Prim Sch RH17 .... 34 B4
Danehill La RH17 .... 33 E5
Danehill Rd BN2 .... 164 F5
Daniel Way TN31 .... 94 F2
Dannfields Ho BN25 .... 180 E3
Danny Sheldon Ho **14** BN2 .. 164 C4
Danum Cl BN7 .... 129 C3
Danworth La BN6 .... 72 B3
Darby's La TN5 .... 30 B2
Darcey Dr BN1 .... 143 A6
Daresbury Cl TN39 .... 157 B6
Darley Rd BN20 .... 188 D7
Dart Ct RH19 .... 2 A3
Dartmouth Cl BN2 .... 143 F1
Dartmouth Cres BN2 .... 143 F1
Darvel Down TN33 .... 86 B2
Darwall Dr BN25 .... 181 A3
Darwell Cl Hastings TN38 ...... 135 E1
  Robertsbridge TN32 .... 64 B3
Darwell Dr BN24, BN26 .... 174 A5
Davey Dr BN1 .... 143 B1
Davey's La BN7 .... 123 E2
David Lloyd Club The BN2 .... 184 F8
David Saloman's Ho TN3 ...... 7 D8
Davids Heights BN21 .... 184 E5
Davigdor Cty Inf Sch BN3 .... 163 D6
Davigdor Rd BN3 .... 163 E7
Davis Cl TN39 .... 157 A7
Dawber Bldgs BN27 .... 152 B7
Dawlish Cl BN2 .... 143 F1
Dawson Terr BN2 .... 164 C6
Daynes Way RH15 .... 72 C1
De Cham Ave TN37 .... 159 D8
De Cham Rd TN37 .... 159 C8
De Chardin Dr TN34 .... 137 A5
De Courcel Rd BN2 .... 164 E3
De Grey Cl BN7 .... 123 D2
De La Warr Par TN40 .... 157 E2
De La Warr Rd Bexhill TN40 .. 157 E5
  East Grinstead RH19 .... 1 F1
De Moleyns Cl TN40 .... 157 D4
De Montfort Rd Brighton BN2 .. 164 C7
  Lewes BN7 .... 123 B1
De Roos Rd BN21 .... 184 E4
De Walden Mews BN20 .... 188 E8
De Warrenne Rd BN7 .... 123 B1
Deacons Dr BN41 .... 141 C2
Deadman's Cross TN21 .... 83 B5
Deadmans La TN31 .... 93 C6
Deadmantree Hill BN8 .... 101 B3
Deal Ave BN25 .... 181 C5
Deals The TN31 .... 93 B5
Dean Cl BN41 .... 141 C2
Dean Court Rd BN2 .... 177 A6
Dean Gdns BN41 .... 141 C2
Dean Rd BN25 .... 180 F2
Dean St BN1 .... 163 E5
Dean Wood Cl BN23 .... 174 A4
Deanery Cl BN7 .... 123 D3
Deans Cl Bexhill TN39 .... 157 B6
  Woodingdean BN2 .... 165 E8
Deans Dr TN39 .... 157 A6
Deans Meadow BN8 .... 101 E5
Deans Rd BN26 .... 170 F3

Deanway BN3 .... 142 B3
Decimus Burton Way **10**
  TN37 .... 159 C7
Decoy Dr BN22, BN21 .... 173 D1
Deepdene TN5 .... 30 A6
Deepdene Gdns TN34, TN35 .. 137 C3
Deepdene Sch BN3 .... 162 D7
Deer Paddock La **7** BN27 .. 152 C7
Deerswood La TN38 .... 156 E5
Deeside The BN1 .... 143 A7
Delavall Wlk BN23 .... 185 F6
Delaware Dr TN38 .... 135 F6
Delaware Rd BN7 .... 146 A8
Delfryn BN41 .... 140 F3
Dell Cl TN38 .... 136 A1
Dell Dr TN2 .... 8 D4
Dell The East Grinstead RH19 .. 2 B1
  Haywards Heath RH16 .... 50 C5
Dellney Ave RH16 .... 50 F3
Dellsfoot Cotts TN6 .... 28 A3
Delves Ave TN2 .... 8 C1
Delves Cl BN8 .... 124 D6
Delves Ho BN8 .... 124 D6
Delves Way BN8 .... 124 D6
Den Hill BN20 .... 184 A4
Denbigh Cl TN39 .... 156 E4
Denbigh Rd TN4 .... 8 C7
Dencher Rd BN7 .... 145 E3
Dene Cl BN20 .... 183 B1
Dene Dr BN22 .... 173 C1
Dene Path TN22 .... 55 D1
Dene Side BN20 .... 183 B2
Dene The Hastings TN34 ...... 137 A5
  Hove BN3 .... 141 D3
  Lower Willingdon BN20 ...... 173 A3
  Uckfield TN22 .... 55 D1
Dene Vale BN1 .... 142 D5
Dene Way TN3 .... 7 A7
Denecroft BN1 .... 142 D5
Denehurst Gdns TN34 .... 137 A5
Deneside BN1 .... 142 D5
Deneway The BN1 .... 142 D4
Denham Cl TN38 .... 135 F4
Denham Rd BN6, RH15 .... 72 D3
Denham Way TN31 .... 94 E2
Denman's Cl RH16 .... 51 A8
Denman's La
  Haywards Heath RH16 .... 51 A7
  Haywards Heath RH16 .... 51 B7
Denmark Pl TN34 .... 159 F7
Denmark Rd BN41 .... 162 C7
Denmark Terr BN1 .... 163 E6
Denmark Villas BN3 .... 163 B7
Dennis Hobden Cl BN2 .... 143 E1
Denton Cl TN31 .... 93 A6
Denton Cty Prim Sch BN9 .... 168 E1
Denton Dr Brighton BN1 ...... 143 A6
  Newhaven BN9 .... 168 E1
Denton Rd Eastbourne BN20 .. 188 D8
  Newhaven BN9 .... 168 E1
Denton Rise BN9 .... 168 E2
Dentons The BN20 .... 188 D8
Derby Ct **3** BN3 .... 163 E7
Derby Pl **6** BN2 .... 189 B5
Derek Ave BN3, BN41 .... 162 D6
Derek Ho BN3 .... 162 F6
Derwent Cl BN27 .... 129 A1
Derwent Ct BN1 .... 189 F6
Derwent Dr TN4 .... 7 E5
Derwent Lodge Sch TN1 ...... 8 B4
Derwent Rd BN20 .... 188 E8
Desmond Rd BN22 .... 185 D5
Desmond Way BN2 .... 164 F6
Devil's Dyke Rd
  BN1, BN3, BN41, BN45 ...... 141 E7
Devonian Ct TN2 .... 189 B7
Devonshire Cl TN2 .... 16 F8
Devonshire Ct **1** BN3 ...... 163 C7
Devonshire Lodge **1** BN22 .. 185 C5
Devonshire Pl Brighton BN2 .. 189 B5
  Eastbourne 185 A2
Devonshire Rd Bexhill TN40 .. 157 C3
  Hastings TN34 .... 159 F8
Devonshire Sq TN40 .... 157 C3
Dew La TN31 .... 92 A8
Dewe Rd BN2 .... 143 C1
Dewhurst Cotts TN5 .... 29 A7
Dewhurst La TN5 .... 29 B8
Dewlands Hill TN20 .... 38 F2
Dewpond The BN10 .... 167 B1
Dexter Dr RH19 .... 10 E8
Diana Cl TN40 .... 158 A6
Dickens Cl RH19 .... 1 C1
Dickens Way BN23 .... 174 E3
Dicklands The BN7 .... 167 D8
Diggers The BN1 .... 143 B3
Dillingburgh Rd BN20 .... 184 C4
Dillon Way TN1 .... 8 D6
Dinapore Ho **10** BN2 ...... 189 B7
Diplock Cl BN26 .... 172 F6
Diplocks Bldgs BN27 .... 152 A7
Diplocks The BN27 .... 152 A8
Diplocks Way BN27 .... 152 A7
Diplocks Wlk BN27 .... 152 A8
Dirty La RH19 .... 11 E7
Ditchling Bostall BN6 .... 120 D7
Ditchling Common Ctry Pk
  BN6 .... 73 F1
Ditchling Cres BN1 .... 143 C5
Ditchling Ct **4** BN1 .... 164 B8
Ditchling Dr TN35 .... 137 E4
Ditchling Gdns BN1 .... 143 B1
Ditchling Mus BN6 .... 98 C3
Ditchling Rd
  Brighton BN1, BN2 .... 143 B4
  Westmeston BN1, BN6 .... 120 D4
Ditchling Rise BN1 .... 164 A8

Ditchling Way BN27 .... 152 B6
Ditton's Cnr BN26 .... 173 C6
Ditton's Rd BN26 .... 173 D6
Dittons BN26 .... 173 C6
Dittons Mews TN38 .... 135 E2
Dittons Rd Eastbourne BN21 .. 184 B5
  Stone Cross BN24 .... 174 B5
Dixter La TN31 .... 67 B8
Dixter Rd TN31 .... 67 A6
Dock The BN8 .... 148 C3
Dodshill TN6 .... 26 A1
Dog Cotts RH19 .... 3 B1
Dog Kennel La TN22 .... 57 F6
Dogs Hill Rd TN36 .... 118 B5
Doleham Cotts TN35 .... 115 D5
Doleham Hill TN35 .... 115 D5
Doleham La TN35 .... 115 B6
Doleham Sta TN35 .... 115 C5
Dolphin Ct Eastbourne BN20 .. 188 E7
  5 Hove BN3 .... 163 A6
Dolphin Ind Est BN43 .... 161 B7
Dolphin L Ctr The RH16 ...... 50 D6
Dolphin Rd
  Haywards Heath RH16 .... 50 D4
  Shoreham-by-Sea BN43 ...... 161 B7
Dolphin Way BN43 .... 161 B7
Donald Hall Rd BN2 .... 164 D5
Donald Way BN2 .... 118 A5
Donkey Mews BN3 .... 163 D5
Donnington Rd BN2 .... 165 E6
Dorchester TN4 .... 8 B6
Dordrecht Way TN34 .... 136 E1
Dorin Ct TN2 .... 8 C3
Dorking Rd TN1 .... 8 C6
Dorman's Cl RH7 .... 2 A8
Dormans Gdns RH19 .... 1 E6
Dormans High St RH7 .... 2 A8
Dormans Park Rd
  Dormans Park RH19 .... 1 E6
  East Grinstead RH19 .... 1 D3
Dormans Sta RH7 .... 1 F8
Dormans Station Rd RH7 ...... 1 F7
Dormansland Prim Sch RH7 .. 2 A8
Dornden Dr TN3 .... 7 A4
Dorothy Ave BN10 .... 178 C7
Dorothy Ave N BN10 .... 178 C8
Dorothy Rd BN3 .... 162 D8
Dorothy Stringer Sch BN1 .... 142 F3
Dorset Ave RH19 .... 1 C3
Dorset Cl TN7 .... 14 B4
Dorset Ct **6** Eastbourne BN22 .. 185 B3
  Hove BN41 .... 162 F6
Dorset Gdns Brighton BN2 .... 189 B5
  East Grinstead RH19 .... 1 C3
Dorset Pl Brighton BN2 .... 189 B5
  Hastings TN34 .... 159 E7
Dorset Rd Bexhill TN40 .... 157 D4
  Bexhill TN40 .... 157 E5
  Lewes BN7 .... 146 D8
  Royal Tunbridge Wells TN2 .. 8 D2
Dorset Rd S TN40 .... 157 D4
Dorset St BN2 .... 189 A5
Doubledays RH15 .... 73 B2
Doucegrove TN38 .... 136 A1
Douglas Cl BN27 .... 129 B2
Douglas Rd TN6 .... 27 D1
Dove Cl TN22 .... 78 C8
Dovedale Gdns BN22 .... 173 F2
Dover Cl BN25 .... 181 C5
Dover Rd Brighton BN1 .... 143 A2
  Polegate BN26 .... 173 B7
Dower Cl BN2 .... 165 D3
Down Ave TN3 .... 20 A4
Down La TN3 .... 28 C8
Down Rd TN39 .... 157 A5
Down St TN22 .... 54 C5
Down Terr BN2 .... 164 C6
Down The BN3 .... 141 D4
Down's Rd TN34 .... 136 F3
Downash Cl BN2 .... 164 E6
Downash Ho TN5 .... 32 A3
Downes Ct **9** BN43 .... 161 C8
Downey Ho TN37 .... 136 B6
Downland Ave
  Peacehaven BN10 .... 178 E6
  Southwick BN42 .... 140 E1
Downland Cl Southwick BN42 .. 140 D1
  Woodingdean BN2 .... 165 B8
Downland Copse TN22 .... 78 C8
Downland Cres BN3 .... 141 F3
Downland Ct BN41 .... 141 A2
Downland Dr BN3 .... 141 F3
Downland Rd BN2 .... 165 B8
Downlands Ave TN39 .... 157 B4
Downlands Cl TN39 .... 157 A4
Downlands Sch BN6 .... 97 F3
Downlands Way BN3 .... 183 B1
Downline Cl TN21 .... 106 F7
Downs Ave BN20 .... 184 B6
Downs Cl BN7 .... 123 A2
Downs Cty Jun Sch BN1 ...... 143 A1
Downs Park Sch BN41 .... 140 C4
Downs Rd Burgess Hill RH15 .. 72 E4
  Seaford BN25 .... 181 A3
  Willingdon BN22 .... 173 B2
Downs Sch The BN20 .... 184 B4
Downs Valley Rd BN2 .... 165 C8
Downs View Ninfield TN33 .... 133 B5
  North Chailey BN8 .... 75 E7
  Peacehaven BN10 .... 167 D2
Downs View Cl
  East Dean BN20 .... 183 C1
  North Chailey BN8 .... 75 E7
Downs View La BN20 .... 183 C1
Downs View Rd BN6 .... 97 F3
Downs View Sch BN2 .... 165 C8

Downs Villas BN9 .... 168 E3
Downs Wlk BN10 .... 167 B2
Downscroft RH15 .... 73 D6
Downside Brighton BN1 .... 142 D5
  Hove BN3 .... 142 B3
  Lewes BN7 .... 146 A8
  Shoreham-by-Sea BN43 ...... 140 A1
Downside Cl Eastbourne BN20 .. 184 C3
  Shoreham-by-Sea BN43 ...... 140 A1
Downsmeade BN21 .... 184 E3
Downsvalley Rd BN20 .... 173 A4
Downsview Heathfield TN21 .. 82 B8
  Hove BN3 .... 141 D3
  Hurstpierpoint BN6 .... 97 A5
Downsview Ave BN2 .... 165 C8
Downsview Cotts BN2 .... 123 A4
Downsview Cres TN22 .... 78 D8
Downsview Dr RH17 .... 74 C4
Downsview Rd
  Lower Willingdon BN20 ...... 173 A3
  Portslade-by-Sea BN41 ...... 141 A2
  Seaford BN25 .... 181 A3
Downsview Way BN27 .... 152 B7
Downsway Berwick BN26 ...... 150 B3
  Southwick BN42 .... 140 F1
  Woodingdean BN2 .... 144 D1
Draffin La TN31 .... 94 D3
Drake Ave BN23 .... 185 E7
Drake Ct BN25 .... 180 E2
Drapers Way TN38 .... 136 B2
Draxmont Way BN1 .... 142 F3
Drayton Rise TN4 .... 8 C6
Drive Lodge **10** BN3 .... 163 C7
Drive The Burgess Hill RH15 .. 73 B4
  Crowborough TN6 .... 25 D2
  Hailsham BN27 .... 152 B6
  Hastings TN38 .... 158 F8
  Hove BN3 .... 163 C7
  Maresfield TN22 .... 55 A5
  Maresfield Park TN22 .... 55 A7
  Newhaven BN9 .... 179 C5
  Royal Tunbridge Wells TN2 .. 8 B1
  Southwick BN42 .... 140 E1
  Uckfield TN22 .... 78 C8
Drockmill Cl BN26 .... 173 C6
Drove Ave BN2 .... 144 D2
Drove Cres BN41 .... 141 A2
Drove Rd Newhaven BN9 ...... 179 D8
  Portslade-by-Sea BN41 ...... 141 A1
  Woodingdean BN2 .... 165 B8
Drove The Brighton BN1 ...... 142 D1
  Falmer BN1 .... 144 C5
  Newhaven BN9 .... 179 E8
  Offham BN8 .... 123 A5
Drovers Cl BN41 .... 141 C2
Drovers Way RH15 .... 73 C1
Droveway The
  Haywards Heath RH16, RH17 .. 50 C6
  Hove BN3 .... 142 B2
  Hove BN3 .... 142 C1
Drummond Cl RH16 .... 50 D4
Drummond Ct RH16 .... 50 D4
Drury La TN38 .... 136 A2
Drusilla's Zoo Park BN26 ...... 171 A6
Dryden Wlk BN23 .... 174 E3
Duchess Dr BN25 .... 180 E6
Dudeney Lodge BN1 .... 143 B1
Dudley Inf Sch TN35 .... 160 C5
Dudley Lodge TN2 .... 8 C4
Dudley Rd Brighton BN1 ...... 143 B1
  Eastbourne BN22 .... 185 B4
  Hastings TN35 .... 160 C5
  Royal Tunbridge Wells TN1 .. 8 A4
Dudwell Rd BN2 .... 165 E7
Duke Bernard Ct **7** BN22 .. 185 C5
Duke Mews **2** TN37 .... 136 B2
Duke Rd TN37 .... 136 B2
Duke St Bexhill TN39 .... 156 F5
  Brighton BN1 .... 189 F5
  Hastings TN37 .... 136 B2
Duke Terr TN37 .... 136 B2
Duke's Dr BN20 .... 188 C2
Duke's Mound BN2 .... 164 D4
Dukes Barn Ct RH16 .... 51 B7
Dukes Cl BN25 .... 180 D5
Dukes Hill TN33 .... 112 D6
Dukes La BN1 .... 189 F5
Dukes Rd Haywards Heath RH16 .. 51 B8
  Royal Tunbridge Wells TN1 .. 8 A4
Dulwich Cl BN25 .... 181 B4
Dumb Woman's La TN31 ...... 92 D3
Dumbrell Cl BN27 .... 146 B8
Dumbrells Court Rd BN6 ...... 98 D4
Dumbrells Ct BN6 .... 98 D4
Dumbrills Cl RH15 .... 73 A5
Dunbar Dr BN27 .... 129 A1
Duncan Ho BN10 .... 167 D1
Dunclutcha Rd TN34 .... 136 F4
Duncton Cl RH16 .... 50 D4
Duncton Ho BN2 .... 97 A4
Dundale Rd TN3 .... 9 E1
Dunes Ave TN31 .... 94 F2
Dunning's Rd RH19 .... 10 E7
Dunnings Mill L Complex RH19 .. 10 E6
Dunorlan Farm Cotts TN2 .... 8 E4
Dunstall Ave RH15 .... 72 E4
Dunstall Farm Rd RH15 .... 72 F4
Dunstan Gr TN4 .... 8 B6
Dunstan Rd TN4 .... 8 B6
Dunstans Croft TN20 .... 40 C3
Dunster Cl BN1 .... 143 B1
Dunvan Cl BN7 .... 123 C3
Durham Cl BN2 .... 144 A1
Durham Ct Eastbourne BN20 .. 184 B6
  Hove BN3 .... 163 B6
Durkins Rd RH19 .... 1 D3
Durrell Cl BN23 .... 174 F2
Dursley Rd BN22 .... 185 A4

Dutchells Way BN22 .... 173 E4
Dyall Cl RH15 .... 72 E4
Dyke Cl BN3 .... 142 B4
Dyke Rd BN1, BN3 .... 163 E7
Dyke Road Ave BN1, BN3 .... 142 C4
Dyke Road Dr BN1 .... 163 F8
Dyke Road Pl BN1, BN3 ...... 142 C4
Dymchurch Cl Polegate BN26 .. 173 C7
  Seaford BN25 .... 181 C5
Dymock Cl BN25 .... 181 C4
Dymock's The BN6 .... 98 D3
Dymond Rd TN4 .... 136 A3
Dynevor Rd TN4 .... 8 C7

Eagle Cl TN22 .... 78 E5
Eagle Rd TN31 .... 93 C6
Earl St TN34 .... 159 F8
Earl's Rd TN4 .... 7 F4
Earls Cl BN22 .... 180 C5
Earls Gdn **5** BN7 .... 123 D1
Earwig Cnr BN8 .... 123 E3
East Albany Rd BN25 .... 180 F3
East Ascent TN38 .... 159 C6
East Beach St TN34 .... 160 B4
East Beeches Rd TN6 .... 26 B2
East Bourne St **22** TN34 .. 160 B4
East Brighton Golf Course
  BN2 .... 165 B5
East Cl BN26 .... 173 B6
East Cliff TN31 .... 93 C6
East Cliff Rd TN4 .... 8 A6
East Dean Rd BN20 .... 184 B2
East Dean Rise BN25 .... 181 A4
East Dr BN2 .... 164 C5
East Gdns BN6 .... 98 D3
East Grinstead Sta RH19 ...... 1 D1
East Hill TN34 .... 160 B4
East Hill Pas **7** TN34 ...... 160 B4
East Hoathly CE Prim Sch
  BN8 .... 104 F5
East Mascalls Rd RH16 .... 51 E6
East Meadway BN43 .... 161 A6
East Par TN34 .... 160 A3
East Point **6** BN43 .... 161 A6
East St Brighton BN1 .... 189 A4
  Coggins Mill TN20 .... 40 D3
  Falmer BN1 .... 144 C6
  Hastings TN34 .... 160 A4
  Lewes BN7 .... 123 D1
  Portslade-by-Sea BN41 ...... 162 C7
  Rye TN31 .... 93 C5
  Seaford BN25 .... 180 F3
East Sussex F HQ TN7 .... 123 B2
East Sussex Music Sch BN7 .. 146 C8
East Sussex Music Sch
  (Annexe) BN7 .... 123 D1
East Sussex National
  Golf Club TN22 .... 103 C7
East View TN21 .... 82 B6
East View Fields BN7 .... 99 E5
East View Terr TN33 .... 88 F1
East Way BN7 .... 122 F2
East Wick RH16 .... 51 C7
Eastbank BN42 .... 140 F1
Eastbourne Ave BN24 .... 175 D5
Eastbourne Coll BN21 .... 184 F5
Eastbourne Coll of
  Arts & Tech Eastbourne BN21 184 E7
  Eastbourne, Upperton BN21 .. 184 E4
  Eastbourne, Upperton BN21 .. 184 F4
Eastbourne Coll of
  Food & Fashion BN20 .... 185 A1
Eastbourne District
  General Hospl BN21 .... 184 E7
Eastbourne Rd Brighton BN2 .. 143 D1
  Felbridge RH19 .... 1 A5
  Halland BN8 .... 104 C6
  Lower Willingdon
  BN20, BN26 .... 173 A6
  Pevensey Bay BN24 .... 175 C4
  Seaford BN25 .... 181 C3
  Uckfield TN22 .... 78 F3
  Westham BN23, BN24 .... 174 F4
Eastbourne Sta BN21 .... 184 E3
Eastbridge Rd BN9 .... 179 E7
Eastbrook Rd BN41 .... 162 B7
Eastbrook Way BN42 .... 162 A7
Eastdale Rd RH15 .... 73 D4
Eastend La BN6 .... 98 D3
Eastergate TN39 .... 156 D6
Eastergate Rd BN2 .... 143 F4
Eastern Ave Polegate BN26 .. 173 B7
  Shoreham-by-Sea BN43 ...... 161 A7
Eastern Cl BN43 .... 161 A7
Eastern Cotts RH16 .... 51 B7
Eastern Pl BN2 .... 164 E4
Eastern Rd Brighton BN2 ...... 164 D4
  Haywards Heath RH16 .... 50 F3
  Haywards Heath, Lindfield RH16 .. 51 C7
  Wivelsfield RH17 .... 74 B4
Eastern Ring Rd BN1 .... 144 C7
Eastern Terr BN2 .... 164 D4
Eastern Terrace Mews **9**
  BN2 .... 164 D4
Eastfield Cres BN1 .... 143 B4
Eastgate St BN7 .... 123 D1
Eastgate Wharf **9** BN7 .... 123 D1
Easthill Dr BN41 .... 141 B2
Easthill Way BN41 .... 141 B1
Eastlands Cl TN2, TN4 .... 16 E8
Eastlands Rd TN4 .... 7 E1
Eastport La BN7 .... 146 C8
Eastview Cotts BN8 .... 124 E5
Eastway TN39 .... 156 D4
Eastwell Pl BN27 .... 152 B8
Eastwick Cl BN1 .... 143 B7
Eastwood Rd TN39 .... 157 A4
Eatenden La TN32, TN33 ...... 87 B3

Eaton Ct **9** BN3 .... 163 B7
Eaton Gardens Mansions **20**
BN3 .... 163 C7
Eaton Gate **17** BN3 .... 163 C7
Eaton Gdns BN3 .... 163 C7
Eaton Gr BN3 .... 163 C7
Eaton Hall **18** BN3 .... 163 C7
Eaton Manor **11** BN3 .... 163 B7
Eaton Pl BN2 .... 164 D4
Eaton Rd BN3 .... 163 C7
Eaton Villas BN3 .... 163 B7
Ebden's Hill TN33, TN34 .... 136 B8
Ebenezer Rd TN34 .... 160 B4
Ecclesden **6** BN2 .... 189 B6
Ecmod Rd BN22 .... 185 C6
Edburton Ave BN1 .... 143 A1
Eden Dr TN39 .... 156 F4
Eden Rd TN1 .... 8 A2
Eden Vale Dormans Park RH19 .... 1 F5
East Grinstead RH19 .... 1 D4
Edenbridge Rd TN7 .... 13 E6
Edensor Rd BN20 .... 188 D7
Edgar Rd TN35 .... 160 C6
Edgehill Cl TN21 .... 81 F7
Edgehill Way BN41 .... 140 F2
Edgeland Terr TN22 .... 173 F1
Edinburgh Ct Eastbourne BN20 .... 184 C5
Seaford BN25 .... 180 D3
Edinburgh Rd Bexhill TN40 .... 157 C5
Brighton BN2 .... 164 B8
Hastings TN38 .... 158 E7
Seaford BN25 .... 180 D3
Edinburgh Way RH19 .... 10 F7
Edison Rd BN22, BN23 .... 174 A1
Edith Ave BN10 .... 178 B7
Edith Ave N BN10 .... 178 C8
Edith Rd TN35 .... 137 D3
Edmond Cl BN23 .... 185 F8
Edmonton Rd TN39 .... 157 B7
Edmund Rd TN35 .... 160 C6
Edward Ave Hove BN3 .... 142 A3
Saltdean BN2 .... 166 D3
Edward Cl Hove BN3 .... 142 A3
Seaford BN25 .... 180 A6
Edward Ho BN3 .... 162 F6
Haywards Heath RH16 .... 50 E2
Edward Rd Hastings TN37 .... 159 D7
Edward St Brighton BN2 .... 189 B5
6 Lewes BN2 .... 123 C1
Royal Tunbridge Wells TN4 .... 7 F8
Rusthall TN4 .... 7 C4
Edward Terr TN38 .... 136 A4
Edward Way RH15 .... 72 D2
Edwin Rd TN35 .... 160 C6
Effingham Cl BN2 .... 177 C6
Effingham Dr TN39 .... 156 D3
Egbert Cl BN23 .... 185 F8
Egerton Rd TN39 .... 157 B3
Egginton Cl BN1 .... 144 A5
Egginton Rd BN1, BN2 .... 144 A5
Egles Gr TN22 .... 78 B8
Egmont Rd BN3 .... 141 B7
Egremont Pl Brighton BN2 .... 189 B5
Hastings TN34 .... 160 B6
Eight Acre La TN35 .... 115 D1
Eight Bells Cl TN22 .... 56 C4
Eileen Ave BN2 .... 177 B5
Eisenhower Dr TN38 .... 135 F6
Elder Cl BN41 .... 141 B2
Elder Pl BN1 .... 189 A7
Elderwood Cl Bexhill TN39 .... 157 C7
Eastbourne BN22 .... 173 D2
Eldon Rd BN21 .... 184 C5
Eldred Ave BN1 .... 142 D5
Eleanor Cl Lewes BN7 .... 123 B2
Seaford BN25 .... 180 D5
Eleanor Terr TN35 .... 137 D4
Eley Cres BN2 .... 165 E4
Eley Dr BN2 .... 165 E3
Elford St **3** TN34 .... 159 F8
Elgar Way BN23 .... 174 E3
Elgin Gdns BN25 .... 181 C3
Elim Court Gdns TN6 .... 25 E4
Elim Wlk TN34 .... 136 F2
Eliot Ho **4** RH16 .... 50 E3
Elizabeth Ave BN3 .... 142 A3
Elizabeth Cl Hove BN3 .... 142 A3
Seaford BN25 .... 180 A6
Elizabeth Cres RH19 .... 1 F3
Elizabeth Ct Eastbourne BN20 .... 184 C5
2 Hailsham BN27 .... 152 C7
7 Hove BN3 .... 163 C7
Polegate BN26 .... 173 A6
Elizabeth Garlick Ct **1** TN1 .... 8 B4
Elizabeth Rd Hastings TN38 ..... 136 A2
Shoreham-by-Sea BN43 .... 161 C8
Elizabethan Cl TN33 .... 132 F2
Ellen Ho **3** BN3 .... 163 B7
Ellen St Hove BN3 .... 163 B7
Portslade-by-Sea BN41 .... 162 C7
Ellenslea Rd TN37 .... 159 C7
Ellenwhorne La TN32 .... 89 A7
Ellerslie La TN39 .... 156 F6
Elliots Way TN21 .... 82 A8
Ellis Gordon Ct BN9 .... 179 B7
Ellis Way TN22 .... 78 A7
Elm Cl Hove BN3 .... 142 C2
Laughton BN8 .... 126 C7
Seaford BN25 .... 181 C3
Elm Cotts Hailsham BN27 .... 151 A8
Laughton BN8 .... 126 C6
Elm Ct Brighton BN1 .... 163 E8
Newhaven BN9 .... 179 B7
Polegate BN26 .... 173 A6
Portslade-by-Sea BN41 .... 162 B8
Elm Dr East Grinstead RH19 .... 2 A1
Hove BN3 .... 141 E1
Elm Gn **4** BN27 .... 129 B1

Elm Gr Brighton BN2 .... 164 C7
Eastbourne BN22 .... 173 F1
11 Lewes BN7 .... 146 C8
Elm Grove Cty Prim Sch 164 C7
Elm Rd BN1 .... 162 B8
Elm Way TN21 .... 82 B6
Elmhurst Ave TN2 .... 9 D8
Elmore Rd TN2 .... 189 B6
Elms Ave BN21 .... 185 B2
Elms La TN35 .... 116 F1
Elms Lea Ave BN1 .... 142 E3
Elms Rd BN21 .... 185 B2
Elms The BN8 .... 124 C5
Elmstone Pl BN27 .... 152 C7
Elmstead BN19 .... 10 E8
Elmstead Rd TN19 .... 10 E8
Elmstead Rd TN40 .... 157 E5
Elmwood **9** BN21 .... 184 F4
Elmwood Cl BN23 .... 174 C4
Elmwood Gdns BN23 .... 174 C4
Elphick Rd Broyle Side BN8 .... 124 F7
Newhaven BN9 .... 179 C8
Elphick's Pl TN2 .... 17 B8
Elphinstone Ave TN34 .... 136 F2
Elphinstone Cty Prim Sch
TN34 .... 160 A6
Elphinstone Gdns TN34 .... 136 F3
Elphinstone Inf Sch TN34 .... 136 F2
Elphinstone Rd TN34 .... 136 F2
Elsted Cl BN22 .... 174 A1
Elsted Cres BN1 .... 143 C6
Elstone Rd TN39 .... 156 C2
Elven Cl BN20 .... 183 C1
Elven La BN20 .... 183 C1
Elvin Cres BN2 .... 165 E4
Elwood Cl RH15 .... 72 F1
Ely Ct TN2 .... 8 B4
Embassy Ct BN3 .... 163 D5
Emerald Quay BN43 .... 161 A6
Emmanuel Rd TN34 .... 160 A5
Encore Ho TN21 .... 81 F8
Endcliffe Ct BN20 .... 188 E8
Endwell Rd TN40 .... 157 C4
Engalee RH19 .... 1 C2
English Cl BN3 .... 162 E8
English's Pas **10** BN7 .... 123 D1
Enterprise Est BN1 .... 143 C7
Enys Rd BN21 .... 184 F4
Epsom Cl TN38 .... 159 A8
Erica Cl BN22 .... 174 B2
Eridge Cl TN39 .... 157 A4
Eridge Dr TN6 .... 26 A3
Eridge Gdns TN6 .... 26 A3
Eridge Gn BN7 .... 123 B2
Eridge Rd Boarshead TN3, TN6 .... 26 D7
Crowborough TN6 .... 26 D7
Eastbourne BN21 .... 184 D7
Hove BN3 .... 142 A2
Royal Tunbridge Wells TN2, TN4 .... 7 E1
Steel Cross TN6 .... 26 C4
Eridge Sta TN3 .... 15 E2
Erin Way RH15 .... 72 E3
Erroll Rd BN3, BN41 .... 162 C6
Ersham Rd BN27 .... 152 B5
Ersham Way BN27 .... 152 B6
Erskine Park Rd TN4 .... 7 C4
Eshton Rd BN25 .... 180 F4
Eskbank Ave BN1 .... 143 A7
Eskdale Cl BN23 .... 174 C4
Esplanade BN25 .... 180 E2
Esplanade The BN10 .... 177 F3
Essenden Rd TN38 .... 159 A7
Essex Cl TN2 .... 16 F8
Essex Ct BN20 .... 184 B6
Essex Pl **3** Brighton BN2 ..... 164 C5
Newhaven BN9 .... 179 C7
Essex Rd TN38 .... 136 A4
Essex St BN2 .... 164 C4
Estate Rd BN9 .... 179 E7
Estcots Cty Prim Sch RH19 .... 2 A1
Estcots Dr RH19 .... 2 A1
Etchingham CE Prim Sch
TN19 .... 44 D2
Etchingham Rd BN19 .... 174 E1
Etchingham Sta TN19 .... 44 C1
Ethel St BN3 .... 163 B7
Etherington Rd BN23 .... 185 E8
Etherington Hill TN3 .... 7 C8
Etherton Way BN25 .... 181 A4
Ethnam La TN18 .... 47 E4
Eton Mews **2** BN21 .... 185 A3
Eurythmy Sch RH19 .... 10 E6
Evelyn Ave BN9 .... 179 C7
Evelyn Ct BN41 .... 162 A8
Evelyn Glennie Ct **7** BN2 .... 164 C5
Evelyn Rd BN7 .... 123 B2
Evelyn Terr BN2 .... 164 C5
Everest Ho **2** BN3 .... 162 F7
Eversfield Ct TN37 .... 159 D7
Eversfield Hospl TN38 .... 159 A6
Eversfield Mews N **5** TN37 .... 159 C7
Eversfield Pl TN37 .... 159 D7
Eversfield Rd BN21 .... 184 F4
Eversley Cl TN37 .... 136 C2
Eversley Cres TN37 .... 136 C2
Eversley Rd Bexhill TN40 .... 157 C3
Hastings TN37 .... 136 C2
Everton Cotts TN19 .... 62 B6
Evesham TN38 .... 136 A3
Ewart St BN2 .... 189 B6
Ewehurst La TN3 .... 6 F6
Ewell Ct TN40 .... 157 E4
Ewhurst Cl TN34 .... 136 F4
Ewhurst La TN31 .... 66 F4
Ewhurst Rd BN2 .... 143 C1

Excelsior The BN1 .... 142 D4
Exeat Cl Brighton BN2 .... 164 E6
Eastbourne BN23 .... 174 B4
Exeter Cl BN22 .... 173 B2
Exeter St **1** BN1 .... 163 E8
Exmouth Pl TN34 .... 160 A4

Factory La BN27 .... 152 A6
Fair La Robertsbridge TN32 ...... 64 B4
Robertsbridge TN32 .... 64 C4
Fair Meadow TN31 .... 93 C7
Fair Oak Cl TN21 .... 82 A7
Fair View TN5 .... 30 A6
Fairbanks BN16 .... 50 E4
Fairbridge Way RH15 .... 72 F5
Faircrouch La TN5 .... 29 B5
Fairdene BN42 .... 140 F1
Fairfax Ave BN1 .... 143 A8
Fairfield Herstmonceux BN27 .... 130 E6
Peacehaven BN10 .... 178 B7
Fairfield Ave TN1, TN2 .... 8 C5
Fairfield Chase TN39 .... 156 F4
Fairfield Cl Burgess Hill RH15 .... 72 F4
Shoreham-by-Sea BN43 .... 140 C1
Fairfield Cotts BN26 .... 149 D2
Fairfield Cres TN6 .... 97 A6
Fairfield Gdns
Burgess Hill RH15 .... 72 F4
Portslade-by-Sea BN41 .... 141 B1
Fairfield Lodge BN20 .... 188 E8
Fairfield Rd Burgess Hill RH15 .... 72 F4
East Grinstead RH19 .... 10 F8
Eastbourne BN20 .... 184 E1
Hastings TN37 .... 136 C6
Fairfield Way RH16 .... 50 D8
Fairford Cl RH16 .... 50 E5
Fairglen Cotts TN5 .... 29 B4
Fairglen Rd TN5 .... 29 B4
Fairholme **6** BN7 .... 146 C8
Fairholme Rd BN9 .... 168 F1
Fairhurst BN10 .... 177 F3
Fairisle Cl BN27 .... 129 A2
Fairlawn **1** RH16 .... 50 E4
Fairlawn Cres RH19 .... 1 B2
Fairlawn Dr RH19 .... 1 B2
Fairlawns **8** Hove BN3 .... 163 A6
Shoreham-by-Sea BN43 .... 161 A8
Fairlawns Dr BN27 .... 130 E6
Fairlea Cl RH15 .... 72 F4
Fairlie Gdns BN1 .... 142 E3
Fairlight TN22 .... 55 E1
Fairlight Ave Hastings TN35 .... 137 D3
Telscombe Cliffs BN10 .... 177 F3
Fairlight Cl Bexhill TN40 .... 158 A5
Polegate BN26 .... 173 A6
Fairlight Ct TN40 .... 177 F4
Fairlight Cty Prim Sch TN35 .... 164 C8
Fairlight Field BN8 .... 124 D5
Fairlight Gdns TN35 .... 138 F4
Fairlight Pl **4** BN2 .... 164 C8
Fairlight Rd
Eastbourne BN22 .... 185 C5
Fairlight TN35 .... 138 A4
Fairmile Rd TN2 .... 8 E5
Fairmount Rd TN40 .... 157 D5
Fairplace RH17 .... 74 C2
Fairstone Cl TN35 .... 137 E4
Fairview Cotts TN6 .... 25 E4
Fairview La TN6 .... 25 E4
Fairview Rise BN1 .... 142 D5
Fairway Cl BN20 .... 184 C2
Fairway Cres BN41 .... 141 C2
Fairway The Bexhill TN39 .... 156 F6
Hastings TN38 .... 158 F8
Newhaven BN9 .... 179 A7
Fairway Trad Est BN2 .... 143 E4
Fairways BN1 .... 163 E8
Fairways Cl BN25 .... 181 C2
Fairways Rd BN25 .... 181 B2
Fairways The TN4 .... 8 A7
Falaise Rd
Hastings TN34, TN37 .... 159 D7
Newhaven BN9 .... 168 F1
Falcon Cl BN43 .... 161 C6
Falcon Way BN27 .... 129 B3
Falconbury Dr TN39 .... 156 D3
Falconer Dr TN33 .... 112 F4
Fallowfield Cl BN3 .... 141 F2
Fallowfield Cres BN3 .... 141 F2
Falls Ct TN38 .... 135 F6
Falmer Ave BN2 .... 177 C6
Falmer Cl BN20 .... 184 B7
Falmer Gdns BN2 .... 165 D8
Falmer Hill BN1 .... 144 B6
Falmer House Rd BN1 .... 144 B6
Falmer Rd Woodingdean BN2 .... 144 D1
Woodingdean BN2, BN1 .... 165 E5
Falmer Sta BN1 .... 144 A5
Falmer Sta BN1 .... 144 B6
Falmouth Cl BN23 .... 185 F8
Faraday Ave RH19 .... 10 F6
Faraday Cl BN22 .... 173 F1
Farlaine Rd BN21 .... 184 C6
Farley Bank TN34, TN35 .... 160 B6
Farley Way TN35 .... 138 E5
Farlington Ave RH16 .... 50 F5
Farlington Cl RH16 .... 50 F5
Farm Cl East Grinstead RH19 .... 11 B8
Hassocks BN6 .... 97 E4
Portslade-by-Sea BN41 .... 141 A2
Seaford BN25 .... 181 B4
Farm Gdns TN31 .... 69 C2
Farm Hill BN2 .... 165 C8
Farm La Camber TN31 .... 94 D3
Ditchling BN6 .... 98 E3
Farm Mews **8** BN3 .... 163 D6
Farm Rd BN3 .... 163 D6
Farm Trail BN26 .... 151 A4

Farm Way Burgess Hill RH15 .... 73 D1
Southwick BN42 .... 162 A7
Farmcombe La TN1 .... 8 B2
Farmcombe Rd TN1, TN2 .... 8 C2
Farmland Way BN27 .... 129 C1
Farmlands Ave BN26, BN20 .... 172 F4
Lower Willingdon BN26 .... 173 A4
Farmlands Cl BN26 .... 173 A4
Farmlands Way BN26 .... 172 F5
Farmway Cl BN3 .... 141 D2
Farncombe Cl RH17 .... 74 D4
Farncombe Rd **5** BN7 .... 123 C1
Farne Cl BN22 .... 129 A2
Farnham Ave BN1 .... 98 A5
Farnham Beeches TN3 .... 7 A3
Farnham Cl TN3 .... 7 A3
Farnham La TN3 .... 7 A3
Farningham Rd TN6 .... 38 C8
Farnley RH15 .... 73 D5
Farnol Ho **4** BN21 .... 184 D4
Farriers Way TN22 .... 78 C6
Farthing Hill TN5 .... 31 E1
Farthing La BN27, TN33 .... 109 E4
Farthings The TN6 .... 26 A3
Faulkners Way RH15 .... 73 A5
Faversham Rd BN23 .... 174 D2
Faygate Cl TN39 .... 157 B8
Faygate Ct BN2 .... 164 E6
Faygate Rd BN22 .... 173 E2
Fayre Meadow TN32 .... 64 C4
Fazan Ct TN5 .... 29 F4
Fearon Rd TN34 .... 136 F2
Felbridge Cl RH19 .... 1 C3
Felbridge Ct RH19 .... 1 A4
Felbridge Ctr The RH19 .... 1 A3
Felcourt Cotts RH19 .... 1 C8
Felcourt La RH19, RH7 .... 1 C8
Felcourt Rd RH19, RH7 .... 1 C7
Fellows Rd TN34 .... 137 B3
Felride RH16 .... 50 E3
Felwater Ct RH19 .... 1 A3
Fennel Wlk BN43 .... 140 B1
Fennell's Cl BN21 .... 184 E5
Ferbies TN3 .... 7 A7
Ferbies Cotts TN3 .... 7 A7
Ferdinand Terr TN3 .... 15 C7
Ferguson Rd TN29 .... 96 D2
Fermor Rd TN6 .... 38 A7
Fermor Row TN6 .... 37 F8
Fermor Way TN6 .... 38 A8
Fern Cl BN23 .... 174 C3
Fern Gn **1** BN21 .... 129 B1
Fern Rd TN38 .... 158 F8
Fernbank Sh Ctr TN6 .... 25 F3
Ferndale TN6 .... 8 D5
Ferndale Cl TN2 .... 8 C4
Ferndale Point TN2 .... 8 C4
Ferndale Rd Burgess Hill RH15 .... 73 C2
Hastings TN34 .... 163 D7
Fernhurst Cl BN1 .... 143 B6
Fernhurst Cres BN1 .... 143 B5
Fernlea TN35 .... 114 E4
Ferns The TN1 .... 8 C4
Fernside Ave TN38 .... 135 F1
Fernwood Rise BN1 .... 142 D5
Ferrers Rd BN27 .... 130 E6
Ferring Cl TN31 .... 93 A6
Ferring Ct BN1 .... 143 C5
Ferring Hill TN36 .... 117 E8
Ferry Rd TN31 .... 93 B5
Festival Gdns TN39 .... 157 C7
Feversham Cl BN43 .... 161 B6
Field Cl Burgess Hill RH15 ...... 72 E4
Seaford BN25 .... 181 B2
Field End TN22 .... 55 A4
Field Sch The BN25 .... 162 D7
Field View TN32 .... 64 B3
Field Way TN38 .... 158 E8
Fielden La TN6 .... 25 D1
Fielden Rd TN6 .... 25 D2
Fieldfare Ct BN27 .... 152 D7
Fields End Cl RH16 .... 50 F4
Fieldway Broad Oak TN31 .... 90 C5
Ditchling BN6 .... 98 D3
Haywards Heath RH16 .... 50 E8
Fiennes Rd BN27 .... 130 E6
Figg La TN6 .... 37 F8
Filching Rd BN26 .... 172 E3
Filching Ct BN20 .... 184 B5
Filching Manor Motor Mus
BN26 .... 172 D2
Filching Rd BN20 .... 184 B5
Filder Cl BN22 .... 185 A6
Filsham Dr TN40 .... 157 A8
Filsham Rd TN38 .... 159 A8
Filsham Valley TN38 .... 158 F7
Filsham Valley Sch TN38 .... 158 F7
Finches Gdns RH16 .... 51 A8
Finches La RH16 .... 51 A8
Finches Park Rd RH16 .... 51 A8
Finches The Bexhill TN40 .... 157 F4
2 Hastings TN38 .... 136 A5
Shoreham-by-Sea BN43 .... 161 A8
Findon Ave BN2 .... 177 C6
Findon Cl Bexhill TN39 .... 156 E3
Hove BN3 .... 141 F3
Seaford BN25 .... 181 C3
Findon Rd BN2 .... 164 F5
Finley Ct TN38 .... 158 F6
Finmere Cl BN22 .... 185 C6
Finmere Rd BN22 .... 185 C6
Finsbury Lodge **1** BN2 .... 164 C6
Finsbury Rd BN2 .... 164 C6
Fir Cl BN2 .... 165 F7
Fir Grove Rd TN21 .... 81 B6
Fir Toll Cl TN20 .... 39 F2

Fir Toll Rd Woolbridge TN20 .... 39 C2
Woolbridge TN20 .... 39 F2
Fir Tree Cl Bexhill TN39 .... 156 C3
Hailsham BN27 .... 129 C2
Fir Tree Rd TN4 .... 7 F3
Fir Tree Way BN6 .... 98 A4
Fircroft Cl BN1 .... 142 E3
Firehills Cotts TN35 .... 138 C3
Firlands RH15 .... 50 F4
Firle Bostal BN8 .... 148 A2
Firle CE Prim Sch BN8 .... 148 B4
Firle Cl Hastings TN35 .... 137 E4
Seaford BN25 .... 180 E5
Firle Cres BN7 .... 122 F5
Firle Dr BN25 .... 180 E5
Firle Gn TN22 .... 55 E1
Firle Grange BN25 .... 180 E5
Firle Place BN8 .... 148 C3
Firle Rd Bexhill TN39 .... 156 D4
Brighton BN2 .... 164 D6
Eastbourne BN22 .... 185 B4
Peacehaven BN10 .... 178 C8
Seaford BN25 .... 180 E6
Firle Terr BN9 .... 168 D2
Firs Ct TN4 .... 7 F6
First Ave Bexhill TN40 .... 157 F5
Camber TN31 .... 94 F2
Hove BN3 .... 163 C6
Newhaven BN9 .... 179 C7
First St TN1 .... 6 F3
Firtoft Cl RH15 .... 73 B3
Firtree Rd TN34 .... 160 A6
Firwood Cl Eastbourne BN22 .... 173 E1
Heathfield TN21 .... 82 A8
Firwood Rise TN21 .... 82 A8
Fisher Cl BN23 .... 185 F7
Fisher St BN7 .... 123 D1
Fisher's Gate Cotts TN7 .... 14 A1
Fishermen's Mus TN34 .... 160 B3
Fishersgate Cty Fst Sch
BN41 .... 162 A7
Fishersgate Sta BN41 .... 162 C8
Fishersgate Terr BN41, BN42 .... 162 A7
Fishmarket Rd TN31 .... 93 C6
Fishponds La TN35 .... 114 E3
Fitch Dr BN2 .... 143 F1
Fitzalan Ho **7** BN21 .... 184 F1
Fitzgerald Ave BN25 .... 180 F2
Fitzgerald Cl BN20 .... 184 F1
Fitzgerald Ho **5** BN25 .... 180 E3
Fitzgerald Pk BN25 .... 180 F2
Fitzgerald Rd BN7 .... 123 D3
Fitzherbert Dr BN2 .... 164 D8
Fitzjohn Cl BN6 .... 97 F3
Fitzjohns Rd BN7 .... 123 B2
Fitzmaurice Ave BN22 .... 185 B5
Fitzroy Rd BN7 .... 123 B2
Five Acre Wlk TN34 .... 136 E1
Five Ashes CE Prim Sch
TN20 .... 58 B6
Five Hos The TN36 .... 117 E8
Five Villages Ho TN36 .... 116 F6
Fiveways TN1 .... 8 A4
Flag Ct BN3 .... 163 B5
Flamsteed Rd BN27 .... 131 A1
Fleetway Ct TN31 .... 94 F2
Fleming Cl BN23 .... 174 F2
Fletcher Ave TN37, TN38 .... 135 F7
Fletching CE Prim Sch TN22 .... 53 F3
Fletching Cl BN2 .... 164 F6
Fletching Rd BN22 .... 174 A2
Fletching St TN20 .... 40 B3
Flimwell Bird Pk TN19 .... 32 E2
Flimwell Cl Brighton BN2 .... 164 E5
Eastbourne BN23 .... 174 A4
Flimwell TN5 .... 32 D4
Hastings TN38 .... 135 D3
Flint Cl Portslade-by-Sea BN41 .... 141 B2
Seaford BN25 .... 180 E6
Flints The BN7 .... 145 E5
Flitterbrook La TN21 .... 83 C4
Florance La TN3 .... 15 B6
Florence Ave BN3 .... 162 D8
Florence Ct BN1 .... 142 F2
Florence Pl BN1 .... 143 B1
Florence Rd BN1 .... 164 A8
Florida Ct TN38 .... 158 F6
Fold Sch The BN3 .... 162 D7
Folders Cl RH15 .... 73 D1
Folders La BN6, RH15 .... 73 D1
Foley Cl BN25 .... 185 E7
Folkestone Cl BN25 .... 181 C5
Folkestone Rd TN31 .... 93 F8
Follett Holt Ho BN8 .... 100 E7
Folly Field BN9 .... 179 C7
Fonthill Rd BN3 .... 163 B8
Fontridge La TN19 .... 62 E3
Fontwell Ave TN39 .... 156 C5
Foords La BN24 .... 174 C7
Foot's La TN19 .... 61 B3
Ford Rd TN38 .... 135 F2
Fordbrook Hill TN6 .... 37 F2
Fordcombe CE Prim Sch TN3 .... 6 B5
Fordcombe La TN3 .... 6 C5
Fordcombe Rd TN3 .... 6 C4
Foredown Cl Eastbourne BN20 .... 184 C2
Portslade-by-Sea BN41 .... 141 B2
Foredown Dr BN41 .... 141 C1
Foredown Rd
Portslade Village BN41 .... 141 B4
Portslade-by-Sea BN41 .... 141 B2
Forest Dene TN6 .... 26 D1
Forest Fold Cotts TN6 .... 25 D5

Forest Lodge
Crowborough Warren TN6 .... 37 D8
2 East Grinstead RH19 .... 10 F8
Forest Pk TN6 .... 25 D2
Forest Pl TN21 .... 80 F6
Forest Rd Brighton BN1 .... 143 E6
Forest Row RH18 .... 12 B2
Royal Tunbridge Wells TN2 ...... 8 C1
Forest Ridge RH19 .... 21 A5
Forest Rise TN6 .... 26 D1
Forest Row Bsns Pk RH18 ...... 11 F4
Forest Row CE Inf Sch RH18 ... 11 F2
Forest View Hailsham BN27 ...... 152 A8
Nutley TN22 .... 35 C3
Forest View Rd RH19 .... 10 E6
Forest Way Hastings TN34 .... 136 E1
Pembury TN2 .... 9 D8
Royal Tunbridge Wells TN2 ...... 8 D1
Forewood La TN33 .... 135 A7
Forewood Rise TN33 .... 134 F6
Forge Cl
Portslade-by-Sea BN41 .... 141 B2
Staplecross TN32 .... 65 E1
Uckfield TN22 .... 78 C6
Forge Field TN5 .... 42 F6
Forge La TN22 .... 65 E1
Forge Lane Cotts TN22 .... 55 A8
Forge Rd TN3, TN6 .... 15 C2
Forge Rise TN22 .... 78 C6
Forge Way Burgess Hill RH15 ..... 73 A4
Hastings TN37 .... 136 C5
Forstal The Cobbarn TN3 .... 15 F3
Pembury TN2 .... 9 E8
Forstall TN3 .... 7 A4
Fort Gate BN9 .... 179 E5
Fort Haven BN43 .... 161 C6
Fort La BN22 .... 185 D6
Fort Newhaven BN9 .... 179 D5
Fort Rd Eastbourne BN22 .... 185 D6
Newhaven BN9 .... 179 D6
Fort Rise BN9 .... 179 D5
Foster Cl BN25 .... 180 E4
Foundry Ct RH15 .... 73 B3
Foundry La BN7 .... 123 E1
Foundry St BN1 .... 189 A6
Fountains Brighton BN1 .... 143 C2
Eastbourne BN22 .... 173 E3
Founthill Ave BN2 .... 177 B5
Founthill Rd BN2 .... 177 B5
Fourteen Acre La TN35 .... 115 D4
Fourth Ave BN3 .... 163 B6
Fowey Cl BN43 .... 161 B6
Fowlers Cl TN39 .... 156 E5
Fowly La TN22 .... 56 C7
Fox Cl RH15 .... 72 F1
Fox Hill RH16 .... 50 E1
Fox Hill Cl RH16 .... 50 F1
Fox Hill Village RH16 .... 50 E1
Fox in the Wood TN5 .... 29 C6
Fox Way BN41 .... 141 B2
Foxcote TN37 .... 136 D5
Foxdown Rd BN2 .... 165 F7
Foxglove Cl BN8 .... 125 A7
Foxglove Rd BN23 .... 174 B3
Foxhill Bexhill TN39 .... 156 E5
Peacehaven BN10 .... 167 B1
Foxhill Ct **3** RH16 .... 50 E3
Foxhole La Four Throws TN18 .... 46 D8
Wadhurst TN5 .... 30 B4
Foxhunters Rd BN41 .... 140 F3
Foxwarren RH16 .... 50 C5
Framelle Mount TN22 .... 79 B6
Framfield **11** BN2 .... 164 F5
Framfield CE Prim Sch TN22 ... 79 B6
Framfield Cl BN1 .... 143 E6
Framfield Rd Buxted TN22 .... 56 B3
Uckfield TN22 .... 78 D6
Framfield Way BN21 .... 184 D6
Francis Rd RH16 .... 51 B8
Francis St BN1, BN2 .... 189 A7
Francislea RH16 .... 50 E2
Frankfield Rise TN2 .... 8 A1
Franklands Cl RH15 .... 73 B1
Franklands Gdns RH15 .... 98 A8
Franklands Way RH15 .... 98 A8
Franklin Rd Brighton BN2 ..... 164 C7
Portslade-by-Sea BN41 .... 140 D1
Shoreham-by-Sea BN43 .... 140 D1
Franklin St BN2 .... 164 C8
Franklynn Rd RH16 .... 50 F3
Frankton Ave RH16 .... 51 A3
Frant Ave TN39 .... 156 C5
Frant CE Prim Sch TN3 .... 17 B4
Frant Cl TN39 .... 156 C5
Frant Rd Hove BN3 .... 142 A2
Royal Tunbridge Wells TN2, TN3 ... 17 A7
Frant Sta TN3 .... 17 F5
Frary Wlk TN21 .... 82 A3
Fraser Ave BN23 .... 185 E7
Fraser Ct **2** BN43 .... 161 C8
Freckley Hollow TN33 .... 111 C1
Fred Emery Ct **10** BN1 .... 163 E5
Freda Gardham Cty Prim Sch
TN31 .... 93 D6
Frederick Cotts RH16 .... 51 B7
Frederick Gdns BN1 .... 189 A6
Frederick Pl BN1 .... 189 A6
Frederick Rd TN35 .... 137 C3
Frederick St BN1 .... 189 A6
Free Heath Rd TN3, TN5 .... 19 C3
Freehold Terr **1** BN2 .... 164 C8
Freek's La RH15 .... 73 A5
Freeland Cl BN25 .... 180 A6
Freeman Ave RH16 .... 50 E2
Freemans Rd BN41 .... 162 A8

Freezeland La TN39 .... 134 A2
Fremlin Cl TN4 .... 7 B4
French Gdns RH16 .... 51 A6
Frenches Farm Dr TN21 .... 82 A5
Frenchgate Cl BN22 .... 173 F2
Frenchgate Rd BN22 .... 173 F2
Freshfield Bank RH18 .... 11 E2
Freshfield Cl BN27 .... 152 B6
Freshfield Halt RH17 .... 52 B8
Freshfield La RH17 .... 33 E2
Freshfield Pl BN2 .... 164 C5
Freshfield Rd BN2 .... 164 D6
Freshfield St BN2 .... 164 C6
Freshfield Way BN2 .... 164 C5
Freshford BN23 .... 174 D2
Freshwater Ave TN34 .... 136 E2
Freshwater Sq BN22 .... 173 B3
Freshway BN22 .... 173 C3
Frewen TN31 .... 67 B7
Frewen Coll TN31 .... 67 C5
Frewyn Cl TN38 .... 135 F4
Friar Cl BN1 .... 143 A4
Friar Cres BN1 .... 143 A3
Friar Rd BN1 .... 143 A3
Friar Wlk BN1 .... 142 F4
Friar's Cres TN35 .... 138 B7
Friar's Hill Terr TN35 .... 138 A7
Friar's Way TN34 .... 136 F4
Friars' Ave BN10 .... 178 E6
Friars Bank TN35 .... 138 B7
Friars Cl BN6 .... 97 E4
Friars Hill TN35 .... 137 F7
Friars Oak Rd BN6 .... 97 E5
Friars Rd TN36 .... 117 F7
Friars Way TN2 .... 8 D6
Friars' Wlk BN7 .... 123 D1
Friday St BN23 .... 174 C3
Fridays The BN20 .... 187 B7
Friezland Rd TN4 .... 7 D1
Frimley Cl BN2 .... 165 F7
Friston Ave BN22 .... 173 C1
Friston Cl Brighton BN2 .... 143 F4
Friston BN20 .... 183 A1
Seaford BN25 .... 180 C4
Friston Downs BN20 .... 183 B2
Frith Pk RH19 .... 1 E3
Frith Rd BN3 .... 163 A8
Frobisher Cl BN23 .... 185 F7
Frobisher Ho BN10 .... 167 D1
Frog Hole La TN20 .... 58 C5
Frog La TN1 .... 8 A2
Front Cotts TN5 .... 31 E1
Fruitfields TN5 .... 32 C3
Fry Cres RH15 .... 72 E5
Fryatts Way TN39 .... 156 F6
Fryman's La TN31 .... 89 D2
FTA (Trng Ctr) TN5 .... 29 D6
Fulford Cl TN38 .... 159 A8
Fuller Cl TN5 .... 29 E5
Fuller Rd BN7 .... 123 A3
Fuller's Pas **18** BN7 .... 123 D1
Fullers La TN31 .... 67 B6
Fullwood Ave BN9 .... 179 B7
Fulmar Cl BN3 .... 142 D1
Fulmar Dr RH19 .... 2 B3
Fulmer Pl **1** TN40 .... 157 C4
Furlongs The BN26 .... 170 F3
Furnace Ave TN1 .... 20 A3
Furnace La
Beckley Furnace TN31 .... 90 D7
Hook Green TN3 .... 19 E4
Horam TN21 .... 106 D8
Warbleton TN21 .... 82 E2
Furnace Way TN22 .... 78 E7
Furness Rd BN20, BN21 .... 184 F2
Furnival Ct TN2 .... 16 F8
Furze Croft Hastings TN38 ..... 159 A8
Hove BN3 .... 163 D6
Furze Hill BN3 .... 163 D6
Furze Hill Ct BN3 .... 163 E6
Furze Hill Ho BN3 .... 163 E6
Furze La RH19 .... 1 B4
Furzedene BN3 .... 163 D6
Furzefield Ave TN3 .... 7 A8
Furzefield Chase RH19 .... 1 E6
Furzefield Rd RH19 .... 1 D4
Fyning Pl TN39 .... 156 C5
Fyrsway TN35 .... 138 E4
Fysie La TN31 .... 44 D3

Gableson Ave BN1 .... 142 B4
Gage Ridge RH18 .... 11 E2
Gages The BN27 .... 152 D7
Gainsborough Cres BN23 .... 174 D1
Gainsborough Ho **16** BN3 ..... 163 C7
Gainsborough La BN26 .... 172 E6
Gainsborough Rd TN40 .... 157 E6
Galley Hill View TN40 .... 157 E4
Galliers Cl BN1 .... 143 B6
Gallipot Hill TN7 .... 13 C3
Gallops The BN7 .... 123 A1
Gallows Cl BN24 .... 174 E6
Gallows La BN24 .... 174 E6
Galveston Cl BN23 .... 185 F7
Gammons Way TN33 .... 88 C1
Gander Cl RH15 .... 73 A5
Gander Gn RH16 .... 50 F7
Gander Hill RH16 .... 50 F7
Gannet Ho **5** Eastbourne BN21 185 A2
Hove BN3 .... 142 B1
Garden Cl Bexhill TN40 .... 157 D4
East Grinstead RH19 .... 10 F7
Portslade-by-Sea BN41 .... 162 C8
Shoreham-by-Sea BN43 .... 140 B1
Garden Cotts **14** TN34 .... 160 B4
Garden Ho The BN1 .... 189 F6
Garden House La RH19 .... 10 F7
Garden Mews BN20 .... 188 D8

Garden Rd TN1 .... 8 B4
Garden St Lewes BN7 .... 146 D8
Royal Tunbridge Wells TN1 ...... 8 B4
Garden Wood Rd RH19 .... 10 C8
Gardener St BN41 .... 162 B8
Gardens The Southwick BN42 .. 161 F7
Gardner Centre Rd BN1 .... 144 B6
Gardner Cl BN23 .... 185 F7
Gardner Rd BN41, BN42 .... 162 A7
Gardner St Brighton BN1 .... 189 A5
Herstmonceux BN27 .... 130 F6
Gardner Way TN38 .... 159 B6
Gardner's Hill TN31 .... 70 B6
Garfield Rd BN27 .... 152 C7
Garland Rd RH19 .... 1 D2
Garnet Dr BN20, BN21 .... 184 C7
Garnet Ho **13** BN2 .... 164 C4
Garston Pk TN19 .... 62 B6
Garth Cl TN39 .... 157 A5
Gatehouse Cl TN39 .... 156 C2
Gatehouse La
Burgess Hill BN6, RH15 .... 72 C4
Framefield TN22 .... 79 C7
Gatelands Dr TN39 .... 157 B6
Gatesmead RH16 .... 50 F8
Gattons Cty Inf Sch The
RH15 .... 72 E3
Gattons The RH15 .... 72 E3
Gatwick Farm Cotts RH19 .... 3 A4
Gaudick Cl BN20 .... 184 E1
Gaudick Rd BN20 .... 184 E1
Gavin Astor Ct TN40 .... 158 A6
Geary Pl TN5 .... 114 E3
Geering Pk BN27 .... 152 D7
Geering Rd BN24 .... 174 B5
Geers Wood TN21 .... 81 F6
Geerswood Cotts **2** TN21 .... 82 A6
Gemma BN27 .... 152 E7
Geneva Rd BN9 .... 179 D6
Genistos The BN6 .... 97 E4
Gensing Rd TN38 .... 159 C7
George Hill TN32 .... 64 B3
George St Brighton BN2 .... 189 A5
Hailsham BN27 .... 152 C7
Hastings TN34 .... 160 A3
Hove BN3 .... 163 B6
Portslade-by-Sea BN41 .... 162 C7
Royal Tunbridge Wells TN2 ..... 8 C3
Southwick BN41 .... 162 A7
Sparrow's Green TN5 .... 29 F5
Georgian Cl TN40 .... 157 E5
Georgian Wlk TN38 .... 158 F8
Gerald Cl RH15 .... 73 D3
Gerald Rd BN25 .... 180 F1
Gerard St BN1 .... 189 A8
German St TN36 .... 117 E7
Ghyll Rd Crowborough TN6 ...... 25 E4
Heathfield TN21 .... 82 A6
Ghyll Side Rd TN31 .... 67 B7
Ghyllside BN2 .... 143 E1
Ghyllside Ave TN34 .... 136 D4
Ghyllside Dr TN34 .... 136 D4
Ghyllside Way TN34 .... 136 D4
Gibb Cl TN40 .... 158 A5
Gibbetts TN3 .... 6 F3
Gibbon Rd BN9 .... 179 C6
Gibraltar Rise TN21 .... 82 A7
Gibson Ct BN7 .... 123 D2
Giffards Cl TN1 .... 1 F1
Gilbert Rd Eastbourne BN22 ... 185 B4
Hastings TN35 .... 159 B8
Gilbert Way BN27 .... 152 B5
Gilberts Dr BN20 .... 187 B8
Gilda Cres BN26 .... 173 A6
Gildredge Rd Eastbourne BN21 184 F2
Seaford BN25 .... 180 F3
Gilham La RH18 .... 11 E2
Gill The TN2 .... 9 E8
Gillham Wood Ave TN39 .... 156 D3
Gillham Wood Rd TN39 .... 156 D3
Gilligans The RH15 .... 72 F5
Gillridge Gn TN6 .... 25 F4
Gillsman's Dr TN38 .... 135 F1
Gillsman's Hill TN38 .... 136 A1
Gillsman's Pk TN38 .... 135 F1
Gimble Way TN3 .... 9 D8
Gingerbread La TN18 .... 32 F2
Gipps Cross La TN3 .... 6 E1
Girton Ho BN41 .... 162 F6
Githa Rd TN35 .... 160 C6
Glade The Hailsham BN27 ...... 151 F6
Mayfield TN20 .... 40 A3
Uckfield TN22 .... 78 D7
Gladepoint **7** RH16 .... 50 E5
Glades The Bexhill TN40 .... 157 E6
East Grinstead RH19 .... 2 B1
Gladstone Bldgs BN8 .... 101 E4
Gladstone Cl BN22 .... 173 F1
Gladstone Pl BN2 .... 164 C8
Gladstone Rd Burgess Hill RH15 .. 73 C4
Crowborough TN6 .... 25 F1
Hastings TN34 .... 160 A5
Portslade-by-Sea BN41 .... 162 B7
Rusthall TN4 .... 7 B4
Gladstone Terr BN2 .... 189 B7
Gladys Ave BN10 .... 178 D6
Gladys Rd BN3 .... 162 D8
Glassenbury Dr TN40 .... 157 F5
Glastonbury Rd BN3 .... 162 D6
Gleave Cl RH19 .... 2 A2
Glebe Cl Bexhill TN39 .... 156 D3
Eastbourne BN20 .... 184 D3
Lewes BN7 .... 145 E5
Southwick BN42 .... 161 F7
Glebe Cotts TN35 .... 134 A7
Glebe Cty Mid Sch BN42 .... 161 D7
Glebe Dr BN25 .... 180 E3

Glebe The Felbridge RH19 .... 1 A4
Hastings TN34 .... 160 B5
Haywards Heath RH16 .... 51 A8
Hurstpierpoint BN6 .... 97 A6
Pembury TN2 .... 9 D8
Pett TN35 .... 116 F1
Glebe Villas BN3 .... 162 D7
Glebelands Cl BN43 .... 161 B8
Glebelands The TN6 .... 25 F2
Glen Cl BN26 .... 172 F4
Glen Rise BN1 .... 142 B5
Glen Rise Cl BN1 .... 142 B5
Glen The TN22 .... 55 D1
Glen Vue RH19 .... 1 E1
Glencoe TN6 .... 25 F2
Glendale Ave BN21 .... 184 C5
Glendale Ct TN1 .... 8 D6
Glendale Rd Burgess Hill RH15 ... 73 B2
Hove BN3 .... 163 D7
Glendor Rd BN3 .... 162 E6
Glendyne Cl RH19 .... 11 A8
Glendyne Way RH19 .... 11 A8
Gleneagles Cl Bexhill TN40 .... 157 E5
Seaford BN25 .... 180 A6
Gleneagles Ct **13** RH16 .... 50 E4
Gleneagles Dr Hailsham BN27 152 A8
Hastings TN38 .... 158 F7
Glenfalls Ave BN1 .... 143 A7
Glengorse TN33 .... 112 F3
Glenham Pl RH19 .... 21 A5
Glenleigh Ave TN39 .... 156 F6
Glenleigh Park Rd TN39 .... 157 A6
Glenleigh Wlk TN32 .... 64 A4
Glenmore Mews **3** BN21 .... 185 A3
Glenmore Pk TN6 .... 16 F8
Glenmore Rd TN6 .... 25 C3
Glenmore Rd E TN6 .... 25 D3
Glenthorn Rd TN39 .... 157 A4
Glenthorne Ho **11** BN21 ...... 184 F4
Glenview TN35 .... 160 D5
Glessing Rd BN24 .... 174 B6
Gleton Ave BN3 .... 141 D6
Gloucester Ave TN40 .... 158 A5
Gloucester Cl
East Grinstead RH19 .... 11 A8
Eastbourne BN22 .... 173 C2
Gloucester Cotts **3** TN34 .... 160 A4
Gloucester Ct BN23 .... 174 E1
Gloucester Pas **2** BN1 .... 189 A6
Gloucester Pl BN1, BN2 .... 189 A6
Gloucester Rd Brighton BN1 ... 189 A6
Burgess Hill RH15 .... 72 F3
Sparrow's Green TN5 .... 29 F6
Gloucester St BN1, BN2 .... 189 A6
Glovers La TN39, TN40 .... 157 C7
Glynde Ave Eastbourne BN22 173 C1
Saltdean BN2 .... 177 D6
Glynde CE Prim Sch BN8 .... 147 F7
Glynde Cl BN9 .... 168 D2
Glynde Ct TN39 .... 156 C3
Glynde Ho BN3 .... 163 D6
Glynde Rd BN2 .... 164 D6
Glynde Sta BN8 .... 147 F6
Glyndebourne Ave BN2 .... 177 C6
Glyndebourne Gdns TN37 ..... 136 C6
Glyndley Manor Cottage Est
BN24 .... 152 F2
Glyne Ascent TN40 .... 157 F5
Glyne Barn Cl TN40 .... 158 A5
Glyne Dr TN40 .... 158 A5
Glyne Gap St TN40 .... 158 A5
Glyne Hall TN40 .... 157 D3
Glynleigh **17** BN2 .... 189 B6
Glynleigh Dr BN26 .... 173 C6
Glynleigh Rd BN24 .... 153 A1
Glynn Rd BN10 .... 167 C1
Glynn Rd W BN10 .... 167 C1
Glynn Rise BN10 .... 167 B1
Goatham La TN31 .... 89 E5
Goathard Gr Cuckfield Hospl Annexe)
BN6 .... 72 B5
Godden Cl TN31 .... 67 B7
Godden Rd BN3 .... 76 C7
Goddens Gill TN31 .... 67 B7
Godfrey Cl TN17 .... 123 C3
Godwin Rd Hastings TN35 ..... 160 C5
Hove BN3 .... 141 D1
Goffs The BN21 .... 184 E3
Golby Ct BN10 .... 178 A7
Gold La BN10 .... 167 C2
Goldbridge Rd BN8, TN22 .... 76 E7
Goldcrest Dr TN22 .... 78 D5
Golden Hill RH15 .... 73 D3
Golden Miller La BN26 .... 172 F6
Goldhurst Gn TN36 .... 116 E5
Golding Rd BN23 .... 174 F2
Goldsmid Rd BN1, BN3 .... 163 E7
Goldsmith Cl BN23 .... 174 E3
Goldsmiths Ave TN6 .... 25 D3
Goldsmiths L Ctr TN6 .... 25 F4
Goldstone Cl BN3 .... 142 A2
Goldstone Cres BN3 .... 142 B2
Goldstone Ct BN3 .... 142 B2
Goldstone Cty Jun Sch BN3 ... 141 E1
Goldstone Ho **4** BN3 .... 163 B7
Goldstone La BN3 .... 163 B8
Goldstone Rd BN3 .... 163 B7
Goldstone St BN3 .... 163 B7
Goldstone Villas BN3 .... 163 B7
Goldstone Way BN3 .... 142 A2
Golf Dr BN1 .... 143 B3
Goods Station Rd TN1 .... 8 B4
Goodtrees La TN8 .... 4 B2
Goodwin Ct BN27 .... 129 A2
Goodwins Ct TN31 .... 1 D3
Goodwins The TN2 .... 7 F1

Goodwood Cl Bexhill TN40 .... 157 D6
Willingdon BN20 .... 173 B2
Goodwood Ct **2** BN3 .... 163 D7
Goodwood Way BN2 .... 143 F3
Gooseberry La TN31 .... 67 A3
Gordon Ave BN43 .... 161 A7
Gordon Cl RH16 .... 50 E6
Gordon Ho RH15 .... 73 C4
Gordon Pl TN39 .... 157 B6
Gordon Rd Brighton BN1 .... 142 F2
Burgess Hill RH15 .... 73 C4
Buxted TN22 .... 56 C3
Crowborough TN6 .... 25 F2
Hailsham BN27 .... 152 B7
Hastings TN34 .... 160 A4
Haywards Heath RH16 .... 50 E6
Portslade-by-Sea BN41 .... 162 C7
Royal Tunbridge Wells TN4 ...... 8 C7
Shoreham-by-Sea BN43 .... 161 A7
Southwick BN41 .... 162 A7
Gore Ave BN2 .... 184 D4
Gore Park Rd BN21 .... 184 D4
Gorham Ave BN2 .... 177 A6
Gorham Cl BN2 .... 177 A6
Gorham Ct BN10 .... 177 E4
Gorham Way BN10 .... 177 E4
Goring Cl BN1 .... 143 F5
Gorringe Cl
Lower Willingdon BN20 .... 173 A3
Shoreham-by-Sea BN43 .... 161 D7
Gorringe Dr BN20 .... 173 A3
Gorringe Rd BN21, BN22 .... 185 A4
Gorringe Valley Rd
BN20, BN22 .... 173 A3
Gorse Cl Eastbourne BN20 .... 184 B5
Portslade-by-Sea BN41 .... 140 F4
Gorse Dr BN25 .... 180 F6
Gorse Hill TN21 .... 59 F1
Gorse Rd TN2 .... 8 E5
Gorselands TN33 .... 88 E1
Gorses The TN39 .... 156 C2
Gorsethorn Way TN35 .... 138 E4
Gorseway The TN39 .... 156 C5
Gosford Way BN26 .... 172 F6
Gote La BN8 .... 124 D4
Goudhurst Cl BN23 .... 174 D1
Gower Rd RH16 .... 50 E3
Gows Croft BN7 .... 145 E5
Grace Ct BN6 .... 97 E5
Gradwell End BN8 .... 100 D7
Graffham Cl BN2 .... 164 E6
Grafton St BN2 .... 189 B4
Graham Ave Brighton BN1 ..... 142 F5
Portslade-by-Sea BN41 .... 140 F4
Graham Cl BN41 .... 140 F4
Graham Cres BN41 .... 140 F4
Grampian Eastbourne BN23 .. 174 C3
Royal Tunbridge Wells TN2 ..... 8 D5
Granary Cotts TN33 .... 112 E4
Grand Ave Bexhill TN40 .... 158 A5
Hassocks BN6 .... 97 F4
Hove BN3 .... 163 C6
Seaford BN25 .... 180 D6
Grand Avenue Mansions **23**
BN3 .... 163 C6
Grand Cres BN2 .... 177 A5
Grand Ct Eastbourne BN21 .... 185 A1
10 Hastings TN37 .... 159 C6
Grand Hotel Bldgs BN20 .... 185 A1
Grand Junction Rd BN1, BN2 .. 189 A4
Grand Par Brighton BN2 ..... 189 A5
Eastbourne BN21 .... 185 B2
Hastings TN37, TN38 .... 159 C6
Polegate BN26 .... 172 F6
Grand Parade Mews BN2 ...... 189 A5
Grange Ave TN34 .... 136 D4
Grange Cl Brighton BN1 .... 142 E1
Burgess Hill RH15 .... 73 C5
Crowborough TN6 .... 25 D1
Horam TN21 .... 106 F6
Grange Court Dr TN39 .... 157 B6
Grange Ct Eastbourne BN21 .. 184 F2
Lewes BN7 .... 146 C8
9 Southwick BN42 .... 161 E7
Grange End BN20 .... 184 F1
Grange Gdns Eastbourne BN20 . 184 F2
Rusthall TN4 .... 7 D4
Grange Ind Est BN42 .... 161 D7
Grange Rd
Barcombe Cross BN8 .... 101 D4
Eastbourne BN20, BN21 .... 184 F1
Hastings TN34 .... 136 E5
Hove BN3 .... 162 E8
Lewes BN7 .... 146 C8
Rusthall TN4 .... 7 D4
Southwick BN42 .... 161 E7
Uckfield TN22 .... 78 C7
Grange The
Barcombe Cross BN8 .... 101 D4
Saltdean BN2 .... 177 D6
Uckfield TN22 .... 78 C7
Grangeways BN1 .... 142 E5
Granoon Cotts BN20 .... 187 A4
Grant St BN2 .... 189 B7
Grantham Bank BN8 .... 101 E4
Grantham Rd BN1 .... 143 A1
Grants Hill Ho TN22 .... 78 C7
Granville Ct
2 Eastbourne BN20 .... 184 F1
10 Hove BN3 .... 163 B7
4 Seaford BN25 .... 180 E2
Granville Rd Eastbourne BN20 .. 184 F1
Hove BN3 .... 163 B7
Royal Tunbridge Wells TN1 ...... 8 C5
Graperies The **3** BN2 .... 164 C5
Grasmere Cl BN23 .... 174 B4
Grassington Rd BN20 .... 184 F1

Grassmere Ave BN10 .... 177 F4
Grassmere Ct BN10 .... 178 A8
Gratton Cl TN39 .... 157 A3
Gravebury BN27 .... 152 C7
Gravelye Cl RH16 .... 51 B5
Gravelye La
  Haywards Heath RH16 .... 51 A4
  Haywards Heath RH16 .... 51 B6
Gravett Ct RH15 .... 72 F2
Graycoats Dr TN6 .... 25 F2
Grays Cotts TN33 .... 112 F3
Grays Cty Inf Sch BN9 .... 179 D6
Graystone La TN35 .... 137 D3
Grazebrook Cl TN39 .... 156 C3
Great Brooms Rd TN4 .... 8 C8
Great Cliffe Rd BN23 .... 174 E1
Great College St BN2 .... 164 C4
Great Courtlands TN3 .... 7 A3
Great Dixter TN31 .... 66 F7
Great Footway TN3 .... 6 F3
Great Hall Arc 3 TN1 .... 8 B3
Great Heathmead RH16 .... 50 D6
Great House Ct 4 RH19 .... 10 F8
Great Knelle Farm
  (Childrens Farm) TN31 ...... 68 A8
Great Oak TN19 .... 45 A3
Great Rough BN8 .... 76 A6
Great Sanders Ho TN33 .... 88 D4
Great Walstead Sch RH16 .... 51 F6
Great Wilkins BN1 .... 144 B5
Greater Paddock BN8 .... 124 E6
Greatham Ct BN1 .... 142 E6
Grecian Rd TN1 .... 8 B2
Greeba Ct 8 TN38 .... 159 B6
Green Cl Ringmer BN8 .... 124 E6
  4 Southwick BN42 .... 161 E7
Green Ct 3 BN42 .... 161 E7
Green Field Cl BN42 .... 161 E8
Green Gate BN10 .... 167 C1
Green Gr BN27 .... 152 B8
Green Hedges TN32 .... 63 E4
Green Hedges Ave RH19 .... 1 D2
Green Hedges Cl RH19 .... 1 D2
Green La Bexhill TN39 .... 156 D5
  Broyle Side BN8 .... 103 B1
  Crowborough TN6 .... 26 B2
  Heathfield TN21 .... 82 B6
  Jevington BN26 .... 172 C1
  Lewes BN7 .... 146 C8
  Seaford BN25 .... 180 E2
  South Chailey BN8 .... 100 E7
  South Street BN8 .... 75 E1
  Woodingdean BN2 .... 165 E6
Green Meadows RH16 .... 51 B8
Green Park Cnr RH17 .... 74 B4
Green Rd RH17 .... 74 B5
Green Ridge BN1 .... 142 B5
Green Sq TN5 .... 29 F5
Green St BN20, BN21 .... 184 C4
Green The Blackboys TN22 ..... 80 A6
  Bodiam TN32 .... 65 E7
  Catsfield TN33 .... 133 E8
  Ewhurst Green TN32 .... 66 B5
  Hastings TN38 .... 159 B8
  Hove BN3 .... 142 C2
  Langton Green TN3 .... 6 E3
  Newick BN8 .... 76 D7
  Ninfield TN33 .... 133 B5
  Ringmer BN8 .... 124 D5
  Rottingdean BN2 .... 165 F2
  Sedlescombe TN33 .... 113 E8
  Southwick BN42 .... 161 E7
Green View RH15 .... 72 E3
Green Way Eastbourne BN20 .. 184 B6
  Royal Tunbridge Wells TN2 ..... 8 E8
Green Wlk Hailsham BN27 .... 129 C1
  Seaford BN25 .... 181 B2
Green Wlk The BN22 .... 173 B3
Greenacres Brighton BN1 ..... 142 F1
  Peacehaven BN10 .... 167 D2
  Telscombe Cliffs BN10 .... 178 A7
  Westfield TN35 .... 114 E3
Greenacres Dr Hailsham BN27 . 152 C7
  Ringmer BN8 .... 124 D4
Greenacres Way BN27 .... 152 C8
Greenbank Ave BN2 .... 177 D6
Greene Ct TN4 .... 146 B8
Greenfield Cl Brighton BN1 .. 143 A5
  Rusthall TN4 .... 7 C5
Greenfield Cres BN1 .... 142 F5
Greenfield Dr TN22 .... 78 D4
Greenfield Rd Burwash TN19 .. 62 C7
  Eastbourne BN21 .... 184 D4
Greenfields BN27 .... 129 A1
Greenfields Cl TN37 .... 136 B6
Greenfields Sch RH18 .... 11 C1
Greenhill Pk RH16 .... 51 A2
Greenhill Way
  Haywards Heath RH16 .... 51 A2
  Peacehaven BN10 .... 167 C2
Greenlands Cl RH15 .... 98 B8
Greenlands Dr RH15 .... 98 B8
Greenleaf Gdns BN26 .... 173 A8
Greenleas Hove BN3 .... 141 D2
  Pembury TN2 .... 9 C6
Greenstede Ave RH19 .... 1 F2
Greenway Ct BN2 .... 177 A5
Greenways Bexhill TN39 .... 156 F7
  Haywards Heath RH16 .... 50 F6
  Ovingdean BN2 .... 165 D3
  Portslade-by-Sea BN41 ..... 141 B1
  Southwick BN42 .... 140 F1
Greenways Cnr BN2 .... 165 D4
Greenways Cres BN43 .... 140 A1
Greenwell Cl BN25 .... 181 B4
Greenwich Rd BN27 .... 152 D7
Greenwich Way BN10 .... 178 C7
Greenwoods La TN21 .... 83 D7

Greggs Wood Rd TN1, TN2 ...... 8 E7
Gregory La BN24 .... 174 F5
Gregory Wlk TN33 .... 113 E8
Grenada TN39 .... 157 A2
Grenada Cl TN39 .... 156 D4
Grenham TN35 .... 137 C3
Grenville Ho BN10 .... 167 D1
Grenville Rd BN24 .... 175 C4
Grenville St BN1 .... 189 F5
Gresham BN24 .... 175 B6
Gresham Cl BN21 .... 184 C6
Gresham Way TN38 .... 159 A8
Gresley Rd TN4 .... 135 F5
Greville Rd TN35 .... 137 C3
Grey Alders RH16 .... 51 B6
Grey Tower Bglws BN24 .... 175 C3
Greyfriars BN3 .... 163 D8
Greyfriars BN7 .... 123 D1
Greyfriars Pl TN38 .... 118 B6
Greyhorses TN39 .... 156 B4
Greys Rd BN20 .... 184 D3
Greystones Ct TN6 .... 25 D4
Grinstead La RH19 .... 21 C7
Grinstead Mount 4 BN2 .... 164 F5
Gromenfield TN3 .... 15 C7
Groombridge Hill TN3 .... 6 D1
Groombridge Place TN3 .... 15 C8
Groombridge Place Gdns TN3 . 15 C8
Groombridge Rd TN3 .... 6 A1
Grosvenor Bridge TN1, TN4 ..... 8 B5
Grosvenor Cl BN26 .... 172 F5
Grosvenor Cres TN38 .... 159 A6
Grosvenor Ct BN1 .... 142 E3
Grosvenor Gdns TN38 .... 158 F6
Grosvenor Pk TN1, TN4 .... 8 A4
Grosvenor Rd
  East Grinstead RH19 .... 1 D1
  Royal Tunbridge Wells TN1 .... 8 A4
  Seaford BN25 .... 180 E4
Grosvenor St BN2 .... 189 B5
Grosvenor Wlk TN1 .... 8 A4
Grove Ave TN1 .... 8 A2
Grove Bank 8 BN2 .... 189 B6
Grove Ct 5 BN3 .... 163 C6
Grove Hill Brighton BN2 .... 189 B6
  Grove Hill BN27 .... 129 D7
Grove Hill Gdns TN1 .... 8 B2
Grove Hill Rd TN1, TN2 .... 8 B3
Grove La TN31 .... 70 C4
Grove Park Sch TN6 .... 25 E1
Grove Rd Burgess Hill RH15 ... 73 B3
  Eastbourne BN21 .... 184 F2
  Hastings TN35 .... 137 D4
  Seaford BN25 .... 180 F3
Grove Sch The TN38 .... 135 F2
Grove St BN2 .... 189 B6
Grove The Battle TN33 .... 112 F3
  Bexhill TN39 .... 156 E5
  Crowborough TN6 .... 25 E1
  Eastbourne BN20 .... 184 B7
  Hailsham BN27 .... 152 B6
  Mayfield TN20 .... 40 A2
  Newhaven BN9 .... 168 E2
  Pembury TN2 .... 9 D8
  Rye TN31 .... 93 C6
  Willingdon BN20 .... 172 F3
Grove Villa 3 BN1 .... 189 F7
Grovelands Cl RH15 .... 72 F1
Grovelands Cty Prim Sch
  BN27 .... 129 A1
Grovelands Rd BN27 .... 129 A1
Grovely La TN21 .... 84 B1
Grover St 3 TN1 .... 8 B4
Growers End BN8 .... 76 D7
Guardian Ct BN26 .... 172 F7
Guardswell Pl BN25 .... 180 F3
Guestling Rd BN22 .... 185 D5
Guestling-Bradshaw Prim Sch
  TN35 .... 138 A8
Guildford Rd 7 TN1, TN2 .... 8 B3
Guildford St BN1 .... 189 F6
Guilford Rd BN1 .... 189 F6
Guinness Ct BN9 .... 168 E1
Guinness Trust
  Holiday Home The BN9 ..... 168 E2
Guldeford La TN29, TN31 ...... 71 F3
Guldeford Lane Cnr TN31 ...... 71 D2
Guldeford Rd TN31 .... 93 E7
Gun Rd TN22 .... 80 A6
Gundreda Rd BN7 .... 123 B2
Gunter's La TN39 .... 157 A6
Gurth Rd TN35 .... 160 C5
Gwent Ct 7 BN22 .... 185 C4
Gwydir Mansions 4 BN3 ...... 163 D6
Gwyneth Gr TN40 .... 157 F7
Gwynne Gdns RH19 .... 1 C2

Hackenden Cl RH19 .... 1 E3
Hackenden La RH19 .... 1 E3
Hackhurst La BN27 .... 128 B4
Hackhurst Lane Ind Est BN27 . 128 B4
Hackwood TN32 .... 63 E4
Haddington Cl BN3 .... 163 B6
Haddington St 11 BN3 .... 163 B7
Hadley Ct Polegate BN26 ...... 173 A6
  Royal Tunbridge Wells TN4 .... 7 F6
Hadley Ho 4 BN1 .... 184 F3
Hadlow Ave BN23 .... 174 B4
Hadlow Cl BN2 .... 164 D6
Hadlow Down Rd TN6 .... 38 B4
Hadrian Ave BN42 .... 162 A8
Hadrian Gdns TN38 .... 136 A6
Haig Ave BN1 .... 143 D6
Hailsham Ave BN2 .... 166 D3
Hailsham Com Coll BN27 ...... 152 B8
Hailsham Rd Eastbourne BN24 . 174 B5
  Heathfield TN21 .... 82 A6

Hailsham Rd
  Herstmonceux BN27 .... 130 E5
  Polegate BN26 .... 172 F7
  Stone Cross BN24, BN26 .... 173 F8
Hairpin Croft BN10 .... 167 C1
Half Mile Dro BN8 .... 125 B7
Hall's Grove Rd TN2 .... 8 D2
Hall's Hole Rd TN2 .... 8 E4
Halland Cl BN20 .... 173 D1
Halland Rd BN2 .... 143 F4
Hallett Rd BN2 .... 164 D7
Halley Rd BN2 .... 152 D7
Halley Rd Cade Street TN21 .... 82 E8
  Wartling BN27 .... 131 B1
Halls Cotts TN5 .... 29 F5
Hallyburton Rd BN3 .... 162 D8
Halsford Croft RH19 .... 1 B3
Halsford Gn RH19 .... 1 B3
Halsford La RH19 .... 1 C3
Halsford Park Cty Prim Sch
  RH19 .... 1 C2
Halsford Park Rd RH19 .... 1 C2
Halton Cres TN34 .... 160 B6
Halton Hts TN34 .... 160 B6
Halton Pl TN34 .... 160 B6
Halton Rd BN2 .... 185 C4
Halton Shaws BN6 .... 97 B5
Halton Terr TN34 .... 160 B6
Ham Bsns Ctr BN43 .... 161 A7
Ham La Burwash TN19 .... 62 B6
  Lewes BN7 .... 146 D8
  Ringmer BN8 .... 124 C6
  Scaynes Hill RH17 .... 51 E3
Ham Rd BN43 .... 161 A7
Hambleton Cl BN23 .... 174 D3
Hambrook RH15 .... 73 C1
Hamelsham Ct BN27 .... 152 A8
Hamilton Cl BN41 .... 141 A3
Hamilton Ct Brighton BN2 .... 165 A3
  Royal Tunbridge Wells TN4 ... 8 A5
Hamilton Gdns TN35 .... 137 D3
Hamilton Ho
  12 Eastbourne BN21 .... 184 E4
  Royal Tunbridge Wells TN4 ... 8 A5
  Seaford BN25 .... 180 E4
Hamilton Lodge Sch BN2 .... 164 D5
Hamilton Mansions BN3 ...... 163 B5
Hamilton Rd BN1 .... 189 F7
Hamilton Terr TN39 .... 157 A4
Hamlands La BN22 .... 173 B3
Hamlin's Cnr BN26 .... 72 A6
Hammer La BN27, TN21 ...... 107 F5
Hammerwood Pk RH19 .... 3 C2
Hammerwood Rd RH19 .... 11 E6
Hammonds Dr BN22, BN23 .. 185 C7
Hammonds Ridge RH15 .... 72 F1
Hammy La BN43 .... 161 C8
Hammy Rd BN43 .... 161 B8
Hammy Way BN43 .... 161 B8
Hampden Ave BN22 .... 173 F1
Hampden Gdns BN9 .... 168 D2
Hampden Park Cty Inf Sch
  BN22 .... 173 F2
Hampden Park Dr BN22 .... 184 E8
Hampden Park Sch BN22 ..... 173 E2
Hampden Park Sports Ctr
  BN22 .... 173 D2
Hampden Park Sta BN22 ...... 173 F1
Hampden Rd BN2 .... 164 C7
Hampden Terr 8 BN22 .... 185 C4
Hampshire Ct Brighton BN2 .. 189 B4
  6 Eastbourne BN23 .... 174 E1
Hampstead Rd BN1 .... 142 D2
Hampton Pl BN1 .... 163 E5
Hampton St 14 BN1 .... 163 E5
Hampton Way RH10 .... 10 F7
Hamsey Cl Brighton BN2 ...... 164 F5
  Eastbourne BN20 .... 184 B6
Hamsey Cres BN7 .... 123 A2
Hamsey Cty Prim Sch BN8 ... 123 A8
Hamsey La Cooksbridge BN8 . 123 B7
  Seaford BN25 .... 181 C2
Hamsey Rd Saltdean BN2 ..... 177 D4
  Sharpthorne RH19 .... 21 A6
Hamshaw Ct TN2 .... 184 F8
Hamsland RH17 .... 33 C4
Hanbury La RH16 .... 51 A5
Hanbury Park Sports Stad
  RH16 .... 51 A5
Hanging Birch La TN21 .... 81 D1
Hangleton Cl BN3 .... 141 D2
Hangleton Cty Inf & Jun Sch
  BN3 .... 141 E2
Hangleton Gdns BN3 .... 141 D1
Hangleton Manor Cl BN3 ..... 141 D2
Hangleton Rd BN3 .... 141 E2
Hangleton Valley Dr BN3 ..... 141 D4
Hangleton Way BN3 .... 141 D3
Hankham Cty Prim Sch BN24 . 174 B8
Hankham Hall Rd BN24 .... 174 D7
Hankham Rd BN24 .... 174 B8
Hankham St BN24 .... 174 B8
Hanlye La RH17 .... 50 B8
Hannington Pl BN6 .... 97 A7
Hanover Cl Bexhill TN40 ...... 157 C5
  Seaford BN25 .... 180 B6
Hanover Cres BN2 .... 189 B7
Hanover Ct Brighton BN2 ..... 189 B7
  Eastbourne BN21 .... 184 D5
  Haywards Heath RH16 .... 50 D4
Hanover Mews BN2 .... 189 B7
Hanover Rd Eastbourne BN22 . 185 C4
  Royal Tunbridge Wells TN1 .... 8 A4
Hanover St BN2 .... 189 B7
Hanover Terr BN2 .... 189 B7

Hanson Rd BN9 .... 179 C6
Harbour Barn TN36 .... 118 B6
Harbour Ct BN42 .... 161 E7
Harbour Farm TN36 .... 118 B6
Harbour Rd TN31 .... 93 D4
Harbour View Cl BN25 .... 180 B6
Harbour View Rd BN9 .... 179 B5
Harbour Way Hastings TN38 . 135 F2
  Shoreham-by-Sea BN43 ..... 161 B6
Harbour's Yd TN33 .... 112 E4
Harcourt Cl TN22 .... 78 C6
Harcourt Rd TN22 .... 78 D6
Harding Ave BN22 .... 185 B6
Hardwick Rd Eastbourne BN21 . 185 A2
  Hove BN3 .... 141 E3
Hardwick Way BN3 .... 141 E3
Hardwicke Rd BN34 .... 160 B6
Hardy Dr BN23 .... 185 F6
Hare Way TN34 .... 136 C5
Harebeating Cl BN27 .... 129 C2
Harebeating Cres BN27 .... 129 C2
Harebeating Dr BN27 .... 129 C2
Harebeating Gdns BN27 ...... 129 C2
Harebeating La BN27 .... 129 D1
Harebell Cl BN23 .... 174 C3
Harebell Dr BN41 .... 141 A3
Harecombe Rd TN6 .... 37 F8
Harecombe Rise TN6 .... 37 F8
Haremere Hall Gdns TN19 .... 44 E2
Haremere Hill TN19 .... 44 D2
Harescroft TN2 .... 16 F7
Harewood Cl TN39 .... 157 A3
Harewood Ct 8 BN3 .... 163 C6
Harfield Cl BN9 .... 168 F2
Hargate Cl TN2 .... 16 F8
Hargreaves Rd BN22 .... 174 A1
Harison Rd BN25 .... 181 A4
Harkness Dr TN34 .... 137 B5
Harlands Cl RH16, RH17 .... 50 C6
Harlands Cty Prim Sch
  Haywards Heath RH16 .... 50 D7
  Uckfield TN22 .... 78 D5
Harlands Rd RH16, RH17 .... 50 D6
Harlequin Gdns TN37 .... 136 A6
Harlequin La TN6 .... 37 A6
Harlequin Pl TN6 .... 37 B8
Harley La TN38 .... 158 E7
Harley Shute Rd TN38 .... 158 E7
Harley Way TN38 .... 158 E6
Harmans Dr RH19 .... 2 B1
Harmans Mead RH19 .... 2 B1
Harmers Hay Rd BN27 .... 129 B1
Harmers Hill BN8 .... 76 C8
Harmony St TN4 .... 7 D4
Harmsworth Cres BN3 .... 141 E3
Harold Cl BN24 .... 175 F7
Harold Dr BN23 .... 185 F8
Harold Mews 2 TN38 .... 159 C6
Harold Pl TN34 .... 159 F7
Harold Rd TN34, TN35 .... 160 C5
Harold Terr TN38 .... 112 F3
Harpers Rd BN9 .... 179 C7
Harrier La TN33 .... 112 F4
Harriers Ct BN27 .... 152 D7
Harries Rd TN1, TN2 .... 8 E7
Harrington Ct 13 BN1 .... 142 E2
Harrington Mansions 12 BN1 . 142 E2
Harrington Pl BN1 .... 143 B2
Harrington Rd BN1 .... 142 E2
Harrington Villas BN1 .... 142 F2
Harris Ct BN21 .... 185 A3
Harrisons La BN8 .... 124 E5
Harrow Cl BN25 .... 181 A4
Harrow La TN37 .... 136 B5
Hart Cl TN22 .... 78 A7
Hartfield Ave BN1 .... 143 A5
Hartfield La BN21 .... 184 F4
Hartfield Meadow TN38 .... 135 D3
Hartfield Rd Bexhill TN39 .... 156 E2
  Cowden TN8 .... 4 C6
  Eastbourne BN21 .... 184 F3
  Forest Row RH18 .... 12 B2
  Saltdean BN2 .... 177 D5
  Seaford BN25 .... 181 A3
Harting Combe TN38 .... 159 B8
Hartington Mansions 7 BN21 . 189 A1
Hartington Pl Brighton BN2 .. 164 C8
  Eastbourne BN21 .... 185 A2
Hartington Rd BN2 .... 164 C8
Hartington Terr BN2 .... 164 C8
Hartington Villas BN3 .... 163 B8
Hartwood Lodge 5 TN40 ..... 157 C4
Harvard Cl BN7 .... 123 C3
Harvard Rd BN8 .... 124 D5
Harvest Cl
  Haywards Heath RH16 .... 51 B7
  Telscombe Cliffs BN10 ...... 167 B2
Harvest Hill RH19 .... 10 E8
Harvest Way TN37 .... 136 C5
Harvesters RH16 .... 50 D2
Harvey Cl TN38 .... 135 F4
Harvey's La BN8, TN22 .... 103 D4
Harveys Way BN7 .... 123 E1
Harvington Bsns Pk BN22 .... 184 F8
Harwood Cl BN23 .... 185 E7
Harwoods Cl 3 RH19 .... 10 F7
Harwoods La RH19 .... 10 F7
Haslam Cres TN40 .... 157 F6
Hasletts Cl TN2 .... 8 B6
Hassocks Cty Inf Sch BN6 ..... 97 F4
Hassocks Lodge BN6 .... 97 F3
Hassocks Rd BN6 .... 97 B5
Hassocks Sta BN6 .... 97 E4
Hastings Bsns Ctr BN25 .... 181 C5
Hastings Castle TN34 .... 160 A4
Hastings Coll of Arts & Tech
  TN38 .... 159 B6

Hastings Mus & Art Gall
  TN34 .... 159 E7
Hastings Mus of Local History
  TN34 .... 160 A4
Hastings Rd Battle TN33 ...... 113 B2
  Bexhill TN40 .... 157 E5
  Bexhill TN40 .... 157 F5
  Brighton BN2 .... 164 C8
  Newenden TN17, TN18 .... 48 C6
  Pembury TN2 .... 9 D6
  Pembury TN12 .... 9 F5
  The Moor TN18 .... 45 F6
Hastings Sea Life Ctr TN34 .. 160 B3
Hastings Sports Ctr TN34 .... 159 D8
Hastings Sta TN34 .... 159 E8
Hatch End RH18 .... 11 F2
Hatchgate Cl RH17 .... 50 A6
Hatchgate La RH17 .... 50 A6
Hatfield Cl 16 BN2 .... 163 D6
Hatherley Rd TN37 .... 159 C7
Havelock Rd Bexhill TN39, TN40 . 157 C6
  Brighton BN1 .... 142 F1
  Eastbourne BN22 .... 185 B4
  Hastings TN34 .... 159 F7
Haven Brow BN25 .... 181 A4
Haven Cl Beachlands BN24 ... 175 C6
  Lower Willingdon BN22 ...... 173 B3
Haven Rd TN38 .... 158 D6
Hawkenbury Cl TN2 .... 8 D2
Hawkenbury Mead TN2 .... 8 D1
Hawkenbury Rd TN2, TN3 .... 8 E1
Hawkenbury Way TN2 .... 8 D2
Hawkes Farm Cty Prim Sch
  BN27 .... 129 B3
Hawkhurst CE Prim Sch TN18 . 45 D4
Hawkhurst Cl BN23 .... 174 D2
Hawkhurst Pl BN1 .... 143 D6
Hawkhurst Rd Brighton BN1 . 143 D6
  Flimwell TN18, TN19, TN5 ... 32 C2
Hawkhurst Way TN39 .... 156 E3
Hawkins Cl BN43 .... 140 D1
Hawkins Cres BN43 .... 140 D2
Hawkins Rd BN43 .... 140 D1
Hawkins Way BN27 .... 152 B8
Hawks Farm Cl BN27 .... 129 B2
Hawks Rd BN27 .... 129 B2
Hawks Town Cres BN27 .... 129 C2
Hawksbridge Cl BN22 .... 173 C3
Hawkstown Cl BN27 .... 129 B3
Hawkstown Gdns BN27 .... 129 B3
Hawkstown View BN27 .... 129 B3
Hawkswood Dr BN27 .... 129 C3
Hawkswood Rd BN27 .... 129 C3
Hawth Cl BN25 .... 180 C4
Hawth Cres BN25 .... 180 C4
Hawth Gr BN25 .... 180 C4
Hawth Hill BN25 .... 180 C5
Hawth Park Rd BN25 .... 180 C4
Hawth Pl BN25 .... 180 C5
Hawth Rise BN25 .... 180 C5
Hawth Valley Ct 1 BN25 ..... 180 C4
Hawth Way BN25 .... 180 D4
Hawthorn Ave TN39 .... 156 D3
Hawthorn Bank BN2 .... 143 F4
Hawthorn Cl Burgess Hill RH15 . 73 D5
  Saltdean BN2 .... 177 C6
Hawthorn Ct BN26 .... 173 B6
Hawthorn Rd Eastbourne BN23 . 185 C7
  Hastings TN35 .... 160 D6
Hawthorn Rise BN9 .... 179 B7
Hawthorn Way BN41 .... 141 A3
Hawthorn Wlk TN2 .... 8 E8
Hawthorne Cl TN21 .... 82 B6
Hawthornes The TN31 .... 90 B4
Hawthorns The
  Burgess Hill RH15 .... 73 A3
  Hailsham BN27 .... 152 A7
Hawthylands Cres BN27 .... 129 B2
Hawthylands Dr BN27 .... 129 B2
Hawthylands Rd BN27 .... 129 B2
Haybourne Cl BN2 .... 164 E7
Haybourne Rd BN2 .... 164 E7
Hayes Cl Portslade-by-Sea BN41 . 162 C8
  Ringmer BN8 .... 124 D5
Hayes La TN31 .... 91 C5
Hayes Plat TN31 .... 67 C5
Hayland Gn BN27 .... 129 C1
Haylind Rd RH16 .... 51 B5
Haystoun Cl BN22 .... 173 C2
Haystoun Pk BN22 .... 173 C2
Hayward Rd BN7 .... 123 A3
Haywards Heath Coll RH16 .... 50 D6
Haywards Heath Hospl RH16 .. 50 E6
Haywards Heath Sta RH16 ..... 50 E6
Haywards Rd Brighton BN1 .. 143 A6
  Haywards Heath RH16 .... 50 E3
Haywood Way TN34 .... 137 C4
Hazel Bank 3 BN2 .... 189 B7
Hazel Cl Newhaven BN9 ...... 179 B7
  Portslade-by-Sea BN41 ..... 141 C3
Hazel Court Sch BN23 .... 174 B3
Hazel Ct TN34 .... 136 F6
Hazel Gr Burgess Hill RH15 ... 73 B1
  Lower Willingdon BN22 ...... 173 A3
Hazelbank TN3 .... 6 F3
Hazeldene BN25 .... 181 B3
Hazeldene Meads BN1 .... 142 D2
Hazeldene La BN8 .... 75 F7
Hazelgrove Gdns 8 RH16 ...... 50 E4
Hazelgrove Rd RH16 .... 50 E4
Hazelwood BN1 .... 142 D3
Hazelwood Ave BN22, BN26 .. 173 C4
Hazelwood Cl Bexhill TN39 .. 156 C3
  Royal Tunbridge Wells TN2 .... 8 E8
Hazelwood Cotts TN5 .... 31 D1

Hazelwood Gdns TN37 .... 136 D5
Hazleden Cross RH19 .... 10 B6
Headland Ave BN25 .... 181 A3
Headlands Cl BN10 .... 178 E7
Heansill La TN18 .... 45 E8
Heath Cl **9** RH16 .... 50 E4
Heath Cl **6** RH16 .... 50 E5
Heath Hill Ave BN2 .... 144 A2
Heath Rd RH16 .... 50 E5
Heath Sq RH16 .... 50 D5
Heathcote Dr RH19 .... 1 C2
Heathdown Cl BN10 .... 167 D2
Heather Bank RH16 .... 50 C5
Heather Cl BN23 .... 174 B3
Heather Ct **9** BN1 .... 163 E6
Heather Way TN35 .... 138 F4
Heather Wlk TN6 .... 26 D1
Heatherdune Rd TN39 .... 157 A5
Heathfield Ave BN2 .... 177 D6
Heathfield CE Prim Sch TN21 . 82 D6
Heathfield Cl TN34 .... 136 F5
Heathfield Cres BN41 .... 140 F3
Heathfield Dr BN41 .... 140 F4
Heathfield Gdns TN32 .... 64 B3
Heathfield L Ctr TN21 ...... 82 D7
Heathfield Rd BN25 .... 180 F3
Heathfield Sch & Com Coll TN21 . 82 E7
Heathfields TN2 .... 8 D4
Heathlands TN35 .... 114 E3
Heathy Brow BN10 .... 167 B1
Heavegate Rd TN6 .... 37 C8
Heaven Farm Mus RH17 .... 34 E1
Heighton Cl TN39 .... 156 D3
Heighton Cres BN9 .... 168 D2
Heighton Rd BN9 .... 168 E2
Heights The Brighton BN1 ... 142 B5
Hastings TN35 .... 137 E4
6 Haywards Heath RH16 ... 50 E4
Helena Cl BN41 .... 141 C2
Helena Ct TN38 .... 159 B7
Helena Rd BN2 .... 144 C1
Helensdene Wlk TN37 .... 159 D8
Helenswood Sch (Lower) TN37 . 136 D6
Helenswood Sch (Upper) TN34 . 137 B4
Hellingly Cl BN2 .... 164 F5
Hellingly Cty Prim Sch TN21 . 128 F5
Helvellyn Dr BN23 .... 174 C4
Hempstead Gdns TN38 .... 159 D7
Hempstead La Hailsham BN27 . 128 F1
Uckfield TN22 .... 78 D7
Uckfield TN22 .... 78 E8
Hempstead Rd Saltdean BN2 .. 166 D3
Uckfield TN22 .... 78 C7
Hempstead Rise TN22 .... 78 C7
Hemsley Ho TN21 .... 81 F8
Henderson Cl TN34 .... 136 F3
Hendon St BN2 .... 164 D5
Henfield Cl BN2 .... 164 F5
Henfield Rd BN22 .... 173 E2
Henfield Way BN1 .... 141 F3
Henge Way BN41 .... 141 B2
Hengist Cl BN23 .... 185 F8
Henleaze BN21 .... 184 E3
Henley Cl
Royal Tunbridge Wells TN2 .. 8 C4
Rye TN31 .... 93 A6
Henley Ct BN2 .... 164 F4
Henley Rd BN2 .... 164 F4
Henley's Hill BN2 .... 131 F7
Henry Terr TN34 .... 160 B4
Henwood Green Rd TN12, TN2 . 9 E6
Henwoods Cres TN2 .... 9 D6
Henwoods Mount TN2 .... 9 E6
Herbert Rd BN1 .... 142 F2
Herbrand Wlk TN39, BN24 .... 156 A1
Hereford Ct **15** Brighton BN2 . 189 B5
1 Eastbourne BN23 .... 174 C1
15 Hove BN3 .... 163 C7
Hereford St BN2 .... 164 C5
Hereward Rd BN23 .... 185 F8
Hereward Way BN7 .... 123 D3
Hermitage La RH19 .... 10 F8
Hermitage Rd RH19 .... 1 D3
Hermitage The TN34 .... 159 E8
Herne Cty Jun Sch TN6 ...... 37 F8
Herne Down TN6 .... 38 A7
Herne Rd TN6 .... 37 F8
Heron Cl Eastbourne BN23 ... 174 C2
Hastings TN38 .... 158 E8
Uckfield TN22 .... 78 D5
Heron Cotts TN18 .... 48 D3
Heron Pl RH19 .... 10 F8
Heron Ridge BN26 .... 173 B6
Heron's Tye BN6 .... 97 F3
Herons Dale Sch BN43 .... 140 C1
Herons The BN43 .... 161 A8
Herons Way TN2 .... 9 E8
Heronsdale Rd BN2 .... 165 F8
Herontye Dr RH19 .... 11 A8
Herring's Rd TN21, TN33 .... 109 F8
Herstmonceux Castle Gdns BN27 . 131 A1
Herstmonceux CE Prim Sch BN27 . 130 E6
Herstmonceux Science Ctr BN27 . 131 C1
Hertford Cl TN34 .... 136 A4
Hertford Cty Inf Sch BN1 ... 143 B2
Hertford Cty Jun Sch BN2 ... 143 C2
Hertford Rd BN1 .... 143 B2
Heskett Pk TN2 .... 9 E6

Hestingas Plat **2** TN34 .... 160 B4
Heston Ave BN1 .... 142 F7
Hever Cl BN23 .... 174 D2
Hever Cres TN39 .... 156 F5
Heyworth Cl BN2 .... 165 F8
Heyworth Cty Prim Sch RH16 . 50 F4
Hickling Cl BN23 .... 174 B4
Hickman Way TN34 .... 136 D4
Hickman's Cl RH16 .... 51 B8
Hickman's La RH16 .... 51 A8
Hide Hollow BN23 .... 174 D3
High Bank TN35 .... 137 C3
High Bank Cl BN35 .... 160 C6
High Beech Cl TN38 .... 135 F6
High Beech Country Club The TN38 . 135 F6
High Beech La RH16 .... 50 F8
High Beeches TN2 .... 8 D6
High Branches TN39 .... 156 E4
High Broom Ind Pk TN4 ...... 8 C8
High Broom La TN6 .... 37 E7
High Broom Rd TN6 .... 37 F7
High Brooms Rd TN4 .... 8 C7
High Brooms Sta TN4 .... 8 C7
High Brooms Sta TN1 .... 8 C7
High Cl East Dean BN20 ..... 183 C2
Portslade-by-Sea BN41 ...... 141 A1
High Cross Fields TN6 ...... 25 F3
High Fords TN36 .... 116 E5
High Fords Cl TN36 .... 116 E5
High Hurst Cl BN8 .... 76 D7
High Hurstwood CE Prim Sch TN22 . 37 A1
High Meadow TN31 .... 67 B7
High Park Ave BN3 .... 141 E3
High Pk TN31 .... 67 A7
High Point RH16 .... 51 A3
High Rocks TN3 .... 7 B1
High Rocks La TN3, TN4 ..... 7 C1
High Sh Hall The **13** BN25 . 180 E2
High St Alfriston BN26 ..... 171 A2
Barcombe Cross BN8 .... 101 E4
Battle TN33 .... 112 D4
Bexhill TN40 .... 157 D5
Brighton BN2 .... 189 B5
Burwash TN19 .... 62 A6
Buxted TN22 .... 56 C3
Cowden TN8 .... 4 B5
Crowborough TN6 .... 25 F3
Ditchling BN6 .... 98 D3
East Grinstead RH19 .... 10 F8
East Hoathly BN8 .... 105 A5
Eastbourne BN21 .... 184 E3
Etchingham TN19 .... 44 C1
Flimwell TN5 .... 32 C3
Frant TN3 .... 17 C4
Hailsham BN27 .... 152 C8
Hartfield TN7 .... 13 D4
Hastings TN34 .... 160 B4
Haywards Heath RH16 .... 51 B8
Heathfield TN21 .... 82 A8
Hurstpierpoint BN6 .... 97 A5
Lamberhurst TN3 .... 20 B5
Lewes BN7 .... 123 C1
Maresfield TN22 .... 55 B4
Mayfield TN20 .... 40 B2
Newhaven BN9 .... 179 C7
Newick BN8 .... 76 D7
Ninfield TN33 .... 133 A6
Nutley TN22 .... 35 C3
Pembury TN2 .... 9 E8
Pevensey BN24 .... 175 B6
Polegate BN26 .... 173 A6
Portslade-by-Sea BN41 ...... 141 A1
Robertsbridge TN32 .... 64 B4
Rotherfield TN6 .... 39 B8
Rottingdean BN2 .... 165 F1
Royal Tunbridge Wells TN1 .. 8 A2
Rye TN31 .... 93 C5
Seaford BN25 .... 180 E2
Ticehurst TN5 .... 31 C1
Uckfield TN22 .... 78 C6
Wadhurst TN5 .... 29 F4
Westham BN24 .... 175 A6
Winchelsea TN36 .... 117 F7
High Trees **3** Eastbourne BN21 . 184 F4
Haywards Heath RH16 .... 50 F5
High View TN21 .... 82 B8
High View Rd TN21 .... 59 E1
High Wickham TN35 .... 160 B5
High Woods La TN2 .... 9 B3
Higham Gdns TN35 .... 138 A8
Higham La TN31 .... 67 A7
Highbank BN1 .... 142 C5
Highbridge La BN7 .... 100 B4
Highbrook Cl BN2 .... 143 D3
Highcliff Ct BN2 .... 177 A5
Highcombe BN20 .... 188 D7
Highcroft Cres TN21 .... 82 A7
Highcroft Lodge BN1 .... 142 E1
Highcroft Rd RH19 .... 21 A6
Highcroft Villas BN1, BN3 .. 163 E8
Highden **2** BN2 .... 164 C6
Highdown BN41, BN42 .... 140 F1
Highdown Cl BN41, BN42 ..... 140 F1
Highdown Cotts TN17 .... 20 F3
Highdown Ct BN1 .... 142 E3
Highdown Rd Hove BN1, BN3 .. 163 E7
Lewes BN7 .... 123 A2
Highfield RH17 .... 33 C4
Highfield Cl TN2 .... 9 C6
Highfield Cres BN1 .... 143 A5
Highfield Ct **7** RH16 .... 50 E4
Highfield Cty Jun Sch BN22 . 174 A1
Highfield Dr Hastings TN38 . 135 D3
Hurstpierpoint BN6 .... 97 C5
Highfield Gdns TN39 .... 157 C7
Highfield Ind Est N BN23 ... 174 A1
Highfield Ind Est S BN23 ... 174 A1

Highfield Rd East Grinstead RH19 . 1 D3
Horam TN21 .... 106 F7
Royal Tunbridge Wells TN4 .. 8 C7
Highfields Brighton BN1 .... 143 E5
Burwash TN19 .... 62 A6
Forest Row RH18 .... 11 F2
Rye TN31 .... 93 B7
Highgate Flats TN6 .... 27 B1
Highgate Rd RH18 .... 11 F1
Highgrove TN2 .... 17 A8
Highland Ct Crowborough TN6 . 25 E3
Haywards Heath RH16 .... 50 E4
Highland Grange TN6 .... 25 E3
Highland Lodge BN21 .... 184 F4
Highland Rd RH16 .... 50 F3
Highlands Ave TN22 .... 78 D4
Highlands Cl Bexhill TN39 .. 156 F7
Crowborough TN6 .... 25 E3
Keymer BN6 .... 98 A3
Highlands Dr Burgess Hill RH15 . 73 A4
Hastings TN38 .... 159 B7
Highlands Gdns TN38 .... 159 B7
Highlands Mews **2** TN38 .. 159 B6
Highlands Rd
Portslade-by-Sea BN41 ...... 141 B1
Seaford BN25 .... 180 F3
Highlands The Bexhill TN39 . 156 F7
Cuckfield RH17 .... 50 A8
Highlea Cl TN37 .... 136 C5
Highleigh **7** BN2 .... 189 B6
Highsted Pk BN10 .... 167 D2
Highview Ave N BN1 .... 142 E6
Highview Ave S BN1 .... 142 E6
Highview Cl Hastings TN37 .. 136 D5
Windmill Hill BN27 .... 131 B5
Highview Ct BN20 .... 184 F1
Highview La TN22 .... 78 D4
Highview Rd Bexhill TN39 ... 156 E6
Telscombe Cliffs BN10 ...... 177 F4
Highview Way BN1 .... 142 E6
Highwater View TN38 .... 135 F7
Highway Cl BN2 .... 143 D2
Highway The Brighton BN2 ... 143 D2
Newhaven BN10, BN9 .... 179 A6
Highways BN1 .... 141 B2
Highwoods Ave TN39 .... 156 C6
Highwoods Cl TN39 .... 156 E5
Highwoods Golf Course TN39 . 156 D6
Hiham Bglws TN36 .... 117 E7
Hiham Gn TN36 .... 117 E7
Hilary Cl BN26 .... 172 F5
Hilary Lodge **2** BN2 ..... 164 C5
Hilbert Cl TN2 .... 8 C5
Hilders Farm Cl TN6 .... 26 B1
Hilgrove Rd BN2 .... 166 D3
Hill Brow BN3 .... 142 B3
Hill Cl TN6 .... 25 E1
Hill Crest Dormans Park RH19 . 1 E6
Royal Tunbridge Wells TN4 .. 8 B8
Hill Crest Ct BN9 .... 179 C6
Hill Crest Rd BN9 .... 179 D6
Hill Dr BN3 .... 142 B3
Hill Farm Way BN42, BN43 ... 140 E2
Hill House Prep Sch TN22 ... 78 C5
Hill Mead TN22 .... 35 C4
Hill Rd Eastbourne BN20 .... 184 B5
Fairlight TN35 .... 138 C4
Lewes BN7 .... 123 B2
Newhaven BN9 .... 168 F2
Saltdean BN2 .... 177 B5
Hill Rise Newhaven BN9 ..... 168 F2
Seaford BN25 .... 180 C5
Hill Side BN9 .... 179 D7
Hill St Hastings TN34 ...... 160 A4
Royal Tunbridge Wells TN1 .. 8 B5
Hill Top BN1 .... 142 B5
Hill Top Cl BN41 .... 140 F2
Hill View Rd TN4 .... 7 C4
Hillary Cl TN2 .... 2 A3
Hillbank Cl BN41 .... 140 F3
Hillbert Rd TN1, TN2 .... 8 C5
Hillborough Cl TN39 .... 156 D4
Hillbrow (Brighton Univ) BN20 . 184 B1
Hillbrow Rd BN1 .... 142 D4
Hillbury Gdns TN5 .... 31 D1
Hillcrest Brighton BN1 ..... 142 C5
Rye TN31 .... 93 B7
Hillcrest Ave TN39 .... 157 A6
Hillcrest Cl RH17 .... 51 F3
Hillcrest Ct BN1 .... 142 C5
Hillcrest Dr TN1 .... 8 D7
Hillcrest La RH17 .... 51 F3
Hillcrest Sch TN35 .... 137 E5
Hillcroft BN41 .... 140 F2
Hillgarth TN4 .... 8 A8
Hillrise TN6 .... 26 B2
Hillside Brighton BN2 ...... 143 E2
Forest Row RH18 .... 11 E3
Friston BN20 .... 183 B1
Mayfield TN20 .... 40 B2
Portslade-by-Sea BN41 ...... 141 C1
Southwick BN42 .... 140 F1
Hillside Ave BN25 .... 181 C5
Hillside Cl RH19 .... 1 E3
Hillside Cotts TN5 .... 30 B8
Hillside Dr TN21 .... 106 F7
Hillside Rd Bexhill TN39, TN40 . 157 C5
Hastings, Silverhill Park TN34 . 136 B3
Hastings, St Helen's Wood TN34 . 136 E3
Hillside Sch BN41 .... 141 B2
Hillside Way
Brighton, Moulsecoomb BN2 . 143 E2
Brighton, Westdene BN1 ..... 142 C4
Hillside Wlk RH17 .... 50 C6
Hilltop Dr TN31 .... 93 B7
Hillview Rd BN2 .... 165 B8

Hillyfield BN7 .... 146 B8
Hillyglen Cl TN34 .... 159 E8
Hindleap Warren Activity Ctr RH18 . 22 C5
Hindover Cres BN25 .... 181 A4
Hindover Rd BN25 .... 181 A4
Hinton Cl BN1 .... 143 C2
Hither Chantlers TN3 .... 7 A2
Hoad Rd BN22 .... 185 B4
Hoad's Wood Rd TN34 .... 137 A3
Hoadleys La TN6 .... 25 D5
Hoadswood Cross TN21 .... 84 B2
Hoath Hill TN32 .... 87 C5
Hoathdown Ave BN9 .... 179 A7
Hobbs La TN31 .... 68 D6
Hoblands RH16 .... 51 B4
Hobney Rise BN24 .... 174 F5
Hockington La BN20 .... 173 B1
Hodcombe Cl BN23 .... 174 B4
Hoddern Ave BN10 .... 178 B8
Hoddern Cty Jun Sch BN10 .. 178 B8
Hodshrove La BN2 .... 143 E3
Hodshrove Pl BN2 .... 143 E3
Hodshrove Rd BN2 .... 143 E3
Hoe The TN37 .... 136 B6
Hogarth Ho TN38 .... 159 A8
Hogarth Rd Eastbourne BN23 . 174 D1
Hove BN3 .... 162 F7
Hoghole La TN3 .... 19 F2
Hogtrough La TN36 .... 117 E7
Holbrook Cl BN20 .... 188 E8
Holden Park Rd TN4 .... 8 A4
Holdings The
Kingston near Lewes BN7 .... 145 F5
Upper Wellingham BN8 .... 124 B7
Hole Farm Cl TN34 .... 136 E2
Hollamby Pk BN27 .... 152 D7
Holland Ave TN39 .... 156 C4
Holland Mews BN3 .... 163 D5
Holland Rd BN3 .... 163 D6
Holland St BN2 .... 189 B6
Hollands The RH15 .... 73 C4
Hollands Way RH19 .... 2 A4
Hollier's Hill TN40 .... 157 C6
Hollies The TN20 .... 40 A2
Hollin Cl TN4 .... 7 F4
Hollingbourne Ct **8** BN2 . 164 E4
Hollingbury Copse BN1 ...... 143 A4
Hollingbury Cres BN1 .... 143 B2
Hollingbury Ind Est BN1 .... 143 C7
Hollingbury Park Ave BN1 ... 143 A3
Hollingbury Park Golf Course BN1 . 143 A3
Hollingbury Pl BN1 .... 143 B2
Hollingbury Rd BN1 .... 143 B1
Hollingbury Rise BN1 .... 143 B2
Hollingbury Rise W BN1 ..... 143 A3
Hollingbury Terr BN1 .... 143 A2
Hollingdean La BN1, BN2 .... 164 B8
Hollingdean Rd BN2 .... 164 B8
Hollingdean St BN1 .... 143 B1
Hollingdean Terr BN1 .... 143 B2
Hollinghurst Ct TN37 .... 136 B5
Hollinghurst Rd TN37 .... 136 B4
Hollington Ct TN38 .... 159 A8
Hollington Cty Inf Sch TN38 . 136 A4
Hollington Cty Jun Sch TN38 . 136 A4
Hollington Old La TN38 ..... 136 A4
Hollington Park Cl TN38 .... 136 A1
Hollington Park Rd TN38 .... 136 A1
Hollow La Blackboys TN22 ... 80 B2
Dormansland RH19, RH7 ...... 2 D6
Hollow The RH16 .... 51 B5
Holly Bank **3** BN2 .... 189 B8
Holly Cl Bexhill TN39 ...... 156 C6
Brighton BN1 .... 142 E3
Hailsham BN27 .... 152 B6
Heathfield TN21 .... 82 A6
Holly Ct TN6 .... 25 E2
Holly Dr TN21 .... 82 A6
Holly Pl BN2 .... 173 E3
Holly Rd BN1 .... 51 A3
Hollybank Gdns TN38 .... 136 B1
Hollycroft BN7 .... 100 A3
Hollydene Rd TN5 .... 29 F6
Hollyshaw Cl TN2 .... 8 C2
Hollywood Ct **10** RH16 ... 50 E5
Holm Oak Cl TN39 .... 156 E3
Holmbush Cl
Haywards Heath RH16 .... 50 E2
Shoreham-by-Sea BN43 .... 140 D2
Holmbush Ct **8** BN43 ..... 161 C8
Holmbush Cty Fst Sch BN43 . 140 D1
Holmbush Way BN42, BN43 ... 140 E1
Holmdale Rd BN9 .... 169 A1
Holmebury Ho **1** TN34 .... 159 E7
Holmes Ave BN3 .... 141 F1
Holmes Cl BN25 .... 180 A6
Holmes Farm Cotts TN39 .... 156 A8
Holmes Hill Cotts BN8 ...... 127 C6
Holmesdale Cl TN5 .... 29 E5
Holmesdale Ct TN34 .... 159 E5
Holmesdale Rd Bexhill TN39 . 157 A4
Burgess Hill RH15 .... 73 A1
Holmewood Ho TN3 .... 7 A2
Holmewood Rd TN4 .... 8 C7
Holmewood Ridge TN3 .... 6 F3
Holmhurst Cl TN4 .... 7 F4
Holmhurst La TN37 .... 136 B5
Holmstead BN2 .... 189 B7
Holmwood Cl BN2 .... 97 F4
Holt Lodge **1** BN2 .... 189 B7
Holt The Burgess Hill RH15 . 73 C2
Hailsham BN27 .... 152 A6
Seaford BN25 .... 180 F5
Holters Way BN25 .... 180 F5
Holton Hill BN2 .... 165 E7

Holtview Rd BN2 .... 165 B8
Holtye Ave RH19 .... 2 A3
Holtye Golf Club TN8 .... 3 F3
Holtye Rd RH19 .... 2 B3
Holy Cross CE Prim Sch TN22 . 78 D7
Holyrood RH19 .... 11 A8
Holywell Cl BN20 .... 188 E7
Holywell Rd BN20 .... 188 E7
Holywell Wlk BN27 .... 152 B7
Home Farm Bsns Ctr BN7 .... 145 F5
Home Farm Ct Frant TN3 .... 17 C4
Horsted Keynes RH17 .... 33 C5
Home Farm La TN6 .... 8 E8
Home Farm Rd BN1 .... 143 D3
Home Platt TN3 .... 21 A6
Home Rd BN1 .... 142 E1
Homebush Ave Saltdean BN2 .. 177 D5
Telscombe BN2 .... 166 F3
Homecoast Ho BN10 .... 178 B7
Homedale Ho **8** TN34 ..... 159 F7
Homedrive Ho BN3 .... 163 C8
Homefield Cl BN25 .... 180 F4
Homefield Rd BN25 .... 180 F4
Homegate Ho **3** BN2 ...... 184 F3
Homeglade Ho BN20 .... 188 E8
Homehill Ho **6** TN40 ..... 157 C4
Homelands TN39 .... 157 A6
Homelatch Ho **1** BN20 .... 185 A3
Homelawn Ho TN40 .... 157 E4
Homeleigh BN1 .... 142 E5
Homeridge Ho BN2 .... 177 D5
Homestall Rd RH19 .... 11 E8
Homestead The TN3 .... 15 C7
Hometye Ho BN25 .... 180 D3
Homewarr Ho TN40 .... 157 E4
Homewood Cl BN22 .... 185 B6
Homeoenathic Hospl TN1 .... 8 A3
Honey Croft BN3 .... 141 D4
Honey La BN8 .... 149 D7
Honeycrag Cl BN26 .... 173 A7
Honeypot La BN7, BN8 .... 100 B7
Honeysuckle Cl
Eastbourne BN23 .... 174 B3
Hailsham BN27 .... 152 B5
Hastings TN37 .... 136 D5
Honeyway Cl BN26 .... 172 F3
Honies Ct TN39 .... 157 C6
Hoo Gdns BN20 .... 173 B1
Hoo The BN20 .... 173 B1
Hood Cl BN23 .... 185 E7
Hooe Rd TN33 .... 133 A3
Hook Hill TN5 .... 31 A6
Hookswood Cl TN6 .... 26 A3
Hoopers Cl BN7 .... 123 C3
Hoover Cl TN38 .... 135 F7
Hop Gdn TN22 .... 36 C2
Hope Cotts BN42 .... 161 E8
Hopehouse La TN17, TN18 .... 47 E7
Hopfield Gdns TN22 .... 78 E8
Hopgarden Cl TN34 .... 159 E8
Hoppers Croft La TN19 ..... 62 B6
Hopwood Gdns TN4 .... 8 A6
Horam Park Cl TN21 .... 106 F7
Horebeech La TN21 .... 107 A6
Horizon Cl TN4 .... 8 B8
Horleigh Green Rd TN20 .... 39 C1
Horley Pl BN2 .... 164 E6
Hornblower Cotts TN19 ..... 44 C1
Hornbuckles Cl BN8 .... 100 E7
Hornby Pl BN2 .... 144 A1
Hornby Rd BN2 .... 144 A1
Horning Cl BN23 .... 174 B4
Horns Rd TN18 .... 45 D8
Hornshurst Rd TN37 .... 136 C1
Horntye Rd TN37 .... 136 C1
Horsa Cl BN23 .... 185 F8
Horsegrove Ave TN5 .... 31 F1
Horsegrove La TN6 .... 39 B8
Horseshoe Cl TN38 .... 136 B2
Horseshoe La TN31 .... 68 A1
Horsewalk BN27, TN33 ...... 154 E7
Horsfield Rd BN7 .... 123 B3
Horsgate Ho RH17 .... 50 A8
Horsgate La RH17 .... 50 A6
Horsham Ave BN10 .... 178 C7
Horsham Ave N BN10 .... 178 C8
Horsham Cl BN2 .... 164 F6
Horsted Ho **1** RH16 ...... 50 F3
Horsted Keynes Ind Est RH17 . 33 B7
Horsted Keynes Sta RH17 ... 33 A7
Horsted La Danehill RH17 .. 34 A4
Isfield TN22 .... 102 F7
Sharpthorne RH19 .... 21 B3
Horsted Sq TN22 .... 78 A6
Horsye Rd BN22 .... 185 B7
Horton Rd BN1 .... 143 B1
Hoskins Pl RH19 .... 2 A4
Hosmers Field TN6 .... 39 D8
Hospital Villas **5** RH16 . 50 F3
Houghton Green La TN31 .... 70 C2
Houghton La TN31 .... 70 C5
Houndean Cl BN7 .... 146 A8
Houndean Rise BN7 .... 145 F8
Hova Villas BN3 .... 163 B6
Hove Bsns Ctr BN3 .... 163 B8
Hove Ent Ctr BN41 .... 162 C6
Hove General Hospl BN3 .... 163 A7
Hove Manor **7** BN3 .... 163 A6
Hove Mus & Art Gall BN3 ... 163 A6
Hove Nuffield Hospl BN3 ... 162 C7
Hove Park Gdns Hove BN3 ... 142 B1
Hove BN3 .... 163 B8
Hove Park Rd BN3 .... 142 B1
Hove Park Sch (Lower) BN3 . 141 D2
Hove Park Sch (Upper) BN3 . 142 A1
Hove Park Villas BN3 ...... 163 B8

Hove Park Way BN3 .... 142 C1
Hove Pl BN3 .... 163 B5
Hove St BN3 .... 163 A6
Hove Sta BN3 .... 163 B8
Hovedene BN3 .... 163 C7
How's Cl TN31 .... 90 B5
Howard Ave RH15 .... 72 E4
Howard Cl BN27 .... 152 D6
Howard Ct Hove BN3 .... 142 A2
  Peacehaven BN10 .... 178 B7
Howard Gdns TN2 .... 8 A1
Howard Ho Bexhill TN39 .... 156 E4
  Peacehaven BN10 .... 167 D1
Howard Pl BN1 .... 189 F7
Howard Rd BN1 .... 164 C7
Howard Sq BN21 .... 185 A2
Howard Terr BN1 .... 189 F7
Howards Cres TN39 .... 156 C4
Howbourne La TN22 .... 56 E5
Howes Cotts TN18 .... 45 F8
Howey Cl BN9 .... 168 F1
Howlett Cl TN38 .... 135 F4
Howlett Dr BN27 .... 129 B2
Howletts Cl BN22 .... 173 F1
Hoyle Rd BN10 .... 178 C7
Hudson Cl BN23 .... 185 G7
Hudson Ct BN26 .... 185 C6
Huggett's La BN20, BN22 ...... 173 B3
Hughenden Ct 2 TN34 .... 136 F2
Hughenden Pl 1 TN34 .... 136 F2
Hughenden Rd TN34 .... 160 A6
Hughes Rd BN2 .... 164 B8
Hugletts La TN21 .... 83 A7
Humboldt Ct TN4 .... 8 D5
Humphrey Lodge RH15 .... 73 D3
Humphrey's Gap RH15 .... 161 A7
Hundred Acre La BN6, RH17 .. 74 B2
Hundredhouse La TN31 .... 90 F4
Hungershall Pk TN4 .... 7 E2
Hunloke Ave BN22 .... 185 B6
Hunston Cl RH15 .... 165 F7
Hunt's Gate BN8 .... 52 E3
Hunters Way
  Royal Tunbridge Wells TN2 ... 7 F1
  Uckfield TN22 .... 78 B8
Hunting Cl TN40 .... 157 C5
Huntingdon Rd TN6 .... 25 F1
Huntingdon Way RH15 .... 73 D5
Huntley Mill Rd TN5 .... 31 E3
Huntleys Pk TN4 .... 7 F5
Hurdis Rd BN25 .... 180 A6
Hurrell Rd TN34 .... 160 B6
Hurst Cres BN41 .... 162 B8
Hurst Farm Rd RH19 .... 10 D7
Hurst Green CE Sch TN19 ...... 45 A2
Hurst Hill BN1 .... 143 C5
Hurst La Eastbourne BN21 .... 184 D4
  Sedlescombe TN33 .... 88 F3
  Windmill Hill BN27 .... 131 B5
Hurst Rd Eastbourne BN21 .... 184 D5
  Hassocks BN6 .... 97 D4
Hurst Shaw TN21 .... 107 C8
Hurst The TN2 .... 8 E7
Hurst Way TN34 .... 137 A6
Hurst Wickham Cl BN6 .... 97 C5
Hurstfield RH16 .... 51 A2
Hurstpierpoint Coll BN6 .... 97 B8
Hurstwood 6 BN2 .... 164 F5
Hurstwood Cl TN40 .... 158 B5
Hurstwood La
  Haywards Heath RH16 .... 51 A2
  Royal Tunbridge Wells TN4 ..... 7 F3
  Sharpthorne RH17, RH19 ...... 21 D1
Hurstwood Pk TN4 .... 7 F3
Hurstwood Rd TN22 .... 56 A6
Hurtis Hill TN6 .... 37 E7
Hutton Rd BN1 .... 143 B3
Hyde Cl BN7 .... 145 E5
Hyde Gdns BN21 .... 185 A2
Hyde Rd BN21 .... 184 F2
Hyde The BN2 .... 164 F8
Hyde Tynings Cl BN20 .... 188 D8
Hydehurst Cl TN6 .... 25 F1
Hydney St BN22 .... 185 C5
Hydneye The BN22 .... 173 F1
Hylden Cl BN2 .... 165 B8
Hyperion Ave BN26 .... 172 E6
Hythe Ave TN38 .... 158 B5
Hythe Cl Polegate BN26 .... 173 C7
  Seaford BN25 .... 181 C5
Hythe Cres BN25 .... 181 C4
Hythe Rd BN1 .... 143 A2
Hythe View BN25 .... 181 C4

Ian Cl TN40 .... 157 F7
Icklesham CE Prim Sch
  TN36 .... 116 E6
Icklesham Dr TN38 .... 135 D3
Iden Cl BN26 .... 164 E5
Iden Ct TN34 .... 136 C3
Iden Hurst BN6 .... 97 A7
Iden Rd TN31 .... 70 B3
Iden St BN22 .... 174 A2
Iden's La TN21 .... 82 D8
Ifield Cl BN2 .... 177 E6
Ifield Mill Ho BN24 .... 174 B5
Iford Cl BN9 .... 168 D1
Iford & Kingston CE Prim Sch
  BN7 .... 145 F5
Ilex Ct BN42 .... 141 A1
Ilex Gn 6 BN21 .... 129 B1
Image Cross Flats RH19 .... 21 A5
Imberhorne La RH19 .... 1 B2
Imberhorne Lower Sch RH19 .... 1 D3
Imberhorne Sch RH19 .... 1 B3
Imberhorne Way RH19 .... 1 B3
Impala Gdns TN4 .... 8 B6
Imperial Arc BN1 .... 189 F5

Independent Bsns Pk The
  RH19 .... 1 A3
Ingham Dr BN1 .... 143 D6
Ingleside Sch TN38 .... 135 F4
Ingleside Dr TN6 .... 25 E2
Inglewood Gdns TN38 .... 135 E4
Ingram Cres E BN3 .... 162 E8
Ingram Cres W BN3 .... 162 E8
Ingram Ct BN3 .... 162 E7
Ingrams Ave TN39 .... 157 C7
Ingrams Way BN27 .... 152 A6
Inholmes Cl RH15 .... 73 C3
Inholmes Park Rd RH15 .... 73 B3
Ink Pen La RH18 .... 11 E1
Innham's Wood TN6 .... 25 E4
Innings Dr BN24 .... 175 C4
Insley Ct TN39 .... 156 F3
Inverness Rd BN2 .... 164 C8
Inwood Cres BN1 .... 142 E1
Iona Way 12 RH16 .... 50 E4
Irelands La BN7 .... 123 B1
Ironlatch Ave TN38 .... 135 F2
Ironlatch Cl TN38 .... 135 F2
Ironstone Way TN22 .... 78 E7
Ironstones TN3 .... 7 B3
Irving Ho TN1 .... 8 B5
Isaac's La RH16, RH15 .... 50 A2
Isabel Cl BN26 .... 180 E5
Isabel Cres BN3 .... 162 E8
Isfield Rd Brighton BN1 .... 143 C2
  Isfield TN22 .... 102 E5
Isle of Thorns (Univ of Sussex)
  RH17 .... 22 D1
Islingword Pl BN2 .... 164 C6
Islingword Rd BN2 .... 164 C7
Islingword St BN2 .... 189 B6
Ismay Lodge TN39 .... 156 D3
Iveagh Cres BN9 .... 168 D2
Ivor Rd BN2 .... 144 C1
Ivory Pl BN2 .... 189 B6
Ivy Cotts BN8 .... 104 C6
Ivy Dene La RH19 .... 11 D6
Ivy Pl BN1, BN3 .... 163 D5
Ivy Terr BN21 .... 184 F3
Ivyhouse Employment Area
  TN34 .... 137 B4
Ivyhouse La TN34, TN35 .... 137 B6
Ivylands Yd TN31 .... 93 B5

Jack O'Dandy Cl BN21 .... 184 C7
Jackdaws The TN22 .... 78 E4
Jackies La BN8 .... 76 B7
Jacks Hill TN7 .... 13 D2
Jackson Mews BN9 .... 179 C7
Jackson St BN2 .... 189 B7
Jacobs Acre TN40 .... 157 C5
Jacqueline Du Pre Ct 6 BN2 164 C5
James Ave BN27 .... 130 E6
Jameson Cres TN38 .... 136 A3
Jameson Rd TN40 .... 157 D4
Jane Murray Way
  Burgess Hill BN6, RH15 .... 72 D5
  Burgess Hill RH15 .... 72 E1
Jane's La RH15 .... 73 E4
Janes Cl RH15 .... 73 C5
Janes La RH15 .... 73 D4
Janeston Ct 4 BN3 .... 163 C7
Japonica Ct TN4 .... 140 B1
Jardine Ct TN6 .... 25 F2
Jarvis Brook Cty Prim Sch
  TN6 .... 38 B8
Jarvis Brook Cty Prim Sch
  TN6 .... 38 C7
Jarvisbrook Cl TN39 .... 156 D3
Jasmine Cotts TN3 .... 15 C7
Jasmine Ct BN1 .... 142 F5
Jasmine Gn 2 BN27 .... 129 B1
Jason Cl BN10 .... 178 C7
Jay Cl BN23 .... 174 C2
Jay Rd BN10 .... 178 E6
Jays The Burgess Hill RH15 .... 72 E4
  Uckfield TN22 .... 78 D4
Jefferies RH17 .... 33 C4
Jefferies Way TN6 .... 25 F4
Jefferson Way TN38 .... 135 F6
Jeffreys Way TN22 .... 55 D1
Jellicoe Cl BN23 .... 185 F7
Jenner's La TN35 .... 137 E6
Jephson Cl BN20 .... 188 F8
Jerome Cl BN23 .... 174 E2
Jersey St BN2 .... 189 B6
Jervis Ave BN23 .... 185 A8
Jesmond Cl BN3 .... 162 E7
Jesmond Rd BN3 .... 162 E7
Jesters RH15 .... 73 C7
Jevington Cl TN39 .... 156 D2
Jevington Dr BN43 .... 161 D6
Jevington Dr Brighton BN2 ... 143 D1
  Seaford BN25 .... 180 D4
Jevington Gdns BN20 .... 185 A1
Jevington Ho 7 BN21 .... 184 D4
Jevington Rd BN26 .... 172 D2
Jew St BN1 .... 189 A5
Jireh Ct 4 RH16 .... 50 C4
Joan Hughes Ct BN26 .... 173 A6
Joan Nightingale Ho RH16 ..... 50 C4
Job's La BN6 .... 72 A6
Joe's La BN27 .... 131 B5
John Dann Cl TN22 .... 80 A6
John Macadam Way TN37 ..... 136 A6
John Spare Ct TN4 .... 8 B6
John St Brighton BN2 .... 189 B6
  Royal Tunbridge Wells TN4 ..... 8 A5
John Whittle Lodge 4 BN2 .. 143 C1
John's Cross Rd TN32 .... 87 C8
Johns Cl BN10 .... 167 C2
Johnson Bank 4 BN2 .... 164 C7
Johnson Dr RH15 .... 73 D3

Jonas Dr TN5 .... 29 E5
Jonas La TN5 .... 29 E5
Jordan Ct BN3 .... 162 E8
Jordans La BN22 .... 173 D3
Jordans La E BN22 .... 173 D3
Jordans La W BN22 .... 173 C3
Jordans The RH19 .... 10 E8
Joyce Villas TN21 .... 106 E5
Jubilee Cl RH16 .... 51 A4
Jubilee Ct BN2 .... 143 E2
Jubilee Gdns BN25 .... 181 A5
Jubilee Ho BN9 .... 179 C7
Jubilee Rd Bexhill TN39 .... 157 A7
  Burgess Hill RH15 .... 72 E2
  Portslade-by-Sea BN41 .... 162 A8
Jubilee St BN1 .... 189 A6
Judge's Terr RH19 .... 10 E8
Jugg's Rd BN7 .... 146 B7
Juggs Cl BN7 .... 146 B8
Juggs Rd BN7 .... 146 A7
Julian Ct 5 BN43 .... 161 C8
Julian Rd BN3 .... 163 E7
Junction Cl RH15 .... 73 C4
Junction Rd
  Bodiam TN18, TN32 .... 46 A3
  Brighton BN1 .... 189 F6
  Burgess Hill RH15 .... 73 B3
  Cripp's Corner TN32 .... 65 C5
  Cripp's Corner TN32, TN33 ... 88 D5
  Eastbourne BN21 .... 185 A3
  Hastings TN37 .... 136 B7
Junction St BN26 .... 173 B6
Juniper Cl Hastings TN38 ..... 135 C4
  Portslade-by-Sea BN41 .... 141 B3
  Seaford BN25 .... 181 C3
Juniper Wlk BN43 .... 140 C1
Jury's Gap Coastguard Cotts
  TN31 .... 95 E1
Jury's Gap Rd TN29 .... 96 F5

Kammond Ave BN25 .... 181 B5
Kane Hythe Rd TN33 .... 111 D6
Karenza Ct BN1 .... 164 A8
Katherine Way BN25 .... 180 D5
Keats Cl TN38 .... 158 F6
Keats Pl RH19 .... 1 D1
Keats Wlk BN23 .... 174 E3
Kebbell Lodge 12 BN2 .... 189 B5
Kedale Rd BN25 .... 180 E4
Keel Gdns TN4 .... 7 E8
Keere St BN7 .... 146 C8
Keith Wlk BN23 .... 185 F6
Keld Ave TN22 .... 78 D6
Keld Cl TN22 .... 78 D6
Keld Dr TN22 .... 78 D6
Kelly Rd BN3 .... 142 D1
Kelsey Cotts BN8 .... 124 E6
Kelsey Ct RH15 .... 73 D3
Kemble Ct BN2 .... 8 E7
Kemp Ct BN2 .... 164 E4
Kemp St BN1 .... 189 A6
Kemp Town Pl 18 BN2 .... 164 D4
Kemps Farm Rd TN6 .... 26 B1
Kemps Way TN32 .... 64 C5
Kemptown Mews 11 BN2 ...... 164 E4
Kendal Cl BN9 .... 179 E7
Kendal Pk TN4 .... 7 E5
Kendal Rd BN3 .... 162 F8
Kenilworth Cl BN22 .... 144 A2
Kenilworth Rd TN38 .... 159 B7
Kenmure Ave BN1 .... 143 A7
Kennard Ct RH18 .... 11 E3
Kennedy Ave RH19 .... 1 D3
Kennedy Cl TN21 .... 82 B6
Kennedy Ct TN38 .... 136 B3
Kennedy Rd TN40 .... 157 E4
Kennedy Way BN9 .... 179 B8
Kennel Cnr BN8 .... 124 F6
Kennel La TN39 .... 156 C4
Kennett Cl BN26 .... 173 F5
Kenrith Ct TN34 .... 136 E2
Kensington Gdns BN1 .... 189 A6
Kensington Pl BN1 .... 189 A6
Kensington St BN1 .... 189 A6
Kent Cl Bexhill TN40 .... 158 A5
  Shoreham-by-Sea BN43 ...... 161 C7
  Winchelsea TN36 .... 117 E7
Kent Ct BN20 .... 184 B6
Kent & East Sussex Rly TN17 . 49 D5
Kent Fields BN7 .... 145 E5
Kent La TN32 .... 85 F6
Kent Rd Hastings TN38 .... 135 F4
  Royal Tunbridge Wells TN4 ..... 8 A6
Kent St TN33 .... 114 A3
Kent & Sussex Hospl TN4 .... 8 A4
Kent's La BN6 .... 99 C7
Kentish Gdns TN39 .... 16 E8
Kenton Cl TN39 .... 157 A5
Kenton Ct BN21 .... 185 A1
Kenton Rd BN3 .... 162 D7
Kents Rd RH16 .... 50 F3
Kenwards BN1 .... 143 D7
Kenwood Cl TN34 .... 137 B4
Kenya Ct 3 BN1 .... 163 E6
Keppel Rd TN34 .... 136 F2
Kepplestone BN20 .... 188 E8
Kerrara Terr BN22 .... 185 B5
Kerrison Mews BN3 .... 163 D5
Kestrel Cl Bexhill TN40 .... 157 E4
  Hove BN3 .... 163 D8
Kestrel Ct BN27 .... 152 D7
Kestrels The Hastings TN38 .. 135 F5
  Shoreham-by-Sea BN43 .... 161 A8
Ketcham Cnr BN24 .... 174 E6
Ketche's La RH17,TN22 .... 52 E7
Kevin Gdns BN2 .... 165 E8
Kew St BN1 .... 189 F6
Kewhurst Ave TN39 .... 156 D3

Keymer Ave BN10 .... 178 D7
Keymer Cl Eastbourne BN23 . 174 E1
  Hastings TN38 .... 158 E6
Keymer Ct RH15 .... 73 B2
Keymer Gdns RH15 .... 73 B1
Keymer Par RH15 .... 73 B2
Keymer Pk BN6 .... 98 B3
Keymer Rd Brighton BN1 ...... 143 B6
  Burgess Hill RH15 .... 98 B8
  Hassocks BN6 .... 97 F3
Kibbles La TN4 .... 7 E8
Kidbrook RH16 .... 51 B6
Kidbrooke Park
  (Michael Hall Sch) RH18 ...... 11 D1
Kidbrooke Rise RH18 .... 11 E2
Kidd's Hill TN22, TN7 .... 24 A4
Kilbarn Ct RH16 .... 50 D2
Kilbarn Way RH16 .... 50 D2
Kilburn Terr 5 BN21 .... 185 A3
Kilda St 1 BN2 .... 185 B4
Kildare Cl TN34 .... 137 B4
Kildare St BN20 .... 184 C3
Kiln Cl TN22 .... 78 D4
Kiln Dr TN31 .... 93 B8
Kiln La Haywards Heath RH16 . 51 B5
  Hooe TN33 .... 155 B7
  Isfield TN22 .... 102 E5
Kiln Rd BN8 .... 125 A8
Kiln The RH15 .... 73 C3
Kilnwood La BN8 .... 100 E7
Kilpatrick Cl BN23 .... 174 D3
Kimberley Rd Brighton BN2 .. 143 D1
  Seaford BN25 .... 180 C4
Kindersley Cl RH19 .... 2 B3
Kinfauns Ave BN22 .... 185 B6
King Alfred (Swimming Pool
  & Sports Ctr) BN3 .... 163 A5
King Charles Pl 8 BN43 .... 161 A6
King Edward Ave TN37 .... 136 C3
King Edward Cl TN37 .... 136 C3
King Edward's Par
  BN20, BN21 .... 188 F8
King George Ave RH19 .... 1 C3
King George Rd BN43 .... 161 D8
King George V Hill TN1 .... 8 C5
King George VI Ave BN1, BN3 142 A3
King George VI Dr BN3 .... 142 A4
King George VI Mansions
  BN3 .... 141 F2
King Henry's Rd BN7 .... 123 B2
King John Ct 4 BN43 .... 161 A6
King Offa Cty Prim Sch TN39 157 B5
King Offa Way TN39, TN40 ... 157 C5
King Pl BN1 .... 189 F5
King St Brighton BN1 .... 189 A5
  East Grinstead RH19 .... 1 E1
King Wood Hill TN31 .... 90 A3
King's Ave Eastbourne BN21 . 184 E5
  Newhaven BN9 .... 168 E1
  Rye TN31 .... 93 D6
King's Bank La TN31 .... 68 A3
King's Cl BN21 .... 184 E5
King's Dr BN20, BN21, BN22 . 184 D7
King's Espl BN43 .... 163 A5
King's Gdns BN3 .... 163 B5
King's Hill Rd TN19 .... 62 B3
King's Manor Sch BN43 .... 161 D8
King's Mead La BN25 .... 180 D4
King's Rd Brighton BN1, BN3 . 163 E5
  Hastings TN37 .... 159 C7
  Haywards Heath RH16 .... 50 F3
Kingfisher Cl TN22 .... 78 E5
Kingfisher Ct BN27 .... 152 D7
Kingfisher Dr BN27 .... 174 C2
Kingfisher Rise RH19 .... 10 F8
Kings Chase TN6 .... 25 D3
Kings Cl Bexhill TN40 .... 157 C4
  Eastbourne BN21 .... 184 F5
Kings Copse 9 RH19 .... 10 F8
Kings Ct TN6 .... 25 E2
Kings Dr BN6 .... 97 F4
Kings Gate BN3 .... 163 C8
Kings Mews BN3 .... 163 B6
Kings Par BN1 .... 143 A2
Kings Pk TN2 .... 8 D3
Kings Rd BN42 .... 140 E1
Kings Ride Alfriston BN26 .... 170 F3
  Burgess Hill RH15 .... 73 D1
  Seaford BN25 .... 180 D4
Kings Toll Rd TN2 .... 9 F6
Kings Way RH15 .... 73 D2
Kings Wlk 10 BN3 .... 159 F8
Kingsbury Rd TN34 .... 189 A7
Kingsbury St BN1, BN2 .... 189 A7
Kingscliffe Sch BN2 .... 164 C5
Kingscote Lodge BN1 .... 143 F5
Kingscott Cl TN39 .... 157 B8
Kingsdale Cl Battle TN33 ...... 112 F3
  Hastings TN37 .... 136 C6
Kingsfield BN42 .... 161 E8
Kingsfield Cotts BN8 .... 149 E8
Kingsfold Ct 1 BN25 .... 180 F2
Kingsford 2 BN23 .... 185 E7
Kingsland Cl BN43 .... 161 B7
Kingsley Cl TN37 .... 136 A5
Kingsley Ct 11 Brighton BN1 163 E5
  Wadhurst TN5 .... 30 A4
Kingsley Rd Brighton BN1 .... 142 D1
  Lewes BN7 .... 123 B2
Kingsmarsh Cotts TN20 .... 58 B6
Kingsmead BN25 .... 180 E5
Kingsmead Ct BN25 .... 180 E4
Kingsmead Way BN25 .... 180 E5
Kingsmead Wlk BN25 .... 180 E4
Kingsmere BN1 .... 142 E2
Kingsmere Ct 2 BN21 .... 184 D4
Kingsmere Way BN23 .... 185 F8

Kingsthorpe Rd BN3 .... 162 F8
Kingston Ave BN25 .... 181 B3
Kingston Bay Rd BN43 .... 161 C6
Kingston Broadway
  BN42, BN43 .... 140 D1
Kingston Buci Cty Fst Sch
  BN43 .... 161 B8
Kingston Cl Brighton BN1 ..... 143 E6
  Hove BN3 .... 141 E2
  Seaford BN25 .... 181 B3
  Shoreham-by-Sea BN43 ...... 161 C8
Kingston Ct 17 BN43 .... 161 C8
Kingston Gn BN25 .... 181 B3
Kingston La BN41, BN42, BN43 161 C8
Kingston Rd Eastbourne BN22 173 F2
  Lewes BN7 .... 146 B7
Kingston Ridge BN7 .... 145 D6
Kingston Villas TN21 .... 106 E5
Kingston Way Seaford BN25 .. 181 B3
  Shoreham-by-Sea BN42, BN43 140 D1
Kingsway Hove BN3, BN41 ... 163 B5
  Seaford BN25 .... 180 D4
Kingsway Ct BN3 .... 163 C5
Kingswood Ave TN39 .... 156 F6
Kingswood Cl TN2 .... 8 C3
Kingswood Flats BN2 .... 189 B5
Kingswood Rd TN2 .... 8 C3
Kingswood St BN2 .... 189 A5
Kinross Ct 3 BN22 .... 185 A4
Kinsale Ct 5 BN3 .... 163 D7
Kinver La TN40 .... 158 A6
Kipling Ave BN2 .... 165 E7
Kipling Ct Bexhill TN40 .... 157 C6
  3 Haywards Heath RH16 ...... 50 D5
  Rottingdean BN2 .... 177 A5
Kipling Way RH19 .... 1 C1
Kipling Wlk 1 BN23 .... 174 E2
Kirby Dr BN10 .... 167 A1
Kirdford Cl RH15 .... 73 C1
Kirk Way BN20 .... 184 B5
Kirkdale Rd TN1 .... 8 B4
Kirkstall Cl BN22 .... 173 E3
Kitchenour La TN31 .... 68 E5
Kite Cl TN38 .... 158 E8
Kitilear Ct 5 BN3 .... 163 D6
Knebworth Rd TN39 .... 156 F5
Knelle Rd TN32 .... 64 A4
Knelle View 2 TN31 .... 67 B7
Knepp Cl BN2 .... 143 F2
Knight's Ridge TN2 .... 9 D7
Knights Cl TN2 .... 9 D7
Knights Gate Rd BN1 .... 144 C7
Knights Gdn BN27 .... 152 B6
Knights Meadow TN22 .... 78 E8
Knightsbridge Cl TN4 .... 7 F5
Knole Cl TN40 .... 157 D3
Knole Gr RH19 .... 1 C3
Knole Rd Bexhill TN40 .... 157 D3
  Rottingdean BN2 .... 177 A5
Knoll Bsns Ctr The BN3 .... 162 D8
Knoll Cl BN3 .... 141 D1
Knoll Cres BN22 .... 174 A1
Knoll Cty Inf Sch BN3 .... 141 D1
Knoll Rd BN22 .... 174 A1
Knoll Rise TN38 .... 159 A7
Knowle Cl Crowborough TN6 .. 38 C8
  Langton Green TN3 .... 6 F3
Knowle Cotts TN3 .... 17 E1
Knowle Ct TN38 .... 136 E1
Knowle Hill Bodiam TN32 ...... 65 D8
  Mayfield TN20 .... 40 A1
Knowle La BN8 .... 104 A6
Knowle Park Rd TN20 .... 40 A1
Knowle Pk TN6 .... 25 D2
Knowle Rd TN35 .... 138 E5
Knoyle Rd BN1 .... 142 E2
Knyveton Ct RH15 .... 73 B3
Kylemore BN24 .... 175 B6
Kymer Gdns BN6 .... 98 A3

La Marne Ct TN34 .... 136 E2
Laburnam Wlk BN22 .... 173 D3
Laburnham Gn 5 BN27 .... 129 B1
Laburnum Ave BN3 .... 141 E1
Laburnum Ct TN1 .... 8 C7
Laburnum Gdns TN40 .... 157 F6
Laburnum Gr BN1 .... 143 B3
Laburnum Way RH16 .... 51 B4
Lacys Hill BN8 .... 147 F8
Ladies Mile Brighton BN1 ..... 143 B7
  Withyham TN3 .... 14 D4
Ladies Mile Cl BN1 .... 142 F6
Ladies' Mile Ct BN1 .... 142 E6
Ladies' Mile Rd BN1 .... 142 F6
Lady Bee Ind Est BN42 .... 161 E6
Lady Oak La TN17, TN18, TN5 .. 32 C7
Lady's Gift Rd TN4 .... 7 F8
Ladycross Cl BN25 .... 181 C3
Ladyfern Ct TN2 .... 8 C4
Ladymead RH15 .... 73 C5
Ladysmith Rd BN2 .... 164 D8
Lagwood Cl BN6 .... 97 F3
Laine Cl BN1 .... 142 E3
Laines The 2 BN26 .... 170 F3
Lake Dr BN10 .... 178 B8
Lake House Cl TN39 .... 156 D4
Lake Rd TN4 .... 7 E4
Lake St TN20, TN6 .... 40 D7
Lake View 1 BN2 .... 164 C5
Lakelands Cl BN22 .... 174 A1
Lakeside TN2 .... 8 E6
Lakeside BN22 .... 174 A1

Laleham Cl Eastbourne BN21 .... 184 E4
Hastings TN37 .... 136 C5
Lamberhurst CE Prim Sch
TN3 .... 20 B6
Lamberhurst Golf Course TN3 20 C5
Lamberhurst Rd TN3, TN12 ... 20 C8
Lamberhurst Vineyard TN3 .... 20 A4
Lambert Pl BN7 .... 123 D3
Lambert Rd BN23 .... 174 E3
Lamberts Cotts TN33 .... 112 E3
Lamberts Rd TN1, TN2 .... 8 D3
Lambourn Cl RH19 .... 1 E3
Lambourn Way TN2 .... 8 D1
Lambourne Cl BN1 .... 143 C2
Lambourne Rd BN1 .... 143 C2
Lampington Row TN3 .... 6 E3
Lampool Cnr TN22 .... 55 A7
Lanark Ct BN20 .... 184 B6
Lancaster Ct **11** BN43 .... 163 A6
Lancaster Dr RH19 .... 2 A3
Lancaster House Rd BN1 .... 144 B7
Lancaster Rd Brighton BN1 ..... 189 F7
Hastings TN38 .... 135 F5
Lancaster St BN7 .... 123 D1
Lancing Cl TN34 .... 136 D3
Lancing Ct **5** BN42 .... 164 F5
Lancing Way BN26 .... 172 F4
Landgate TN31 .... 93 C6
Landport Farm Rd BN7 .... 123 A3
Landport Rd Lewes BN7 .... 123 B3
Lewes BN7 .... 123 C2
Landsdown Rd BN25 .... 181 C5
Landsdowne Way TN40 .... 157 E5
Landseer Rd BN3 .... 163 A8
Langdale Cl BN23 .... 174 C4
Langdale Ct BN41 .... 162 F6
Langdale Gdns BN3 .... 162 F6
Langdale Rd BN3 .... 162 F6
Langham Cl Hastings TN34 ..... 136 F4
Ringmer BN8 .... 124 D5
Langham Rd Hastings TN34 .... 136 F4
Robertsbridge TN32 .... 63 F4
Langholm Rd TN3 .... 6 F3
Langley Cl TN3 .... 157 B8
Langley Cres BN2 .... 144 E1
Langney Cty Prim Sch BN23 .. 174 E1
Langney Gn BN23 .... 185 E8
Langney Rd BN21, BN22 .... 185 B3
Langney Rise TN31 .... 174 D2
Langney Sh Ctr BN23 .... 174 C2
Langridge Dr
East Grinstead RH19 .... 10 E8
Portslade-by-Sea BN41 .... 141 B3
Langridge La RH16 .... 51 A5
Langridge Way RH15 .... 72 E5
Langridges Cl BN8 .... 76 C7
Langton Cl TN33 .... 112 E4
Langton Green Cty Prim Sch
TN3 .... 6 E4
Langton Rd Rusthall TN3, TN4 .. 7 C3
Speldhurst TN3 .... 7 A7
Langton Ridge TN3 .... 7 B3
Langtye La BN26, BN8 .... 149 E6
Lansdown Terr TN1 .... 82 B6
Lansdowne Cres BN27 .... 129 B2
Lansdowne Dr BN27 .... 129 A2
Lansdowne Gdns BN27 .... 129 B2
Lansdowne Mews **9** BN3 ..... 163 D6
Lansdowne Pl BN3 .... 163 D6
Lansdowne Rd Hailsham BN27 . 129 B2
Hove BN1, BN3 .... 163 D6
Royal Tunbridge Wells TN1, TN2 .. 8 B4
Lansdowne Sq Hove BN3 .... 163 D5
8 Royal Tunbridge Wells TN1 .. 8 B4
Lansdowne St BN3 .... 163 D6
Lansdowne Way BN27 .... 129 B3
Lapierre Rd BN9 .... 179 B7
Lapwing Cl BN23 .... 174 C2
Lapwing Ct BN27 .... 152 D7
Larch Cl Hastings TN38 .... 136 A1
Heathfield TN21 .... 82 B5
Woodingdean BN2 .... 165 F7
Larch Gdns BN22 .... 173 D3
Larch Way RH16 .... 51 B4
Lark Hill BN3 .... 141 E3
Larke Cl BN43 .... 161 C7
Larkfield Cl TN38 .... 136 A3
Larkfield Way BN1 .... 143 A4
Larkhill TN40 .... 157 C4
Larkspur Dr BN23 .... 174 B3
Larnach Cl TN22 .... 78 D8
Lascelles Terr BN21 .... 185 A1
Lashbrooks Rd TN22 .... 78 B7
Latimer Rd BN22 .... 185 C4
Laton Rd TN34 .... 136 F2
Laughton Cl BN23 .... 174 A4
Laughton Cty Prim Sch BN8 .. 126 C6
Laughton Lodge Hospl BN8 .. 126 A8
Laughton Rd Broyle Side BN8 . 125 D6
Woodingdean BN2 .... 165 F8
Laundry La RH17 .... 22 D1
Laurel **2** BN27 .... 50 D6
Laurel Bank Bexhill TN40 .... 157 E5
Royal Tunbridge Wells TN4 ...... 8 B8
Wadhurst TN5 .... 30 A4
Laurel Cl RH15 .... 73 C5
Laurel Dene RH19 .... 1 F1
Laurel La TN36 .... 116 F5
Laurel Rd TN1 .... 8 D7
Laurel Way TN1 .... 8 D7
Laurel Wlk TN38 .... 135 E3
Laurels The **4** Brighton BN2 .. 189 B8
Uckfield TN22 .... 78 E8
Lauriston Rd BN1 .... 142 E2

Lavant Cl TN39 .... 156 C6
Lavender Cl BN23 .... 174 B3
Lavender Gdns TN5 .... 31 E1
Lavender Hill BN43 .... 140 B1
Lavender Ho BN2 .... 189 B4
Lavender Line TN22 .... 102 E8
Lavender St BN2 .... 189 B4
Lavender Ho BN2 .... 179 C7
Lawn The TN38 .... 159 C7
Lawns Ave BN21 .... 184 D4
Lawns The
Eastbourne BN22 .... 185 C5
Hailsham BN27 .... 152 C6
Willingdon BN20 .... 173 B1
Willingdon BN20 .... 173 B2
Lawrence Cl BN23 .... 174 D1
Lawrence Ho TN22 .... 78 C7
Lawrence Rd BN3 .... 162 F7
Lawrie La RH16 .... 51 B5
Laylands Ct BN41 .... 162 A7
Laylands Rd BN41 .... 162 A7
Lazanby Ct TN38 .... 159 B8
Le Brun Rd BN21 .... 184 F5
Lea Ave TN31 .... 93 A6
Lea Ct BN9 .... 179 C8
Lea Rd BN10 .... 178 B8
Leach Ct BN2 .... 164 C5
Leaf Hall Rd **10** BN22 .... 185 B3
Leaf Hospl (Univ of Brighton)
BN21 .... 184 F4
Leaf Rd BN21 .... 185 A3
Leahurst Court Rd BN1 .... 142 E3
Leahurst Ct **4** BN1 .... 142 E3
Lealands Cl TN3 .... 15 C6
Lealands Dr TN22 .... 55 C1
Leamland Wlk BN27 .... 152 B7
Leap Cross Small Bsns Ctr
BN27 .... 129 A1
Leas The Burgess Hill RH15 .... 72 F4
Peacehaven Heights BN10 ..... 178 F6
Turner's Green TN5 .... 30 A6
Leasam La TN31 .... 93 B8
Leasingham Gdns TN39 .... 157 A5
Ledsham Ave TN37 .... 136 B5
Ledsham Cl TN37 .... 136 B5
Ledsham Pk TN37 .... 136 B5
Ledsham Way TN37 .... 136 B5
Lee Rd BN7 .... 123 B2
Lee Way BN9 .... 179 C8
Leeds Ave BN23 .... 185 D7
Leeds Cl TN35 .... 137 D4
Leeds La TN20 .... 58 D6
Leeford Cotts TN33 .... 88 A1
Leeford Vineyard TN33 .... 88 A1
Leeves Cl TN21 .... 82 A6
Leeves Way TN21 .... 82 A6
Leggs' La TN3 .... 6 E5
Legsheath La RH18, RH19 .... 21 F8
Leicester Ct **5** BN22 .... 185 B4
Leicester Dr TN2 .... 16 F8
Leicester Rd BN7 .... 123 B1
Leicester St BN2 .... 189 B5
Leicester Villas BN3 .... 162 D7
Leighton Cl TN4 .... 8 A7
Leighton Rd
Horsted Keynes RH17 .... 33 C5
Hove BN3 .... 163 A8
Leighton Villas RH17 .... 33 C5
Leneda Dr TN2 .... 16 E8
Lenham Ave BN2 .... 177 B5
Lenham Rd E BN2 .... 177 B5
Lenham Rd W BN2 .... 177 A5
Lennox Cl BN20 .... 184 B5
Lennox Ct TN21 .... 82 B8
Lennox Rd Hove BN3 .... 162 F8
Shoreham-by-Sea BN43 .... 161 B8
Lennox St BN2 .... 189 B5
Leopold Rd Bexhill TN39 .... 157 B4
Brighton BN1 .... 189 F6
Lepeland BN27 .... 129 A1
Lesley Cl TN40 .... 157 F7
Leslie St BN2 .... 185 B4
Letheren Pl BN20, BN21 .... 184 D3
Leveller End BN8 .... 76 D7
Leveller Rd BN8 .... 76 D7
Levett Ave BN26 .... 173 C6
Levett Cl BN26 .... 173 C6
Levett Rd BN26 .... 173 C6
Levett Way BN26 .... 173 C6
Levetts La TN32 .... 46 D1

Lewes Tertiary Coll (S Bldg)
BN7 .... 146 D8
Lewinscourt TN33 .... 112 D5
Lewis Ave TN40 .... 158 A5
Lewis Cl BN9 .... 168 F2
Lewis Ct **2** BN2 .... 164 C8
Lewis Rd TN38 .... 136 A3
Lewry Cl BN9 .... 179 B7
Lexden Ct BN25 .... 181 A4
Lexden Dr BN25 .... 181 A5
Lexden Lodge Ind Est TN6 ...... 38 D8
Lexden Rd BN25 .... 180 F6
Leybourne Cl BN2 .... 144 A1
Leybourne Gdns TN37 .... 136 C4
Leybourne Par BN2 .... 144 A2
Leybourne Rd BN2 .... 144 A1
Leyland Rd BN24 .... 175 D4
Leylands Pk RH15 .... 73 B5
Leylands Rd RH15 .... 73 B4
Lichfield Ct **10** BN2 .... 164 F5
Lifeboat Mus BN21 .... 185 A1
Lilac Cl BN23 .... 173 D3
Lillesden Cotts TN18 .... 45 E7
Lillywhite Cl RH15 .... 72 F5
Limden Cl TN5 .... 42 F6
Lime Cl Frant TN3 .... 17 B3
Hastings TN36 .... 136 B1
Uckfield TN22 .... 78 D8
Lime Cross BN27 .... 130 F5
Lime Hill Rd TN1 .... 8 A4
Lime Tree Ave TN22 .... 78 D7
Lime Tree Gr RH16 .... 51 C7
Lime Tree Terr TN19 .... 62 A6
Lime Way TN1 .... 82 B6
Limekiln Ct TN6 .... 26 C3
Limes The Dormans Park RH19 .. 1 A5
13 Eastbourne BN21 .... 184 E4
Limetree Ave BN22 .... 173 D3
Limney Rd BN2 .... 164 E7
Linchmere BN2 .... 164 F7
Linchmere Ave BN2 .... 177 C5
Lincoln Ave BN2 .... 178 A7
Lincoln Ave S BN10 .... 178 A7
Lincoln Cl Eastbourne BN20 ... 188 C8
2 Hastings TN38 .... 136 A4
Lincoln Cotts BN2 .... 189 B6
Lincoln Ct Eastbourne BN20 ... 184 B7
Peacehaven BN10 .... 178 A7
Lincoln Rd BN41 .... 162 B7
Lincoln St BN2 .... 189 B7
Lincoln Wood RH16, RH17 ...... 50 C5
Linden Ave RH19 .... 1 C2
Linden Chase TN2 .... 78 D7
Linden Cl Eastbourne BN22 ..... 173 E2
Royal Tunbridge Wells TN2 .... 8 A2
Linden Ct TN22 .... 78 C7
Linden Gdns TN2 .... 7 F1
Linden Gr Hailsham BN27 .... 129 C3
Haywards Heath RH16 .... 51 B7
Linden Park Rd TN2 .... 8 A2
Linden Rd TN40 .... 157 C3
Lindens The **4** BN2 .... 189 B7
Lindfield BN2 .... 141 A1
Lindfield Ave BN25 .... 181 C2
Lindfield Cl BN2 .... 177 B6
Lindfield Ct **1** BN2 .... 143 C2
Lindfield Cty Inf Sch RH16 ...... 51 A7
Lindfield Cty Jun Sch RH16 .... 51 B7
Lindfield Ent Pk RH16 .... 51 C6
Lindfield Rd Eastbourne BN22 . 173 D1
Lindfield Sch The BN22 .... 173 D2
Lindon Cl BN20 .... 183 B1
Lindsay Cl BN20 .... 184 C2
Lingfield Rd RH19 .... 1 D3
Link Rd BN20 .... 184 D1
Link The Friston BN20 .... 183 C2
Rye TN31 .... 93 A5
Link Way TN2 .... 8 E8
Linkden Cotts TN18 .... 47 E5
Links Ave BN10, BN9 .... 179 A7
Links Cl Crowborough TN6 .... 25 D2
Portslade-by-Sea BN41 .... 162 C8
Seaford BN25 .... 181 A2
Links Dr TN40 .... 157 E4
Links (Golf Course) The
BN20 .... 184 D2
Links Rd Portslade-by-Sea BN41 162 C8
Seaford BN25 .... 181 A2
Links The Bexhill TN40 .... 157 D3
Hastings TN38 .... 158 F8
Links Way TN31 .... 94 E2
Linkswood BN21 .... 184 E2
Linkway Eastbourne BN20 .... 184 B7
Westham BN24 .... 174 E6
Linkway The BN1 .... 143 B1
Linley Cl Bexhill TN40 .... 157 D4
Hastings TN34 .... 137 A3
Linley Dr TN34 .... 137 A3
Linnet Cl BN23 .... 174 C2
Linnet Gn TN22 .... 78 D5
Linthouse BN10 .... 167 D2
Linton Cres TN34 .... 159 E8
Linton Ct TN34 .... 159 E8
Linton Rd Hastings TN34 .... 159 E8
Hove BN3 .... 162 F8
Lion Hill BN23, BN24 .... 174 B5
Lion La BN27 .... 185 B3
Lion Mews **4** BN3 .... 162 F7
Lion St TN31 .... 93 C5
Lionel Rd TN40 .... 157 E3
Lions Ct BN2 .... 164 E5
Lions Dene BN1 .... 142 D4
Lions Gdns BN1 .... 142 D2
Lions Pl BN25 .... 180 F2
Liphook Cl BN1 .... 143 C1

Lipscombe Rd TN2 .... 8 D6
Liptraps La TN1, TN2 .... 8 D7
Lismore Rd BN21 .... 185 A2
Lister Ave BN23 .... 174 A1
Lister Rd BN23 .... 174 A1
Litlington Ct **4** BN25 .... 180 C4
Little Bayham Cotts TN3 .... 18 F4
Little Bentswood RH16 .... 50 F5
Little Bentswood CHRH16 .... 50 F5
Little Black Hill RH16 .... 51 B7
Little Common Cty Prim Sch
TN39 .... 156 D4
Little Common Rd TN39 .... 156 E5
Little Copse Rd BN6 .... 97 E6
Little Cres TN39 .... 177 B5
Little East St Brighton BN2 ..... 189 A4
Lewes BN7 .... 123 D1
Little Footway TN3 .... 6 F3
Little George St BN2 .... 189 A4
Little Horsted CE Prim Sch
TN22 .... 78 C1
Little Iridge Farm Cotts TN19 .. 45 C1
Little King St RH19 .... 1 E1
Little London Rd TN21 .... 106 F8
Little Mallett TN3 .... 6 F3
Little Mead BN8 .... 123 A7
Little Mount Sion TN1 .... 8 A2
Little Paddock
Crowborough TN6 .... 25 E1
Heathfield TN21 .... 82 A7
Ringmer BN8 .... 124 E6
Little Park Cotts TN33 .... 112 E5
Little Pk TN5 .... 29 E5
Little Preston St BN1 .... 163 E5
Little Ridge Ave TN37 .... 136 C5
Little Ridge Cty Prim Sch
TN37 .... 136 C5
Little Sherwood Ind Pk TN36 .. 116 D5
Little Sunnyside TN6 .... 25 F1
Little Trogers La TN20 .... 40 B4
Little Twitten TN39 .... 156 C3
Little Western St **1** BN1 ...... 163 E5
Littlemead TN22 .... 35 C3
Littleworth Cl BN2 .... 165 F7
Living World The BN25 .... 181 F4
Livingstone Ho **5** BN3 .... 163 B7
Livingstone Rd
Burgess Hill RH15 .... 72 F3
Hove BN3 .... 163 B7
Livingstone St BN2 .... 164 D5
Lloyd Cl BN3 .... 163 C8
Lloyd Rd BN3 .... 163 C8
Lockitt Way BN7 .... 145 E5
Locks Cres BN41 .... 141 B1
Locks Ct **10** BN42 .... 161 E7
Locks Hill BN41 .... 141 B1
Lockwood Cl BN2 .... 165 E7
Lockwood Cres BN2 .... 165 E7
Loder Pl BN1 .... 142 F2
Loder Rd BN1 .... 142 F2
Lodge Ave BN22 .... 173 C1
Lodge Cl East Grinstead RH19 ... 1 D1
Portslade-by-Sea BN41 .... 140 F2
Lodge Hill La BN6 .... 98 C4
Lodge La BN6 .... 98 B2
Lodge Rd TN35 .... 160 C5
Lodge The Brighton BN2 .... 189 B8
14 Eastbourne BN21 .... 185 A2
Lodsworth Cl BN2 .... 164 F7
Lomaria Ct TN2 .... 8 C4
Lomas La TN18 .... 47 F5
Lomond Ave BN1 .... 143 B7
London Meed Cty Prim Sch
RH15 .... 73 A1
London Rd Bexhill TN39, TN40 . 157 B5
Brighton BN1 .... 189 A7
Brighton, Withdene BN1 .... 142 D4
Burgess Hill RH15 .... 72 F5
Crowborough TN6 .... 25 E4
Danehill RH17 .... 34 A4
East Grinstead RH19 .... 1 C3
East Hoathly BN8 .... 105 A5
Flimwell TN5 .... 32 D3
Forest Row RH18 .... 11 E4
Hailsham BN27 .... 129 A2
Hassocks BN6, RH15 .... 97 E6
Hastings TN37, TN38 .... 159 C8
Hurst Green TN19 .... 45 A3
John's Cross TN32, TN33 .... 87 D3
Pyecombe BN1, BN45 .... 119 C4
Royal Tunbridge Wells TN4 ...... 8 A8
Royal Tunbridge Wells,
Mount Sion TN1, TN2, TN4 ...... 8 A3
Uckfield TN22 .... 55 D2
London Road Sta BN1 .... 164 A8
London Terr BN1 .... 189 A7
Loney Ct **1** BN43 .... 161 C8
Long Acre Cl BN21 .... 184 D5
Long Ave TN40 .... 158 A6
Long Barn Motor Mus TN1 ...... 80 F8
Long Hos TN32 .... 85 D5
Long La TN33 .... 88 E1
Long Man The BN26 .... 171 E3
Long Meads TN3, TN4 .... 7 B4
Long Park Cnr BN6 .... 98 D2
Long Slip TN3 .... 7 A3
Long Wlk RH16 .... 51 B4
Longacre Ct TN34 .... 136 C6
Longfield Rd TN2 .... 8 D8
Longhill Cl BN2 .... 165 E4
Longhill Rd BN2 .... 165 E4
Longhill Sch BN2 .... 165 E4
Longhurst **9** Brighton BN2 ... 164 B7
Burgess Hill RH15 .... 73 D2
Longhurst Cotts BN8 .... 75 D7
Longland Rd BN20 .... 184 C4
Longridge Ave BN2 .... 177 D5
Longstone Rd BN21 .... 185 A3

Longview TN21 .... 82 A5
Longview Way TN1 .... 8 D7
Lonsdale Gdns TN1, TN2 .... 8 A3
Lookout The BN10 .... 167 D3
Loose Farm Barns TN33 .... 113 A2
Loose Farm Cotts TN33 .... 113 A2
Lordine La TN32 .... 66 B4
Lords La TN35 .... 137 D3
Lords The BN25 .... 180 E6
Lordslaine Cl BN20 .... 188 D8
Lordswell La TN6 .... 37 E8
Loriners Ct BN3 .... 162 D8
Lorna Rd BN3 .... 163 D7
Lorne Rd BN1 .... 189 A8
Lorraine Ct **7** BN3 .... 163 E7
Lorraine Rd BN9 .... 179 D7
Lossenham La TN18 .... 48 D3
Lottbridge Dr BN22 .... 173 F1
Lottbridge Dro
Eastbourne BN22, BN23 .... 185 B7
Eastbourne BN23 .... 185 D7
Lottbridge Rdbt BN22 .... 185 A8
Lovat Mead TN38 .... 158 E6
Love La Eastbourne BN20 .... 184 D3
Mayfield TN20 .... 39 F2
Rye TN31 .... 93 B6
Lovegrove Ct BN3 .... 162 E8
Lovell Ct BN2 .... 184 D5
Lover's Wlk BN1 .... 163 F8
Lowdells Cl RH19 .... 1 C4
Lowdells Dr RH19 .... 1 D4
Lowdells La RH19 .... 1 C3
Lower Bevendean Ave BN2 .... 143 E1
Lower Chalvington Pl BN2 ..... 164 E5
Lower Church Rd RH15 .... 72 F3
Lower Cross Cotts TN31 .... 91 E2
Lower Dene RH19 .... 2 A1
Lower Dicker BN27 .... 128 C3
Lower Dr Seaford BN25 .... 180 F5
Southwick BN42 .... 140 E1
Lower Glen Rd TN37 .... 136 B4
Lower Green Rd Pembury TN2 ... 9 D7
Rusthall TN3, TN4 .... 7 C6
Lower Hazelhurst TN5 .... 31 A4
Lower High St TN5 .... 30 A4
Lower Lake TN34 .... 112 E4
Lower Market St BN3 .... 163 D5
Lower Mere RH19 .... 10 F8
Lower Park Rd TN34 .... 136 E1
Lower Pl BN9 .... 179 C7
Lower Platts TN5 .... 31 F1
Lower Rd Eastbourne BN21 .... 184 D4
Forest Row RH18 .... 11 F3
Golden Cross BN27 .... 130 E3
Lower Rock Gdns BN2 .... 189 B4
Lower Saxonbury TN6 .... 25 F2
Lower South Rd TN37, TN38 .. 136 C1
Lower Sq RH18 .... 11 E3
Lower St East Dean BN20 ...... 187 B8
Lower Street TN33 .... 133 B5
Lower Waites La TN35 .... 138 F4
Lowfield Rd RH16 .... 50 F3
Lowlands Rd RH15 .... 73 B5
Lowlands The BN27 .... 129 A1
Lowther Cl BN23 .... 174 D3
Lowther Rd BN1 .... 143 A2
Loxdale (The Swedish Folk
High Sch) BN41 .... 141 B1
Loxfield Cl BN20 .... 40 A2
Loxfield Gdns TN6 .... 26 B1
Loxwood Cl Bexhill TN39 .... 156 D5
Eastbourne BN22 .... 173 C1
Lucas RH17 .... 33 D5
Lucas Cl RH19 .... 2 A1
Lucas Grange RH16 .... 50 D5
Lucas Way RH16 .... 50 C5
Lucastes Ave RH16, RH17 .... 50 D6
Lucastes La RH16, RH17 .... 50 C6
Lucastes Rd RH16 .... 50 C5
Lucerne Cl BN41 .... 141 B1
Lucerne Rd BN1 .... 143 A1
Lucinda Way BN25 .... 180 F6
Lucraft Rd BN1, BN2 .... 144 A5
Ludley Hill TN31 .... 91 A6
Ludlow Rise BN2 .... 144 A1
Ludpit La TN19, TN32 .... 63 C6
Luke Lade Ct BN27 .... 152 C7
Lulham Cl BN10 .... 167 B4
Lullington Ave BN22 .... 162 F8
Lullington Cl Bexhill TN40 ..... 158 A6
Eastbourne BN22 .... 184 C7
Seaford BN25 .... 181 B2
Lullington Gdns TN37 .... 136 C5
Lullington Ho **3** BN21 .... 184 E4
Lunce's Hill RH16, RH17 .... 73 F8
Lundy Wlk TN34 .... 129 A2
Lureland Ct BN10 .... 178 C6
Lurgashall RH15 .... 73 C1
Lushington La BN2 .... 185 A2
Lushington Rd BN21 .... 185 A2
Lustrells Cl BN2 .... 177 B6
Lustrells Cres BN2 .... 177 C6
Lustrells Rd BN2 .... 177 A6
Lustrells Vale BN2 .... 177 C6
Luther St BN2 .... 164 C7
Luton Cl BN21 .... 184 C6
Luxford Cl TN22 .... 78 C7
Luxford Dr TN6 .... 38 A8
Luxford La TN6 .... 38 A8
Luxford Rd Crowborough TN6 ... 38 A8
Haywards Heath RH16 .... 51 B7
Luxford's La RH19 .... 11 B6
Lychgates Ct TN40 .... 157 D5
Lydd Cl BN23 .... 174 D2
Lydd Rd TN31 .... 95 C1
Lymden La TN5 .... 43 A7
Lyminster Ave BN1 .... 143 A5

Entry	Ref
Lynchet Cl BN1	143 C3
Lynchet Down BN1	143 C2
Lynchet Wlk BN1	143 C2
Lynchets Cres BN3	141 D3
Lynchets The BN7	123 E3
Lynden Ct 6 BN1	142 E2
Lyndhurst Ave TN34	137 A4
Lyndhurst Ct BN3	163 D7
Lyndhurst Rd BN3	163 D7
Lynholm Rd BN26	173 C6
Lynton Cl East Grinstead RH19	2 A2
Hurstpierpoint BN6	97 B5
Lynton Park Ave RH19	2 A2
Lynton St BN2	164 C7
Lynwood TN3	15 C6
Lynwood Cl TN37	136 D5
Lynwood Rd BN2	177 C4
Lyon Cl BN3	163 D7
Lyoth La RH16	51 C4
Lyoth Villas RH16	51 C4
Lytham Cl TN38	158 F8
Mabb's Hill TN5	42 F7
Maberley Rd TN39, TN40	157 C6
Mackerel Hill TN31	68 F4
Mackerel's Rocks BN8	76 F3
Mackie Ave Brighton BN1	143 A7
Keymer BN6	98 A5
Macmillan Dr BN2	184 C5
Madehurst Cl BN2	164 D5
Madeira Dr BN2	164 C4
Madeira Pk TN1	8 B2
Madeira Pl BN2	189 B4
Maderia Dr TN37	136 C3
Mafeking Rd BN2	143 D1
Magdalen Cl BN2	174 C3
Magdalen Rd Bexhill TN40	157 D4
Hastings TN37	159 D7
Magna Ct TN40	157 B4
Magnolia Cl TN21	82 B5
Magnolia Dr BN22	173 D2
Magnolia Wlk BN22	173 D2
Magpie Cl Bexhill TN39	156 C6
Hastings TN38	158 E8
Magpie Rd BN2	174 C3
Magreed La TN21	59 E2
Maidstone Rd TN2	9 E8
Main Rd Icklesham TN35, TN36	116 D5
Westfield TN35	114 E4
Main St Iden TN31	70 B4
Northiam TN31	67 B5
Peasmarsh TN31	69 B2
Mainstone Rd 1 BN3	162 F7
Maitland Ct TN34	136 E6
Major Cl BN1	143 B1
Major York's Rd TN4	7 F2
Malcolm Gdns BN26	173 A7
Maldon Rd BN1	142 D2
Malines Ave BN10	178 B8
Malines Ave S BN10	178 A7
Mallard Cl BN22	184 F8
Mallard Dr TN22	78 C5
Mallard Pl RH19	10 F8
Mallett Cl 3 BN25	180 E2
Malling BN7	123 D3
Malling Down BN7	123 E3
Malling Hill BN7	123 E2
Malling House	
(Sussex Pol HQ) BN7	123 D3
Malling Ind Est BN7	123 E2
Malling St 1 Lewes BN7	123 E1
Lewes BN7	123 E2
Mallory Rd BN3	142 C2
Malt House Trad Est BN43	161 B7
Malthouse Bsns Pk The TN31	69 C2
Malthouse Ct 14 BN2	189 B5
Malthouse La	
Burgess Hill BN6, RH15	72 C2
Peasmarsh TN31	69 B2
Peasmarsh TN31	69 D2
Malthouse Trad Est BN43	161 B7
Malthouse Way BN2	123 A7
Maltings Barn The 6 BN7	123 E1
Maltings The Burgess Hill BN6	72 D4
Peasmarsh TN31	69 B2
Malton Way TN2	8 F7
Malvern Cl BN22	173 E4
Malvern Ho TN39	157 B3
Malvern St 12 BN3	163 B7
Malvern Way TN34	137 B4
Manaton Cl RH16	50 F4
Manchester Rd TN33	133 A6
Manchester St BN2	189 A4
Mandalay Ct BN1	142 D4
Manhattan Ct BN1	142 D4
Manhattan Gdns TN35	137 D4
Manifold Rd BN22	185 B4
Mann St TN34	159 F8
Manning Cl RH19	1 D2
Manor Ave BN6	98 A5
Manor Cl Brighton BN2	164 E5
Broyle Side BN8	124 F7
Burgess Hill RH15	73 D4
Horam TN21	106 F7
Icklesham TN36	116 F5
Royal Tunbridge Wells TN4	7 F2
Seaford BN25	181 B3
Southwick BN42	162 A8
Uckfield TN22	78 C8
Willingdon BN20	173 B2
Manor Cotts TN3	20 B5
Manor Cres BN2	164 E5
Manor Ct Seaford BN25	181 B3
Southwick BN42	162 A7
Manor Cty Prim Sch TN22	78 D8
Manor Dr BN10	167 B1
Manor End TN22	78 C8
Manor Gdns BN2	164 E5
Manor Gn BN2	164 E5
Manor Hall Cty Fst Sch	
BN42	161 F7
Manor Hall Cty Mid Sch	
BN42	161 F8
Manor Hall Rd BN42	161 F8
Manor Hill BN2	164 E6
Manor Paddock BN2	164 E4
Manor Park BN27	129 A3
Manor Park Rd BN26	173 A6
Manor Park Rd BN27	129 A3
Manor Pk TN4	7 E3
Manor Pl BN2	164 E4
Manor Rd Bexhill TN40	157 D4
Brighton BN2	164 E5
Burgess Hill RH15	73 D4
East Grinstead RH19	1 C2
Eastbourne BN22	174 A2
Hastings TN34	160 A5
Horam TN21	106 F8
Rusthall TN4	7 C4
Seaford BN25	181 B3
Manor Rd N BN25	181 B3
Manor Way Brighton BN2	164 E5
Crowborough TN6	37 E8
Eastbourne BN24	184 B8
Polegate BN26	173 B6
Uckfield TN22	78 C8
Mansell Cl BN2	156 C4
Mansell Ct RH15	73 B3
Mansell Rd BN43	161 B8
Mansers La BN27	128 C3
Mansfield Rd BN3	162 E7
Mansion Cl RH15	73 D3
Manston Way TN34	136 E2
Mantell Cl BN23	185 D8
Mantell Ho 2 BN2	189 B5
Manton Cl BN23	185 D8
Manton Rd BN2	143 E1
Manvers Rd BN20	184 B3
Maple Ave TN39	156 C3
Maple Cl Brighton TN39	156 C3
Burgess Hill RH15	73 B5
Haywards Heath RH16	51 B3
Maresfield TN22	55 A4
Royal Tunbridge Wells TN2	8 A1
Woodingdean BN2	165 E7
Maple Ct BN27	152 A8
Maple Dr Burgess Hill RH15	73 A5
East Grinstead RH19	2 A1
Maple Gdns BN3	141 F1
Maple Hts TN37	136 B7
Maple Leaf Cl BN9	179 B7
Maple Rd Eastbourne BN23	185 D7
Peacehaven Heights BN10	178 F6
Maple Wlk TN39	156 C3
Maplehurst Cl TN37	136 B7
Maplehurst Dr TN37	136 C8
Maplehurst Rd	
Eastbourne BN22	173 D2
Hastings TN37	136 B7
Portslade-by-Sea BN41	141 A1
Maplehurst Rise TN37	136 B7
Mapleleaf Gdns BN26	173 A8
Maples Cotts TN22	80 A6
Maplewood 7 BN1	142 E3
Marbles Rd BN6	76 D7
Marchants Cl BN6	97 A6
Marchants Dr TN31	94 F2
Marchants Rd BN6	97 A6
Marchants Way RH15	72 F5
Marcia Cl BN20	184 A8
Marcus Gdns TN38	136 A5
Mardan Ct TN38	159 B7
Marden Cl BN2	144 E1
Marden Cl BN23	157 A3
Marden's Hill TN6	25 B6
Mare Bay Cl TN38	135 E7
Maresfield Bonners	
CE Prim Sch	55 B4
Maresfield Dr BN24	175 E6
Maresfield Rd BN2	164 E5
Margaret Ct BN10	178 B7
Margaret St BN2	189 B4
Margery Rd BN3	162 D8
Marina Bexhill TN39, TN40	157 C2
Hastings TN38	159 B6
Marina Court Ave TN40	157 C2
Marina Dr Rottingdean BN2	165 C2
Marina Gdns BN2	189 B4
Marina Par Brighton BN2	164 C4
Eastbourne BN21, BN22	185 B3
Hastings TN34	160 A3
Seaford BN25	180 C3
Marine Parade Rd 15 BN22	185 B3
Marine Rd Eastbourne BN22	185 B3
Pevensey Bay BN24	185 D5
Marine Sq BN2	164 C4
Marine Terr BN2	175 D5
Marine Terrace Mews 7 BN2	164 C4
Marine View 3 BN2	189 B5
Mariners Quay BN2	164 F3
Mariteau Ho TN36	117 E7
Marjoram Pl BN43	140 B1
Mark Cl BN25	181 C2
Mark Cross BN8	126 B2
Mark Cross CE Prim Sch TN6	28 A3
Mark La BN21	185 A2
Market La 7 BN7	123 D1
Market Pas 6 Hastings TN34	160 A3
9 Hastings, St Leonards TN38	159 C6
Market Pl Burgess Hill RH15	73 A2
Hailsham BN27	152 C7
Haywards Heath RH16	50 E6
14 Royal Tunbridge Wells TN2	39 F2
Market Rd Battle TN33	112 C5
Rye TN31	93 C5
Market Sq Battle TN33	112 D5
1 Hailsham BN27	152 C7
Royal Tunbridge Wells TN2	8 B4
Market St Brighton BN1	189 A5
Hastings TN37, TN38	159 C6
Lewes BN7	123 D1
13 Royal Tunbridge Wells TN2	8 A2
Rye TN31	93 C5
Market Terr 8 TN38	159 C6
Markland Way TN2	78 A7
Marklye La TN21	59 B1
Markstakes Cnr BN8	75 E1
Markstakes La BN8	75 F1
Marlborough Cl	
Eastbourne BN23	174 D3
Hastings TN38	136 A1
Royal Tunbridge Wells TN4	7 A4
Marlborough Ct	
Burgess Hill RH15	72 E3
1 Hove BN3	163 C6
Marlborough Dr RH15	73 C2
Marlborough Mews BN1	189 F5
Marlborough Pl BN1, BN2	189 A6
Marlborough St BN1	189 F5
Marle Ave RH15	73 A4
Marle Green Cotts TN21	107 B6
Marley Cl TN33	112 F4
Marley Gdns TN33	112 F4
Marley La TN33	113 B6
Marley Lodge BN2	189 B7
Marley Rd TN31	93 A6
Marley Rise TN33	112 F4
Marline Ave TN38	136 A4
Marline Rd TN38	136 A4
Marlinspike The BN43	161 A6
Marlow Ave BN2	185 B6
Marlow Ct BN2	189 B7
Marlow Dr Hastings TN37	136 C5
Haywards Heath RH16	51 C4
Marlow Rd BN2	164 F4
Marlowes The TN40	157 E5
Marlpit Cl RH19	1 E4
Marlpit Gdns TN5	31 E1
Marlpit Rd RH19	21 A6
Marlpit The TN5	29 E5
Marlpits La TN33	133 A7
Marmion Rd BN3	162 F7
Marsden Rd BN23	174 E1
Marsh Ho 3 BN43	161 D7
Marsh Quarter La TN18	47 C3
Marshall Cl BN22	173 D1
Marshall La BN9	179 C7
Marshall Rd BN22	185 A8
Marshall Rdbt BN22	174 A1
Marshalls Row BN1	189 A7
Marshfoot La BN27	152 E8
Marshlands Cty Prim Sch	
BN27	152 D8
Marshlands La TN21	82 A7
Marston Ct 6 BN3	163 E7
Martello Ct Pevensey Bay BN24	175 C3
1 South Heighton BN9	168 D1
Martello Rd Eastbourne BN22	185 D6
Seaford BN25	180 E2
Martello Tower Mus BN25	180 E1
Martens Field TN33	146 E1
Martha Gunn Cl BN2	143 E1
Martin Ct BN22	173 D1
Martin Rd BN3	141 D1
Martineau La TN35	137 F5
Martingale Cl TN37	136 C5
Martins The BN10	167 B1
Martlet Ct TN6	25 F1
Martlet Ho Brighton BN1	164 A8
Saltdean BN2	177 D4
Martlet The BN3	142 D1
Martlets Bexhill TN40	157 E5
Lower Willingdon BN22	173 B3
Martlets The Broad Oak TN31	90 C4
Burgess Hill RH15	73 A3
Crowborough TN6	25 F1
Hailsham BN27	152 A7
Lewes BN7	123 D3
South Chailey BN8	100 D7
Martletts The	
Burwash Common TN19	60 F3
Ringmer BN8	124 E6
Martyn's Cl BN2	165 E4
Martyns Pl RH19	11 A8
Martyns Way TN38, TN40	158 A5
Marwick Ct TN38	159 B8
Marwick Terr TN38	159 B8
Mary Burfield Ct 3 TN21	82 A7
Mary Stamford Gn TN31	94 A3
Maryan Ct BN27	152 B8
Maryland Rd TN2	8 D1
Marylands RH16	50 F5
Maskelyne Rd BN27	131 A1
Mason Cl RH19	1 E2
Mason Rd Rye TN31	93 A5
Seaford BN25	180 F4
Matlock Rd Brighton BN1, BN3	142 D2
Eastbourne BN20	188 E8
Maudlin Ct TN37	159 C8
Maunsell Rd TN38	135 F5
Maurice Rd BN25	180 F1
Maxfield Cl BN20	184 B5
Maxfield La TN35	115 D2
May Ave BN25	181 B3
May Gdns BN2	164 D7
May Rd BN2	164 D7
May Tree Gdns TN40	157 F6
Mayfair Dr BN26	172 F4
Mayfield Ave BN10	178 D6
Mayfield CE Prim Sch TN20	40 B3
Mayfield Cl Brighton BN1	143 A5
Royal Tunbridge Wells TN2	39 F2
Mayfield Coll TN20	40 C6
Mayfield Cres Broad Oak BN27	59 E1
Burgess Hill RH15	73 B3
Saltdean BN2	177 C6
Mayfield Flat TN21, TN22	81 A8
Hastings TN38	135 D2
Mayfield Pk TN5	29 C5
Mayfield Rd BN22	185 A4
Mayfield Rd Mark Cross TN6	28 A2
Rotherfield TN6	39 A7
Royal Tunbridge Wells TN4	7 F4
Mayfield Way TN37	157 C5
Mayflower Ct	
Haywards Heath RH16	50 F4
9 Shoreham-by-Sea BN43	161 A6
Mayflower Rd RH16	50 F4
Mayflower Sq BN1	189 A7
Mayhew Way BN7	123 D2
Maynard's RH15	72 F1
Maynard's Green	
Cty Prim Sch TN21	82 A2
Mayne Waye TN34	137 B4
Mayo Cl 5 BN2	164 B8
Mayo La TN39	157 A8
Mayo Rd BN2	164 B8
Mayo Rise TN39	157 A8
Maypole Cotts TN22	56 B8
Maypole Rd Ashurst Wood RH19	11 E6
East Grinstead RH19	1 D2
Maytham Rd TN17	49 C7
Maytree Cotts BN8	100 C7
Maytree Wlk BN3	141 E1
Mayvern Ct TN6	25 F3
Mayview Cl TN21	59 E1
Maywood Ave BN22, BN26	173 E2
Maze Hill TN38	159 B7
Maze Hill Terr TN38	159 B7
McIndoe Rd RH19	1 D3
McWilliam Rd BN2	144 C1
Meachants Cl BN20	173 B2
Meachants La BN20	173 B2
Mead The Bexhill TN39	156 D4
Royal Tunbridge Wells TN2	8 C2
Meadow Bank TN33	112 E4
Meadow Cl Hailsham BN27	129 B1
Hastings TN38	136 A4
Hove BN3	142 B3
Portslade-by-Sea BN41	141 B2
Rottingdean BN2	165 F3
Southwick BN42	162 A8
Meadow Cres TN39	157 C7
Meadow Dr RH16	51 B6
Meadow Hill Rd 6 TN1, TN2	8 B3
Meadow Ho BN8	100 E7
Meadow La Burgess Hill RH15	72 F1
Haywards Heath RH16	51 B6
Meadow Par BN2	165 F3
Meadow Pl TN22	78 C6
Meadow Rd Groombridge TN3	15 C7
Hailsham BN27	152 A6
Royal Tunbridge Wells TN1	8 A4
Rusthall TN4	7 C4
Meadow The TN2	9 E8
Meadow Vale BN2	165 E5
Meadow View Rotherfield TN6	39 B7
Westfield TN35	114 E4
Meadow View Cotts TN19	45 A3
Meadow Way	
Fairlight Cove TN35	138 E4
Heathfield TN21	82 A6
Seaford BN25	181 B3
Meadowcroft Cl RH19	1 C2
Meadowlands Ave BN22	173 D1
Meadows BN6	97 F5
Meadows Rd BN22	173 B2
Meadows The Crowborough TN6	25 F2
Hastings TN37	136 C5
Hove BN3	141 C3
Lewes BN7	123 E3
Meadowside TN33	88 E1
Meadowside Cotts TN5	31 F1
Meadowview Brighton BN2	143 E1
Lower Street TN33	133 B5
Meads Ave Bexhill TN39	156 C4
Hove BN3	141 C3
Meads Brow BN20	188 D8
Meads CE Prim Sch BN20	188 D7
Meads Cl BN3	141 C3
Meads Cl BN20	184 E1
Meads Cty Prim Sch The RH19	10 E7
Meads Gate BN20	188 E8
Meads Rd Bexhill TN39	156 C4
Eastbourne BN20, BN21	184 E1
Seaford BN25	180 F3
Meads St BN20	188 E8
Meads The Brighton BN1	143 D5
East Grinstead RH19	10 E7
Meadway Cres BN3	141 F2
Meadway Dr BN42, BN43	161 D8
Meadway The Brighton BN2	164 F5
Shoreham-by-Sea BN43	161 A6
Mealla Cl BN7	123 C3
Medina Pl BN3	163 B6
Medina Terr Hastings TN38	159 A6
Hove BN3	163 B5
Medina Villas BN3	163 B6
Medmerry Hill BN2	143 E2
Medway Crowborough TN6	26 C1
Hailsham BN27	129 A2
Medway Dr East Grinstead RH19	10 D6
Forest Row RH18	11 F2
Forest Row RH18	12 A1
Medway La BN24, BN26	174 A5
Medway Rd TN1	8 B5
Meeching Pl BN9	179 C7
Meeching Rd BN9	179 D7
Meeching Rise BN9	179 C7
Meeching Valley	
Cty Prim Sch BN9	179 B7
Meeds Rd RH15	73 A2
Meeting House La BN1	189 A5
Megrims Hill TN18	47 A6
Melbourne Rd BN22	185 B4
Melbourne St BN2	164 C8
Melfort Rd TN6	25 D1
Melrose Ave BN41	141 A1
Melrose Cl Brighton BN1	143 C2
Hailsham BN27	152 A8
Melvill La BN20	173 B1
Melville Rd BN3	163 E7
Mendip Ave BN23	174 D3
Mendip Gdns TN34	137 B3
Mendip Wlk TN2	8 D5
Menzies Rd TN37, TN38	136 B2
Mercatoria TN38	159 C6
Mercer St TN1	8 B5
Mercers TN3	7 A3
Mercia Ct TN40	157 C5
Mercread Rd BN25	180 F3
Meres La TN20	58 D7
Merevale BN1	143 B2
Merewood Ct BN21	184 E4
Mereworth Rd TN4	8 A6
Meridian Ctr BN10	178 C8
Meridian Cty Prim Sch BN10	167 C1
Meridian Ind Est The BN10	178 C7
Meridian L Ctr BN10	178 C7
Meridian Rd BN2	123 B2
Meridian Way	
East Grinstead RH19	1 F3
Peacehaven BN10	178 C7
Merivale TN34	137 A6
Merlin Cl BN3	163 D8
Merlin Ct BN27	152 E7
Merlin Way RH19	2 A3
Merlyn 12 BN21	185 A2
Mermaid Pas TN31	93 B5
Mermaid St TN31	93 B5
Merrimac Ho TN40	157 E4
Merrimede Cl TN38	159 A7
Merriments La TN18, TN19	45 D5
Merrion Cl TN4	8 B7
Merrion Way TN4	8 B7
Merston Cl BN2	165 E6
Merston Ct TN40	157 E4
Meryon Ct TN31	93 C5
Metcalfe Ave BN9	179 B8
Metropole 16 Brighton BN1	163 E5
11 Eastbourne BN23	185 B3
Mewetts Ct BN20	173 B3
Mews Ct RH19	10 F6
Mews Rd TN38	159 C6
Mews The Brighton BN1	142 E2
East Hoathly BN8	105 A5
Pembury TN2	9 C6
5 Royal Tunbridge Wells TN1	8 B3
Seaford BN25	181 B4
Meyners Ct BN2	141 C3
Michael Fields RH18	11 E2
Michael Tetley Hall	
(Nursery Trng Coll,	
Dr Barnardo's Home) TN2	8 D5
Michel Cl BN20	183 C1
Michel Dene Cl BN20	183 C1
Michel Dene Rd BN20	183 C1
Michel Gr BN21	184 E4
Michelbourne Cl RH15	72 E1
Michele Cl 1 TN38	136 B1
Micheham Cl BN23	174 A4
Michelham Priory BN27	151 B7
Michelson Cl TN34	135 F4
Micklefield Sch BN25	181 B3
Micklefield Wadhurst Sch	
TN5	29 C4
Mid Sussex Golf Club The	
BN6	99 A5
Middle Dr TN22	55 A6
Middle Field TN2	9 E8
Middle Furlong BN25	180 F3
Middle Rd Bells Yew Green TN3	18 A5
Brighton BN1	142 E3
Hastings TN35	137 D4
Shoreham-by-Sea BN43	161 B7
Middle Row 1 RH19	10 F8
Middle St Brighton BN1	189 F5
Falmer BN1	144 C6
9 Hastings TN34	159 F8
Portslade-by-Sea BN41	162 B6
Middle Street Cty Prim Sch	
BN1	189 F5
Middle Way Burgess Hill RH15	73 B3
Lewes BN7	123 A1
Middle Wlk TN2	8 E8
Middleham Cl BN20	124 C4
Middlesex Ct 4 BN22	185 B4
Middlesex Rd TN40	157 D3
Middleton Ave BN3	162 D6
Middleton Dr BN23	185 E7
Middleton Rise BN1	143 E5
Middleway BN27	131 B5

Midfields Cl RH15 .... 73 B3
Midfields Dr RH15 .... 73 B3
Midfields Wlk RH15 .... 73 B4
Midhurst Rd BN22 .... 173 F2
Midhurst Rise BN1 .... 143 B6
Midhurst Wlk BN3 .... 141 F3
Midway Rd BN2 .... 165 C8
Midway The TN4 .... 7 D2
Mighell St BN2 .... 189 B5
Milchester Ho BN20 .... 188 E8
Milcote Ave BN3 .... 162 F8
Mildenhall Dr TN37 .... 136 B3
Mildmay Cl BN8 .... 124 D6
Mildmay Rd BN7 .... 123 A1
Mile End Cotts BN1 .... 142 E6
Mile Oak Cres BN42 .... 140 F1
Mile Oak Cty Prim Sch BN41 . 140 F3
Mile Oak Gdns BN41 .... 141 A1
Mile Oak Rd
  Portslade-by-Sea BN41, BN42 .... 140 F3
  Southwick BN41, BN42 .... 140 F1
Milestones TN21 .... 82 B8
Milfoil Dr BN23 .... 174 B3
Military Rd TN30, TN31 .... 70 F3
Mill Brooks BN8 .... 100 D7
Mill Cl East Grinstead RH19 .... 10 E7
  Friston BN20 .... 183 A1
  Hastings TN35 .... 137 E4
  Portslade-by-Sea BN41 .... 141 C1
  Ringmer BN8 .... 124 E5
  South Chailey BN8 .... 100 D7
  Tilsmore TN21 .... 81 F7
  Wannock BN26 .... 172 F4
  Westfield TN35 .... 114 E5
Mill Cnr TN31 .... 67 A3
Mill Cotts RH19 .... 10 E7
Mill Cres TN6 .... 25 F3
Mill Dr Crowborough TN6 .... 25 F3
  Hove BN3 .... 142 A3
  Seaford BN25 .... 181 A3
Mill Dro Seaford BN25 .... 180 A5
  Uckfield TN22 .... 78 C6
Mill Gap Rd BN21 .... 184 F4
Mill Gdns Heathfield TN21 .... 82 A5
  Ringmer BN8 .... 124 D5
Mill Green Rd RH16 .... 50 E5
Mill Hill Cl RH16 .... 50 E5
Mill La Barcombe BN8 .... 101 D2
  Clayton BN45, BN6 .... 119 E7
  Crowborough TN6 .... 25 E2
  Dormansland RH7 .... 1 F8
  East Hoathly BN8 .... 105 A5
  Flackley Ash TN31 .... 68 F3
  Goddards' Green BN6 .... 72 A3
  Hastings TN35 .... 137 E5
  Hellingly BN27 .... 129 A6
  Hooe Common TN33 .... 132 F2
  Mark Cross TN6 .... 28 A3
  Portslade-by-Sea BN41 .... 141 B1
  Rodmell BN7 .... 167 D8
  Uckfield TN22 .... 78 C6
  Westfield TN35 .... 114 E5
Mill Mead BN8 .... 124 E5
Mill Path BN8 .... 124 E5
Mill Pk RH15 .... 73 B3
Mill Race BN6 .... 97 E8
Mill Rd Brighton BN1 .... 142 C6
  Burgess Hill RH15 .... 73 B3
  Eastbourne BN21 .... 184 E5
  Hailsham BN27 .... 152 D6
  Lewes BN7 .... 123 E3
  Ringmer BN8 .... 124 D5
  Rye TN31 .... 93 C7
  Southwick BN41 .... 162 B7
  Tilsmore TN21 .... 81 F7
  Winchelsea TN36 .... 117 E8
Mill Rd Ind Est BN41 .... 162 B7
Mill Rise Brighton BN1 .... 142 C5
  Heathfield TN21 .... 82 A8
  Robertsbridge TN32 .... 64 A3
Mill St BN1 .... 144 C7
Mill Stream Meadow RH16 .... 50 D7
Mill View BN8 .... 124 C4
Mill View Cl BN24 .... 174 D6
Mill View Rd TN39 .... 157 B7
Mill Way East Grinstead RH19 .... 10 E7
  Wannock BN26 .... 172 E4
Mill Wood RH15 .... 73 B3
Milland Cl TN40 .... 157 E6
Milland Rd BN27 .... 129 B1
Millbank BN7 .... 73 B4
Millberg Rd BN25 .... 181 C4
Millbrook Bsns Pk TN6 .... 38 D8
Millbrook Cl TN21 .... 107 A7
Millbrook Gdns BN20 .... 184 B6
Millbrook Ind Est TN6 .... 38 D8
Millbrook Rd TN6 .... 26 A3
Millcroft BN1 .... 142 C5
Millcroft Ave BN42 .... 140 E1
Millcroft Gdns BN42 .... 140 E1
Millcross Rd BN41 .... 141 B1
Milldown Rd BN25 .... 180 F3
Miller's Hill TN35 .... 114 E6
Miller's Rd BN1 .... 142 E1
Millers Rise BN27 .... 152 A6
Millers Way RH15 .... 73 B4
Millfield TN33 .... 133 A6
Millfield Cl Newick BN8 .... 76 C7
  Seaford BN25 .... 181 B4
Millfield Cotts BN2 .... 164 D4
Millfield Rise TN40 .... 157 C4
Millfields BN25 .... 181 B4
Millfields Ct BN26 .... 173 A7
Millham Cl TN39 .... 156 F5
Millington Ct TN22 .... 78 C6

Millrace The BN26 .... 172 F4
Millstream Cl TN3 .... 5 D2
Millstream Gdns BN26 .... 172 F4
Millward Rd BN24 .... 175 C3
Millwood Cl TN22 .... 55 D4
Millwood La TN22 .... 55 C4
Millwood Rd TN39 .... 157 A8
Millyard Cres BN2 .... 165 D7
Milner Flats BN2 .... 189 B5
Milner Rd BN2 .... 143 D1
Milnthorpe Gdns BN20 .... 188 E8
Milnthorpe Rd
  Eastbourne BN20 .... 188 E8
  Hove BN3 .... 162 F8
Milton Cres East Grinstead RH19 10 C8
  Eastbourne BN21 .... 184 C4
Milton Ct RH16 .... 50 D5
Milton Dr
  Royal Tunbridge Wells TN1, TN2 ... 8 D7
  Southwick BN42 .... 161 F8
Milton Rd Brighton BN2 .... 189 B7
  Eastbourne BN20, BN21 .... 184 C4
  Haywards Heath RH16 .... 50 D6
  St BN24 .... 174 B7
Milward Cres TN34 .... 160 A4
Milward Ct BN43 .... 161 C8
Milward Rd TN34 .... 160 A5
Mimosa Cl BN26 .... 173 A7
Mimosa Ct BN1 .... 143 B3
Mindleheim Ave RH19 .... 2 B2
Minnels The BN6 .... 98 A3
Minsted Sq TN39 .... 156 C2
Minster Cl BN24 .... 173 A7
Mint The TN31 .... 93 B5
Mistley Cl TN40 .... 158 A6
Mitchelldean BN10 .... 167 C1
Mitre Ho BN1 .... 163 E5
Mitten Rd TN40 .... 157 C4
Moat Croft TN20 .... 184 E3
Moat Croft Rd BN21 .... 184 E4
Moat Farm TN2 .... 17 A7
Moat La Cowden TN8 .... 4 E7
  Waldron TN21, BN8 .... 80 D2
  Westfield TN33 .... 114 B3
Moat Rd RH19 .... 1 E2
Mocatta Way RH15 .... 72 D5
Modena Rd BN3 .... 162 F7
Moira House Sch BN20 .... 188 D8
Molesey Ct TN22 .... 78 C7
Molesworth St BN3 .... 162 F8
Molyneux Almshouses TN4 .... 7 B4
Molyneux Ct TN4 .... 7 F4
Molyneux Park Rd TN4 .... 7 F4
Mona Rd BN2 .... 185 B5
Monarch Gdns
  Eastbourne BN23 .... 174 F1
  Seaford BN25 .... 181 A5
Monarch Ho BN22 .... 185 E5
Monastery Gdns TN6 .... 39 B8
Monceux Rd
  Eastbourne BN20, BN21 .... 184 C4
  Herstmonceux BN27 .... 130 E6
Monckton Way BN7 .... 145 E5
Monger's Mead BN8 .... 101 E4
Monk Cl BN1 .... 143 E6
Monk's House BN7 .... 146 E1
Monks La Lewes BN7 .... 146 C8
  Newbury's TN5 .... 30 B8
Monks Way Lewes BN7 .... 123 C3
  Northiam TN31 .... 67 B8
Monks' Wlk TN36 .... 117 E7
Monmouth St BN3 .... 163 B7
Monson Rd TN1 .... 8 B4
Monson Way TN1 .... 8 B4
Montacute Gdns TN2 .... 7 F2
Montacute Rd Lewes BN7 .... 146 A8
  Royal Tunbridge Wells TN2 .... 8 A1
Montacute Way TN22 .... 78 D8
Montague Cl BN43 .... 161 D7
Montague Ct BN2, BN43 .... 164 C4
  Shoreham-by-Sea BN43 .... 161 D7
Montague Pl BN2 .... 164 C4
Montague St BN2 .... 164 C4
Montague Way BN24 .... 174 F5
Montargis Way TN6 .... 26 A1
Montefiore Rd BN3 .... 163 E7
Monteith Cl TN3 .... 7 A3
Monterey Cl TN39 .... 156 E3
Monterey Ct BN1 .... 142 E3
Monterey Gdns TN39 .... 156 E3
Montes Hill RH16 .... 51 F8
Monteswood La RH16, RH17 .... 52 B8
Montford Cl BN43 .... 161 D8
Montfort Cl BN24 .... 174 F6
Montfort Rd BN24 .... 174 F6
Montgomery Rd Hastings TN35 137 D5
  Royal Tunbridge Wells TN4 .... 8 B7
Montgomery St BN3 .... 163 A7
Montpelier Cres BN1 .... 163 E6
Montpelier Lodge BN1 .... 163 E6
Montpelier Pl BN1 .... 163 E6
Montpelier Rd BN1 .... 163 E6
Montpelier St BN1 .... 163 E6
Montpelier Terr BN1 .... 163 E6
Montpelier Villas BN1 .... 163 E6
Montreal Rd BN2 .... 189 B6
Montserrat TN39 .... 157 A2
Monument View BN2 .... 164 D6
Moon's La RH19, RH7, TN8 .... 2 E8
Moons Hill TN33 .... 133 B6
Moor Hall Dr TN33 .... 132 F6
Moor Hill TN18 .... 45 F8
Moor La Ashton Green BN8 .... 125 B3
  Westfield TN35 .... 114 E3
Moor Pl RH19 .... 1 D2
Moor Rd TN35 .... 114 E3
Moor The TN18 .... 45 F8
Moore Pk BN27 .... 152 D7

Moore's La TN31 .... 90 E8
Moorhurst Rd TN38 .... 135 F5
Moorings The
  East Grinstead RH19 .... 1 A3
  Eastbourne BN20 .... 188 E8
  Shoreham-by-Sea BN43 .... 161 C6
Moray Wlk BN27 .... 129 A2
Morecambe Rd BN1 .... 143 A6
Morestead BN10 .... 167 D1
Morgan Cl TN39 .... 157 B8
Morgay Wood La TN35 .... 115 E2
Morlais Pl TN36 .... 118 B6
Morlais Ridge TN36 .... 118 B6
Morland Dr TN3 .... 20 B5
Morlands Cl TN33 .... 133 B5
Morley Cl BN7 .... 146 B7
Morley St BN2 .... 189 B6
Morningside Cl BN25 .... 180 F4
Mornington Cres BN3 .... 162 D7
Mornington Mansions BN3 ... 162 D7
Morris Rd BN7 .... 123 A1
Mortain Pk BN7 .... 152 D7
Mortain Rd BN24 .... 174 F6
Mortimer Gdns BN24 .... 174 F4
Mortimer Rd Eastbourne BN22 185 A6
  Hove BN3 .... 163 A8
Morton Rd RH19 .... 10 E7
Moscow Rd TN35 .... 137 C3
Motcombe Ct TN40 .... 157 D3
Motcombe La BN21 .... 184 D4
Motcombe Pl BN21 .... 184 D4
Motcombe Rd BN21 .... 184 D4
Motte Field TN7 .... 13 E4
Mottins Hill TN6 .... 38 D8
Moulsecoomb Cty Inf Sch
  BN2 .... 143 E3
Moulsecoomb Cty Jun Sch
  BN2 .... 143 E3
Moulsecoomb Sta BN2 .... 143 D2
Moulsecoomb Way BN2 .... 143 F4
Mount Caburn Cres BN10 .... 167 C2
Mount Cl BN9 .... 179 F8
Mount Dr BN2 .... 177 D6
Mount Edgcumbe Rd TN4 .... 8 A3
Mount Ephraim TN1, TN4 .... 8 A4
Mount Ephraim Ct TN4 .... 7 F4
Mount Ephraim Rd TN1 .... 8 A4
Mount Harry Rd BN7 .... 123 A2
Mount Idol View TN39 .... 157 A8
Mount Joy TN33 .... 112 D5
Mount Pl BN7 .... 123 C1
Mount Pleasant Blackboys TN22 80 A6
  Brighton BN2 .... 189 B5
  Crowborough TN6 .... 38 B7
  Hastings TN38 .... 159 C6
  Hook Green TN3 .... 19 E6
  Mount Pleasant BN8 .... 101 E6
  Sparrow's Green TN5 .... 29 E5
  The Moor TN18 .... 45 F8
  Uckfield TN22 .... 78 C6
Mount Pleasant Ave TN2 .... 8 B3
Mount Pleasant Cres TN34 136 F1
Mount Pleasant Ct TN34 .... 160 A6
Mount Pleasant Hospl TN3 ... 137 C3
Mount Pleasant La TN3 .... 20 A6
Mount Pleasant Rd
  Hastings TN34 .... 160 A6
  Royal Tunbridge Wells TN1, TN2 .... 8 A3
Mount Rd Eastbourne BN20 .... 188 F3
  Hastings TN35 .... 160 C6
  Newhaven BN9 .... 179 F8
Mount Sion TN1 .... 8 A3
Mount St Battle TN33 .... 112 D5
  Lewes BN7 .... 146 C8
Mount The Hailsham BN27 .... 152 C6
  Hastings TN38 .... 159 B7
  Uckfield TN22 .... 78 C6
Mount View Terr BN27 .... 152 C6
Mount Zion Pl BN1 .... 189 F6
Mountain Ash Cl BN27 .... 152 A8
Mountbatten Cl TN35 .... 137 D5
Mountbatten Dr BN23 .... 185 F7
Mountfield Ct TN1 .... 8 B3
Mountfield Gdns TN2 .... 8 B3
Mountfield La TN32 .... 86 C8
Mountfield Rd
  Eastbourne BN22 .... 173 F1
  Lewes BN7 .... 146 D8
  Royal Tunbridge Wells TN2 .... 8 B3
Mountfield Villas TN32 .... 87 C5
Mountfield & Whatlington
  CE Prim Sch TN32 .... 87 D7
Mountfields BN1 .... 143 C2
Mountney Bridge Bsns Pk
  BN24 .... 174 F4
Mountney Dr BN24 .... 175 F2
Mountney Rd BN21 .... 184 C4
Mountreed TN20 .... 58 B7
Mowden Sch BN1 .... 142 D1
Moy Ave BN22 .... 185 B5
Moyne Cl BN3 .... 141 E1
Muirfield Cl RH16 .... 50 E4
Muirfield Rise TN38 .... 158 F8
Mulberry Cl Bexhill TN39 .... 156 C4
  Brighton BN1 .... 142 F3
  Eastbourne BN22, BN26 .... 173 E3
  Shoreham-by-Sea BN43 .... 140 D1
Mulberry Ct BN26 .... 173 A6
Mulberry La BN6 .... 98 B3
Mulberry Way TN21 .... 82 B5
Mulberry Wlk TN37 .... 136 D5
Munns Dr RH15 .... 73 B4
Munster Cotts BN8 .... 101 E4
Munster Gn BN8 .... 101 E4
Murray Ave BN9 .... 179 C7
Museum of Rural Life TN32 ... 64 B4
Museum of Shops BN21 .... 185 A2

Musgrave Ave RH19 .... 10 E3
Mushroom Field BN7 .... 145 E5
Muster Cl RH16 .... 50 D4
Muster Gn N RH16 .... 50 D4
Muster Gn S RH16 .... 50 D4
Mutton Hall Hill TN21 .... 82 B8
Mutton Hall La TN21 .... 82 B8
Mutton Hill RH7 .... 2 B8
Myrtle Rd Crowborough TN6 .... 25 F1
  Eastbourne BN22 .... 185 D6

Namrik Mews BN3 .... 163 A6
Nan Kemp's Grave BN7 .... 145 E6
Nan Tucks La TN22 .... 56 C2
Nanson Rd BN1 .... 143 D6
Naomi Cl BN26 .... 184 E1
Napier Ho BN2 .... 164 C7
Napier Rd Hastings TN38 .... 135 E4
  Royal Tunbridge Wells TN2 .... 8 D2
Nash La RH17 .... 52 B4
Natal Rd BN2 .... 143 D1
Neale Cl RH19 .... 1 B3
Neath Rd TN29 .... 96 A2
Neaves La BN8 .... 125 A5
Neill's Cl BN9 .... 179 C7
Neills Rd TN3 .... 19 D2
Nellington Ct TN4 .... 7 B4
Nellington Rd TN3, TN4 .... 7 B4
Nelson Dr BN23 .... 185 E6
Nelson Ho TN39 .... 156 E4
Nelson Pl BN2 .... 189 B6
Nelson Rd Hastings TN34 .... 160 A5
  Royal Tunbridge Wells TN2 .... 8 D2
Nelson Row BN2 .... 189 B5
Nesbitt Rd BN2 .... 143 D1
Nestor Ct BN1 .... 142 E1
Nether La TN22 .... 35 C3
Netherfield Gn BN2 .... 165 F8
Netherfield Hill TN33 .... 112 B7
Netherfield Hill Cotts TN33 .... 112 B7
Netherfield Rd TN33 .... 111 F8
Netherfield Way TN33 .... 86 D2
Netherwood Cl TN34 .... 136 F5
Nettleton Ct BN1 .... 143 B1
Nevill Ave Eastbourne BN22 173 E1
  Hove BN3 .... 141 F1
Nevill Cl
  Crowborough Warren TN6 .... 37 C8
  Hove BN3 .... 142 A2
Nevill Cotts BN3 .... 98 D2
Nevill Cres BN7 .... 123 A1
Nevill Ct
  Crowborough Warren TN6 .... 37 C8
  Hove BN3 .... 142 A1
Nevill Gate TN2 .... 8 B1
Nevill Gdns BN3 .... 142 A2
Nevill Gn TN22 .... 55 D1
Nevill Golf Course TN2, TN3 .... 17 D7
Nevill Lodge TN2 .... 8 C4
Nevill Pk TN2 .... 7 E3
Nevill Pl BN3 .... 142 A2
Nevill Rd Crowborough TN6 .... 25 F3
  Hove BN3 .... 142 A2
  Lewes BN7 .... 123 A2
  Rottingdean BN2 .... 165 F1
  Uckfield TN22 .... 55 D1
Nevill Ridge TN4 .... 7 D3
Nevill St TN1, TN2 .... 8 A2
Nevill Terr TN2 .... 7 F2
Nevill Way BN3 .... 142 A2
Neville Rd Eastbourne BN22 . 185 B4
  Peacehaven BN10 .... 178 D6
New Barn Cl Hailsham BN27 . 152 C6
  Portslade-by-Sea BN41 .... 141 B2
  Shoreham-by-Sea BN43 .... 140 B1
New Barn La TN22 .... 78 C5
New Barn Rd Rottingdean BN2 . 165 F3
  Shoreham-by-Sea BN43 .... 140 B1
New Church Rd BN3, BN41 .... 162 E7
New College Cl BN23 .... 174 C4
New Cotts Crowborough TN6 ..... 38 C8
  Five Ashes TN20 .... 58 B6
  Scaynes Hill RH17 .... 51 F1
New Cut Mountfield TN32 .... 87 C5
  Westfield TN35 .... 114 E4
New Dorset St BN1 .... 189 F6
New England Ho BN1 .... 189 A7
New England La Rye TN31 .... 93 C8
  Sedlescombe TN33 .... 113 F6
New England Rd Brighton BN1 189 F7
  Haywards Heath RH16 .... 50 F4
  Royal Tunbridge Wells TN4 .... 8 A2
New England Rise BN41 .... 141 A4
New England St BN1 .... 189 A7
New Farthingdale RH7 .... 2 B8
New Forest Lodge TN6 .... 37 C8
New Life Sch RH19 .... 1 D2
New Lydd Rd TN31 .... 94 E2
New Moorsite TN35 .... 114 F3
New Park Ave TN40 .... 157 C4
New Pl Eastbourne BN21 .... 184 D3
  Uckfield TN22 .... 78 C5
New Pond Hill TN21 .... 81 D6
New Rd Brighton BN1 .... 189 A5
  Crowborough TN6 .... 25 F3
  Eastbourne BN22 .... 185 B4
  Fairlight TN35 .... 138 D4
  Hailsham BN27 .... 129 C4
  Hastings TN35 .... 160 D6
  Keymer BN6 .... 98 B2
  Lewes BN7 .... 146 B7
  Mill Corner TN31 .... 67 B3
  Polegate BN26 .... 173 B6
  Ringmer BN8 .... 124 D3
  Rotherfield TN6 .... 39 C8
  Rye TN31 .... 93 D6

New Rd
  Saint's Hill TN11 .... 6 A8
  South Heighton BN9 .... 168 D1
  Uckfield TN22 .... 78 D3
New Steine BN2 .... 189 B4
New Steine Mews BN2 .... 189 B5
New Sussex Hospl BN3 .... 163 E6
New Upperton Rd BN21 .... 184 E4
New Way La BN6 .... 97 B2
New Winchelsea Rd
  TN31, TN36 .... 93 B3
Newark Pl BN2 .... 189 B6
Newbury Cotts TN5 .... 30 B8
Newbury La TN5 .... 30 C8
Newcomen Rd TN4 .... 8 A5
Newells Cl BN2 .... 144 E1
Newfield La BN9 .... 179 C7
Newfield Rd BN9 .... 179 C7
Newgate Rd TN37 .... 136 C1
Newhaven Harbour Sta BN9 .. 179 D6
Newhaven Local &
  Maritime Mus BN9 .... 168 D1
Newhaven Marine Sta BN9 .... 179 E6
Newhaven Rd BN25 .... 180 B5
Newhaven Sq BN9 .... 179 D7
Newhaven St BN2 .... 189 B6
Newhaven Town Sta BN9 .... 179 D8
Newick CE Prim Sch BN8 .... 76 C6
Newick Cl BN25 .... 181 C2
Newick Dr BN8 .... 76 C7
Newick Hill BN8 .... 76 C7
Newick House Sch RH15 .... 73 C1
Newick La TN20, TN21 .... 59 C5
Newick Rd Brighton BN1 .... 143 E4
  Eastbourne BN20, BN21 .... 184 C6
Newington Ct TN5 .... 31 E1
Newlands TN3 .... 7 A3
Newlands Ave TN39 .... 157 B5
Newlands Cl Hastings TN34 ... 136 E5
  Keymer BN6 .... 98 B3
Newlands Cres RH19 .... 1 D2
Newlands Manor Sch
  (Senior) BN25 .... 181 A4
Newlands Park Way BN8 .... 76 C7
Newlands Pl RH18 .... 11 F3
Newlands Rd Rottingdean BN2 . 177 A5
  Royal Tunbridge Wells TN4 .... 8 B7
Newlands Rise RH19 .... 8 A6
Newlands Sch BN25 .... 181 B4
Newlands Way TN4 .... 8 B7
Newmans Way TN35 .... 137 D4
Newmarket Rd BN2 .... 164 C8
Newmarket Terr BN2 .... 164 C8
Newnham Rd TN21 .... 82 A6
Newnham Way TN21 .... 82 A7
Newport Rd RH15 .... 72 F3
Newport St BN2 .... 189 B7
Newstead Pl BN1 .... 189 F7
Newtimber Dr BN41 .... 141 A1
Newton Ave RH19 .... 10 F6
Newton Cl RH16 .... 51 B7
Newton Ct RH16 .... 50 E5
Newton Pk BN27 .... 152 D7
Newton Rd
  Haywards Heath RH16 .... 51 C7
  Lewes BN7 .... 123 B2
  Peacehaven BN10 .... 178 C7
  Royal Tunbridge Wells TN1 .... 8 B4
Newton Willows TN3 .... 15 C7
Newton's Hill TN7 .... 13 D3
Newtown Rd BN3 .... 163 B8
Nicholson Ct BN23 .... 174 E1
Nicolson Dr BN43 .... 161 A7
Nightingale Cl
  East Grinstead RH19 .... 10 D7
  Eastbourne BN23 .... 174 C2
Nightingale Cotts TN35 .... 114 D4
Nightingale La RH15 .... 97 F8
Nightingale Rd TN22 .... 78 C2
Nightingales The
  Royal Tunbridge Wells TN4 .... 8 A5
  Uckfield TN22 .... 78 C5
Nile St BN1 .... 189 A5
Ninfield CE Prim Sch TN33 .... 133 B5
Ninfield Pl BN2 .... 164 E7
Ninfield Rd TN39, TN40 .... 157 B7
Nizells Ave BN3 .... 163 E7
Noahs Ark La RH16 .... 51 C7
Nodes La BN27 .... 129 F4
Noel Gn RH15 .... 73 B4
Noel Rise RH15 .... 73 B4
Nolan Rd BN2 .... 165 E7
Nook Cl TN35 .... 137 D3
Norbury Cl TN6 .... 25 E4
Nore Rd BN9 .... 179 B6
Norfolk Bldgs BN1 .... 163 E5
Norfolk Cl BN1 .... 157 B7
Norfolk Ct BN22 .... 185 C4
Norfolk Dr TN38 .... 135 F5
Norfolk Ho BN1 .... 159 C7
Norfolk Mews BN1 .... 163 E5
Norfolk Rd Hove BN1 .... 163 E6
  Royal Tunbridge Wells TN1 .... 8 B2
Norfolk Sq BN1 .... 163 E5
Norfolk St BN1 .... 163 E5
Norfolk Terr BN1 .... 163 E6
Norfolk Way TN22 .... 78 C8
Norlington Ct BN8 .... 124 D6
Norlington Fields BN8 .... 124 D6
Norlington La BN8 .... 124 D7
Norman Cl Battle TN33 .... 112 F4
  Seaford BN25 .... 180 B6
Norman Ct TN34 .... 159 E7
Norman Rd Burgess Hill RH15 .. 73 A3
  Hastings TN37, TN38 .... 159 C6
  Hove BN3 .... 162 E6
  Newhaven BN9 .... 179 C7

Norman Rd
Pevensey Bay BN24 .... 175 D4
Royal Tunbridge Wells TN1 ...... 8 B5
Normandale TN39 .... 156 F3
Normandale Ho TN39 .... 156 F3
Normandy Cl 7 RH19 .... 10 F8
Normandy Ct TN39 .... 157 B3
Normandy Ho 3 BN3 .... 163 C6
Normandy Rd TN37 .... 136 C3
Normanhurst 8 BN2 .... 189 B6
Normans TN39 .... 156 F3
Normans' Bay Sta BN24 .... 176 C8
Normansal Cl BN25 .... 181 A6
Normansal Park Ave BN25 ... 181 A6
Normansland TN22 .... 36 B2
Normanton St 8 BN2 .... 164 C7
Norstead Gdns TN4 .... 8 B7
North Ave BN20 .... 184 B5
North Bank BN6 .... 97 E4
North Barnes La BN7 .... 100 A5
North Beeches Rd TN6 .... 26 A2
North Camp La BN25 .... 180 F5
North Cl Polegate BN26 .... 173 B7
Portslade-by-Sea BN41 .... 141 A2
North Cnr TN21 .... 107 C4
North Common Rd BN8, RH17 .. 74 E5
North Crescent Ind Est BN27 . 152 A7
North Ct Hassocks BN6 .... 97 E4
Lewes BN7 .... 123 E1
North Dr BN2 .... 164 C6
North End BN6 .... 98 D4
North Farm La TN1, TN2 .... 8 C8
North Farm Rd TN1, TN4 .... 8 C8
North Gdns BN1 .... 189 F6
North Heath Cl BN27 .... 129 C2
North La Lidham Hill TN35 ...... 115 E5
Portslade-by-Sea BN41 .... 141 A3
North Pl BN1 .... 189 A5
North Point 1 BN43 .... 161 A6
North Quay Rd BN9 .... 179 D8
North Rd Alfriston BN26 .... 170 F3
Bexhill TN39 .... 157 C7
Bodle Street Green BN27 .... 109 C2
Brighton BN1 .... 189 A6
Brighton, Preston BN1 .... 142 E1
Hastings TN37, TN38 .... 136 C1
Haywards Heath RH16 .... 51 A4
Pevensey Bay BN24 .... 175 D5
Portslade-by-Sea BN41 .... 141 A2
Ringmer BN8 .... 124 D6
North Road Cotts BN8 .... 124 D6
North Row TN22 .... 78 C8
North Salts TN31 .... 93 C6
North St Alfriston BN26 .... 171 A3
Brighton BN1 .... 189 A5
Cowden TN8 .... 4 A6
Eastbourne BN21 .... 185 B3
Hailsham BN27 .... 152 B8
Hastings TN37, TN38 .... 159 C7
Hellingly BN27 .... 129 A7
Lewes BN7 .... 123 D2
Lower Horsebridge BN27, TN21 . 107 A2
Lower Horsebridge BN27 .... 128 F4
Mayfield TN20 .... 40 B3
Portslade-by-Sea BN41 .... 162 C7
Punnett's Town TN21 .... 83 D6
Roser's Cross TN21 .... 80 F5
Rotherfield TN6 .... 39 B8
Royal Tunbridge Wells TN2 ...... 8 C3
Winchelsea TN36 .... 117 E8
North Terr TN34, TN35 .... 160 C6
North Trade Rd TN33 .... 112 B4
North Way Lewes BN7 .... 123 A2
Newhaven BN9 .... 179 C8
Seaford BN25 .... 180 F5
North–South Rd BN1 .... 144 B7
Northampton Way 1 TN38 ... 136 A4
Northbourne Rd BN22 .... 185 C6
Northbridge St TN32 .... 64 B5
Northcliffe Cl BN25 .... 180 F4
Northcote La BN10 .... 167 A1
Northdown Cl BN9 .... 179 C6
Northdown Rd BN9 .... 179 B6
Northdown Terr RH19 .... 1 D3
Northease Cl BN3 .... 141 D2
Northease Dr BN3 .... 141 E3
Northease Gdns BN3 .... 141 E3
Northerlea BN41 .... 141 A1
Northern Ave BN26 .... 173 B7
Northfield BN26 .... 172 F5
Northfield Cl BN25 .... 180 F5
Northfield Cotts TN22 .... 102 D8
Northfield Rise Hove BN3 .... 141 D4
Rottingdean BN2 .... 177 A6
Northfield Way BN1 .... 143 A4
Northfields TN3 .... 7 A8
Northfields Bsns Pk BN27 .... 128 A4
Northgate BN2 .... 165 F2
Northiam CE Prim Sch TN31 ... 67 B5
Northiam Rd Broad Oak TN31 ... 90 A6
Eastbourne BN20, BN21 .... 184 C4
Northiam Rise TN38 .... 135 D2
Northiam Sta TN31 .... 48 C2
Northlands Ave RH16 .... 51 B4
Northlands Cotts TN32 .... 46 C1
Northlands Wood
Cty Prim Sch RH16 .... 51 B4
Northridge TN31 .... 67 A7
Northumberland Ct BN22 ..... 174 A2
Northway RH15 .... 73 C4
Northwood Ave BN2 .... 177 E5
Norton Cl BN3 .... 163 B6
Norton Dr BN2 .... 144 E1
Norton Rd Hove BN3 .... 163 B6
Newhaven BN9 .... 179 E7
Norton Terr BN9 .... 179 E7
Norway Rd BN22 .... 185 D6
Norway St BN41 .... 162 C7

Norwich Cl BN2 .... 144 A2
Norwich Cres BN2 .... 143 F2
Norwich Dr BN2 .... 144 A2
Norwich House Rd BN1 .... 144 B7
Norwood BN1 .... 143 A4
Nottidge Rd TN4 .... 7 D1
Novington La BN7 .... 100 A3
Nuffield Hospl TN2 .... 8 C3
Nunnery La TN11 .... 5 F8
Nunnery Stables BN7 .... 123 B1
Nursery Cl Hailsham BN27 ..... 152 C8
Haywards Heath RH16 .... 50 D5
Polegate BN26 .... 173 B6
Portslade-by-Sea BN41 .... 140 E4
Shoreham-by-Sea BN43 .... 161 B8
Union Street TN5 .... 32 B3
Nursery Field TN22 .... 56 C4
Nursery La Maresfield Park TN22 . 55 B7
Nutley TN22 .... 35 C4
Uckfield TN22 .... 78 D4
Waldron Down TN21, TN22 ...... 80 E8
Windmill Hill BN27 .... 131 B5
Nursery Path BN27 .... 152 B6
Nursery Rd TN4 .... 8 B8
Nursery The RH15 .... 73 C4
Nursery Way TN21 .... 81 E7
Nutbourne Cl BN23 .... 174 E2
Nuthatch Rd BN23 .... 174 C2
Nuthurst Cl BN2 .... 164 F6
Nuthurst Pl BN2 .... 164 F5
Nutley Ave BN2 .... 177 D4
Nutley CE Prim Sch TN22 ...... 35 C5
Nutley Cl Hove BN3 .... 141 F3
Rye TN31 .... 93 A6
Nutley Mill Rd BN24 .... 174 B5
Nye Cl TN6 .... 25 F1
Nye La Ditchling BN6 .... 98 D1
Westmeston BN6 .... 120 D8
Nye Rd RH15 .... 73 C3
Nyetimber Hill BN2 .... 143 E2
Nym Cl BN8 .... 100 E7

Oak Bank RH16 .... 50 F7
Oak Cl BN1 .... 142 E3
Oak Croft RH19 .... 11 A8
Oak Field The TN35 .... 116 F1
Oak Hall Pk RH15 .... 73 B1
Oak Hall Sch TN21 .... 60 B1
Oak Pas 8 TN34 .... 160 A4
Oak Rd TN1 .... 8 D7
Oak Terr TN31 .... 67 B6
Oak Tree Cl Eastbourne BN24 .. 174 C4
Royal Tunbridge Wells TN1 ...... 8 A1
Oak Tree Cotts
Burgess Hill RH15 .... 73 B3
Danehill RH17 .... 34 A4
Oak Tree Ct TN22 .... 78 D8
Oak Tree La BN23, BN24 .... 174 C4
Oak Tree Way BN27 .... 129 C2
Oakapple Rd BN42 .... 140 E1
Oakdale Rd
6 Haywards Heath RH16 ...... 50 F3
Royal Tunbridge Wells TN4 ...... 7 F4
7 Haywards Heath RH16 .... 50 D5
Oakdene Ave BN41 .... 140 E3
Oakdene Cl BN41 .... 140 E3
Oakdene Cres BN41 .... 140 E3
Oakdene Gdns BN41 .... 140 E3
Oakdene Rise BN41 .... 140 E4
Oakdene Way BN41 .... 140 E4
Oakdown Ct TN19 .... 61 A4
Oakenfield RH15 .... 73 A5
Oakfield Court Rd TN2 .... 8 C3
Oakfield Rd TN35 .... 137 C3
Oakfield The TN31 .... 93 B8
Oakfield Way Bexhill TN39 ... 156 C6
East Grinstead RH19 .... 1 F3
Oakhill Cotts TN31 .... 68 C4
Oakhill Dr TN31 .... 90 B5
Oakhurst RH16 .... 50 D8
Oakhurst Cl TN34 .... 136 E5
Oakhurst Dr TN6 .... 26 A3
Oakhurst Gdns RH19 .... 1 C2
Oakhurst La RH16 .... 50 D8
Oakhurst Rd TN33 .... 112 D7
Oakland Dr TN32 .... 63 D4
Oakland Villas TN3 .... 15 B7
Oaklands Crowborough TN6 ..... 26 B1
South Chailey BN8 .... 100 C4
Westham BN24 .... 174 D6
Oaklands Ave TN22 .... 177 D5
Oaklands Cl BN26 .... 173 B6
Oaklands Rd Groombridge TN3 .. 15 B6
Haywards Heath RH16 .... 50 D5
Oaklands Way BN27 .... 152 A6
Oaklea Cl TN37 .... 136 C4
Oaklea Ct TN7 .... 13 D4
Oaklea Way TN22 .... 78 C7
Oakleaf Cl BN26 .... 173 A7
Oakleaf Dr BN26 .... 173 A7
Oakleigh Annexe
(Queen Victoria Hospl) RH19 . 11 C7
Oakleigh Dr TN21 .... 82 B6
Oakleigh Rd TN39 .... 156 C4
Oakley Cl RH19 .... 11 B7
Oakley Cotts RH19 .... 11 C7
Oakmead Rd RH15 .... 72 F1
Oakmede Way BN8 .... 124 D5
Oakmeeds Com Sch RH15 ...... 73 A2
Oakroyd Cl TN31 .... 73 D5
Oaks Cl TN19 .... 63 B8
Oaks Forstal TN18 .... 47 C5
Oaks The Burgess Hill BN6 ...... 72 C4
East Grinstead RH19 .... 11 B8
Hastings TN37 .... 136 D5
Haywards Heath RH16 .... 51 A4

Oaks The
Haywards Heath RH16 .... 51 C4
Heathfield TN21 .... 82 B6
Oaktree BN8 .... 101 E4
Oakwood RH16 .... 50 D4
Oakwood Ave TN39 .... 157 B7
Oakwood Cl Burgess Hill RH15 .. 73 B2
Hastings TN34 .... 136 F3
Oakwood Dr TN22 .... 78 E8
Oakwood Pk Forest Row RH18 ... 11 F2
Nutley TN22 .... 35 C4
Oakwood Rd Burgess Hill RH15 .. 73 B2
Haywards Heath RH16 .... 50 D4
Oakwood Rise TN2 .... 8 E7
Oast Cl TN1 .... 8 D7
Oast House Dr TN31 .... 92 F4
Oast House Field TN36 .... 116 F6
Oast House Rd TN36 .... 116 F5
Oasthouse Cl TN37 .... 136 D5
Oathall Ave RH16 .... 50 F6
Oathall Com Coll RH16 .... 50 F6
Oathall Rd RH16 .... 50 E5
Oban Rd TN37 .... 136 B3
Observatory View BN27 .... 152 D7
Ochiltree Cl TN34 .... 137 A4
Ochiltree Rd TN34 .... 137 A4
Ockenden Way BN6 .... 97 E3
Ockley Hill BN6, RH15 .... 98 B6
Ockley La Burgess Hill RH15 ..... 98 B7
Keymer BN6 .... 98 B4
Ockley Way BN6 .... 98 A5
Ocklynge Ave 1 BN21 .... 184 D4
Ocklynge Cl TN39 .... 156 C5
Ocklynge Cty Jun Sch BN21 ... 184 C6
Ocklynge Rd BN21 .... 184 D4
Ockman La TN31 .... 93 C5
Octagon The BN2 .... 164 F3
Offa Cl TN1 .... 8 D7
Offa Rd TN35 .... 137 D3
Offham Cl BN25 .... 180 F5
Offham Ct 3 BN25 .... 180 C4
Offham Rd BN7 .... 123 B2
Okehurst Rd BN20, BN21 .... 184 C3
Old Barn Cl BN20 .... 173 B1
Old Barn Ct TN4 .... 50 D2
Old Barn Way BN42 .... 162 A7
Old Ben Homes BN25 .... 180 F4
Old Boat Cnr BN1 .... 143 C7
Old Boat Wlk BN1 .... 143 B7
Old Brickyard TN31 .... 93 A5
Old Camp Rd BN20 .... 184 C2
Old Church Rd
Hastings TN37, TN38 .... 136 A4
Pembury TN2 .... 9 D8
Old Clergy Ho (NT) BN26 .... 171 A2
Old Coastguard Cotts BN9 ..... 179 D6
Old Coastguards TN35 .... 139 C7
Old Convent The RH19 .... 1 C4
Old Court Cl BN1 .... 142 F4
Old Dr BN26 .... 172 F6
Old Dro BN23 .... 174 C3
Old Farm Rd Bexhill TN39 ...... 157 B6
Brighton BN1 .... 142 F5
Old Fire Station The 4 BN22 . 185 A3
Old Foord Cl BN8 .... 100 D7
Old Forest La TN6 .... 38 E8
Old Forewood La TN33 .... 134 F7
Old Forge La TN22 .... 36 A1
Old Fort Rd BN43 .... 161 B6
Old Gardens Cl TN2 .... 17 B8
Old Ghyll Rd TN21 .... 82 A5
Old Harrow Rd TN37 .... 136 B4
Old Heath Cl BN8 .... 104 C6
Old Hop Garden The TN31 ...... 69 C2
Old House Gdns TN34 .... 136 F4
Old House La TN3 .... 6 D4
Old Humphrey Ave 1 TN34 .. 160 B4
Old La Crowborough,
Crowborough Warren TN6 ...... 25 D3
Crowborough, Poundfield TN6 ... 26 B1
Mayfield TN20 .... 40 A2
Old London Rd Brighton BN1 .. 142 E6
Hastings TN34, TN35 .... 160 C6
Old Lydd Rd TN31 .... 94 E2
Old Malling Way BN7 .... 123 C3
Old Manor Cl TN40 .... 157 D4
Old Mansion Cl BN20 .... 184 A8
Old Mill Cl Brighton BN1 .... 142 E5
Hailsham BN27 .... 129 A3
Southwick BN41 .... 162 A7
Old Mill Ct TN6 .... 25 E2
Old Mill La BN26 .... 172 E3
Old Mill Pk TN39 .... 157 A6
Old Mint House BN24 .... 175 B6
Old Motcombe Mews 9
BN21 .... 184 D4
Old Orchard Pl BN27 .... 152 B7
Old Orchard Rd BN21 .... 184 F2
Old Parish La BN2 .... 165 C8
Old Park Cl RH17 .... 50 A6
Old Patcham Mews BN1 .... 142 E6
Old Place Ct BN2 .... 165 F1
Old Rd East Grinstead RH19 ..... 1 F1
Magham Down BN27 .... 130 A4
Old Rectory Gdns BN43 .... 161 D8
Old Riding School The TN3 ...... 15 B2
Old River Way TN36 .... 118 B7
Old Roar Rd TN37 .... 136 C5
Old School Cl BN8 .... 124 E6
Old School Cotts BN7 .... 99 E5
Old School Ho BN27 .... 131 B5
Old School La BN26 .... 173 A4
Old School Pl RH15 .... 72 F2
Old Shoreham Rd
Portslade-by-Sea BN3, BN41 .. 162 C8
Southwick BN41 .... 140 E1
Old Station Rd TN5 .... 29 E6
Old Steine BN1, BN2 .... 189 A5

Old Swan La BN27 .... 152 D6
Old Timbers La TN22 .... 78 C6
Old Top Rd TN35 .... 137 D4
Old Viaduct Ct 6 BN2 .... 164 C8
Old Wardsdown TN5 .... 32 B3
Old Wickham La RH16 .... 50 E7
Old Willingdon Rd BN20 .... 183 B2
Old Wish Rd BN21 .... 184 F1
Old World Cotts TN31 .... 94 F2
Oldaker Rd BN8 .... 76 D7
Olde Place Mews BN2 .... 165 F1
Oldfield Ave BN20 .... 173 A4
Oldfield Cres Hailsham BN27 ... 129 B1
Southwick BN42 .... 161 E8
Oldfield Rd BN20 .... 173 A4
Oldlands Ave BN6 .... 98 A4
Oldlands Hall TN22 .... 36 D4
Oldlands Hill TN22 .... 36 C2
Olive Rd BN3 .... 162 D8
Oliver Cl Brighton BN2 .... 164 C5
Crowborough TN6 .... 26 A1
Oliver Ho BN3 .... 163 B5
Olives Meadow BN22 .... 78 D7
Onslow Rd BN3 .... 142 C2
Open Mkt The BN1 .... 189 A7
Orange Row BN1 .... 189 A5
Orchard Ave BN3 .... 142 A1
Orchard Bsns Ctr TN4 .... 8 D8
Orchard Cl Fairwarp TN22 ...... 36 B2
Hastings TN34 .... 136 F2
Haywards Heath RH16 .... 50 D8
Royal Tunbridge Wells TN1 ...... 8 B6
Scaynes Hill RH17 .... 51 F3
Southwick BN42 .... 161 F8
Orchard Cnr RH16 .... 51 B5
Orchard Cotts TN6 .... 39 B8
Orchard Gdns BN3 .... 142 B1
Orchard Gr TN1 .... 8 B5
Orchard La Ditchling BN6 ...... 98 D4
Hassocks BN6 .... 97 F4
Orchard Mews 2 BN9 .... 168 E2
Orchard Par BN20 .... 173 A3
Orchard Rd Bexhill TN40 .... 157 C6
Burgess Hill RH15 .... 72 E3
Hove BN3 .... 142 B1
Lewes BN7 .... 123 E2
Orchard Rise TN3 .... 15 B7
Orchard The Broad Oak TN31 .... 90 B4
Hassocks BN6 .... 97 F3
Nutley TN22 .... 35 C4
Orchard Way Burgess Hill RH15 . 72 F3
East Grinstead RH19 .... 1 E1
Haywards Heath RH16 .... 50 D8
Peasmarsh TN31 .... 69 C1
Orchards The Brighton BN2 ..... 143 E3
11 Haywards Heath RH16 ...... 50 E4
Orchid Cl BN23 .... 174 B3
Orchid Pk RH16 .... 51 C4
Orchid View BN23 .... 143 C6
Orchidhurst TN2 .... 8 D7
Oriental Pl BN1 .... 163 E5
Orion Cl BN27 .... 152 D7
Orion Par BN6 .... 97 F3
Orkney Ct BN20 .... 184 B6
Ormerod Ave TN38 .... 136 A4
Ormerod Ct 5 RH16 .... 50 E5
Orpen Rd BN3 .... 142 D1
Osbern Cl TN3 .... 156 C3
Osborne Cl TN34 .... 136 E2
Osborne Ct 7 BN43 .... 161 C8
Osborne Hill TN6 .... 38 C8
Osborne Rd Brighton BN1 ...... 143 A2
Crowborough TN6 .... 38 C8
Eastbourne BN20 .... 184 B4
Osborne Villas BN3 .... 163 B6
Osmers Hill TN5 .... 29 F7
Osmond Rd BN3 .... 163 E7
Osmunda Bank RH19 .... 1 E6
Osmunda Ct TN2 .... 8 C4
Osprey Ct TN22 .... 78 E5
Osprey Ho 8 BN1 .... 163 E5
Oswald Ct TN4 .... 157 C4
Otham Court La BN26 .... 173 B8
Otham Pk BN27 .... 152 D7
Otham Rd BN22 .... 174 A2
Ottafield Ct RH16 .... 50 F6
Otteham Ct TN22 .... 173 B6
Oulton Cl BN23 .... 174 B4
Our Lady of Lourdes
RC Prim Sch BN7 .... 165 F1
Ousedale Cl BN7 .... 123 B1
Outlook Ave BN10 .... 178 F6
Outlook The BN20 .... 183 A1
Oval Cl BN10 .... 167 C2
Over St BN1 .... 189 A6
Overdown Rise BN41 .... 140 F4
Overhill BN42 .... 140 E1
Overhill Dr BN1 .... 142 E5
Overhill Gdns BN1 .... 142 E5
Overhill Way BN1 .... 142 E6
Overton Shaw RH19 .... 1 E4
Ovingdean Cl BN2 .... 165 D5
Ovingdean Grange Cotts BN2 . 165 D4
Ovingdean Hall Sch BN2 .... 165 D5
Ovingdean Rd BN2 .... 165 D5
Owen Cl RH15 .... 72 F1
Owl House Gdns TN3 .... 19 E7
Owls Gdns TN5 .... 42 F5
Owlsbury Cross TN21 .... 83 B5
Ox Lea TN3 .... 7 A3
Oxbottom Cl BN8 .... 76 B6
Oxenbridge La TN19 .... 63 C8
Oxenbridge Row TN19 .... 63 C8
Oxendean Gdns BN22 .... 173 B4
Oxford Ct BN1 .... 189 A7
Oxford Mews BN3 .... 163 C7
Oxford Pl BN1 .... 189 A7

Oxford Rd 8 Eastbourne BN22 . 185 B4
Hastings TN38 .... 136 A3
Oxford St BN1, BN2 .... 189 A7
Oxford Terr 9 TN34 .... 160 B4
Oxshott Ct TN40 .... 157 F4

Packer Cl RH19 .... 2 A3
Packham Way RH15 .... 72 F4
Paddock Cl Bexhill TN40 .... 157 D6
Fordcombe TN3 .... 6 B5
Paddock Ct BN41 .... 140 F3
Paddock Gdns
East Grinstead RH19 .... 10 E7
Polegate BN26 .... 172 F4
Paddock La BN7 .... 123 C1
Paddock Rd Hastings TN37 ..... 136 C5
Lewes BN7 .... 123 C1
Paddock The Eastbourne BN22 . 173 F2
Hove BN3 .... 142 C1
Maresfield TN22 .... 55 A4
4 Northiam TN31 .... 67 B7
Pembury TN2 .... 9 C6
Paddockhall Rd RH16 .... 50 D5
Paddocks The Cowden TN8 .... 4 B7
Hailsham BN27 .... 129 A2
Plumpton Green BN7 .... 99 E6
Rodmell BN7 .... 167 D8
Padgham Cnr TN21 .... 109 D8
Padgham La TN21 .... 109 D8
Padua Ho BN2 .... 165 F8
Padua House Flats BN2 .... 165 F8
Page's Cotts TN39 .... 156 F2
Pages Ave TN39 .... 156 F2
Pages Cl TN21 .... 81 E7
Pages Hill TN21 .... 81 E7
Pages La TN39 .... 156 E3
Pagets The BN8 .... 76 D7
Pagham Cl BN23 .... 174 B4
Pain's Flat RH15, RH17 .... 72 D8
Paine's Cnr TN21 .... 60 C4
Paines Cotts TN31 .... 94 A3
Palace Pl BN1 .... 189 A5
Palesgate La TN6 .... 26 C2
Palliser Cl BN23 .... 185 E6
Palma Cl BN20 .... 173 A7
Palmeira Ct 2 BN3 .... 163 C6
Palmeira Ho 6 BN3 .... 163 D7
Palmeira Mansions 18 BN3 .. 163 C6
Palmeira Pl BN3 .... 163 D7
Palmeira Sq BN3 .... 163 C6
Palmer Ho BN8 .... 100 E7
Palmers Row BN27 .... 152 B7
Palmerston Rd BN9 .... 168 F1
Pangdean La BN6 .... 72 C4
Pangdene Cl RH15 .... 72 F1
Pankhurst Ave BN2 .... 164 D6
Pankhurst Cl TN39 .... 157 A8
Pankhurst Rise TN39 .... 157 A8
Pannel La TN35 .... 116 E2
Pannell Cl RH19 .... 1 D1
Pannett RH15 .... 72 E4
Pantiles The
Royal Tunbridge Wells TN4 ...... 7 F2
17 Royal Tunbridge Wells TN2 .. 8 A2
Parade The Beachlands BN24 .. 175 F6
Hove BN3 .... 141 E2
Pevensey Bay BN24 .... 175 E5
Paradise Cl BN20 .... 184 D2
Paradise Dr Brighton BN20, BN21 . 184 D2
Paradise Family L Pk BN9 ..... 168 D1
Paragon The BN20 .... 172 F3
Parham Cl BN2 .... 164 D5
Park Ave Bexhill TN39 .... 157 B3
Eastbourne BN21, BN22 .... 184 D7
Hastings TN34 .... 136 D3
Hove BN3 .... 162 E7
Keymer BN6 .... 98 A2
Shoreham-by-Sea BN43 .... 161 A8
Telscombe Cliffs BN10 .... 178 A8
Park Cl Brighton BN1 .... 143 E5
Burgess Hill RH15 .... 72 F4
Eastbourne BN20 .... 184 D3
Hailsham BN27 .... 152 B6
Hastings TN34 .... 136 D3
Hove BN3 .... 141 E3
Hurstpierpoint BN6 .... 97 A6
Portslade-by-Sea BN41 .... 141 B1
Park Cnr BN2 .... 104 F2
Park Coll BN21 .... 184 E7
Park Cres Brighton BN2 .... 189 B7
Crowborough TN6 .... 25 F3
Forest Row RH18 .... 12 A2
Hastings TN34 .... 136 D2
Portslade-by-Sea BN41 .... 162 A8
Rottingdean BN2 .... 165 F1
Park Crescent Pl BN2 .... 189 B7
Park Crescent Rd BN2 .... 189 B7
Park Crescent Terr BN2 .... 189 B7
Park Croft BN26 .... 173 A5
Park Ct Brighton, Patcham BN1 . 142 E6
Brighton, Preston BN1 .... 142 F1
Burgess Hill RH15 .... 73 A3
4 Haywards Heath RH16 ...... 50 E4
Park Dr TN34 .... 136 D2
Park Drive Cl BN9 .... 168 F2
Park Farm Cl TN19 .... 63 B8
Park Gate Hailsham BN27 ..... 129 D3
Hove BN3 .... 163 D6
Park Gates 16 BN21 .... 185 A2
Park Hill BN2 .... 189 B5
Park La Ashurst Wood RH19 ..... 11 D6
Battle TN33 .... 112 D4
Bexhill TN39 .... 157 A6
Crowborough TN6 .... 25 F3

Park La
Eastbourne BN21 .... 184 C8
Southwick BN42, BN43 .... 161 D7
Whatlington TN32, TN33 .... 88 A5
Park Lodge
🔟 Eastbourne BN21 .... 185 A2
Hove BN3 .... 163 D8
Park Lodge Ct TN38 .... 159 B7
Park Manor BN1 .... 142 D4
Park Mead Cty Prim Sch
BN27 .... 151 A7
Park Rd Bexhill TN39 .... 157 B3
Brighton BN1 .... 143 E5
Burgess Hill RH15 .... 73 A3
Crowborough TN6 .... 25 F3
Dormans Park RH19 .... 1 D1
East Grinstead RH19 .... 1 D1
Forest Row RH18 .... 12 A2
Hailsham BN27 .... 129 B4
Haywards Heath RH16 .... 50 E4
Heathfield TN21 .... 82 B7
Heathfield TN21 .... 82 C6
Lewes BN7 .... 123 C1
Peacehaven Heights BN10 ..... 178 F6
Rottingdean BN2 .... 165 F1
Royal Tunbridge Wells TN4 .... 8 B5
Seaford BN25 .... 180 D3
Shoreham-by-Sea BN43 .... 161 A8
Park Rise BN1 .... 141 E3
Park Road Terr 🔲 BN2 .... 189 B5
Park Royal BN1 .... 163 E6
Park Shaw TN33 .... 88 E1
Park St Brighton BN2 .... 189 B5
Falmer BN1 .... 144 C6
Royal Tunbridge Wells TN2 .... 8 C3
Park Terr BN2 .... 165 F1
Park The Crowborough TN6 ... 25 F2
Rottingdean BN2 .... 177 A5
Park View Brighton BN1 ...... 163 E8
Brighton BN2 .... 164 C6
Buxted TN22 .... 56 C4
Hastings TN34 .... 136 D2
Haywards Heath RH16 .... 50 E6
Northiam TN31 .... 67 A6
Peasmarsh TN31 .... 69 B2
Park View Cl BN10 .... 167 A1
Park View Rd BN3 .... 142 B1
Park View Rise BN10 .... 178 A8
Park View Terr Brighton BN1 ... 163 E8
Westfield TN35 .... 114 E4
Park Village Rd BN1 .... 144 B8
Park Village The BN1 .... 144 A8
Park Villas TN21 .... 82 B6
Park Way Hastings TN34 .... 136 D3
Southwick BN42 .... 161 F8
Park Way Cl BN42 .... 161 F8
Park Wood Rd TN34 .... 136 F6
Parker BN21 .... 184 E5
Parker Ct BN41 .... 141 B2
Parker TN34 .... 137 A3
Parkfield Ave BN22 .... 173 E1
Parkhurst Rd TN39, TN40 ... 157 C3
Parkland Cty Inf Sch BN22 ..... 173 E1
Parkland Cty Jun Sch BN22 .... 173 D1
Parklands Maresfield TN22 ... 55 A5
Royal Tunbridge Wells TN4 .... 7 E8
Shoreham-by-Sea BN43 .... 161 C8
Parklands Rd BN6 .... 97 F3
Parkmead BN2 .... 189 B7
Parkmore Terr BN1 .... 189 F8
Parks Yd TN33 .... 112 D4
Parkside Burgess Hill RH15 ... 72 F3
East Grinstead RH19 .... 1 C1
Heathfield TN21 .... 82 B6
Keymer BN6 .... 98 A4
Portslade-by-Sea BN43 .... 140 A1
Parkside Cty Prim Sch TN21 .... 82 C5
Parkside Rd BN5 .... 180 F4
Parkstone Par TN34 .... 136 D4
Parkstone Rd TN34 .... 136 D4
Parkview BN6 .... 97 A5
Parkview Rd TN22 .... 55 D1
Parkway BN20 .... 184 B8
Parkwood TN31 .... 70 B4
Parkwood Cl TN1 .... 8 C6
Parrock La TN7 .... 12 E2
Parry Cl BN23 .... 174 E3
Parsonage Cl TN4 .... 7 B5
Parsonage La Icklesham TN36 ... 116 F6
Lamberhurst TN3 .... 20 B6
Westfield TN33, TN35 .... 114 C4
Parsonage Rd
Eastbourne BN21 .... 184 D4
Rusthall TN4 .... 7 B5
Parsons Cl TN38 .... 135 F4
Partridges La TN5, TN6 .... 28 E6
Pashley Down Cty Inf Sch
BN20 .... 184 B4
Pashley Manor Gdns TN19 ...... 44 B7
Pashley Rd BN20 .... 184 C2
Paston Pl BN2 .... 164 D4
Pasture Hill Rd RH16 .... 50 D6
Patcham By-Pass BN1 .... 142 E6
Patcham Cty Inf Sch BN1 .... 142 E6
Patcham Cty Jun Sch BN1 ...... 142 F6
Patcham High Sch BN1 .... 142 F6
Patcham House Sch BN1 .... 142 E6
Patcham Mill Rd BN24 .... 174 B5
Patchdean BN1 .... 142 F5
Patching Lodge 🔲 BN2 ...... 164 C5
Paton Rd TN39 .... 157 B2
Paul Cl BN27 .... 129 A3
Pavilion Bldgs BN1 .... 189 A5
Pavilion Ct BN6 .... 97 C5
Pavilion Ct 🔢 BN1 .... 163 E7

Pavilion Par BN2 .... 189 A5
Pavilion Rd BN1 .... 144 C7
Pavilion Ret Pk BN2 .... 143 C1
Pavilion St BN2 .... 189 A5
Pavilion Way RH19 .... 10 E8
Paxhill Cl TN38 .... 135 E4
Paxhill Park Golf Course RH16 ... 51 E8
Paygate Rd TN33 .... 113 E7
Payne Ave BN3 .... 162 F8
Payne Terr BN1 .... 143 B1
Paynsbridge Way TN21 .... 107 A7
Paynters Way BN8 .... 76 C7
Paynton Rd TN37 .... 136 B3
Paythorne Cl BN42 .... 140 D1
Payton Dr RH15 .... 72 E2
Payton Ho RH15 .... 73 D3
Peace Cl BN1 .... 143 C1
Peacehaven Cty Inf Sch
BN10 .... 178 B7
Peacehaven Golf Course
BN9 .... 179 A7
Peacock Ind Est BN3 .... 163 D7
Peacock La BN1 .... 142 E4
Peakdean Cl BN20 .... 183 B2
Peakdean La BN20 .... 183 B2
Pearl Ct 🔳 BN21 .... 185 A2
Pearse Ho BN1 .... 20 B5
Peartree Cl RH15 .... 72 E3
Peartree Field TN36 .... 116 F6
Peartree Hill TN5 .... 42 E4
Peartree La TN39 .... 156 D6
Peasmarsh CE Prim Sch TN31 ... 69 B1
Pebble Rd BN24 .... 175 E5
Pebsham Cty Prim Sch TN40 ... 158 A5
Pebsham Dr TN40 .... 158 A6
Pebsham La TN38, TN40 ..... 158 A6
Peckham Cl BN7 .... 123 C3
Peel Rd BN2 .... 164 F4
Peelings La BN24 .... 174 D6
Peeps La TN6 .... 39 A6
Pegasus Way RH19 .... 2 B3
Pegler Ave BN9 .... 179 B6
Pegwell Cl TN34 .... 136 E2
Pelham Arc 🔳 TN34 .... 160 A3
Pelham Cl Peacehaven BN10 ... 167 D1
Westham BN24 .... 174 F5
Pelham Cres Hailsham BN27 ... 152 C6
Hastings TN34 .... 160 A3
Pelham Ct 🔢 BN25 .... 180 E2
Pelham Pl TN34 .... 160 A3
Pelham Place Cotts RH16 .... 51 A7
Pelham Rd
Haywards Heath RH16 .... 51 A6
Seaford BN25 .... 180 E2
Pelham Rise BN10 .... 167 D1
Pelham Sq BN1 .... 189 A6
Pelham St Brighton BN1 ...... 189 A6
Hastings TN34 .... 159 F7
Pelham Terr Brighton BN2 ... 143 C1
Lewes BN7 .... 123 C2
Pelham Yd 🔢 BN25 .... 180 E2
Pell TN5 .... 30 A6
Pellbrook Rd BN7 .... 123 B3
Pells CE Prim Sch Lewes BN7 . 123 C1
Lewes BN7 .... 123 C2
Pelwood Rd TN31 .... 95 A2
Pembroke Ave BN3 .... 163 A7
Pembroke Cl BN27 .... 129 C3
Pembroke Cres BN3 .... 163 A7
Pembroke Ct 🔳 BN3 .... 163 A6
Pembroke Gdns BN3 .... 163 A6
Pembury Cl
Haywards Heath RH16 .... 51 B3
Pembury TN2 .... 9 D7
Pembury Cty Prim Sch TN2 .... 9 D8
Pembury Gr TN39 .... 157 A7
Pembury Grange TN2 .... 9 A6
Pembury Hospl TN2 .... 9 B3
Pembury Rd Eastbourne BN23 . 174 D1
Royal Tunbridge Wells TN2 .... 8 E4
Pendean RH15 .... 73 C1
Pendragon Ct BN3 .... 163 A8
Pendrill Pl TN5 .... 29 F5
Penhale Rd BN22 .... 185 D5
Penhurst Cl Eastbourne BN22 . 174 A1
Hastings TN37 .... 136 D5
Penhurst Dr TN40 .... 158 A6
Penhurst La TN33 .... 110 E6
Penhurst Pl BN2 .... 164 F6
Penland Cl RH16 .... 50 D7
Penland Ct 🔟 TN40 .... 157 E4
Penland Rd Bexhill TN40 ..... 157 D5
Haywards Heath RH16, RH17 ... 50 D7
Penn Cres
Haywards Heath RH16 .... 51 A5
Ringmer BN8 .... 124 D5
Penn Yd TN2 .... 9 C6
Pennine Rise TN34 .... 137 B4
Pennine Way BN23 .... 174 D3
Pennine Wlk TN2 .... 8 D5
Pennington Ho RH16 .... 51 A3
Penny La TN40 .... 158 A5
Pennybridge La TN20 .... 40 D5
Pensford Dr BN23 .... 174 D3
Penshurst Rd TN11, TN3 .... 6 E8
Penstone Ct 🔳 BN43 .... 161 C8
Pentland Ct Eastbourne BN23 ... 174 E3
Hastings TN37 .... 136 C5
Pentlands BN26 .... 183 C7
Pepper Dr RH15 .... 72 F1
Pepper Hall Cotts RH17 .... 174 F4
Peppercombe Rd BN20 .... 184 B4
Pepys Wlk BN23 .... 174 C3
Percival Cres BN22, BN26 ... 173 F3
Percival Rd BN22 .... 173 F3
Percival Terr 🔢 BN2 .... 164 D4
Percy Rd TN35 .... 137 C3
Perry Ave RH19 .... 1 E3

Perry Hill BN2 .... 166 C3
Perryfields RH15 .... 72 E4
Perryhill Cotts TN7 .... 13 E8
Perryhill La TN7 .... 13 E8
Perryman's La RH17 .... 34 D3
Perrymans La TN22 .... 36 F1
Perrymount Rd RH16 .... 50 E5
Perth Cl BN25 .... 181 C3
Perth Ct 🔳 BN22 .... 185 A4
Perth Rd TN37 .... 136 B3
Peter Gladwin Cty Prim Sch
BN41 .... 141 B2
Peter James Cl TN31 .... 94 E2
Peter James La TN35 .... 138 C6
Petersfield TN2 .... 9 E7
Petlands Gdns 🔲 RH16 .... 50 F3
Petlands Rd RH16 .... 50 E3
Pett La TN35, TN36 .... 117 A4
Pett Level Rd TN35, TN36 ... 139 B7
Pett Rd TN35 .... 138 C8
Petworth Dr RH15 .... 73 A4
Petworth Pl BN22 .... 173 E2
Petworth Rd BN1 .... 143 B6
Pevensey Bay Rd BN23 ...... 175 A2
Pevensey Bay Sta BN24 .... 175 C6
Pevensey Castle BN24 .... 175 A6
Pevensey Cl BN25 .... 181 B4
Pevensey Ct TN39 .... 157 B3
Pevensey Park Rd BN24 ..... 174 F6
Pevensey Rd 🔳 Brighton BN2 . 164 C8
Eastbourne BN21, BN22 .... 185 B3
Hastings TN37, TN38 .... 159 B7
Newhaven BN9 .... 179 B5
Polegate BN26 .... 173 C6
Pevensey & Westham
CE Prim Sch BN24 .... 175 A4
Pevensey & Westham Sta
BN24 .... 174 F5
Peverells The BN25 .... 181 B4
Peyton Cl BN23 .... 185 F7
Philip Cole Cl 🔟 TN34 .... 160 B4
Philip Ct 🔲 BN1 .... 163 C7
Phoenix Brewery Halls BN2 ... 189 B7
Phoenix Cl BN27 .... 152 E7
Phoenix Cres BN42 .... 161 D8
Phoenix Cswy BN7 .... 123 D1
Phoenix Ct 🔟 BN22 .... 185 B3
Phoenix Way BN10 .... 11 E6
Phoenix Pl Brighton BN2 ..... 189 B6
Lewes BN7 .... 123 D1
Phoenix Way BN42 .... 161 D8
Phyllis Ave BN10 .... 178 B8
Picardy Cl TN33 .... 112 E4
Piccadilly La TN20 .... 40 C1
Pickers Gn RH16 .... 51 A8
Picketts La TN22 .... 54 D8
Pickforde La TN5 .... 31 D1
Picton St BN2 .... 164 C7
Piddinghoe Ave BN10 .... 178 D6
Piddinghoe Cl BN10 .... 178 D7
Piddinghoe Mead BN9 .... 168 B1
Pilgrim Ct RH16 .... 51 A5
Pilgrims Old Sch BN7 .... 146 A7
Pilgrims Sch BN25 .... 180 E6
Pilmer Rd TN6 .... 25 F4
Pilot Ho 🔟 BN2 .... 189 B5
Pilot Rd TN34 .... 137 B4
Piltdown Cl Bexhill TN39 ..... 157 B4
Hastings TN34 .... 136 E1
Piltdown Rd BN2 .... 164 F6
Piltdown Rise TN22 .... 78 D8
Piltdown Way BN22 .... 174 A4
Pinders Rd TN35 .... 160 D6
Pinders Wlk TN35 .... 137 D3
Pine Ave TN34 .... 137 B4
Pine Gr Crowborough TN6 .... 25 E3
East Grinstead RH19 .... 1 B3
Pine Tree Cl Hurstpierpoint BN6 . 97 B5
Newhaven BN9 .... 179 C7
Pine Tree Rd TN21 .... 82 A6
Pine Trees Ct BN6 .... 97 D4
Pine Way BN27 .... 152 A7
Pine Way Cl RH19 .... 10 E7
Pine Wlk TN22 .... 78 D8
Pineham Copse RH16 .... 50 F4
Pinehurst RH15 .... 73 A1
Pines The 🔲 Brighton BN2 . 189 B7
Haywards Heath RH16 .... 51 B4
Hove BN3 .... 163 E6
Pinewood 🔲 BN1 .... 142 E3
Pinewood Chase TN6 .... 25 D3
Pinewood Cl Eastbourne BN22 . 173 D2
Seaford BN25 .... 180 F4
Pinewood Ct RH16 .... 50 D2
Pinewood Rd TN2 .... 8 D5
Pinewood Way Hastings TN38 . 135 E3
Haywards Heath RH16 .... 50 D2
Pinewoods TN39 .... 156 E4
Pinewoods Ct TN39 .... 156 E4
Pinfold 🔲 RH16 .... 50 D6
Pinfold Cl BN23 .... 165 E6
Pinton Hill TN5 .... 31 B3
Pinwell Rd BN7 .... 146 D8
Pipe Pas 🔳 BN7 .... 123 C1
Piper's Gate TN22 .... 78 D4
Pipers Cl Bexhill TN40 .... 157 C5
Hove BN3 .... 141 C3
Pipers Field TN22 .... 78 D4
Pipers La TN32 .... 64 B3
Pit Rd BN6 .... 97 A5
Pitreavie Dr BN27 .... 152 A8
Pitt Dr BN25 .... 181 A5
Pitt Gdns BN2 .... 165 D7
Place La BN25 .... 180 E3
Plainfields Ave BN1 .... 143 A7
Plaistow Cl BN2 .... 164 F6

Plat The TN31 .... 67 B6
Platt The Dormansland RH7 ... 2 A8
Frant TN3 .... 17 B1
Haywards Heath RH16 .... 51 B5
Plaw Hatch La RH18, RH19 ... 21 E5
Playden Cl 🔟 BN2 .... 164 E4
Playden Gdns BN34 .... 137 B4
Playden La TN31 .... 70 C3
Playden St Michael's
CE Prim Sch TN31 .... 70 C2
Pleasant View Cotts TN6 ..... 25 E4
Pleasant View Rd TN6 .... 25 F4
Plemont Gdns TN39 .... 157 A6
Pleyden Rise TN39 .... 155 F6
Plough La TN37 .... 136 B5
Plover Cl BN23 .... 174 C2
Plover Ct Hailsham BN27 ..... 152 D7
Hastings TN38 .... 135 E3
Plum Tree Cotts TN18 .... 45 E8
Plumey Feather Cotts TN3 ... 14 E3
Plumpton Bostall BN7 .... 121 E6
Plumpton Cl Bexhill TN40 .... 157 C6
Eastbourne BN23 .... 174 A4
Plumpton Cross BN7 .... 99 E3
Plumpton Crossways BN7, BN8 . 74 F1
Plumpton Cty Prim Sch BN7 .... 99 F5
Plumpton La BN7 .... 99 E3
Plumpton Race Course BN7 .... 99 E4
Plumpton Rd BN2 .... 164 D6
Plumpton Sta BN7 .... 99 E5
Plymouth Ave BN2 .... 143 F1
Plymouth Cl BN23 .... 185 F8
Plynlimmon Rd TN34 .... 160 A4
Pocock's Rd BN21 .... 184 D5
Pokes Cott TN17 .... 20 F2
Polegate By-Pass BN26 ...... 8 D2
Polegate Cty Prim Sch BN26 . 173 A7
Polegate Sta BN26 .... 173 A6
Polesden Rd TN2 .... 8 D2
Polley Cl TN2 .... 9 D7
Pomper La BN6 .... 72 A2
Pond Cl TN31 .... 90 B5
Pond Way RH19 .... 2 B1
Pondcroft Rd RH16 .... 51 B7
Pondsyde Ct BN25 .... 180 F4
Ponswood Rd TN38 .... 136 B2
Pont Cl TN21 .... 83 C6
Pook Reed Cl TN21 .... 81 F6
Pook Reed La TN21 .... 81 F6
Pool Valley BN1 .... 189 A4
Poona Rd TN1, TN2 .... 8 B2
Poplar Ave BN3 .... 141 E3
Poplar Cl Brighton BN1 .... 142 F2
Hove BN3 .... 141 E3
Poplar Wlk BN22 .... 173 D3
Poplars The BN6 .... 98 A3
Poppinghole La TN32 .... 87 E8
Popps La TN39 .... 156 C3
Poppyfield TN31 .... 70 C1
Port Hall Ave BN1 .... 163 E8
Port Hall Mews BN1 .... 163 E8
Port Hall Pl BN1 .... 163 E8
Port Hall Rd BN1 .... 163 E8
Port Hall St BN1 .... 163 E8
Port Rd BN24 .... 174 A1
Porters Way BN26 .... 173 B6
Portfield Ave BN1 .... 143 A6
Portfield Cl TN40 .... 157 D5
Portland Ave BN3 .... 162 E7
Portland Ct BN27 .... 129 A1
Portland Cotts 🔳 TN34 ...... 159 F8
Portland Gate BN3 .... 162 E7
Portland Ho 🔳 RH19 .... 10 F8
Portland Pl 🔢 Brighton BN2 . 164 C4
🔢 Hastings TN34 .... 159 F8
Portland Rd Burgess Hill RH15 . 72 F3
East Grinstead RH19 .... 10 F8
Hove BN3 .... 162 D7
Portland Road Trad Est BN3 ... 162 D8
Portland Sq TN21 .... 82 D7
Portland St BN1 .... 189 F5
Portland Terr
🔢 Hastings TN34 .... 159 F8
South Heighton BN9 .... 168 D2
Portland Villas
🔢 Hastings TN34 .... 159 F8
Hove BN3 .... 162 D7
Portlands BN23 .... 185 G7
Portside BN2 .... 164 F3
Portslade Com Coll
(Lower) BN41 .... 141 A3
Portslade Com Coll
(Sixth Form) BN41 .... 141 A1
Portslade Cty Inf Sch BN41 ... 140 F2
Portslade Sta BN3 .... 162 C8
Portsmouth La RH16 .... 50 E8
Portsmouth Wood RH16 .... 50 F8
Portsmouth Wood Cl RH16 ... 50 F8
Posey Cotts BN27 .... 131 B5
Possingworth Cl TN21 .... 80 F8
Post Horn Cl RH18 .... 12 B1
Post Horn La RH18 .... 12 B2
Post Office Par 🔟 TN34 .... 160 A4
Potato La BN8 .... 124 F5
Potman's La TN33, TN39 ..... 133 F4
Pottens Mill La TN20 .... 59 F4
Potteries Cotts BN27 .... 128 D3
Potteries The TN22 .... 78 D4
Potters Field BN8 .... 124 D6
Potters La RH15 .... 72 F1
Pottery Cl TN31 .... 90 A2
Pottery Cotts BN6 .... 74 A1
Pottery La TN31 .... 90 A2
Pottingfield Rd TN31 .... 93 A6
Potts Marsh Ind Est BN24 ..... 174 F4
Pouchlands Dr BN8 .... 100 C7

Pound Cl BN23 .... 185 F6
Pound Cnr BN8 .... 101 D4
Pound Gate BN6 .... 97 D3
Pound La Framefield TN22 ... 79 E7
Laughton BN8 .... 126 C7
Pound The RH15 .... 72 F4
Poundfield Farm TN6 .... 26 B2
Poundfield Rd Crowborough TN6 . 26 B2
Sandhurst TN18 .... 47 B5
Poundsbridge Hill TN11, TN3 .. 6 D7
Poveys CT RH15 .... 72 D3
Powder Mill La TN4 .... 8 B8
Powdermill Cl TN4 .... 8 C8
Powdermill La Battle TN33 .. 112 C1
Goatham Green TN31, TN33 ... 89 D3
Powell Gdns BN9 .... 168 D1
Powell Rd BN8 .... 76 D7
Powis Gr BN1 .... 189 F6
Powis Rd BN1 .... 163 E6
Powis Sq BN1 .... 163 E6
Powis Villas BN1 .... 189 F6
Poynings Cl BN25 .... 181 C2
Poynings Dr BN3 .... 141 F3
Poynter Rd BN3 .... 163 A8
Pratt's Folly La TN6 .... 25 E1
Prescott Gdns RH15 .... 73 A3
Preston Cir BN1 .... 189 A7
Preston Dro BN1 .... 142 F2
Preston Gr TN22 .... 79 B6
Preston Grange BN1 .... 142 E1
Preston Manor (Mus) BN1 .... 142 E1
Preston Park Ave BN1 .... 142 F1
Preston Park Sta BN1 .... 142 D2
Preston Rd Bexhill TN39 ...... 157 B7
Brighton BN1 .... 163 F8
Preston St BN1 .... 163 E5
Prestonville Ct 🔟 BN1 .... 189 F7
Prestonville Rd BN1, BN3 .... 189 F7
Prideaux Rd BN21 .... 184 E5
Primrose Cl BN23 .... 174 B3
Primrose Hill Bexhill TN39 .. 156 F6
Fairlight Cove TN35 .... 138 F5
Primrose La RH18 .... 12 A1
Prince Albert St BN1 .... 189 A5
Prince Charles Cl BN41, BN42 . 141 A1
Prince Charles Rd BN7 .... 123 E3
Prince Edward's Rd BN7 ..... 123 B1
Prince Of Wales Ct BN41 .... 162 F6
Prince Regent's Cl BN2 ...... 164 E4
Prince Regent's Ct 🔲 BN2 .. 164 E4
Prince William Par
BN22, BN23 .... 185 F6
Prince's Cres BN2 .... 189 B8
Prince's Pl BN1 .... 189 A5
Prince's Rd Brighton BN1, BN2 . 164 B8
Hastings TN37 .... 159 D7
Prince's St Brighton BN2 ..... 189 A5
Royal Tunbridge Wells TN2 .... 8 C3
Prince's Terr BN2 .... 164 E4
Princes Ave BN3 .... 163 A6
Princes Cl Seaford BN25 ..... 180 E5
Uckfield TN22 .... 78 A7
Princes Cres BN3 .... 163 A6
Princes Ct 🔲 BN3 .... 163 A6
Princes Field BN26 .... 150 B3
Princes Rd BN1 .... 185 E7
Princes Sq BN3 .... 163 A6
Princess Dr BN25 .... 180 D5
Princess Royal Hospl The
RH16 .... 50 F2
Prinkle La BN27 .... 109 C1
Prinsep Rd BN3 .... 163 A8
Prior's Way TN8 .... 4 A6
Priory Ave TN34 .... 136 E1
Priory Cl Hastings TN34 .... 136 E1
Pevensey Bay BN24 .... 175 D5
Priory Cres TN37 .... 146 C8
Priory Ct Brighton BN1 .... 163 F8
🔟 Eastbourne BN20 .... 184 F1
Lewes BN7 .... 146 D8
Priory Flats 🔢 BN7 .... 146 C8
Priory Ho BN20 .... 184 F1
Priory Hts BN20 .... 184 A5
Priory La BN23 .... 174 E3
Priory Meadow Sh Ctr TN34 ... 159 F8
Priory Orch BN23 .... 174 E1
Priory Rd Burgess Hill RH15 .. 73 A1
Eastbourne BN23 .... 174 E2
Forest Row RH18 .... 11 D2
Hassocks BN6 .... 97 E5
Hastings TN34, TN35 .... 160 B5
Priory Sch BN7 .... 146 E8
Priory St Hastings TN34 ..... 159 F7
Lewes BN7 .... 146 C8
Priory The Brighton BN1 ..... 142 D5
Hove BN3 .... 163 B5
Priory Way RH16 .... 50 F4
Promenade BN10 .... 178 C6
Promenade The BN24 .... 175 D4
Prospect Cotts TN3 .... 20 A3
Prospect Gdns 🔟 BN21 ..... 184 D4
Prospect Pl TN34 .... 159 F7
Prospect Rd Heathfield TN21 . 82 B6
Royal Tunbridge Wells TN4 .... 7 F8
Royal Tunbridge Wells TN1, TN2 . 8 C3
Prospect Terr TN21 .... 82 A7
Providence Cotts
Crowborough TN6 .... 25 D4
Groombridge TN3 .... 15 C7
Providence Pl BN1 .... 189 A7
Prowting Mead TN39 .... 156 C4
Pudding Cake La TN22 .... 78 C2
Pulborough Ave BN22 .... 173 E2
Pulborough Cl BN2 .... 164 F7
Pump Ho The BN3 .... 162 D8
Pump La TN22 .... 79 D4
Punnetts Town Cty Prim Sch
TN21 .... 83 B6

Purbeck Cl BN23 .... 174 C4
Putlands Cres TN39 .... 157 A8
Pyecombe Golf Course BN45 .. 119 E6
Pyecombe St BN45 .... 119 A6

Quadrangle The BN8 .... 105 C5
Quadrant BN1 .... 189 F5
Quadrant The BN6 .... 98 A4
Quail Cl BN27 .... 152 D7
Quakers La RH16 .... 51 A5
Quantock Cl BN23 .... 174 C4
Quantock Gdns TN34 .... 137 B3
Quarry Bank Rd BN1 .... 143 B2
Quarry Cl RH15 .... 73 C3
Quarry Cotts TN5 .... 29 D7
Quarry Cres TN34 .... 160 A5
Quarry Farm TN32 .... 65 D6
Quarry Hill Hastings TN38 .... 159 B7
 Haywards Heath RH17 .... 50 C6
Quarry Ho TN38 .... 159 B6
Quarry La BN25 .... 181 A5
Quarry Rd Hastings TN34 ...... 160 A5
 Newhaven BN9 .... 179 D5
Quarry Rise RH19 .... 2 A3
Quay Ct BN43 .... 161 B6
Quay The 5 BN3 .... 161 A6
Quebec Cl Bexhill TN39 .... 157 A5
 Eastbourne BN23 .... 185 F7
Quebec Mansions TN38 .... 159 A8
Quebec Rd TN38 .... 136 A4
Quebec St BN2 .... 189 B6
Queen Alexandra Ave BN3 .... 142 A3
Queen Anne's Cl BN7 .... 123 C1
Queen Caroline Cl BN3 .... 142 A3
Queen Elizabeth Ave RH15 ... 73 A2
Queen Mary Ave BN3 .... 142 A3
Queen Sq BN1 .... 189 F5
Queen St TN18 .... 47 B5
Queen Victoria Ave BN3 .... 142 A3
Queen Victoria Hospl The
 RH19 .... 1 F3
Queen's Ave 4 TN34 .... 159 F7
Queen's Cres BN23 .... 185 E7
Queen's Ct RH16 .... 50 F6
Queen's Gdns Brighton BN1 .. 189 A6
 Eastbourne BN21, BN22 ...... 185 B3
 Hove BN3 .... 163 C5
 Royal Tunbridge Wells TN4 .... 8 B6
Queen's Par Eastbourne BN22 .. 173 F1
 Hove BN3 .... 141 E2
Queen's Park Cty Prim Sch
 BN2 .... 164 C5
Queen's Park Rd BN2 .... 164 C6
Queen's Park Rise BN2 .... 164 C6
Queen's Park Terr BN2 .... 164 C6
Queen's Pl Brighton BN1 ...... 189 A7
 Hove BN3 .... 163 C6
Queen's Rd Brighton BN1 ..... 189 F6
 East Grinstead RH19 .... 1 E1
 Eastbourne BN23 .... 185 D7
 Hastings TN34 .... 159 F8
 Lewes BN7 .... 123 D3
 Royal Tunbridge Wells TN4 .... 8 B6
Queens App TN22 .... 55 D1
Queens Cotts TN5 .... 29 E6
Queens Cres RH15 .... 73 A2
Queens Ct TN39 .... 157 B3
Queens Dr Hassocks BN6 ...... 97 F4
 Maresfield TN22 .... 54 F4
Queens Park Gdns BN25 ...... 180 C4
Queens Sq TN34 .... 159 F8
Queensbury Mews BN1 .... 163 E5
Queensdown Sch BN1 .... 143 C3
Queensdown School Rd
 BN1, BN2 .... 143 D2
Queensmount TN20 .... 58 B7
Queensway Brighton BN2 .... 164 D6
 East Grinstead RH19 .... 1 E1
 Hastings TN37, TN38 .... 135 E5
 Seaford BN25 .... 181 A6
Querneby Cl BN43 .... 161 C7
Quickbourne La TN31 .... 67 C7
Quinnell Dr BN27 .... 129 B2
Quintin Cl BN27 .... 152 A5
Quintins The BN27 .... 152 C8

Radcliffe Cl TN37 .... 136 C3
Radinden Dr BN3 .... 142 D1
Radinden Manor Rd BN3 ...... 163 D8
Radnor Mews TN38 .... 135 E2
Ragged Dog La TN21 .... 81 B3
Raglan Ct Brighton BN1 .... 189 F5
 Pevensey Bay BN24 .... 175 C3
Railway App
 East Grinstead RH19 .... 1 E1
 Newhaven BN9 .... 179 D7
Railway Cotts Cowden TN8 ..... 4 D8
 Hastings TN38 .... 158 F6
 Horsted Keynes RH19 .... 33 A8
Railway La BN7 .... 123 D1
Railway Rd BN9 .... 179 D7
Railway St BN1 .... 189 F6
Railway View TN6 .... 38 C8
Raleigh Cl BN23 .... 185 E7
Ramsay Way BN23 .... 185 F7
Ramslye Rd TN2, TN4 .... 16 E8
Ranalah Est BN9 .... 179 D8
Randiddles Cl BN6 .... 97 B4
Randolph La TN31 .... 70 B3
Ranelagh Ct BN23 .... 185 E6
Ranelagh Villas BN3 .... 163 B8
Rangemore Dr BN21 .... 184 D6
Rankine Rd TN1 .... 8 D7

Ranmore Cl TN34 .... 136 E6
Rannoch Rd TN6 .... 25 D2
Rannoch Rd W TN6 .... 25 D2
Ranscombe Hill BN8 .... 147 A6
Ranscombe La BN8 .... 147 D6
Ranworth Cl BN23 .... 174 B4
Raphael Rd BN3 .... 162 F7
Rapson's Rd BN20 .... 173 A3
Rastrick Cl RH15 .... 72 F1
Rattle Rd BN24 .... 174 D6
Ratton Dr BN20 .... 184 B7
Ratton Gdn BN20 .... 184 B7
Ratton Rd BN21 .... 184 E4
Ratton Sch BN21 .... 184 C7
Ratton Village BN20 .... 184 B8
Raven Cl Battle TN33 .... 112 F4
 Hastings TN38 .... 135 E3
Ravens Cl TN39 .... 156 C3
Ravens Croft BN20 .... 188 F8
Ravens Dr BN20 .... 188 F8
Ravenside Ret & L Pk TN38 ... 158 A4
Ravenswood Ave TN1, TN2 ..... 8 D6
Ravenswood Dr BN2 .... 165 F6
Ravenswood Rd RH15 .... 73 B3
Raving Cl TN34 .... 137 A3
Rayford Cl BN10 .... 178 C7
Rayford Ct Bexhill TN40 .... 157 D4
 6 Seaford BN25 .... 180 E2
Raymond Cl BN25 .... 181 A5
Raystede Ctr for Animal
 Welfare BN8 .... 103 D1
Readers La TN31 .... 69 F5
Reading Rd BN2 .... 164 F4
Reba Ct BN2 .... 177 D4
Rectory Cl Burwash TN19 ...... 62 B6
 East Hoathly BN8 .... 105 A5
 Eastbourne BN20 .... 184 D3
 Hastings TN38 .... 136 B2
 Hove BN3 .... 162 D7
 Newhaven BN9 .... 179 C6
 Shoreham-by-Sea BN43 ...... 161 D7
Rectory Ct 15 BN43 .... 161 C8
Rectory Field TN7 .... 13 E4
Rectory La Beckley TN31 .... 67 F4
 Iden TN31 .... 70 B4
 Rye TN31 .... 93 C8
 Winchelsea TN36 .... 117 E7
Rectory Rd Newhaven BN9 ... 168 E2
 Shoreham-by-Sea BN43 ...... 161 D7
Rectory Way TN40 .... 157 D5
Red Dyke Cotts BN26 .... 173 F6
Red Lake Cty Prim Sch TN35 .. 137 D4
Red Lake Terr TN35 .... 137 D4
Red Oak TN18 .... 45 E8
Red Oast Cotts TN5 .... 32 C3
Redbridge La TN6 .... 37 D5
Redbrook La BN2 .... 56 D4
Redford Cl BN23 .... 174 E1
Redgarth Ct RH19 .... 1 B3
Redgeland Rise TN38 .... 135 F2
Redgill La BN8 .... 53 B1
Redhill Cl BN1 .... 142 C5
Redhill Dr BN1 .... 142 C5
Redleaf Cl TN2 .... 8 D6
Redman King Ho BN20 .... 184 F2
Redoubt Mus & Aquarium The
 BN22 .... 185 C4
Redoubt Rd BN22 .... 185 C4
Redshank Ct BN27 .... 152 D7
Redvers Rd BN2 .... 143 D1
Redwood Dr RH16 .... 50 D3
Reed Ct BN7 .... 123 D3
Reed Ho BN8 .... 100 E7
Reed Pond Wlk RH16 .... 51 A4
Reedham Rd BN23 .... 174 B4
Reedswood Rd
 Broad Oak TN31 .... 90 B4
 Hastings TN38 .... 158 E8
Reeves Ct TN3 .... 6 B5
Reeves Hill BN3 .... 143 D5
Reeves Terr TN5 .... 31 E1
Refectory Rd BN1 .... 144 B7
Regal Dr 10 RH19 .... 10 F8
Regency Cl TN22 .... 78 C8
Regency Gdns TN38 .... 159 A8
Regency Hall 19 TN2 .... 8 A2
Regency Mews
 18 Brighton BN1 .... 163 E5
 Eastbourne BN20 .... 185 A1
Regency Rd BN1 .... 189 F5
Regency Sq BN1 .... 163 E5
Regent Arc BN1 .... 189 A5
Regent Bsns Pk RH15 .... 72 E2
Regent Hill BN1 .... 189 F5
Regent Pl Hastings TN38 ...... 135 F7
 Royal Tunbridge Wells TN2 .... 8 D3
Regent Row BN1 .... 189 F5
Regent Sq TN31 .... 93 C6
Regent St BN1 .... 189 A5
Regents Cl BN25 .... 180 E5
Regina Ct TN4 .... 7 F4
Reginald Rd TN39 .... 157 B4
Regnum Cl BN22 .... 173 E4
Reigate Rd BN1 .... 142 D1
Renfrew Ct BN2 .... 185 D6
Resting Oak Hill BN8 .... 100 F3
Reynolds Dr TN40 .... 157 E5
Reynolds La TN4 .... 7 F6
Reynolds Rd Eastbourne BN23 .. 174 E1
 Hove BN3 .... 162 F7
Reynoldstown La BN26 .... 172 F6
Ribbetts Ho BN6 .... 97 A5
Ribbetts The BN6 .... 97 A5
Riccards La TN33 .... 88 A2
Rices Hill RH19 .... 1 E1
Richard Allen Ct 2 BN2 .... 143 C1
Richardson Ct 5 BN3 .... 162 F7

Richardson Rd Hove BN3 ...... 162 F7
 Royal Tunbridge Wells TN4 .... 8 A5
Richborough Cl TN34 .... 136 D4
Richington Way BN25 .... 181 B5
Richland Cl TN35 .... 137 D3
Richmead Gdns TN20 .... 40 B2
Richmond Ave TN39 .... 156 F3
Richmond Cl TN39 .... 157 A3
Richmond Ct 5 BN3 .... 163 E7
Richmond Gr TN39 .... 157 A2
Richmond Hts 11 BN2 .... 189 B6
Richmond Par BN2 .... 189 B6
Richmond Pl Brighton BN2 .. 189 A6
 Eastbourne BN21 .... 184 F4
Richmond Rd Bexhill TN39 ... 157 A3
 Brighton BN2 .... 164 B8
 Pevensey Bay BN24 .... 175 D5
 Seaford BN25 .... 180 E3
Richmond Sq RH19 .... 1 D2
Richmond St Brighton BN2 .. 189 B6
 Hastings TN34, TN35 .... 160 C6
Richmond Terr Brighton BN2 ... 189 B7
 1 Seaford BN25 .... 180 E3
Richmond Way RH19 .... 10 F8
Rickland Cotts TN22 .... 53 B6
Riddens Cl BN7 .... 99 E5
Riddens La BN7 .... 99 E6
Riddens The BN7 .... 99 E5
Riddlesdale Ave TN4 .... 8 A6
Ride The BN1 .... 142 F1
Riders Bolt TN39 .... 156 E5
Ridge Cl Nutley TN22 .... 35 C5
 Portslade-by-Sea BN41 ...... 141 A4
Ridge Rd BN1 .... 144 C7
Ridge The Groombridge TN3 .. 15 A6
 Hastings TN34, TN35, TN37 .. 136 D6
 Winchelsea Beach TN36 ...... 118 C6
Ridge View BN1 .... 143 E5
Ridge W The TN37, TN38 ..... 136 A7
Ridge Way RH16 .... 51 B2
Ridgelands Cl BN20 .... 184 C3
Ridgeside Ave BN1 .... 142 E5
Ridgeway East Grinstead RH19 .. 10 E7
 Hurst Green TN19 .... 45 A3
 Pembury TN2 .... 9 D7
 Southwick BN41, BN42 ...... 140 F1
 The Moor TN18 .... 45 E8
Ridgeway Cl Heathfield TN21 ... 82 A8
 Southwick BN42 .... 140 F1
Ridgeway Gdns BN2 .... 165 E7
Ridgeway The Burgess Hill RH15 .. 73 B4
 Friston BN20 .... 183 B1
 Herstmonceux BN27 .... 130 E6
 Seaford BN25 .... 180 F4
Ridgewood Ave BN2 .... 166 C3
Ridgewood Cl TN22 .... 78 D4
Ridgewood Gdns TN40 .... 157 F4
Ridgewood Ind Pk TN22 .... 78 E4
Ridgway Cl BN2 .... 165 D8
Ridgway Paddock BN7 .... 145 E6
Ridgway The BN2 .... 165 D8
Ridings The Bexhill TN39 ..... 156 F8
 Burgess Hill RH15 .... 73 C2
 Hastings TN37 .... 136 C5
 Newick BN8 .... 76 C7
 Royal Tunbridge Wells TN2 .... 8 F6
 Seaford BN25 .... 180 F5
 Telscombe Cliffs BN10 .... 167 B2
Rigden Rd BN3 .... 142 C1
Riley Rd BN2 .... 143 C1
Rill Wlk RH19 .... 2 B1
Ringle Gn TN18 .... 47 C5
Ringmer Bsns Pk BN8 .... 124 F6
Ringmer Cl BN1 .... 143 E4
Ringmer Com Coll BN8 .... 124 E6
Ringmer Cty Prim Sch BN8 .. 124 E7
Ringmer Rd Brighton BN1 .... 143 E4
 Brighton BN1 .... 143 F4
 Newhaven BN9 .... 179 B6
 Seaford BN25 .... 180 E2
Ringmer Way BN23 .... 174 A4
Ringwood Cl BN22 .... 185 B5
Ringwood Ct 5 BN22 .... 185 C5
Ringwood Rd Bexhill TN39 ... 157 C7
 Eastbourne BN22 .... 185 B5
Ripe La BN8 .... 126 E2
Ripley Chase BN21 .... 184 E3
Ripsley Cl BN23 .... 174 E2
Risden La TN18 .... 46 D7
Rise Park Gdns BN23 .... 174 E2
Rise The East Grinstead RH19 ... 10 F8
 Haywards Heath RH16 .... 51 B5
 Portslade-by-Sea BN41 ...... 140 F2
Riseden Rd TN5 .... 29 C1
Rising The BN23 .... 174 E2
Rissom Ct BN1 .... 142 E2
River La BN26 .... 171 A3
River Way TN22 .... 78 C6
Riverbourne Ho 10 BN22 ... 185 B4
Riverdale BN7 .... 123 C2
Riverhall Hill TN5 .... 28 E7
Riverside Forest Row RH18 ... 11 E3
 Newhaven BN9 .... 179 D6
 Southwick BN42 .... 161 E7
Riverside Ind Est BN7 .... 123 D2
Riverside Rd BN43 .... 161 A6
Rixons Cl RH17 .... 33 C5
Rixons Orch RH17 .... 33 C5
Roadean Cl BN25 .... 181 A4
Robert Lodge BN2 .... 164 F4
Robert Mitchell Sch TN39 ... 157 B7
Robert St BN1 .... 189 A6
Robert Tressell Cl TN34 ...... 159 F8
Robert Tressell Workshops 7
 TN34 .... 159 F8
Robert's Hill TN36 .... 117 A8
Roberts Row TN31 .... 68 C5
Richardson Ct 5 BN3 .... 162 F7

Robertson Pas TN34 .... 159 F7
Robertson Rd BN1 .... 142 D1
Robertson St TN34 .... 159 F7
Robertson Terr 1 TN34 .... 159 F7
Robertsons Hill TN34 .... 160 B6
Robin Cl East Grinstead RH19 .... 1 F2
 Eastbourne BN23 .... 174 C2
Robin Ct TN39 .... 157 A3
Robin Davis Cl BN2 .... 143 E1
Robin Dene BN2 .... 164 E4
Robin Hill TN39 .... 156 D4
Robin Post La BN26 .... 151 B1
Robin Rd BN6 .... 72 D2
Robinia Lodge 1 BN1 .... 142 E2
Robins Row BN1 .... 141 A1
Robinson Rd BN9 .... 179 C8
Robinsons Ct BN22 .... 185 C6
Roborough Cl BN22 .... 185 A4
Robsack Ave TN34 .... 135 E2
Robsack Wood Cty Prim Sch
 TN38 .... 135 C2
Rochdale Rd TN1 .... 8 C6
Rochester Cl Eastbourne BN20 .. 188 C8
 2 Hove BN3 .... 163 D6
Rochester Ct 3 BN3 .... 163 D6
Rochester Gdns BN3 .... 163 D6
Rochester Ho TN6 .... 26 C4
Rochester Rd 4 TN37 .... 136 B2
Rochester St BN2 .... 164 D5
Rochester Way TN6 .... 26 B1
Rochford Way BN25 .... 180 B6
Rock Channel TN31 .... 93 C5
Rock Channel Quay TN31 ..... 93 C5
Rock Cl Hastings TN35 .... 137 C4
 12 Southwick BN42 .... 161 E7
Rock Cotts TN3 .... 17 B1
Rock Gr BN2 .... 164 E4
Rock La TN35 .... 137 D7
Rock Pl BN2 .... 189 B4
Rock St BN2 .... 164 E4
Rock Villa Rd TN1 .... 8 A4
Rock's Hill TN35 .... 114 E7
Rock-a-Nore Par TN34 .... 160 B4
Rock-a-Nore Rd TN34 .... 160 B3
Rockall Dr BN27 .... 129 A2
Rockhurst Dr BN20 .... 184 B6
Rockington Way TN6 .... 38 B8
Rocklands Cotts BN27 .... 131 B5
Rocklands La TN35 .... 160 C5
Rockmead Rd TN35 .... 138 F4
Rocks Hill TN32 .... 64 E6
Rocks La TN22 .... 55 F7
Rocks Park Cty Prim Sch
 TN22 .... 78 B8
Rocks Park Rd TN22 .... 78 B7
Rocks The TN19 .... 11 D6
Rocky La RH16, RH15 .... 50 D1
Roderick Ave Peacehaven BN10 .. 178 B7
 Peacehaven BN10 .... 178 C8
Roderick Ave N BN10 .... 167 C2
Rodmell Ave BN2 .... 177 D5
Rodmell CE Prim Sch BN7 ... 146 E1
Rodmell Ct 5 BN25 .... 180 C4
Rodmell Ho BN9 .... 168 D3
Rodmell Pl BN1 .... 143 A6
Rodmell Rd
 Royal Tunbridge Wells TN1 .... 8 A2
 Seaford BN25 .... 181 B2
Rodmill Dr BN21 .... 184 D6
Rodmill Rd BN21 .... 184 D5
Rodney Cl BN23 .... 185 F7
Rodwell TN6 .... 26 C1
Roebuck St 18 TN34 .... 160 B4
Roedale Rd BN1 .... 143 B1
Roedean Cl TN39 .... 157 A5
Roedean Cres BN2 .... 165 A4
Roedean Hts BN2 .... 165 A4
Roedean Path BN2 .... 165 A3
Roedean Rd Brighton BN2 ... 164 F4
 Royal Tunbridge Wells TN1, TN2 .. 8 A1
Roedean Sch BN2 .... 165 C3
Roedean Terr BN2 .... 165 B3
Roedean Vale BN2 .... 165 B3
Roedean Way BN2 .... 165 B3
Roeheath BN8 .... 75 F4
Roffrey Ave BN22 .... 173 D1
Rolfe Dr RH15 .... 73 D3
Romaine Cl RH15 .... 73 D5
Roman Cl BN25 .... 180 B6
Roman Cres BN42 .... 161 E8
Roman Rd Hove BN3 .... 162 D6
 Southwick BN42 .... 161 E8
Roman Way Southwick BN42 .. 161 E8
 Uckfield TN22 .... 78 E7
Romans Way BN24 .... 174 E6
Romany Cl BN41 .... 162 B8
Romford Rd TN2, TN12 .... 9 F7
Romney Cl BN25 .... 181 C4
Romney Rd Polegate BN26 ... 173 B7
 Rottingdean BN2 .... 177 A5
Romney St BN22 .... 185 C5
Romsey Cl BN1 .... 143 C2
Rookery Cl BN9 .... 168 E2
Rookery La TN36 .... 117 F7
Rookery The BN23 .... 174 C4
Rookery Way
 Haywards Heath RH16 .... 50 E1
 Newhaven BN9 .... 168 F2
 Seaford BN25 .... 180 B5
Rookhurst Rd TN40 .... 157 F6
Rookley Cl TN2 .... 8 D2
Rookwood Cl TN22 .... 78 E8
Roopers TN3 .... 7 A7
Roosevelt Ct TN38 .... 136 B3
Rope Wlk Hailsham BN27 ... 152 B8
 Rye TN31 .... 93 C6
Rope Wlk The TN18 .... 47 B5

Pur – Roy 209

Roper's Gate TN2 .... 7 E1
Rosary Ct RH15 .... 73 B2
Rose Cotts RH17 .... 34 A4
Rose Ct BN6 .... 97 E4
Rose Hill BN2 .... 189 B7
Rose Hill Cl BN1, BN2 .... 189 A7
Rose Hill Ct BN1 .... 189 A7
Rose Hill Sch TN4 .... 7 E5
Rose Hill Terr BN1 .... 189 A7
Rose Walk Cl BN9 .... 179 C7
Rose Wlk BN25 .... 180 F4
Rose Wlk The BN9 .... 179 C7
Rosebarn Cl RH15 .... 73 C1
Rosebery Ave Eastbourne BN22 173 E1
 Woodingdean BN2 .... 165 C8
Rosedale Pl BN22 .... 173 D3
Rosedene Cl BN2 .... 165 E6
Rosefield Cotts TN6 .... 26 C1
Rosehill Wlk TN1 .... 8 A3
Roselands Bexhill TN39 ...... 156 F6
 Sedlescombe TN33 .... 88 E1
Roselands Ave
 Eastbourne BN22 .... 185 C5
 Wellbrook TN20 .... 39 F1
Roselands Cl BN22 .... 185 C5
Roselands Cty Inf Sch BN22 .. 185 B5
Roseleigh Gdns RH17 .... 51 F3
Rosemary Cl
 Haywards Heath RH17 .... 50 B6
 Peacehaven BN10 .... 167 C1
Rosemary Dr BN43 .... 140 C1
Rosemary La
 Shellies Green TN35 .... 138 D6
 Stonecrouch TN5 .... 32 A5
Rosemount BN25 .... 180 A6
Rosetti Rd BN24 .... 175 D4
Roseveare Rd BN22 .... 185 C6
Rossdale TN2 .... 8 D5
Rosslyn Ave BN3 .... 161 A7
Rosslyn Rd BN43 .... 161 A7
Rotary Lodge BN1 .... 143 E6
Rotary Point BN41 .... 141 B1
Rothbury Rd BN3 .... 162 D7
Rother Ave BN26 .... 173 F5
Rother Cl Burwash TN19 ...... 62 B6
 Crowborough TN6 .... 38 A7
Rother Ct TN39 .... 157 B6
Rother Rd BN25 .... 181 A2
Rother View TN19 .... 62 B7
Rotherfield Ave Bexhill TN40 .. 157 D4
 Eastbourne BN22, BN23 ..... 174 A4
 Hastings TN34 .... 160 B5
Rotherfield Cl BN1 .... 143 B6
Rotherfield Cres BN1 .... 143 B5
Rotherfield La TN20 .... 39 F4
Rotherfield Rd TN6 .... 38 E8
Rotherhill Rd TN6 .... 38 A7
Rotherhurst La TN6 .... 39 B6
Rothermead TN20 .... 39 F1
Rotherview TN32 .... 64 C5
Rothley Chase RH16 .... 50 F4
Rothsay Rd TN38 .... 159 B7
Rothwell Ct BN9 .... 179 A7
Rotten Row BN7 .... 146 B8
Rottingdean CE Prim Sch
 BN2 .... 177 A6
Rottingdean Pl BN2 .... 165 F4
Rotunda Rd BN23 .... 185 D8
Rotyngs The BN2 .... 165 F2
Rough Brow BN25 .... 181 A4
Rough Field RH19 .... 1 D4
Rough The BN2 .... 76 C7
Round Hill Rd 2 BN1, BN2 ... 164 B8
Round Hill St 3 BN2 .... 164 B8
Roundacres Way TN40 .... 157 E6
Roundel The TN37 .... 136 D5
Roundhay Ave BN10 .... 178 B6
Roundhill Cres BN2 .... 164 B8
Roundhill Rd TN2 .... 8 D1
Roundhouse Cotts TN21 .... 82 D7
Roundway BN1 .... 143 E5
Roundwood La RH16 .... 50 F8
Roundwood Rd TN37 .... 136 B5
Rowan Ave Eastbourne BN22 .. 173 D3
 Hove BN3 .... 141 E1
Rowan Cl Hastings TN37 ..... 136 D6
 Haywards Heath RH16 .... 51 B4
 Heathfield TN21 .... 82 A5
 Portslade-by-Sea BN41 ...... 141 A1
 Seaford BN25 .... 181 C3
Rowan Ct BN26 .... 173 A6
Rowan Gdns TN40 .... 157 F6
Rowan Tree Rd TN2 .... 7 E1
Rowan Way BN2 .... 165 E4
Rowan's Ct 1 BN7 .... 123 C1
Rowanden Ct BN2 .... 177 C4
Rowbarns TN33 .... 112 C6
Rowe Ave BN10 .... 178 B7
Rowe Ave N BN10 .... 178 B8
Rowsley Rd BN20 .... 188 D7
Royal Alexandra Hospl for
 Sick Children The BN1 ...... 189 F6
Royal Ashdown Forest
 Golf Course RH18 .... 12 A1
Royal Chase TN4, TN1 .... 7 F4
Royal Cres BN2 .... 164 C4
Royal Crescent Mansions 10
 BN2 .... 164 C4
Royal Crescent Mews 8 BN2 164 C4
Royal Dr BN25 .... 180 E6
Royal George Par BN43 ...... 140 C1
Royal George Rd RH15 .... 72 E3
Royal Mews TN38 .... 159 A6
Royal Military Rd TN36 .... 118 A8

Royal Oak La TN22 .... 56 B8
Royal Par Eastbourne BN22 ... 185 C4
  Eastbourne BN22 .... 185 D5
Royal Pavilion BN1 .... 189 A5
Royal Sovereign View BN23 ... 185 F6
Royal Sussex Cres BN20 ...... 184 B5
Royal Sussex Ct BN7 .... 146 D8
Royal Sussex Cty Hospl
  (General) BN2 .... 164 D4
Royal Terr 4 TN37 .... 159 C7
Royal Victoria Place Sh Ctr
  TN2 .... 8 B4
Royles Cl BN2 .... 177 A6
Royston Cl BN20 .... 183 A1
Royston Gdns TN40 .... 157 F6
Rudyard Cl BN2 .... 165 E8
Rudyard Kipling
  Cty Prim Sch BN2 .... 165 E7
Rudyard Rd BN2 .... 165 E8
Rue De Bayeux TN33 .... 112 D5
Ruffet Ct TN2 .... 7 E1
Rufus Cl BN7 .... 123 C1
Rugby Cl BN25 .... 181 B4
Rugby Ct 5 BN2 .... 164 E4
Rugby Pl BN2 .... 164 E4
Rugby Rd BN1 .... 143 A1
Rumbolds La RH16 .... 50 D2
Rumsey Ct TN6 .... 25 F1
Rusbridge La 3 BN7 .... 123 E1
Rush Ct 4 BN22 .... 185 B3
Rushers Cross TN20 .... 40 E5
Rushes The RH16 .... 51 C4
Rushetts TN5 .... 6 F4
Rushey Cl BN8 .... 124 E5
Rushlake Cl BN1 .... 143 E5
Rushlake Cres BN21 .... 184 D6
Rushlake Rd BN1 .... 143 E5
Rushlye Cl TN3 .... 17 F5
Rushmere Rise TN38 .... 135 E1
Rushwood Cl RH16 .... 51 B4
  Willingdon BN20, BN22 ..... 173 E1
Rusper Rd Brighton BN1 ... 143 D6
  Eastbourne BN20 .... 184 B6
Ruspers RH15 .... 73 D2
Russell Cotts 4 BN21 ..... 184 E4
Russell Cres 2 BN1, BN3 ... 189 F7
Russell Ct 5 TN34 .... 160 A3
Russell Mews 17 BN1 ...... 163 E5
Russell Pl BN1 .... 189 F5
Russell Rd BN1 .... 189 F5
Russell Row BN7 .... 123 C3
Russell St TN34 .... 159 F8
Russet Cl BN26 .... 173 C6
Rusthall Grange TN4 .... 7 D4
Rusthall High St TN4 .... 7 C4
Rusthall Pk TN4 .... 7 D4
Rusthall Rd TN4 .... 7 D4
Rustic Cl BN10 .... 167 B1
Rustic Rd BN10 .... 167 B2
Rustington Ct BN20 .... 188 F8
Rustington Rd BN1 .... 143 A5
Rustlings Cl RH16 .... 51 B5
Rustwick TN4 .... 7 D4
Rutherfords Bsns Pk TN33 ... 113 B7
Rutland Cl BN21 .... 184 D6
Rutland Ct 3 Eastbourne BN23 174 E1
  Hove BN3 .... 162 F6
Rutland Gdns BN3 .... 162 F7
Rutland Rd BN3 .... 163 A7
Rutley Cl TN32 .... 64 C5
Ruxley Ct BN23 .... 174 D2
Rydal Cl TN4 .... 7 E5
Rydal Dr TN4 .... 7 E5
Rydal Way BN23 .... 174 C4
Ryde Cl BN3 .... 141 D1
Ryde Rd BN2 .... 164 D7
Ryders TN3 .... 7 A3
Rye Cl Polegate BN26 .... 173 C7
  Saltdean BN2 .... 177 F6
  Seaford BN25 .... 181 C4
Rye Golf Links TN31 .... 94 B2
Rye Harbour Nature Reserve
  TN31 .... 94 B1
Rye Ind Est TN31 .... 93 D4
Rye Rd Four Throws TN18 ... 46 D8
  Hastings TN35 .... 137 D5
  Iden TN30, TN31 .... 70 A8
  Rye Foreign TN31 .... 69 E2
Rye St BN22 .... 185 D6
Rye Sta TN31 .... 93 B6
Ryecroft 12 Brighton BN2 ... 164 F5
  Haywards Heath RH16 .... 50 E3
Ryefield Cl BN21 .... 184 C7
Ryelands Dr BN2 .... 143 D3
Rylstone Rd BN22 .... 185 C4
Rymers Cl TN1 .... 8 D7
Rymill Rd TN38 .... 136 A3
Ryst Wood Rd RH18 .... 12 B1

Sackville Cl East Grinstead RH19 ... 1 C3
  Lewes BN7 .... 123 C1
Sackville Coll RH19 .... 1 F1
Sackville Ct East Grinstead RH19 ... 157 D5
  3 East Grinstead RH19 .... 10 F8
Sackville Gdns
  East Grinstead RH19 .... 1 C3
  Hove BN3 .... 162 F6
Sackville La RH19 .... 1 C3
Sackville Rd Bexhill TN39 ... 157 B3
  Eastbourne BN22 .... 173 F2
  Hailsham BN27 .... 152 C6
  Hove BN3 .... 163 A7
Sackville Sch RH19 .... 2 A1

Sackville Trad Est BN3 .... 163 B8
Sacred Heart RC Prim Sch
  TN35 .... 160 B5
Sacred Heart Sch TN5 .... 29 D5
Saddler's Ct 6 TN38 .... 159 B6
Saddlers Cl RH15 .... 73 D1
Sadler Way BN2 .... 164 F6
Sadlers Way BN8 .... 124 D4
Saffron Cl BN43 .... 140 C1
Saffron Gdns BN26 .... 170 F3
Saffrons Ct BN21 .... 184 E2
Saffrons Mead BN20 .... 184 F2
Saffrons Pk BN20 .... 184 E1
Saffrons Rd BN21 .... 184 E2
Saffrons The RH15 .... 72 F5
Saint Hill Rd RH19 .... 10 C5
Saints Hill TN11 .... 6 A8
St Agnes Rd RH19 .... 1 E2
St Andrew's CE Inf Sch BN22 185 D6
St Andrew's CE Prim Sch
  BN3 .... 163 B6
St Andrew's Ct BN9 .... 179 B7
St Andrew's Dr BN25 .... 180 B6
St Andrew's La 11 BN7 .... 123 D1
St Andrew's Rd Bexhill TN40 157 C5
  Brighton BN1 .... 143 A1
  Portslade-by-Sea BN41 .... 162 C7
St Andrew's Sq 6 TN34 ... 159 F8
St Andrews Cl BN27 .... 129 A1
St Andrews Rd RH15 .... 73 D3
St Ann's Ct 12 BN3 .... 163 D7
St Anne's Cl TN40 .... 157 D5
St Anne's Cres BN21 .... 123 B1
St Anne's Ct 9 Brighton BN2 ... 164 C4
  6 Brighton BN1 .... 189 F7
St Anne's Gdns BN6 .... 98 A3
St Anne's Ho 7 BN1 .... 189 F7
St Anne's Rd BN21 .... 184 F4
St Anne's Sch BN7 .... 146 B8
St Annes Gn TN19 .... 62 A6
St Annes Rd BN22 .... 173 B3
St Annes Well Ho 7 BN3 ... 163 D6
St Anthony's Ave BN23 .... 185 E8
St Anthonys BN8 .... 124 E6
St Aubyn's Cres BN41 ...... 162 B7
St Aubyn's Mead BN2 ...... 177 A5
St Aubyn's Rd
  Eastbourne BN22 .... 185 B3
  Portslade-by-Sea BN41 .... 162 C7
  Southwick BN41 .... 162 A7
St Aubyns BN3 .... 163 B6
St Aubyns St BN3 .... 163 A5
St Augustine Cl RH17 .... 51 F3
St Augustine's Cl TN39 .... 156 F3
St Augustine's RC Prim Sch
  TN4 .... 8 A7
St Barnabas CE Prim Sch TN1 ... 8 B5
St Barnabas' Cl TN1 .... 8 B5
St Bartholomew's
  CE Prim Sch BN1 .... 189 A7
St Bede's Prep Sch BN20 ... 188 E7
St Bede's Sch BN27 .... 151 A8
St Bernadette's
  RC Prim Sch BN2 .... 142 E2
St Brelades BN21 .... 185 B2
St Catherine's Cl TN37 ..... 159 D8
St Christopher's Rd BN6 .... 97 A6
St Christopher's Sch BN3 ... 163 A6
St Christopher's (Trng Coll,
  Dr Barnardo's Home) TN2 ... 8 D4
St Clement's Caves TN34 ... 160 A4
St Clement's Sch BN21 .... 184 D6
St Clements Pl 5 TN38 .... 159 C6
St Crispians BN25 .... 180 D3
St Crispians Cl BN25 .... 180 D3
St Cuthmans Cl BN2 .... 164 F6
St David's Ave TN40 .... 157 C5
St David's Cl BN10 .... 178 B8
St David's Rd TN4 .... 8 B6
St Davids Cl BN22 .... 173 D4
St Dominic Cl TN38 .... 159 A8
St Edmund's Rd RH16 .... 50 F3
St Edward's Cl RH19 .... 1 C1
St Elizabeth's BN25 .... 180 F4
St Francis Chase TN39 ..... 157 A5
St Francis Cl RH16 .... 50 F2
St George's La BN6 .... 97 B5
St George's Mews BN1 .... 189 A6
St George's Pk TN2 .... 16 F8
St George's Pl Brighton BN1 ... 189 A6
  Hurstpierpoint BN6 .... 97 B5
St George's Rd
  Bexhill TN39, TN40 .... 157 C5
  Brighton BN2 .... 164 D4
  Eastbourne BN22 .... 185 B4
  Hastings TN34 .... 160 A5
St George's Sch TN2 .... 9 A5
St George's Terr 5 BN2 ... 164 C4
St Georges Ct RH19 .... 1 C3
St Georges Vineyard TN21 ... 80 F3
St Giles CE Prim Sch RH17 ... 33 C6
St Margaret's Rd
St Giles Cl
  Shoreham-by-Sea BN43 ... 161 B8
  Winchelsea TN36 .... 117 F7
St Gregory's
  Catholic Comp Sch TN4 ..... 8 A7
St Helen's La TN34 .... 136 E3
St Helen's Cres Hastings TN34, TN36 136 E2
  Hove BN3 .... 141 D3
St Helen's Ct TN34 .... 136 E2
St Helen's Down TN34 ..... 137 A3
St Helen's Dr BN3 .... 141 D3
St Helen's Park Rd TN34 ... 136 E3
St Helen's Rd Brighton BN2 ... 164 D7
  Hastings TN34, TN37 .... 136 D2
St Helena's Ct 11 BN21 ... 184 E4
St Helens's Wood Rd TN34 ... 136 E5

St Heliers Ave BN3 .... 162 E7
St James' Ave TN40 .... 157 D6
St James' CE Inf Sch TN2 ... 8 C4
St James' CE Jun Sch TN2 ... 8 C4
St James' Cl TN40 .... 157 C7
St James' Cres TN40 .... 157 D7
St James' Ho 13 BN2 .... 189 B5
St James La TN22 .... 35 C4
St James' Pk TN1, TN2 .... 8 C5
St James' Rd Bexhill TN40 ... 157 C6
St James Rd Eastbourne BN22 ... 185 C4
St James' Rd
  Royal Tunbridge Wells TN1 TN2 ... 8 C5
St James St BN7 .... 146 C8
St James Wlk BN8 .... 75 E1
St James's Ave BN8 .... 189 B5
St James's Ct TN1 .... 8 B4
St James's Rd
  East Grinstead RH19 .... 1 D1
  Hastings TN34 .... 136 F1
St James's St BN2 .... 189 B5
St James's Street Mews BN2 189 B5
St John Bank TN40 .... 100 D8
St John St 4 BN7 .... 123 D1
St John the Baptist
  RC Prim Sch BN2 .... 164 D5
St John's Ave RH15 .... 72 F4
St John's CE Prim Sch
  Crowborough TN6 .... 25 C4
  Royal Tunbridge Wells TN4 ... 8 A5
St John's Cl Crowborough TN6 ... 25 E3
  East Grinstead RH19 .... 1 E2
  South Chailey BN8 .... 100 C7
St John's Dr BN24 .... 174 E6
St John's Hill 2 BN7 .... 123 C1
St John's Ho BN20 .... 188 F8
St John's Mount 8 BN2 ... 189 B5
St John's Pk TN4 .... 8 A8
St John's Pl Brighton BN2 ... 189 B5
  10 Hove BN3 .... 163 C6
St John's Rd Bexhill TN40 ... 157 B6
  Crowborough TN6 .... 25 D4
  East Grinstead RH19 .... 1 E2
  Eastbourne BN20 .... 188 F8
  Hastings TN37 .... 159 C7
  Haywards Heath RH16 ...... 50 E2
  Hove BN3 .... 163 C5
  Polegate BN26 .... 173 A6
  Royal Tunbridge Wells TN1, TN4 ... 8 A6
  Seaford BN25 .... 180 E2
St John's Sch TN37 .... 123 C1
St Johns CE Prim Sch TN4 ... 8 B7
St Johns Ct RH15 .... 73 A3
St Johns Rd RH15 .... 73 A3
St Joseph's Cl BN3 .... 163 A8
St Joseph's RC Cty Prim Sch
  BN23 .... 143 C1
St Joseph's RC Prim Sch
  RH16 .... 50 E4
St Joseph's Trad Est BN3 ... 163 A8
St Josephs Way RH16 .... 50 E4
St Julian's La BN43 .... 161 D7
St Julians Cl BN43 .... 161 C7
St Keyna Ave BN3, BN41 ... 162 C6
St Kitts TN39 .... 157 A2
St Laurence Cl BN10 .... 167 A1
St Lawrence CE Prim Sch BN6 97 A6
St Lawrence Rd TN39 .... 157 B7
St Lawrence Way BN6 .... 97 A7
St Leonard's Ave BN21 .... 162 C7
St Leonard's Gdns BN3, BN41 162 D7
St Leonard's Pl BN20 .... 184 C3
St Leonard's Rd
  5 Brighton BN2 .... 164 C8
  Eastbourne BN21 .... 185 A3
  Hove BN3, BN41 .... 162 C7
  Newhaven BN9 .... 168 F2
St Leonards CE Prim Sch
  TN38 .... 159 A7
St Leonards Cl BN9 .... 168 F2
St Leonards Ct TN38 .... 159 A6
St Leonards Pk RH19 .... 1 E1
St Leonards Rd TN40 .... 157 C3
St Leonards Terr TN26 ..... 172 F7
St Leonards
  (Warrior Square) Sta TN38 ... 159 C7
St Louie Cl BN42 .... 162 A8
St Lucia TN39 .... 157 A2
St Luke's CE Inf Sch TN4 ..... 8 C7
St Luke's Cty Inf Sch BN2 ... 164 C6
St Luke's Cty Jun Sch BN2 ... 164 C6
St Luke's La BN9 .... 179 C7
St Luke's Rd Brighton BN2 ... 164 C6
  Royal Tunbridge Wells TN4 ... 8 B6
St Luke's Terr BN2 .... 164 C6
St Lukes Ct RH15 .... 73 A3
St Margaret CE Prim Sch BN6 98 D3
St Margaret's Ave RH19 .... 1 F6
St Margaret's Pl BN1 .... 189 F5
St Margaret's Rd
  East Grinstead RH19 .... 1 F3
  Hastings TN37 .... 159 D7
St Margaret's Rise BN25 ... 180 A6
St Margaret's Terr TN37 ... 159 D7
St Margarets BN2 .... 177 A5
St Margarets Cres TN39 ... 156 B8
St Margarets Terr TN31 ..... 93 C5
St Mark's CE Prim Sch
  Brighton BN2 .... 164 E5
  Hadlow Down TN22 .... 57 C5
  Royal Tunbridge Wells TN4 ... 7 D1
St Mark's Rd TN4 .... 16 F7
St Mark's St BN2 .... 164 E4
St Marks TN39 .... 156 D5
St Marks Field TN22 .... 57 B5
St Martin's Flats 6 BN2 ... 164 C7
St Martin's La 4 BN7 ...... 146 C8

St Martin's Pl BN2 .... 164 C7
St Martin's St BN2 .... 189 B8
St Martins TN33 .... 112 D5
St Martins CE Prim Sch BN2 ... 164 C8
St Martins Cres BN9 .... 168 D1
St Martins Ho BN8 .... 124 E6
St Martins Rd BN22 .... 173 D3
St Mary Magdalen
  RC Prim Sch BN1 .... 163 E5
St Mary Magdalen's
  RC Prim Sch TN40 .... 157 F6
St Mary Magdalene St BN2 189 B8
St Mary Star of the Sea
  RC Prim Sch TN37 .... 159 D8
St Mary the Virgin
  CE Prim Sch TN2 .... 13 D4
St Mary's CE Sch RH19 .... 1 D2
St Mary's Cl Cackle Street TN31 ... 90 A2
  Ticehurst TN5 .... 31 D1
  Willingdon BN22 .... 173 B2
St Mary's Cnr 3 BN21 ..... 184 D3
St Mary's Cotts Battle TN33 ... 112 E3
  Bexhill TN39 .... 156 F8
  4 Eastbourne BN20 .... 184 D3
St Mary's Ct
  2 Eastbourne BN21 .... 184 D3
  8 Hastings TN37 .... 159 C7
St Mary's Farmhouse TN33 112 E3
St Mary's Gdns TN33 .... 112 E3
St Mary's La Bexhill TN39 ... 156 F8
  Speldhurst TN3 .... 7 A8
  Ticehurst TN5 .... 31 D1
St Mary's Pl BN2 .... 189 B5
St Mary's RC Prim Sch
  Crowborough TN6 .... 26 A2
  Portslade-by-Sea BN41 .... 162 C7
St Mary's Rd Burgess Hill RH15 ... 72 F4
  Eastbourne BN21 .... 184 D4
  Hastings TN34 .... 160 A5
St Mary's Rd W RH15 .... 72 E4
St Mary's Sch Bexhill TN40 ... 157 E6
  Maynard's Green TN21 ...... 82 A1
St Mary's Sq 17 BN2 .... 164 D4
St Mary's Terr Battle TN33 ... 112 F3
  Hastings TN34 .... 160 A5
St Mary's Villas TN33 ...... 112 E3
St Mary's Wlk BN27 .... 152 C7
St Mary-in-the-Fields TN20 40 B2
St Marys TN21 .... 80 E7
St Marys Ave BN27 .... 152 C7
St Marys Garth BN22 .... 56 C4
St Marys Pl 3 BN43 .... 161 A6
St Matthew's Dr TN38 ..... 136 C1
St Matthew's Gdns TN38 ... 136 B1
St Matthew's High Brooms
  CE Prim Sch TN4 .... 8 B8
St Matthew's Rd TN38 ..... 136 B1
St Matthews Ct BN2 .... 164 C5
St Mellion Ct TN38 .... 151 F8
St Michael's Cty Prim Sch
  TN7 .... 14 B5
St Michael's Pl Brighton BN1 ... 163 E6
  8 Hastings TN34 .... 159 E7
St Michael's Rd
  Portslade-by-Sea BN41 .... 162 B7
  Royal Tunbridge Wells TN4 ... 8 B7
St Michael's Terr BN7 ...... 123 C3
St Michaels Cl TN6 .... 38 B8
St Michaels Rd RH19 .... 1 E2
St Nicholas' CE Jun Sch
  BN41 .... 162 B8
St Nicholas Ct RH16 .... 51 A6
St Nicholas La 13 BN7 .... 123 D1
St Nicholas Lodge BN1 .... 189 F5
St Nicholas Pl 2 BN43 .... 161 A6
St Nicholas Rd Brighton BN1 ... 189 F6
  Portslade-by-Sea BN41 .... 162 B7
St Nicolas Cl BN24 .... 175 B6
St Nicolas & St Mary CE Sch
  BN43 .... 161 A8
St Olive's Cl TN21 .... 81 C7
St Pancras Gdns BN7 .... 146 B8
St Pancras Gn BN7 .... 145 E5
St Pancras RC Prim Sch BN7 123 B1
St Pancras Rd BN7 .... 146 B8
St Patrick's Cres TN40 ..... 157 C5
St Patrick's Rd BN3 .... 163 A7
St Paul's CE Prim Sch
  Brighton BN2 .... 189 F6
St Paul's CE Prim Sch
  Hastings TN37 .... 136 D1
St Paul's Cl RH16 .... 50 F5
St Paul's Ct Hastings TN37 ... 159 D8
  Rusthall TN4 .... 7 C4
St Paul's Pl TN37 .... 159 D8
St Paul's RC Sec Sch RH16 ... 50 F5
St Paul's Rd TN37 .... 136 C1
St Paul's St Brighton BN2 ... 189 B8
  Rusthall TN4 .... 7 C4
St Pauls CE Inf Sch TN4 ...... 7 B4
St Pauls CE Jun Sch TN4 ..... 7 B4
St Pauls Cl BN22 .... 173 D3
St Peter & St Paul
  CE Prim Sch TN40 .... 157 C4
St Peter's Ave BN10 .... 178 A8
St Peter's CE Prim Sch TN2 ... 8 C3
St Peter's Cl Hove BN3 ..... 141 F2
  Seaford BN25 .... 180 E5
St Peter's Cres TN40 .... 157 D5
St Peter's Cty Inf Sch BN41 ... 162 B7
St Peter's Mews TN40 ..... 157 D5
St Peter's Pl BN1, BN2 ..... 189 A6
St Peter's RC Prim Sch
  BN43 .... 161 A8
St Peter's RC Sch RH19 .... 1 C3
St Peter's Rd Hastings TN37 ... 159 C8
  Portslade-by-Sea BN41 .... 162 B7
  Seaford BN25 .... 180 E5

St Peter's Sch RH15 .... 73 A4
St Peter's St Brighton BN1 ... 189 A7
  Royal Tunbridge Wells TN2 ... 8 C3
St Peters Meadow TN6 .... 39 A7
St Peters Pl BN7 .... 123 C1
St Peters Rd RH15 .... 73 A4
St Peters Row TN3 .... 6 A5
St Philip's Ave BN22 .... 185 B5
St Philip's RC Prim Sch TN22 ... 78 C5
St Philips Ct TN1 .... 8 D6
St Philips Mews 3 BN3 .... 162 F7
St Richard's Ct BN3 .... 141 D1
St Richard's Flats BN41 .... 162 B7
St Richard's RC Sch TN40 ... 157 E4
St Richard's Rd BN41 ...... 162 B7
St Richards Ho 3 TN38 .... 159 C7
St Richards Rd TN6 .... 38 A7
St Saviour's Rd TN38 .... 158 F6
St Saviours Ct 1 BN1 ...... 164 B8
St Stephens Ct TN1 .... 8 B5
St Swithun's Cl RH19 .... 1 F1
St Swithun's La 1 BN7 .... 146 C8
St Swithun's Terr 5 BN7 ... 146 C8
St Thomas TN39 .... 157 A2
St Thomas a' Becket
  RC Inf Sch BN2 .... 184 F5
St Thomas a' Becket
  RC Jun Sch BN21 .... 184 F5
St Thomas Ct 2 BN7 .... 123 E1
St Thomas of Canterbury Ct
  TN20 .... 40 A2
St Thomas's CE Prim Sch TN3 15 C6
St Thomas's Rd TN34 .... 160 A5
St Thomas's St TN36 .... 117 F7
St Vincent's Ct BN2 .... 165 A3
St Vincent's Dr TN38 .... 158 F7
St Vincents Flats TN37 ..... 136 B4
St Vincents Pl BN20 .... 184 E1
St Vincents Rd TN38 .... 158 F7
St Wilfred's Ct 5 RH16 ..... 50 E4
St Wilfred's Pl BN25 .... 181 B3
St Wilfreds Rd RH15 .... 73 B4
St Wilfrid's CE Prim Sch RH16 50 F4
St Wilfrid's Gn BN27 .... 152 C8
St Wilfrid's Way RH16 .... 50 F4
St Wilfrids RC Prim Sch RH15 72 F2
Salcey Ct TN38 .... 135 E2
Salehurst CE Prim Sch TN32 64 B4
Salehurst Gdns TN38 .... 135 D2
Salehurst Rd BN20, BN21 ... 184 C4
Salisbury Cl BN22 .... 173 C2
Salisbury Rd
  Bexhill TN39, TN40 .... 157 B5
  Eastbourne BN20 .... 188 C8
  Hastings TN37 .... 136 C1
  Hove BN3 .... 163 C6
  Langton Green TN3 .... 6 F3
  Royal Tunbridge Wells TN4 ... 8 C8
  Seaford BN25 .... 180 E3
Salisbury Terr TN21 .... 81 B8
Sally Ct 3 BN22 .... 185 B3
Salomons Rd TN4 .... 7 C4
Saltcote Mews TN31 .... 93 C7
Saltdean Cl TN39 .... 156 E3
Saltdean Cty Prim Sch BN2 ... 177 C6
Saltdean Dr BN2 .... 177 B5
Saltdean Park Rd BN2 ..... 177 C5
Saltdean Vale BN2 .... 177 D6
Saltdean Way TN39 .... 156 D3
Salters La TN34 .... 160 B4
Saltwood Rd BN25 .... 181 C4
Salvador Cl BN23 .... 185 F7
Salvington Cres TN39 ...... 156 F4
San Feliu Ct RH19 .... 2 B2
San Jose Cl TN35 .... 160 C6
Sancroft Rd BN20 .... 184 B3
Sanctuary The BN20 .... 184 B4
Sand Hill La BN8 .... 104 B8
Sand Rd TN3 .... 20 A4
Sandbanks BN27 .... 152 A5
Sandbanks Gdns BN27 ..... 152 B5
Sandbanks Gr BN27 .... 152 B6
Sandbanks Rd BN27 .... 152 A6
Sandbanks Way BN27 ...... 152 B6
Sandbrook TN6 .... 97 F3
Sanders Ho BN3 .... 162 E8
Sanderstead 1 BN27 .... 164 F5
Sandfield Rd TN11 .... 6 A7
Sandgate Cl BN25 .... 181 C5
Sandgate Rd BN1 .... 143 A2
Sandhawes Hill RH19 .... 2 A4
Sandhill La Boarshead TN6 ... 26 E7
  Churches Green BN27, TN21 ... 109 B6
Sandhurst Ave Pembury TN2 ... 9 E6
  Woodingdean BN2 .... 144 D1
Sandhurst Cl
  Royal Tunbridge Wells TN1 ... 8 C5
  Sandhurst Cross TN18 .... 47 A4
Sandhurst Cty Prim Sch TN18 ... 47 C5
Sandhurst Gdns TN38 .... 136 F6
Sandhurst Ho TN2 .... 8 D5
Sandhurst La TN39 .... 156 B6
Sandhurst Pk TN1 .... 8 C6
Sandhurst Rd TN1, TN2, TN4 ... 8 D6
Sandore Cl BN25 .... 181 A4
Sandore Rd BN25 .... 181 A4
Sandown Cl Eastbourne BN23 174 B4
  Royal Tunbridge Wells TN2 ... 8 F5
Sandown Ct BN3 .... 141 D1
Sandown Cty Prim Sch TN35 137 C4
Sandown Gr TN2 .... 8 F6
Sandown Pk TN2 .... 8 F6
Sandown Rd Brighton BN2 ... 164 D7
  Hastings TN35 .... 137 C3
  Southwick BN42 .... 161 E8
Sandown Way TN40 .... 157 E6
Sandpiper Wlk BN23 .... 174 C2

Sandridge TN6 .... 25 F1
Sandringham Cl
 East Grinstead RH19 .... 11 A8
 Hove BN3 .... 142 A3
 Seaford BN25 .... 181 A6
Sandringham Dr BN3 .... 142 A3
Sandringham Hts TN38 .... 135 D3
Sandringham Lodge 15 BN3 .. 163 C6
Sandrock Hall TN34 .... 136 F5
Sandrock Hill TN33 .... 135 A4
Sandrock Ho TN2 .... 8 D4
Sandrock Pk TN34 .... 136 F5
Sandrock Rd TN2 .... 8 C4
Sandrocks Way RH16 .... 50 E2
Sandwich Dr TN38 .... 158 F8
Sandwich St BN22 .... 185 C6
Sandy Cl TN37 .... 136 B5
Sandy Cross Cotts TN21 .... 82 A5
Sandy Cross La TN21 .... 82 B5
Sandy La Coleman's Hatch TN7 .. 23 D6
 East Grinstead RH19 .... 1 F1
 Framefield TN22 .... 79 A7
 Lions Green TN21 .... 81 E2
Sandy Vale BN25 .... 50 E2
Sanshaw Ct BN21 .... 184 E3
Santa Cruz Dr BN23 .... 185 F7
Santer Ho TN18 .... 45 E8
Sanyhils Ave BN1 .... 142 F7
Saunders Cl Hastings TN34 .... 160 A5
 Uckfield TN22 .... 78 A8
Saunders Hill BN1 .... 143 D7
Saunders Park Rise 3 BN2 .. 143 C1
Saunders Park View BN2 ...... 143 C1
Saunders Rd TN4 .... 7 E1
Saunders Way TN31 .... 95 A2
Savill Rd RH16 .... 51 A8
Sawyard Cotts TN22 .... 53 C5
Sawyers Cl RH15 .... 73 D1
Saxby Cl BN23 .... 174 E1
Saxby Rd Bexhill TN39 .... 157 A5
 Burgess Hill RH15 .... 72 D4
Saxon Cl BN2 .... 177 C6
Saxon Ct Hastings TN37 .... 159 C8
 Hove BN3 .... 162 D6
Saxon La BN25 .... 180 E2
Saxon Mount Sch TN38 .... 158 E7
Saxon Pl BN21 .... 184 C6
Saxon Pl Hastings TN35 .... 137 D3
 Hove BN3 .... 162 D6
 Newhaven BN9 .... 179 C7
Saxon Rise TN40 .... 157 E4
Saxon St TN37 .... 159 C6
Saxonbury 15 BN2 .... 189 B6
Saxonbury Cl TN6 .... 25 F2
Saxonhurst Ct TN37 .... 136 B4
Saxons TN39 .... 156 F3
Saxonwood Rd TN33 .... 112 C5
Sayerland La BN26 .... 173 A8
Sayerland Rd BN26 .... 173 A8
Sayers The 6 RH19 .... 1 C1
Scamps Hill RH16 .... 51 C6
Scanlon Cl BN20 .... 173 A3
Scarborough Rd BN1 .... 142 D1
Scarletts Cl TN22 .... 78 B7
Scaynes Hill CE Prim Sch
 RH17 .... 51 F3
Sceptre 2 BN1 .... 142 E2
Schofield Way BN23 .... 185 F7
School Cl Burgess Hill RH15 ... 72 F2
 1 Southwick BN42 .... 161 E7
School Cotts
 East Chiltington BN7 .... 100 B3
 Maresfield TN22 .... 55 B4
School Field BN8 .... 101 E5
School Hill
 Barcombe Cross BN8 .... 101 E4
 Lamberhurst TN3 .... 20 B6
 Maresfield TN22 .... 55 B4
 Old Heathfield TN21 .... 82 D5
 Winchelsea TN36 .... 117 E8
School La Ashurst Wood RH19 .. 11 E6
 Blackboys TN22 .... 80 A6
 Crowborough, Blackness TN6 . 25 F1
 Crowborough, St John's TN6 .. 25 D4
 Danehill RH17 .... 34 B5
 Hadlow Down TN22 .... 57 B5
 Nutley TN22 .... 35 C5
 Peasmarsh TN31 .... 69 B2
 Polegate BN26 .... 173 A7
 Pyecombe BN45 .... 119 C6
 Saltdean BN2 .... 177 C6
School Path BN8 .... 101 D4
School Pl TN40 .... 158 A5
School Rd Hastings TN35 .... 137 C3
 Hove BN3 .... 162 F8
School Rise Brighton BN2 ..... 164 E6
 Royal Tunbridge Wells TN2 .... 7 F1
School Terr TN32 .... 64 C5
Schwerte Way 5 TN37 .... 159 E7
Science Park Rd BN1 .... 144 B7
Science Park Sq BN1 .... 144 B6
Scotland St BN2 .... 189 B6
Scotney Cl TN3 .... 20 D3
Scotney Castle Gdns TN3 ...... 20 D3
Scotsford Cl TN21 .... 59 F1
Scotsford Hill TN20 .... 40 E1
Scotsford Rd TN21 .... 59 F2
Scott Rd BN3 .... 162 F7
Scotts Acre TN31 .... 94 E2
Scotts Way TN2 .... 16 E8
Scrace Hill Terr RH16 .... 73 F8
Scraper's Hill BN8 .... 128 A8
Scrase Lodge RH15 .... 73 D3
Scutes Cl TN34 .... 137 A3
Sea Ho 14 BN2 .... 161 E7
Sea Rd Bexhill TN40 .... 157 D3
 Camber TN31 .... 94 F2
 Fairlight Cove TN35 .... 139 A5

Sea Rd
 Hastings TN38 .... 158 F6
 Pevensey Bay BN24 .... 175 D5
 Winchelsea Beach TN36 .... 118 B7
Seabeach La BN22 .... 185 C5
Seabourne Rd Bexhill TN40 ... 158 A6
 Bexhill TN40 .... 158 B5
Seacliffe BN10 .... 177 F3
Seafield Cl BN25 .... 181 B5
Seafield Rd BN3 .... 163 B6
Seaford Cty Prim Sch BN25 .. 180 E4
Seaford Head Com Coll
 (Lower) BN25 .... 180 F2
Seaford Head Com Coll
 (Upper) BN25 .... 181 A2
Seaford Rd Eastbourne BN22 .. 185 C5
 Hove BN3, BN41 .... 162 C6
 Newhaven BN9, BN25 .... 179 F8
Seaford Sta BN25 .... 180 E3
Seagrave Cl BN25 .... 180 A6
Seagrove Way BN25 .... 180 F5
Searle Ave BN10 .... 178 E6
Seasaw Way BN2 .... 164 F7
Seaside BN22, BN23 .... 185 C5
Seaside Rd
 Eastbourne BN21, BN22 .... 185 B3
 Hastings TN38 .... 158 F6
Seaside Rdbt BN22 .... 185 D7
Seaside Way TN38 .... 158 F6
Seaview Ave BN10 .... 178 E6
Seaview Cotts BN27 .... 129 D3
Seaview Est BN42 .... 161 F7
Seaview Rd Newhaven BN9 ... 168 F1
 Peacehaven BN10 .... 178 E6
 Woodingdean BN2 .... 165 B8
Seaview Terr Icklesham TN36 .. 116 E5
 Rye TN31 .... 93 C5
Seaville Dr Eastbourne BN23 .. 185 D8
 Pevensey Bay BN24 .... 175 D5
Second Ave Bexhill TN40 .... 157 F5
 Camber TN31 .... 94 F2
 Hove BN3 .... 163 C6
 Newhaven BN9 .... 179 C6
Second Rd BN10 .... 178 A7
Sedgecombe Gdns TN34 ...... 136 E2
Sedgewick Rd TN39, TN40 ... 157 C6
Sedlescombe CE Prim Sch
 TN33 .... 88 E1
Sedlescombe Gdns TN38 ..... 136 B2
Sedlescombe Rd N TN37 ...... 136 B4
Sedlescombe Rd S TN38 .... 136 B1
Sefton Chase TN6 .... 26 A3
Sefton Rd BN41 .... 140 F3
Sefton Way TN6 .... 26 A3
Segrave Cl BN7 .... 123 B2
Selba Dr BN2 .... 143 E3
Selborne Pl BN3 .... 163 C7
Selborne Rd BN3 .... 163 C6
Selby Cl RH16 .... 50 E3
Selby Gdns TN22 .... 78 D5
Selby Rd Eastbourne BN21 .... 184 D5
 Uckfield TN22 .... 78 D6
Selby Rise TN22 .... 78 D5
Selham Cl BN1 .... 143 D6
Selham Dr BN1 .... 143 D6
Selham Pl BN1 .... 143 D6
Selhurst Rd BN2 .... 165 E6
Sellbourne Pk TN3 .... 17 C4
Selmeston Cl TN34 .... 136 D1
Selmeston Ct 2 BN25 .... 180 C4
Selmeston Ho 6 BN21 .... 184 D4
Selmeston Pl BN2 .... 164 F6
Selmeston Rd BN21 .... 184 C7
Selmestone Rd BN2 .... 164 F5
Selsey Cl BN1 .... 143 E6
Selsfield Cl BN21 .... 184 D6
Selsfield Dr BN2 .... 143 D3
Selwyn Dr BN21 .... 184 E4
Selwyn Ho 9 BN21 .... 184 E4
Selwyn Park Ct 8 BN21 .... 184 E4
Selwyn Rd BN21 .... 184 E4
Semley Rd Brighton BN1 ...... 143 A1
 Hassocks BN6 .... 97 E4
Sempstead La TN31, TN32 ...... 66 C4
Senlac Ct TN33 .... 112 D5
Senlac Gdns TN33 .... 112 E4
Senlac Green TN22 .... 78 E8
Senlac Pl TN3 .... 15 C7
Senlac Rd BN9 .... 179 D7
Senlac Way TN37 .... 136 C5
Sergison Cl RH16 .... 50 D5
Sergison Rd RH16 .... 50 D5
Setfords Field BN8 .... 75 E1
Sevelands Cl BN2 .... 164 F7
Seven Acre Cl TN37 .... 136 A5
Seven Dials BN1 .... 189 F7
Seven Sisters Ctry Pk BN25 .. 182 A2
Sevenfields BN2 .... 72 D4
Sevenoaks Rd BN23 .... 174 D2
Seville St BN2 .... 164 C7
Sewell Ave TN40 .... 157 C5
Seymour Ho 5 BN2 .... 164 D4
Seymour Sq 3 BN2 .... 164 D4
Seymour St 4 BN2 .... 164 D4
Shaftesbury Ct TN22 .... 78 C8
Shaftesbury Pl BN1 .... 164 A8
Shaftesbury Rd Brighton BN1 .. 189 A8
 Royal Tunbridge Wells TN4 .... 8 A5
Shakespeare St BN3 .... 163 A8
Shakespeare Wlk BN23 .... 174 D2
Shalesbrook La RH18 .... 12 A1
Shalfleet Ct BN23 .... 174 B3
Shandon Cl TN2 .... 8 C4
Shands BN6 .... 97 F3
Shanklin Cl BN23 .... 174 B4
Shanklin Ct 7 Brighton BN2 .. 164 C8
 Hove BN3 .... 141 D1

Shanklin Rd BN2 .... 164 C8
Shannon Cl BN10 .... 167 B1
Shannon Way BN23 .... 185 F8
Sharp's Cnr TN21 .... 106 E8
Sharpthorne Cres BN41 .... 141 C1
Sharrow Ct 9 RH16 .... 50 E5
Shaw The TN2 .... 8 C2
Shawcross Ho 10 BN1 .... 142 E2
Shawfield TN6 .... 26 B2
Shaws Cnr 6 TN31 .... 67 B7
Shedden Ct TN21 .... 82 A8
Sheddingdean Bsns Ctr RH15 .. 72 F5
Sheddingdean Cl RH15 .... 73 A4
Sheddingdean Ct RH15 .... 72 F4
Sheddingdean Cty Inf Sch
 RH15 .... 73 A5
Sheddingdean Cty Prim Sch
 RH15 .... 73 A5
Sheen Rd BN22 .... 185 B4
Sheep Pen La 3 BN25 .... 181 A3
Sheep Plain TN6 .... 37 D8
Sheep Wlk BN2 .... 165 F1
Sheepbell Cl BN41 .... 141 B3
Sheepfair BN7 .... 123 A2
Sheepfold The BN10 .... 167 C1
Sheepsetting La TN21 .... 81 E7
Sheepstreet La TN19, TN5 .... 43 E5
Sheerwater Cres TN34 .... 136 D4
Sheffield Mill La TN22 .... 53 C8
Sheffield Park Gdns TN22 ...... 53 D5
Sheffield Park Sta TN22 .... 53 A4
Sheffield Park Way TN34 ...... 174 A4
Sheiling Rd TN6 .... 25 E3
Shell La TN34 .... 160 A3
Shelldale Ave BN41 .... 162 B7
Shelldale Cres BN41 .... 162 B7
Shelldale Rd BN41 .... 162 B8
Shelley Cl BN7 .... 123 B1
Shelley Ct 4 RH16 .... 50 D5
Shelley Pk 4 TN21 .... 82 A7
Shelley Rd East Grinstead RH19 .. 1 D1
 Hove BN3 .... 162 F7
Shelley Wood BN6 .... 72 D4
Shelly Wlk 3 BN23 .... 174 E2
Shenfield Way TN39 .... 143 B3
Shenstone RH16 .... 51 B8
Shepham Ave BN2 .... 177 D6
Shepham La BN24, BN26 .... 173 C8
Shepherd St 3 TN37, TN38 .. 159 C6
Shepherd's Cl TN39 .... 156 D4
Shepherd's Hill TN7 .... 23 D8
Shepherd's Way TN35 .... 138 E4
Shepherds Cl
 Eastbourne BN22, BN26 .... 173 F3
 Piddinghoe BN9 .... 168 B2
 Ringmer BN8 .... 124 E5
Shepherds Cot BN10 .... 167 D2
Shepherds Croft BN1 .... 142 C4
Shepherds Ct TN35 .... 138 E4
Shepherds Mead RH15 .... 72 F4
Shepherds Way Ringmer BN8 .. 124 E5
 South Chailey BN8 .... 100 C7
 Uckfield TN22 .... 78 C5
Shepherds Wlk
 Crowborough TN6 .... 26 C1
 Hassocks BN6 .... 97 F5
 Royal Tunbridge Wells TN2 .... 8 D4
Shepherdsgrove La RH19 .... 3 A4
Sheppard Way BN41 .... 141 A3
Sheppey Wlk BN27 .... 129 A3
Sheppeys RH16 .... 50 D2
Shepway The BN25 .... 181 B4
Sheraton Cl BN21 .... 184 F2
Sherborne Ct 3 BN21 .... 184 D4
Sherborne Cl Hove BN3 .... 141 D3
 Royal Tunbridge Wells TN2 .... 8 D2
Sherborne Rd BN3 .... 141 D3
Sherborne Way BN3 .... 141 D3
Sheridan Cl RH19 .... 1 C1
Sheridan Mansions BN3 .... 163 A8
Sheridan Terr BN3 .... 163 A8
Sheriff's La TN6 .... 39 C7
Sheringham Cl TN32 .... 65 E2
Sherrington Rd BN22 .... 165 F8
Sherwood Cl TN34 .... 136 F1
Sherwood Dr RH6 .... 50 C5
Sherwood Gn BN27 .... 152 B6
Sherwood Park Cty Prim Sch
 .... 8 D6
Sherwood Rd
 Royal Tunbridge Wells TN2 .... 8 E5
 Seaford BN25 .... 180 F4
Sherwood Rise BN23 .... 180 F4
Sherwood Way TN2 .... 8 D6
Shinewater Ct BN23 .... 174 B3
Shinewater Cty Prim Sch
 BN23 .... 174 B4
Shinewater La BN23 .... 174 B4
Shinewater Rdbt BN23 .... 174 B1
Shingle Ct TN38 .... 135 E2
Shingle Rd BN43 .... 161 A6
Ship St Brighton BN1 .... 189 F5
 East Grinstead RH19 .... 10 E8
 Newhaven BN9 .... 179 C8
Ship Street Gdns BN1 .... 189 F5
Shipley La TN39 .... 156 D3
Shipley Rd BN2 .... 165 E7
Shipwreck Heritage Ctr (Mus)
 TN34 .... 160 D3
Shipyard La TN31 .... 93 C5
Shirlea View TN33 .... 112 E4
Shirley Ave BN3 .... 142 B2
Shirley Cl BN43 .... 161 D8
Shirley Dr Hastings TN37 .... 136 C2
Shirley Gdns TN4 .... 7 C5
Shirley Gr TN4 .... 7 C5

Shirley Rd BN3 .... 163 C8
Shirley St BN3 .... 163 C8
Shirleys BN6 .... 98 E2
Shoreham Beach Cty Fst Sch
 BN43 .... 161 A6
Shoreham By-Pass
 BN41, BN42, BN43, BN15 ... 140 D2
Shoreham Coll BN43 .... 161 D7
Short Brow BN25 .... 181 A4
Short Brow Cl BN22 .... 173 B3
Shortdean Pl BN21 .... 184 D4
Shortgate Rd BN2 .... 143 F4
Shortlands Cl BN22 .... 173 C1
Shotters RH15 .... 72 E1
Shovelstrode La RH19 .... 11 D8
Showfields Rd TN2 .... 7 F1
Shropshire Ct BN20 .... 184 B7
Shrub La TN19 .... 62 C7
Shrublands Ct TN2 .... 8 C4
Shrublands The TN39 .... 156 E3
Sicklehatch La TN21 .... 82 B2
Sidcup Ct BN23 .... 174 D2
Sidehill Dr BN41 .... 140 F2
Sidley Cty Prim Sch TN39 ..... 157 C7
Sidley Gn TN39 .... 157 C7
Sidley Rd BN22 .... 185 C5
Sidley St TN39 .... 157 C7
Sidney Cl TN2 .... 16 F8
Silchester Rd TN37, TN38 ..... 159 C7
Sillwood Ct 7 BN1 .... 163 E5
Sillwood Hall 6 BN1 .... 163 E5
Sillwood Pl BN1 .... 163 E5
Sillwood Rd BN1 .... 163 E5
Sillwood St BN1 .... 163 E5
Silva Cl TN40 .... 158 A6
Silvan Rd TN38 .... 135 E4
Silver Bank Cotts TN32 .... 64 B8
Silver Birches RH16 .... 51 A4
Silver Hill TN37 .... 45 B1
Silverdale BN6 .... 98 B3
Silverdale Ave BN3 .... 163 D7
Silverdale Ct BN27 .... 152 B8
Silverdale Cty Prim Sch TN38 136 B3
Silverdale La TN4 .... 8 B6
Silverdale Rd Burgess Hill RH15 .. 73 C2
 Eastbourne BN20 .... 184 F1
 Hove BN3 .... 163 D7
 Royal Tunbridge Wells TN4 .... 8 B6
Silverden Cotts TN18 .... 46 F4
Silverhill Ave TN37 .... 136 C4
Silverlands Rd 1 TN37 .... 136 B2
Silvester Rd TN40 .... 157 C5
Silwood Cl TN2 .... 8 E7
Simmonds Ct TN4 .... 7 B4
Simons Cl TN6 .... 26 A1
Singleton Rd BN1 .... 143 A6
Singleton Way TN34 .... 73 C1
Sinnock Sq 17 TN34 .... 160 B4
Sir Henry Fermor
 CE Prim Sch TN6 .... 26 A2
Six Bells Mews TN31 .... 67 C5
Skinner's La TN33 .... 133 D8
Skinners' Sch The TN4 .... 8 A6
Skippers Hill Manor Prep Sch
 TN20 .... 58 B7
Skyline View BN10 .... 167 D1
Slade The TN2 .... 20 A3
Sleeches Cross TN3 .... 17 B2
Sleepers Stile Rd TN5 .... 19 B1
Slider's La TN22 .... 53 A7
Slides The TN38 .... 135 F3
Slimbridge Rd RH15 .... 72 F5
Slindon Ave BN10 .... 178 D6
Slindon Cres BN23 .... 174 E1
Slinford Cl TN2 .... 8 D2
Sliverick's La TN21, TN33 .... 109 F7
Sloane Ct 4 BN2 .... 164 C5
Sloe La BN26 .... 171 A3
Slonk Hill Rd BN43 .... 140 A1
Slugwash La RH17 .... 74 B7
Smeatons La TN36 .... 118 B5
Smith Cl TN33 .... 133 B5
Smithy's Cl TN37 .... 136 C5
Smolletts RH19 .... 10 C8
Smugglers Cl BN26 .... 170 F3
Smugglers La TN6 .... 25 D5
Smugglers Way TN35 .... 138 F4
Snape View TN5 .... 29 F4
Snatt's Rd TN22 .... 55 C1
Snednore BN7 .... 145 F5
Snipe Cl TN2 .... 9 E8
Snowdon Cl BN23 .... 174 D3
Snowdrop La RH16 .... 51 C4
Snowflakes La TN6 .... 51 D6
Soames Ct RH15 .... 72 F4
Solomon's La TN32 .... 87 C4
Solway BN27 .... 129 A2
Solway Ave BN3 .... 142 F7
Somerhill Ave BN3 .... 163 D7
Somerhill Ct 10 BN3 .... 163 D7
Somerhill Cty Jun Sch BN3 .. 163 D6
Somerhill Lodge 6 BN3 .... 163 D6
Somerhill Rd BN3 .... 163 D6
Somerset Ct Eastbourne BN23 .. 174 E1
 3 Hove BN3 .... 163 C7
Somerset Point 1 BN2 .... 164 C4
Somerset Rd TN4 .... 8 A6
Somerset St BN2 .... 164 C5
Somerset Villas TN3 .... 15 C7
Somerville Ct BN23 .... 185 E7
Somerville Gdns TN4 .... 7 F4
Sompting Cl TN22 .... 164 F7
Sompting Ct 3 BN43 .... 161 B8
Sorrel Cl BN23 .... 174 C3
Sorrel Dr BN23 .... 174 C3
South Ave Brighton BN2 .... 164 C5
 Eastbourne BN20 .... 184 B5
 Hurstpierpoint BN6 .... 97 A5

South Bank BN6 .... 97 E3
South Brooks Rd TN29 .... 96 F7
South Cl Beachlands BN24 .... 175 F6
 Burgess Hill RH15 .... 72 E3
 Hailsham BN27 .... 152 B6
South Cliff Bexhill TN39 .... 156 F2
 Eastbourne BN20 .... 188 F8
South Cliff Ave Bexhill TN39 .. 156 E2
 Eastbourne BN20 .... 184 F1
South Cliff Tower BN20 .... 188 F8
South Cliffe 7 BN7 .... 123 E1
South Coast Rd
 Peacehaven BN10, BN9 .... 178 D6
 Telscombe Cliffs BN10, BN2 .. 177 E4
South Ct 4 BN7 .... 123 E1
South Downs TN7 .... 99 E5
South Downs Bsns Pk BN7 .. 123 E2
South Downs Rd BN7 .... 123 D2
South Dr RH15 .... 72 E3
South Gr TN1 .... 8 A2
South La Newhaven BN9 .... 179 C7
 Wood's Corner TN21 .... 84 C2
South Lodge 9 BN2 .... 164 F5
South Lodge Cl RH15 .... 72 F4
South Lynn Dr BN21 .... 184 F4
South Malling CE Prim Sch
 BN7 .... 123 E3
South Pl 8 BN7 .... 123 D1
South Point 7 BN43 .... 161 A6
South Rd Brighton BN1 .... 142 E1
 Hailsham BN27 .... 152 B6
 Haywards Heath RH16 .... 50 E4
 Newhaven BN9 .... 179 D7
 Wivelsfield Green RH17 .... 74 D4
South Rough BN8 .... 76 C7
South Side TN21 .... 59 E1
South St Brighton BN1 .... 189 F5
 Crowborough TN6 .... 25 E1
 Ditchling BN6 .... 98 D3
 East Hoathly BN8 .... 104 F4
 Eastbourne BN21 .... 185 A2
 Falmer BN1 .... 144 C6
 Hastings TN37 .... 159 C7
 Lewes BN7 .... 123 C2
 Mayfield TN20 .... 40 B2
 Portslade-by-Sea BN41 .... 141 A1
 Rotherfield TN6 .... 39 B8
 Seaford BN25 .... 180 E2
South Terr Broad Oak TN21 .... 59 E1
 Hastings TN34 .... 159 F6
 Westfield TN35 .... 114 E3
South Undercliff TN31 .... 93 C5
South View Ditchling BN6 .... 98 E5
 10 Eastbourne BN21 .... 184 E4
 1 South Heighton BN9 .... 168 E2
 South View TN19 .... 44 F3
South View Rd
 Crowborough TN6 .... 25 E1
 Royal Tunbridge Wells TN4 .... 8 B8
 Turner's Green TN5 .... 29 F6
South Way Lewes BN7 .... 123 A1
 Newhaven BN9 .... 179 D7
 Seaford BN25 .... 181 C1
South Woodlands BN1 .... 142 E5
Southall Ave BN2 .... 143 D2
Southampton Cl BN23 .... 185 F8
Southampton St BN2 .... 189 B6
Southborough CE Prim Schs
 TN4 .... 7 F8
Southbourne Rd BN22 .... 185 C6
Southcourt Ave TN39 .... 156 F2
Southdown Ave Brighton BN1 .. 143 A1
 Hastings TN34 .... 137 B3
 Lewes BN7 .... 146 A8
 Lower Willingdon BN20 .... 173 A3
 Peacehaven BN10 .... 178 E6
 Portslade-by-Sea BN41 .... 162 C8
Southdown Cl
 Haywards Heath RH16 .... 50 D2
 Newhaven BN9 .... 179 B6
Southdown Cotts BN20 .... 173 B3
Southdown Ct
 3 Hailsham BN27 .... 152 C7
 Polegate BN26 .... 172 F6
Southdown Cty Jun Sch BN9 .. 179 C7
Southdown Ho 4 BN20 .... 184 F1
Southdown Pl BN1 .... 143 A1
Southdown Rd Brighton BN1 .. 143 A1
 Eastbourne BN20, BN21 ...... 184 C7
 Newhaven BN9 .... 179 B6
 Portslade-by-Sea BN41 .... 141 A2
 Seaford BN25 .... 181 A2
 Southwick BN42 .... 161 E7
Southease Sta BN9 .... 168 E2
Southerden Cl BN27 .... 152 C7
Southern Ave BN26 .... 173 B6
Southern Rd BN22 .... 173 F2
Southern Ring Rd BN1 .... 144 B6
Southfield BN26 .... 172 F5
Southfield Rd
 Royal Tunbridge Wells TN4 .... 8 A6
 Speldhurst TN3 .... 7 A7
Southfields TN5 .... 29 F6
Southfields Ct 5 BN21 .... 184 F3
Southfields Rd BN21 .... 184 F3
Southfields Way TN4 .... 8 B8
Southgate TN4 .... 7 F3
Southlands RH19 .... 10 E7
Southlands Ave TN39 .... 157 A2
Southlands Cl 1 BN43 .... 161 B8
Southlands General Hospl
 BN43 .... 161 B8
Southlands Rd TN39 .... 157 A7
Southmead Cl TN20 .... 40 D1
Southmount BN1 .... 143 B1

Southon Cl BN41 .... 140 F3
Southover CE Prim Sch BN7 .. 146 C8
Southover High St BN7 .... 146 C8
Southover Pl BN2 .... 189 B7
Southover Rd BN7 .... 146 C8
Southover St BN2 .... 189 B6
Southridge Rd TN6 .... 37 E8
Southridge Rise TN6 .... 37 E8
Southview RH17 .... 51 F3
Southview Cl Crowborough TN6 . 25 E1
Southwick BN42 .... 140 E1
Southview Dr TN22 .... 78 D8
Southview Rd
  Peacehaven BN10 .... 178 C8
  Southwick BN42 .... 161 E8
Southwater Cl BN2 .... 164 D6
Southwater Rd TN37 .... 159 C8
Southway RH15 .... 72 D3
Southway Cty Jun Sch RH15 .... 72 D3
Southwick Cl RH19 .... 1 D2
Southwick Ho RH19 .... 1 D2
Southwick Sq BN42 .... 161 E7
Southwick St BN42 .... 161 E8
Southwick Sta 161 E7
Southwood Ave TN4 .... 8 A6
Southwood Cl TN38 .... 136 A1
Southwood Rd TN4 .... 7 B5
Sovereign Ct Hastings TN34 .... 137 A4
  Seaford BN25 .... 181 A5
Sovereign Ct BN22 .... 185 C5
Sovereign Jr BN22 .... 185 E6
Spa Ct BN3 .... 163 B5
Spa Golf Course TN4 .... 7 E3
Spa Ind Est TN2 .... 8 E8
Spa Valley Rly TN4 .... 7 D1
Spaldings The TN38 .... 135 E1
Spanish Ct RH15 .... 73 B4
Sparks Gdns TN33 .... 133 A6
Sparrow Way BN6 .... 72 D3
Sparrows Green Rd TN5 .... 29 F5
Sparrows The BN10 .... 167 D1
Spatham La BN6 .... 98 F4
Speldhurst CE Prim Sch TN3 .. 7 A7
Speldhurst Hill TN3 .... 7 B8
Speldhurst Rd Langton Green TN3 6 F4
  Royal Tunbridge Wells TN3, TN4 .. 7 E8
Spencer Ave BN1 .... 141 D3
Spencer Mews TN1 .... 8 A2
Spencer Rd BN21 .... 185 A2
Spencer's Mews TN1 .... 8 B4
Spences Field BN7 .... 123 E2
Spences La BN7 .... 123 E2
Spicers Cl RH15 .... 72 F5
Spindlewood Dr TN39 .... 156 C4
Spinnals Gr BN42 .... 161 D7
Spinney Cl BN6 .... 97 C5
Spinney The Battle TN33 .... 112 F3
  Bexhill TN39 .... 156 D3
  Burgess Hill RH15 .... 73 B5
  Hassocks BN6 .... 97 C5
  Hastings TN35 .... 136 E1
  Haywards Heath RH16, RH17 .. 50 D8
  Hove BN3 .... 142 C3
  Robertsbridge TN32 .... 63 F3
Spinneys The Heathfield TN21 ... 82 B6
  Lewes BN7 .... 123 E2
Spital Rd BN7 .... 123 B1
Spithurst Rd BN8 .... 101 E6
Spode La TN8 .... 4 A7
Sponden La TN18 .... 47 A7
Sportcentre Rd BN1 .... 144 A6
Spotted Cow La TN22 .... 56 E5
Spout Hill TN6 .... 27 D1
Spray Hill TN3 .... 20 B4
Spray's La TN33, TN35, TN35 .. 114 B4
Spring Cl BN20 .... 173 B1
Spring Copse RH19 .... 1 D3
Spring Gdns Brighton BN1 ...... 189 A5
  Glynde BN8 .... 147 F5
  Lewes BN7 .... 123 D1
  Rusthall TN4 .... 7 B4
  Southwick BN42 .... 161 E7
Spring Hill Northiam TN31 .... 67 B7
  Saint's Hill TN11, TN3 .... 6 A7
Spring Hill Wildfowl Pk RH18 .. 11 A1
Spring La Bexhill TN39 .... 156 C5
  Burwash TN19 .... 61 F6
  Clayton BN6 .... 119 E8
Spring Lodge Cl BN23 .... 174 E2
Spring Meadow RH18 .... 11 F1
Spring Park TN21 .... 82 A8
Spring St Brighton BN1 .... 163 E5
  Hastings TN37 .... 136 C1
Spring Steps TN36 .... 117 F8
Spring Way RH19 .... 2 A4
Springate Rd BN42 .... 161 E8
Springett Almshouses TN18 .... 45 E8
Springett Ave BN8 .... 124 D5
Springett Cotts BN8 .... 124 D5
Springfield RH19 .... 1 D4
Springfield Ave BN10 .... 177 F4
Springfield Cl Crowborough TN6 26 B2
  Westham BN24 .... 174 F6
Springfield Cotts
  Cackle Street TN31 .... 90 A2
  Rotherfield TN6 .... 39 B8
Springfield Rd Bexhill TN40 .... 157 C6
  Brighton BN1 .... 164 A8
  Eastbourne BN22 .... 185 B4
  Groombridge TN3 .... 15 C7
  Hastings TN38 .... 136 B1
Springfield Valley Rd TN38 .... 136 A1
Springfields TN5 .... 31 E1
Springfields Farm Ind Est
  RH17 .... 73 F5

Springhead TN2 .... 8 D5
Springhead Way TN6 .... 37 E8
Springside Wlk TN38 .... 135 F1
Springview Apartments TN1 ...... 8 D6
Springwood Rd TN21 .... 82 A8
Spruce Cl BN22 .... 173 D2
Spur Rd BN26 .... 173 B5
Spurway Pk BN26 .... 173 B5
Squab La BN27 .... 130 A5
Square The Beachlands BN24 .. 175 F6
  Brighton BN1 .... 142 E6
  Cowden TN8 .... 4 B6
  Hailsham BN27 .... 152 A7
  Wadhurst TN5 .... 30 A4
Squirrel Cl Bexhill TN39 .... 156 E5
  Hastings TN38 .... 135 F3
Squirrel Way TN2 .... 8 E5
Stable Ctyd TN22 .... 23 A1
Stable Mews TN37 .... 136 C5
Stabledene Way TN2 .... 9 D6
Stablefield TN35 .... 114 E4
Stables La BN21 .... 185 A3
Stacey's Cnr TN21 .... 85 A5
Stafford Ct BN23 .... 174 E1
Stafford Cty Jun Sch BN22 .... 185 A6
Stafford Ho BN21 .... 184 F3
Stafford House F Ed Ctr BN6 .. 98 A3
Stafford Rd Brighton BN1 .... 163 E8
  Royal Tunbridge Wells TN2 .... 8 E4
  Seaford BN25 .... 180 F3
Stafford Way BN6 .... 98 A3
Stag Rd TN2 .... 8 D8
Stainsby St TN37 .... 159 C7
Stamford RH16 .... 50 D6
Stamford Ct TN35 .... 160 D6
Stamford Lodge BN1 .... 142 E2
Stanam Rd TN2 .... 9 E6
Standard Hill Cl TN33 .... 132 F6
Standean Cl BN1 .... 143 D6
Standen Cl RH19 .... 1 A4
Standen (NT) RH17 .... 10 D4
Standen St
  Royal Tunbridge Wells TN4 .... 8 A5
  Standen Street TN17, TN18 ...... 47 E8
Stanford Ave Brighton BN1 ..... 143 A1
  Hassocks BN6 .... 97 E4
Stanford Cl Hassocks BN6 .... 97 E4
  Hove BN3 .... 142 C1
Stanford Ct BN1 .... 163 F8
Stanford Cty Inf Sch BN1 .... 163 E8
Stanford Cty Jun Sch BN1 ...... 163 F8
Stanford Rd BN1 .... 163 F8
Stanford Terr BN6 .... 97 E4
Stanhope Pl TN38 .... 159 C6
Stanhope Rd TN1 .... 8 B2
Stanier Rd TN38 .... 135 F5
Stanley Ave BN41 .... 140 F3
Stanley Deason L Ctr BN2 ...... 164 F5
Stanley Deason Sch BN2 .... 164 F5
Stanley Rd Brighton BN1 .... 189 A7
  Eastbourne BN22 .... 185 B4
  Hastings TN34 .... 159 E8
  Peacehaven BN10 .... 167 B1
  Portslade-by-Sea BN41 .... 162 A8
  Royal Tunbridge Wells TN1 .... 8 B5
Stanley St BN2 .... 189 B6
Stanmer BN1 .... 143 F8
Stanmer Ave BN2 .... 166 D3
Stanmer Dr BN22 .... 173 D1
Stanmer Park Rd BN1 .... 143 B2
Stanmer St BN1 .... 143 B2
Stanmer Villas BN1 .... 143 B2
Stansfield Rd BN2 .... 123 B2
Stanstead Cres BN2 .... 165 F6
Stansted Rd BN22 .... 185 A4
Staplecross Methodist
  Prim Sch TN32 .... 65 E2
Staplefield Dr BN2 .... 143 F3
Stapley Cl BN3 .... 162 D8
Stapley Rd BN3 .... 141 D1
Star La Alfriston BN26 .... 171 A3
  Blackboys BN22 .... 80 B6
  Mayfield TN20 .... 40 B2
Star Mews TN20 .... 40 B2
Star Rd BN2 .... 184 E4
Starboard Ct BN2 .... 164 F3
Starborough Cotts RH7 .... 1 F7
Starfield TN6 .... 25 E1
Starr's Cotts TN34 .... 160 B4
Starr's Green La TN33 .... 113 A3
Starrs Mead TN33 .... 113 A3
Starvecrow La TN31 .... 91 D6
Starwell Cl TN34 .... 136 D3
Station App Battle TN33 .... 112 E3
  Eastbourne BN22 .... 173 F1
  Etchingham TN19 .... 44 C1
  Falmer BN1 .... 144 B6
  Hassocks BN6 .... 97 F4
  Hastings TN34 .... 159 E8
  Hastings, St Leonards TN37 .... 159 C7
  Heathfield TN21 .... 82 A7
  Horsted Keynes RH17 .... 33 A7
  Hove BN3 .... 163 B8
  Mayfield TN20 .... 39 F2
  Seaford BN25 .... 180 E3
Station Cl Plumpton Green BN7 .. 99 E5
  Town Row TN6 .... 27 D1
Station Cotts Crowhurst TN33 .. 135 A6
  Hassocks BN6 .... 97 F4
  Winchelsea TN36 .... 92 D1
Station Par BN21 .... 184 F3
Station Rd Bexhill TN40 .... 157 C4
  Brighton BN1 .... 142 D3
  Burgess Hill RH15 .... 73 B2
  Crowhurst TN33 .... 134 F5
  East Grinstead RH19 .... 1 D1
  Forest Row RH18 .... 11 F3
  Groombridge TN3 .... 15 C7

Station Rd
  Hailsham BN27 .... 152 C6
  Hastings TN34 .... 159 F8
  Heathfield TN21 .... 82 A7
  Horsted Keynes RH17 .... 33 C5
  Hurst Green TN19 .... 45 A3
  Isfield TN22 .... 102 D8
  Lewes BN7 .... 146 D8
  Mayfield TN20 .... 40 A2
  Newhaven BN9 .... 168 F1
  North Chailey BN8 .... 75 F7
  Northiam TN31 .... 67 B8
  Plumpton Green BN7 .... 99 E6
  Polegate BN26 .... 173 A6
  Portslade-by-Sea BN3, BN41 .. 162 C7
  Robertsbridge TN32 .... 64 B4
  Rockrobin TN5 .... 29 C6
  Seaford BN25 .... 180 B5
  Sharpthorne RH19 .... 21 A6
  Southwick BN42 .... 161 E7
  Stonegate TN5 .... 42 E5
  Town Row TN6 .... 27 C1
  Winchelsea TN36 .... 92 E1
  Withyham TN7 .... 14 B5
Station Road Ind Est BN27 .... 152 C6
Station St Brighton BN1 .... 189 A6
  Eastbourne BN21 .... 185 A3
  Lewes BN7 .... 123 D1
Staveley Rd BN20 .... 188 E8
Steep Hill Brede La TN31 .... 89 E2
Steep Rd TN20, TN6 .... 38 D3
Steine Gdns BN2 .... 189 A5
Steine La BN1, BN2 .... 189 A5
Steine St BN2 .... 189 A4
Stephen's Rd TN4 .... 8 B6
Stephens Cl BN8 .... 124 D5
Stephens Rd BN1 .... 143 B2
Stephenson Dr RH19 .... 10 F7
Stevens Cl TN39 .... 157 C7
Stevens Ct BN3 .... 162 E7
Stevenson Cl BN23 .... 174 E3
Stevenson Rd Brighton BN2 .. 164 C5
  Hastings TN37 .... 136 B3
Stewards Inn La BN7 .... 146 C8
Stewart Rd TN4 .... 8 C7
Steyne Cl BN25 .... 180 F2
Steyne Ct BN25 .... 180 E2
Steyne Rd BN25 .... 180 F2
Steyne The BN25 .... 180 E2
Steyning Ave Hove BN3 .... 141 F3
  Peacehaven BN10 .... 178 C7
Steyning Cl BN25 .... 181 C2
Steyning Ct BN3 .... 163 B7
Steyning Rd Rottingdean BN2 .. 177 A5
  Seaford BN25 .... 181 C2
Stiles The BN27 .... 152 C7
Stirling Ave BN25 .... 181 C4
Stirling Cl Burgess Hill RH15 ... 73 C4
  Seaford BN25 .... 181 C3
Stirling Court Rd RH15 .... 73 C4
Stirling Ct BN3 .... 163 C7
Stirling Pl BN3 .... 163 A6
Stirling Rd TN38 .... 135 F5
Stirling Way RH19 .... 2 B3
Stock Dale TN5 .... 138 F4
Stockland Green Rd TN3 .... 7 B8
Stockleigh Rd TN38 .... 159 C7
Stocks Meadow TN33 .... 133 B5
Stockwell Ct Burgess Hill RH15 .. 72 F3
  Haywards Heath RH16 .... 50 E3
Stockwell Rd RH19 .... 10 E6
Stoddards La TN31 .... 67 F6
Stoke Brunswick Sch RH19 .... 11 E7
Stoke Cl BN25 .... 181 B3
Stoke Manor Cl BN25 .... 181 B4
Stokes Cotts TN19 .... 60 F3
Stokes Ho TN39 .... 157 A4
Stone Cotts TN3 .... 19 F4
Stone Court La TN2 .... 9 E8
Stone Cross Eastbourne BN24 .. 174 B5
  Mayfield TN20 .... 39 F2
Stone Cross Cty Prim Sch
  BN24 .... 174 A5
Stone Cross Rd
  Crowborough TN6 .... 38 A7
  Wadhurst TN5 .... 30 A4
Stone Pit La TN18 .... 47 E5
Stone Quarry Rd RH17 .... 34 D7
Stone Row TN3 .... 6 B5
Stone Row Cotts TN3 .... 6 D1
Stone St Brighton BN1 .... 163 E5
  Hastings TN34 .... 159 F8
  Royal Tunbridge Wells TN1 .... 8 B4
Stone Works Cotts TN31 .... 93 F3
Stonebeach Rise TN38 .... 135 F7
Stonecott Cl TN6 .... 37 F8
Stonecroft Cl BN3 .... 141 E4
Stonecross Rd BN2 .... 143 F4
Stonedene Ct RH18 .... 12 B2
Stonefield Pl TN34 .... 159 F8
Stonefield Rd TN34 .... 159 F8
Stonefield Way RH15 .... 72 F5
Stonegate CE Prim Sch TN5 ... 42 F5
Stonegate Cl BN23 .... 174 A4
Stonegate Ct TN5 .... 42 F5
Stonegate Rd TN5 .... 30 C1
Stonegate Sta TN5 .... 42 D3
Stonegate Way TN21 .... 82 B8
Stoneham Cl BN7 .... 123 C3
Stoneham Rd BN3 .... 162 F7
Stonehouse Dr
  Hastings TN38 .... 136 A1
  Hastings, Beauport Park
  TN33, TN38 .... 113 F1
Stonehurst Ct BN2 .... 164 C6
Stonehurst La TN20, TN22 ...... 57 D7
Stoneleigh Ave BN1 .... 142 F6

Stoneleigh Cl Brighton BN1 ... 142 F6
  East Grinstead RH19 .... 1 F1
Stonelink Cl TN38 .... 135 F7
Stonepark Dr RH18 .... 12 A2
Stonepound Crossroads BN6 ... 97 D4
Stonepound Rd BN6 .... 97 E4
Stonery Cl BN41 .... 141 A2
Stonery Rd BN41 .... 141 A2
Stonestile La TN34, TN35 ...... 136 F8
Stonewall Park Rd TN3 .... 6 F3
Stonewood Cl BN25 .... 181 C4
Stoney La Hailsham BN27 .... 152 C7
  Shoreham-by-Sea BN43 .... 161 C8
Stoneywish Ctry Pk BN6 .... 98 E3
Storrington Cl BN3 .... 141 E2
Straight Half Mile TN22 .... 55 B5
Strand TN31 .... 93 B5
Strand Ct TN31 .... 93 B5
Strand Hill TN36 .... 117 F7
Strand Meadow TN19 .... 62 B7
Strand The BN2 .... 165 A3
Stratford St TN1 .... 8 C5
Strathenden Ct BN25 .... 180 E2
Strathfield Cl RH16 .... 50 F4
Strawberry Cl TN2 .... 16 E7
Strawberry Fields TN31 .... 67 A7
Strawlands BN7 .... 99 E6
Stream La Sedlescombe TN33 ... 88 C2
  The Moor TN18 .... 46 A7
Stream Lane Cotts TN18 .... 46 A7
Stream Pit La TN18 .... 47 B6
Stream Pk RH19 .... 1 A3
Streamside Cl TN34 .... 136 E5
Streat Bostall BN6, BN7 .... 121 C6
Streat La BN6 .... 99 C4
Streatfield Gdns TN21 .... 81 F8
Streatfield Ho TN22 .... 78 C8
Streatfield Rd Tilsmore TN21 ... 81 F8
  Uckfield TN22 .... 78 B7
Streele View TN22 .... 78 E8
Street End La Broad Oak TN21 .. 59 E1
  Broad Oak TN20 .... 59 E5
Street The Framefield TN22 ...... 79 B6
  Kingston near Lewes BN7 .... 145 E5
  Sedlescombe TN33 .... 88 E1
  West Firle BN8 .... 148 B3
  Westmeston BN6 .... 120 F8
Streetlands TN33 .... 88 E1
Stringer Way TN33 .... 142 F3
Stringwalk The TN22 .... 152 C7
Stroma Gdns BN27 .... 128 F2
Strome Ho TN39 .... 157 C7
Strongs Pas TN34 .... 160 B4
Strood Gate RH17 .... 74 C5
Strood Rd TN37 .... 136 C2
Stuart Ave BN21 .... 184 C6
Stuart Cl TN2 .... 16 F8
Stuart Way RH19 .... 10 F7
Stubb La TN31 .... 90 D2
Stubbygrove Cotts TN3 .... 17 E4
Stud Cotts BN27 .... 151 A8
Studdens La BN27 .... 108 D1
Sturdee Cl BN23 .... 185 F7
Sturdee Pl TN34 .... 160 A3
Sturton Pl BN27 .... 152 B7
Sudeley Pl BN2 .... 164 D4
Sudeley St BN2 .... 164 D4
Sudeley Terr BN2 .... 164 D4
Suffolk Cl BN22 .... 185 C4
Suffolk Rd TN39 .... 157 C7
Suffolk St BN3 .... 162 F8
Sugar La RH17 .... 33 C4
Sugworth Cl RH16 .... 50 D7
Sullington Cl BN2 .... 143 F4
Sullington Way BN43 .... 161 A8
Sumach Cl BN22 .... 173 E2
Summer Cl BN41 .... 162 A7
Summer Ct BN20 .... 188 D7
Summer Hill TN38 .... 159 A8
Summer Hill Rd TN39 .... 156 F6
Summercourt BN27 .... 152 B8
Summerdale Rd BN3 .... 141 D2
Summerdown Cl BN20 .... 184 D3
Summerdown La BN20 .... 183 C1
Summerdown Rd BN20 .... 184 D3
Summerfields Ave BN27 .... 152 A8
Summerfold House Sch RH15 .. 73 A4
Summerheath Rd BN27 .... 152 B8
Summerhill Cl RH16 .... 50 F7
Summerhill Dr RH16 .... 51 A7
Summerhill Grange RH16 .... 50 F7
Summerhill La RH16 .... 50 F7
Summerlands Rd BN22 .... 173 C2
Summersdeane BN42 .... 140 F1
Summervale Rd TN2, TN4 .... 7 E1
Sun La TN34 .... 160 A3
Sun St BN7 .... 123 C1
Sunhill Ct TN2 .... 9 C6
Sunningdale Cl Bexhill TN40 .. 157 E4
  Hailsham BN27 .... 129 A1
  Seaford BN25 .... 181 A2
Sunningdale Dr TN38 .... 158 F7
Sunninghill Ave BN3 .... 141 F2
Sunninghill Cl BN3 .... 141 E2
Sunnybank Cl BN2 .... 40 B2
Sunnycroft Cl RH17 .... 51 E2
Sunnydale Ave BN1 .... 143 A6
Sunnydale Cl BN1 .... 143 A6
Sunnyside Rd TN4 .... 7 C4
Sunnywood Dr RH16 .... 50 D3
Sunset Cl Beachlands BN24 ... 175 F6
  Telscombe Cliffs BN10 .... 167 B1
Sunstar La BN26 .... 172 E6
Sunte Ave RH16 .... 50 F7
Sunview Ave BN10 .... 178 D6
Surrenden Cl BN1 .... 142 F4

Surrenden Cres BN1 .... 142 E4
Surrenden Holt BN1 .... 142 F3
Surrenden Lodge BN1 .... 142 F2
Surrenden Pk BN1 .... 143 A4
Surrenden Rd BN1 .... 142 F3
Surrey Cl
  Royal Tunbridge Wells TN2 .... 16 E3
  Seaford BN25 .... 180 C4
Surrey Ho BN2 .... 164 D4
Surrey Rd BN25 .... 180 C4
Surrey St BN1 .... 189 F6
Susan's Rd BN21 .... 185 A3
Susans Cl BN8 .... 105 A5
Sussex Ave BN27 .... 152 B8
Sussex Chambers BN34 .... 159 F8
Sussex Ct Bexhill TN39 .... 156 F5
  Hailsham BN27 .... 152 B8
  Royal Tunbridge Wells TN2 .... 8 C1
Sussex Ct Eastbourne BN22 ... 185 B5
  Haywards Heath RH16 .... 50 E3
  Hove BN3 .... 163 C6
Sussex Cty Cricket Gd BN3 ... 163 C7
Sussex Eye Hospl BN2 .... 164 D4
Sussex Gdns East Dean BN20 .. 183 C1
  Haywards Heath RH16 .... 51 B3
Sussex Ho Eastbourne BN21 ... 185 A4
  Telscombe Cliffs BN10 .... 177 F3
Sussex Hts BN1 .... 163 E5
Sussex House Ind Est BN3 .... 162 F8
Sussex Mews Brighton BN2 .. 164 E4
  Royal Tunbridge Wells TN2 .... 8 A2
Sussex Nuffield Hospl BN2 .... 165 C8
Sussex Pl BN2 .... 189 B6
Sussex Rd Hastings TN38 .... 159 A6
  Haywards Heath RH16 .... 50 E3
  Hove BN3 .... 163 B5
Sussex Sq Brighton BN2 .... 164 E4
  Haywards Heath RH16 .... 50 E4
Sussex St BN2 .... 189 B5
Sussex Terr BN2 .... 189 B6
Sussex Toy & Model Mus
  BN1 .... 189 A6
Sussex Way Burgess Hill RH15 .. 72 E5
  Telscombe Cliffs BN10 .... 177 F3
Sutherland Ave TN39 .... 157 A4
Sutherland Cl TN39 .... 157 A4
Sutherland Rd Brighton BN2 .. 164 C5
  Royal Tunbridge Wells TN1 .... 8 B3
Sutton Ave Peacehaven BN10 .. 178 B7
  Seaford BN25 .... 181 A3
Sutton Ave N BN10 .... 178 B8
Sutton Cl BN22 .... 144 E1
Sutton Cotts BN7 .... 146 B3
Sutton Croft La BN25 .... 180 E3
Sutton Dro BN25 .... 180 F4
Sutton Park Rd BN25 .... 180 E3
Sutton Pl TN40 .... 157 E7
Sutton Rd Eastbourne BN21 ... 185 A3
  Seaford BN25 .... 181 A3
Suttons Ind Pk TN36 .... 118 A7
Suttons The Camber TN31 .... 95 A1
  Hastings TN38 .... 135 F2
Swaine's Pas TN34 .... 160 B4
Swaines Way TN21 .... 82 A6
Swainham La TN33 .... 135 B4
Swainsthorpe Cl RH16 .... 50 F3
Swallow Bank TN38 .... 135 F2
Swallow Cl BN23 .... 174 C2
Swallow Dr Battle TN33 .... 112 F4
  Royal Tunbridge Wells TN2 .... 8 F6
Swallows The BN10 .... 167 B1
Swan Ave BN34 .... 160 A4
Swan Bsns Ctr BN27 .... 152 D6
Swan Cl BN8 .... 100 E7
Swan Rd BN27 .... 152 D6
Swan Terr TN34 .... 160 A4
Swanborough Dro BN2 .... 164 F7
Swanborough Dro BN7 .... 145 F4
Swanborough Hollow BN7 .... 146 A4
Swanborough Pl BN2 .... 164 F7
Swanley Cl BN23 .... 174 D2
Swann Cl RH15 .... 73 D3
Swannee Cl BN10 .... 167 D1
Swans Ghyll RH18 .... 11 E3
Swaylands Ave TN6 .... 37 F7
Sweda Ct BN2 .... 164 D4
Sweeps Hill Cl TN2 .... 9 D7
Sweethaws La TN6 .... 37 C6
Sweetings La TN3, TN5 .... 19 D1
Sweetlands BN6 .... 98 B5
Swife La TN21 .... 60 D5
Swift Cl Crowborough TN6 .... 25 D1
  Uckfield TN22 .... 78 D5
Swiftsden Cotts TN19 .... 44 F6
Swinburne Ave BN22 .... 173 C3
Swingate Cross BN27 .... 129 C5
Swissland Hill RH19, RH7 .... 1 E7
Swynford Dr TN38 .... 136 A5
Sybron Way TN6 .... 38 D8
Sycamore Cl Bexhill TN39 ...... 156 C4
  Eastbourne BN23 .... 173 D3
  Hastings TN38 .... 136 A1
  Heathfield TN21 .... 82 B6
  Portslade-by-Sea BN41 .... 141 C3
  Seaford BN25 .... 181 C3
  Woodingdean BN2 .... 165 E8
Sycamore Cotts TN2 .... 9 C6
Sycamore Ct TN22 .... 78 D8
Sycamore Dr
  East Grinstead RH19 .... 2 A1
  Hailsham BN27 .... 152 B5
Sycamores The BN10 .... 167 D1
Sydenham Cl TN40 .... 157 D3
Sydney CI TN37, TN38 .... 136 B3
Sydney Little Rd TN38 .... 135 D4
Sydney Rd Eastbourne BN22 ... 185 B4
  Haywards Heath RH16 .... 50 E6

Sydney St BN1 .... 189 A6
Sydney Tidy Ho **5** BN2 .... 164 C6
Sylvan Cl RH16 .... 51 B4
Sylvester Way BN3 .... 141 C3
Symbister Rd BN41 .... 162 C7
Syresham Gdns RH16 .... 50 F4

Tackleway TN34 .... 160 B4
Taddington Ho **2** BN22 .... 185 C4
Taddington Rd **1** BN22 ...... 185 C4
Tainter's Brook TN22 .... 78 E8
Talbot Cres BN1 .... 143 D6
Talbot Pk TN2 .... 8 D5
Talbot Rd TN18 .... 45 F8
Talbot Terr BN1 .... 123 C1
Tall Ash Dr TN37 .... 136 C4
Talland Par **15** BN25 .... 180 E2
Tamarack Cl BN22 .... 173 D2
Tamerisk Stps **24** TN34 ...... 160 B4
Tamworth Rd BN3 .... 162 F7
Tan Yard Cotts TN36 .... 117 F8
Tanbridge Rd BN23 .... 174 F2
Tandridge Rd BN3 .... 162 E6
Tangier La TN3 .... 17 B6
Tanglewood Coppice TN39 .... 156 E3
Tangmere Cl TN39 .... 156 E3
Tangmere Rd BN1 .... 143 A6
Tanhouse La TN31 .... 68 F2
Tanners' Brook BN7 .... 146 D8
Tanners Field RH17 .... 74 A5
Tanners Way TN6 .... 26 A1
Tanyard TN18 .... 47 B5
Tanyard Ave RH19 .... 11 A8
Tanyard Cotts Battle TN33 .... 112 E7
  Buxted TN22 .... 56 C1
Tanyard La
  Chelwood Common RH17 ..... 34 C4
  Winchelsea TN36 .... 117 F8
Tapsell's La TN5 .... 29 D5
Tarner Rd BN2 .... 189 B6
Tarragon Way BN43 .... 140 C1
Tarring Cl BN9 .... 168 D2
Tas Combe Way BN20, BN22 ... 173 B2
Tate Cres RH15 .... 72 F5
Taunton Gr BN2 .... 144 A1
Taunton Pl BN2 .... 144 A1
Taunton Rd BN2 .... 143 F1
Taunton Way BN2 .... 144 A1
Tavistock **8** BN21 .... 185 A2
Tavistock Down BN1 .... 143 C2
Tavistock & Summerhill Sch
  RH16 .... 50 F7
Taylor Cl TN38 .... 135 F4
Taylor St TN4 .... 8 A8
Tea Garden La TN3, TN4 .... 7 C2
Teal Cl TN38 .... 135 E3
Teasley Mead TN3 .... 5 C4
Tedder Rd TN4 .... 8 B7
Tedder Terr TN35 .... 137 D5
Teg Cl BN41 .... 141 C2
Teknol Ho RH15 .... 72 E2
Telegraph St **12** BN2 .... 164 C4
Telford Rd TN38 .... 136 A5
Telham Cl TN34 .... 137 A5
Telham La TN33 .... 112 E1
Telscombe Cliffs
  Cty Prim Sch BN10 .... 178 A8
Telscombe Cliffs Way BN10 ... 178 A8
Telscombe Pk BN10 .... 167 C2
Telscombe Rd
  Eastbourne BN23 .... 174 F2
  Peacehaven BN10 .... 167 D2
Temple Gdns BN1, BN3 .... 163 E6
Temple Gr RH15 .... 72 D4
Temple Grove Sch TN22 .... 36 E3
Temple St BN1 .... 163 E6
Tenantry Down Rd BN2 .... 164 E8
Tenantry Rd BN2 .... 164 D8
Tennis Cl BN27 .... 152 B7
Tennis Rd BN3 .... 162 E6
Tennyson Ct **5** RH16 .... 50 D5
Tennyson Rise RH19 .... 10 C8
Tennyson Wlk BN23 .... 174 E3
Tenterden Cl BN23 .... 174 D2
Tenterden Rise TN34 .... 136 E2
Terminus Ave TN39 .... 157 A3
Terminus Pl
  9 Brighton BN1 .... 189 F7
  6 Hailsham BN27 .... 152 C7
Terminus Rd Bexhill TN39 .... 157 B3
  Brighton BN1 .... 189 F7
  Eastbourne BN21 .... 185 A3
Terminus St BN1 .... 189 F6
Terrace Rd TN37 .... 159 C7
Tescombe Grange BN10 ...... 177 F3
Teynham Ho BN2 .... 177 C4
Thackeray Cl BN23 .... 174 E3
Thakeham Cl TN40 .... 158 A6
Thalia Ho TN40 .... 157 B4
Thames Cl BN23 .... 189 B5
Thanet Way TN34 .... 136 E2
Thatchers Cl RH15 .... 73 D1
Thatchings The BN26 .... 173 A5
Theaklen Dr TN38 .... 136 B2
Theobalds Gn TN21 .... 82 A5
Theobalds Rd RH15 .... 73 D6
Theobold Ho **1** BN1 .... 189 A6
Theodore Cl TN2 .... 8 E7
Third Ave Bexhill TN40 .... 157 F6
  Hove BN3 .... 163 B6
  Newhaven BN9 .... 179 C6
Third Rd BN10 .... 178 A7
Third St TN9 .... 6 F3
Thirlmere Rd TN4 .... 7 E5
Thomas Brassey Cl TN37 ..... 136 B5
Thomas Peacocke Com Coll
  TN31 .... 93 B6
Thomas Peacocke Sch TN31 ... 93 B6

Thomas St Lewes BN7 .... 123 E2
  Royal Tunbridge Wells TN4 .... 8 A5
Thomas Turner Dr BN8 .... 105 A5
Thompson Rd Brighton BN1 .. 143 C1
  Newhaven BN9 .... 168 F2
Thorn Cotts TN35 .... 116 A4
Thornbank Cres TN39 .... 156 F3
Thornbush Cres BN41 .... 141 B3
Thorndean Rd BN2 .... 143 D3
Thornden Ct TN17 .... 49 A8
Thornden La TN17 .... 49 A8
Thorne Cres TN39 .... 133 E1
Thornfield Gdns TN2 .... 8 F5
Thornhill Ave BN1 .... 143 A7
Thornhill Cl BN3 .... 141 E2
Thornhill Rise BN41 .... 141 A4
Thornhill Way BN41 .... 141 A3
Thorns The TN35 .... 138 A8
Thornsdale **4** BN2 .... 189 B6
Thornton Ct **5** BN22 .... 185 B3
Thornwell Rd BN26 .... 171 F7
Thornwood Cl BN22 .... 173 E2
Thorny Cl TN21 .... 82 A7
Thorpe Works TN4 .... 7 F8
Three Gables TN2 .... 35 C4
Three Oaks & Guestling Halt
  TN35 .... 115 D2
Three Oaks La TN5 .... 29 D7
Thurrock Cl BN20, BN22 ...... 173 B4
Thyme Cl BN43 .... 140 C1
Thyssel La TN31 .... 67 B6
Tibbs Mill La TN22, TN6 .... 37 E2
Ticehurst Ave TN39 .... 155 F5
Ticehurst CE Prim Sch TN5 .... 43 D8
Ticehurst Cl TN39 .... 155 F4
Ticehurst Rd BN2 .... 164 F5
Tichborne Cotts RH16 .... 51 C6
Tichborne St BN1 .... 189 A5
Tickerage La TN22 .... 79 F6
Tidebrook TN5, TN20 .... 40 F7
Tidebrook Gdns BN23 .... 174 F2
Tideswell Rd BN21 .... 185 A3
Tideway Sch & Sixth Form Ctr
  BN9 .... 179 B6
Tidy St BN1 .... 189 A6
Tilbury Cl BN2 .... 189 B5
Tilbury Way BN2 .... 189 B6
Tile Barn Cl TN22 .... 102 D8
Tile Barn Rd TN38 .... 135 F4
Tilehurst Dr TN27 .... 152 A8
Tilekiln La TN35 .... 137 E4
Tilers Cl RH15 .... 73 D3
Tilford Ct TN40 .... 157 F4
Tilgate Cl Brighton BN2 ...... 164 D6
  Eastbourne BN23 .... 184 D7
Tilgate Dr TN39 .... 156 D3
Tilley La BN27 .... 131 E6
Tilling Green Cty Inf Sch TN31 .. 93 A5
Tillingham Ave TN31 .... 93 B6
Tillingham La TN31 .... 92 A6
Tillingham View TN31 .... 90 B5
Tillingham Way BN24 .... 174 A5
Tillington BN2 .... 164 F7
Tillington Terr TN35 .... 160 C6
Tillstone Cl BN2 .... 143 D2
Tillstone St BN2 .... 189 B5
Tilsmore Cnr TN21 .... 81 F7
Tilsmore Rd TN21 .... 81 F7
Timber Yard Cotts BN7 .... 123 E1
Timberlaine Rd BN24 .... 175 C4
Timberley Rd BN27 .... 173 D1
Timbers Ct BN27 .... 152 C8
Tindal Cl RH15 .... 73 D3
Tinker's La TN22 .... 57 E3
Tinkers La TN5 .... 31 E3
Tintern Cl Brighton BN1 ...... 143 B1
  Eastbourne BN22 .... 173 E3
Tisbury Rd BN3 .... 163 C6
Titchfield Cl RH15 .... 73 D1
Tithe Barn Field TN36 .... 116 F5
Titian Rd BN3 .... 162 F7
Tiverton Dr TN40 .... 157 E5
Tivoli **3** BN1 .... 142 E2
Tivoli Cres BN1 .... 142 D1
Tivoli Cres N BN1 .... 142 D2
Tivoli Pl BN1 .... 142 D2
Tivoli Rd BN1 .... 142 D2
Tobago TN39 .... 157 A2
Tobias Sch of Art RH19 .... 10 E6
Tolkien Rd BN23 .... 174 F2
Toll Wood Rd TN21 .... 106 F7
Tollgate Haywards Heath RH16 .. 51 B8
  Peacehaven BN10 .... 167 B1
Tollgate Gdns BN23 .... 185 D7
Tollgate Lock TN31 .... 93 B4
Tollgates TN33 .... 112 B4
Tollwood Pk TN6 .... 26 B1
Tollwood Rd TN6 .... 38 B8
Tompset's Bank RH18 .... 11 F1
Tonbridge Rd TN2, TN11 .... 9 A7
Tonbridge Way TN31 .... 94 E2
Tongdean Ave BN3 .... 142 C2
Tongdean Ct BN1 .... 142 D4
Tongdean La
  Brighton BN1, BN3 .... 142 C4
  Brighton BN1 .... 142 D4
Tongdean Rd BN3 .... 142 C3
Tongdean Rise BN1 .... 142 C4
Top Cross Rd TN40 .... 158 A7
Top Dr TN22 .... 55 A6
Top Rd RH19 .... 21 B5
Tor Rd BN10 .... 167 C1
Tor Rd W BN10 .... 167 C1
Torcross Cl BN2 .... 143 E1
Torfield Cl TN34 .... 160 B4
Torfield Ct BN21 .... 184 E4
Torfield Ho TN34 .... 160 B4

Torfield Rd BN21 .... 184 E4
Torfield Sch TN34 .... 160 B5
Toronto Terr Brighton BN2 ... 164 C6
  Lewes BN7 .... 123 C1
Torrance Cl BN3 .... 141 F1
Totland Rd BN2 .... 164 D7
Tott Hill BN6 .... 97 B5
Tott Yew Rd BN20 .... 173 A4
Tottington Way BN43 .... 140 B1
Tovey Cl BN21 .... 184 D6
Tower Cl Beachlands BN24 ... 175 F7
  East Grinstead RH19 .... 1 E2
  Tower Rd TN19 .... 1 E2
Tower Ho **4** Brighton BN1 .. 142 E2
Tower Mill Rd BN15 .... 73 B2
Tower Mill Pl BN26 .... 173 A5
Tower Rd Brighton BN2 .... 164 C6
  Hastings TN37, TN38 .... 136 C1
Tower Rd W TN38 .... 159 B8
Tower Ride Uckfield TN22 ...... 55 D1
  Uckfield TN22 .... 55 E1
Tower St Heathfield TN21 ...... 82 B8
  Rye TN31 .... 93 C6
Tower View TN22 .... 78 D8
Towergate BN1 .... 142 E2
Towerscroft Ave TN37 .... 136 C5
Town Hill TN3 .... 20 A4
Town Place Farm Cotts RH17 .. 52 C7
Towner Art Gall & Mus BN21 .. 184 D3
Townlands Rd TN5 .... 29 F4
Toy & Model Mus TN3 .... 20 C7
Tozer Cl BN41 .... 162 B7
Traders Pas TN31 .... 93 B5
Trafalgar Cl Hastings TN38 ... 135 F7
  Peacehaven BN10 .... 167 C1
Trafalgar Cotts **8** TN34 ... 160 B4
Trafalgar Gate BN2 .... 164 F3
Trafalgar La BN1 .... 189 A6
Trafalgar Pl BN1 .... 189 A6
Trafalgar Rd BN41 .... 162 B8
Trafalgar St BN1 .... 189 A6
Trafalgar Terr BN1 .... 189 A6
Tram Rd TN31 .... 94 A2
Transit Rd BN9 .... 179 D7
Travellers La TN35 .... 137 C4
Trebilco Cl TN1 .... 8 D7
Treblers Rd TN20, TN6 .... 38 E6
Tredcroft Rd BN3 .... 142 C2
Tree Tops Cl BN2 .... 165 E8
Treemaines Rd BN23 .... 174 F2
Treemans Rd RH17 .... 33 B2
Tremola Ave BN2 .... 177 C6
Trenches Rd TN6 .... 25 F1
Trevor Gdns BN8 .... 147 F6
Treyford Cl BN2 .... 144 E1
Triangle Rd RH16 .... 50 E3
Triangle The BN20 .... 173 B3
Trickland Cotts TN22 .... 53 C5
Trinity Cl TN2 .... 8 D4
Trinity Field BN8 .... 124 E6
Trinity Mews **3** TN34 ...... 159 E7
Trinity Pl BN2 .... 185 B2
Trinity Rd BN6 .... 97 A6
Trinity St Brighton BN2 ...... 189 B7
  10 Hastings TN34 .... 159 E7
Trinity Trees BN21 .... 185 A2
Trinity Villas **2** TN34 ...... 159 E7
Tristan Gdns TN4 .... 7 D4
Trojans Platt TN36 .... 117 E7
Troon Cl BN25 .... 180 A6
Trossachs Cl BN23 .... 174 D3
Troy Cl TN6 .... 26 A1
Truleigh Cl BN2 .... 165 F7
Truleigh Dr BN41 .... 141 A4
Truleigh Way BN43 .... 140 A1
Truman Dr TN38 .... 135 F6
Tudor Ho TN34 .... 159 A7
Tudor Cl East Grinstead RH19 .. 10 F8
  Hove BN3 .... 141 F2
  Rottingdean BN2 .... 177 A6
  Seaford BN25 .... 180 D4
Tudor Ct TN2 .... 7 E1
Tudor Gdns RH15 .... 72 F4
Tudor Wlk TN22 .... 79 B5
Tugwell Rd BN22 .... 173 F2
Tumulus Rd BN2 .... 166 C3
Tunbridge Wells Golf Club
  TN4 .... 7 E3
Tunbridge Wells
  Gram Sch for Boys TN4 .... 8 A7
Tunbridge Wells
  Gram Sch for Girls TN4 .... 8 A6
Tunbridge Wells Ind Hospl The
  TN3 .... 6 B3
Tunbridge Wells Mus TN1 ..... 8 B4
Tunbridge Wells Rd
  Argos Hill TN20, TN6 .... 39 E5
  Mark Cross TN3,TN6 .... 28 A5
Tunnel Rd TN1 .... 8 B4
Tuppen Ho BN7 .... 145 E5
Turkey Cock La TN31 .... 93 C6
Turkey La RH15 .... 73 B3
Turkey Rd TN39 .... 156 E7
Turley Cotts TN3 .... 7 A8
Turnberry Cl TN38 .... 158 F7
Turnberry Ct **14** RH16 ...... 50 E4
Turnberry Dr BN27 .... 152 A8
Turner Cl Bexhill TN40 .... 157 C5
  Eastbourne BN23 .... 174 D1
Turner Ct TN19 .... 2 A3
Turner's Hill Rd RH19 .... 10 B1
Turners Cotts TN31 .... 68 C5
Turners Green La TN5 .... 29 F6
Turners Green Rd TN5 .... 29 F6
Turners Mill Cl RH16 .... 50 D7

Turners Mill Rd RH16 .... 50 D6
Turners Way RH15 .... 72 F4
Turnpike Cl Broyle Side BN8 ... 125 A8
  Peacehaven BN10 .... 167 C1
Turnpike Piece BN1 .... 144 B6
Turret Ct RH19 .... 1 C3
Turton Cl BN2 .... 164 D5
Tuscan Ct BN10 .... 177 F3
Tutts Barn La BN22, BN21 .... 185 A5
Tuxford Rd TN4 .... 7 B5
Tweedsmuir Cl BN23 .... 174 C3
Twineham Cl BN2 .... 164 F7
Twineham Rd BN2 .... 184 D7
Twitten Cl **2** BN42 .... 161 E7
Twitten The Bexhill TN39 .... 156 D4
  Burgess Hill BN15 .... 73 B4
  Crowborough TN6 .... 25 E1
  Ditchling BN6 .... 98 D3
  Southwick BN42 .... 161 E7
Twyford Cres TN37 .... 136 C4
Twyford Rd BN1 .... 143 E6
Twyfords TN6 .... 25 E1
Twyhurst Ct RH19 .... 1 D3
Twysden Cotts TN18 .... 47 A4
Tye Cl BN2 .... 177 D4
Tye Hill Rd BN26 .... 151 A4
Tye View BN10 .... 167 A1
Tyedean Rd BN10 .... 177 F4
Tyler's Gn RH16, RH17 .... 50 B4
Tylers La TN22 .... 35 E1
Tyndale Ave TN39 .... 156 C3
Tyson Pl **9** BN2 .... 189 B5

Uckfield Cl BN2 .... 164 F6
Uckfield Com Coll TN22 .... 78 D8
Uckfield Com Hospl TN22 ...... 78 D6
Uckfield Rd Poundgate TN6 ... 37 B7
  Upper Wellingham BN8 ...... 124 B7
Uckfield Sta TN22 .... 78 C6
Uckham La TN33 .... 112 E6
Udiam Cotts TN32 .... 65 C5
Udimore Rd TN31 .... 91 C3
Under Rd BN27 .... 130 B3
Undercliff Hastings TN38 .... 159 B6
  Hastings TN38 .... 159 C6
Undercliff Terr **7** TN38 ... 159 C6
Underdown Rd BN42 .... 161 E8
Underhill TN22 .... 55 B5
Underhill La Clayton BN45, BN6 .. 119 E8
  Westmeston BN6 .... 120 C8
Unicorn Ho **1** TN34 .... 160 A4
Union Cl BN27 .... 129 B3
Union Rd BN2 .... 189 B7
Union Sq **18** TN2 .... 8 A2
Union St Brighton BN1 .... 189 A5
  11 Hastings TN38 .... 159 C7
  Union Street TN5 .... 32 B3
Univ of Brighton BN2 .... 189 A5
  Eastbourne BN20 .... 188 D8
  Falmer BN1 .... 144 B6
Univ of Brighton (Belgrave St
  Annexe) BN2 .... 189 A6
Univ of Brighton (Cockcroft/
  Watts Annexes) BN2 .... 143 D2
Univ of Brighton (Finsbury Rd
  Annexe) BN2 .... 189 B6
Univ of Brighton
  (St Peter's Ho) BN2 .... 189 A6
Univ of Sussex BN1 .... 144 A7
Upland Rd BN20 .... 184 C3
Uplands Cl Bexhill TN39 ..... 156 F6
  Uckfield TN22 .... 55 C1
Uplands Com Coll TN5 .... 30 A4
Uplands Pk TN5 .... 59 E1
Uplands Rd BN1 .... 143 C2
Uplands Sch BN2 .... 143 C2
Uplands The TN38 .... 159 B7
Upper Abbey Rd BN2 .... 164 D4
Upper Ave BN21, BN22 .... 185 A4
Upper Bedford St BN2 .... 164 C4
Upper Belgrave Rd BN25 ..... 180 F5
Upper Bevendean Ave BN2 ... 143 E1
Upper Broomgrove Rd TN34 .. 137 B3
Upper Carlisle Rd BN20 ...... 188 D8
Upper Chalvington Pl BN2 ... 164 E5
Upper Church Rd TN37 .... 136 B4
Upper Chyngton Gdns BN25 .. 181 B4
Upper Cl RH18 .... 11 F2
Upper Clarence Rd TN37 ..... 136 C1
Upper Cotts BN2 .... 165 D4
Upper Cumberland Wlk TN1 .... 8 B1
Upper Dene BN3 .... 163 D8
Upper Duke's Dr BN20 .... 188 C7
Upper Dunstan Rd TN4 .... 8 B2
Upper Gardner St BN1 .... 189 A6
Upper Glen Rd TN37 .... 136 A5
Upper Gloucester Rd BN1 .... 189 A6
Upper Greenwoods La TN21 ... 83 C6
Upper Grosvenor Rd TN1, TN4 .. 8 B6
Upper Hamilton Rd BN1 ..... 189 F8
Upper Hollingdean Rd
  BN1, BN2 .... 143 B1
Upper Horsebridge Rd BN27 .. 129 A3
Upper King's Dr BN20 .... 173 B1
Upper Kingston La
  BN42, BN43 .... 140 D1
Upper Lake TN33 .... 112 E4
Upper Lewes Rd BN2 .... 189 B7
Upper Lodges BN1 .... 143 D8
Upper Market St BN3 .... 163 D5
Upper Maze Hill TN38 .... 159 B7
Upper Nellington TN3 .... 7 B4
Upper North St BN1 .... 189 F5
Upper Park Pl **7** BN2 ...... 189 B5
Upper Park Rd TN34, TN37 .. 159 A7
Upper Platts TN5 .... 31 F1
Upper Profit TN3 .... 7 A3
Upper Ratton Dr BN20 .... 184 B8

Upper Rock Gdns BN2 .... 189 B5
Upper Roedale Cotts BN1 .... 143 B4
Upper Sea Rd TN40 .... 157 D4
Upper Sherwood Rd BN25 ... 181 A4
Upper Shoreham Rd
  Shoreham-by-Sea BN43 ...... 140 B1
  Shoreham-by-Sea BN42, BN43 .. 140 D1
Upper South Rd TN37 .... 136 C1
Upper Sq RH18 .... 11 E3
Upper St East Dean BN20 .... 187 B8
  Rusthall TN4 .... 7 D4
Upper St James's St BN2 ..... 189 B4
Upper St Johns Rd RH15 ...... 73 A4
Upper Station Rd TN21 .... 82 A7
Upper Stephens TN3 .... 7 A3
Upper Sudeley St **7** BN2 ... 164 D4
Upper Valley Rd BN9 .... 179 B6
Upper Wellington Rd **5** BN2 . 164 C7
Upper Winfield Ave BN1 ..... 142 F6
Upper Wish Hill BN20 .... 184 B8
Upperton Gdns BN21 .... 184 F3
Upperton La BN21 .... 184 F3
Upperton Rd BN21 .... 184 E4
Upton Ave BN22 .... 140 E1
Upton Quarry TN3 .... 6 F3
Upwick Rd BN20 .... 184 C3

Val Prinseps Rd BN24 .... 175 C4
Vale Ave Brighton BN1 .... 142 E7
  Royal Tunbridge Wells TN1 .... 8 A3
Vale Cl BN25 .... 181 B4
Vale Ct BN41 .... 162 B7
Vale Gdns BN41 .... 162 B7
Vale Rd Battle TN33 .... 112 B5
  Hastings TN37 .... 136 C2
  Haywards Heath RH16 .... 50 E2
  Mayfield TN20 .... 40 B2
  Portslade-by-Sea BN3, BN41 .. 162 C7
  Royal Tunbridge Wells TN1 .... 8 A3
  Saltdean BN2 .... 166 D3
  Seaford BN25 .... 181 A4
Vale The BN2 .... 165 E5
Vale View Rd TN21 .... 82 B6
Valebridge Cl RH15 .... 73 C6
Valebridge Dr RH15 .... 73 C5
Valebridge Rd RH15 .... 73 C6
Valence Rd BN7 .... 123 B1
Valentine Ct
  2 Eastbourne BN21 .... 185 A2
  11 Hove BN3 .... 163 C7
Valentine Dr RH15 .... 72 E4
Valerie Cl BN41 .... 141 C2
Vallance Cl RH15 .... 72 E4
Vallance Gdns BN3 .... 163 A6
Vallance Rd BN3 .... 163 A6
Vallensdean Cotts BN41 ..... 141 C2
Valley Cl Brighton BN1 .... 142 C4
  Newhaven BN9 .... 179 B8
Valley Dene BN9 .... 179 B7
Valley Dr Brighton BN1 .... 142 C4
  Seaford BN25 .... 181 A5
Valley Rd Crowborough TN6 ... 25 F1
  Lewes BN7 .... 146 A8
  Newhaven BN9 .... 179 A7
  Newhaven BN9 .... 179 B7
  Peacehaven BN10 .... 167 C2
  Portslade-by-Sea BN41 ...... 141 A4
  Rusthall TN4 .... 7 D4
Valley Rise BN25 .... 180 F4
Valley Side Rd TN34, TN35 .. 137 C3
Valley View TN22 .... 53 A8
Valley View Cl TN6 .... 25 F1
Valverde Ho **13** BN3 ...... 163 C7
Vanbrugh Ct **21** BN3 ...... 163 C7
Vantage Wlk TN38 .... 136 B2
Varndean Cl BN1 .... 142 E3
Varndean Coll BN1 .... 142 F3
Varndean Dr BN1 .... 142 E3
Varndean Gdns BN1 .... 142 E3
Varndean Holt BN1 .... 142 F3
Varndean Rd BN1 .... 142 E3
Varndean Sch BN1 .... 143 A3
Vega Cl BN27 .... 152 D7
Ventnor Cl BN23 .... 174 B4
Ventnor Villas BN3 .... 163 B6
Venture Cl TN40 .... 157 F4
Verbania Way RH19 .... 2 B1
Verdant Cl TN34 .... 159 D8
Vere Rd BN1, BN2 .... 189 A8
Veric **12** BN3 .... 163 C7
Vermont Rd TN4 .... 7 C4
Vermont Way TN38 .... 135 F6
Vernon Ave Peacehaven BN10 . 178 D6
  Woodingdean BN2 .... 165 C8
Vernon Cl BN23 .... 185 E7
Vernon Ct **4** BN1 .... 163 E6
Vernon Lodge **9** BN21 ..... 185 A2
Vernon Rd
  Royal Tunbridge Wells TN1 .... 8 C6
  Uckfield TN22 .... 78 D6
Vernon Terr BN1 .... 163 E7
Vernons Rd BN8 .... 76 C7
Veronica Way BN2 .... 189 B4
Verrall's Wlk **9** BN7 .... 146 C8
Verulam Pl TN37 .... 159 E7
Viaduct Rd BN1, BN2 .... 189 A7
Vian Ave BN23 .... 185 F7
Vicarage Cl Newhaven BN9 .. 168 E2
  Ringmer BN8 .... 124 D5
  Seaford BN25 .... 180 F3
Vicarage Dr BN21 .... 184 D3
Vicarage Field BN27 .... 152 C8
Vicarage La
  Burwash Common TN19 ...... 61 A3
  Eastbourne BN20 .... 184 D3

Vicarage La
Hailsham BN27 .... 152 C8
Hellingly BN27 .... 129 A6
Rottingdean BN2 .... 165 F1
Scaynes Hill RH17 .... 51 F3
Westfield TN35 .... 114 D3
Vicarage Rd
Burwash Common TN19 .... 61 A3
Eastbourne BN20, BN21 .... 184 D3
Hailsham BN27 .... 152 C7
Hastings TN34 .... 160 A5
Vicarage Terr BN2 .... 165 F1
Vicarage Way
Hurst Green TN19 .... 45 A3
Ringmer BN8 .... 124 D5
Viceroy Lodge 9 BN3 .... 163 A6
Victor Cl BN25 .... 180 E5
Victoria Ave Burgess Hill RH15 ... 72 E3
Hastings TN35 .... 137 C4
Peacehaven BN10 .... 178 C7
Victoria Cl Burgess Hill RH15 ... 72 E3
Burgess Hill RH15 .... 72 F2
Polegate BN26 .... 172 F7
Victoria Cotts TN6 .... 39 C6
Victoria Ct Hastings TN38 ... 159 B6
21 Hove BN3 .... 163 C6
Portslade-by-Sea BN41 .... 162 C8
Victoria Dr BN20, BN21 ...... 184 C4
Victoria Gdns Burgess Hill RH15 72 F2
Eastbourne BN20 .... 184 C4
Victoria Gr 9 BN3 .... 163 C6
Victoria Ind Est RH15 .... 72 E2
Victoria Mews BN2 .... 165 F1
Victoria Pl 11 BN1 .... 163 E6
Victoria Rd Bexhill TN39, TN40 .. 157 B4
Brighton BN1 .... 163 E6
Burgess Hill RH15 .... 72 E2
Crowborough TN6 .... 38 C8
Eastbourne BN20 .... 184 C5
Hailsham BN27 .... 152 C7
Hastings TN37 .... 159 D7
Haywards Heath RH16 .... 51 A3
Mayfield TN20 .... 40 A3
Polegate BN26 .... 172 F7
Portslade-by-Sea BN3, BN41 ... 162 C8
Royal Tunbridge Wells TN1 .... 8 B4
Southwick BN41, BN42 .... 161 D7
Windmill Hill BN27 .... 131 B5
Victoria St BN1 .... 163 E6
Victoria Terr TN19 .... 62 A6
Victoria Way Burgess Hill RH15 .. 72 F2
East Grinstead RH19 .... 10 F7
Winchelsea Beach TN36 .... 118 A5
Victory Mews BN2 .... 165 A3
View Bank TN35 .... 160 D6
View Rd BN10 .... 178 C8
View Terr RH7 .... 2 A4
Views Path RH16 .... 51 B4
Views Wood Path TN22 .... 55 D1
Viking Cl BN25 .... 180 B6
Viking Way BN23 .... 185 F8
Villa Rd TN37 .... 159 D7
Village Barn The BN1 .... 142 E7
Village Mews TN39 .... 156 C4
Village The BN20 .... 188 D8
Village Way BN1 .... 144 C6
Village Wks BN8 .... 105 A5
Villiers Cl BN2 .... 165 E8
Villiers Ct BN1 .... 189 A6
Vincent Cl BN23 .... 185 F7
Vine Cotts TN6 .... 38 C7
Vine Farm Cotts BN8 .... 104 A5
Vine Pl BN1 .... 189 F6
Vine Sq BN22 .... 185 D6
Vine St BN1 .... 189 A6
Vinehall Cl TN34 .... 137 A5
Vinehall (Prep Sch for Boys)
TN32 .... 87 E6
Vinehall Rd TN32 .... 87 E5
Vineries The Burgess Hill RH15 .. 73 D3
Eastbourne BN23 .... 174 D2
11 Hove BN3 .... 163 E6
Vines Cross Rd Brighton BN2 .. 164 F7
Horam TN21 .... 107 B7
Vineyard La TN5 .... 31 C2
Vintry The Eastbourne BN21 .. 184 C7
Nutley TN22 .... 35 C4
Virgin's Croft TN33 .... 112 D6
Virgin's La TN33 .... 112 D6
Volks Electric Rly BN1, BN2 .. 164 C4
Vue Gris Nez TN36 .... 118 B5

Wade Cl BN23 .... 185 F7
Wadhurst Bsns Pk TN5 .... 29 B7
Wadhurst CE Prim Sch TN5 ..... 29 F5
Wadhurst Cl Eastbourne BN22 .. 173 F2
Hastings TN37 .... 136 B5
Wadhurst La TN33 .... 111 E6
Wadhurst Par TN5 .... 29 F4
Wadhurst Rd TN6 .... 28 C3
Wadhurst Rise BN2 .... 164 F5
Wadhurst Sta TN5 .... 29 C6
Wadlands Brook Rd RH19 .... 1 D5
Wagg Cl RH19 .... 2 A1
Waghorns La TN22 .... 57 C6
Wainwright Cl TN38 .... 135 D3
Wainwright Rd TN39 .... 157 B4
Waite Cl BN7 .... 123 D2
Waites La TN35 .... 138 E5
Wakefield Rd BN2 .... 189 B8
Waldegrave Rd BN1 .... 143 A1
Waldegrave St 4 TN34 .... 159 F8
Walden Terr TN33 .... 112 E4
Waldene Cl TN34 .... 136 F2
Waldron Ave BN1 .... 143 D6

Waldron Cl BN22 .... 184 D8
Waldron Ct TN21 .... 82 B8
Waldron Pl BN1 .... 143 D6
Waldron Rd BN8 .... 105 A5
Waldron Thorns TN21 .... 82 A7
Waldshut Rd BN7 .... 123 A3
Wales Farm Cotts BN7 .... 121 C7
Walesbeech Rd BN23 .... 177 D4
Walker Cl BN23 .... 185 F7
Walks The TN3 .... 15 C8
Wall Hill Rd RH18, RH19 .... 11 E5
Wallace Cl TN2 .... 17 A8
Wallands Cres BN7 .... 123 C1
Wallands Cty Prim Sch BN7 .. 123 A2
Walled Garden The TN22 .... 55 D4
Wallers TN3 .... 7 A8
Wallington Towers TN40 .... 157 F4
Wallis Ave BN23 .... 185 E7
Wallis Cl TN6 .... 26 A1
Wallis Field TN3 .... 15 B6
Wallis Ho RH19 .... 1 E1
Wallis Pl BN23 .... 185 E8
Wallis Way RH15 .... 72 E4
Wallsend Rd BN24 .... 175 C6
Walmer Cres BN2 .... 144 B1
Walmer Rd BN25 .... 181 C4
Walnut Cl Brighton BN1 .... 142 E3
Heathfield TN21 .... 82 B6
Walnut Pk RH16 .... 51 B4
Walnut Tree Wlk BN20 .... 184 B8
Walnut Wlk BN26 .... 173 A6
Walpole Rd BN2 .... 164 D5
Walpole Terr BN2 .... 164 D5
Walpole Wlk BN23 .... 174 E3
Walshes Rd TN6 .... 38 B7
Walsingham Cl BN22 .... 173 D3
Walsingham Rd BN3 .... 162 F6
Walter May Ho 13 BN2 .... 164 F5
Walters Green Rd TN11, TN3 ... 5 F6
Walton Bank BN1 .... 143 E5
Walton Cl Eastbourne BN23 ... 174 E3
Hastings TN37 .... 136 C5
Walton Pk TN39 .... 156 F4
Walwers La 14 BN7 .... 123 D1
Wanderdown Cl BN2 .... 165 E4
Wanderdown Dr BN2 .... 165 E4
Wanderdown Rd BN2 .... 165 D4
Wanderdown Way BN2 .... 165 E4
Wannock Ave BN20 .... 172 F3
Wannock Cl TN40 .... 158 A6
Wannock Dr BN26 .... 172 F5
Wannock Gdns BN20 .... 172 F3
Wannock La BN20, BN26 ...... 172 F3
Wannock Rd
Eastbourne BN22 .... 185 D5
Polegate BN26 .... 172 F5
War Memorial Hospl TN6 ...... 25 E1
Warbleton Cl BN2 .... 164 E5
Warburton Cl
East Grinstead RH19 .... 11 A8
Eastbourne BN21 .... 184 C8
Uckfield TN22 .... 78 D8
Ward Cl TN5 .... 29 E5
Ward Way TN39 .... 157 A6
Ward's La TN5 .... 30 E4
Warden Ct RH17 .... 50 A4
Wardsbrook Rd TN5 .... 43 D7
Ware Ct RH15 .... 73 D3
Warelands RH15 .... 72 F1
Warenne Rd BN3 .... 141 C4
Wares Field TN22 .... 78 D4
Wares Rd TN22 .... 78 D4
Warleigh Rd BN1, BN2 .... 189 A8
Warmdene Ave BN1 .... 142 F6
Warmdene Cl BN1 .... 142 F5
Warmdene Rd BN1 .... 142 F6
Warmdene Way BN1 .... 142 F6
Warminster Rd BN24 .... 175 D5
Warner Ct RH15 .... 73 A3
Warnham BN3 .... 163 C5
Warnham Gdns TN39 .... 156 E2
Warnham Rise BN1 .... 143 A5
Warr Gn BN7 .... 123 B3
Warren Ave BN2 .... 165 C8
Warren Cl Crowborough TN6 ... 25 E2
Eastbourne BN20 .... 188 C8
Friston BN20 .... 183 B1
Hastings TN38 .... 158 E8
Lewes BN7 .... 146 B8
Roser's Cross TN21 .... 81 A6
Woodingdean BN2 .... 165 B8
Warren Cnr TN21 .... 81 A8
Warren Cotts Mayfield TN20 .... 40 C3
North Chailey BN8 .... 75 F7
Warren Dr BN7 .... 146 A8
Warren Farm La TN3 .... 16 B4
Warren Gdn TN6 .... 25 E2
Warren Hill BN20 .... 184 A1
Warren La Beacon Down TN21 .. 81 A7
Friston BN20 .... 183 B1
North Chailey BN8 .... 75 E8
Warren Lodge BN10 .... 167 A1
Warren Rd Crowborough TN6 ... 25 C1
Fairlight TN35 .... 138 C4
Woodingdean BN2 .... 165 B8
Warren Ridge TN3 .... 17 C3
Warren Rise BN2 .... 165 B8
Warren The Burgess Hill RH15 .. 73 C1
Mayfield TN20 .... 40 C2
Ticehurst TN5 .... 31 E1
Warren Way North Chailey BN8 .. 75 F8
Telscombe Cliffs BN10 .... 167 A1
Woodingdean BN2 .... 165 D8
Warrenwood BN8 .... 53 A1
Warrior Cl BN41 .... 141 B2
Warrior Gdns TN37 .... 159 C7
Warrior Ho BN1 .... 188 E3

Warrior Sq
6 Eastbourne BN22 .... 185 C4
Hastings TN37 .... 159 D7
Warrs Hill La BN8 .... 75 E8
Wartling Cl TN38 .... 135 F3
Wartling Dr TN39 .... 155 F5
Wartling Rd Eastbourne BN22 .. 185 D6
Wartling BN27 .... 131 C2
Warwick Ct
4 Eastbourne BN23 .... 174 E1
4 Hove BN3 .... 163 E7
Warwick Mount BN2 .... 164 C4
Warwick Pk TN1, TN2 .... 8 B1
Warwick Rd Bexhill TN39 ...... 156 F5
4 Royal Tunbridge Wells TN1 ... 8 A2
Seaford BN25 .... 180 E3
Washington Ave TN38 .... 135 F6
Washington Rd RH16 .... 51 A5
Washington St BN2 .... 189 B7
Washwell La TN5 .... 29 F3
Wassall La TN17 .... 48 E7
Watchbell La TN31 .... 93 C5
Watchbell St TN31 .... 93 C5
Waterbury Mill RH17 .... 33 B5
Waterdown Rd TN4 .... 7 E1
Waterdyke Ave BN42 .... 161 E7
Waterfield TN2 .... 17 A7
Waterford Cl BN10 .... 167 C2
Waterfrets Cotts TN3 .... 6 F5
Watergate TN39 .... 157 B8
Watergate La BN2 .... 146 C8
Waterhall Golf Course BN1 ... 142 A7
Waterhall Rd BN1 .... 142 C6
Waterloo Cl TN37 .... 135 F7
Waterloo Pas 15 TN34 .... 160 B4
Waterloo Pl 1 Brighton BN1 .. 189 B6
13 Hastings TN34 .... 160 B4
2 Lewes BN7 .... 123 D1
Waterloo Sq BN26 .... 171 A3
Waterloo St BN3 .... 163 D5
Watermen's Cl TN34 .... 136 F3
Watermill Cl Bexhill TN39 ...... 157 B7
Lower Willingdon BN26 .... 173 A5
Watermill Dr TN38 .... 135 D3
Watermill La Clayhill TN31 ...... 67 D2
Icklesham TN35, TN36 .... 116 C3
Watermill TN39 .... 134 B2
Waters Cotts TN5 .... 30 A4
Waterside RH19 .... 2 B1
Waterside Cl TN34 .... 137 C3
Waterworks Cotts
Friston BN20 .... 183 A1
1 Hastings TN34 .... 159 F8
Waterworks Rd
Eastbourne BN22 .... 185 A4
1 Hastings TN34 .... 136 F1
Watling Cl 5 BN42 .... 161 E7
Watling Ct 8 BN42 .... 161 E7
Watling Rd BN42 .... 161 E7
Wattle's Wish TN33 .... 112 C6
Watts Cl TN5 .... 29 F4
Watts La BN21 .... 184 E4
Watts Lodge RH15 .... 73 D3
Watts' Palace La TN31 .... 89 D7
Waverley Cres BN1 .... 143 C1
Waverley Ct 4 TN34 .... 159 E7
Waverley Dr TN2 .... 8 F6
Waverley Gdns BN24 .... 175 D5
Wayfaring Down BN26 .... 172 D3
Wayfield Ave BN3 .... 141 F1
Wayford Ct BN23 .... 174 D2
Wayland Ave BN1 .... 142 C3
Wayside Brighton BN1 .... 142 D6
East Dean BN20 .... 183 B1
Wayside Wlk TN21 .... 81 F6
Weald Ave BN3 .... 162 F8
Weald Cl Barcombe Cross BN8 .. 101 E4
Lewes BN7 .... 123 C2
Weald Rd RH15 .... 72 E3
Weald Rise RH16 .... 50 E1
Weald The RH19 .... 1 F4
Weald View
Barcombe Cross BN8 .... 101 E4
Staplecross TN32 .... 65 E2
Turner's Green TN5 .... 29 F6
Wealden Cl TN6 .... 25 F3
Wealden Cotts TN19 .... 61 C3
Wealden Ind Est TN6 .... 38 C8
Wealden Pk BN22 .... 173 C1
Wealden View TN19 .... 62 B7
Wealden Way Bexhill TN39 ... 156 C6
Haywards Heath RH16 .... 50 D4
Wealdview Rd TN21 .... 81 F7
Weare Rd TN4 .... 8 C8
Weatherby Cl BN21 .... 184 C8
Weavers Cl RH15 .... 73 D1
Weavers La BN26 .... 170 F3
Wedderburn Rd BN20 .... 173 B1
Week La BN8 .... 124 D2
Weir Wood Resr
(Nature Reserve) RH19 .... 10 D1
Welbeck Ave Hastings TN38 .. 159 A7
Hove BN3 .... 162 E6
Royal Tunbridge Wells TN4 .... 8 C3
Welbeck Cl Burgess Hill RH15 .. 73 D4
Eastbourne BN22 .... 173 D3
Welbeck Ct 3 BN25 .... 180 E3
Welbeck Dr RH15 .... 73 D4
Welesmere Rd BN2 .... 166 A3
Welkin (Brighton Univ) BN20 184 E1
Welkin The RH16 .... 51 B8
Well House Pl BN2 .... 123 C1
Wellcombe Cres BN20 .... 188 D7
Weller Rd TN4 .... 7 C4
Wellesley Cl Bexhill TN39 ..... 156 D3
Crowborough TN6 .... 25 D1
Wellesley Ct 19 TN34 .... 160 B4
Wellesley Rd 6 BN21 .... 185 A3

Wellfield RH19 .... 11 C7
Wellgreen La BN7 .... 145 F5
Wellhouse La RH15 .... 98 C7
Wellingham La BN8 .... 124 A7
Wellington Ct Brighton BN2 ... 165 A3
3 Eastbourne BN22 .... 185 C5
Wellington Gdns TN33 .... 112 C5
Wellington Ho 17 TN34 .... 159 F8
Wellington Lodge TN34 .... 160 A4
Wellington Mews TN34 .... 159 F8
Wellington Pk 1 BN25 .... 181 A3
Wellington Pl
7 Hastings TN34 .... 159 F7
Sparrow's Green TN5 .... 29 F5
Wellington Rd Brighton BN2 .. 189 B7
Hastings TN34 .... 160 A4
Newhaven BN9 .... 168 F2
Peacehaven BN10 .... 178 E6
Portslade-by-Sea BN41 .... 162 B6
Wellington Sq TN34 .... 159 F8
Wellington St Brighton BN2 ... 164 C7
1 Lewes BN7 .... 123 D1
Wellington Terr 14 TN34 ...... 159 F8
Wellington Town Rd RH19 ...... 1 D2
Wellingtonia Cl 11 BN1 .... 142 E3
Wellis Ct TN38 .... 159 A8
Wellis Gdns TN38 .... 159 A8
Wellplace Cotts TN36 .... 116 F5
Wells Chase BN7 .... 99 E6
Wells Cl Eastbourne BN20 ..... 188 C8
Plumpton Green BN7 .... 99 E6
Royal Tunbridge Wells TN1 .... 8 A3
Wells Lea RH19 .... 1 D3
Wells Meadow RH19 .... 1 D3
Wellsbourne 8 BN2 .... 164 F5
Wendale Dr BN10 .... 167 D2
Wendover Grange 3 BN3 ..... 163 A6
Went Hill Gdns BN22 .... 173 B3
Went Hill Pk BN25 .... 181 A3
Went La BN20 .... 183 C1
Went Way BN20 .... 187 B8
Wenthill Cl BN20 .... 187 B8
Wentworth Cl Bexhill TN40 ... 157 F5
Hailsham BN27 .... 129 A1
Wentworth Ct BN23 .... 185 E6
Wentworth St BN2 .... 189 B4
Wentworth Way TN38 .... 158 F8
West Ascent TN38 .... 159 B6
West Beeches Rd TN6 .... 26 B2
West Blatchington Inf Sch
BN3 .... 141 E4
West Blatchington Jun Sch
BN3 .... 141 E4
West Cl Alfriston BN26 .... 170 F3
Polegate BN26 .... 173 B7
West Comm RH16 .... 50 F6
West Common Dr RH16 .... 51 A7
West Dean Rise BN25 .... 181 A4
West Down Rd TN39 .... 157 A5
West Dr BN2 .... 164 C6
West End Rd BN27 .... 130 E6
West End Cotts TN19 .... 60 F3
West Furlong Cl BN6 .... 97 A5
West Furlong La BN6 .... 97 A5
West Gate BN7 .... 99 E6
West Hill Dormans Park RH19 ... 1 C6
East Grinstead RH19 .... 10 D8
West Hill Arc 3 TN34 .... 160 A3
West Hill Cl 4 TN38 .... 159 B6
West Hill Cliff Rly TN34 .... 160 A4
West Hill Mews TN38 .... 158 F6
West Hill Pl BN1 .... 189 F6
West Hill Rd Brighton BN1 .... 189 F6
Hastings TN38 .... 159 A6
West Hill St BN1 .... 189 F7
West Ho 15 BN21 .... 185 A2
West Hoathly Rd RH19 .... 10 D4
West Hove Cty Inf Sch BN3 ... 162 F7
West Hove Cty Jun Sch BN3 .. 162 F7
West Hove Golf Course BN3 .. 141 C5
West Kent Coll of F Ed TN4 ..... 8 A7
West La RH19 .... 10 E7
West Leigh RH19 .... 10 E7
West Mallion RH16 .... 50 F3
West Par TN39 .... 157 B2
West Park Cres RH15 .... 72 D4
West Rd BN41 .... 162 A7
West Rise Cty Inf Sch BN23 ... 174 C2
West Rise Cty Jun Sch BN23 .. 174 C2
West St Alfriston BN26 .... 170 F3
Brighton BN1 .... 189 F5
Burgess Hill RH15 .... 72 E4
Ditchling BN6 .... 98 D3
Dormansland RH7 .... 2 A4
East Grinstead RH19 .... 10 E8
Eastbourne BN21 .... 184 F2
Hastings TN34 .... 160 A3
Lewes BN7 .... 123 D1
Mayfield TN20 .... 40 A2
Portslade-by-Sea BN41 .... 162 C7
Rottingdean BN2 .... 165 F1
Rye TN31 .... 93 C5
Seaford BN25 .... 180 E2
West St Leonards
Cty Prim Sch TN38 .... 158 F8
West St Leonards Sta TN38 ... 158 F7
West Street La TN21 .... 81 F2
West Terr Eastbourne BN21 ... 184 F2
Herstmonceux BN27 .... 130 E6
West Undercliff TN31 .... 93 A5
West View Hastings TN34 ...... 160 B6
Haywards Heath RH16 .... 51 B6
Hove BN3 .... 163 C8
Seaford BN25 .... 180 E2
Uckfield TN22 .... 78 E7
West View Cotts RH16 .... 51 B6
West View Ct 8 BN25 .... 180 E2
West View Gdns RH19 .... 10 E8

West View Terr BN9 .... 168 D2
West Way BN3 .... 141 D2
Westaway Dr TN39 .... 157 A4
Westbourne Ct TN39 .... 156 C2
Westbourne Gdns BN3 .... 163 A7
Westbourne Gr BN3 .... 163 A7
Westbourne Pl BN3 .... 163 A6
Westbourne St BN3 .... 163 A7
Westbourne Villas BN3 .... 162 F6
Westbrook Forest Row RH18 ... 11 E3
Saltdean BN2 .... 177 C6
Westbrook La TN35 .... 114 E5
Westbrook Terr TN37 .... 8 D1
Westbrook Way BN42 .... 161 F7
Westcliff Mansion BN20 ...... 188 F8
Westcombe 1 BN1 .... 163 E7
Westcourt Dr TN39 .... 156 F3
Westdean Ave BN9 .... 179 A5
Westdene Cl TN37 .... 159 C7
Westdene Cty Prim Sch BN1 . 142 C5
Westdene Dr BN1 .... 142 C5
Westdown Ho 4 BN21 .... 185 A2
Westdown La TN19 .... 61 A3
Westdown Rd BN25 .... 180 D4
Westergate Rd BN2 .... 143 E4
Westerham Rd BN23 .... 174 D1
Westerings The 4 TN21 .... 82 A6
Westerleigh Cl TN38 .... 159 A8
Western Ave BN26 .... 173 B7
Western Espl BN3, BN41 .... 162 D6
Western Gdns TN6 .... 38 D8
Western Rd
Bexhill TN39, TN40 .... 157 C3
Burgess Hill RH15 .... 72 E3
Crowborough TN6 .... 38 C7
Eastbourne BN22 .... 185 B4
Hailsham BN27 .... 152 B7
Hastings TN37 .... 159 C7
Haywards Heath RH16 .... 50 F4
Hove BN1, BN3 .... 163 E5
Hurstpierpoint BN6 .... 97 A7
Lewes BN7 .... 123 B1
Newhaven BN9 .... 179 C6
Newick BN8 .... 76 C7
Pevensey Bay BN24 .... 175 D4
Royal Tunbridge Wells TN1 .... 8 C5
Turner's Green TN5 .... 29 F6
Western Road Cty Prim Sch
BN7 .... 146 C8
Western St BN1 .... 163 D5
Western Terr 5 BN1 .... 163 E5
Westfield Ave BN2 .... 166 D3
Westfield Ave N BN2 .... 166 D3
Westfield Ave S BN2 .... 166 D3
Westfield Cl Brighton BN1 .... 143 A4
Five Ashes TN20 .... 58 B6
Polegate BN26 .... 173 A7
Westfield Cres BN1 .... 143 A5
Westfield Ct BN26 .... 173 A6
Westfield Cty Prim Sch TN35 . 114 E4
Westfield La TN34, TN35 .... 136 C8
Westfield Rd BN2 .... 184 D6
Westfield Rise BN2 .... 166 E3
Westgate St BN7 .... 123 C1
Westham Cl TN39 .... 156 E3
Westham Dr BN24 .... 175 F6
Westhill Dr RH15 .... 72 E3
Westland Ct BN41 .... 162 A7
Westlands Rd RH16 .... 51 B5
Westmeston Ave BN2 .... 177 B6
Westminster Cl BN2 .... 173 D4
Westminster Cres TN34 .... 137 A4
Westmoreland Ct TN38 .... 135 F3
Westmorland Ct
Eastbourne BN20 .... 184 B7
12 Hove BN1 .... 163 E7
Westmount 3 BN2 .... 164 C6
Westmount Ct BN42, BN43 ... 161 D8
Westpoint BN8 .... 76 C7
Westville Rd TN39 .... 157 A4
Westway TN2 .... 9 D7
Westway Cl BN41 .... 140 E4
Westway Gdns BN41 .... 140 E4
Westwood Rd TN4 .... 7 C5
Wharf Rd Eastbourne BN21 ... 184 F3
Hove BN3 .... 162 D6
Whatlington Rd TN33 .... 112 E7
Whatlington Way TN38 .... 135 D2
Wheatfield Ct TN37 .... 136 C5
Wheatfield Way BN2 .... 143 F3
Wheatland Cl BN10 .... 167 B2
Wheatsheaf Cl RH15 .... 72 E5
Wheatsheaf Gdns BN7 .... 123 E2
Wheatsheaf La RH17 .... 50 A6
Wheel Farm Bsns Pk TN35 ... 114 D4
Wheel La TN35 .... 114 D3
Wheelers La TN22 .... 57 D6
Wheelers Lane Cotts TN22 ..... 57 D5
Wheelwright Cl BN22 .... 173 D4
Wheelwright La RH15 .... 73 D1
Whichelo Pl BN2 .... 164 C6
Whin Croft Pk TN6 .... 37 D8
Whipping Post La BN2 .... 165 F1
Whippingham Rd BN2 .... 164 C7
Whippingham St BN2 .... 164 C8
Whistler Ct BN1 .... 142 F1
Whitbread Cl BN23 .... 174 B4
White Bear Pas 3 TN1, TN4 ..... 8 A2
White Ct BN26 .... 170 F2
White Hill Ho BN7 .... 123 C1
White Hill Ave TN39 .... 156 F4
White Hill Dr TN39 .... 156 V6
White House Cty Prim Sch
BN27 .... 152 B8
White Lodge Brighton BN3 ... 163 C8
Royal Tunbridge Wells TN1 .... 8 C4
White Rock TN34, TN37 .... 159 E7
White Rock Gdns 7 TN34 ..... 159 E7

White Rock Pleasure Grounds
TN34 .... 159 E7
White Rock Rd TN34, TN37 ...... 159 E7
White St BN2 .... 189 B5
White Way Alfriston BN26 .... 170 F1
Lewes BN7 .... 146 B1
White's Cl BN6 .... 97 A7
Whitebread La TN31 .... 67 E8
Whitecross St BN1 .... 189 A6
Whitefield Rd TN4 .... 8 A6
Whitefriars Rd TN34 .... 160 A5
Whitegate Cl TN4 .... 8 A8
Whitegates Cl BN8 .... 100 E7
Whitegates La TN5 .... 29 D8
Whitegates Pk TN35 .... 114 D2
Whitehawk Cl BN2 .... 164 E5
Whitehawk Cres BN2 .... 164 E5
Whitehawk Cty Inf Sch BN2 .. 164 E6
Whitehawk Cty Jun Sch BN2 . 164 E6
Whitehawk Hill Rd BN2 .... 164 D5
Whitehawk Rd Brighton BN2 .... 164 E6
Brighton BN2 .... 164 F5
Whitehawk Way BN2 .... 164 F6
Whitehill Cl TN6 .... 25 F1
Whitehill Cty Inf Sch TN6 ...... 25 F1
Whitehill Rd TN6 .... 37 F8
Whitehouse Ave TN39 .... 157 B7
Whitehouse La TN21 .... 81 B4
Whitelot Cl BN42 .... 140 E2
Whitelot Way BN42 .... 140 E2
Whiterock Pl BN42 .... 161 E7
Whitethorn Dr BN1 .... 142 B4
Whiteway Cl BN25 .... 180 E6
Whiteway La BN2 .... 177 A6
Whiteways Cotts BN7 .... 146 D2
Whitfield La BN8 .... 123 C6
Whitley Rd BN22 .... 185 B5
Whittingehame Gdns BN1 ...... 142 F3
Whittington Coll RH19 .... 1 A4
Whittington's Way TN34 .... 137 B4
Whittle Dr BN23 .... 174 A1
Whittlewood Cl TN38 .... 135 E2
Whitworth Rd TN37 .... 136 B7
Whybourne Crest TN2 .... 8 D1
Whydown Hill TN33 .... 113 E6
Whydown Rd TN39 .... 156 B7
Wick Hall BN3 .... 163 D6
Wickets The RH15 .... 72 F5
Wickham Ave TN39 .... 157 B3
Wickham Cl RH16 .... 50 E7
Wickham Dr BN6 .... 97 C5
Wickham Gdns TN4 .... 7 D5
Wickham Hill BN6 .... 97 C4
Wickham La BN7, BN8 .... 100 E3
Wickham Rock La TN36 .... 117 C5
Wickham Way RH16 .... 50 E7
Wickhurst Cl BN41 .... 140 F2
Wickhurst Rd BN41 .... 141 A2
Wickhurst Rise BN41 .... 140 F3
Wicklands Ave BN2 .... 177 D5
Widbury Cl TN3 .... 6 F2
Widdicombe Way BN2 .... 143 E2
Wigmore Cl BN1 .... 143 B1
Wilbury Ave BN3 .... 163 C8
Wilbury Cres BN3 .... 163 D7
Wilbury Gdns BN3 .... 163 C8
Wilbury Gr BN3 .... 163 C6
Wilbury Grange BN3 .... 163 C6
Wilbury Lodge BN3 .... 163 C6
Wilbury Rd BN3 .... 163 C6
Wilbury Villas BN3 .... 163 C7
Wilby Ave BN42 .... 140 E1
Wild Park Cl BN2 .... 143 E3
Wilderness Gdns BN31 .... 67 B7
Wilderness La TN22 .... 57 C3
Wilderness Pk TN6 .... 25 E2
Wilderness Rd BN6 .... 97 A6
Wilderness Rise RH19 .... 2 A6
Wilderness The RH16 .... 51 B8
Wilderness Wood
(Adventure Pk) TN22 .... 57 D4
Wilderwick Rd RH19, RH7 .... 2 A5
Wilfrid Rd BN3 .... 141 D1
Wilkins Way TN40 .... 157 F6
Wilkinson Cl TN2 .... 165 F3
Wilkinson Way BN25 .... 180 E4
Willard Cl BN22 .... 185 A6
Willetts Cotts TN3 .... 5 C4
Willetts Field BN8 .... 127 E8
Willetts La TN3 .... 5 C4
William Allen La RH16 .... 51 B6
William Parker Sch (Lower)
TN34 .... 136 D3
William Parker Sch (Upper)
TN34 .... 136 D4
William Rd TN38 .... 158 E7
William St Brighton BN2 .... 189 A5
Royal Tunbridge Wells TN4 ...... 8 A5
Southwick BN41 .... 162 B7
William Sutton Ho BN1 .... 189 A5
Williams Ct BN23 .... 174 E1

Williams Rd BN43 .... 161 C8
Willingdon Ave Bexhill TN39 .. 157 A4
Hastings TN38 .... 136 A5
Willingdon Cl Hastings TN38 .. 136 A5
Willingdon BN20 .... 173 B1
Willingdon Ct BN20 .... 173 B3
Willingdon Cty Prim Sch
BN20 .... 173 A3
Willingdon Dro BN23 .... 174 B2
Willingdon La BN26 .... 183 C7
Willingdon Park Dr BN22 ...... 173 D2
Willingdon Rd Brighton BN2 .. 143 E1
Eastbourne BN20, BN21 ...... 184 C6
Willingdon Sch BN20 .... 172 F4
Willingdon Trees
Cty Prim Sch BN22 .... 173 D3
Willington Way
Hastings TN38 .... 136 A5
Willingdon BN22 .... 173 B2
Willingford La TN19 .... 61 C2
Willoughby Cres BN22 .... 185 C6
Willow Ave BN27 .... 129 B1
Willow Bank TN32 .... 64 B3
Willow Cl East Grinstead RH19 .. 1 D3
Etchingham TN19 .... 63 B8
Heathfield TN21 .... 82 B8
Woodingdean BN2 .... 165 E8
Willow Ct Hove BN3 .... 163 D7
Polegate BN26 .... 173 A6
Willow Dr Bexhill TN39 .... 156 C5
Polegate BN26 .... 173 A5
Seaford BN25 .... 181 C3
Willow End TN34 .... 136 F4
Willow Est The BN9 .... 179 E8
Willow Gdns BN6 .... 97 A7
Willow Ho BN6 .... 97 C5
Willow La TN36 .... 118 B6
Willow Mead RH19 .... 10 F8
Willow Mews TN32 .... 64 B3
Willow Pk RH16 .... 51 B4
Willow Stream Cl TN35 .... 115 E3
Willow Tree Rd TN4 .... 7 F1
Willow Way BN6 .... 97 A8
Willow Wlk Eastbourne BN22 .. 173 D2
Newhaven BN9 .... 179 C8
Royal Tunbridge Wells TN2 ...... 8 E8
Willowbed Wlk TN34 .... 136 E5
Willowbrook Way BN6 .... 98 A3
Willowdowne Cl BN26 .... 173 A5
Willowfield Rd BN22 .... 185 B4
Willowfield Sq BN22 .... 185 B3
Willowmead TN6 .... 37 E8
Willows Rise TN22 .... 79 B5
Willows The Brighton BN2 .... 189 B8
Burgess Hill RH15 .... 73 C5
Hassocks BN6 .... 97 E4
Hastings TN37 .... 136 A6
Wilman Rd TN4 .... 8 B7
Wilmington Cl Brighton BN1 .. 143 A5
Hassocks BN6 .... 97 F4
Wilmington Gdns BN21 .... 185 A1
Wilmington Par BN1 .... 142 F5
Wilmington Rd Hastings TN34 . 137 A3
Newhaven BN9 .... 179 B6
Seaford BN25 .... 180 D4
Wilmington Sq BN21 .... 185 A1
Wilmington St BN26 .... 171 F6
Wilmington Way Brighton BN1 . 143 A5
Haywards Heath RH16 .... 51 A5
Wilmot Ct BN43 .... 161 C8
Wilmot Rd BN43 .... 161 C8
Wilson Ave BN2 .... 164 F6
Wilson Gr TN22 .... 78 A7
Wilson's Cross BN27 .... 131 F7
Wilton RH16 .... 50 D6
Wilton Ave BN22 .... 173 F2
Wilton Rd TN40 .... 157 C3
Wiltshire Cl BN23 .... 174 E1
Wiltshire Ho BN2 .... 189 B5
Wiltshire Way TN1 .... 8 D7
Winceby Cl TN39 .... 156 E2
Winchcombe Rd BN22 .... 185 A4
Winchelsea Cl BN25 .... 181 C5
Winchelsea La
Cock Marling TN31, TN36 ...... 92 C1
Hastings TN35 .... 137 E5
Winchelsea Mus TN36 .... 117 E7
Winchelsea Rd
Eastbourne BN22 .... 185 D6
Guestling Green TN35 .... 137 F7
Hastings TN35 .... 137 D4
Rye TN31 .... 93 B5
Winchelsea St Thomas
CE Prim Sch TN36 .... 117 F7
Winchelsea Sta TN36 .... 92 D1
Winchester Ho BN22 .... 173 E3
Winchester St BN1 .... 189 A8
Winchester Way BN22 .... 173 C2
Wincombe Rd BN1, BN3 .... 142 D1
Windermere Cres BN22 .... 185 C5
Windermere Rd BN2 .... 164 C6

Windermere Rd RH16 .... 50 F4
Windgrove Cotts TN33 .... 112 D6
Windgrove Ho TN33 .... 112 D6
Winding St TN34 .... 160 B4
Windlesham Ave BN1, BN3 .... 163 E6
Windlesham Ct BN41 .... 141 A1
Windlesham Ct BN1 .... 163 E7
Windlesham Gdns BN1, BN3 .. 163 E7
Windlesham Rd BN1 .... 163 E6
Windlesham Sch BN1 .... 163 E8
Windmill Ave BN6 .... 97 F3
Windmill Cl Eastbourne BN21 .. 184 D6
Heathfield TN21 .... 82 B8
Hove BN3 .... 141 F2
Windmill Ct
Royal Tunbridge Wells TN2 ...... 8 C3
Winchelsea Beach TN36 ...... 118 B6
Windmill Dr Bexhill TN39 ...... 157 B6
Brighton BN1 .... 142 D6
Burgess Hill RH15 .... 73 A4
Windmill Gn BN24 .... 174 C5
Windmill La
Ashurst Wood RH19 .... 11 C7
Cousley Wood TN5 .... 30 C8
Durgates TN5 .... 29 E4
East Grinstead RH19 .... 1 D3
Friston BN20 .... 183 A1
Windmill Par BN42 .... 140 E1
Windmill Pl BN26 .... 173 A5
Windmill Rd Hastings TN38 .. 136 B2
Polegate BN26 .... 173 A6
Southwick BN42 .... 140 E1
Windmill St Brighton BN2 .... 189 B6
Royal Tunbridge Wells TN2 ...... 8 C3
Windmill Terr BN1 .... 189 B6
Windmill View BN1 .... 143 B7
Windmill Way TN6 .... 118 B7
Windmills Cty Jun Sch BN6 .. 98 A3
Windover Cres BN7 .... 123 A2
Windover Way BN22 .... 173 B3
Windsor Cl Eastbourne BN23 .. 174 C3
Hove BN3 .... 142 A3
Seaford BN25 .... 180 B6
Windsor Dr Brighton BN1 .... 189 F5
Brighton, Withdean BN1 ...... 142 D4
Crowborough TN6 .... 38 C8
Eastbourne BN22 .... 185 B3
Polegate BN26 .... 173 A7
Windsor Lodge BN3 .... 163 B6
Windsor Pl Crowborough TN6 .. 38 C8
East Grinstead RH19 .... 11 A8
Hastings TN34 .... 136 C2
Windsor Rd Bexhill TN39 ...... 157 B4
Crowborough TN6 .... 38 C8
Hailsham BN27 .... 152 B6
Hastings TN37 .... 136 B3
Windsor St BN1 .... 189 F5
Windsor Way Polegate BN26 .. 173 A7
Winchelsea Beach TN36 ...... 118 A5
Wineham Way TN40 .... 157 F4
Winfield Ave BN1 .... 142 F6
Winfield Cl Brighton BN1 ...... 142 F5
Portslade-by-Sea BN41 .... 141 A3
Wingate Cl TN38 .... 136 A1
Wingle Tye Rd RH15 .... 98 A3
Winkfield Ct RH16 .... 50 D5
Winkhurst Way RH15 .... 73 D1
Winkney Rd BN22 .... 173 F3
Winnals Pk RH16 .... 50 D5
Winston BN27 .... 152 B7
Winston Cres BN23 .... 185 D7
Winston Dr TN39 .... 156 F4
Winstone Scott Ave TN3 .... 6 E4
Winterbourne Cl
Hastings TN34 .... 159 D8
Lewes BN7 .... 146 A8
Winterbourne Hollow BN7 .... 146 B8
Winterbourne La BN7 .... 146 A8
Winterbourne Mews BN7 ...... 146 B8
Winterton Way BN43 .... 161 B6
Winton Ave BN2 .... 166 C3
Winton St BN26 .... 171 A4
Wireless Mus RH16 .... 51 B7
Wisden Ave RH15 .... 72 E5
Wiseacre TN3 .... 20 A3
Wish Ct BN3 .... 162 E8
Wish Hill BN20 .... 173 B1
Wish Rd Eastbourne BN21 .... 185 A2
Hove BN3 .... 162 E6
Wish St TN31 .... 93 B5
Wish Tower Mus BN21 .... 185 A1
Wish Ward TN31 .... 93 B5
Wishing Tree Cl TN38 .... 135 F2
Wishing Tree La TN38 .... 135 F1
Wishing Tree Rd TN38 .... 135 F2
Wishing Tree Rd N TN38 ...... 136 A4
Wiston Ct BN43 .... 161 C8
Wiston Rd BN2 .... 164 F6
Wiston Way BN2 .... 164 F7
Withdean Ave BN1 .... 142 D2
Withdean Cl BN1 .... 142 D3

Withdean Court Ave BN1 ...... 142 D3
Withdean Cres BN1 .... 142 E3
Withdean Ct BN1 .... 142 E3
Withdean Hall BN1 .... 142 E3
Withdean Rd BN1 .... 142 D3
Withdean Rise BN1 .... 142 E3
Witherenden Rd TN20 .... 41 A1
Withy Bush RH15 .... 72 E5
Withyham Ave BN2 .... 177 C5
Withyham Cl BN22 .... 173 F1
Withyham Rd Bexhill TN39 .. 156 C2
Groombridge TN3 .... 15 A6
Wittersham Rd TN17, TN30 .. 49 D4
Potman's Heath TN17, TN30 .. 49 D4
Wittersham Road Sta TN17 .. 49 D6
Wivelsfield Cty Prim Sch
RH16 .... 73 F6
Wivelsfield Rd
Haywards Heath RH16 .... 50 E2
Saltdean BN2 .... 166 C3
Wivelsfield Sta RH15 .... 73 C4
Woburn Cl BN27 .... 129 A1
Woburn Pl BN1 .... 143 F5
Woburn Way BN22 .... 173 D3
Wolfe Cl TN6 .... 38 A8
Wolseley Rd Brighton BN1 .... 143 D6
Portslade-by-Sea BN41 .... 162 A8
Royal Tunbridge Wells TN4 ...... 8 C7
Wolstead Lodge RH16 .... 50 F3
Wolstonbury Cl BN6 .... 97 B4
Wolstonbury Ct RH15 .... 73 B2
Wolstonbury Rd BN3 .... 163 E7
Wolstonbury Way RH15 .... 73 B2
Wolverstone Dr BN1 .... 143 C2
Wood La BN27 .... 131 D2
Wood Ride RH16 .... 50 D3
Wood Rise Comm TN6 .... 25 F4
Wood St East Grinstead RH19 .. 1 D1
Royal Tunbridge Wells TN1 ...... 8 A8
Wood's Pas TN34 .... 160 B4
Woodbourne Ave BN1 .... 143 A4
Woodbrook Rd TN34 .... 136 F2
Woodbury Ave RH19 .... 2 B1
Woodbury Cl
East Grinstead RH19 .... 11 B8
Royal Tunbridge Wells TN4 ...... 8 A5
Woodbury Park Gdns TN4 ...... 8 B5
Woodbury Park Rd TN4 .... 8 B5
Woodcombe TN34 .... 136 F4
Woodcote Rd RH18 .... 11 F2
Woodcrest Rd RH15 .... 72 F1
Woodcroft RH15 .... 72 F5
Woodcroft Dr BN21 .... 184 C7
Woodcutters RH17 .... 51 F3
Woodgate Meadow BN7 .... 99 E7
Woodgate Rd BN22 .... 185 C5
Woodhams TN33 .... 112 D5
Woodhill Pk TN2 .... 9 C6
Woodhouse Cl BN3 .... 162 E7
Woodhouse Rd BN3 .... 162 E7
Woodingdean Cty Prim Sch
BN2 .... 165 C8
Woodland Ave
Burgess Hill RH15 .... 73 C4
Eastbourne BN22, BN21 ...... 173 C1
Hove BN3 .... 142 B3
Woodland Cl Burgess Hill RH15 . 73 C4
Hove BN3 .... 142 B2
Royal Tunbridge Wells TN4 ...... 8 B7
Woodland Cres RH15 .... 73 C4
Woodland Ct BN3 .... 142 B4
Woodland Dr BN3 .... 142 B3
Woodland Mews TN21 .... 82 B6
Woodland Par BN3 .... 142 B3
Woodland Rd TN4 .... 8 C7
Woodland Rise TN40 .... 157 E4
Woodland Vale Rd
TN37, TN38 .... 159 C8
Woodland Way Brighton BN1 .. 142 F4
Crowborough TN6 .... 37 F8
Crowhurst TN33 .... 134 F4
Fairlight Cove TN35 .... 138 E4
Heathfield TN21 .... 82 B6
Woodland Wlk BN2 .... 165 D4
Woodlands Hove BN3 .... 142 C2
Romford TN2 .... 9 F7
Woodlands Cl Hailsham BN27 .. 129 C2
Heathfield TN21 .... 82 B5
Peacehaven BN10 .... 167 B1
Uckfield TN22 .... 78 D8
Woodlands Rd
East Grinstead RH19 .... 2 A4
Haywards Heath RH16 .... 50 F4
Woodlands The Brighton BN1 .. 142 E5
Hastings TN34 .... 136 E5
Woodlands Way TN34 .... 136 E6
Woodleigh Rd RH15 .... 73 C4
Woodmans Oak TN33 .... 88 A3
Woodpecker Cres BN6 .... 72 D3
Woodpecker Dr BN27 .... 152 A8
Woodpecker Rd BN23 .... 174 B2

Woodridge Cl RH16 .... 51 A3
Woodruff Ave BN3 .... 142 C2
Woods Green Cotts TN5 .... 29 F7
Woods Hill Cl RH19 .... 11 B6
Woods Hill La RH19 .... 11 D6
Woods Ho BN3 .... 163 A8
Woodsgate Ave TN39, TN40 .. 157 C6
Woodsgate Pk TN39 .... 157 B6
Woodsgate Way TN2 .... 9 B6
Woodside TN6 .... 25 E2
Woodside Ave BN1 .... 142 D2
Woodside Cl TN2 .... 9 E6
Woodside Lodge BN1 .... 142 D2
Woodside Rd Pembury TN2 .... 9 E6
Rusthall TN4 .... 7 D4
Woodside Terr BN26 .... 151 F4
Woodside Way BN27 .... 152 A4
Woodslands Cl BN6 .... 97 F4
Woodslands Rd BN6 .... 97 F4
Woodspring TN37 .... 136 B5
Woodstock RH19 .... 1 C2
Woodstock Rd TN39 .... 156 C6
Woodview Cl BN1 .... 143 D6
Woodville Rd TN39 .... 157 B3
Woodward Cl BN23 .... 185 E7
Woodwards Cl RH15 .... 73 B1
Woolven Ct RH15 .... 72 E1
Worcester Ct
Eastbourne BN23 .... 174 E1
Hove BN3 .... 163 E6
Worcester Villas BN3 .... 162 C7
Wordsworth Dr BN23 .... 174 E2
Wordsworth Rise RH19 .... 1 C1
Wordsworth St BN3 .... 163 A7
Workhouse La TN36 .... 116 F5
Worsham La TN40 .... 157 F7
Worsted La RH19 .... 11 B8
Wray Cl RH19 .... 11 D6
Wren Cl TN21 .... 82 A7
Wren Ct Battle TN33 .... 112 F4
Hastings TN38 .... 135 E3
Wrentham Ho RH15 .... 73 B3
Wrestwood Ave BN20 .... 173 C1
Westwood Cl TN40 .... 157 D6
Westwood Rd TN40 .... 157 D6
Wrotham Cl Eastbourne BN23 . 174 D1
Hastings TN34 .... 136 E5
Wroxham Rd BN23 .... 174 B4
Wyatts La RH17 .... 33 D5
Wyberlye Rd RH15 .... 73 A4
Wybourne Rise TN2 .... 17 B8
Wychperry Rd RH16 .... 50 D5
Wychurst Gdns TN40 .... 157 D6
Wyck Ct BN41 .... 162 A7
Wykeham Rd TN34 .... 159 E8
Wykeham Terr BN1 .... 189 F5
Wykeham Way RH15 .... 73 C2
Wynberg Cotts TN6 .... 39 C6
Wyndham St BN2 .... 189 B4
Wynnes Mews BN3 .... 163 A4
Wynnstay RH15 .... 73 B2
Wyshe The BN45 .... 119 C6
Wythwood RH16 .... 50 E1

Yardley St BN1 .... 189 A8
Yates Cl TN31 .... 95 A2
Yeomans BN8 .... 125 A7
Yew La RH19 .... 1 B3
Yew Tree Cl Broyle Side BN8 .. 124 F7
Hastings TN34 .... 136 E6
Heathfield TN21 .... 82 A6
Yew Tree Cotts
Burgess Hill RH15 .... 73 B3
Groombridge TN3 .... 15 F8
Yew Tree Rd TN4 .... 8 B8
Yewtree La TN6 .... 39 E8
Yielding's Cl BN21 .... 184 D5
York Ave East Grinstead RH19 .. 11 A8
Hove BN3 .... 163 E6
York Bldgs BN34 .... 159 F7
York Ct BN3 .... 163 E7
York Gdns BN34 .... 159 F7
York Gr BN1 .... 189 F7
York Hill BN1 .... 189 A7
York Ho BN41 .... 162 A7
York Pl BN1, BN2 .... 189 A6
York Rd Bexhill TN40 .... 158 A5
Burgess Hill BN6, RH15 .... 72 D2
Eastbourne BN21 .... 184 F2
Hastings TN37 .... 136 C2
Hove BN1, BN3 .... 163 E6
Peacehaven BN10 .... 178 E6
Royal Tunbridge Wells TN1 ...... 8 A4
York Villas BN1 .... 189 F7
Yorkshire Ct BN20 .... 184 B7
Youl Grange BN20 .... 184 D1
Youngsmere Cl BN1 .... 143 C2
Yvonne Robertson Ho TN40 .. 157 D5

Town and village index

Alciston 170 D8
Alfriston 170 F2
Argos Hill 39 E5
Arlington 150 F4
Ashton Green 125 A5
Ashurst 5 D2
Ashurst Wood 11 E6
Barcombe 101 E2
Barcombe Cross 101 E4
Battle 112 D5
Beachlands 175 F6
Beacon Down 81 A7
Beckley 68 A4
Beckley Furnace 90 D7
Beddingham 147 D4
Bells Yew Green 17 F5
Berner's Hill 32 A2
Berwick 170 F7
Bewlbridge 20 D1
Bexhill 157 A2
Bishopstone 180 C6
Blackboys 80 A5
Blackham 5 A4
Boarshead 26 C6
Bodiam 65 E8
Bodle Street Green 109 C2
Boreham Street 131 F3
Brede 90 B2
Brightling 85 C7
Brighton 164 B4
Brighton 189 A4
Broad Oak
  (nr Heathfield) 59 F1
Broad Oak
  (nr Westfield) 90 C4
Broyle Side 125 A7
Buckland Hill 19 A1
Bullingstone 6 F7
Burgess Hill 73 D2
Burwash 62 B6
Burwash Common 61 A4
Buxted 56 B4
Cackle Street 90 A2
Cade Street 82 E6
Camber 94 F2
Catsfield 133 F8
Chailey 75 E4
Chalvington 150 A7
Chelwood Common 34 D6
Chelwood Gate 34 D8
Chiddingley 105 F1
Churches Green 109 B8
Clayhill 67 D3
Clayton 119 E8
Cliff End 139 B7
Cobbarn 15 F3
Cock Marling 92 A2
Coggins Mill 40 D4
Coghurst 137 C6
Coleman's Hatch 23 E7
Cooksbridge 123 A8
Cooper's Green 55 D4
Cousley Wood 30 C7
Cowbeech 108 C1

Cowden 4 A6
Cripp's Corner 88 D7
Cross-in-Hand 81 C7
Crowborough 26 C1
Crowhurst 134 F6
Cuckfield 50 A6
Dallington 84 D3
Danehill 34 A4
Ditchling 98 D3
Dodd's Hill 35 D2
Dormans Park 1 E6
Dormansland 2 B8
Durgates 29 E5
East Chiltington 100 A3
East Dean 187 B8
East Grinstead 1 E2
East Hoathly 105 B5
Eastbourne 185 B2
Eridge Green 16 B3
Etchingham 44 B1
Etchingwood 56 D1
Ewhurst Green 66 B5
Fairlight 138 C4
Fairlight Cove 138 F5
Fairwarp 36 B2
Falmer 144 D6
Felbridge 1 A6
Felcourt 1 C8
Five Ashes 58 B7
Flackley Ash 68 F3
Fletching 53 F4
Flimwell 32 C3
Flowers Green 130 F3
Folkington 172 B4
Fordcombe 6 B5
Forest Row 11 F3
Four Oaks 68 C5
Four Throws 46 D8
Framfield 79 B6
Frant 17 C3
Friar's Gate 25 B7
Friston 183 A2
Ginger's Green 130 C6
Glynde 147 E7
Goatham Green 89 E5
Goddard's Green 72 A5
Golden Cross
  (nr Hailsham) 127 D6
Golden Cross
  (nr Herstmonceux) 130 E3
Green Street 135 B4
Groombridge 15 C7
Grove Hill 107 E1
Guestling Green 138 A8
Guestling Thorn 116 A4
Hadlow Down 57 C5
Hailsham 152 C8
Halland 104 C5
Hammerwood 3 B3
Hamsey 123 C6
Hankham 174 B8
Hartfield 13 D4
Hassocks 97 E4
Hastings 160 B3

Haywards Heath 50 C3
Heathfield 82 B7
Hellingly 129 A5
Henwood Green 9 E6
Heron's Ghyll 36 E3
Herstmonceux 130 E6
High Hurstwood 37 A1
Holtye 3 F3
Hooe 155 D8
Hooe Common 132 F2
Hook Green 19 C4
Horam 106 E7
Horsted Keynes 33 D5
Hove 163 B5
Hurst Green 45 B3
Hurst Wickham 97 C6
Hurstpierpoint 97 B6
Icklesham 116 E6
Iden 70 B4
Iford 146 B3
Isfield 102 E7
Jevington 183 C8
John's Cross 87 C7
Keymer 98 B4
Kilndown 20 F3
Kingston near Lewes 145 E5
Lamberhurst 20 B5
Langton Green 6 E3
Laughton 126 C6
Lewes 123 F1
Lidham Hill 115 E6
Linkhill 47 E4
Lions Green 81 B1
Litlington 182 B8
Little Horsted 78 C1
Lower Cousley Wood 30 E8
Lower Dicker 128 D3
Lower Horsebridge 128 F3
Lower Street 133 B5
Lower Willingdon 173 C4
Lunsford Cross 133 E2
Magham Down 129 F4
Maresfield 55 A5
Mark Cross 28 A4
Mayfield 40 A2
Maynard's Green 82 A1
Mill Corner 67 A3
Milton Street 171 D5
Mount Pleasant 101 F6
Mountfield 87 A5
Muddles Green 127 F8
Netherfield 86 C2
Newbury's 30 B8
Newenden 48 D3
Newhaven 179 E6
Newick 76 C8
Ninfield 133 B6
Norman's Bay 176 D8
North Chailey 75 E6
Northbridge Street 64 C6
Northiam 67 B6
Norton 180 C8
Nutley 35 C4
Offham 122 F5

Old Heathfield 82 D5
Ovingdean 165 D3
Oxley's Green 85 E8
Peacehaven 178 D7
Peacehaven Heights 178 F5
Peasmarsh 69 B2
Pell Green 30 A7
Pembury 9 C6
Penhurst 110 E6
Pett 138 E8
Pevensey 175 B6
Pevensey Bay 175 E4
Piddinghoe 168 A2
Piltdown 54 C1
Plumpton 121 E8
Plumpton Green 99 E6
Polegate 173 B5
Ponts Green 110 B4
Portslade-by-Sea 162 B5
Potman's Heath 49 E4
Poundgate 37 A6
Poundsbridge 6 D8
Punnett's Town 83 C5
Pyecombe 119 B6
Quaker's Platt 2 A8
Ringmer 124 C6
Ripe 126 D1
Robertsbridge 64 B4
Rockrobin 29 D6
Rodmell 146 D1
Romford 9 F7
Roser's Cross 80 F6
Rotherfield 39 B7
Rottingdean 177 A6
Royal Tunbridge Wells 8 D3
Rushlake Green 83 D2
Rusthall 7 C4
Rye 93 B6
Rye Foreign 69 E1
Rye Harbour 93 F2
Saint's Hill 6 A8
Salehurst 64 D5
Saltdean 177 D6
Sandhurst 47 C6
Sandhurst Cross 46 F4
Scaynes Hill 51 E3
Seaford 180 D2
Sedlescombe 88 D1
Selmeston 149 D2
Sharpthorne 21 A6
Sheffield Green 53 C7
Shellies Green 138 C8
Shoreham-by-Sea 161 A5
Shortbridge 77 E8
Shortgate 104 B3
Shover's Green 30 C1
Smart's Hill 6 A8
South Chailey 100 D7
South Heighton 168 E2
South Street 75 E1
Southease 167 F1
Southwick 161 F7
Sparrow's Green 29 F5
Speldhurst 7 B7

Spithurst 101 F7
Standen Street 47 D8
Staplecross 65 E2
Stone Cross
  (nr Eastbourne) 174 C6
Stone Cross
  (nr Royal
  Tunbridge Wells) 6 A2
Stonebridge 29 E6
Stonecrouch 31 F6
Stonegate 42 F6
Streat 99 C3
Tarring Neville 168 D4
Teasley Mead 5 C4
Telscombe 167 B3
Telscombe Cliffs 178 A8
The Moor
  (nr Hurst Green) 45 F8
The Moor
  (nr Westfield) 114 E2
Three Cups Corner 83 F5
Three Leg Cross 31 D3
Three Oaks 115 E2
Ticehurst 31 E1
Tidebrook 41 A8
Town Row 27 C2
Turner's Green 29 F6
Udimore 91 C2
Union Street 32 B3
Upper Dicker 151 A8
Upper Wellingham 124 B8
Vinehall Street 87 C7
Wadhurst 30 A4
Waldron 80 F3
Waldron Down 80 D8
Walter's Green 5 D7
Wannock 172 E4
Warbleton 83 A1
Wartling 154 D7
Watermill 134 B4
Wellbrook 39 E1
West Firle 148 C3
Westdean 182 B4
Westfield 114 F4
Westham 174 E5
Westmeston 120 F8
Whatlington 88 A1
White Post 5 D7
Whitesmith 127 B8
Willingdon 173 A1
Wilmington 171 F5
Winchelsea 117 E7
Winchelsea Beach 118 A5
Windmill Hill 131 B6
Withyham 14 A3
Wivelsfield 74 B5
Wivelsfield Green 74 D5
Wood's Corner 84 F3
Woodingdean 165 D7
Woolbridge 39 D2
Wych Cross 22 E5

The Street Atlases are available from all good bookshops or by mail order direct from the publisher. Orders can be made in the following ways. **By phone** Ring our special Credit Card Hotline on **01933 443863** during office hours (9am to 5pm) or leave a message on the answering machine, quoting your full credit card number plus expiry date and your full name and address. **By post or fax** Fill out the order form below (you may photocopy it) and post it to: **Philip's Direct, 27 Sanders Road, Wellingborough, Northants NN8 4NL** or fax it to: **01933 443849.** Before placing an order by post, by fax or on the answering machine, please telephone to check availability and prices.

STREET ATLASES
ORDER FORM

COLOUR LOCAL ATLASES

	PAPERBACK	
	Quantity @ £3.50 each	£ Total
CANNOCK, LICHFIELD, RUGELEY	☐ 0 540 07625 2	➤ ☐
DERBY AND BELPER	☐ 0 540 07608 2	➤ ☐
NORTHWICH, WINSFORD, MIDDLEWICH	☐ 0 540 07589 2	➤ ☐
PEAK DISTRICT TOWNS	☐ 0 540 07609 0	➤ ☐
STAFFORD, STONE, UTTOXETER	☐ 0 540 07626 0	➤ ☐
WARRINGTON, WIDNES, RUNCORN	☐ 0 540 07588 4	➤ ☐

COLOUR REGIONAL ATLASES

	HARDBACK	SPIRAL	POCKET	
	Quantity @ £10.99 each	Quantity @ £8.99 each	Quantity @ £5.99 each	£ Total
BERKSHIRE	☐ 0 540 06170 0	☐ 0 540 06172 7	☐ 0 540 06173 5	➤ ☐
	Quantity @ £10.99 each	Quantity @ £8.99 each	Quantity @ £4.99 each	£ Total
MERSEYSIDE	☐ 0 540 06480 7	☐ 0 540 06481 5	☐ 0 540 06482 3	➤ ☐
	Quantity @ £12.99 each	Quantity @ £9.99 each	Quantity @ £4.99 each	£ Total
DURHAM	☐ 0 540 06365 7	☐ 0 540 06366 5	☐ 0 540 06367 3	➤ ☐
EAST KENT	☐ 0 540 07483 7	☐ 0 540 07276 1	☐ 0 540 07287 7	➤ ☐
WEST KENT	☐ 0 540 07366 0	☐ 0 540 07367 9	☐ 0 540 07369 5	➤ ☐
	Quantity @ £12.99 each	Quantity @ £9.99 each	Quantity @ £5.50 each	£ Total
GREATER MANCHESTER	☐ 0 540 06485 8	☐ 0 540 06486 6	☐ 0 540 06487 4	➤ ☐
TYNE AND WEAR	☐ 0 540 06370 3	☐ 0 540 06371 1	☐ 0 540 06372 X	➤ ☐
	Quantity @ £12.99 each	Quantity @ £9.99 each	Quantity @ £5.99 each	£ Total
BIRMINGHAM & WEST MIDLANDS	☐ 0 540 07603 1	☐ 0 540 07604 X	☐ 0 540 07605 8	➤ ☐
BUCKINGHAMSHIRE	☐ 0 540 07466 7	☐ 0 540 07467 5	☐ 0 540 07468 3	➤ ☐
CHESHIRE	☐ 0 540 07507 8	☐ 0 540 07508 6	☐ 0 540 07509 4	➤ ☐
DERBYSHIRE	☐ 0 540 07531 0	☐ 0 540 07532 9	☐ 0 540 07533 7	➤ ☐
EDINBURGH & East Central Scotland	☐ 0 540 07653 8	☐ 0 540 07654 6	☐ 0 540 07656 2	➤ ☐
GLASGOW & West Central Scotland	☐ 0 540 07648 1	☐ 0 540 07649 X	☐ 0 540 07651 1	➤ ☐

STREET ATLASES
ORDER FORM

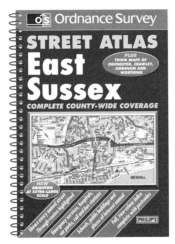

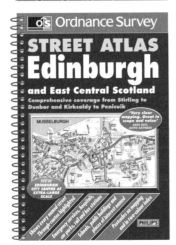

COLOUR REGIONAL ATLASES

	HARDBACK	SPIRAL	POCKET	£ Total
	Quantity @ £12.99 each	Quantity @ £9.99 each	Quantity @ £5.99 each	
NORTH HAMPSHIRE	☐ 0 540 07471 3	☐ 0 540 07472 1	☐ 0 540 07473 X	➤ ☐
SOUTH HAMPSHIRE	☐ 0 540 07476 4	☐ 0 540 07477 2	☐ 0 540 07478 0	➤ ☐
HERTFORDSHIRE	☐ 0 540 06174 3	☐ 0 540 06175 1	☐ 0 540 06176 X	➤ ☐
OXFORDSHIRE	☐ 0 540 07512 4	☐ 0 540 07513 2	☐ 0 540 07514 0	➤ ☐
SURREY	☐ 0 540 06435 1	☐ 0 540 06436 X	☐ 0 540 06438 6	➤ ☐
EAST SUSSEX	☐ 0 540 07306 7	☐ 0 540 07307 5	☐ 0 540 07312 1	➤ ☐
WEST SUSSEX	☐ 0 540 07319 9	☐ 0 540 07323 7	☐ 0 540 07327 X	➤ ☐
WARWICKSHIRE	☐ 0 540 07560 4	☐ 0 540 07561 2	☐ 0 540 07562 0	➤ ☐
SOUTH YORKSHIRE	—	☐ 0 540 07667 8	☐ 0 540 07669 4	➤ ☐
WEST YORKSHIRE	☐ 0 540 07671 6	☐ 0 540 07672 4	☐ 0 540 07674 0	➤ ☐
	Quantity @ £14.99 each	Quantity @ £9.99 each	Quantity @ £5.99 each	£ Total
LANCASHIRE	☐ 0 540 06440 8	☐ 0 540 06441 6	☐ 0 540 06443 2	➤ ☐
NOTTINGHAMSHIRE	☐ 0 540 07541 8	☐ 0 540 07542 6	☐ 0 540 07543 4	➤ ☐
STAFFORDSHIRE	☐ 0 540 07549 3	☐ 0 540 07550 7	☐ 0 540 07551 5	➤ ☐

BLACK AND WHITE REGIONAL ATLASES

	HARDBACK	SOFTBACK	POCKET	£ Total
	Quantity @ £11.99 each	Quantity @ £8.99 each	Quantity @ £3.99 each	
BRISTOL AND AVON	☐ 0 540 06140 9	☐ 0 540 06141 7	☐ 0 540 06142 5	➤ ☐
	Quantity @ £12.99 each	Quantity @ £9.99 each	Quantity @ £4.99 each	£ Total
CARDIFF, SWANSEA & GLAMORGAN	☐ 0 540 06186 7	☐ 0 540 06187 5	☐ 0 540 06207 3	➤ ☐
EAST ESSEX	☐ 0 540 05848 3	☐ 0 540 05866 1	☐ 0 540 05850 5	➤ ☐
WEST ESSEX	☐ 0 540 05849 1	☐ 0 540 05867 X	☐ 0 540 05851 3	➤ ☐

Post to: Philip's Direct, 27 Sanders Road, Wellingborough, Northants NN8 4NL

◆ Free postage and packing

◆ All available titles will normally be dispatched within 5 working days of receipt of order but please allow up to 28 days for delivery

☐ Please tick this box if you do not wish your name to be used by other carefully selected organisations that may wish to send you information about other products and services

Registered Office: 2-4 Heron Quays, London E14 4JP

Registered in England number: 3597451

I enclose a cheque / postal order, for a **total** of ☐ made payable to *Octopus Publishing Group Ltd,* or please debit my

☐ MasterCard ☐ American Express ☐ Visa

account by ☐

Account no ☐☐☐☐ ☐☐☐☐ ☐☐☐☐ ☐☐☐☐

Expiry date ☐☐ ☐☐

Signature..

Name...

Address..

....

....

....POSTCODE